Crime Victims

AN INTRODUCTION TO VICTIMOLOGY

CONTEMPORARY ISSUES IN CRIME AND JUSTICE SERIES

1987   Wilbanks, *The Myth of a Racist Criminal Justice System*

1990   Johnson, *Death Work: A Study of the Modern Execution Process*
        Pollock–Byrne, *Women, Prison, and Crime*
        Poveda, *Lawlessness and Reform: The FBI in Transition*

1991   Vetter and Perlstein, *Perspectives on Terrorism*
        Hickey, *Serial Murderers and Their Victims*
        Westermann and Burfeind, *Crime and Justice in Two Societies*

1992   Surrette, *Media, Crime, and Criminal Justice: Images and Realities*
        Levine, *Juries and Politics*
        Chesney-Lind and Shelden, *Girls, Delinquency, and the Juvenile Justice System*

1993   Inciardi, *Street Kids, Street Drugs, Street Crime*

1994   Walker, *Sense and Nonsense about Crime and Drugs: A Policy Guide*, 3rd ed.
        Irwin and Austin, *It's about Time*
        Pollock, *Ethics in Crime and Justice: Dilemmas and Decisions*, 2nd ed.

1995   Close and Meier, *Morality in Criminal Justice: An Introduction to Ethics*
        Klofas and Stojkovic, *Crime and Justice in the Year 2010*
        Silberman, *A World of Violence*
        Wooden, *Renegade Kids, Suburban Outlaws*

1996   Belknap, *The Invisible Woman: Gender, Crime, Justice*
        Johnson, *Hard Time: Understanding and Reforming the Prison*, 2nd ed.
        Karmen, *Crime Victims: An Introduction to Victimology*, 3rd ed.
        Walker, Spohn, and DeLone, *The Color of Justice*

Crime Victims

AN INTRODUCTION TO VICTIMOLOGY

THIRD EDITION

ANDREW KARMEN

John Jay College of Criminal Justice

Wadsworth Publishing Company

I(T)P® An International Thomson Publishing Company

Belmont • Albany • Bonn • Boston • Cincinnati • Detroit • London • Madrid • Melbourne •
Mexico City • New York • Paris • San Francisco • Singapore • Tokyo • Toronto • Washington

Criminal Justice Editor: *Sabra E. Horne*
Assistant Editor: *Claire Masson*
Editorial Assistant: *Louise Mendelson*
Production Services Coordinator: *Debby Kramer*
Production: *Scratchgravel Publishing Services*
Print Buyer: *Karen Hunt*
Permissions Editor: *Jeanne Bosschart*
Copy Editor: *Stephanie Prescott*

Cover Designer: *Stephen Rapley*
Cover Illustration: *Paul Klee, Komposition mit Fenstern
    (Komposition mit dem B') 1919.156. Kunstmuseum Bern,
    Paul-Klee-Stiftung, Bern. © via ARS, New York.*
Interior Illustrations: *Scratchgravel Publishing Services*
Compositor: *Scratchgravel Publishing Services*
Printer: *Malloy Lithographing, Inc.*

*This book is printed on
acid-free recycled paper.*

For more information, contact Wadsworth Publishing Company:

Wadsworth Publishing Company
10 Davis Drive
Belmont, California 94002, USA

International Thomson Publishing Europe
Berkshire House 168-173
High Holborn
London, WC1V 7AA, England

Thomas Nelson Australia
102 Dodds Street
South Melbourne 3205
Victoria, Australia

Nelson Canada
1120 Birchmount Road
Scarborough, Ontario
Canada M1K 5G4

International Thomson Editores
Campos Eliseos 385, Piso 7
Col. Polanco
11560 México D.F. México

International Thomson Publishing GmbH
Königswinterer Strasse 418
53227 Bonn, Germany

International Thomson Publishing Asia
221 Henderson Road
#05-10 Henderson Building
Singapore 0315

International Thomson Publishing Japan
Hirakawacho Kyowa Building, 3F
2-2-1 Hirakawacho
Chiyoda-ku, Tokyo 102, Japan

Library of Congress Cataloging-in-Publication Data

Karmen, Andrew.
    Crime victims : an introduction to victimology / Andrew Karmen. —
3rd ed.
        p.   cm. — (Contemporary issues in crime and justice series)
    Includes bibliographical references (p.   ) and index.
    ISBN 0-534-23772-X (alk. paper)
    1. Victims of crimes—United States.   I. Title.   II. Series.
HV6250.3.U5K37 1995
362.88'0973—dc20   95-19959

To everyone whose suffering is needlessly intensified
or prolonged because of ignorance about
crime victims or a lack of commitment to them

ABOUT THE AUTHOR

Andrew Karmen earned a Ph.D. in sociology from Columbia University in 1977, and he has been teaching sociology, criminology, and criminal justice courses since 1970. Since 1978 he has been a member of the sociology department at the John Jay College of Criminal Justice of the City University of New York, where he is an associate professor. In 1983, Donal MacNamara and Dr. Karmen edited *Deviants: Victims or Victimizers?,* a book that explored the overlap between criminology and victimology. Dr. Karmen has published articles on victim issues, research taboos, news media ethics, the Rosenberg spy case, agent provocateurs, the use of deadly force by police, drug abuse, auto theft, and vigilantism.

Brief Contents

Contents

5   SPECIAL KINDS OF VICTIMS: PROBLEMS AND SOLUTIONS

Boxes

Preface

In revising this book, I have retained the basic structure of the previous two editions and added a wealth of new material to expand and update the coverage of many subjects. When I wrote the first edition during the early 1980s, it was difficult to locate either reliable social science data or well-informed speculation about a number of crucial aspects of criminal victimization. When I prepared the second edition in the late 1980s, I encountered the opposite problem. Instead of a scarcity of material, there was literally too much: massive amounts of data, including insightful analyses of such topics as murder, rape, spouse abuse, child abuse, elder abuse, hate crimes, deaths and injuries caused by drunk drivers, and victims' rights. By the early 1990s, when I began to prepare this third revision, this "knowledge-explosion problem" had become even more serious. Entire issues of scholarly journals have been devoted to, and whole books have been written on, topics that I glossed over in the previous editions and can allot only several pages in this text—topics such as retrieving repressed memories of childhood sexual abuse and handling cases of date rape on college campuses. Finding more data and analyses than could be easily digested, adequately summarized, or even thoroughly cited, I was forced to be highly selective. Of course, there can never be too much information about crime victims, but a great deal must be omitted from an introductory textbook, even one that tries to be systematic, comprehensive, and up-to-date.

As in the first and second editions, I have tried in this edition to be objective as I examine the controversies surrounding victims and their relations with offenders, the news media, social movements, profit-oriented enterprises selling security products and services, and criminal justice officials and agencies. Whenever possible, I succinctly summarize every side of emotionally gripping, passionately debated, and politically divisive issues. I do not necessarily endorse the points of view that I present or their implications for social policy. But I believe it is my obligation to call attention to sharp differences of opinion and interpretation whenever it is relevant to victim issues.

In the prefaces of both the first and second editions, I listed my "credentials" as a crime victim. My personal experiences are as relevant to my understanding of the book's subject matter as my academic training and research. I know from first-hand encounters what it is like to be a victim of a street crime. Before the first edition was written,

- I was held up twice (in one month!) by pairs of knife-wielding robbers in the hallway of my apartment building.
- I lost a car to thieves. (The police discovered it completely stripped, burned, and abandoned.)
- I endured a series of thefts of car radios, hubcaps, and batteries.
- I suffered a break-in that left my home in shambles and the burglar about $100 richer.

By the time the second edition of this textbook was written, my already impressive résumé as a street crime victim had grown considerably:

- A thief stole the bicycle that I used to ride to the train station by cutting the fence to which it was chained.
- Someone ran off with a fishing rod I left unattended on a pier for a few minutes while I was buying more bait.
- A teenager singled out my car in a crowded parking lot and smashed the rear window with a rock. An eyewitness pointed out the youngster to the police, and his foster parents volunteered to pay my bills for the damage. I minimized their expenses by going to a salvage yard to find a replacement window.
- A thief broke into the trunk of my car and stole my wallet and my wife's pocketbook while we spent an afternoon at the beach. Our wallets were later recovered from a nearby mailbox, emptied of our cash and credit cards.
- One hot summer night, an intruder entered our kitchen through an unlocked screen door. He ran off with a purse while we talked to guests in the living room.
- A car I was riding in was sideswiped by a vehicle driven by a fugitive with a patrol car in hot pursuit. No one was hurt, but the offender escaped.
- A thief smashed the side window of my car, which was parked a block away from the college where I was teaching. Sitting in the passenger's seat, he began to remove the radio. When the alarm went off, he fled, leaving his screwdriver behind.

Almost five years have passed, and (fortunately) I have very few misfortunes to add to the list:

- My car was broken into two more times (on busy streets during the daytime). In each incident, the alarm sounded and apparently scared off the thief, cutting short his or her depredations and minimizing my losses. One thief got away with an ashtray full of quarters I accumulate for parking meters and tolls; the second thief bent and ruined the inside latch that pops open the trunk. The most serious consequence was that both intruders damaged the door locks (the first on the driver's side, the second on the passenger's side), which cost me about $75 to repair (each!). Since then, the car alarm that has done its job three times over a span of six years has finally broken and is not worth fixing, given the advanced age of the vehicle. But it was a good investment and has served me well.

Although others have suffered much more severely than I, these many brushes with offenders have sensitized me to the kinds of financial losses, emotional stresses, and physical injuries that taken together constitute the "victim's plight." I suspect that many victimologists and victim advocates have been drawn to this humanistic discipline because their own painful experiences inspired them to try to alleviate the suffering of others.

Acknowledgments

In the first edition I acknowledged the assistance of my John Jay College colleagues Edward Sagarin, David Sternberg, Fred Kramer, Sidney Harring, and Donal MacNamara; of Henry Staat, Cindy Stormer, Bill Waller, and Penelope Sky at Brooks/Cole Publishing Company; and of Gilbert Geis, Brent Smith, C. Ron Huff, J. L. Barkas, Herman and Julia Schwendinger, and Roy Roberg for reading drafts of various chapters and offering constructive criticisms.

In preparing the second edition, I benefited again from Roy Roberg's insights and from comments by reviewers William Doerner, Florida State University, Tallahassee; Eric W. Hickey, Ball State University; Jackye McClure, San Jose State University; Stanley Saxton, University of Dayton; and Joseph Victor, Mercy College. I greatly appreciated Lynne Fletcher's copyediting and the support and guidance provided by Claire Verduin, Cindy Stormer, and Penelope Sky, all editors at Brooks/Cole.

This third edition was begun at Brooks/Cole and then transferred to Wadsworth. At Brooks/Cole, I was helped by my editor Cindy Stormer. At Wadsworth, I want to thank my editor Sabra Horne, her assistant Louise Mendelson, production coordinator Debby Kramer, permissions editor Jeanne Bosschart, print buyer Karen Hunt, marketing representative Tricia Schumacher, and cover designer Stephen Rapley. I also appreciate the production work of the Scratchgravel team, Anne and Greg Draus, and free-lancers Stephanie Prescott, Linda Dane, and Jan Erie.

Finally, my thanks to the following reviewers of this edition for all their helpful comments: Lin Huff-Corzine, Kansas State University; Janet L. Lauritsen, University of Missouri–St. Louis; Michael Maxfield, Indiana University; and Joseph Victor, Mercy College.

Andrew Karmen

Introduction

Victimology Becomes a "Dirty Word"

A peculiar thing has happened to the term *victimology* in the past few years. It used to refer to an obscure branch of criminology that most people never heard of unless they took a college course on crime or criminal justice. Now the term has entered everyday parlance. But somehow in the process of being incorporated into the language of the mainstream culture, *victimology* (undeservedly!) has become a "dirty word."

Consider the following sampling of how the term *victimology* has been used in the 1990s as an epithet, spit out between clenched teeth:

- During a nationally televised interview, a harsh critic of contemporary feminism (Paglia, 1993) declared . . .

  "I hate *victimology*. I despise a victim-centered view of the universe. Do not teach young women that their heritage is nothing but victimization." (emphasis added)

- In a best-seller, the author decries what he describes as the fragmentation of America brought on by multiculturalism. Denouncing various groups that loudly complain about their plight and demonstrate little commitment toward maintaining a cohesive society, the author (Hughes, 1993: 9) argues . . .

  "Meanwhile, the new orthodoxy of feminism is abandoning the image of the independent, existentially responsible woman in favor of woman as helpless victim of male oppression—treat her as equal before the law, and you are compounding her victimization. Conservatives have been delighted to cast their arguments in the same terms of *victimology*, with the difference that, for them, what produces victims is feminism itself, in league with the opportunist phallus." (emphasis added)

- In a newspaper opinion piece about the controversy over lifting the ban on homosexuals serving in the military, the author (Sullivan, 1993: A21) observes that . . .

"And the effect that ending the ban could have on the gay community is to embolden the forces of responsibility and integration and weaken the impulses of *victimology* and despair. . . . A defeat would send a signal to a gay community at a crossroads between hopeful integration and a new relapse into the *victimology* of the ghetto." (emphasis added)

- In his syndicated column, a leading conservative partisan (Buckley, 1994: 30A) condemns the thinking of the 1960s Woodstock generation . . .

"The countercultural music is the perfect accompaniment for the culture of sexual self-indulgence, of exhibitionism, of crime and illegitimacy and ethnic rancor and *victimology*." (emphasis added)

- In an angry denunciation of several different jury verdicts that found defendants "not guilty," a newsmagazine commentator (Leo, 1994) complains . . .

"We are deep into the era of the abuse excuse. The doctrine of *victimology*—claiming victim status means you are not responsible for your actions—is beginning to warp the legal system. . . . The irony of this seems to escape victimologists. A movement that began with the slogan, 'Don't blame the victim' now strives to blame murder victims for their own deaths." (emphasis added)

Why is victimology being singled out for such harsh criticisms and bitter attacks? Apparently, victimology is being confused with "victim mentality."

Victimology is just one of many "ologies" (including such narrowly focused fields as penology, suicidology, and sociobiology). The suffix *-ology* merely means "the study of." The misuse of the term *victimology* in these excerpts parallels the mistaken usage of the term *sociology* in casual speech, when, for example, people talk about "sociological conditions" (the study of societal conditions?) rather than "social conditions" (such as poverty, unemployment, and homelessness). In the same vein, if the phrase "the study of victims" is substituted for "victimology" in the citations above, the usage makes no sense. Evidently the angry individuals quoted are railing at something other than research into the situation of people harmed by criminals.

It appears that what they are deriding is a victim-oriented outlook on life, which can be categorized as the ideology of "victimism" (see Sykes, 1992). An ideology is a coherent, integrated set of beliefs that shapes interpretations and leads to political action. Whether it is justifiable, understandable, and politically potent or not, victimism seems to be a popular contemporary ideological current. It is a point of view held by a group of people who share a sense of common "victimhood." Victimists believe that they and their fellow group members have been severely harmed by some other group or by an unfair system of roles and relationships. They maintain that their genuine, well-documented grievances arising from past horrors justify their reasonable demands for mechanisms to compensate for past wrongs. Because victims expect, demand, and sometimes receive special treatment and benefits, public and official recognition of "victim status" has become highly desirable. Therefore, when victimists assert that their constituents have been and still are oppressed (kept down) and/or exploited (taken unfair advantage of) and/or alienated (excluded), their accusations usually provoke an intense reaction. An acrimonious debate breaks out with opponents who resist their calls for compensatory measures. Critics of the ideology of victimism condemn what they deem to be a mind-set that broods over outrages that took place long ago and nurses resentments about injustices that are imagined to continue. The result is a highly politicized trading of charges and countercharges about who are the real victims today and a further polarization between these opposing groups.

As an "ology" and not an "ism," victimology is a neutral, evenhanded, nonpartisan, ongoing scientific endeavor that does not take sides, play favorites, or speak with just one voice. So there is no reason to condemn the whole scholarly enterprise of victimology and dismiss it as flawed, distorted, or biased, as the authors quoted above do.

The current spate of denunciations of victimology as too "provictim"—inclined to side with and to offer excuses in behalf of groups that perceive themselves as victims—is particularly ironic, since the academic discipline is still recovering from a series of attacks launched during the 1970s from the opposite direction! In those days, the entire scientific enterprise of victimology was (unfairly) branded by critics with a provictim bent as being inherently antivictim. There was a kernel of truth in these charges; the first few victimologists to gain recognition in academic circles were intrigued by the possibility that some crimes could be the "fault" of victims. Their research into the issue of shared responsibility provoked some detractors to charge that the entire discipline of victimology really just furnished scientific trappings to cover up a mean-spirited impulse to blame the victim for his or her own plight. But as the field evolved, matured, and diversified, accusations about alleged antivictim biases faded away.

Only one of the angry quotes cited above (the last) pertains solely to criminal victimization. Claims about social victimization—exploitation, oppression, alienation, and discrimination—that do not specifically involve illegal interpersonal acts go far beyond the confines of criminological victimology and fall outside the scope of this textbook, which focuses exclusively on persons harmed by illegal acts of violence and theft.

In sum, victimology has received a "bum rap" in common, everyday political speech by those who mistakenly mock it. Read on, and this confusion will be dispelled. Victimology will emerge as a challenging, meaningful, balanced, and relevant field of study focusing on an increasingly threatening, stubbornly resistant, and deep-seated social problem: criminal victimization.

Crime Victims

AN INTRODUCTION TO VICTIMOLOGY

1

The History of Victimology and the Rediscovery of Crime Victims

- **The History of Victimology**
  Victims and Offenders ▪ The Need for Objectivity ▪ The Emergence of a New Focus ▪ Victimology Compared to Criminology ▪ What Victimologists Do

- **The Neglect and Rediscovery of Crime Victims**
  The Decline of Crime Victims ▪ Renewed Interest ▪ Stages in the Process of Rediscovering Victims ▪ The Continuing Process of Rediscovery

THE HISTORY OF VICTIMOLOGY

Victims and Offenders

The word *victim* can be traced back to ancient cultures and the earliest languages. Its roots lie in the notion of sacrifice. In the original meaning of the term, a victim was a person or an animal put to death during a ceremony in order to appease some supernatural power or deity. Over the centuries, the word has picked up additional meanings. Currently, in everyday usage, the term refers to all those who experience injury, loss, or hardship due to any cause. People commonly speak of accident victims, cancer victims, flood victims, and victims of discrimination and similar injustices. Crime victims are individuals or groups that suffer because of illegal activities. Direct, or primary, victims experience the criminal act and its consequences firsthand. Indirect, or secondary, victims (such as family members) also suffer emotionally or financially but are not immediately involved or injured. Survivors are the relatives of people killed by murderers.

Victimology, the scientific study of crime victims, focuses on the physical, emotional, and financial harm people suffer at the hands of criminals. Victimologists study the victim–offender relationship, the public's reaction to the victim's plight, the criminal justice system's handling of victims, and victims' attempts to recover from their negative experiences. Victimization is an asymmetrical relationship that is parasitical, abusive, destructive, and unfair. Criminals force their victims to play roles (almost as if following a script) that mimic the dynamics between predator and prey, winner and loser, even master and slave, if only temporarily, while the crime is in progress.

The scientific study of victimization requires research into the relationships between victims and offenders, the interactions between victims and criminal justice agencies and officials (especially police departments, prosecutors, defense attorneys, judges, probation departments, parole boards), and the connections between victims and other societal groups and institutions (such as the news media, businesses selling anticrime hardware and protective services, and social movements concerned about the crime problem). Victimologists want to know how victims have been physically injured, economically hurt, robbed of self-respect, emotionally traumatized, socially stigmatized, politically oppressed, collectively exploited, personally alienated, manipulated, co-opted, neglected, ignored, blamed, defamed, demeaned, or vilified. Victimologists are equally curious to learn how victims can be empowered, strengthened, assisted, served, accommodated, placated, rehabilitated, educated, excused, celebrated, memorialized, honored, and even idolized.

The suffering of victims (and of survivors) has always been a theme that artists and writers interpret and that political and religious leaders address. The dominant tendency has been to stereotype victims as weak, defenseless, unsuspecting, innocent "lambs" who, through ironic circumstances or just plain bad luck, wind up exploited by cunning, vicious "wolves." But this long and rich tradition embodies what might be categorized as the "subjective" approach to the plight of victims, since victim–offender relationships were explored from the standpoint of morality, ethics, philosophy, and emotion. Now the plight of crime victims is being examined from a new, fresh angle, as social scientists try to cultivate an "objective" approach to the study of victimization.

Scientific objectivity means that when victimologists study clashes that arise from interpersonal conflict and illegal activities, they should try to be fair, open-minded, evenhanded, dispassionate, neutral, and unbiased. Like other social scientists, victimologists should not take sides, show favoritism, allow personal prejudices to affect their analyses, permit their emotions to cloud their reasoning, or let the shifting values of the times color their conclusions and recommendations. These scientific tenets are extremely difficult to live up to when the subject matter—criminally inflicted injuries and losses—draws upon widely held beliefs about what is good and evil, right and wrong, just and unjust. Prescriptions to remain neutral are easier to abide by when the incidents under scrutiny happened to people long ago and far away. It's much harder to maintain social distance when investigating the plight of real flesh-and-blood people right here and now. Impartiality is virtually impossible to attain because the crime problem has become such a subject of intense concern and heated debate. It is so easy to slide into subjectivity and partiality. Basic human decency demands that observers side with the downtrodden and the underdog and denounce the behavior of wrongdoers.

It is not easy to remain unmoved when confronted by injustices. In the following real-life examples, consider how "natural" it is to feel sorry for the victims and to feel hostility toward the aggressors who showed such callous disregard and depraved indifference toward the human beings they cold-bloodedly targeted and treated as depersonalized objects:

An intruder walks into an evening biology class on a college campus and forces the instructor and the seven students to lie flat on the floor and hand over their valuables. The victims lose a total of $655 in cash, plus jewelry. "Being held up in class is unprecedented. It's a surrealistic situation. It was like a movie, watching it go on before your eyes," says the laboratory assistant. (Purdum, 1986)

Two college freshmen returning to their Jeep in a shopping center parking lot are confronted by a junior from another college who is home for Christmas break. The premed major draws a gun and forces his two hostages to drive to a deserted area. There, he orders his captives out, reassuring them, "Don't be nervous. I'm not going to hurt you." But when they are lying face down in the snow, he shoots each of them in the back of the head, killing one young man and injuring the other, and drives off with his prize—the Jeep. (Hanley, 1994b)

Two armed men accost a graduate student working a summer job as an ice cream vendor. Without saying a word, they shoot him twice, take his money, and flee. He collapses in a pool of blood near his truck on the edge of a housing project. A crowd of over a hundred children and teenagers gather. But instead of helping him, they help themselves to his ice cream, leaving him bleeding on the ground for over an hour until the police arrive. "Some of them were happy that such a thing would happen, that an opportunity would come up, that they'd be getting something free," the victim says from his hospital bed. (Associated Press, 1984b)

It is difficult enough to try to avoid being swept up by powerful emotions when examining a situation in which an innocent, law-abiding person, minding his or her own business, is harmed by a gunman who is clearly committing a vicious crime. But, as the following actual cases illustrate, when robbery victims do the right thing and their reactions under incredibly difficult circumstances are so understandable, or really clever, or particularly admirable, taking a pro-victim and anti-offender stance is virtually unavoidable:

A bank teller is handed a note that reads "This is a stickup. Put all the money in a bag and no one will get hurt." The teller hands over bundles of bills but is too panicky to slip in a specially prepared package of currency that, triggered by an electronic beam at the entrance, would shoot red dye and tear gas on the robber as he tries to make his getaway. As a result, he escapes with the money. The next morning, bank officials order the teller to either accept a demotion and cut in pay or take an unpaid, indefinite leave of absence. Instead, she quits, saying, "I did what any normal person would do—I gave the man the money. For three years I've been a loyal employee and this is what I get." (Maier, 1984)

An author of a book that urges its readers to commit "random acts of kindness" toward strangers is mugged and beaten by three teenagers. True to his principle of accentuating the positive, he praises the police officers and hospital staff who attended to his wounds, and notes optimistically that one of the teens did not assault him and that the trio did not get away with the bicycle he was riding. (Associated Press, 1994b)

A college student is cornered outside a campus building by a robber who demands her purse and car keys. She asks if he wants her ATM card too so he can empty out her bank account at a cash machine. He says he wants it so badly that he will let her go into her dormitory and upstairs to her room to get it. While he waits outside, she calls the campus police, who swiftly arrive and arrest him. (Edwards, 1994)

A passenger jams a gun barrel to a cabdriver's neck and announces a stickup. Dissatisfied with the amount of money the driver hands over, the robber demands more. Pretending that he is driving to a bank to withdraw additional cash, the cabbie tricks him and screeches to a stop in front of a police station. When he sees that there are no cops in sight, he crashes his cab into a line of police cars parked outside. As the startled cops come charging out, they see the robber fleeing from the scene and tackle him. (James, 1993)

A court officer is waiting for a train home late one night when he feels someone's arm closing in on him. Suddenly he realizes he is being stabbed in the chest. He draws his service revolver and fires all six rounds, hitting his assailant three times. But the two men continue to fight over the gun and the knife and fall onto the tracks. When the robber grows weak from his wounds, he surrenders and asks for help. The officer, wobbling and dripping blood, drags the offender off the tracks, onto the platform, and then up a staircase, looking for a telephone, until he collapses. "I could hear the life was draining out of him," says the victim, who did not think twice about trying to save the man who tried to kill him, once he was no longer a threat. (Fisher, 1992)

An elderly man is beaten up and robbed on a train platform by several teenagers. A policeman arrives upon the scene and shoots one of the fleeing youths in the back, severing his spinal cord and paralyzing him for life. The robber serves nearly three years in prison but upon release sues the transit authority, arguing that the officer used undue force in capturing him. A jury awards the wheelchair-bound ex-convict nearly $5 million. The victim, who was never even reimbursed for his broken eyeglasses, denounces the court's ruling as sending "the idiotic message to young men that crime frequently pays!" He then launches a civil suit against the offender and vows that if he wins back some of the millions, he will donate it to the hiring of more railroad police. (Perez-Pena, 1993)

As these incidents clearly demonstrate, when examining the basic subject matter of victimology—cases that arouse strong emotional reactions—it will be very difficult to attain and then maintain the necessary objectivity that is the hallmark of social science.

The Need for Objectivity

The importance of reserving judgments, refraining from jumping to conclusions, and resisting the urge to take sides might not be self-evident at first. An angry gut reaction might be to ask, "What decent person could possibly side with criminals against their law-abiding, totally innocent victims? What is wrong with championing the interests of people who have been hurt by unjust and illegal actions?"

There are several good answers to these crucial questions.

First of all, victimization arises from conflicts between people with opposing interests. The initial clash occurs between victims and offenders, of course. But victims may also become embroiled in disputes and find themselves at odds with persons and groups besides the perpetrators: journalists reporting about their cases; police officers and detectives investigating their complaints; prosecutors representing them, as well as defense attorneys working on behalf of those they accuse; lawyers handling their lawsuits in civil court; juries and judges deciding how to resolve their cases; probation, parole, and corrections officers supervising convicts who harmed them; governmental agencies and legislative bodies shaping their legal rights; social movements ostensibly rallying to their side or openly opposing their wishes; businesses seeking to sell them security products and services; and other law-abiding people. Impartiality aids the observer in understanding the reasons for this friction and in finding solutions to these antagonistic relations.

Allegiances to causes (like freedom of the press) or positions toward groups (such as probusiness or antipolice) must be put aside when gathering and interpreting data. Advocacy, whether for or against some policy or practice, should be kept separate from any analysis or assessment of its effectiveness in reaching its intended goals. Scientific skepticism—not self-interest—should also prevail when evaluating whether preventive and rehabilitative programs actually work in behalf of victims, as intended, or are ineffective or even counterproductive.

Consider, for example, the importance of remaining neutral when examining the grievances victims might have against journalists. Rather than defend the way the news media cover crime stories or side with victims who feel that their privacy has been invaded or their plight sensationalized, why not strive to be a detached and disinterested observer who can develop guidelines for fair reporting? As another illustration, note the need for keeping an open mind when investigating whether car alarms actually provide the protection their purchasers want and their manufacturers claim. Rather than agreeing with those motorists whose cars have been stolen that the wailing sirens did no good, or trying to defend the alarm industry's reputation (and profits), nonpartisan victimologists can independently evaluate the effectiveness of these antitheft devices in deterring break-ins by amateurs, minimizing the loss of possessions like car stereos, and aiding in the apprehension of thieves who get caught in the act. Looking at yet another possibility, consider the charges leveled by some victims that the officers who responded to their calls for help showed disrespect or insensitivity. Shouldn't victimologists approach the controversy from a neutral stance, rather than from a provictim or propolice orientation?

Second, impartiality is called for when injured parties turn out to be offenders themselves. What could it possibly mean to be faithfully "provictim" in those rather common cases in which criminals victimize other criminals? To put it bluntly, predators prey upon each other, as well as upon innocent, law-abiding members of the general public. When rival factions of organized crime families engage in a "mob war" and a gangster is "hit" or "rubbed out," the dead man in this case is not an unsuspecting target of random violence. Similarly, when a turf battle erupts between drug dealers and one attacks the other, the loser aspired to be the victor. When youth gangs feud with each other by carrying out "drive-by" shootings, the young gang members who get gunned down are casualties of their own brand of retaliatory street justice. In shoot-outs between the police and heavily armed bank robbers, the dead crooks are not "murder victims" but rather "justifiable homicides." Researchers (see Singer, 1981; Fattah, 1990) have noted that people routinely engaged in lawbreaking are more likely to be harmed than their law-abiding counterparts and that a considerable proportion of the people who get robbed, assaulted, or killed were engaged in illegal activities at the time. Hustlers, con men, smugglers, high-stakes gamblers, and others living life in the fast lane on the fringe of the underworld often are hurt because they find themselves in volatile situations and in the company of persons known to be dangerous.

To further complicate matters, consider the possibility of a "cycle of violence" over time, in which a victim transforms into a victimizer (see Fagan, Piper, and Cheng, 1987). For example, a group of picked-on children may band together to beat up a bully; a physically abused child may grow up to parent his sons in the same punitive way he was raised; or a battered wife may launch a vengeful surprise attack against her brutal husband. In one study that tracked the fortunes and fates of about 900 abused children over a follow-up period of from fifteen to twenty years, researchers estimated that being victimized increased their odds of future delinquency and criminality by 40 percent (Widom, 1992).

Even more confusing are the situations of certain groups of people who continuously switch roles as they lead their twisted daily lives. For instance, desperate heroin addicts are repeatedly victims of consumer fraud (dealers constantly cheat them by selling heavily adulterated packets of this forbidden substance), but then the addicts routinely go out and commit property crimes to raise the cash that pays for their habits (see Kelly, 1983). Of course, it is possible for lawbreakers to be genuine victims deserving of protection and redress through the courts. For example, prostitutes who illicitly trade sexual favors for money are frequently beaten by sadistic "johns" and are robbed of their earnings by exploitive "pimps" (see Boyer and James, 1983). Suspects (who may, in fact, be guilty) all too often become victims of police brutality when they are unlawfully beaten by the arresting officers who use far more force than the law allows to subdue and take them into custody, or who apply force to extract a confession. Convicts become victims when they are assaulted, gang-raped, or robbed by other, more vicious, inmates with whom they are locked up.

The third and final answer to the question "Why shouldn't victimologists be openly and squarely provictim?" is that on occasion this allegiance provides no real guidance. Some situations are not so simple and clear-cut. There is a constant stream of cases coming to public attention over which observers may have honest and legitimate disagreements over who should be labeled the victim and who should be designated the offender. These real-life situations dramatize the necessity for impartiality in analyzing and untangling convoluted relationships in order to make a rational argument, as well as a reasonable legal determination, that one person or the other should be arrested, prosecuted, and punished. Unlike the dramatic examples presented at the beginning of this chapter (which depicted obvious wrongdoers harming clearly innocent, law-abiding citizens), these more complicated incidents reflect clashes between two people who are both victims, or both offenders, or victims and offenders (to some degree) simultaneously. Consider the following news accounts, which, though admittedly atypical, illustrate just how difficult it can be to try to establish exactly who did the wrong thing and who acted appropriately:

Two brothers, eighteen and twenty-one, barge in upon their wealthy parents as they are watching television in their mansion and slay them with fifteen shotgun blasts. For months, the police search for the murderers until the brothers concede they did it. Putting them on trial for first-degree murder (which carries the death penalty), the prosecution contends that the sons killed their parents in order to get their hands on their $14 million inheritance (they quickly spent $700,000 on luxury cars, condos, and fashionable clothing). But the brothers contend they acted in self-defense, believing that their parents were about to attack them. The two college students give tearful, haunting, emotionally compelling testimony that denigrates their dead parents with vivid (but uncorroborated) descriptions of how their father sexually molested and emotionally abused them as boys. When the jurors become deadlocked over whether to find them guilty of murder or only the lesser charge of voluntary manslaughter, the judge declares a mistrial and the prosecution vows to retry the case. (Berns, 1994; Mydans, 1994)

An ex-marine who works as a bouncer in a bar wakes up and discovers to his horror that his wife has sliced off his penis with a kitchen knife. She drives off and tosses his "extremity" into a weed-filled lot as a friend rushes him to a hospital to have it reattached. Arrested for "malicious wounding," she tells the police that her mutilation of his body followed his attack on her earlier that evening when, in a drunken stupor, he awakened her and forced himself upon her. Arrested and put on trial for marital sexual abuse, he is acquitted by a jury that does not believe her testimony about a history of beatings, involuntary rough sex, and other humiliations. But when she is put on trial (ironically, by the same prosecutor) for the bloody bedroom assault, many people rally to her side. To her supporters, she is seen as undermining the debilitating stereotype of female passivity with a single stroke; she literally disarmed him and threw the symbol of male sexual dominance out the window. To her detractors, she is a master at manipulation, publicly playing the role of sobbing, sympathetic victim to divert attention from her act of rage against a sleeping husband who lost sexual interest in her. Facing up to twenty years in prison, she declines to negotiate a guilty plea and demands her day in court. The jury accepts her defense that she was a traumatized battered wife, deeply depressed, beset by flashbacks, and susceptible to "irresistible impulses" because of years of cruelty and abuse, and finds her not guilty by reason of temporary insanity. After forty-five days of observation in a mental hospital, she is released, the couple divorces, and then they both cash in on all the international media coverage, sensationalism, titillation, voyeurism, and sexual politics. (Margolick, 1994; Sachs, 1994)

A man riding a subway train is approached by two teenagers who ask him for $5 while two of their friends look on. Fearing that he is about to be robbed and injured as in a previous incident, the man rises from his seat, draws an unlicensed revolver, and empties it of the bullets he hollowed out for greater impact, shooting two of the teens in the chest, one in the side, and the fourth youth twice, once in the back at close range. Dubbed the "Subway Vigilante" by reporters, he is widely hailed as a hero who stood up and fought back, striking a symbolic blow on behalf of all victims against all criminals. Others, however, including some high officials, depict him as a trigger-happy gunman who overreacted to stereotypes and mowed down four unarmed teenagers, two of them fleeing, before they made their intentions clear. He is arrested, indicted, and tried for attempted murder, assault, and reckless endangerment. His lawyer puts on a prosecutorial defense, arguing that the four wounded victims are really injured criminals, and that the accused is actually an intended victim who justifiably resorted to deadly force to protect himself. The jury convicts him only of possessing an unlicensed handgun. The judge sentences him to a jail term followed by probation, community service, psychiatric observation, and a fine (Fletcher, 1988b). The young man who was shot twice ends up in a wheelchair, paralyzed from the waist down. He sues the man who shot him for millions of dollars; after ten years, the matter is still pending in civil court.

In each of the above cases, the persons officially designated as the victims by the police and prosecutors—the slain parents, the slashed husband, the wounded teenagers—could be considered deserving victims, and, indeed, they were viewed by substantial segments of the public and of the juries just that way, as wrongdoers who got what was coming to them. The individuals who got in trouble with the law—the brothers, the wife, the subway rider—denied that they were criminals and insisted that they were victims: abused children, a battered woman, or an innocent commuter about to be robbed. When opinion differs sharply over who is the genuine victim and who is the actual victimizer, any simple provictim or anticriminal allegiance loses its meaning. The confusion inherent in the unrealistically simplistic labels of "offender" and "victim" underscores the need for objectivity when trying to sort out who is responsible for what happened.

Three types of biases undermine the ability of any social scientists (not just victimologists) to achieve objectivity (Myrdal, 1944). The first may arise from personal experiences, taking the form of individual preferences and prejudices. For example, victimologists who have been personally victimized in some way (by a burglary, auto theft, or rape, for example) might become so sensitized to the plight of their fellow victims that they can see issues only from the victim's point of view. Conversely, those who have never been through such an ordeal might be unable to truly grasp what the victim must endure. In either case, the victimologist may develop a bias, whether it be oversensitivity and overidentification or insensitivity and lack of identification.

A second type of bias derives from the discipline itself. The language, concepts, theories, and research priorities of the discipline reflect the collective biases of its founders and their followers. For example, many victimologists acknowledge today that the pioneers in the field betrayed an antivictim bias. They were drawn to the study of the victim–offender relationship because they were convinced that certain victims were partly at fault. These early victimologists were thus guilty of a victim-blaming approach to the question of crime causation. At present, the tide has decisively turned, and the vast majority of victimologists make no secret of their commitment to aiding and supporting victims.

A third type of bias, though subtle, can be traced back to the mood of the times. Victimologists, like other people, are influenced by their surroundings and social environment. The events that shape public opinion during different periods in history can also affect scientific thought. During the 1960s and early 1970s, for example, many people asked how the government could help victims recover financially and emotionally. These questions were rarely asked before these decades and were voiced less often during the 1980s and early 1990s, when the themes of "less social spending by government and lower taxes" prevailed.

The study of how victims suffer at the hands of criminals and others in society is unavoidably a value-laden pursuit that raises deep moral concerns and arouses intense passions. As a result, some researchers conclude that objectivity is an impossible and unrealistic goal that should be abandoned in favor of a forthright affirmation of values and allegiances: Victimologists (and other social scientists) should acknowledge their biases at the outset to alert their audiences to the slant their analyses and policy recommendations will take. Others argue that objectivity is worth striving for because its opposite, subjectivity, thwarts attempts to accurately describe, understand, and explain what is happening, why it came about, and how conditions can be improved.

For the author of a textbook, the best course of action is to present as balanced a view as possible by examining all sides of controversial issues. Nevertheless, space limitations impose hard choices.

This book focuses almost entirely on victims of street crimes (murder, rape, robbery, assault, burglary, larceny, and motor vehicle theft). There are many other categories of lawbreaking: crimes in the "suites" by high government officials against their "enemies" or the general public, and by corporate executives against their company's competitors, workers, or customers; white-collar crimes by employees against their employers or by citizens against government programs; organized rackets run by mobsters; crimes without complainants ("victimless crimes" to some, "vice" to others); political crimes, including acts of terrorism; and status offenses committed by juveniles. These other types of crime are serious and merit attention from scholars, law enforcement agencies, and concerned citizens. But they are not the lawless deeds that come to mind when people talk about the crime problem or express fears about being victimized. Street crime scares the public, preoccupies the police, and captures the notice of politicians. These conventional, ordinary, depressingly familiar and all-too-common predatory acts have tangible, visible, readily identifiable victims, individuals and their families, who are directly affected and immediately aware of their injuries and losses. In contrast, in the other categories of crime, harm might befall abstractions (like the public order or national security) or impersonal entities (like the U.S. Treasury or insurance companies) or vaguely defined collectivities (like taxpayers or consumers). It's harder to grasp who or what has suffered in these cases, and it's also more difficult to describe or measure their characteristics or responses. But victims of street crimes can be easily observed, contacted, interviewed, and studied, so a wealth of statistical data has accumulated about their injuries, losses, and reactions. For these reasons, victims of interpersonal violence and theft will be the primary focus of attention and concern throughout this text.

Note: This decision immediately introduces a bias into this study of victimology, one that reflects the author's experiences, the collective priorities of victimology's founders and researchers in the field, and the mood of the times!

The Emergence of a New Focus

The origins of the academic discipline of victimology can be traced back to several articles, books, and research projects initiated by criminologists during the 1940s and 1950s. At that time, the focus of attention was squarely on those who violated the law: who they were, why they engaged in illegal activities, how they were handled by the criminal justice system, why they were incarcerated, and how they might be rehabilitated. Eventually, perhaps through the process of elimination, several criminologists searching for solutions to the crime problem were drawn to—or stumbled on—the subject of victims. Victims were considered to be worthy of serious study primarily because they were the completely overlooked half of the "dyad" (pair). The first scholars to consider themselves victimologists examined the resistance put up by rape victims (Mendelsohn, 1940); the presumed vulnerabilities of certain kinds of people, such as the very young, the very old, recent immigrants, and the mentally disturbed (Von Hentig, 1948); and the kinds of people, in terms of factors like age, sex, and race, whose actions contributed to their own violent deaths (Wolfgang, 1958). The first use of the term *victimology* in English to refer to the scientific study of people harmed by criminals appeared in a book about murderers written by a psychiatrist (Wertham, 1949).

During the 1960s, as the problem of street crime intensified, the President's Commission on Law Enforcement and the Administration of Justice urged criminologists to pay more attention to victims (and, in effect, to become victimologists):

> One of the most neglected subjects in the study of crime is its victims: the persons, households, and businesses that bear the brunt of crime in the United States. Both the part the victim can play in the criminal act and the part he could have played in preventing it are often overlooked. If it could be determined with sufficient specificity that people or businesses with certain characteristics are more likely than others to be crime victims, and that crime is more likely to occur in some places rather than in others, efforts to control and prevent crime would be more productive. Then the public could be told where and when the risks of crime are greatest. Measures such as preventive police patrol and installation of burglar alarms and special locks could then be pursued more efficiently and effectively. Individuals could then substitute objective estimation of risk for the general apprehensiveness that today restricts—perhaps unnecessarily and at best haphazardly—their enjoyment of parks and their freedom of movement on the streets after dark. (Task Force on Assessment, 1967: 80)

In this call for action, the Commission's Task Force on Assessment stressed the potential practical benefits of a science of victimology: More crimes could be prevented and more criminals caught, unrealistic fears could be calmed and unwarranted complacency dispelled, and needless expenditures could be eliminated or reduced. These ambitious goals have not yet been attained. Other goals not cited by the commission have been added over the years: to reduce suffering, to make the criminal justice system more responsive, and to restore victims to the financial condition they were in before the crime occurred.

During the 1960s and 1970s, criminologists, reformers, and political activists argued persuasively that offenders themselves were in some sense victims—of poverty, inferior schooling, run-down housing, job shortages, discrimination, disrupted family relations, and other social injustices. In reaction, many people asked, "But what about the real flesh-and-blood victims they preyed upon, who were innocent, law-abiding, and vulnerable? What can be done to ease their suffering?" In trying to answer that question, people of good will came to recognize that such individuals were being systematically abandoned to their fates. Many acknowledged that institutionalized neglect had prevailed for too long. A consensus that certain categories of people harmed by illegal acts deserved better treatment began to emerge. Plans for financial assistance were the focus of early discussions; campaigns for enhanced political rights soon followed.

By the 1970s, victimology had become a recognized area of specialization within criminology, with its own national and international professional organizations, conferences, and journals. Today, victimology is studied at over 240 colleges and universities. (See Box 1.1 for a compilation of the major events in victimology's short history.)

Victimology Compared to Criminology

Victimology is an interdisciplinary field that benefits from the contributions of sociologists, psychologists, social workers, political scientists, doctors, nurses, lawyers, police officials, judges, and other professionals, advocates, and activists. Academically and organizationally, victimology is best conceived of as an area of specialization within criminology, on par with the other fields of intensive study like delinquency, drug abuse, and terrorism.

Victimology parallels criminology along many dimensions. Criminologists ask why some individuals become lawbreakers while others do not. They study the offenders' motives in order to uncover the root causes of crime. Victimologists ask why some individuals, households, and entities are victimized while others are not. They seek to discover the sources of vulnerability to criminal attack and examine the reasons (if any) some victims might have for acting carelessly, behaving recklessly, or even instigating trouble. Criminologists recognize that most people occasionally break certain laws (especially during adolescence) but are otherwise law-abiding; only some who engage in delinquent acts graduate to become hardcore offenders and career criminals. Victimologists realize that anyone can suffer the misfortune of being at the wrong place at the wrong time, but wonder why some categories of people are targeted much more frequently than other groups. Although the law holds offenders personally accountable for their illegal conduct, criminologists explore how social, economic, and political conditions generate criminal activity. Similarly, although certain victims might be accused of sharing some degree of responsibility with offenders for specific crimes, or of exposing themselves to unnecessary risks, victimologists examine personal and social factors and cultural imperatives that compel some people to put their lives in danger. Just as criminal behavior can be learned, victims may have been taught to play (and accept) their subordinate roles.

As social scientists, both criminologists and victimologists place a great emphasis on carefully gathering and interpreting data. Criminologists collect and analyze data about offenders, such as their ages and social backgrounds. Victimologists look over statistics about the ages and social backgrounds of people who are harmed by

---

BOX 1.1   Highlights in the Brief History of Victimology

1941   Hans Von Hentig publishes an article focusing on the interaction between victims and criminals.

1947   Benjamin Mendelsohn coins the term *victimology* in an article in French.

1957   In Great Britain, Margery Fry proposes legislation that would reimburse victims for their losses.

1958   Marvin Wolfgang studies the circumstances surrounding the deaths of murder victims.

1964   The U.S. Congress holds hearings on the plight of crime victims but rejects legislative proposals to cover their losses.

1965   California becomes the first U.S. state to set up a special fund to repay victims for crime-inflicted expenses.

1966   A research team carries out a nationwide survey to find out about crimes that were not reported to the police.

1967   A presidential commission recommends that criminologists study victims.

1968   Stephen Schafer writes the first textbook about victims.

1972   The federal government initiates a yearly *National Crime Victimization Survey* of the general public to uncover firsthand information about street crimes.

1973   The first international conference of victimologists is convened in Jerusalem.

1976   The first scholarly journal devoted to victimology begins publication.

1979   The World Society of Victimology is founded.

1981   President Reagan proclaims April 8–14 Victims' Rights Week.

1982   Congress passes a Victim and Witness Protection Act that suggests standards for fair treatment of victims within the federal court system.

1983   The President's Task Force on Victims of Crime recommends changes in the Constitution and in federal and state laws to guarantee victims' rights.

1984   Congress passes the Victims of Crime Act, which provides federal subsidies to state victim compensation and assistance programs.

1985   The United Nations General Assembly unanimously adopts a resolution that urges all members to respect and extend the rights of victims both of crimes and of abuses of power.

1986   Victims' rights activists host a conference to develop strategies to secure the passage of constitutional amendments on the federal and state levels guaranteeing victims' rights.

1987   The U.S. Department of Justice opens a National Victims Resource Center in Rockville, Maryland, to serve as a clearinghouse for information.

1990s   Victimology is mistakenly characterized by some commentators as an ideology that excuses victims rather than a scientific discipline that studies victims.

Sources: Galaway and Hudson, 1981; Schneider, 1982; Lamborn, 1985; National Organization for Victim Assistance (NOVA), 1989.

---

criminals. Criminologists apply their findings to devise crime-prevention strategies; victimologists use the patterns and trends in their data to develop and test out victimization-prevention strategies—ways people can avoid or at least minimize the risks they face. For example, persons holding jobs in which they could be captured by hostage-takers—ranging from convenience store clerks and bank tellers to diplomats and jet-set corporate executives—want to be trained about how to act, what to say, and what not to do if they are taken as prisoners and used as bargaining chips (see Turner, 1990). In terms of academic disciplines and college courses, the scientific study of spatial crime patterns and of geographical and local factors that influence target selection (where and why) is the focus of environmental criminology. The application and evaluation of victimization prevention measures leads to risk analysis and loss prevention. Techniques of safeguarding employees, customers, visitors, buildings, factories, and inventories fall under the headings of security management, industrial security, or private security.

Both criminologists and victimologists study how the criminal justice system *really* works, in contrast to the way the system is *supposed* to work according to agency regulations, official roles, federal and state legislation, and court decisions. Just as criminologists scrutinize how suspects, defendants, and convicts are actually handled, victimologists examine the way victims are really treated by police officers, prosecutors, judges, and parole boards.

Criminologists assess the needs of offenders for individual and group counseling, more intensive forms of psychotherapy, additional education, job training, and drug treatment. In addition, criminologists evaluate the effectiveness of various rehabilitation programs available behind bars or offered to probationers or parolees that are intended to reduce recidivism rates. Whereas criminologists seek to discover the psychological problems that burdened lawbreakers before they violated the law, victimologists want to diagnose the emotional problems that beset people after they have been harmed by offenders. For example, severely abused children might suffer from posttraumatic stress disorder, dysfunctional interpersonal relationships, personality disorders, and self-destructive impulses (see Briere, 1992).

Just as criminologists want to discover what works to transform lawbreakers into law-abiding citizens, victimologists want to determine which kinds of services and policies benefit the injured parties the most (see Roberts, 1990; and Lurigio, 1990). For instance, victimologists study how well or how poorly the police, prosecutors, judges, mediators, and family therapists respond to the plight of battered wives (see Hilton, 1993). (Psychiatrists, psychologists, therapists, counselors, doctors, nurses, other physical and mental health professionals, lawyers, and officers provide the actual services; victimologists evaluate their effectiveness in terms of how quickly and thoroughly victims recover from their wounds, emotional suffering, and losses. In this area, victimology interfaces with the academic disciplines of law, police science, psychology, social work, nursing, and medicine.)

Criminologists try to calculate the social and economic costs of crime to a community or society as a whole. Victimologists estimate the personal losses individuals incur and gauge the efficiency of efforts to reimburse these expenses. For example, in 1992, the typical person stabbed or shot received medical and therapy bills and lost earnings that added up to about $41,000 ("New Studies," 1994).

Criminologists agree among themselves that they should limit their studies to illegal activities (and not all forms of social deviance). Victimologists do not agree among themselves about the appropriate boundaries of their field. Some victimologists argue that criminal victimization should not be the only form of suffering worthy of systematic study. Those who advocate adopting a broader definition and a more inclusive scope want to transcend artificial and arbitrary boundaries in order to integrate studies of crime victims with studies of victims of natural disasters (such as floods and earthquakes), human-made disasters (like wars and famines), and sheer accidents. The common goals would be to develop effective strategies for crisis intervention, short-run relief, and long-term solutions in order to alleviate human suffering (see Viano, 1990a: xii). The line dividing harmful behaviors that are illegal (crimes causing suffering and loss) and harmful behaviors that are perfectly legal (but lead to starvation, ill health, impoverishment, and other social problems) is artificial and politically determined. By going further and embracing all kinds of victims of all sorts of injustices, such as those harmed by repressive governments and oppressive social conditions, the need for a more ambitious goal—respecting, extending, and safeguarding "human rights"—becomes evident (see Elias, 1986).

But the majority of victimologists believe that the discipline should be limited to criminal victimization so that there are precise, readily identifiable limits and a sharp focus for research and theorizing. Even though criminal victimization is not more serious (financially) or more injurious (medically) or more traumatic and longer lasting (psychologically) than other types of victimization, it is necessary to circumscribe the field in order to make it manageable for the practical purposes of holding conferences, publishing journals, writing textbooks, and teaching college courses. If victimology were to cut its historical ties to criminology, break away, and cast itself adrift to inquire into any and all sources and expressions of human suffering, its subject matter would evolve into victimization in a generic sense and on a global scale. Then the discipline would become unfocused, diffuse, stretched thin without a center, unable to make measurements or generalizations, unscientific, and unavoidably judgmental (see Flynn, 1982; and Fattah, 1991).

Victimology does not have the distinct schools of thought that divide criminologists into opposing camps, probably because victimology lacks its own well-developed theories of human behavior. The major split in victimology concerns priorities: What should be the main thrust of the field? Should victimologists concentrate their efforts on uncovering what victims did wrong and how they may share responsibility with offenders for crimes, or should they devote their energies to discovering ways to help victims recover? Many of the pioneers in the field during the 1950s and 1960s were attracted by the prospect of finding evidence that some victims could be faulted for contributing to their own downfall. Since the 1970s, most of the theorists, researchers, and practitioners drawn to victimology hope that their work can be used to alleviate the suffering of individuals harmed by criminals.

Finally, in both criminology and victimology, political ideologies—conservative, liberal, or radical–critical—can play a significant role in influencing the choice of research topics and in shaping policy recommendations. As victimology matures and attracts more scholars and activists, competing political outlooks are becoming more evident.

The conservative tendency within victimology focuses primarily upon street crimes. A basic tenet of conservative thought is that individuals—both victims and offenders—must be held strictly accountable for their decisions and actions. This translates into an emphasis on self-reliance rather than governmental assistance. Individuals should strive to take personal responsibility for preventing, avoiding, resisting, and recovering from criminal acts and for defending themselves, their families, and their homes. Lawbreakers must be punished in behalf of their victims (retribution or suffering their "just deserts"), as well as for general and specific deterrence.

The liberal tendency sees the scope of the field as stretching beyond street crime to include criminal harm inflicted on persons by reckless corporate executives and corrupt government officials. A basic theme within liberal thought is to endorse governmental intervention to try to ensure fair treatment and to alleviate needless suffering. This position leads to efforts to extend the "safety net" mechanisms of the welfare state to cushion shocks and losses due to misfortunes, including crime. To "make the victim whole again," aid must be available from such programs as state compensation funds, subsidized crime insurance plans, rape crisis centers, and shelters for battered women. Some liberals are enthusiastic about experiments that attempt to make wrongdoers repay their victims so that reconciliation between the two parties might become possible, instead of punishing offenders by imprisoning them.

The radical–critical tendency seeks to demonstrate that the problem of victimization arises from the exploitive and oppressive relations that run through the entire social system. Therefore, the scope of the field should not be limited simply to the casualties of criminal activity in the streets. The inquiry must be extended to cover the harm inflicted by industrial polluters, owners and managers of hazardous workplaces, fraudulent advertisers, brutal police forces, and discriminatory institutions. Victims might not be particular individuals but whole groups of people, such as factory workers, minority groups, consumers, or neighborhood residents. From the radical–critical perspective, victimology can be faulted for preferring to study the more obvious, less controversial kinds of harmful behaviors, mostly acts of violence and crude theft, instead of the more fundamental injustices that mar everyday life: the inequitable distribution of wealth and power that results in poverty, malnutrition, homelessness, structural unemployment, and other social problems. The legal system and the criminal justice apparatus are considered part of the problem because they primarily safeguard the interests of influential groups and privileged classes (see Birkbeck, 1983; Friedrichs, 1983; Viano, 1983; Elias, 1986, 1993; Fattah, 1986, 1990, 1992a, 1992b; Miers, 1989; Reiman, 1990; Walklate, 1991; and Mawby and Walklate, 1993).

One other similarity between criminology and victimology needs to be highlighted. Criminology and victimology are not well-paying fields ripe with opportunities for employment and advancement. Becoming a criminologist or a victimologist rarely leads to fame and fortune and certainly doesn't make a person invincible to physical attacks, thefts, or swindles. Yet, for several reasons, a growing number of people are investing time, energy, and money to study victimology. First of all, victimologists benefit intellectually, as do all social scientists, by gaining insights, solving puzzles, appreciating life's subtleties, seeing phenomena more clearly, and understanding complex situations more profoundly. Second, individuals profit from pursuits that expand their horizons, transcend the limits of their own experiences, free them from irrational fears and unfounded concerns, and enable them to overcome gut reactions of fatalism, emotionalism, and deep-seated prejudice. Third, the findings generated from theorizing and research have humanistic applications that simultaneously ease the suffering of others and give the victimologist a sense of purpose, worth, and satisfaction.

Victimology is not the cold or dismal discipline it might appear to be at first glance. Victimologists are not morbidly curious about or preoccupied with misfortune, loss, death, tragedy, pain, and grief. Of course, because of its negative subject matter, the discipline is, by nature, problem oriented. Furthermore, victimologists and criminologists can lapse into, and be guilty of, impersonal detachment, when, for example, they study murder victims by counting corpses and noting the circumstances of death. But the dilemma of treating tragedies as mere "cases" or "statistics" is largely unavoidable and arises just as sharply in other fields, such as medicine, military history, police science, and suicidology. The redeeming value of victimology lies in its potential for human betterment. Victimology's allegiance to the principle of striving for objectivity doesn't detract from the discipline's overall commitment to alleviate needless suffering.

What Victimologists Do

Once the term *victimology* was coined to refer to the scientific study of victims, a debate erupted over the boundaries of the field. As is clear from the previous discussion, the issue has still not been resolved. Some want the scope of inquiry limited to victims of illegal acts; others want to go well beyond the province of the law to compare the plight of crime victims with the suffering of victims of accidents, illnesses, natural disasters, and social calamities (such as war, mass starvation, and genocide). (For the pros and cons of these alternative visions of what the scope of victimology ought to be, see Schafer, 1968; Viano, 1976 and 1983; Galaway and Hudson, 1981; Scherer, 1982; Schneider, 1982; Friedrichs, 1983; and Elias, 1986.)

The current parameters of the field are evident in the kinds of questions victimologists try to answer. In general, these questions transcend the basic "who, how, where, and when." Victimologists explore the complex interaction between victims and offenders, victims and the criminal justice system, and victims and society. In the process, victimologists, like all social scientists, gather data to test hypotheses and refine theories. They display a critical spirit and adopt a skeptical stance, declaring, "Prove it!" and "Show me, I doubt it!" In the search for truth, myth must be separated from reality by rejecting unfounded claims, dismissing public relations propaganda, and challenging commonsense notions. The following guidelines outline the step-by-step process that victimologists follow when carrying out their research (see Parsonage, 1979; Birkbeck, 1983; and Burt, 1983).

1. Identify, define, and describe the problem. A definition identifies essential characteristics and also marks boundaries. A working definition tells the researcher which cases should be counted and which excluded. In order to conduct their studies, victimologists might have to clarify or reformulate existing definitions or invent their own. For example, when trying to determine how many high school students have been victims of violence, should individuals who have been threatened (for example, with a gun), but not physically injured, be counted?

Sometimes, a group is hard to study because there isn't a good word to capture the nature of their plight. For example, in recent years, the terms *carjackings, battered women, elder abuse,* and *bias crimes* have entered everyday speech to fill the void that previously existed when discussing the harms inflicted upon specific groups. On occasion, victimologists assist others in breaking the silence about situations that long have been considered taboo topics, such as incestuous sexual impositions, sibling abuse, and marital rape.

Victimologists analyze how membership in the category "victims" is socially defined and constructed. They explore why only some of the people who suffer physical, emotional, or economic harm are designated and treated as full-fledged, bona fide, and officially recognized victims, while other injured parties are left to fend for themselves. Key questions include "Who decides what kinds of harm are unacceptable and, therefore, illegal?" "Whose definition of a situation determines whether deception is permissible or whether an act of theft or fraud has been committed?" "What interpretations of events determine whether the use of force is an appropriate response as part of the right to self-defense?" and, "In what ways are the social standing of the initiator of the action and of the recipient taken into account when people (officials or members of the general public) evaluate whether or not anyone should get in legal trouble for what happened?"

Throughout history, people of higher status have not tolerated any violence against them by persons of lower status; on the other hand, powerful figures have been able to legitimize their use of force against individuals beneath them in the social hierarchy. For example, a Supreme Court decision granted teachers legitimate authority to employ corporal punishment (with parental consent) to bring unruly students under control. If school authorities act within reasonable limits, their resort to physical force ("paddling") will not be deemed to be an assault or an act of child abuse. The teacher, dean, or headmaster who administers the beating will not be considered an offender and the misbehaving student who is "disciplined" will not be viewed as a victim, in the eyes of the law.

When describing victim–offender relationships, all the different ways that victims might suffer must be accurately gauged: the extent of any physical injuries, psychological trauma, and economic costs, plus any social consequences (such as loss of status). The perspectives of all the participants in these dramas have to be presented with objectivity. For instance, any accusations that the victim might in some way share responsibility for the crime with the offender must be analyzed evenhandedly.

2. Measure the true dimensions of the problem. Since policymakers and the general public want to know how often different incidents occur, victimologists devise ways to keep track of their frequency. Statistics kept by government officials and private agencies must be critically examined to ferret out any bias that might inflate or deflate the estimates to the advantage of those who, for some self-serving reason, wish to either exaggerate or downplay the real extent of the problem.

Once victimologists can measure frequency per year with reasonably good precision and reliability, they can begin to search for changes over time. A downward trend might indicate that a type of criminal activity is claiming fewer and fewer victims each year; a sharp upward trend signals that this kind of lawbreaking is touching more and more lives with each passing year.

To grasp the importance of making accurate measurements, detecting trends in the data, and analyzing changes over time, consider the problem of child abuse. Official statistics (gathered by government agencies) indicate a huge increase in the number of reported instances of suspected child abuse over the last generation or so. How can this upsurge be explained? One possibility is that parents are neglecting, beating, and molesting their children these days like never before. But another explanation is that new compulsory reporting requirements recently imposed by law on physicians, school nurses, and teachers are bringing many more cases to the attention of child protection bureaus. Thus, the sharp rise in reports might not reflect a crime wave directed at children by their caretakers but just improvements in detecting and record keeping. Given the circulation of horror stories in the news media, the public's well-founded fears about the mistreatment of the next generation and growing parental concerns about being falsely accused and stigmatized, victimologists can make a real contribution toward resolving conflicts by estimating the actual dimensions of the problem.

Other questions whose answers require accurate statistics include: Are huge numbers of children being snatched up by kidnappers? Or are abductions by strangers very rare? Are husbands assaulted by their wives about as often as wives are battered by their husbands? Or is female aggression of minor importance compared to male violence? Is forced sex a common outcome at the end of an evening, or is date rape less of a problem than some people believe?

After measuring how often a type of victimization takes place, victimologists must establish what categories of people are preyed upon the most and the least. They can then draw a "profile" (statistical portrait of the characteristics of the typical victim) of people who fall into high-risk and low-risk groupings. Victimologists can also estimate "prevalence rates" (the proportion of the population that has ever experienced this type of misfortune) and project "lifetime likelihoods" (the proportion of the population that will someday suffer in this way, if current rates prevail into the future).

3. Investigate how the criminal justice system handles the problem.
Victimologists scrutinize how the police, prosecutors, judges, juries, and probation and parole officials respond to the victims' requests for help. They evaluate programs designed to elicit cooperation with law enforcement and test the effectiveness of plans to repay victims for their losses, to rehabilitate them mentally and physically, and to prevent repeat victimizations. Victimologists seek to identify just what the injured parties want, need, and get from the criminal justice system and from the social service delivery system. They try to pinpoint the sources of tension, conflict, mistreatment, and dissatisfaction that alienate victims from criminal justice agencies and officials allegedly on their side.

Sharp disagreements break out over the way the system handles certain kinds of cases. For example, should children generally be trusted when they report that they were physically or sexually abused? Or are child witnesses quite impressionable and open to suggestion and, therefore, notoriously unreliable when testifying in court? And, are large numbers of adults now able to remember incidents of incest that occurred years ago when they were little children because of new techniques developed by skilled therapists? Or are their distraught parents telling the truth when they assert that their grown children are suffering from "false memory syndrome" and are imagining things that never happened? These are the kinds of controversies that the studies conducted by victimologists can help to resolve.

4. Examine the societal response to the problem. Victimologists chronicle the emergence, growth, and development of self-help groups that provide mutual aid and support to their members and of coalitions that link up to form a larger victims' rights movement. Victimologists investigate the impact of these groups and movements on the plight of the individuals they seek to assist and try to assess the short-term effects and long-term consequences of the rights that victims and their allies advocate, are fighting for, or have won. Victimologists also analyze the politicization of criminal justice issues—how candidates running for office, government agencies, and officials address, ignore, co-opt, or exploit the demands of victims. In addition, as social scientists, they assess and evaluate legislation (proposed and passed), recent procedural changes, and funding provisions.

Victimologists also examine the commercial response to the needs and desires of victims—how businesses, entrepreneurs, advertisers, and various professions develop new products and services to satisfy the unmet needs of victims, while also taking advantage of their wants, yearnings, hopes, fantasies, fears, and pain.

A sampling of the wide range of intriguing and imaginative studies carried out by victimologists appears in Box 1.2.

BOX 1.2	The Kinds of Studies Victimologists Undertake

Identifying the Cues That Trigger a Mugger into Action

Pedestrians may signal to prowling robbers by their body language that they are "easy marks."

Men and women walking down a New York City street were secretly videotaped for several seconds, about the time it takes a criminally inclined person to size up a potential victim. The tapes were then shown to a panel of "experts"—prisoners convicted of assaulting strangers—who sorted out those who looked as if they would be easy to corner from those who might give them a hard time. Individuals who received high "muggability" ratings tended to move along awkwardly, unaware that their nonverbal communication might cause them trouble (Grayson and Stein, 1981).

Explaining the Indifference Toward Victims of Fraud and Con Games

People who have lost money to swindlers and con artists often are portrayed as undeserving of sympathy in the media, and they encounter callousness, suspicion, or contempt when they turn to the police or consumer fraud bureaus for help. This second-class treatment seems to be due to negative stereotypes and ambivalent attitudes that are widely held by the public as well as criminal justice officials. A number of aphorisms place blame on the victims themselves: fraud only befalls those of questionable character; an honest man can't be cheated; and people must have larceny in their heart to fall for a con game. The stereotype of cheated parties is that they disregard the basic rules of sensible conduct regarding fi-

(continued on next page)

BOX 1.2   *continued*

---

nancial matters. They don't read contracts before signing and don't demand that guarantees be put in writing before making purchases. Their perceived stupidity, carelessness, or complicity undermines their credibility and makes others reluctant to activate the machinery of the criminal justice system on their behalf, to formally condemn and punish those who harmed them, and to validate their claims to be treated as authentic victims worthy of support rather than as mere dupes, losers, or suckers who were outsmarted (Walsh and Schram, 1980; Moore and Mills, 1990).

Examining How Victims Are Viewed by Pickpockets

According to twenty *class cannons* (professional pickpockets) working the streets of Miami, Florida, their preferred *marks* (victims) are tourists who are relaxed, off guard, loaded with money, and lacking in clout with criminal justice officials. Some pickpockets choose *paps* (elderly men), because their reaction time is slower, but others favor *bates* (middle-aged men), because they tend to carry more valuables. A *moll buzzer,* or *hanger binger* (sneak thief who preys on women), is looked down on in the underworld fraternity as one who acts without skill or courage.

Interaction with victims is kept to a minimum. Although pickpockets may *trace a mark* (follow an intended victim) for some time, they need just a few seconds to *beat him of his poke* (steal his wallet). This is done quietly and deftly, without a commotion or any jostling. They rarely *make a score* (steal a lot in a single incident). The class cannon *passes* (hands over) the *loot* (wallet, wad of bills) to a member of his *mob* (an accomplice) and swiftly leaves the scene of the crime. Only about one time in a hundred do they get caught by the mark. When the theft is detected, they can usually persuade their victims not to call the police. They give back what they took (maybe more than they stole) and point out that pressing charges can ruin a vacation because of the need to surrender the wallet as evidence and the time wasted in court appearances. Cannons show no hatred or contempt for their marks. They rationalize their crimes as impersonal acts directed at targets who can easily afford the losses or who would otherwise be fleeced or swindled by businessmen and other exploitive *legal types* (Inciardi, 1976).

Exploring the Bonds between Captives and Their Captors

Hostages (of terrorists, skyjackers, kidnappers, bank robbers, rebelling prisoners, and gunmen who go berserk) are used by their captors to exert leverage on a third party—perhaps a family, the police, or a government agency. These victims frequently react in a surprising way to being trapped. Instead of showing anger and seeking revenge, these pawns in a larger drama may emerge from the siege feeling warmth for, and attachment to, the lawbreakers. Their outrage is directed at the authorities who rescued them, presumably for acting with life-threatening indifference during the protracted negotiations. This surprising emotional realignment has been termed the *Stockholm Syndrome,* because it was first noted after a 1973 bank holdup in Sweden.

Several psychological explanations for this *pathological transference* are plausible: the hostages may be identifying with the aggressor; they may be sympathetic to acts of defiance aimed at the Establishment; as survivors, they may harbor intense feelings of gratitude toward their keepers for sparing their lives; or as helpless dependents, they may cling to the powerful figures who are endangering them because of a primitive emotional response called *traumatical infantilism.* After the ordeal, these terrorized victims need to be welcomed back and reassured that they did nothing wrong during—and right after—their captivity (Fattah, 1979; Ochberg, 1978; Symonds, 1980a).

THE NEGLECT AND REDISCOVERY OF CRIME VICTIMS

Laws create criminals and formally define persons as victims at the same time. The outlawing of specific harmful activities thus always marks, in a sense, the discovery of another set of victims. The laws prohibiting what are now called street crimes are among the very oldest on the books.

The Decline of Crime Victims

Legal historians report that there was a time centuries ago when victims played a leading role in the resolution of criminal matters. To discourage retaliation and endless feuding, simple societies around the world established direct repayment schemes that enabled victims and their families to receive money or valuables from the persons who wronged them to compensate them for the pain, suffering, and losses. This type of victim-oriented justice process prevailed when social relations were based on family ties, personal obligations, strong emotions, and sacred traditions and when people lived in small villages and engaged in farming. But the victim's role diminished as industrialization and urbanization brought about social relations that were voluntary, secular, impersonal, rationalized, and contractual. Victims lost control over the process of determining the fate of the individuals who harmed them. The government dominated judicial proceedings and extracted fines from criminals and/or physically punished or executed them. The seriousness of the wounds and losses inflicted by the offender was of importance only insofar as it determined the charges and penalties upon conviction. Restoring victims to the condition they were in before the crimes occurred was no longer the main concern. In fact, the recovery of damages became a separate matter to be handled in another arena (civil court) according to different rules (tort law), after criminal proceedings were concluded (Schafer, 1968).

In the history of the United States, this same rise and fall can be observed. Over the course of several hundred years, victims went from central figures to passive spectators relegated to the sidelines. In colonial America, police forces and public prosecutors had not yet been established. Victims conducted their own investigations, paid for warrants to have sheriffs make arrests, and hired private attorneys to indict and prosecute their alleged attackers. Convicts were forced to repay victims up to three times as much as they damaged or stole. Victims were key decision makers within and direct beneficiaries of the criminal justice process. But after the Revolutionary War and the adoption of the Constitution and Bill of Rights, crimes were considered hostile acts directed against the authority of the state, as the representative of the people. Addressing the suffering of victims was deemed to be less important than dealing with the symbolic threat posed by lawbreakers to the social order. Public prosecutors, as representatives of the government and of society, took over the powers and responsibilities formerly assumed by victims. Federal, state, and district attorneys were granted the authority to decide whether or not to press charges against defendants and what sanctions to ask judges to invoke against convicts. The goals of deterring crime through punishment, protecting society by incapacitating dangerous persons, and rehabilitating deviants through treatment began to overshadow the demands of victims that they be restored to financial, emotional, and physical health.

Over the next two centuries, the government increasingly assumed the obligation of providing detainees and inmates with food, housing, medical care, recreational opportunities, schooling, job training, psychological counseling, and legal representation while leaving victims to fend for themselves. As victims lost control over their cases, their role was limited to two contributions: initiating investigations by complaining to the police, and testifying for the prosecution as just another piece of evidence in the state's presentation of damning facts against the accused. When plea bargaining replaced trials as the means of resolving the overwhelming majority of cases, most victims lost their last opportunity to actively participate in the process by telling their stories on the witness stand. Victims became so routinely overlooked in criminal justice proceedings that they were rarely asked what actions the prosecution should take; often were never even informed of the outcomes of "their" cases. Thoroughly marginalized, victims often sensed that they had been harmed twice, the second time by a system ostensibly set up to help them but in reality more intent on satisfying the needs of its constituent agencies and officials (McDonald, 1977; Davis, Kunreuther, and Connick, 1984).

Renewed Interest

The rediscovery of the plight of crime victims was initiated in the late 1950s and early 1960s by a small number of self-help advocates, social scientists, crusading journalists, enlightened criminal justice officials, and responsive lawmakers. They started to make the public aware of what they defined as problematic: systematic neglect of victim issues. Through writings, meetings, and events such as petition drives and demonstrations, these activists communicated to a wider audience their message that victims were forgotten persons who needed to be rediscovered. Discussion and debate emerged in the late 1960s and intensified throughout the 1970s and 1980s over why the situation existed and what could be done about it. Various groups with their own distinct agendas formed coalitions and mobilized to campaign for changes. As a result, criminal justice policies are being reformed and new laws favorable to victims are being passed.

The News Media: Portraying the Victim's Plight   The news media—newspapers, magazines, and radio and television stations—deserve a great deal of credit for contributing to the rediscovery of victims. Featuring accounts of crimes as front-page items or as lead stories in broadcasts is a long-standing journalistic tradition. Today, everyone is familiar with America's crime problem—not because of firsthand experience but because of secondhand accounts relayed through the news media. In the past, the offender received the lion's share of attention. But now details about the injured party are routinely included to inject some "human interest." Drawing upon an inexhaustible source—a steady flow of new cases emanating from a crime-ridden society—the news media are saturated with stories about deception, loss, brutality, death, and tragic irony. Administered this daily dose of horror stories, members of the general public might well be expected to be experts about how, when, and where illegal acts are committed and what it is like to be victimized. But if the media's historical preoccupation with violence and mayhem spreads misinformation and perpetuates false stereotypes, the public may harbor illusions.

At its best, crime reporting can explain the plight of victims in precise detail: how they are harmed, what losses they incur, what emotions they feel, how they are handled by the legal system, and what helps or hinders their recovery. By remaining faithful to the facts, journalists can enable their audiences to transcend their own limited experiences with criminals and to see emergencies, tragedies, triumphs, and dangers through the victims' eyes. Skillful reporting can convey a sharp picture of the consequences of lawlessness, from the raw emotion and drama of the situation to the institutional responses that make up the criminal justice process. Accurate information and well-grounded, insightful interpretations allow nonvictims to better understand and empathize with the actions and reactions of victims.

But often the news media's coverage can be misleading instead of enlightening, a source of fallacies and myths instead of the truth. First of all, almost by definition, the items considered newsworthy must be attention grabbers; that is, some aspect of the act, the perpetrator, or the target must be unusual, unexpected, strange, perverse, or shocking. What is typical, commonplace, or predictable is just not news. As a result, as soon as some pattern of victimization becomes "routine" and well known, it loses its "shelf life." The media's roving eye has a notoriously short attention span. For example, victims of drive-by shootings who are caught in the cross fire between rival gang members might be the subject of lead stories for a week or so. Then this topic will disappear from the news, and a spate of incidents in which motorists get shot on congested highways might seize center stage. After that, a series of mysterious deaths among hospital patients might be featured. These events could then be superseded by coverage of a rash of poisonings due to product tampering. Then stories might dwell on the slayings of taxi drivers by robbers, or on holdups of elderly women by teenage boys, or on murders of children by abusive parents, or on attacks on teachers by angry students. The procession of grisly, depressing, and infuriating tidbits never ceases, although eventually the subjects begin to be repeated. Such "pack journalism" can create the impression that a particular kind of crime is on the rise, when actually it is temporarily the focus of a number of competing reporters who generate variations of each other's stories until the topic is exhausted. The rediscovery of a group of victims by one news department can inspire imitators to search for additional newsworthy stories on the same theme. As editors scour the press releases of police departments for still more cases of this type, a "crime wave" can be created.

Superficiality of coverage characterizes much crime reporting. Space and time limitations (meeting deadlines) dictate that items be short and quick, making fast-paced news more entertaining but less informative. Complex issues must be oversimplified, caricatured, reduced to cliches, edited out, or simply ignored. As a result, the intricacies of the victim–offender relationship, and the complicated reactions of victims to crimes, are rarely examined in any depth. For example, in covering rapes, reporters tend to portray the victims as either "virgins" (good, pure, innocent, unsuspecting) or as "vamps" (evil, seductive, wanton). A woman is likely to be pictured as a vamp if she knew her assailant, if no weapon was used to intimidate her, if she belongs to the same racial or ethnic group and social class as the aggressor, if she is young and considered "pretty," and if she does not fit the traditional image of a housewife and mother preoccupied with her family. Greater interest is shown toward the plight of white women than minority women, especially if the offenders are not white. Rapes are more likely to be written off as isolated, bizarre, and exceptional events than to be attributed to deeply rooted and long-standing social problems involving gender roles, power relationships, race and class tensions, child-rearing practices, and misogynist themes pervading popular culture. In their moralistic narratives, reporters keep old myths alive, sympathizing with virgins ravished by depraved monsters while blaming vamps for arousing the lust of regular guys (Benedict, 1992).

Sensationalism is another problem. For a case to receive exaggerated importance and undue attention, some aspect of the victim–offender relationship must stand out. Historically, the heinous crimes that have received the most coverage have one or more of these elements in common: a child or woman as the victim or the defendant; a high-class or well-known victim or defendant; intimations of promiscuous behavior by the victim or defendant; and some doubts about the guilt of the accused (Stephens, 1988). Editors and journalists sift through an overwhelming number of real-life tragedies that come to their attention (largely through their contacts with the local police department) and select out the cases they anticipate will shock people out of their complacency or arouse the public's social conscience. The stories that are featured strike a responsive chord in their audiences because the incidents symbolize some significant theme—for example, that anyone can be chosen at random to be brutally attacked (simply for being at the wrong place at the wrong time); that bystanders may not come to a victim's aid, especially in anonymous, big-city settings; or that complete strangers cannot be trusted (Roberts, 1989).

Another bias that colors media coverage is a tendency to accentuate the negative. Bad news sells better than good news. However, dwelling on defeat, destruction, and tragedy breeds cynicism, pessimism, even a sense of despair. The public is led to believe that victims suffer endless misery, that extreme reactions are typical responses, that crime is spiraling out of control, and that nothing positive can be done or is being tested to counteract the damage inflicted by offenders.

The kind of coverage that can be called "scandal-mongering," "pandering," "yellow journalism," and "tabloidism" occurs primarily because the news media that employ the journalists are commercial enterprises. Newspapers, magazines, radio stations, and television networks are profit-oriented businesses. Shocking stories attract readers, listeners, and viewers. Blaring headlines, gripping accounts, colorful phrasing, memorable quotes, and other forms of media "hype" build the huge audiences that permit media firms to charge sponsors high rates for advertising. But other factors are operating as well, such as considerations of personal gain (getting an "inside story" and "scooping" the competition, for example) and organizational imperatives (meeting inflexible deadlines and space limitations). Producers, editors, and reporters seeking to play up the human-interest angle have rediscovered the victims' plight because they have found that crime stories attract large crowds if they are spiced up with a heavy dose of sex, gore, and raw emotions. As a result, readers and viewers are increasingly confronted with tasteless images of slain policemen and their grieving widows, missing children and their distraught parents, wounded teenage gang members and their vengeful friends, and surveillance camera footage of fleeing robbers leaving behind shopkeepers lying in pools of blood. Overzealous journalists are frequently criticized for maintaining deathwatch vigils at victims' homes or for shoving microphones in the faces of bereaved, dazed, or hysterical persons. When reporters turn a personal tragedy into a media event, and thus into a public spectacle, the victim's right to privacy is invaded. The injured party receives unwanted publicity and exposure and experiences a loss of control as others comment on, interpret, draw lessons from, and impose judgments on the case.

And yet, it can be argued that this media reaction is a necessary evil. Criminal acts not only harm particular victims but also threaten society as a whole. The public has a right and a need to know about the emergence of dangerous conditions and threatening developments. The news media have a right to carry crime stories, perhaps even a duty to probe into, disclose fully, and disseminate widely all relevant details regarding significant violations of the law. Reporters and news editors have a constitutional right arising from the First Amendment's guarantee of a free press to present the facts to the public without interference from the government. The problem is that the public's right to know about news and the media's right to report it clash with the victim's right to privacy.

Questions of fairness and ethics concerning how members of the media portray the plight of victims and survivors are being addressed by editors, journalists, and victims' advocates and organizations in confrontations, in court, and at conferences. Several remedies have been proposed to curb the abusive treatment of victims by insensitive journalists. One approach would be to enact new laws to protect victims from needless public exposure, such as the unnecessary disclosure of their names and addresses. An alternative approach would be to rely on the self-restraint of journalists and their editors. The fact that most news accounts of rapes no longer reveal the victims' names is an example of this approach in action. A third remedy would be for the media to adopt a code of professional ethics. Journalists who abide by the code would "read victims their rights" at the outset of interviews, just as police officers read suspects their Miranda rights when taking them into custody (see Thomason and Babbilli, 1987; Karmen, 1989). Victimologists could play an important role by studying how frequently and how seriously news reporters offend the subjects of their stories, and by monitoring how successfully the different reform strategies prevent abuses or minimize harm.

Businesses: Selling Products and Services to Victims Some businesses have discovered in victims an untapped market for goods and services. After suffering through an unpleasant experience, many victims become willing, even eager consumers, searching for products that will protect them from any further harm. Potential victims—essentially everyone else—constitute a far larger market, if they can be convinced that the personal security industry can reduce the odds of their becoming a statistic.

But the attention paid to the victim's plight by businesses may turn out, like media coverage, to be a mixed blessing. Along with the development of this new market for antitheft devices and protective services comes the possibility of commercial exploitation. Profiteers can engage in false advertising and fear mongering to cash in on the crime problem and capitalize on the legitimate concerns and needs of vulnerable and sometimes panicky customers.

As industries producing security products and services for personal, automobile, and home use experience dramatic growth, private efforts based on these commercial services and products (such as guards, guns, bullet-proof clothing, and alarms) to deter and reduce crime are becoming increasingly important. Individuals and small groups equipped with the latest in technological gadgetry are enlisted as troops in the "war on crime" as responsibility shifts away from the corporate and governmental sources of the problem and away from collective, societal solutions.

Social Movements: Taking Up the Victims' Cause Aside from having been harmed by criminals, victims as a group may have very little in common. They differ in age, gender, race, class, political orientation, and in many other important ways. However, sustained efforts are being made to organize them into self-help groups and to recruit these groups into a larger social movement. This victims' movement is now a broad alliance of activists, support groups, and advocacy organizations that lobbies for increased rights and expanded services, demonstrates at trials, educates the public, trains criminal justice professionals and care givers, sets up research institutes and information clearinghouses, designs and evaluates experiments, and holds conferences to share ideas and experiences. The guiding principle holding this diverse coalition together is that victims who otherwise would feel powerless, guilty, and enraged can regain a sense of control over their lives through practical assistance, mutual support, and involvement in the criminal justice process (Friedman, 1985).

The emergence, growth, and development of the victims' movement have been influenced by other social movements. The most important contributions have been made by the law-and-order movement, the women's movement, and the civil rights movement.

The conservative, hard-line, law-and-order movement was the first to proclaim that victims deserve better treatment and formal rights. Alarmed by an upsurge in street crime during the late 1960s, law-and-order advocates argued that the average American should be more worried about becoming a victim than about being falsely accused, mistakenly convicted, and unjustly punished (Hook, 1972). The rediscovered victim was portrayed as a solitary figure who lacked rights (but deserved them), in sharp contrast to the presumably guilty person who seemed well protected by loopholes and technicalities that undermined the government's efforts to arrest, detain, convict, incapacitate, and punish. The scales of justice were said to be unfairly tilted in favor of the bad guys and to the disadvantage of innocent, law-abiding citizens and their allies on the police force and in the prosecutor's office. In the victim-oriented justice system that law-and-order advocates envisioned, punishment would be swift and sure. Permissiveness (unwarranted leniency) and the coddling of criminals would be ended; more offenders would be locked up for longer periods of time; and fewer would be granted bail, probation, or parole. Opponents of these hard-line policies were branded as "procriminal" and "antivictim" (see Carrington, 1975).

Activists in the women's movement helped to launch both the antirape and the antibattering movements. The antirape movement originated when radical feminists set up the first rape crisis centers in Berkeley, California, and Washington, D.C., in 1972. The centers were not only places of aid and comfort; they were also rallying sites for outreach efforts, consciousness raising, and political organizing (see Rose, 1977; Largen, 1981; and Schechter, 1982). Some antirape activists went on to protest street harassment, uniting behind the slogan "Take back the night" (see Lederer, 1980), while others helped to organize the battered women's movement and set up the first "safe house," or refuge, in St. Paul, Minnesota, in 1974. The movement to shelter battered women paralleled the provictim, antirape movement in a number of ways. Both were initiated for the most part by former victims. Both viewed the victims' plight as an outgrowth of societal and institutional problems rather than personal troubles and individual weaknesses. Both sought to empower women by confronting established male authority, challenging existing procedures, providing peer support and advocacy, and devising alternative places to go for assistance. The overall analysis that originally guided the women's movement was that male-versus-female offenses (such as rape, wife beating, sexual harassment in the streets and at work, and incest) pose a threat to all women and slow down progress toward equality and liberation. The gravest dangers are faced by women who are socially disadvantaged because of economic insecurity, racial discrimination, and separation or divorce. The men at the helm of the criminal justice system have demonstrated that they cannot be counted on to effectively protect or assist victimized girls and women.

The civil rights movement (a loose coalition composed of organizations representing the interests of a wide range of racial and ethnic minority groups) campaigns for equality and fair treatment in the face of deeply entrenched discriminatory practices. Earlier in this century, the major problem was racist violence, which took the form of thousands of lynchings of minority males by vicious mobs. These murders usually went unsolved and unpunished. At present, the movement's major concern centers upon hate-motivated *bias crimes*. These acts range from vandalism and harassment (such as cross burnings) to physical violence (such as beatings, bombings, and assassinations). Civil rights groups have been instrumental in setting up antibias task forces and human rights commissions and in establishing specialized police squads and prosecutorial teams to deter or solve these divisive and inflammatory crimes that otherwise would polarize communities along racial and ethnic lines (see Levin and McDevitt, 1993).

Civil rights groups argue that a discriminatory double standard still infects the operations of the criminal justice system. They maintain that crimes by perpetrators from minority groups against victims drawn from the white majority are taken very seriously (thoroughly investigated, solved, vigorously prosecuted), whereas crimes by whites against minorities, and by minorities against minorities, are routinely assigned a lower priority (unless the offenders were obviously motivated by bias and the incidents are likely to cause interracial conflict). "Black-on-black crime" was rediscovered during the 1970s, when representatives of minority communities pointed out that blacks were victimized more often than whites in nearly every category of serious street crime; that fear levels were higher in minority ghettos than in more affluent neighborhoods; that intraracial victimization was undermining the solidarity needed for political progress; and that the problem of street crime and arson was destroying housing, driving away jobs, and closing down services (see *Ebony,* 1979). Activists in the civil rights movement also point out that members of minority groups face greater risks of becoming victims of official misconduct, in the form of police brutality (or even worse, the unjustified use of deadly force), false accusations, frame-ups, and other miscarriages of justice.

Other social movements, besides those concerned with law and order, women's equality, and civil rights, have contributed to the public's awareness of the victims' plight. Most notable among the social movements that have rallied to the defense of specific kinds of street crime victims, starting in the 1960s and 1970s, are those that champion the causes of civil liberties, children's rights, senior citizens' rights, homosexual rights, and self-help.

The civil liberties movement's main focus is to preserve constitutional safeguards and due-process guarantees that protect the rights of suspects, defendants, and prisoners from abuses of governmental power by criminal justice officials. However, civil liberties organizations have won court victories that have benefited victims of street crime in two ways: by furthering police professionalism and by extending the doctrine of "equal protection under the law." In professionalized police departments, officers must meet higher educational and training requirements and must abide by more stringent written regulations. As a result, victims are more likely to receive prompt responses, effective service, and sensitive (nonracist, nonsexist) treatment. If they don't, channels now exist through which they can redress their grievances. The extension of equal-protection guarantees, as ordered by the courts, improves the chances that people whose calls for help were largely ignored in the past will no longer have to fend for themselves and will gain access to police and prosecutorial assistance (Walker, 1982; Stark and Goldstein, 1985).

Members of the children's rights movement campaign against the physical abuse, sexual abuse, and neglect of children. Their successes include more effective parenting programs; stricter reporting requirements; improved procedures for arrest, prosecution, and conviction; greater sensitivity to the needs of victimized children as complaining witnesses; and enhanced protection and prevention services.

Activists in the senior citizens' movement are concerned about the abuse of older persons by care givers as well as street crimes. As a result of their campaigns, in some jurisdictions special police squads have been formed to protect older persons from younger persons; stiffer penalties apply when victims are over sixty; and extra benefits and forms of assistance are available to victims of "elder abuse" who are mistreated financially, emotionally, and physically (see Smith and Freinkel, 1988).

The gay rights movement originally called attention to the vulnerability of homosexuals and lesbians to blackmail, to exploitation by organized crime syndicates that ran some of the bars and clubs, and to police harassment of those who needed police protection (see Maghan and Sagarin, 1983). Currently, the movement's antiviolence task forces point out that "gay-bashing" street attacks against suspected homosexuals and lesbians have escalated since the outbreak of the AIDS epidemic; nevertheless, they contend, such acts, motivated by the offenders' hatred for the victim's presumed sexual orientation, are not consistently classified and prosecuted as serious bias crimes. Although the killers of gay men and women tend to use "excessive violence" ("overkill" in the form of sadistic beatings and/or multiple stab or gunshot wounds), the police solve these murders less often than other homicides, according to a nationwide survey of about 150 cases in 30 states during 1992–1994 (Dunlap, 1994).

Groups that are part of the "self-help movement" can be given credit for making some substantial contributions toward alleviating needless suffering. These groups unite the participatory spirit of the grass roots protest movements of the 1960s and the self-improvement ideals of the human-potential movement of the 1970s. Self-help groups tend to be impatient with and distrustful of large, distant bureaucracies and detached professional care givers. Their simple organizing principle is to bring together individuals who share the same problems. The groups provide mutual assistance and dependable support networks. Their underlying assumption is that the most effective aid and insights come from people who have directly experienced and overcome similar hardships themselves. By accepting the role of helper and caring for others, victims facilitate their own recoveries. They empower themselves to cope with the distressing situations that arise in everyday life, and they engage in political activism to spare others such anguish in the future (Gartner and Riessman, 1980).

The social movements that have stimulated the growth of the victims' movement, and the self-help groups that form its base, need to be studied more closely by victimologists. The demographic characteristics of their membership and backers, their alliances, and their rivalries must be analyzed objectively, and their effectiveness as advocates for their constituents assessed. Public opinion polls indicate that the goals of the victims' movement are endorsed by large majorities of respondents. Females, older persons, better-educated people, and former victims with firsthand experience are the most supportive of the movement's legislative initiatives (Smith, 1985; Smith, Sloan, and Ward, 1990).

Stages in the Process of Rediscovering Victims

The sequential model of the rediscovery process proposed below incorporates observations drawn from several other models: the notion of *developmental stages,* from the self-definition of the victimization process (Viano, 1989) as well as the *natural history, career,* or *life-cycle* approach to examining ongoing social problems (see Fuller and Myers, 1941; Ross and Staines, 1972; Spector and Kitsuse, 1987); the focus on how concerns about victimization are first raised, framed, and publicized, from the *constructionist* approach (see Best, 1989b); the idea of inevitable clashes of opposing interest groups battling over governmental resources and legislation, from sociology's *conflict* approach; and the realization that there is an ongoing struggle by victimized groups for respect and support in the court of public opinion, from the concept of *stigma contests* (Schur, 1984).

The rediscovery process is not just a well-meaning, idealistic, humanitarian undertaking; it is a serious business with far-reaching consequences. The stakes are high: Groups of victims who gain the mantle of "legitimacy" and win public backing are in a position to make compelling claims on government resources (for compensation payments to cover the expenses incurred from physical wounds, for example). They also can make persuasive arguments for reforming criminal justice policies concerning arrest, prosecution, trial procedures, sentencing standards, and custodial control over prisoners. Finally, rediscovered victims can argue that preventing others from suffering their fate requires a change in prevailing cultural values—prescriptions about the ways people should and should not behave (for instance, how husbands should treat their wives; how closely parents should supervise their children; how vigilant grade school teachers and pediatricians should be about detecting and reporting suspected cases of physical abuse) and philosophies about the proper role of government (such as how readily the state should intervene in "private" matters within violent families; and whether agencies should attend to the welfare of victimized members of society).

Stage One: Calling Attention to an Overlooked Problem The rediscovery process is set into motion whenever activists begin to raise the public's consciousness about some type of illegal situation that "everybody knows" happens but few have cared enough about to investigate or try to correct. These *moral entrepreneurs* (who lead campaigns to win people over to their point of view) usually have firsthand experience with the problem and direct, personal knowledge of the pain and suffering it causes. People deserving credit for arousing an indifferent public include the parents of kidnapped children; women brutally raped by men they trusted; and wives viciously beaten by their husbands. They called attention to a state of affairs that people took for granted as harmful but shrugged off with a "What can anyone do?" attitude. They responded, "Things don't have to be this way!" Exploitive and hurtful relationships don't have to be tolerated—they can be prevented, avoided, and outlawed; governmental policies can be altered; and the criminal justice system can be made more accountable and responsive to its "clients."

As Stage One moves along, activists function as the inspiration and nucleus for the formation of self-help groups that provide mutual aid on a personal level and undertake campaigns for reform on a political level. These support groups tend to organize themselves in accord with several principles. The first is that only other people who have suffered through this same ordeal can really be trusted to understand and appreciate what they are going through (a basic tenet borrowed from therapeutic communities that assist substance abusers to recover from drug addiction). The second is that their troubles stem from larger social problems that are beyond any individual's control (and so they are not to be blamed for their misfortunes). And finally self-help activists maintain that, to recover, they need to join together with other victims in a political struggle for empowerment within the criminal justice process, so that they can pursue what they define as their own best interests (whether to see that the offender receives the maximum punishment permitted by law, or is compelled to undergo treatment, and/or is ordered to pay their bills). Effective self-help groups have been set up by parents of murdered children and by adult survivors of childhood incest, among others.

To build wider support for their causes, moral entrepreneurs and self-help groups organize themselves into loosely structured social movements (like the child-search movement, which hunts for missing children). Usually, one or two well-publicized cases are pointed to as symbolic of the problem. Soon, many other victims come forward to tell of their personal experiences. Then, experts like social workers, detectives, and lawyers testify about the routine injustices these kinds of victims endure and to plead that legal remedies are urgently needed.

Extensive media coverage is a prerequisite for success. The group's plight becomes the subject of exposés by investigative reporters, Sunday morning TV news discussions, magazine cover stories, newspaper editorials, and letters to the editor. Soon the topic becomes grist for radio and TV talk shows and is interwoven into the plot of ground-breaking movies and then even mundane sitcoms and soap operas. Meanwhile, press conferences, demonstrations, marches, candlelight vigils, petition drives, ballot initiatives, lawsuits, and lobbying campaigns keep the issue alive.

Sociologically speaking, what happens during the first stage can be termed the *social construction of a social problem* along with *claims-making* and *typification* (Spector and Kitsuse, 1987; Best, 1989). A consensus about a pattern of behavior that is harmful and should be subjected to criminal penalties is "constructed." This crystallization of public opinion is a product of the activities of the moral entrepreneurs, the support groups, and their allies. Spokespersons for the victims' cause engage in a claims-making process through which they air their grievances; estimate how many people are hurt in this manner and how seriously they are harmed; suggest what the appropriate remedies to facilitate recovery would be; and recommend what should be done to prevent this kind of physical, emotional, and/or financial suffering from happening to others. Through the process of typification, advocates point out classic cases and perfect examples that illustrate the menace to society against which they are campaigning.

Stage Two: Winning Victories, Implementing Reforms The rediscovery process enters its second stage when the activists and advocacy groups begin to make progress toward their goals.

At first, it might be necessary to set up independent demonstration projects to prove the need for special services. Then either government grants can be secured or federal, state, and local agencies can copy successful models or take over some of the responsibilities for providing information, assistance, and protection. For instance, the battered women's movement set up shelters and the antirape movement established crisis centers. Eventually city and county governments funded safe houses where women and their young children could seek refuge, and hospitals (and even some colleges) organized their own twenty-four-hour rape hotlines and crisis-intervention services. Originally, private organizations monitored incidents of hate-motivated violence and vandalism directed against racial and religious minorities, as well as gays and lesbians; in 1990, Congress passed the Hate Crime Statistics Act, which authorized the FBI to undertake the task of collecting reports from local police departments about bias crimes (see Levin and McDevitt, 1993).

Achievements that mark this second stage in the rediscovery process include legislative hearings that lead to new laws (for instance, to punish more severely hate-motivated bias crimes, which polarize communities and undermine the mutual respect and good will needed to make multiculturalism viable); special law-enforcement and prosecution units (such as those that investigate, solve, and pursue bias crimes); and updated training programs for professionals (in which they are trained, for example, to recognize whether an assault was motivated by the offender's hatred of the "kind" of person the victim symbolizes).

The best example of a campaign that has won victories and secured reforms is that waged since the early 1980s by an organization of mothers who are outraged about drunk driving. It has brought about a recognition that their sons and daughters injured or killed by drunk drivers are bona fide "crime victims," not merely "accident victims." These anguished survivors argued that for too long, the "killer drunk" was able to get away with a socially acceptable and judicially excusable form of homicide because more people identified with the intoxicated driver than with the innocent person who died from injuries sustained in the collision. Viewing themselves as part of the victims' rights movement, these crusaders were able to move the issue from the obituary page to the front page by using a wide range of tactics to mobilize public support, including candlelight vigils, pledges of responsible behavior and family cooperation between students and their parents, and demonstrations outside courthouses. Local chapters of their national self-help organizations offered concrete services: Pamphlets were distributed through hospital emergency rooms and funeral parlors; bereavement support groups assisted grieving relatives; and volunteers accompanied victims and their families to police stations, prosecutors' offices, trials, and sentencing hearings. With the help of unprecedented favorable media coverage, their lobbying campaigns brought about a crackdown on DUI and DWI offenders (roadblocks, license suspensions and revocations, more severe criminal charges) and reforms of drinking laws (raising the legal age to twenty-one, lowering the blood-alcohol concentration levels that officially define impairment and intoxication) (Thompson, 1984). Along with the 55-MPH speed limit, mandatory seat belt laws, improved vehicle safety engineering, better roads, and breakthroughs in emergency medical services, their efforts saved lives. In 1982, when they started to raise public consciousness, 30 percent of all drivers involved in fatal crashes were determined to be intoxicated; by 1992, the proportion of deadly collisions caused by drunk drivers had dropped to 22 percent (Ayres, 1994).

Stage Three: Emergence of an Opposition and Development of Resistance to Further Changes The third stage in the rediscovery process is marked by the emergence of groups that oppose the goals of the rediscovered victims. Whereas these victims had to overcome public apathy during Stage One and bureaucratic inertia during Stage Two, they encounter resistance from other quarters during Stage Three. A backlash arises against perceived excesses in their demands. The general argument of their opponents is that the pendulum is swinging too far in the other direction, that people are uncritically embracing a point of view that is too extreme, imbalanced, and one-sided; and that special interests are trying to advance an agenda that does not benefit the law-abiding majority.

Spokespersons for the victims' cause might come under fire for a number of reasons. They may be criticized for overestimating the numbers of people harmed, when the actual threat to the public, according to the opposition, is much smaller (for example, not all crashes involving drunk drivers are entirely due to intoxication). Advocates may be condemned for portraying all victims as totally innocent of any blame—and therefore deserving of unqualified support—when in reality some are partly at fault and shouldn't get all the help that they ask for from criminal justice agencies. Activists may be castigated for making unreasonable demands that will cost the government (and taxpayers) too much money. Advocates may also be denounced for demanding new policies that would undermine cherished constitutional rights (such as free expression, which is penalized by hate crime penalty enhancements).

Many other examples illustrate the polarization during Stage Three that results in struggles for support in the court of public opinion. When the antirape movement claimed that there was an outbreak of date rapes on college campuses, an opposition arose, asking why federally mandated statistics about crimes reported to security directors showed no such upsurge and contending that hard-to-classify liasons were being redefined as full-fledged "sexual assaults," thereby maligning some admittedly sexually aggressive and exploitive college men as hard-core criminals (see Gilbert, 1991; and Hellman, 1993). When the battered women's movement organized a clemency drive to free certain wives who had slain their abusive husbands (allegedly in self-defense), opponents charged that some female killers would be getting away with murder. When thousands of adults (usually women) began to identify themselves as "incest survivors" and insist that, with the help of new memory-retrieval techniques, they were now able to recall repressed visions of sexual exploitation by their parents and stepparents, some of the family members they accused banded together and insisted they were being mistakenly slandered because of therapist-induced delusions they labeled a "false memory syndrome." Claims by some child-search organizations that tens of thousands of children were being kidnapped each year by complete strangers created near hysteria among parents until some journalists challenged their estimates as gross exaggerations.

Stage Four: Research and Temporary Resolution of the Dispute   It is in the fourth and final stage of the rediscovery process that victimologists can make valuable contributions. By getting involved, they can become a source of accurate assessments, helping to evaluate the competing claims issued by those who assume the worst and generate estimates on the high end and by those who come up with very low estimates. If they can attain and maintain objectivity, victimologists can serve as arbiters of the truth by offering their expertise and employing the methods of social science. (For instance, a blue-ribbon panel of experts was convened by the U.S. Department of Justice in the late 1980s to make sense out of competing claims and ascertain just how many children really are kidnapped by strangers each year. The researchers concluded that long-term abductions by complete strangers were—thankfully—very rare and did not pose such a dire threat to the well-being of the next generation.)

During Stage Four, a standoff, deadlock, or truce might develop between advocates for the victims' cause who want more changes and opponents who resist any further demands. But the fourth phase is not necessarily the final phase. The findings and policy recommendations of neutral parties like victimologists and criminologists do not settle questions once and for all. Concern about some type of victimization can recede from public consciousness for years, only to reappear when social conditions are ripe for a new cycle of the rediscovery process of claims-making/opposition/temporary resolution.

The Continuing Process of Rediscovery

There is no end in sight to the process of rediscovering victims. All kinds of "new" victims are being constantly rediscovered—that is, there is a steady stream of fresh revelations reminding the public about neglected groups with unmet needs, compelling stories to tell, and legitimate demands for assistance and support. Some groups of victims whose plight is beginning to be examined scientifically include:

- People whose attackers cannot be arrested and prosecuted because they are members of foreign delegations that have been granted diplomatic immunity (Ferrigno, 1987; Trescott, 1987).

- Recipients of crank phone calls, laced with threats or obscenities, from "heavy-breathers" and bored teenagers (Savitz, 1986).
- Unsuspecting consumers who lose money, time, and their reputations because of credit card scams in which thieves purchase goods and then falsely bill their victims' charge accounts (Berreby, 1988; Hinds, 1988).
- Illegal aliens who feel they cannot come forward and ask the police for help without revealing that they lack the proper documents and run the risk of being deported.
- Children who are sexually molested by religious ministers they respected and their parents trusted (Berry, 1992; Woodward et al., 1993).
- Students assaulted, robbed, even fatally shot by fellow students or by intruders in school buildings and yards. (More than 3 million crimes of all kinds are committed each year in or near the nation's 85,000 public schools. But these figures are probably undercounts, since principals tend to cover up incidents to make it appear that the intermediate and high schools they preside over are more orderly. Nearly 25 percent of all students and 10 percent of their teachers report they have been victims of violence on or near school property. Whereas, in the recent past, teachers complained about students talking out of turn, chewing gum, making noise, or running through the halls, now the top disciplinary concerns include sexual harassment, robbery, fights, and the smuggling of guns into school buildings (Bastian and Taylor, 1991; Associated Press, 1993; Toby, 1983; and Dillon, 1994).
- Homeless persons robbed and assaulted on the streets and in shelters (Holloway, 1995).
- Hotel guests who suffer thefts and assaults at the hands of intruders when security measures are lax (Prestia, 1993).
- Tourists who blunder into dangerous situations avoided by street-wise locals (Rohter, 1993a) and are easy prey because they let their guard down (Boyle, 1994).
- Delivery-truck drivers, who may wear bulletproof vests and illegally carry weapons to protect themselves against robbers and hijackers (Sexton, 1994).
- Good Samaritans who try to break up a crime in progress and rescue the intended victim but are injured or killed themselves (McFadden, 1993b).
- Innocent bystanders wounded or killed by stray bullets intended for others, often when caught in the cross fire between rival street gangs or drug dealers fighting over turf. (For example, in New York City prior to 1984, there were fewer than 10 reports in newspapers of such shootings per year; by 1988, there were 54 [Sherman, Steele, Laufersweiler, Hoffer, and Julian, 1989]. Then the police department began to track these incidents; after

peaking in 1991 at 535, the number of bystanders hit by bullets meant for other targets dropped to 342 in 1992, 335 in 1993, and about 170 during the first six months of 1994 [Onishi, 1994].)

■ People deceived and then held up by robbers impersonating plainclothes detectives. (In New York City during 1993, 1,300 complaints were received about impostors flashing false credentials and then committing crimes; about 400 were holdups by fake cops [Sanchez, 1994. The problem was deemed serious enough to merit the formation of a special detective squad, the first of its kind in the nation, to investigate these complaints [Holloway, 1994].)

■ Motorists and pedestrians slammed into by fugitives seeking to avoid arrest, or by squad cars, during high-speed chases. (An estimated 500,000 police pursuits result in almost 300 accidental civilian deaths per year ["Justice by the numbers," 1993]. In some states, the police department can be sued if bystanders are injured or killed because of Hollywood-style hot-pursuit crashes [Gray, 1993].)

■ Unsuspecting persons grabbed as hostages by desperate criminals seeking to escape by using the captive as a bargaining chip or a human shield (Wolff, 1993a).

■ Individuals injured or killed by explosives. (According to the Treasury Department's Bureau of Alcohol, Tobacco, and Firearms, approximately 2,500 bombs and incendiary devices claimed 45 lives, injured nearly 470 people, and caused $22.6 billion in damage during 1992 [Clark, 1994].)

■ Workers murdered on the job. (Cabdrivers, who must take complete strangers to remote destinations where these passengers might rob or even kill them, have the most dangerous of all jobs [Wolff, 1993b]. About 15 of every per 100,000 are slain each year ["Justice by the numbers," 1993]).

■ Unrelated individuals whose lives are snuffed out by vicious and demented serial killers. (Some unknown proportion of the over 5,000 unsolved murders per year are the work of an estimated 350 serial killers still on the prowl, who claim an average of about ten lives each over a period of years [Holmes and DeBurger, 1988; Hickey, 1991].)

■ Suspects subjected to police brutality (unjustifiably beaten and shot by officers) and prisoners assaulted by guards or gang-raped and murdered by other inmates (see Lockwood, 1980; and Silberman, 1995).

In recent years, certain groups of victims have begun to receive the attention they deserve (as the process of rediscovery enters Stage Two): law enforcement officers killed in the line of duty; drivers whose vehicles are taken by carjackers; individuals shadowed by stalkers; young women beaten by their dates; and college students harmed right on their campuses. (See Box 1.3 for descriptions of their situations.)

BOX 1.3   Groups of Victims That Have Been Recently Rediscovered

---

Law Enforcement Officers Wounded and Killed in the Line of Duty

Killing a police officer has always been considered one of the most heinous crimes. In many states, it carries the death penalty. A patrolmen's benevolent association to take care of the widows and orphans of slain officers was set up as early as 1894 in New York City.

Officers who work for law enforcement, probation, parole, or corrections agencies on the local, state, and federal level face unusual challenges and threats. Their jobs require them to come into daily contact with persons known to be armed and dangerous and to knowingly and willingly enter into risky situations. They are called upon to deal with convicts, patrol high-crime locations, break up crimes in progress, search suspicious persons, and track down fugitives. Additional risks arise because uniforms are viewed as symbols of governmental authority. The police, in particular, as the first line of defense for the "system," serve as a lightning rod, absorbing the bolts of discontent emanating from hostile groups within the general public.

In 1993, the FBI recorded seventy felonious slayings of law enforcement officers in the line of duty. That translates to a murder rate for police officers of about 9 per 100,000, making law enforcement the second most dangerous occupation, after driving taxicabs ("Justice by the numbers," 1993). However, contrary to widespread impressions, deadly assaults on police officers are subsiding. The number of officers killed in the line of duty peaked in 1979 and since then has been dropping, even though there are now more people engaged in law enforcement (see Figure 1.1). Reasons for the decline include regulations requiring officers to wear bulletproof vests, better

(continued on next page)

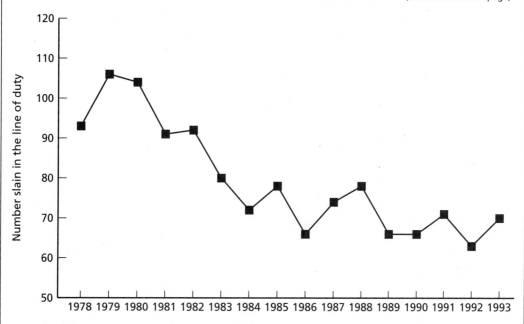

FIGURE 1.1   Trends in Murders of Law Enforcement Officers, 1978–1993

Note: Includes federal, state and local officers feloniously killed.
Source: FBI's annual *Uniform Crime Reports,* 1978–1993.

BOX 1.3   *continued*

training, and improved weaponry ("Line-of-duty deaths," 1994).

In a study of slayings committed from 1983 to 1992, FBI analysts discovered that a deadly mix was a common element: An easy going, good-natured officer who was less inclined to use force than his colleagues entered into a fatal encounter with a suspect afflicted with a personality disorder and armed with a handgun. The homicides were often facilitated by some kind of procedural miscue (such as improperly approaching a vehicle pulled over for a traffic infraction). Most of the murders were committed when an officer was responding to a crime-in-progress or a report of a disturbance (a bar fight or a family quarrel, for instance), investigating a suspicious circumstance, or stopping a vehicle. The typical law enforcement casualty was a white southern male, thirty-six years old, married, with a high school education and an average of nine years of on-the-job experience. The typical assailant was a twenty-nine year-old white man, with a record of a previous arrest (*Uniform Crime Reports* Section, 1993).

Although the average officer goes through a twenty-year career without ever firing a shot (except for target practice), undercover officers face much greater chances than their uniformed colleagues of shooting their revolvers or getting shot. African-American officers in undercover and plainclothes assignments run an additional risk of being hit by "friendly fire" from the guns of officers who mistake them for armed criminals (Geller, 1992).

During the 1980s, probation and parole officers grew concerned about line-of-duty injuries when carrying out spot checks and home interviews. To lessen their vulnerability to assault, robbery, and car theft, probation and parole officers making field visits are getting firearms, bulletproof vests, body alarms, portable phones, armed escorts, and training in self-defense tactics and crisis management techniques (Lindner and Koehler, 1992; Del Castillo and Lindner, 1994).

The families of law enforcement agents were assumed to be stronger emotionally and better prepared than civilians to cope with loss and grief because they are part of a tightly knit community which "takes care of its own." But the inadequate responses of many police departments has brought about the establishment of counseling units, death-notification training (Sawyer, 1987; Stillman, 1987), and peer support groups for injured and disabled officers (Martin, 1989) and grieving families.

Carjacked Drivers

In the movies as well as in real life, motorists have been yanked out of their cars by highwaymen who hop in behind the wheel and then make their getaway. In the early 1990s, the catchy term *carjacking* was coined to describe this kind of robbery of a motor vehicle directly from a driver. Once the crime had a name, police departments began to keep track of it (instead of merging such incidents of thefts or attempted thefts of vehicles by force or threat into the general category of "robberies of all types"); the news media started to report the most outrageous cases (such as the death of a woman who was dragged over a mile because she became tangled in her seat belt while trying to rescue her toddler from the back seat of her commandeered BMW); and legislators began to impose stiffer penalties for the crime (see Gibbs, 1993a).

A carjacking is a type of violent confrontational crime with a dangerous potential for escalation from a robbery into aggravated assault, abduction, rape, and even murder. This kind of robbery is very difficult for victims to anticipate and defend against, since there are no easy precautions to follow and so many different scenarios to be alert for when starting, when stopping, and while underway.

The first attempt to measure how often carjackings took place drew upon data from a federally sponsored annual national survey of the

(continued on next page)

BOX 1.3   continued

general public. It yielded the estimate that about 35,000 carjackings were carried out against motorists each year between 1987 and 1992. Mathematically speaking, that figure translated to about 20 carjacked drivers out of every 100,000 people per year. As for the chances of being accosted, the groups facing the highest risks were men, young drivers under thirty-five, African Americans, and city people. In about half of all confrontations, the victim did not lose the vehicle to the robber; of those who did suffer a completed theft, the average value of the vehicle driven away was close to $4,000. Robbers injured drivers in 24 percent of the completed carjackings and 18 percent of the unsuccessful attempts; 4 percent of the motorists suffered serious injuries, like gunshot and knife wounds or broken bones that required medical attention and hospitalization. In most (77 percent) of the incidents, drivers were confronted by robbers armed with weapons (usually handguns). The majority (67 percent) of the attacks took place after dark. Nearly half (45 percent) were carried out right on the street (such as at a stoplight); most of the remaining confrontations occurred in a parking lot or garage (29 percent) or near the driver's home (18 percent). Motorists reported only 60 percent of the attempts but as many as 90 percent of the completed thefts to the police (Rand, 1994a). Official complaints were filed in order to collect reimbursement from insurance companies, so that the police might be able to catch the perpetrators and recover the stolen property, and so that the owners wouldn't be held responsible for accidents or crimes involving their lost vehicles.

In 1992, Congress made carjackings ("robbery auto theft") carried out with a firearm a federal offense, since vehicles and guns are involved in interstate commerce.

Individuals Menaced by Stalkers

It's standard police procedure for detectives to stake out a suspect's residence or place of work, to tail him if he acts suspiciously, and to maintain surveillance around the clock. But when one person does this to another because of some real or imagined grievance, the target who feels hounded can now turn to the law for help.

The term *stalking* was coined in the late 1980s and entered into everyday language in 1990 when California's legislature made it a crime. Spurred on by victims' rights groups, by 1994 all fifty states had outlawed the act of willfully, maliciously, and repeatedly following and harassing a person. To have the stalker arrested before an attack is actually carried out, many state laws require that the targeted individual have a "reasonable fear of death or great bodily injury" arising from a credible threat of violence made by the perpetrator. Antistalking laws fill a void in the patchwork of laws forbidding menacing, trespassing, and threatening.

Two victim–offender relationships account for most complaints to the police of being stalked. In the first type of pattern, a well-known person (celebrity, star performer, media personality, professional athlete, political figure) receives continuing unwanted attention and intrusions from some unknown "admirer" or enemy. In the second type of pattern, which is much more common, the victim knows the offender and is shadowed in a frightening way after a dispute. Frequently, the terrorized party is a young woman pursued by her violence-prone ex-boyfriend or ex-husband who refuses to accept the fact that a romantic relationship is definitely over. However, many variations on a "fatal attraction" or "murderous obsession" theme are possible; a man might be stalked by a woman who was formerly his lover, or a young man's new girlfriend can be trailed and threatened by his old girlfriend, or a boss might be stalked by a disgruntled worker whom he fired.

In some jurisdictions, stalking is a misdemeanor; in others, it is a felony. Most states provide for both: First offenses are misdemeanors, and repeated convictions or violations of orders of

(continued on next page)

BOX 1.3   *continued*

protection and injunctions to stay away are felonies. Stiffer punishments can be imposed if the offender actually carries out threats and inflicts bodily harm or confines or restrains the person being pursued. In most states, stalking is defined as a face-to-face confrontation, but in one state telephone harassment counts, and in another unwelcome fax transmissions can be considered threatening. The police department in Los Angeles was the first to set up a Threat Management Division to specifically investigate stalking complaints (Beck et al., 1992; Hunzeker, 1992; Kolarik, 1992; Lewin, 1993a).

Young Women Battered during Courtship

Today, the plight of battered women is well known, as is the problem of date rape. Now a growing number of researchers are exploring the phenomenon of physical violence during courtship (especially, for the sake of convenience, among college students).

Courtship is the training ground for marriage, so controlling behaviors (like slapping, grabbing, shaking, kicking, choking, threatening with a weapon, and throwing things) that begin during dating may persist, and perhaps escalate, after the couple ties the knot. But in several crucial ways, violence during courtship differs from violence within marriage. First of all, less force is used over shorter periods of time. Second, young women are more likely to initiate violence against their dates/boyfriends/fiancés than wives are against their husbands (or unmarried women against their live-in lovers). Perhaps these young women feel they can assert themselves more freely because they are not trapped in a day-after-day cohabitation situation and can break off the relationship if the spiral of violence gets out of hand. Of course, much of the physical force exerted by females can, in all fairness, be classified as examples of "fighting back"—either acts of immediate self-defense, or of retaliation for earlier male aggression, or even as preemptive strikes to forestall impending

assaults. However, when women are the victims, not the aggressors, the question "Why does she stay?" inevitably arises. Clearly, some of the reasons married women cite as most important do not apply to dating situations: staying in the relationship for the sake of the children; depending upon the husband financially; or believing that divorce is wrong and a failed marriage is a shameful thing. So other explanations need to be tested. Perhaps some young women tolerate abuse because rules and behavioral limits in romantic relationships are currently in a state of confusion as traditional norms are challenged and rejected. Other women battered during courtship may interpret beatings as demonstrations of "deep feelings" and fits of jealous rage as signs of "really caring." Still others may consider violence within intimate relationships the norm because they were mistreated as children or their parents behaved abusively toward each other. A few might even feel comfortable being dominated by a "virile" man.

Even when the female is the aggressor and the male is the victim, or when mutual combat breaks out, the adversaries are not evenly matched and it is not a fair fight. Young men usually have several advantages—larger size, greater strength, and better hand-to-hand combat skills—which protect them from serious harm and endanger their girlfriends' well-being. Male-initiated violence remains the more frequent and more serious problem (see Makepeace, 1981; Laner and Thompson, 1982; Allbritten and Allbritten, 1985; Stets and Pirog-Good, 1987; Demaris, 1992; and Follingstad et al., 1992).

College Students Harmed on Campus

College and university campuses used to be viewed as sanctuaries from the problems of the "mean streets" and "real world." But a number of highly publicized crimes and a spate of negligence lawsuits filed by distraught parents have forced administrators, faculties, and student govern-

(continued on next page)

BOX 1.3   *continued*

ments to address questions of personal safety within the ivory towers. Despite opposition by college administrators, Congress passed a Student Right-to-Know and Campus Security Act in 1990 (amended by the Higher Education Act of 1992) that required all institutions receiving federal aid to issue annual crime reports.

Students can be victimized by other students or by outsiders. Interpersonal offenses usually take the form of assaults (including violence against pledges during hazing), drunken brawls (at fraternity parties or sports events), gang rapes (at parties), date rapes, and hate crimes (gay bashings, racial fights). As for property crimes, an abundance of bicycles, stereos, and personal computers in an open, unguarded environment attracts robbers, burglars, and thieves. According to statistics collected by the Department of Education, during 1991, 30 murders, almost 1,000 rapes, more than 1,800 robberies, 32,000 burglaries, and 9,000 car thefts took place on 2,400 of the nation's college and university campuses (McLarin, 1994).

But, for a number of reasons, official figures may not reveal the full extent of the growing problem. Many students do not report incidents to either the local police or the campus security force. Crimes that occur in the area immediately surrounding the campus are not counted. Image-conscious administrators devise ways to downplay the risks their students actually face for fear that such revelations will damage their schools' reputa-

tions, scare away potential candidates from applying for admission, and hurt fund-raising campaigns. For example, cases involving allegations of date rape, assault, or threats with a weapon don't have to be publicly reported if they are handled by the campus judicial system and don't lead to an arrest.

Comparisons among campuses, although tempting to make, can be misleading, since their populations differ greatly in size. Furthermore, some institutions are situated in idyllic rural settings while others are located in dense urban neighborhoods or have several satellite centers, branches, or affiliated teaching hospitals. At some institutions, most students live in residence halls, while in others they are all commuters. Finally, a growing number of colleges, especially public ones, have professionalized security forces that check out visitors and seek out incidents to investigate, while the remainder rely mostly on a few guards and on student/faculty judicial committees. To prevent incidents, many campuses now have gates and checkpoints, ID systems, better lighting, more patrols, outdoor emergency phones, evening shuttle buses and student escort services, crisis counseling centers, crime-on-campus columns in student newspapers, and workshops on date rape and crime prevention as part of first-year orientation (Purdum, 1988; Smith, 1988; Graham, 1993; Mathews, 1993; and Lederman, 1994).

2

Digging Up the Facts about Crime Victims

CRIME IN THE STREETS: THE BIG PICTURE

Victimologists gather and interpret data in order to answer certain fundamental questions. For example, they want to find out how many people are harmed by street crimes each year, how rapidly their ranks are growing as time goes by, and which groups are targeted the most and the least. Victimologists want to find out where and when most crimes occur, whether offenders typically carry weapons and, if so, what kinds. Victimologists also want to determine whether attackers tend to be complete strangers, how people act when confronted by assailants, what proportion try to fight back or escape, how many individuals are injured, how many need to be hospitalized, and how much money they lose.

Separate measurements like these, when taken together, constitute what can be termed the "big picture," an overview of what is really happening. The big picture serves as an antidote to limited personal experiences, false impressions, misleading media images, baseless stereotypes, self-serving reports circulated by organizations with vested interests, and widely held myths. But putting together the big picture is not easy. Careful planning, formulation of the right questions, proper data-collection techniques, and insightful analyses are required. Until the 1970s, few efforts were made to routinely and systematically measure various indicators of the victims' plight. By the 1980s, a great many social scientists and agencies were conducting the research needed to bring the big picture into focus. By the 1990s, all sorts of special-interest groups began keeping count and disseminating estimates about a wide variety of victims, including innocent persons hit by stray bullets, police officers killed in the line of duty, children reported missing by their parents, and people attacked by assailants who hate their "kind."

Most of the statistics and analyses presented in this chapter concern the dreaded crimes of murder and robbery. Statistics about murders are more complete, consistent (over time and from place to place), accurate, and detailed than those for any other crime. Robbery statistics are far less precise and reliable but are still extremely important because robberies fuel the public's fears about crime in the streets.

The Use and Abuse of Statistics

Statistics are meaningful numbers that reveal important information. Victimologists need accurate statistics about crimes and victims in order to calculate the odds individuals face of being harmed, to estimate their personal financial losses and societal costs, to anticipate how many people might need help, to test theories that purport to explain why some groups experience higher rates of predation than others, and to evaluate the effectiveness of prevention strategies and recovery efforts. By collecting, computing, and analyzing statistics, victimologists can discover what kinds of people are robbed or killed the most, the ways in which individuals protect themselves when robbers attack, the chances of being slain during a robbery, and whether robberies are becoming more or less of a threat.

Victimologists look at *raw numbers, computed rates, detected patterns, demonstrable trends,* and *statistically derived profiles. Raw numbers* indicate the actual incidence of victimization. For example, more than 20,000 people are murdered each year in the United States. *Rates* are expressed as fractions or ratios that project the odds, chances, or risks of victimization. The numerator of the fraction counts the number of individuals harmed while the denominator is a standardized base (e.g., 1,000 households, 100,000 people, or 100,000 vehicles). During the early 1990s, about 8 out of every 100,000 Americans were murdered annually. Rates are necessary referents when comparing the incidence of crime in populations of unequal size, such as murders in a big city versus a small town. *Patterns* reflect relationships or connections revealed by the data. For instance, data indicate that murders occur at a higher rate in urban neighborhoods than in rural areas. *Trends* reveal how conditions change as the years roll by. For example, since the early 1960s, the murder rate has increased dramatically. *Profiles* are statistical portraits that yield an impression of what is usual or typical in a given situation. The profile of the typical murder victim is a young man from a city neighborhood.

Using data, victimologists can answer interesting questions. What are the chances of becoming a victim during a single year? Victimization rates indicate the odds. Does crime burden all kinds of people equally? No. Victimization patterns result in *differential rates:* Certain groups are targeted much more often than others. Which unwanted event is a person more likely to experience—an accident, an illness, or a crime? *Comparative rates* enable people to assess the relative threat posed by each kind of misfortune. Is the crime problem as severe in other societies as it is in the United States? *International comparisons* rank countries according to their victimization rates. What are the chances that a person will become a victim during an entire lifetime (not just during a single year)? *Cumulative risks* estimate these odds. Are the dangers of being victimized increasing or decreasing with each passing year? *Trends* highlight changes in rates over time.

Statistics are of crucial importance to social scientists, policy analysts, and decision makers because they replace vague adjectives like "many," "most," and "few" with more precise numbers. Criminologists and victimologists collect their own data and pore over official statistics (gathered and published by government agencies). Yet, as useful and necessary as statistics are, they should always be viewed with a healthy dose of skepticism. Whenever statistics are presented to underscore or clinch some point in an argument, their accuracy and interpretation must be questioned. What is the source of the data? How are key concepts defined? How precise are the measurements? What kinds of inaccuracies could creep into the data? What might the margin of error be? Are different estimates available from other sources? Though some mistakes are honest and unavoidable, it is easy, as the expression goes, to "lie" with statistics, to use these impressive and scientific-sounding numbers to manipulate or mislead the public.

Officials, agencies, and interest groups that release statistics might seek to influence the way decision makers or the general public interpret these numbers for several reasons. A leading reason is to demonstrate that those in charge are doing their jobs well (for example, solving murders or preventing robberies) or, on the contrary, are incompetent and need to be replaced. Statistics might be cited to prove that existing laws and policies are having the intended effects (such as reducing the number of carjackings) or, conversely, to persuade people that new approaches are necessary. Data can be assembled to support the argument that more personnel, equipment, and money are needed to successfully combat crime and serve victims; different figures can be marshaled to convince people that current budgets are adequate or even bloated. Numbers can be used to calm the public down (for example, by reassuring people that almost all robbery victims survive their confrontations without any physical injuries) or to arouse alarm (by emphasizing that some robbers kill victims who surrender their valuables and offer no resistance).

Statistics never "speak for themselves." The numbers must be placed within some context or put into some kind of perspective. Usually, the same numbers can be interpreted quite differently, depending on what "spin" commentators give them—what is stressed and what is downplayed.

Consider the figures summarizing the big picture that are compiled by the Federal Bureau of Investigation and illustrated under the heading of the "Crime Clock," presented every year in the Bureau's authoritative *Uniform Crime Report* (see the discussion below). The crime clock dramatizes the FBI's dire reminder that each hour, the toll is mounting. Every few seconds or minutes, another person becomes a victim. The statistics are computed in a straightforward manner: The number of crimes of each kind (reported to police departments across the country in the past year) is divided into the total number of minutes ($60 \times 24 \times 365 = 525,600$) or seconds ($60 \times 60 \times 24 \times 365 = 31,536,000$) in a year. For instance, during 1993, 24,530 people were murdered; the calculation $525,600/24,530 = 21$ yields a ratio of one murder every 21 minutes (FBI, *Uniform Crime Report,* 1994). (Note that when working with impersonal statistics, as in this exercise in counting corpses, it is easy to forget that each case represents a terrible tragedy and devastating loss for the real people involved.) The latest available crime clock is presented in Figure 2.1.

Even glancing at the crime clock figures, the casual reader cannot miss its frightening message. The chilling landscape it paints of the big picture is one in which serious crimes are all too common. According to the crime clock method of presenting statistics, a steady stream of casualties flows into morgues, hospital

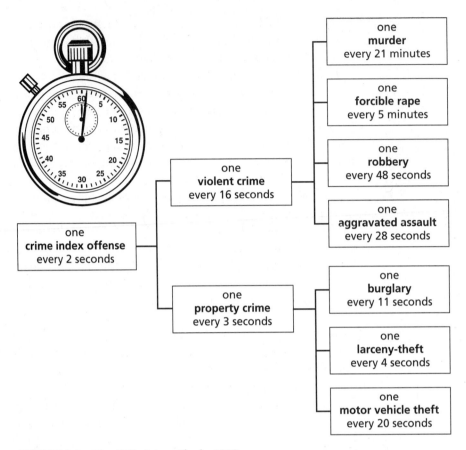

FIGURE 2.1 The FBI's Crime Clock, 1993

Source: Reprinted from the FBI's, *Uniform Crime Report,* 1994.
The FBI adds this note: "The crime clock should be viewed with care. Being the most aggregate representation of *UCR* data, it is designed to convey the annual reported crime experience by showing the relative frequency of occurrence of the index offenses. This mode of display should not be taken to imply a regularity in the commission of the Part I offenses; rather, it represents the annual ratio of crime to fixed time intervals."

emergency rooms, and police stations (and the police surely do not find out about every street crime; see the discussions below and in Chapter 4 about reporting incidents to the police). The reader is reminded by the crime clock that practically every moment—somewhere in the United States—another person is joining the growing ranks of crime victims. For example, the FBI estimated that during 1993:

- Every 4 seconds of each day, some kind of a theft (either a grand or petty larceny) was committed.
- Every 11 seconds, one more family experienced the shock and distress of discovering its home had been burglarized.

- Every 21 seconds, a motorist returned to a parking spot to find that the car had vanished.
- Every 28 seconds, someone was seriously assaulted by an attacker intent on inflicting severe injury.
- Every 47 seconds, another person was held up by robbers.
- Every 5 minutes, a girl or woman was forcibly raped.
- Every 21 minutes, someone was murdered.

Grim statistics such as these make being victimized seem inevitable. Sooner or later, everyone will be harmed in every one of these different ways, or so it appears. The crime clock format implies that it is just a matter of time before disaster strikes. Not surprisingly, this crime clock kind of presentation is frequently used in sales pitches for insurance policies, burglar alarms, or automobile antitheft devices because it sounds so ominous.

However, this "spin" is overly dramatic and pessimistic and, therefore, misleading. What the statistics do not indicate is that many of the incidents were unsuccessful attempts—not completed to the offender's satisfaction (to the victim's relief)—and that many of the crimes (especially burglaries and thefts) were committed against commercial establishments (like stores and warehouses) and not individuals. Most important of all, the crime clock is a misleading way of presenting crime rates because it uses the wrong formula. Instead of seconds and minutes, the other half of the fraction should be "per 100,000 people." Since there are so many millions of people in the United States (and so many homes, cars, and other possessions), the actual chances of any specific person becoming a victim during a single year are rather slim.

While the FBI's crime clock gives the reader the impression that crime is a shockingly frequent and common occurrence, a different set of authoritative figures, circulated by another branch, the Bureau of Justice Statistics (BJS), of the same U.S. Department of Justice, gives the opposite impression. Whereas crime clock statistics are alarming, victimization rates compiled by the BJS seem relatively reassuring. For example, estimates of victimization rates indicate that:

- Only about 6 out of every 1,000 people in the United States are robbed; despite their fears, 994 out of every 1,000 persons will not be threatened or robbed in a year, based on 1993 figures.
- During their entire lifetimes, 700 out of every 1,000 persons now twelve years old probably will never be robbed (if current levels of criminal activity remain constant).
- Each year, accidents and diseases inflict much more suffering (injuries and deaths) than violent crimes do (BJS, 1993, 1994).

Both sets of data from sources in the federal government are trustworthy and reasonably accurate. What differs is the slant, or spin, in the presentation of the data that suggests a particular interpretation. Crime clock figures accentuate the negative and emphasize the number of people harmed per hour, minute, or second, ignoring the huge numbers of individuals who go about their lives without interference. The BJS victimization figures indicate the small numbers who are preyed upon compared to the huge numbers that get away unscathed. Crime statistics, then, are analogous to the classic partially filled glass of water that may be seen as half empty or half full. Clearly, statistics do not and can not "speak for themselves."

Statistics from Official Sources

As highlighted above, there are two main sources of facts and figures about crime and its victims disseminated by the Department of Justice. The first is the Federal Bureau of Investigation's *Uniform Crime Report (UCR)*, subtitled *Crime in the United States* and issued yearly. The second is the *National Crime Victimization Survey (NCVS)* carried out annually by the Census Bureau. The report containing the findings is titled, *Criminal Victimization in the United States* and is published each year by the Bureau of Justice Statistics (BJS).

The *Uniform Crime Report* The FBI's *UCR* is much older and better known than the BJS's *NCVS*. The *UCR* traces its origins back to a committee formed in 1927 by the International Association of Chiefs of Police to develop a standard ("uniform") set of definitions and reporting forms to be used to gather crime statistics. In 1930, the FBI began publishing national crime data based on the records voluntarily sent to Washington by some (but not all) of the nation's police departments. Since 1958, the annual reports have included information drawn from nearly all of the more than 15,000 village, municipal, county, and state police and sheriff's departments across the country that serve about 97 percent of the population.

From its inception in 1930 until the early 1990s, the *UCR* was of limited value to those interested in studying crime victims. Over those decades, the number of incidents, rather than the actual number of victims (except murders, as noted below), were available from the *UCR's* compilation of "index crimes" in Part 1. The index crimes include the range of acts most people think of as "street crime." Four crimes denote acts of violence directed against persons: murder, rape, robbery, and aggravated assault. The other four represent crimes against property: burglary, larceny (thefts of all kinds), motor vehicle theft, and arson (added, at the request of Congress, in 1979). The FBI compiles information about the number of reported cases of each of these eight crimes known to the police, the proportion of each of these types of cases solved by arrest, and the characteristics of the persons arrested for these offenses. Unfortunately, nothing about the victims of these crimes against persons and property, except in murder cases, is requested from the police departments' files. The *UCR* includes descriptions of homicide victims (in terms of sex, age, and race) and their relationships to the offenders (whether strangers or relatives, for example) if detectives can figure this out. In Part 2, the *UCR* furnishes data about the number of people arrested (but not the number of illegal acts committed) for a wide variety of offenses, including some crimes with specific victims, like fraud and vandalism. Information about law enforcement officers assaulted and killed in the line of duty is also published each year.

From a victimologist's point of view, the *UCR*'s method of data collection suffers from several shortcomings that undermine its accuracy and usefulness (see Savitz, 1982; and O'Brien, 1985). First of all, underreporting is a major problem. Because considerable proportions of victims do not inform their local authorities about illegal acts committed against them and their property (see Chapter 4), the FBI's compilation of "crimes known to the police" is invariably lower than the actual (unknown) number of crimes carried out in a jurisdiction. Second, the *UCR* does not provide any information at all about the victims who filed the complaints with the police, except for murders. Third, the *UCR* mixes together reports of attempted crimes (usually not as serious for victims) with completed crimes (in which offenders were successful in achieving their goals). Finally, when computing crime rates, the FBI counts incidents directed against all kinds of targets, without distinguishing between individuals and households, on the one hand, and impersonal entities and commercial establishments, on the other. For example, figures for robberies include bank holdups as well as muggings of elderly persons; and figures for burglaries mix together warehouse break-ins with ransackings of homes.

But the *UCR* is being overhauled and is quickly becoming a more useful source of statistics for victimologists as the FBI converts its data-collection format to a National Incident Based Reporting System (NIBRS). Instead of just eight index offenses, FBI computers now keep track of forty-six Group A offenses derived from twenty-two categories of crimes. In addition to the four crimes against persons and the four against property that were included in Part 1, the new Group A incorporates several crimes with individual victims that formerly were listed in Part 2. These crimes for which victim-oriented data are becoming available include vandalism (property damage and destruction); blackmail (extortion); fraud (swindles and con games); and kidnapping (abduction). Also, details are now being collected about intimidation (categorized as a type of assault); justifiable homicide and negligent manslaughter (classified as types of homicides); and sexual attacks other than rape (forcible sodomy, sexual assault with an object, and forcible fondling).

FBI computers are also storing a number of additional data elements (details) about each incident, including the time and location of the occurrence; the weapons used; any injuries sustained; the kind of property stolen, its value, and whether it was recovered; the age, sex, and race of both the offender and the victim;

and the nature of the relationship between them. Previously, only in cases of homicide were some of these details preserved from police files. Another major change is the abolition of the hierarchy rule in classifying and counting incidents. All the crimes committed during a single incident are recorded, instead of just the most serious offense, making it possible to determine how often one crime evolves into another, such as a robbery culminating with a rape (Reaves, 1993). As more and more local law enforcement agencies and data-collection divisions of the state police phase in the NIBRS, the FBI's *Uniform Crime Report* will increasingly resemble the *National Crime Victimization Survey* report. But one major difference will persist: *UCR* figures will continue to be based solely on crimes reported to the police.

The *National Crime Victimization Survey* Public officials began keeping records about crimes during the 1800s to gauge the "moral health" of society. Then, as now, high crime rates were taken as signs of "social pathology"—indications that something was desperately wrong. The criminologists of the time, as they do now, used crime statistics to build and test theories about the kinds of people breaking the law and the reasons for their lawless deeds. But criminologists, and later victimologists, had deep reservations about the accuracy of the official records kept by the police, the courts, and the prisons. The tallies were known to be incomplete and were suspected of being periodically either inflated or deflated by powerful groups intent on proving some point by manipulating the numbers churned out for public consumption.

Dissatisfaction with official record keeping led criminologists to collect their own data. The first method they used was that of "self-reporting." Small samples of people were promised anonymity if they would "confess" to crimes they had committed. This type of study consistently revealed greater numbers of illegal acts than were indicated by official statistics and confirmed the hypothesis that a lot of lawbreaking occurred among people who were never investigated, arrested, or convicted, especially among members of the middle and upper classes.

After these small self-report studies of criminality had been conducted, the next logical step for criminologists was to survey people from all walks of life about any offenses that may have been committed against them, rather than by them. These studies originally were called "victim surveys," although that label was somewhat misleading, since most respondents answered that they had not been harmed by criminals. But these surveys about past victimizations immediately confirmed one suspicion: A sizable percentage of the individuals in the sample who told interviewers that they had been harmed acknowledged that they had not reported the incident to the police. This additional proof of the existence of unreported crimes undercut confidence in the accuracy of the FBI's *UCR* statistics.

The first national poll (of 10,000 households) was conducted in 1966 for the President's Commission on Law Enforcement and the Administration of Justice. It uncovered a crime rate that was about twice as high as the official *UCR* rate, because many incidents not reported to the authorities were disclosed to the interviewers. In 1972, the federal government initiated a yearly survey of residents in twenty-six large cities; the survey was conducted until 1976. Also in 1972, a national sample of households and businesses was drawn. Surveying the roughly 50,000 businesses was discontinued in 1976, but the interviewing of members of a nationwide panel of households every six months for up to three years has been carried out every year by the Bureau of Justice Statistics. Until 1992, it was known as the *National Crime Survey (NCS)*; it is now called the *National Crime Victimazation Survey (NCVS)*.

At the outset, the idea of surveying people about their recent victimizations was hailed as a major breakthrough by those researchers who distrusted official statistics. But the technique of polling people about the offenses committed against them has not turned out to be the foolproof method for measuring the "actual" crime rate that some victimologists hoped it would be, for a number of reasons (for methodological criticisms, see Levine, 1976; Garofalo, 1981; Skogan, 1981b, 1986; Lehnen and Skogan, 1981; Reiss, 1981, 1986; Schneider, 1981; O'Brien, 1985; Mayhew and Hough, 1988; and Fattah, 1991).

First of all, the findings of this survey, like any other, are reliable only to the extent that the national sample is truly representative of the population of the whole country. If the sample is biased, in terms of age, gender, race, class, geographical mix, or some other important factor, then the projections made about the experiences of the 200 million people who were not questioned will be either too high or too low.

Second, the credibility of what people tell pollsters is a constant subject for debate and a matter of continuing concern in this survey. Some respondents may conceal, while others may exaggerate, or deliberately lie, for a host of personal motives. Experienced detectives filter out from police statistics accounts that do not sound believable (the charges are deemed to be "unfounded," and no further investigation is warranted). But there is no such quality control over what people tell *NCVS* interviewers. (For example, if a person in the sample discusses a crime that was supposedly reported to the police, there is no attempt to check and see if the respondent's recollections coincide with the information in the police files.) Underreporting occurs whenever communication barriers inhibit respondents from discussing incidents with interviewers (that they also refused to bring to the attention of the police). Forgetting ("memory decay") also results in an undercount. Any systematic suppression of facts, such as wives' unwillingness to reveal that their husbands are beating them or teenage girls' reluctance to disclose date rapes, will throw off the survey's projection of the true state of affairs. Furthermore, crimes committed against children under twelve are not probed (so no information is forthcoming about physical and sexual abuse or kidnappings).

Overreporting can occur as well. The police don't accept all reports of crimes at face value, but pollsters must. "Stolen" objects actually may have been misplaced, and an accidentally broken window may be mistaken as evidence of an attempted burglary. Respondents may also commit "forward telescoping," the tendency to believe that a crime occurred within the reference period (the previous six months) and should be counted, when actually it was committed long before and ought to be excluded.

Other, more complicated methodological problems also undermine the accuracy of victimization surveys. The premise that guides this research—to find out the true scope and frequency of crime, ask people if they have been victimized lately—turns out to be deceptively simple and disturbingly costly. Since being victimized within the previous six months is a relatively rare event, tens of thousands of people must be polled to meet the requirements for statistical soundness (estimates derived from small subsamples have large margins of error). The surveys thus become very expensive to carry out.

Over the years, the survey has undergone a number of changes. To cut expenses, the sample size was trimmed down on several occasions from its original size of 72,000 households to about 50,000 households or roughly 100,000 people by the late 1980s. To cut costs further, phone interviews have been progressively substituted for home visits. Before 1980, only 20 percent of the sample were interviewed over the phone; from 1980 to 1986, about 50 percent were called up; by the early 1990s, 75 percent were queried by telephone, some with the assistance of computerized messages.

Several other limitations are worth noting (see Fattah, 1991). First, the survey is person-centered. It is geared toward uncovering the misfortunes of individuals and families (households) but does not attempt to measure offenses committed against organizations or entities, like burglaries or robberies committed against commercial establishments. That undertaking was discontinued in 1977. In addition, the findings of the survey describe the situation in the nation as a whole, but the seriousness of the crime problem in a particular city, county, or state cannot be determined from the limited national sample. Intensive local surveys of residents of twenty-six major metropolitan areas were phased out in the mid-1970s, a few years after they were initiated. Finally, the "actual" figures (x number of robberies committed in 19—) and the rates (y robberies per 1,000 people) are only projections that are derived from the answers given by the respondents in the sample. Therefore, the "true" figures and rates are somewhere within a range (confidence interval); these estimates should always be regarded as approximations, plus or minus a certain correction factor (margin of error) that depends in part upon the size of the sample or subsample (what statisticians consider unavoidable "sampling error").

The *NCVS* has been improved over the years. Beginning in 1986, questions probing several new subject areas were added: whether the victim thought the offender was high on drugs or alcohol at the time of the crime; how the victim behaved, including what self-protective measures the victim took while under attack; what the victim was doing when trouble struck (commuting to work or school, shopping, etc.); and what contacts victims had with agents of the criminal justice system (Taylor, 1989). During the early 1990s, the "state of the art" survey was fine-tuned once again. An advisory panel of criminal justice policymakers, social scientists, victim advocates, and statisticians approved the work of criminologists and survey experts who redesigned some questions to provide cues that could help victims to recall events and details. Also, more explicit questions were added about sexual assaults (involving unwanted or coerced sexual contact) that fell short of the legal definition of rape, and about outbreaks of domestic violence (simple assaults) (Hoover, 1994).

NCVS participants are selected at random and constitute a stratified, multistage cluster sample. They answer questions from a survey that runs over twenty pages. It begins with a series of "screen" questions such as, "During the last six months, did anyone break into your home?" If the respondent answers "Yes," a set of follow-up questions is asked to collect details about the crime. When completed, the survey provides data about the number of violent and property crimes committed against the respondents; the location and date of the incidents; the extent of any injuries or losses they suffered; the nature of any resistance they put up; their descriptions of the offenders; reasons the crime was or was not reported to the police; and the age, sex, race and ethnicity, marital status, income level, education, and place of residence of the individuals disclosing their misfortunes to survey interviewers.

The survey focuses on four crimes of violence (rape, robbery, and two types of assault—simple and aggravated), two kinds of theft against persons (personal larceny with and without contact), and three types of stealing directed at the common property of households (burglary, larceny, and motor vehicle theft).

Drawing on the UCR and the NCVS   For victimologists, the statistics published in the NCVS offer many more possibilities for analysis and interpretation than the data in the UCR. But both official sources have their strengths and weaknesses and can be considered to complement each other.

The UCR is the only source to turn to for information about murder victims (besides public health statistics based on coroners' records, which are also valuable, detailed, and accurate). The UCR is also the place to look up geographical breakdowns, since it provides tallies of index crimes reported to the police in different cities, counties, states, and regions of the country. But the UCR doesn't distinguish between attempted and completed acts, and it doesn't keep track of simple assaults (which includes many wife-beatings, for example).

The NCVS findings can be considered to be more inclusive or complete, since information is recovered about crimes that were not reported to the police. The yearly survey findings are not affected by any changes in the degree of cooperation between the public and the police, or by improvements in recordkeeping by law enforcement agencies, or by temporary police crackdowns. But the *NCVS* has nothing to offer about offenses committed against children under twelve, robberies and burglaries directed at commercial establishments, intentionally set fires (arson), and homicides. Nor are statistics for particular cities and states routinely available.

Even when both sources collect data about the same crimes, the findings may not be strictly comparable. For instance, the definitions of certain crimes (such as rape) can vary. The FBI computes incidents per 100,000 people; the BJS calculates incidents per 1,000 people, or, for property crimes, per 1,000 households. So, when making comparisons, some minor statistical conversions are necessary. Further, *NCVS* findings are estimates and are subject to sampling error, which means that the true value lies within a range (confidence interval), plus or minus a little correction factor (standard error), of the reported value (BJS, 1994). Finally, *UCR* statistics for a given year usually are released to the public several months ahead of *NCVS* findings.

USING OFFICIAL DATA TO ANALYZE THE INTERACTION BETWEEN VICTIMS AND OFFENDERS

The first criminologists attracted to victimology were drawn to the study of the interaction between victims and offenders. They were especially curious about the relationship between the two parties in cases of interpersonal violence or theft. For example, they wondered whether the victim and the offender previously knew each other (as intimates, adversaries, or casual acquaintances), and whether the victim resisted the attack in any way.

Murderers and Their Victims

Murder is the most terrible crime of all. The damage visited upon the victim cannot be undone. The loss suffered by the victim's survivors is total and irreparable. But the social reaction to the taking of a person's life is determined by a number of factors, including the offender's state of mind, the victim's possible contribution to the escalation of hostilities, and the social standing of each party.

Homicide is defined as the willful (nonnegligent) killing of one human being by another. Deaths caused by carelessness, accidents, and suicide are not classified as homicides. Acts of self-defense and failed attempts to kill (which turn out to be aggravated assaults) are also excluded from the body counts. The law takes into account whether the killing was carried out intentionally (malice aforethought), with deliberation (pros and cons weighed), and with premeditation (advance planning). These first-degree murders carry the most severe punishments, including execution or life imprisonment without parole, depending on the state. Homicides committed in the heat of passion, when the perpetrator intended to kill the victim (malice at the moment, but with no advanced planning); or in response to the victim's provocations; or because of reckless disregard for human life or gross negligence, are classified as either second-degree murders, voluntary manslaughter, or involuntary manslaughter. Offenders convicted of these categories of slayings are punished less severely. Some types of killings have special names: vehicular homicide (one caused by the driver of a car); justifiable homicide (a legally excusable act of self-protection); infanticide (the slaying of a child by a parent); parricide (the slaying of a parent by a child); domestic homicide (murder of a spouse); serial killing (several or more victims dispatched one at a time, over an extended period); mass murder (the killing of several people at the same time and place); felony murder (a killing committed as the culmination of another crime, like robbery, rape, or kidnapping); and contract killing (a professional "hit" for a fee) (see Holmes, 1994).

Relationships between Murderers and Their Victims The issue of the victim's prior relationship with the offender is of particular interest in murder cases. Although the *NCVS* has nothing to offer victimologists about the crime of murder, the FBI's *UCR* contains data summarized from *Supplementary Homicide Reports* based on police investigations. Information from public health officials, such as coroners' offices and medical examiners, also enables researchers to reconstruct what happened during the final moments of the lives of many homicide victims.

The specific relationship between the victim and the offender can be broadly categorized to shed light on certain patterns within slayings. Three main categories can be distinguished: The victim and the offender were members of the same family (nuclear or extended); were acquaintances or even friends (including a girlfriend or a boyfriend) before the tragedy; or they were complete strangers brought together by fate. According to police investigations compiled in the FBI's *UCR*s during the early 1990s, in the most common situation (ranging from 34 to 38 percent), the murder victim was killed by a friend or acquaintance. Killings of one family member by another fluctuated from 12 to 14 percent. Slayings by strangers accounted for about 14 or 15 percent of all the cases for which the relationship could be surmised by detectives. The proportion of homicides that were not only unsolved but also "of unknown relationship" hovered between 35 and 39 percent. Combining the percentage of homicides perpetrated by acquaintances with the percentage committed by the victims' family members confirms the old adage that "a person is more likely to be killed by someone he or she knows than by a total stranger."

However, some of the murders categorized as "of unknown relationship," are suspected to be killings committed by complete strangers. Studies conducted by researchers seem to indicate that the proportion of this category of murder is rising, although this trend is not clear from the FBI figures, probably because of the large percentage of cases the police cannot solve (Riedel, 1987).

Most murders arise from outbursts of impulsive violence. In a study of nearly 13,000 homicides committed in Chicago from 1965 to 1981, researchers determined that almost 70 percent of the killings started out as a heated argument between the victim and offender. About 17 percent of the murders began as robberies, but less than 2 percent arose out of burglaries, rapes, or contract killings. The remaining 12 percent or so of the cases were of unknown origin, according to police reconstructions of the events leading up to the crimes (Block, Felson, and Block, 1985).

Some murders that arise from conflicts can be viewed as the outcome of a sequence of events in a transaction. The initial incident might be a personal affront, perhaps something as minor as a slur or gesture. Both the offender and the victim contribute to the escalation of a "character contest." As the confrontation unfolds, at least one party, but usually both, attempts to "save face" at the other's expense by not backing down. The battle turns into a deadly showdown if both participants are steeped in a tradition that favors violence as the way to settle bitter disputes (Luckenbill, 1977).

The relationship between the victim and the offender greatly influences how the case is handled within the criminal justice system. When victims are killed by complete strangers, the prosecution is much more inclined to press serious charges. If convicted, such offenders are also more likely to receive severe prison sentences. In contrast, in cases of homicides arising out of domestic disputes or quarrels between friends or acquaintances, prosecutors are inclined to lodge charges that are less serious than first-degree murder. When persons who were friends and acquaintances of the slain victim are convicted, they tend to receive lighter sentences. Perpetrators who were related to the dead victim usually receive even more lenient treatment. These patterns, discovered in a study of about 270 homicides in Houston, can be summarized as follows: The severity of the penalty for homicide varies inversely with the closeness of the victim–offender relationship (as closeness increases, severity decreases, and vice versa) because of the way police, prosecutors, judges, and juries interpret and apply factors like malice, state of mind, intent, and self-defense (Lundsgaarde, 1977).

An analysis of murder cases adjudicated during 1988 determined that about 75 percent of all defendants and 44 percent of all victims had been arrested for or convicted of some offense in the past. Although most of the victims and offenders were poor young urban men, only a small percentage of those who died were gang members killed in a turf dispute or as a result of a drive-by shooting. Only 4 percent of the slayings were believed to be premeditated, according to this survey of prosecutions carried out in the nation's 75 largest counties (Dawson, 1993).

During the early 1990s, the majority of murders were committed with firearms (rising from 64 percent in 1990 to just about 70 percent in 1993). Most of the gunfire came from revolvers, with shotguns and rifles taking a much smaller toll.

It has become evident in recent years that illicit drugs play a role in many victim–offender altercations leading to murder. Several distinct scenarios ending in someone's death are possible: clashes between rival drug sellers (fights over turf); conflicts between buyers and sellers (quarrels over high prices, money owed, misrepresentation of the contents, and scams surrounding inferior quality); and robberies of dealers or customers. Drug-related murders falling into these categories, taken together, can add up to significant proportions in certain metropolitan areas. In a study of over one hundred robberies that led to murders in Chicago during 1983, researchers found circumstantial evidence that the killing involved drugs in about 16 percent of the cases—either the dead person was a known drug dealer or abuser, or the offender was a drug dealer or abuser, or traces of controlled substances were found at the scene of the crime (Zimring and Zuehl, 1986). A study of more than 570 murders committed in Manhattan turned up even greater proportions of drug-related homicides: 38 percent of the male victims and 14 percent of the female victims were believed to be involved in the street drug scene (Tardiff, Gross, and Messner, 1986). Police experts estimated that roughly 40 percent of all killings in New York City were drug related in 1987 (James, 1988) and 1988 ("Homicide Also Up," 1988). In Washington, D.C., drug-related murders contributed to the overall homicide rate even more strikingly during the late 1980s. In 1985, the Office of Criminal Justice in the District of Columbia estimated that 21 percent of all murders (in which the motive was known to the police) were drug related (either the coroner determined that the victim was under the influence of drugs, or drug traces or paraphernalia were discovered at the crime scene, or the killing occurred in a drug hangout such as a "shooting gallery" or "crack house"). This proportion rose to 34 percent the following year; jumped to 51 percent in 1987; soared to 80 percent in 1988; and climbed to 85 percent during the first part of 1989 (Berke, 1989; Martz, et al., 1989). For the country as a whole, about 16 percent of all victims died under drug-related circumstances during 1988, according to a survey of cases prosecuted in the nation's 75 largest counties (Dawson, 1993).

However, using a restricted definition of "narcotics related" that counted only homicides tied to trafficking or manufacturing activities (but not, for instance, arising from armed robberies), the FBI's *UCR* reported much lower estimates. In 1986, the *UCR* reported that about 4 percent of all murders were tied to narcotics felonies; the figure rose to more than 7 percent in 1989 and then dropped to less than 6 percent in 1992 (Timrots and Snyder, 1994). Of course it is possible that the attention paid to drug-related slayings reflects a desire by various interest groups to prove something about the "war on drugs" (either that it is failing or succeeding, or that it is absolutely necessary, or that it causes more harm than good). The motive can cause definitions of "drug related" to expand or contract and investigations to be carried out more or less thoroughly, in order to "produce" the desired statistics about this aspect of the victim–offender relationship.

Alcohol is even more consistently implicated than drugs in interpersonal violence leading to fatal outcomes. Reports from medical examiners in eight cities in 1978 revealed that the percent of corpses testing positive for alcohol ranged from a low of 38 percent to a high of 62 percent (Riedel and Mock, 1985). In a study of nearly 5,000 homicides committed in Los Angeles between 1970 and 1979, researchers reported that alcohol was detected in the blood of nearly half the bodies autopsied. The blood-alcohol content in about 30 percent of these 5,000 murder victims was high enough to classify the person as "intoxicated" by legal standards at the time of death. The typical alcohol-related slaying involved a young man who was stabbed to death on a weekend, in a bar, as the result of a fight with an acquaintance or friend (Goodman et al., 1986).

Robbers and Their Victims

Robbers are among the most feared and hated of all street criminals. Their offense combines stealing with extortion or outright violence, so it carries some of the stiffest prison sentences permissible under law. Throughout history, bandits were considered much more interesting than their victims, and their exploits were often romanticized. The highwaymen of Robin Hood's band, the pirates who plundered ships laden with treasure, the frontier outlaws who ambushed stagecoaches and trains, and the gangsters who held up banks during the Great Depression—all were the subjects of stories and songs sympathetic to, or at least understanding of, the impulse that drove their dramatic deeds. But now the glitter has largely faded, and in its place is the image of the mugger or gunman as a vicious thug, a cruel predator, and an exploiter of weakness, whose random violence casts a shadow over everyday life. This decline in the popularity of robbers has sparked renewed concern for their victims.

Since robbery victims live to tell about their experiences, more detailed data exist about them than about people who were murdered. Some information about robberies that were reported to the police appears in the FBI's *UCR,* but the data describes the incidents and the arrestees, not the victims. The BJS's *NCVS* can be tapped to find out about "who, where, when," losses, injuries, stolen property recovery rates, and reactions during the confrontations.

Interactions between Robbers and Their Victims All victim–offender interactions can be described in terms of a set of complementary roles. Each person plays a part. Robbers are the initiators and aggressors; victims are usually passive, at least at the start. But targeted individuals can refuse to play their "assigned" role, reject the "script," and overturn the scenario imposed on them. The intended prey might even gain the upper hand, switch roles, and disrupt the interaction or end it in a way dreaded by the aggressors. In other words, the incident may or may not proceed according to the offenders' plan.

Successful or completed robberies are those face-to-face confrontations in which perpetrators take something of value directly from victims against their will, either by force or by threats of violence. The law considers armed robberies more serious than unarmed ones ("strong-arm robberies," "muggings," or "yokings"). Successful robbers, whether armed or unarmed, must be skilled at what has been termed "target manipulation" or "victim management" (Letkemann, 1973).

When analyzed as a transaction based on "instrumental coercion" (applying force to accomplish a goal), a typical robbery proceeds through five stages, or phases: planning, establishing copresence, developing co-orientation, transferring valuables, and leaving (Best and Luckenbill, 1982). During the planning stage, the offenders prepare to strike by choosing accomplices, weapons, sites, and getaway routes. The robbers also choose their targets. They look for certain desirable characteristics, such as valuable possessions, vulnerability to attack, relative powerlessness to resist, and isolation from potential protectors. Strangers are preferred because they will have greater difficulty in providing descriptions to the police and in identifying suspects from pictures or lineups.

During the second phase of the interaction, the offenders establish copresence by moving into striking distance. The robbers try not to arouse the victims' suspicion or to provoke either unmanageable opposition or fright and flight. Some offenders rely on speed and stealth to rush up to unsuspecting persons. Others employ deceit to trick people into letting down their guard.

When the transaction enters the third stage, the robbers announce their intentions to dominate the situation and exploit their advantages. They order victims to surrender valuables, and they demand compliance. Their intended prey either acquiesce or contest the robbers' move to take charge, depending on their assessment of the robbers' punitive resources (ability to inflict injury). Robbers who fail to develop co-orientation (secure compliance) through threats may resort to violence to subdue, incapacitate, or intimidate their targets.

If the robbers successfully gain and maintain the upper hand, the interaction moves into its fourth phase. Victims are searched, and their valuables are seized. But the interaction is terminated prematurely (from the offenders' point of view) if the individuals stubbornly resist, have no valuables, are unexpectedly rescued, or escape.

The fifth and final stage is marked by the robbers' attempts to break off the relationship at a time and under conditions of their choosing. As they prepare to leave the scene, they may inflict additional injuries in order to prevent interference with the getaway. Or, they may issue threats about the dangers of pursuing them or reporting the crime to the authorities (Best and Luckenbill, 1982).

This breakdown of robbery "transactions" into distinct stages and discrete steps facilitates the recognition of possible outcomes. Targeted individuals may or may not suffer financial losses from stolen (or damaged) property. Robbers may or may not injure their victims. Injured persons may or may not need medical attention and hospital care. The intended prey may or may not be able to resist their aggressors' advances and prevent successful completions. And some victims who resist may be killed in incidents that escalate from robbery to homicide.

Findings from the *NCVS* That Shed Light on Robberies Respondents in the sample who confide that they have been recently robbed provide *NCVS* interviewers with a wealth of data. They describe the people who robbed them and the weapons they used, and they discuss whether the robbers got what they were after, where and when the crimes took place, if they resisted, whether they got hurt, and if so, how seriously. These answers from the individuals in the sample are analyzed to provide reasonably accurate estimates of the experiences of the 1.3 million Americans over the age of eleven who were robbed during 1992.

The primary motive behind robbery is theft. But offenders do not always get what they want. A little more than one-third of all robberies were unsuccessful attempts to steal cash, valuables, or both. Failed attempts comprised about a third of the roughly 14.7 million robberies reported to the *NCVS* interviewers from 1973 to 1984, as well (Harlow, 1987), so the success to failure ratio of 2:1 seems to persist. For the roughly two-thirds of victims who were robbed of money or possessions, the mean loss averaged out to about $555 in 1992, a figure skewed, however, by a relatively small number of huge hauls. If the median, instead of the arithmetic mean, is calculated, then in about half of all robberies, the victims lost $90 or less (Klaus, 1994).

In 1992, victims told survey interviewers that about 80 percent of the individuals who held them up were complete strangers that they had never seen before. Half of the incidents involved multiple offenders (two or more persons working together). Almost all the perpetrators were males (96 percent), and most (62 percent) were younger than twenty-nine years old. A little more than half (56 percent) were described as black. About 25 percent of all assailants were suspected of being high at the time of the crime, either on drugs or alcohol. The majority of the incidents (59 percent) took place between 6 P.M. and 6 A.M. As for the scene of the crime, of all the categories listed on the questionnaire, the one cited most often (40 percent) was "on the street" (but not near home or a friend's home); other common locations were in a parking lot or garage (14 percent); near home (11 percent); at home or in the immediate vicinity (10 percent); and in a yard, park, playground, or field (6 percent). Very few victims were robbed on school grounds, on public transportation or in transit stations, or in bars or nightclubs. In answer to the question about what they were doing at the moment of the confrontation, victims most frequently responded was that they were engaged in a leisure activity away from home (29 percent); another sizable category was "shopping or running errands" (11 percent). Only small percentages told interviewers they were on their way to school or work, or were attending school or at work, when the robbers struck.

A little more than half (54 percent) of all the incidents were armed robberies. In about half of these armed robberies, offenders used knives, blunt instruments, and other weapons to intimidate and subdue their targets. The remainder (47 percent) involved a gun (mostly revolvers), so overall, victims faced the prospect of being shot in about 25 percent of all robberies in 1992. Robbers brandished firearms in only about 20 percent of the incidents from 1973 to 1984 (Harlow, 1987; BJS, 1994d).

Robbers may hurt their victims for a number of reasons. They may do so initially to intimidate the target into submission. They may become violent during the holdup in reaction to any perceived resistance, noncooperation, or stalling. Offenders may relish taking advantage of a helpless person or may seize the opportunity to show off to accomplices. Injuring victims may be a sign of anger, disappointment in the haul, scorn, contempt, sadism, fear, or loss of self-control. It may also be instrumental: Wounding victims can render them incapable of later identifying the robbers, pursuing them, or even calling for help. Violent outbursts at the end of the interaction may be intended to shock, stun, or preoccupy the victims, their associates, and any bystanders so that they will hesitate to call the police.

Despite all these possible motives for harming victims, robbers usually don't inflict injuries, however. About 36 percent of all robbery victims were wounded in 1992 (up a little from 33 percent of all cases in 1973–1984). (Some who escaped injuries were grabbed, shoved, and otherwise roughed up.) Of this 36 percent who were injured, most experienced minor wounds, such as cuts, scratches, bruises, and swellings. About one in twelve (8 percent) suffered serious injuries, such as broken bones, lost teeth, loss of consciousness, or gunshot wounds that required medical care in a hospital emergency room. Just 3 percent of all robbery victims were hurt so badly that they had to remain in a hospital overnight or longer; 10 percent missed at least one day of work because of the consequences of the crime (BJS, 1994b).

The issue of resistance to attack is one of the more interesting subjects probed by interviewers carrying out the *National Crime Victimization Survey*. A number of different self-protective strategies are covered in the questionnaire, under two headings: forceful means of repelling an attacker (including brandishing and perhaps using a gun, knife, or other weapon, or fighting back bare-handed to resist or capture the assailant); and nonviolent strategies (such as trying to escape, screaming to frighten off the offender and summon help, and threatening or reasoning with the offender). Of course, during a confrontation a victim might resort to more than one of these strategies. Combining the different kinds of self-protective measures, nearly 60 percent of robbery victims tried to defend themselves in 1992. The most common strategy was trying to physically resist or even capture the offender, followed by trying to run away or hide, trying to reason with or scare off the offender, or shouting for help. Fighting back bare-handed was also a common reaction, but drawing a weapon in self-defense was rare (BJS, 1994b).

According to the data, victims who were injured during a robbery were more likely to have taken some self-protective measures, as were victims who thwarted the robbers' intentions (the acts of theft were not successfully completed). Since the survey data are cross-sectional (representing a snapshot at one point in time), they do not reveal whether victims who ended up injured started out by acquiescing to the robbers' demands or whether they resisted right from the outset. The conjunction between injury and resistance also depended on a number of other situational factors, especially the presence of weapons, of other robbers, and of other victims. Several researchers have tried to make sense of the complicated web of interconnections (two- and three-variable relationships) between the weapons brandished, the outcome in regard to theft, forms of resistance, and extent of injury.

According to a study of cases reported to the *NCVS* between 1973 and 1979 (Cook, 1987), certain types of victims were more likely to be injured than other types, depending in part on the kind of robbers they faced (armed or unarmed, alone or in groups) and the form of resistance, if any, they offered (violent versus nonviolent tactics). Victims were more likely to be physically harmed and need medical attention if they were attacked by three or more robbers or by a robber who was not a stranger to them, were alone when accosted, and were older than fifty-five.

The type of weapon wielded by the robber was the most significant factor determining whether or not a victim was wounded or killed. Although gunmen slay their victims three times as often as knife-wielding robbers, a different pattern prevails when death is not the outcome. In several studies, researchers have concluded that an inverse relationship exists between the likelihood of victim injury and the use of deadly weaponry; that is, victims are more likely to be hurt by unarmed robbers. Apparently, weaponless "muggings," "yokings," or "strong-arm" robberies often begin with an unprovoked attack meant to demonstrate the aggressors' determination to prevail. Conversely, the victim might resist an unarmed robber until the robber uses force. Armed robberies that begin with the brandishing of a gun or knife are less likely to escalate into bloodshed because the threat of the deadly weapon is sufficient to convince most victims to surrender without a struggle (Cook, 1987).

Different resistance strategies also lead to different outcomes. People targeted by robbers must make a split-second decision—whether to flee, fight, or otherwise resist, or to cooperate. A study of nearly 3,000 stranger-to-stranger incidents reported to *NCVS* interviewers between 1973 and 1979 yielded these observations: Nonforceful resistance (which included reasoning with, arguing with, and verbally threatening the offender, as well as yelling for help or trying to run away) was statistically linked to both lower monetary losses and reduced levels of physical attack and injury. Forceful resistance (fighting back, bare-handed or with a weapon), though also associated with lower property losses, was tied to higher injury rates (Block and Skogan, 1986). Similarly, an analysis of over 4,500 incidents reported to interviewers from 1979 to 1985 came to these conclusions: Any form of self-protective tactic reduced the chances that the robber would get away with any valuables. Armed resistance was a more effective form of self-protection than unarmed resistance, and drawing a gun was the most effective response of all, in terms of thwarting the robbers' intentions and avoiding injuries, but it was very rarely attempted. Fighting back without a weapon and calling for help (to attract attention and scare off the attacker) tend to result in victim wounds. Facing a gun inhibits resistance, but since the weapon is rarely fired, most victims wind up losing possessions but escaping injury (Kleck and DeLone, 1993).

Starting in 1986, items were added to the *National Crime Victimization Survey* that inquired about how victims responded to their attackers' initiatives and how they judged the consequences of their self-protective measures. In 1992, recalling the incident, 55 percent of all robbery victims told *NCVS* interviewers that their self-protective actions probably helped their situation, whereas about 9 percent concluded their reactions hurt them; in the opinion of the remainder of the sample, their actions both helped and hurt, neither helped nor hurt, or had an unknown effect on their offenders. Of those who believed their actions helped, nearly half judged that the beneficial impact was to minimize or totally avoid injuries to themselves. The rest answered that their resistance served to ward off their attackers, to facilitate their escape, and to safeguard the property the offender was after. The most frequent unwanted outcome (59 percent) cited by those who felt, in retrospect, that their actions had worsened their plight was that their self-protective measures had made their offenders angrier and more aggressive (BJS, 1994).

It is tempting but dangerous to offer people advice based on the successes and failures of previous robbery victims. The outcomes of robberies in terms of injury and loss are determined by a complex web of interactions among offenders' initiatives (choice of weapon and target), victims' responses (willingness to resist), offenders' responses (willingness to escalate or to give up and disengage), bystanders' reactions (willingness to intervene), and other situational factors (number of offenders, number of victims, location, time, value of property at risk). Furthermore, the sequence of events cannot be reconstructed from cross-sectional survey data. It cannot be established, for example, whether the victims resisted forcefully before, during, or after the robbers physically attacked them. As a result, no simple rules of thumb or successful stratagems can be derived from the data.

Since some studies seem to indicate that victims who comply with robbers' demands are more likely to escape injury, criminal justice officials tend to recommend trading valuables for personal safety. Some experts suggest that potential robbery targets should always carry sums of money they feel they can afford to lose and should hand over these "crime taxes" immediately to appease robbers' demands. But others assert that such strategies deny victims an active role in efforts to control crime. These critics maintain that, instead of encouraging crime, victims can deter would-be robbers by using various strategies, tempered by circumstances, to make robbery attempts unprofitable, frustrating, and dangerous for aggressors (see Ziegenhagen and Brosnan, 1985; Kleck and DeLone, 1993).

CALCULATING VICTIMIZATION RATES

The benefit of survey research is that it eliminates the necessity of attempting the impossible: to interview everyone to find out how they fared in the past year. The experiences of the over 100,000 individuals in the randomly selected sample (as long as they closely mirror the population as a whole in terms of important variables linked to victimization, like sex, age, race, income, and location of residency) can be generalized to derive estimates of the approximate number of persons in the entire country of over 200 million who were robbed, raped, beaten, or suffered thefts.

Based on the incidents disclosed by members of the sample to survey interviewers, the Bureau of Justice Statistics projected that in 1992, the grand total of violent crimes committed against individuals and property crimes carried out against individuals and households (but not commercial establishments) added up to roughly 33,649,340 incidents throughout the nation. Of these, about 6,621,000 were robberies, rapes, and assaults. The approximately 12,211,000 other crimes directed at individuals were thefts—larcenies with or without contact between the offenders and their victims. An additional 14,817,000 acts of stealing were aimed against households that year—burglaries, household larcenies, and motor vehicle thefts (BJS, 1994b).

Two useful sets of numbers can be derived from these projections of the total number of victimizations occurring in a single year throughout the nation. The first set indicates approximately how many people "join the ranks of victims annually." For example, each year another 140,930 persons (mostly females) are raped; roughly 1,225,000 individuals are robbed; over 5,250,000 people are assaulted, more than 150,000 women have their purses snatched, and about 330,000 men and women have their pockets picked. (In each category, some of these crimes were completed while other incidents were unsuccessful attempts. See the figures for "completed" and "attempted" in Table 2.1.) The second set of figures reveals the proportional breakdown or relative percentage of each kind of crime. Personal thefts (overwhelmingly of unguarded property, plus contact thefts like purse snatchings and pocket pickings) come in first as the most common type of victimization, at 36 percent (12,211,000/33,649,340). Another category of thefts, household larcenies, is rather common, at 24 percent. Assaults are the most frequent expression of violence, making up 16 percent of all the estimated incidents during 1992. Burglaries comprised 14 percent of all the incidents disclosed to *NCVS* interviewers, motor vehicle thefts 6 percent, robberies 4 percent, and rapes just 0.4 percent. These estimates of the actual numbers show that most of the street crimes committed each year are thefts, whether of personal possessions or of household property (80 percent), rather than acts of violence (20 percent).

Discovering How Often People Are Harmed

By now, one problem should be obvious: huge numbers are difficult to grasp, remember, analyze, and compare. For these reasons, crime rates, or, more precisely, *victimization rates,* are calculated and disseminated by the BJS in its yearly report of *NCVS* findings. The rates indicate just how common or rare a particular kind of crime is. The rates are computed by constructing ratios whose numerators equal the number of victimizations per year, projected from the survey results, and whose denominators equal the number of persons or households in the nation. These ratios are then converted into decimals by dividing the denominators into the numerators. The tiny decimals are then changed back into fractions with standard denominators of 1,000.

For example, in calculating the victimization rate for crimes of violence committed in 1992, the 6,621,000 completed or attempted robberies, rapes, and assaults constitute the numerator. The denominator, 206,414,000, equals the U.S. population estimate of individuals twelve years old or older provided by the U.S. Census. Dividing the denominator into the numerator yields the decimal 0.03208. Multiplying this decimal by 1,000 produces a violent crime victimization rate of 32.1 persons for every 1,000 people (see Table 2.1).

Victimization rates are easier to use and recall than the huge numbers of incidents and victimized people. For example, it can be seen at a glance in Table 2.1 that assaults are committed much more often than robberies. Household larcenies turn out to be the most common of all victimizations disclosed to interviewers, touching the lives of about 8 percent (83 per 1,000, or 8.3 per 100) of all families a year. The definition of household larcenies includes all thefts and attempted thefts of property and cash from a residence by persons invited in (such as maids, repairmen, or party guests, as opposed to burglars) or thefts of possessions from a home's immediate vicinity (such as lawn furniture) by trespassers. Completed car thefts mar the year for 12.5 households out of every 1,000. Rapes appear to be extremely rare, afflicting less than one person (male or female) in a thousand, a year. (See Table 2.1 for the major categories, working definitions, typical examples, and findings of the 1992 survey.)

TABLE 2.1 *National Crime Victimization Survey:* Definitions and Rates

CRIME	DEFINITION	EXAMPLE	ESTIMATED NUMBER OF INCIDENTS	RATE PER 1,000 PEOPLE, 1992
Crimes of violence against persons				
Rape	"Carnal knowledge" through the use of force or threats. Includes attempts; excludes statutory rape of minors.	A woman thwarts a sexual assault by a stranger. A teenage girl is overpowered by her boyfriend and compelled to have intercourse with him.	140,930	0.7 overall 0.2 completed 0.5 attempted
Robbery	Completed or attempted theft, directly from a person, of property or cash, by force or threat of force, with or without a weapon.	A man's wallet is taken by a knife-wielding bandit. A stranger grabs a woman and pulls at her gold chain but is scared away by her screams.	1,225,510	5.9 overall 3.9 completed 2.0 attempted
Aggravated assault	Attack with a weapon, whether or not the victim is injured. Attack without a weapon that results in serious injury. Includes attempts with weapons.	A man is hit by a chair in a bar and suffers a broken leg. A husband beats his wife unconscious with his fists.	1,848,530	9.0 overall 3.2 with injury 5.8 attempted
Simple assault	Attack without a weapon, resulting in minor injury. Includes attempts.	A 13-year-old boy is pushed to the ground by another youth in a quarrel.	3,406,160	16.5 overall 4.4 with injury 12.1 attempted
Total			6,621,140*	32.1 crimes of personal violence
Crimes of theft against persons				
Personal larceny with contact	Theft of a purse, wallet, or cash directly from the victim, by stealth but without force or threat of harm. Includes attempts.	A man's wallet is picked; a woman's pocket-book is snatched from her grip.	484,810	2.3 overall 0.7 purse snatching 1.6 pocket pickings
Personal larceny without contact	Theft or attempted theft of cash or possessions from any place other than the victim's home or its immediate vicinity.	A bicycle is stolen from a rack; clothing is taken from a parked car.	11,726,020	56.8 overall
Total			12,210,830	59.2 crimes of personal theft*

CRIME	DEFINITION	EXAMPLE	ESTIMATED NUMBER OF INCIDENTS	RATE PER 1,000 PEOPLE, 1992
Crimes of theft against households				
Burglary	Unlawful entry, by force if necessary, of a residence for the purpose of theft. Includes attempts.	A teenager slashes a screen and breaks into a garage to steal tools.	4,757,420	48.9 overall 16.5 forcible entries 22.4 unlawful entries without force 10.0 attempted forcible entries
Household larceny	Theft or attempted theft of property or cash from a residence or its immediate vicinity, by a person who is not trespassing.	A maid steals jewelry from a drawer; a guest at a party steals the host's rare coin collection.	8,101,150	83.2 overall 77.9 completed 5.3 attempted
Motor vehicle theft	Stealing or taking without authorization any motorized vehicle. Includes attempts.	A driver finds that the ignition of his car was tampered with; a snowmobile is stolen.	1,958,780	20.1 overall* 12.5 completed 7.6 attempted
Total			14,817,360*	152.2 crimes of household theft

*Subcategories may not exactly add up to overall rates because of rounding.
Source: BJS, 1994.

EXAMINING VICTIMIZATION TRENDS

Searching for Crime Waves

Trends refer to changes that occur over time. Sharp increases in rates over several years are commonly known as "crime waves." Downward trends, indicating reductions in the level of criminal activity, can occur as well. In bringing the big picture into focus, a key question is whether the situation is becoming worse or getting better.

From the early 1960s into the 1970s, the country was in the grip of a major crime wave, according to the FBI's *UCRs*, which were the only sources of nationwide data during those years. Since 1973, the findings of the BJS's *National Crime Victimization Survey* have served as an additional set of figures to monitor the upward and downward shifts in victimization rates.

Is the United States still in the midst of a crime wave? Few politicians or journalists advance the argument that the sharp deterioration in public safety is over. But what do the statistics derived from the yearly surveys reveal? Are victimization rates leveling off, or even dropping? Graphs are particularly useful for spotting trends at a glance. The graphs shown in Figure 2.2a and 2.2b depict the estimated rates for the violent crimes of robbery and aggravated assault from 1973 to 1992.

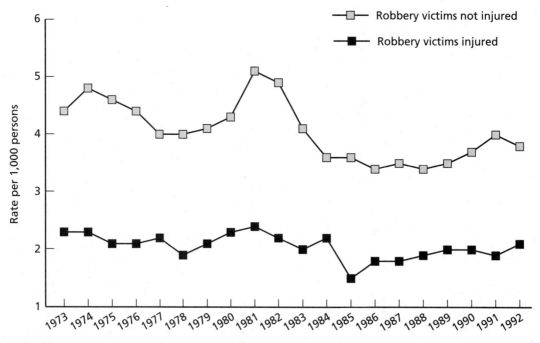

FIGURE 2.2a   Trends in Robbery Rates, *NCVS*, 1973–1992

Note: Includes both attempted and completed robberies.

Source: BJS, 1994a.

As for robberies, the graph in Figure 2.2a shows that no dramatic changes have taken place over time. The line depicting the rate of robberies in which victims sustained no injuries shows that there were a little more than 4 uninjured robbery victims for every 1,000 people in 1973 and fewer than 4 in 1992, with 1981 peaking at around 5. The line indicating the estimated rate for robberies in which victims were wounded shows less fluctuation from year to year, hovering around 2 per 1,000 people per year. Mathematically, robbers use force and hurt their victims in about one-third (2 out of 6 [4+2]) of all confrontations.

Robbery and murder are the two crimes that continue to be the focus of this chapter, but a look at aggravated assault would be appropriate at this point. By definition, aggravated assaults result in serious injuries or involve the use or threatened use of a dangerous or deadly weapon. Therefore, some aggravated assaults are attempted murders in which the victims barely survived (a bullet missed its mark, a knife wound was not fatal, emergency medical care saved a life). The graph in Figure 2.2b shows that aggravated assaults slightly declined in frequency over the twenty-year period. In the early 1970s, about 10 people in every 1,000 were badly injured or threatened with serious harm. By 1983, the rate of aggravated assaults hit a low of 8; by 1992 the rate was close to 9.

To conclude from this analysis of trends in robberies and aggravated assaults that the "worst is over" would be overly optimistic. However, neither of these

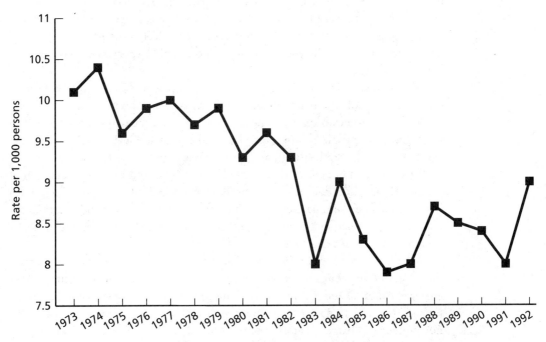

FIGURE 2.2b Trends in Aggravated Assault Rates, *NCVS*, 1973–1992

Note: Includes both attempted attacks with weapons and completed acts causing serious injuries
Source: BJS, 1994a.

crimes is "getting out of hand" (for the nation as a whole, although specific communities may experience serious upsurges in lawlessness). But these crimes are not being effectively brought under control either. The graphs could be interpreted as indicating that violent crime rates have stabilized, or plateaued, at historically high (and publicly intolerable) levels. As for the future, another crime wave could break out, or the slow rate of improvement might continue.

Households Touched by Crime   To further clarify the big picture about the impact and seriousness of street crime in American society, the findings of the *National Crime Victimization Survey* can be analyzed with the help of an additional statistical indicator called "households touched by crime." The rationale for defining households, in addition to individuals, as a unit of analysis is that the effects of crime are not limited to the lives of the immediate victims. Their families suffer, too, sharing their pain, hardships, sense of violation, and fears. Other people living with the victims also experience to some degree the injuries, economic losses, inconveniences, and feelings of vulnerability.

A household is counted as "touched" by crime if once or more during the year any member is a victim of rape, robbery, assault, or personal larceny, with or without contact, or if the living unit's common property is lost due to a burglary, household larceny, or motor vehicle theft (unsuccessful attempts are counted). For example, a family in which a parent was robbed at gunpoint has been touched by crime, as has a household in which a child's tricycle was stolen from the driveway. (Note that a household is counted as touched regardless of the number of crimes committed against it; the average touched household experiences between one and two incidents in a year.)

"Households touched by crime" is the most inclusive of any crime statistic. It combines, or pools, the experiences of all its members. (About a fourth of households are single-person units.) Besides adding together incidents that occurred to several different people, it lumps together (and counts as equal) all sorts of victimizations: rapes, severe beatings, and automobile hubcap thefts. This practice of "adding apples and oranges," like that performed by the FBI in the calculation of its crime index, is of dubious value and has been criticized for years. (The *UCR*'s huge crime index summarizes millions of incidents of the eight index crimes reported to the police in a single year, ranging from murders to attempts to steal a hat from a restaurant coat rack.)

In 1992, the survey interviewers for the *NCVS* discovered that more than three out of every four households they visited or telephoned had nothing to discuss with them. Only 23 percent of the households reported they had been touched by at least one crime of violence or theft that year (most often by thefts, not violence). That was the lowest percentage recorded since the indicator of households touched by crime was devised in 1975. Over the seventeen-year time span, burglaries were down 45 percent and personal thefts without contact, 42 percent. Rapes, robberies, and assaults (taken together) had declined by 13 percent. Only completed and attempted motor vehicle thefts had increased, by 14 percent, over those years (Rand, 1993).

Trends in Homicide Rates Homicide data drawn from death certificates has been gathered by the National Center for Health Statistics throughout the twentieth century. Graphing this data, as shown in Figure 2.3, facilitates the identification of steep rises and sharp drops in the murder rate over the years. Long-term trends can then be considered against a backdrop of major historical events affecting the nation as a whole.

As the graph clearly indicates, homicide rates climbed rapidly shortly after the statistical reporting system was initiated at the start of the century. In the three decades from 1903 to 1933, the murder rate soared from barely 1 person in every 100,000 each year to nearly 10 per 100,000 annually at the height of the Great Depression. Even though the economic hardships of the depression continued throughout the 1930s, the murder rate plummeted, reaching a low point during the years of World War II. Following a short upsurge immediately after the war, when most of the soldiers returned home, the murder rate continued to decline, reaching a low of about 4.5 per 100,000 persons by 1958. From the end of the 1950s to the late 1970s, it shot up again, reflecting the crime-prone teenage and young adult years of the postwar baby boom generation. A new record high was recorded in 1980 when the homicide rate hit 11 per 100,000 persons per year (BJS, 1988); after reaching that peak, murder rates dropped until the early 1990s, when once again they were close to their highest levels for the century.

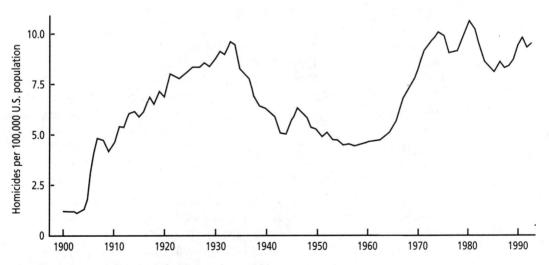

FIGURE 2.3   Trends in Murder Rates since 1900
Sources: BJS, 1988; FBI, *UCR*, 1986–1992.

Checking Whether More Robberies Are Turning into Murders One more set of trend data merits attention. How often do robberies evolve into murders? In other words, what are the chances of being killed by a robber?

Researchers investigating trends in murders arising out of robberies in major U.S. cities from 1968 to 1983 concluded that from 1968 to 1973, the proportion of victims killed by robbers increased, remained roughly at the same level from 1973 until 1979, and then, after 1979, began to decline (Cook, 1985). A detailed study of over one hundred criminal homicides occurring in Chicago during 1983 and classified by the police as robbery-related revealed that different kinds of robberies carry varying risks of victim fatality. Victims were murdered in less than 0.7 percent of all the cases under review. Classified by setting, 36 percent of the killings occurred within homes; another 29 percent were committed indoors at locations such as schools, lobbies, or elevators; and 16 percent took place within commercial establishments. Whereas half of all robbery victims were accosted on the street, only about 20 percent of all slayings occurred there. Hence, being confined indoors during the confrontation seems to increase the danger. Guns were the weapons used in 60 percent of robbery murders. Concerning resistance, the study revealed that a higher percentage of slain victims, compared to victims who were injured less severely or not at all, were actively resisting when they died. The researchers concluded that when confronted by an armed offender who growls "Your money or your life!" the correct response, as dictated by the data, is to hand over your money (Zimring and Zuehl, 1986).

But some people have the impression that robbers kill their victims more readily "these days" than in the past. It is part of a despairing perception that American society is "falling apart," that "civilization is collapsing"; or that offenders used to be of a "higher caliber" and are more depraved, vicious, and unpredictable today than ever before.

Journalists like to play up this theme. For example, in a news magazine cover story titled "The Plague of Violent Crime" the following observation appeared: "Another frightening difference in the crime picture is that life is now pitifully cheap. Law enforcement officials think they have witnessed a shift toward gratuitous slaughter. 'It used to be "Your money or your life," says an assistant Bronx district attorney. . . . Now it's "Your money and your life" ' " (Press et al., 1981:48).

For many people discussing crime, "the way it used to be" refers to the 1940s and 1950s, when street crime was not perceived to be a pressing problem or a major campaign issue. Yet, even during those "good old days," some people feared robbers would kill them even if they cooperated. A reporter at the time wrote, "The hoodlum will bash in your head with a brick for a dollar and ninety-eight cents. The police records of our cities are spotted with cases of 'murder for peanuts' in which the victims, both men and women, have been slugged, stabbed, hit with iron pipes, hammers, or axes, and in a few cases kicked to death—the loot being no more than the carfare a woman carried in her purse or the small change in a man's pocket" (Whitman, 1951:5).

Is it true, as some people suspect, that more and more robberies are turning into murders? *UCR* statistics on murders and *NCVS* findings about robberies assembled in Box 2.1 can shed some light on this grisly question of whether there is an upward trend in felony murders that started out as robberies.

Several tentative conclusions can be drawn from the data assembled in Table 2.2. In roughly 10 percent of all murders (except those in 1988, for some unknown reason), the offender's motive was to take something of value and then escape. So getting away with a robbery as an underlying motivation for taking a life is fairly common. But robberies definitely do not end up as murders in the overwhelming proportion of cases. Thankfully, slayings committed during the course of robberies are rare events. The number of robbery victims tragically and outrageously killed each year hovers around 2,000 (reaching a low of 1,716 in 1988 and a high of 2,519 in 1991). But each year, there are about a million confrontations (ranging from a low of 985,000 in 1985 to a high of 1,381,000 in 1981) in which a life could be taken. Hence, murdered victims constitute a tiny fraction—about one-fifth of 1 percent—of all robbery victims (as few as 0.16 percent in 1984, and as many as 0.22 percent in 1991). That means that about 99.8 percent of all victims survive robberies. Furthermore, there is no obvious upward trend, which means that there is no evidence to support the contention that, as time passes, robbers are becoming more and more inclined to murder their victims.

UNCOVERING VICTIMIZATION PATTERNS

Recognizing Differential Risks

In Table 2.1, victimization rates for the entire population are presented. These statistics indicate how frequently robbery, burglary, and other kinds of crimes are committed against all sorts of people. These overall, or general, victimization rates summarize the experiences of and project the risks faced by "average Americans," or "typical households." They are derived by pooling the responses of all the participants in the *National Crime Victimization Survey*. However, "average Americans" and "typical households" are artificial statistical constructs that real people and families resemble to a greater or lesser degree. It is reasonable to hypothesize that the threat of victimization is not spread evenly across the population (just as different categories of people do not face the same risk of getting hurt accidentally, say from a skiing mishap, or face the same chance of contracting a particular disease, such as AIDS). Certain categories of people, in terms of attributes like gender and age, may be burdened by crime much more or much less than others. If these suspicions can be documented, then composite rates for all Americans might conceal important variations by subgroups. In other words, general victimization

BOX 2.1   "Your Money or Your Life!"

The number of persons killed by robbers can be estimated from *UCR* figures on the numbers of murders and the motives for murder, as surmised by the police. (A study of robbery-related homicides in Baltimore during 1983, however, revealed serious problems in the way deaths are classified. In a considerable proportion of murders, police investigations cannot uncover the motive for the slaying. And in some robbery-murders, the killer robbed the victim's corpse as an afterthought [see Loftin, 1986]). The number of robberies committed each year can be estimated from *NCVS* fig-

ures. (*UCR* figures are much smaller, representing only those robberies known to the police; however, because *NCVS* figures exclude robberies of commercial establishments, they are also underestimates of the actual but unknown grand total of personal and commercial robberies.)

Acknowledging the problems of uncertainty and incompatibility cited above, crude calculations can be performed to roughly estimate how often victims are murdered by robbers (see the computations in Table 2.2).

TABLE 2.2   Yearly Estimates of Murders Committed during Robberies

	1980	1981	1982	1983	
Number of persons murdered	23,040	22,520	21,010	19,310	
Percentage of murders where robbery was the motive	10.8	10.4	10.7	10.6	
Number of robbery victims killed	2,488	2,342	2,248	2,046	
Total number of robbery victims	1,179,000	1,381,000	1,334,000	1,149,000	
Murdered victims as a percentage of all robbery victims	0.21	0.17	0.17	0.18	

	1984	1985	1986	1987	1988
Number of persons murdered	18,690	18,980	20,610	20,096	20,675
Percentage of murders where robbery was the motive	9.3	9.2	9.5	9.4	8.3
Number of robbery victims killed	1,738	1,746	1,958	1,889	1,716
Total number of robbery victims	1,117,000	985,000	1,009,000	1,030,000	1,030,460
Murdered victims as a percentage of all robbery victims	0.16	0.18	0.19	0.18	0.17

	1989	1990	1991	1992	1993
Number of persons murdered	21,500	23,440	24,700	23,760	24,520
Percentage of murders where robbery was the motive	9.1	9.2	10.2	10.0	9.9
Number of robbery victims killed	1,957	2,156	2,519	2,376	2,301
Total number of robbery victims	1,092,000	1,150,000	1,145,000	1,225,500	1,307,000
Murdered victims as a percentage of all robbery victims	0.18	0.19	0.22	0.19	0.18

Sources: FBI, *UCR*, 1981–1994; BJS, *NCVS*, 1981–1994.

rates can mask or obscure substantial differences in the rates that apply to particular categories.

A pattern within a victimization rate is recognizable when one subcategory suffers significantly more than another (the most obvious example is the incidence of rape: females are much more likely to be sexually violated than are males). Searching for patterns means looking for regularities within a seemingly chaotic mass of information and finding predictability within apparently random events. To discover patterns, researchers must break down the data collected each year into its component parts—the various groupings of people and households that participated in the survey. *NCVS* interviewers record the gender, age, marital status, race, income, and area of residence of the roughly 100,000 individuals in the nearly 50,000 households in the *NCVS* sample. Patterns emerge when rates are calculated separately for each subcategory and then compared. Once a pattern has been established over the years, then differential risks observed in the past can be projected into the future. Since men have been assaulted more often than women (according to recent surveys), it can be concluded that men face greater risks of being attacked than women (this year and in the foreseeable future, unless major social changes affecting interpersonal violence occur in the years ahead).

Victimization patterns, and the differential risks derived from them, will be investigated for the crimes of robbery and murder.

Differential Risks of Being Robbed

When the overall *NCVS* robbery rates are broken down into their constituent parts, distinct patterns emerge that reveal that different categories of people face widely varying risks (see Harlow, 1987). Table 2.3 presents the differential rates by subcategory for robberies committed from 1973 to 1984 and during 1992. (Note the numbers in the second and third columns.)

Table 2.3 shows that when the general population is broken down into subcategories according to various attributes, striking differences in robbery rates become evident. Certain groupings of people are robbed much more often and have much more reason to be fearful than others.

Patterns in robbery rates were uncovered by combining the findings of yearly surveys conducted between 1973 and 1984 into one massive data file containing details on nearly 14.7 million incidents (Harlow, 1987). Over this span of twelve years, an average of about 1.2 million persons were robbed annually, yielding a general rate of almost 7 robberies for every 1,000 people twelve years of age and over per year. This overall figure of 7 serves as a standard for comparison for the breakdowns shown in the second column of Table 2.3 (*Average annual rate, 1973–1984*).

Starting with gender, the first pattern that stands out is that the rate at which males were robbed (9.3 per 1,000 per year) was more than twice that of females

TABLE 2.3   Robbery Rates for Various Groups

VICTIM CHARACTERISTICS	PERCENTAGE OF ALL VICTIMS, 1973–1984	AVERAGE ANNUAL RATE, 1973–1984	1992 RATE
Overall rate	100%	7.0	5.9
Sex			
Male	65	9.3	8.1
Female	35	4.6	3.9
Race			
White	75	5.9	4.7
Black	23	14.2	15.6
Other	2	7.2	5.1
Ethnicity			
Hispanic	8	10.4	10.6
Non-Hispanic	92	6.7	5.4
Age			
12–15 years old	14	11.3	9.8
16–19	15	11.3	15.4
20–24	19	11.7	11.4
25–34	20	7.2	7.7
35–49	15	5.0	3.8
50–64	10	4.0	2.8
65 and older	6	3.3	1.5
Marital status			
Married	28	3.4	2.4
Widowed	5	4.6	2.5
Divorced or separated	17	16.0	9.5
Never married	51	11.9	11.8
Family income			
Less than $7,500	38	10.8	11.1
$7,500–14,999	29	6.7	9.5*
$15,000–24,999	19	5.1	5.4
$25,000 and above	14	4.7	5.0*

Notes: Rates are per 1,000 people with these characteristics per year.
*Estimated by combining new categories in the 1992 report.
Percentages for subcategories may not total exactly 100% because of rounding.
Source: Average annual figures based on *NCVS* findings for 1973–1984 were adapted from Harlow, 1987; 1992 rates are from BJS, 1994a.

(4.6 per 1,000 per year). As for race and ethnicity, the rate for black people was more than twice as high as that for white people. Hispanics also were burdened by very high robbery rates. With regard to age, the survey analysis revealed that younger persons (between the ages of twelve and twenty-four) suffered the highest robbery rates. For those over twenty-five, rates declined steadily with increasing age, with senior citizens over sixty-five preyed upon the least often of any age group. Family income exhibited a pattern similar to that found in relation to age: As income increased, the chances of being robbed decreased. In addition to gender, race, income, and age, marital status made a big difference: People who were divorced or separated faced the highest risks (16 per 1,000) of any subcategory in the study. Those who had never been married were also robbed more often than the norm. Married persons and widowed individuals were victimized much less frequently.

Differential rates and risks for robbery also appear in Table 2.3. In the third column (headed *1992 RATE*), breakdowns extracted from the 1992 *NCVS* are presented. By 1992, the overall rate had declined from 7 to 5.9 per 1,000 individuals. But the BJS's calculations indicated that males still were robbed at more than twice the rate for females (8.1 compared to 3.9). African Americans endured risks that were more than three times higher (at 15.6), and Hispanic Americans more than two times higher (at 10.6) than for non-Hispanic whites (at about 5). As for age, in the period 1973–1984, younger teens (twelve to fifteen) were tied with older teens (sixteen to nineteen); but by 1992, the sixteen-to-nineteen-year-old age group clearly stood out as facing the gravest dangers. Teenagers and young adults were still robbed many times more often than were middle-aged and elderly people. Unlike the 1973–1984 period, in 1992, single persons who were never married were robbed more often than those who were separated or divorced. But both these subcategories experienced far greater risks than married couples or widows/widowers. Persons from lower-income families were more likely to be robbed than were persons from middle-income families. Some other patterns (which are not shown in Table 2.3) indicate that less-educated people were robbed more often than better-educated people. Also, residents of urban areas were robbed at a much higher rate than their rural, small-town counterparts; the rate for suburbanites was somewhere in between (Bachman, 1992; BJS, 1994).

To summarize the findings in columns two and three of Table 2.3, the data suggest that the higher risks are faced by men rather than women, minorities rather than members of the white majority, young persons more than middle-age or elderly people, single or divorced individuals over married couples, poor people rather than those who are better off financially (and, not shown, less-educated persons more than those with better educations, and city residents rather than people living in suburbs or small towns). Combining these factors, the profile of the person facing the highest risks of all is that of a poor, African-American young man living in an inner-city neighborhood who dropped out of high school. The *NCVS* report does not calculate a victimization rate for an individual who falls into all of these high-risk subcategories. The highest robbery rate suffered by any BJS grouping listed in the government report was for black teenagers between the ages of sixteen and nineteen, who suffered nearly 47 attempted and completed muggings and holdups per 1,000 in 1992.

The detailed analysis of all the nearly 14.7 million known robbery victims from 1973 to 1984 yields another profile (see the first column in Table 2.3, *Percentage of all victims, 1973–1984*). This additional statistical portrait describes the "average" or "typical" robbery victim. It is drawn by choosing the modal (most common) subcategory from among each set of attributes. The picture that emerges of the typical robbery victim during that period is of a male (65 percent), white (75 percent), non-Hispanic (92 percent), between twenty-five and thirty-four years of age (20 percent) who had never married (51 percent) and came from a very low income household (38 percent).

This profile of the typical victim (male/white/25–34/single/poor) does not exactly match the profile cited earlier of the subcategories of people facing the greatest risks of being robbed (male/black/20–24/divorced/poor). The reason for the discrepancy involves the concepts of *proportionality* and *disproportionality*. Proportionality exists when a group represents roughly the same percentage of the sample as it does of the entire population. Disproportionality exists when the two percentages are substantially different. For example, males constitute about 50 percent of the U.S. population, but made up 65 percent of the robbery victims represented by Table 2.3. Therefore, it can be said that males ran a disproportionately high risk of being robbed (and females, a disproportionately low risk). Similarly, African Americans, who according to census figures constitute about 12 percent of the nation's population, were disproportionately represented among robbery victims (23 percent of whom were black). Families living below the poverty line set by government agencies (approximately $11,000 for an urban family of four during the mid-1980s, raised to about $14,750 by 1994 because of increases in the cost of living) made up from 10 to 15 percent of the country's population, but more than half of all robbery victims, so poor people were also disproportionately burdened by this type of crime.

One additional variable is worthy of consideration—occupation. Robbery rates differ substantially by the victim's occupation. Statistics from the *NCVS* over the years indicate that people holding the following (generally less desirable) jobs are much more likely to be robbed: taxidrivers, gardeners, busboys, dishwashers, carnival and amusement park workers, car wash attendants, messengers, newspaper carriers, peddlers, and certain kinds of construction workers. However, persons who are musicians and composers, painters and sculptors, and photographers are also victimized at above-average rates. Those least likely to be robbed work as inspectors, line workers, bank tellers, opticians, farmers, professional athletes, elementary school teachers, engineers, and psychologists (Block, Felson, and Block, 1985).

Differential Risks of Being Murdered

The statistics compiled by the FBI and published in the *UCR* reveal a number of striking patterns within homicides (especially alarming for those who fall into some of the high-risk categories, somewhat reassuring for all others). The risks of being murdered vary greatly by geographic location (region of the country), area of residence (urban, suburban, or rural), gender, age, and race.

First of all, different parts of the country have substantially different murder rates. The highest homicide rates are found in the states categorized as Southern by the FBI (11 out of every 100,000 southerners were killed in 1993). The lowest rates were noted in those states in the Northeast or Midwest (8 per 100,000). The murder rate in the Western states fell in between the two extremes (10 per 100,000). The state with the highest murder rate was Louisiana (at nearly 20 per 100,000), followed by Texas, Georgia, Mississippi, Alabama, California, and New York (all with rates close to 12 or 13 per 100,000). The states with the lowest homicide rates (less than 5 per 100,000) were generally rural with small urban populations: Hawaii, Utah, Montana, Idaho, Wyoming, Nebraska, Iowa, Minnesota, Wisconsin, North and South Dakota, Maine, New Hampshire, Vermont, Rhode Island, and Massachusetts.

Besides region of the country, another geographic factor makes a great deal of difference: area of residence. Homicide risks are much greater for residents of metropolitan areas (11 per 100,000) than for suburbanites and persons living in small towns in the countryside (about 5 per 100,000). A closer look at the problem faced by city people, as revealed by the FBI's data from urban police departments, shows that rates vary dramatically from one metropolitan area to another. The disparities are not a function of size but seem to be determined by local conditions such as the area's economy (including its unemployment rate and wage scales), its special problems (such as the availability of handguns, the extent of drug trafficking, and outbreaks of "wars" between rival street gangs and mob families), local traditions and customs, and demographic factors (especially the proportion of the population that is poor, male, young, and of minority group background) (Tardiff, Gross, and Messner, 1986; Chilton, 1987). As a result, the risks of being murdered are many times greater for the residents of certain cities than for other urban dwellers. Urban homicide rates may fall or rise considerably from year to year as these local conditions improve or deteriorate.

The compilation presented in Figure 2.4 illustrates how different murder rates can be from one urban area to another. The rates were computed by dividing the number of murders committed within the city limits by the number of people living within the city limits (excluding murders committed and persons living in surrounding counties).

Complex statistical analyses have isolated some of the factors that account for the striking variations in homicide rates from city to city. It appears that high

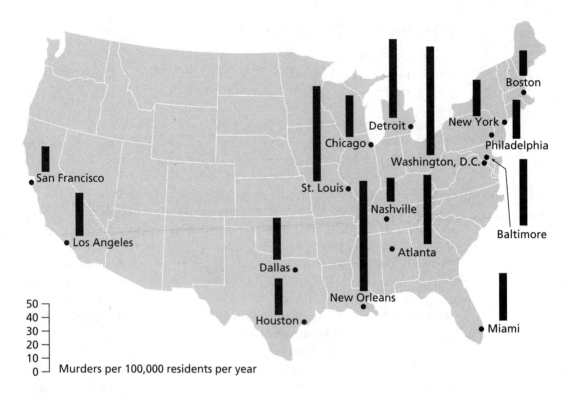

FIGURE 2.4   Murder Rates in Major Cities

Note: Murder rates were calculated on the basis of the population living within city limits and not for the entire metropolitan area of surrounding counties.
Source: FBI, 1994; FBI, *UCR,* 1993.

urban murder rates are associated with high population densities, high poverty rates, high divorce rates, social inequalities between different racial groups, and possibly a subculture of violence that is stronger in the South (see Land, McCall, and Cohen, 1990; and Messner and Golden, 1992). The rise and fall of yearly homicide rates are probably largely due to sharp increases and decreases in the level of competition among drug dealers and the level of conflict among street gangs.

As for gender, 78 percent of the people murdered were males (a proportion that has remained roughly the same since at least the early 1960s). Expressed as rates, males are killed about four times as often as females (14 per 100,000 compared to 3.5 per 100,000).

Besides varying by geographical location and gender, murder rates vary dramatically by age (see Akiyama, 1981). Ten-year-olds are the least likely to be murdered, and twenty-five-year-olds the most. After rising during the teenage years and peaking at age twenty-five, the risks of dying violently drop rapidly. Relatively high rates shown for infants and toddlers reflect deaths caused by physical abuse, often by parents.

Statistically, race turns out to be the most important of all the demographic factors associated with differential risks. Members of minority groups, especially African Americans, confront much higher dangers of violent death. Half of all murder victims were African American in 1993. Since people who identify themselves as "black" on the 1990 census constitute 12 percent of the U.S. population, black representation among the ranks of the dead is disproportional by a factor of more than four. Calculating homicide rates by race, 5 whites out of every 100,000 are slain each year. The comparable figure for blacks is 31 per 100,000, about six times higher (Whitaker, 1990). (Of the incidents investigated during 1993 involving a single killing by a single offender, the vast majority were intraracial: Most whites were slain by other whites [84 percent of the cases], and most blacks were murdered by other blacks [94 percent of the time].For exceptions to this pattern, see Wilbanks, 1987.) As for gender, most males were murdered by other males (about 88 percent of all killings of males). However, most females were not killed by other females; 90 percent of all female victims were slain by males (FBI, 1994).

From this review of the demographic factors that are correlated with higher murder rates, a profile can be derived. The people who run the gravest risks are southerners, urban residents, males, teenagers and young adults between eighteen and twenty-four, and African Americans. (Low-income persons are probably in this high-risk group as well, but police files and FBI compilations do not preserve information about social class.)

Another shocking set of sharply different homicide rates emerges when geography (state of residence) as well as race, gender, and age are taken into account. According to statistics calculated by researchers at the National Center for Health Statistics, using 1987 data, for young black males between the ages of fifteen and twenty-four, the most dangerous state to live in was Michigan, where the homicide rate was 232 slain for every 100,000. Other high-risk locales were California (155 young black males killed per 100,000), the District of Columbia (139), and New York State (137). For young white males between fifteen and twenty-four, the most dangerous state was California (22 killed for every 100,000), followed by Texas (21), New York (18), and Arizona (17). For young white males, Minnesota (2) and Massachusetts (3) were the safest states to live in. For young African-American males, the lowest death tolls occurred in North Carolina (34) and Kentucky (35) (Rosenthal, 1990).

Trends in the Differential Risks of Being Murdered

Patterns can persist or they can change over time, becoming either more prominent or fading away.

As noted above, the differential risks of being killed vary dramatically by age, gender, and race. Teenagers and young adults are slain at rates much higher than those for younger or older people. Boys are murdered more often than girls.

Blacks are killed much more often than whites, especially poor young black males in inner cities (see Wood, 1990; Finerhut, Ingram, and Feldman, 1992a).

Some disturbing trends appear in the graphs in Figure 2.5, which track homicide rates over the years for black and white males of different ages. The upper graph depicts homicide rates for four age groups of African-American males. The patterns of the four lines reveal that black men twenty-five to thirty-four years old faced the gravest risks of any age group from 1950 until 1989; since that year, teenagers and young adults fifteen to twenty-four years old have faced the highest risks. Starting in the mid-1980s and persisting into the early 1990s, the odds of getting killed have soared for black youth, reaching the unprecedented rate of about 160 violent deaths for every 100,000 males of this age and racial group. But for black males older than twenty-five, the risk of being murdered was higher in the early 1970s than in the early 1990s. The lower graph reveals that the murder rates for white males of different ages have been much lower, roughly one-tenth as high, throughout the years. White males died at record rates around 1980; since then the rate for fifteen- to twenty-four year-olds reached an all-time high in 1991.

Since World War II, the most ominous change in homicides has been the trend toward the decreasing age of both killers and their victims. The escalation in the level of lethal violence among teenagers is largely attributed by criminologists to the revival of street gangs and the formation of drug-dealing crews, their willingness to resort to force to settle even minor disputes, their easier access to handguns, and their involvement with drugs and alcohol ("The New American Epidemic," 1994).

PROJECTING CUMULATIVE RISKS

Estimating Lifetime Likelihoods

Yearly victimization rates might lull some people into a false sense of security. Annual rates give the impression that crime is a rare event. Only a handful of people out of every thousand fall prey to offenders; most people get through the year unscathed. But fears do not conform to a January-to-December cycle; people worry that they will be robbed, raped, or murdered at some point in their lifetimes. For that reason, the Bureau of Justice Statistics occasionally provides estimates of the likelihood of a person's being harmed during the course of a lifetime. Estimates of the cumulative risks of victimization, viewed over a span of 60+ years (from age twelve into the seventies, the average life expectancy in the United States today), yield a very different picture of the seriousness of the contemporary crime problem in the United States. What appears to be a rare event in any given year looms as a real threat over the course of an entire lifetime (Koppel, 1987).

Homicide Rates for Black Males

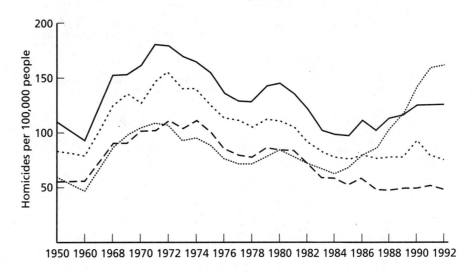

Homicide Rates for White Males

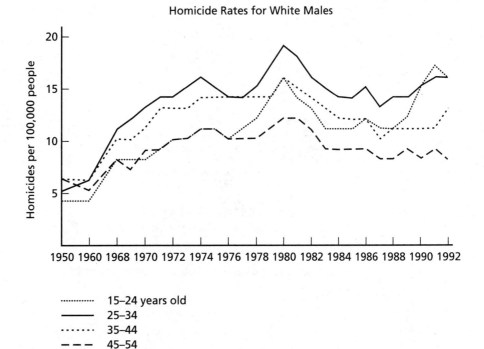

.... 15–24 years old
——— 25–34
· · · · · · 35–44
– – – 45–54

FIGURE 2.5 Trends in Murder Rates by Age and Race for Males

Source: National Center for Health Statistics; graphed in Press, McCormick, and Wingert, *NEWSWEEK,* August 15, 1994, p. 32.

TABLE 2.4   Chances of Becoming a Victim over a Lifetime

TYPE OF VICTIMIZATION AND PERSON'S RACE, SEX, AND AGE	PERCENTAGE OF PERSONS WHO WILL BE VICTIMIZED			
	ONCE OR MORE	ONCE	TWICE	THREE OR MORE TIMES
Rape				
All females age 12	8	8	—	—
White	8*	7	—	—
Black	11	10	1	—
Robbery				
All persons age 12	30*	25	5	1
Males	37	29	7	1
Females	22*	19	2	-
Whites	27	23	4	-
Blacks	51	35	12	4
Assault				
All persons age 12	74	35	24	15
Males	82	31	26	25
Females	62	37	18	7
Whites	74*	35	24	16
Blacks	73*	35	25	12
Personal theft				
All persons age 12	99	4	8	87
All 40-year-olds	82*	31	19	33
All 60-year-olds	43	32	9	2

Note: Estimates are based on average victimization rates calculated by the *National Crime Survey* for the years 1975–1984; for rape, 1973–1982.
*Figures do not exactly add up to total shown because of rounding.
Source: Adapted from Koppel, 1987.

In Table 2.4 the probability that an individual will be victimized at some point in his or her lifetime is estimated for several different kinds of personal crimes.

Cumulative Risks of Rape, Robbery, and Assault

The statistics in Table 2.4 can be interpreted as follows: Over a span of about sixty years, 99 percent—nearly everybody now twelve years old—will experience theft, most eventually three or more times, according to the projections.

Although the chance that a girl or woman will be raped in a given year is minuscule, it rises to a lifetime threat of 80 per 1,000, or 8 percent, or about 1 female in every 12. For black females, the risks are somewhat greater, at 11 percent, or nearly 1 in 9, over a lifetime. Of these 11 black females who will be raped out of every 100, 1 will suffer this outrage twice in a lifetime.

Robbery is a more common crime than sexual assaults. Thirty percent of the population, 3 out of every 10 people, will be robbed at least once in a lifetime. Of this group, 5 percent will be robbed twice, and 1 percent robbed three or more times over the years (25 + 5 + 1 = 31, because of rounding). Taking differential risks by gender and race into account, males are more likely to be robbed at least once in their lives (37 percent) than females (22 percent); and blacks are more likely to be robbed than whites (51 percent compared to 27 percent).

When it comes to assault, the terms *likelihood* and *probability* take on their everyday meanings, as well as their special statistical connotations. Being assaulted at least once is likely or probable for most people, roughly 3 out of every 4 persons. (However, this alarming prediction includes failed attempts to inflict physical injury, threats of bodily harm that were not carried out, minor scuffles, and intrafamily violence.) Males are more likely to become embroiled in fights than females (82 percent compared to 62 percent).

The mathematical and sociological assumptions underlying these crude projections are very complex and subject to challenge. The calculations were based on constants derived by averaging victimization rates for the years 1975 to 1984. If crime rates drop substantially over the next sixty years or so, these estimates will turn out to be overly pessimistic; conversely, if the crime problem intensifies in the first few decades of the twenty-first century, the real odds will be much greater than the percentages shown in Table 2.4. In addition, because the estimates project the future experiences of persons now twelve years old, they must be scaled down to reflect the shorter remaining life spans of those who are much older. For example, it is estimated that 99 percent of today's twelve-year-olds will experience at least one personal theft in the many years they have ahead of them. But of those who are now forty and have lived more than half their lives already (based on actuarial calculations), only 82 percent will become victims of personal theft. For people currently sixty years old, the lifetime likelihood of a personal theft during their remaining years shrinks to 43 percent (Koppel, 1987).

Cumulative Risks of Being Murdered

Lifetime likelihoods of being murdered also have been computed. Unlike the projections discussed above, which were based on *NCVS* findings, murder risk estimates are derived from *UCR* data. The risks vary tremendously, depending on personal attributes, especially gender and race. Differential cumulative risks are presented as ratios, such as "one out of every x people will be murdered." All the $x - 1$ remaining individuals within this category are expected to die from accidents, diseases, other natural causes, or suicides. In general, males are more likely to die violently than are females, and blacks more likely than whites. But when the effects of both gender and race are taken into account, black females turn out to be in greater danger of being slain than white males (BJS, 1988). White females

TABLE 2.5   Projected Risks of Being Murdered over a Lifetime

PERSONAL ATTRIBUTES	PREDICTED LIFETIME RISK OF BECOMING A HOMICIDE VICTIM
White females	1 out of every 495 will be murdered
White males	1 out of every 179 will be murdered
Black females	1 out of every 132 will be murdered
Black males	1 out of every 30 will be murdered

Note: Based on *UCR* homicide data for the mid–1980s.
Source: BJS, 1988.

are in the least danger (relatively speaking) of being murdered. But the prospects facing black males are frightening: One out of every 30 black males (about 3 percent of those alive today) will eventually become a victim of homicide if mid-1980s conditions continue. (In the early 1980s, the threat was even greater: One out of every 21 black males (nearly 5 percent) was likely to die violently [Langan, 1985].) (Table 2.5 presents the cumulative risks of being murdered, by gender and race.)

As with the lifetime likelihoods (discussed above) of becoming the victim of a lesser crime, these government estimates presume that current levels of violence won't change significantly in the future. Although it is necessary to make this assumption in order to perform the calculations, if the murder rate goes up or down substantially over the decades, these projections will be way off.

MAKING INTERNATIONAL COMPARISONS

Victimization rates vary from society to society, as well as from time to time and group to group. Contrasting the rates of victimization in selected countries is another aspect of the study of differential risks. Cross-national comparisons can yield clues about the causes of criminal behavior and suggestions for crime prevention and control.

The two main sources of data about victimization rates in other countries are the United Nations (UN), which periodically surveys its members, and the International Police Organization (Interpol), which has cooperative relationships with law enforcement agencies around the world.

But making international comparisons can be difficult and misleading for a number of reasons. First of all, many governments do not disclose any reliable data on crime or publish figures that seem unrealistic, probably because they fear that high rates and rankings near the top will damage their nation's public image. Even when governments make an effort to be cooperative and accurate, problems arise because of differences in definitions (for example, of rape, robbery, and burglary) and in reporting and record-keeping practices. One study of cross-national crime data yielded these conclusions: U.S. victimization rates for violent crimes were very high; those for auto theft were fairly high; and those for burglary were near the middle of the range for countries furnishing trustworthy data (Kalish, 1988).

Comparing the Murder Rates in Different Societies

The World Health Organization (WHO), an agency of the United Nations, keeps track of homicides in most countries across the globe. But statistics on murder in various societies must be interpreted with great caution. For international comparisons to be valid, definitions of what constitutes a crime must be consistent. Each country's definitions, however, reflect laws and local customs that govern the way acts leading to death are classified. The murder statistics in certain countries count attempted murders (in which the victims survived); these crimes are classified as aggravated assaults in the United States. Other inconsistencies arise because certain countries include deaths from legal interventions (such as the use of deadly force by police officers and executions), unintentional deaths (manslaughter), and self-induced deaths (suicides), all of which are excluded from U.S. figures (Kalish, 1988).

Most industrialized, technologically advanced nations have low murder rates. Some industrializing nations in Asia, Africa, and Latin America have very low rates of interpersonal violence, while others have very high rates. War-torn and conflict-ridden societies have high rates, of course. In fifteen countries, the murder rate is higher than that of the United States; but more than 150 countries have lower murder rates than that of the United States (Deane, 1987).

Two additional factors confound cross-national rankings. First of all, some societies are strikingly different from other societies in terms of economic systems, laws, criminal justice systems, and cultural traditions. It might make more sense to limit any comparative analysis of murder rates to fairly similar highly industrialized societies. Second, a key determinant of the murder rate in any country is simply the proportion of people in the high-risk group (young males). In some countries, a greater proportion of the population is youthful, and in others the ratio of males to females may depart from 50–50. One way to deal with this variation is to calculate the homicide rate for every 100,000 teenage boys and young men in a society. Following this procedure, and then restricting the comparison to only other highly industrialized societies, the United States stands out as having the highest murder rate (Rosenthal, 1990), as is shown in Table 2.6.

According to an analysis of demographic factors in the various countries, higher murder rates are associated with great economic inequality (huge gaps between the wealthy and the poor); limited government funding of social pro-

Table 2.6   Rates of Killings of Young Males in
Different Industrialized Countries

INDUSTRIALIZED COUNTRY	HOMICIDE RATE PER 100,000 MALES, 15–24
Austria	0.3
Japan	0.5
Germany (West)	1.0
Denmark	1.0
Portugal	1.0
England	1.2
Poland	1.2
Ireland	1.3
Greece	1.4
France	1.4
Switzerland	1.4
Netherlands	1.4
Belgium	1.7
Sweden	2.3
Australia	2.5
Canada	2.9
Finland	3.0
Norway	3.3
Israel	3.7
New Zealand	4.4
Scotland	5.0
United States	21.9

Note: Comparisons are based on homicide rates and population estimates for 1987.
Source: Fingerhut and Kleinman, cited in Rosenthal, 1990.

grams; cultural supports for official, legitimate violence (executions and war
deaths); family breakdown (high divorce rates); high rates of female participation
in the labor force; and ethnic heterogeneity (see Gartner, 1990).

ASSEMBLING COMPARATIVE RISKS

Putting Crime into Perspective

An important part of putting the crime problem into perspective involves weighing the threats posed by different kinds of misfortunes. That is, the chance of being harmed by a criminal can be compared to the odds of being hurt in an accident or contracting a serious illness. The study of comparative risks rests on
estimates of the relative likelihood of experiencing various unwanted, negative life

events. One purpose of studying comparative risks is to determine which types of threats (crimes, accidents, or diseases) merit greater precautionary measures by both individuals and government-sponsored campaigns. (A more comprehensive list of calamities could be expanded to include fires and natural disasters such as floods, tornadoes, earthquakes, and hurricanes.) Table 2.7 compares the chances, expressed in a standardized way as rates per 1,000 people, of being stricken by an unwanted event.

The rates shown in Table 2.7 reveal that the most common negative event is to suffer an injury from an accident. Each year, 22 percent (220/1,000) of all adults get hurt unintentionally. A comparison of the estimated rates shows that a person is much more likely to be injured in an accident that takes place at home (which happens to nearly 7 percent of all adults each year), at work (nearly 5 percent), or on the road (about 2 percent) than during a violent crime (0.8 percent, which counts any attack by any assailant, whether an acquaintance, a family member, or a complete stranger).

As for death rates, Table 2.7 indicates that the highest toll is brought about by illnesses, especially cardiovascular disease (such as heart attacks) and cancer which, together, claim 8 lives (5+3) per 1,000 people per year. Accidental deaths of all kinds (including those from car crashes, chokings, falls, and drownings) kill more

TABLE 2.7 Comparing the Risks Posed by Crime, Accidents, and Diseases

TYPE OF MISFORTUNE	ESTIMATED YEARLY RATE PER 1,000 ADULTS
Injury from all kinds of accidents	220
Injury from an accident at home	66
Theft of a personal possession	61
Injury from an accident at work	47
Injury from a motor vehicle accident	22
Injury from a violent crime	11
Aggravated assault	8
Robbery	6
Death from heart problems	5
Death from cancer	3
Rape of a female	1
Death from all kinds of accidents	0.4
Death from pneumonia or influenza	0.2
Death from a motor vehicle accident	0.2
Death by suicide	0.2
Death from AIDS HIV infection	0.1
Death from a murderous assault	0.1

Note: Estimated rates for crimes, accidents, and diseases are for 1991.
Source: BJS, 1993.

people than suicide or AIDS. Becoming a victim of a homicide is the least likely negative event on the list.

Putting this risk comparison into perspective raises interesting policy implications. It could be argued that the public ought to be more concerned about unsafe conditions at home, in school, on the job, and on highways and less preoccupied with crime, which receives so much more media coverage.

However, several problems undermine the usefulness of attempts to assess comparative risks. First of all, the mathematical calculations do not indicate the seriousness of some of these negative events (except, of course, for those that result in death). For example, the extent of physical pain, psychological trauma, and economic loss resulting from injuries due to car crashes or assaults can range from trivial to devastating. But when rates are calculated, incidents resulting in minor injuries are counted the same as events causing serious injuries.

Another weakness is that the overall rates used in the comparisons once again describe the risks faced by the "average American." As was stressed earlier in the discussion of differential risks, the odds vary tremendously, depending upon certain key attributes. For natural disasters, geographical location is the primary determinant: on the West Coast, people need to be concerned about earthquakes; on the East Coast, hurricanes; and in the interior of the country, tornadoes. As for the threat of crime, accidents, and diseases, the most important factors are gender, age, race, income, marital status, and place of residence. If matchups are to be meaningful, comparative risks need to be assessed separately for specific groups. For example, risk levels are closely associated with age levels. The list of the leading causes of death for people between the ages of fifteen and twenty-four is entirely different from the ranking of lethal threats facing the elderly. For persons over sixty-five years of age, heart attacks, cancer, and strokes loom as the most worrisome life-ending events. Being murdered is so highly unlikely that it doesn't even appear on their list of the fifteen leading causes of death. But for individuals in their late teens and early twenties, homicide, far from being a negligible threat, turns out to be the second most common reason for dying, behind accidents (especially car crashes) and ahead of suicides. Murder is the leading cause of death for young black males between the ages of fifteen and twenty-four (BJS, 1988; "A Fair Chance," 1989; Fingerhut, Ingram, and Feldman, 1992a).

To further complicate the picture, when comparing the risks of becoming a crime victim to the risk of suffering an injury or death at work, it is necessary to take into account the job and the offense. *NCVS* data reveals that from 1987 to 1992, an estimated 8 percent of all rapes, 7 percent of all robberies, and as many as 16 percent of all assaults were committed against people who were working or on duty at the time of the attack (Bachman, 1994b). Naturally, risks are closely tied to occupation; some jobs are much more dangerous than others. Focusing on deaths in the workplace, studies conducted by the National Institute for Safety and Health and by the federal government's Bureau of Labor Statistics established that fatal accidents take place most often in construction (34 deaths per 100,000 workers per year), farming and forestry (26 deaths per 100,000), and transportation (23 deaths per 100,000). Putting accidents aside, researchers discovered that certain lines of work carry much greater risks of being murdered on the job. Taxi drivers and chauffeurs are the most vulnerable of all employees; 15 out of every 100,000 are murdered while driving their vehicles each year (not counting traffic fatalities). Law enforcement officers have the second most dangerous occupation, with 9 slain per 100,000 per year. Other hazardous jobs, compared to the national average of 0.7 homicides per 100,000 workers, include being a hotel clerk (5 murdered per 100,000 per year); a gas station attendant (nearly 5); a security guard (almost 4); a stock handler (3); a store owner or manager (nearly 3); and a bartender (a little more than 2). Throughout the 1980s, about 750 people were murdered while doing their jobs each year; these shootings and stabbings accounted for 12 percent of all on-the-job deaths during that time period. During 1992, about 1,000 people were slain while working, representing 17 percent of all occupational fatalities (the bulk of the deaths were attributed to motor vehicle collisions, falls, fires, explosions, exposure to harmful substances, and assorted other causes). A number of measures might reduce the number of occupational homicides: installing better lighting; minimizing the amount of cash an employee handles; making dangerous work sites visible to more people; installing alarms, bulletproof enclosures, and surveillance cameras; increasing the number of staff on duty; adopting policies that urge employees not to resist robbers; increasing police patrols of work sites; closing establishments late at night; and providing conflict-resolution training so that disgruntled employees and individuals who were fired do not attack supervisors and coworkers (Associated Press, 1993c; "The Feds Make It Official," 1993).

One final problem with risk comparisons needs to be addressed. A compilation of comparative risks (like any report about risks) represents a snapshot image of a fluid situation. Thus, Table 2.7 captures a moment in time, the relative standing of the dangers of accidents, diseases, and crime in 1991; it does not depict trends. For example, an encouraging downward trend in fatal accidents during the 1980s was uncovered in a study by the National Safety Council. Deaths due to plane crashes, falls, drownings, fires, and poisonings all dropped during that decade (probably as a result of greater safety consciousness, as well as new devices like smoke detectors and child car seats and new policies like mandatory seat belt laws and tougher penalties for drunk driving). By the 1990s, the risk of dying in a car crash had fallen to its lowest level since the 1920s (Hall, 1990). If accidental deaths become far less likely as time goes on, then the relative threat posed by crime rises in comparison, even if the murder rate stays about the same over the years.

MAKING SENSE OF VICTIMIZATION STATISTICS

The wealth of statistical information about victims and the extent of their plight is accumulating faster than it can be analyzed and interpreted. To catch up, victimologists need to formulate empirical generalizations that can become the basis for hypothesizing, model testing, and theory construction.

Theoretical explanations answer questions that begin with *why*. For example, data reconstructed from the *NCVS* from 1973 to 1984 confirm earlier observations based on *UCR* police statistics that the rates of commission of certain types of crimes exhibit a predictable cycle of increases and decreases during the course of a year. This empirical generalization about the seasonality of criminal victimization requires an explanation. Why should three crimes—household larcenies, unlawful entries (burglaries accomplished without using force to get in), and rapes—be much more common during the warmer months? A plausible answer is that individual behavior patterns that create opportunities for offenders to commit crimes change with the seasons. During the summertime, people spend more time outdoors and are more likely to leave their doors unlocked, their windows open, and sporting goods and lawn furniture lying about unguarded. As a result, there are more sexual assaults against females by strangers and more thefts of household articles by intruders and prowlers (Dodge, 1988). Robberies and personal larcenies do not show much seasonality, but they do peak in December, when shopping for gifts reaches its height (BJS, 1993).

Victimologists engaged in model building and theory construction have been particularly intrigued by the discovery of patterns of victimization that reflect differential risks. The data in the tables and graphs presented in this chapter indicate that certain groups of people are much more likely than others to be murdered or robbed (or assaulted or raped). Why is that? The answers, some of which follow, can be of use to policymakers as well as individuals in high-risk groups.

The Determinants of Differential Risks

As the above analysis of murder and robbery statistics demonstrates, individuals falling into different categories face very different levels of risk. That observation can be underscored by one additional graphical presentation. Depicted in Figure 2.6 is a line that shows the entire spectrum of possibilities, ranging from very low to very high levels of risk of violent victimizations (rapes, robberies, and assaults, but not murders). Three crucial variables are taken into account: gender, race (white/black), and age group (teenagers = 12–19; young adults = 20–34; adult = 35–64; elderly = 65 and older).

Now it is time to pose several interrelated questions. Why do victimization risks show such a skewed distribution? Why is it that collections of victims do not constitute an unbiased sample or cross-section of people of various kinds drawn at ran-

Combined rape, robbery, and assault rate per 1,000 persons

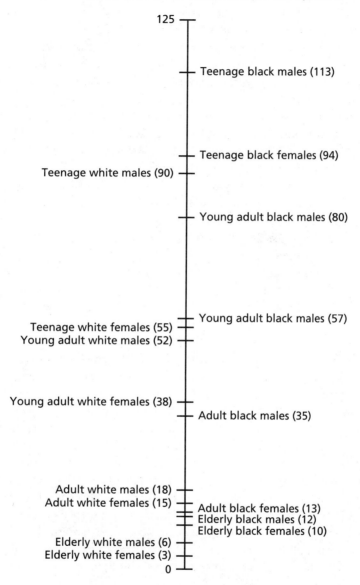

FIGURE 2.6   Violent Victimization Rates By Gender, Age, and Race
Source: BJS, 1994.

dom from the general population? What plausible explanations can be offered to account for the considerable differences in risk levels faced by different groups? What factors explain why the burden of victimization falls more heavily on certain people than others? What is it—if anything—that catches the attention of criminals? Which factors heighten risks, and which reduce the odds of being harmed?

Vulnerability to crime is always a matter of degree. The statistics from victimization surveys confirm the long-held suspicion that particular groups of people are more vulnerable to exploitation and injury than others. But victimologists cannot agree among themselves on exactly what characteristics victims might have in common that make them relatively more susceptible than nonvictims. Inasmuch as the data reveal clear patterns, victimization is definitely not a random process, striking people just by chance. When victims ask, "Why me?" victimologists suggest that the answer may be more than simply "Bad luck."

Someday, it might be possible to compute a personalized vulnerability index to predict the possibility of a given individual's becoming a casualty of a specific type of crime (Galaway and Hudson, 1981). The calculation could take into account a person's sex, age, race, income, occupation, marital status, and area of residence, since these factors have proven to be correlated with victimization rates. But the question remains, why do certain categories of people succumb to victimization at higher rates than others? What differentiates them from the rest of the population?

Certain personal attributes may play a part in determining vulnerability. The mentally retarded, newly arrived immigrants, less-educated people, and very inexperienced persons are attractive targets for exploitation by criminals employing deception and fraud. Con artists swindle the greedy, heartbroken, and lonesome with legendary ease. Physically handicapped people, the elderly and frail, the very young, and perhaps females in general are pictured as "easy" prey for violent attacks. A varied collection of psychological, biological, and social conditions may set whole categories of people apart as particularly vulnerable (Von Hentig, 1941).

From the offenders' standpoint, potential targets (individuals, homes, cars) can be "rated" along several dimensions. One dimension is attractiveness versus repulsiveness; some people and things appear like "fair game" in "open season," just ripe for the taking, while others present a challenge or pose a threat (of being thwarted, even captured). Proximity versus distance describes whether the offender is within striking range, geographically and socially (in terms of interaction and direct contact). Vulnerability versus impregnability is a dimension that reflects whether a potential target is well protected or undefended.

Situational factors may play a major role. People and their possessions are more vulnerable at certain times, periods, or phases than at others. For example, prostitutes are particularly susceptible to robberies, rapes, beatings, and murders (especially by serial killers). These young women are easy targets because they operate in the shadows, are willing to go off with complete strangers to isolated or desolate locations, and often abuse alcohol or other drugs that loosen their inhibitions, increase their desperation for money, and impair their judgment. Crimes committed against them are not taken very seriously by the public or the authorities, and witnesses in their behalf (usually other prostitutes, pimps, or johns) are often disreputable, unreliable, or uncooperative (see Boyer and James, 1983). Similarly, some offenders prefer to prey on tourists. These criminals figure that because of considerations of money, time, or both, few travelers on business trips or vacations will be willing and able to return to the jurisdiction of the crime to take part in legal proceedings, even if their assailants are caught red-handed by the police. A tourist's average length of stay of a few days to a few weeks is invariably too brief to see a case through to its conclusion. As a result, charges against defendants who harm tourists are usually dropped or drastically reduced because of the absence of the complainant. To curtail the attractiveness of tourists as targets, extraordinary policies are needed. For instance, Waikiki Beach in Honolulu, Hawaii, was a haven for muggers and rapists until an apprehensive travel industry, convinced that crime was hurting business, began to fund a victim-witness return project. Free airplane tickets, accommodations, and child care were furnished to visitors who flew back to Hawaii, pressed charges, and testified at trials. Government officials even interceded with victims' employers to assure them of the importance of the trip. As a result, as prosecution and conviction rates went up, tourists reportedly no longer suffered excessively high rates of robbery, theft, and assault ("Hawaii Return-Witness Program," 1982).

But most victimologists are not satisfied with explanations of variations in rates that emphasize discrete vulnerability factors that are biological (like gender, age, and race), psychological (like loneliness or greediness), social (like income and occupation), or situational (like being an immigrant or a tourist). A number of more elaborate answers have been developed to account for differential risks.

One explanation is that observed differences in murder and robbery rates might be the result of differences in lifestyles. The sociological term *lifestyle* refers to how people involve themselves in daily activities and special events on a predictable basis. It encompasses how people spend their time and money at work as well as at leisure, and the social roles (like business traveler, student, or homemaker) they play. Lifestyles are strongly influenced by structural constraints (such as the need to commute to work) and role expectations (for example, how young adults ought to spend their Saturday nights). Lifestyles largely determine the quantity and quality of the contacts between potential victims and criminally inclined individuals who might harm them (in public spaces, like streets and parks at night, for instance, for those who make a habit of congregating in these places). The key factor is that differences in lifestyles lead to variations in exposure to risks. In the long run, exposure is the primary determinant of a group's victimization rate. For example, poor, young, single minority males living in inner cities run the greatest risks of being robbed because of their daily exposure to criminally inclined people living in their midst. Other factors related to lifestyle that affect one's odds of getting in trouble include individual responses to the threat of crime (such as willingness to take precautions) and idiosyncratic personal traits (such as body language) and habits (such as jogging after work) (Hindelang, Gottfredson, and Garofalo, 1978; Garofalo, 1986).

A second, related explanation centers upon "routine activities" and emphasizes how offenders may seize opportunities to strike when attractive, poorly defended targets are in close proximity. Routine activities include commuting to work, shopping, child-rearing responsibilities, pursuing sexual outlets, leisure time hobbies, and socializing with friends. In recent decades, routine activities have shifted away from the home and toward greater interaction with non–household members. Vulnerability increases when people must venture away from their homes and families; predatory strangers are able to isolate suitable targets when they are not adequately guarded (Cohen and Felson, 1979; Cohen, Kluegal, and Land, 1981). The routine-activities explanation ties together several major themes within criminology and victimology: that social conditions continuously generate criminally inclined individuals; that opportunities for committing thefts and robberies multiply as possessions proliferate; that preventive measures in tandem with unofficial guardianship (informal mechanisms of social control in which people assume responsibility for the well-being of others) may be more effective than stepped-up policing and punishment in discouraging offenders from striking; and that certain activities and circumstances expose people and their possessions to heightened risks (see Felson, 1994). The explanation can be strengthened by noting that many incidents tend to be concentrated in a limited number of "hot spots" in urban settings (Sherman, Gartin, and Buerger, 1989); and that everyday routines govern the social ecology of victimization: what kinds of people will be harmed, in what manner, at what time, and at which locations (Messner and Tardiff, 1985). For example, people who spend most of their time at home are not in much danger of being murdered, and certainly not by strangers; but if they do meet a violent end, it is likely to be at the hands of family members or close friends (Messner and Tardiff, 1985; Maxfield, 1987).

Still another explanation for variations in victimization rates portrays victims in a less sympathetic light. It stresses that vulnerability can result from the pursuit of amusement and excitement. Activities such as cruising around, hanging out, partying, and frequenting unlicensed after-hours social clubs incorporate elements of uncertainty and danger. Consequently, those who involve themselves in daring, delinquent, and illicit activities run greater risks of being assaulted, robbed, or raped (Jensen and Brownfield, 1986).

Some offenders select their victims from their own circles of friends and acquaintances. In such cases, victims and their victimizers are not drawn from distinct or mutually exclusive populations, but, on the contrary, come from homogenous or overlapping groups (Fattah, 1991). Adherence to and participation in the norms of certain deviant subcultures can raise an individual's level of risk. For example, in many cases of serious assaults, investigators often discover that both the victims and their assailants were mutual combatants immersed in a subculture of violence in which a willingness to use force in settling disputes is strongly condoned (Singer, 1986). A great deal of violence and theft is known to take place within the drug-oriented subculture when people are intoxicated. For example, a sample of violent offenders incarcerated in state prisons told interviewers that about 30 percent of their victims were under the influence of alcohol or drugs at the time of the crime (Timrots and Snyder, 1994). Even more dramatic are the consequences of the lethal violence that punctuates street-level drug dealing, which caused the homicide rate among teenage boys between fifteen and nineteen years old to soar from the mid-1980s into the early 1990s. The overwhelming majority (about 85 percent) of deaths were from firearms, usually wielded by other young males, reflecting a self-perpetuating cycle of violence in which more and more urban youths were arming themselves. The immediate precursors of many of these killings were thought to be involvement in the crack cocaine trade, carrying a gun for "protection," and a willingness to rely upon bullets to settle disputes. The underlying causes were said to be poverty, poor schooling, limited legitimate job opportunities, family instability, and immersion in a subculture of violence (Fingerhut, Ingram, and Feldman, 1992a; "The New American Epidemic," 1994). The possibility that many of the victims are not selected from the ranks of the generally law-abiding citizenry, but are drawn from social circles that overlapped with their offenders, was underscored by the findings of a study of approximately 8,000 cases prosecuted during 1988 in seventy-five of the nation's most populous jurisdictions. About half (51 percent) of the deceased turned out to have criminal records for arrests or convictions themselves; roughly 85 percent of the people put on trial for murdering them also had been previously in trouble with the law (see Dawson and Langan, 1994).

What all of these explanations have in common is a sociological orientation, rather than a psychological one. They emphasize general patterns of behavior engaged in by entire groups of people, instead of the peculiar propensities of specific individuals (to pick fights or treat valuable possessions carelessly, for instance) (Garofalo, 1986). All of these explanations take "motivation" as a "given" (the reality that some people are inclined to abuse other people), and focus upon informal and formal mechanisms of social control (the ways that potential offenders are enabled to act against their intended victims or are restrained from doing so). As a result, these explanations generate many ideas about how to reduce risks, or better yet, prevent harm. However, observing safety tips and taking precautions may not be enough to meaningfully change the odds some very vulnerable people face (Miethe, Stafford, and Sloane, 1990).

Reducing Risks: How Safe Is Safe Enough?

Life is marred by all sorts of unanticipated, undesirable, and dreaded events. When social scientists estimate risks, they are predicting how many people will experience unwanted events.

The statistical concepts underlying risk estimates can be difficult to grasp. Only three distinct probabilities can be readily understood: "0," which signifies that an event is impossible; "1," which means that an event is inevitable; and "0.5," which indicates a toss-up, or a "50–50" chance (as in hoping for "heads" when flipping a coin). But risks that are 0.1 (1 in 10) or 0.01 (1 in 100) or 0.001 (1 in 1,000) are harder to gauge or evaluate. If the odds of something happening were one in a million, statisticians would advise people not to worry about it (or not to count on it, if the event is desirable). But when 5 people in every 1,000 are robbed each year, should the risk of robbery be taken into account when planning one's daily schedule? How much preparation, fear, and anxiety would be rational in the face of these odds? What sacrifices would be appropriate, in terms of forgoing necessary or welcomed activities (like taking evening classes or walking through the park on a warm spring night)? At what point does disregarding the risks and ignoring precautions become foolhardy?

The proper balance between safety and risk is ultimately a personal decision. But it is also a matter of public debate. In general, more protection can be secured by greater expenditure. Dangers can be reduced if individuals and groups are willing to pay the price (for more police patrols, improved lighting, and other security measures). Any demand for absolute safety (zero risk), however, is irrational, in statistical terms. Probabilities can be reduced but never entirely eliminated. "How safe is safe enough?" is strictly a value judgment. At some point, it is reasonable to declare the odds an "acceptable risk" (Lynn, 1981). When performing a risk-benefit analysis, a point of *diminishing returns* may be discovered. Additional efforts to increase safety are largely futile and wasteful (for example, adding more locks to a door). Risk-benefit analyses seem scientifically sound and precise, but on close inspection they hinge on questionable assumptions and debatable value judgments. How much is a human life worth, in monetary terms? Can the pain and suffering of victims, or the public's fear of crime, be converted by some formula into dollars and cents?

Victimologists and criminologists have coined terms to describe the ways in which people try to alter the risks they face by incorporating risk-reduction activities into their lifestyles and routine activities. *Avoidance strategies* (Furstenberg, 1972) are actions people take to limit their personal exposure to dangerous persons and frightening situations (such as staying home at night, barring strangers from their home, or ignoring passersby who attempt to engage in conversations on deserted streets). *Risk management tactics* (Skogan and Maxfield, 1981) minimize the chances of being harmed when exposure is unavoidable. Examples include walking with others rather than traveling alone, or carrying a weapon instead of going about unarmed. *Crime prevention through environmental design* (abbreviated CPTED) stresses the importance of creating "defensible space" (Newman, 1972) by "target hardening" (improving locks, erecting fences) and maintaining surveillance (limiting the number of entrances, improving visibility by trimming bushes and trees). Risk reduction actions are categorized *as individual* or *collective* (when arranged in concert with others) (Conklin, 1975) or, similarly, as either *private-minded* or *public-minded* (Schneider and Schneider, 1978).

Evaluating the effectiveness of specific precautions to prevent victimization is difficult because it is hard to identify particular instances when using avoidance strategies, practicing risk management tactics, and redesigning the environment have clearly prevented a crime by dissuading a potential offender from his or her intended target. Certain risk-reduction strategies do work to a degree that is plainly observable but not readily quantifiable. Two good examples would be the relatively low robbery rates for women, compared with men, and for the elderly compared to other age groups, even though women and elderly people are pre-sumed to be highly vulnerable to predatory street criminals. The apparent paradox can be explained by noting that women and the elderly routinely incorporate risk-reduction strategies into their lifestyles and routine activities, to the point that the self-imposed restrictions become second nature to these groups and evident to observers. For example, to find young men out late at night drinking in taverns seems normal; to encounter unescorted women or elderly people in such settings at those hours is surprising.

The relatively high rates of robbery (and rape and assault) for divorced, sepa-rated, and unmarried women, compared with rates for married women, can also best be understood as a function of internalizing risk-reduction measures. Married women are more able to avoid or at least manage risks. Their daily rou-tines, social companions, leisure activities, and family-centered obligations are less likely to expose them to danger than the lifestyles of women without hus-bands (except for widows, who tend to be older and follow elderly lifestyles) (Skogan, 1981a).

Deterrence Theory, Applied to Victims

For over two centuries (since the time of Beccaria and Bentham, the originators of the "classical school" of "free will," "choice," or "rational decision-making theory"), a fierce debate has raged over whether would-be offenders are deterred by the prospects of apprehension, conviction, and punishment. But rarely, if ever, is the debate redirected and focused on past and potential victims. The question arises, do victims learn a lesson, and does the public learn from the mistakes of victims?

Simply put, deterrence theory holds that swift and sure punishment is the so-lution to the crime problem. According to the tenets of specific deterrence, pun-ishing an offender teaches him a lesson, so he will not repeat the forbidden act again. According to the logic of general deterrence, punishing an offender creates an example (negative role model) that serves as a warning to others to avoid simi-lar misdeeds.

Proponents and critics argue over whether offenders really learn the intended lesson (especially in jails and prisons, which might actually serve as "schools for crime" that turn out individuals with advanced degrees in criminality); whether would-be lawbreakers actually mull over their decisions rationally, "think twice" and decide not to commit an illegal act (or instead often act impulsively, disregarding the possible consequences, perhaps in the heat of passion); and whether others who hear about the crime and the punishment that followed truly make the connection, think "That could be me!" and are "scared straight" and dissuaded from violating the law.

Applying the principles of general deterrence to law-abiding people, do members of the public closely identify with the innocent victim? Do they also make the connection, "It could have been me!" and profit from someone else's misfortune? Does news media coverage of the crime problem strike fear in the hearts and minds of large numbers of would-be victims, making them think twice before doing anything risky? Does the frightening prospect of becoming a victim lead to constructive responses, in terms of incorporating risk avoidance and risk management precautions into lifestyles?

Applying the principles of specific deterrence, a parallel question arises. Do one-time victims learn their lessons? Do they realize their mistakes, vow not to repeat these errors, take "dos and don'ts" tips more seriously, and change their ways? Or do they disregard the persisting threats, continue to take their chances, plow ahead recklessly, become "repeat victims" and suffer "serial victimizations" (two or more incidents during a relatively short period of time)?

The answers to these queries require careful research. A reasonable hypothesis is that some potential victims are more likely to be deterred than others. Specifically, individuals who are middle class, and middle-aged or older, and female are probably more inclined than others to respond to the fear of being harmed ("punishment") by thinking twice and concluding that the risks outweigh the benefits. They exercise their free will, rationally decide it isn't worth the risk, choose a more prudent course of action, and are deterred from behaving in a way that disregards the potential negative consequences.

From Crime Prevention to Victimization Prevention

The new interest in lifestyles, routine activities, and risk-reduction strategies has contributed to an evolution in prevention strategies. The term *crime prevention* refers to strategies that are pursued to forestall the development of illegal activities, as opposed to *crime control* measures, which are taken in response to acts that have already been committed.

Formerly, crime prevention strategies centered on government programs designed to eradicate the social roots of illegal behavior, such as poverty, unemployment, and discrimination. Crime prevention campaigns used to focus on improving the quality of education in inner-city school systems, providing decent jobs for all those who want to work, and developing meaningful recreational outlets for idle youth. But the campaigns associated with the term have evolved, and broad strategies have been replaced by direct tactics. Crime prevention has come to mean "the anticipation, recognition, and appraisal of a crime risk, and the initiation of some action to remove or reduce it" (National Crime Prevention Institute, 1978). Crime prevention strategies are shifting toward individual and small-group actions and away from large-scale, governmental undertakings. Perhaps a better term than *crime prevention* for these preemptive measures is *victimization prevention* (Cohn, Kidder, and Harvey, 1978). Victimization prevention is much more modest in intent than crime prevention. Its goal is simply to discourage criminals from attacking particular targets, such as a home, warehouse, store, car, or person. Like defensive driving, victimization prevention hinges on the dictum, "Watch the other guy, and anticipate his moves."

The shift from crime prevention on a societal and governmental level to victimization prevention on a neighborhood, small-group, and individual level demands of potential victims that they become crime conscious, or "street smart." The responsibility for keeping out of trouble increasingly falls on the possible targets themselves, who must outmaneuver and keep one step ahead of would-be offenders. Crime conscious individuals are compelled to follow prevention tips, which are long lists of "dos and don'ts," compiled from observations of other people's misfortunes. "Crime resistance," or "target hardening" means making the offender's task more difficult through advanced planning (the opposite of making it easier through carelessness). The aim is to be prepared for an inevitable attack by taking precautions and building defenses (such as installing closed-circuit television monitors).

The plausible hypothesis that "measures that make a person appear well-protected and property well-guarded encourage potential offenders to look elsewhere for easier pickings" (Moore, 1985) must be carefully examined before it can be accepted. If data collected from social experiments support this contention, then effective victimization prevention measures might have far-reaching consequences. A "valve theory of crime shifts" predicts that the number of crimes committed will not drop when targets are hardened but that criminal activity will simply be deflected. If one area of illegal opportunity is shut off (for example, if robbing bus drivers is made unprofitable by the imposition of exact-fare requirements), criminals will shift their attention to more vulnerable targets (such as cabdrivers or storekeepers) (National Commission on the Causes and Prevention of Violence, 1969a). When crime is displaced, the risk of victimization goes down for some but rises for others, assuming that offenders are intent on committing crimes and that they are flexible in terms of time, place, target, and tactics (Allen et al., 1981). In other words, the adoption of victimization prevention strategies by some crime-conscious persons might endanger other unsuspecting people. Victimization will be redistributed, spatially, geographically, and socially. But that is a far cry from genuine crime prevention, which would lower the risks everyone faces.

This distinction is illustrated in the frank acknowledgment, in a pamphlet distributed by the country's largest police department, that self-protective measures merely redirect offenders elsewhere: "No vehicle is theft-proof. You must approach this problem with the attitude that it will not be my car that becomes part of the statistics. As selfish as it may sound, if the thief wants a car of your year, make, and model, let it be someone else's. If you follow these guidelines and take all the necessary precautions to protect your car, the chances are it will not be stolen" (New York Police Department, 1992).

Whether victimization prevention methods really work to cut the crime rate or simply diminish the risks some people and their possessions face, while increasing the threat faced by others, is a question victimologists must examine. One thing is clear: Target-hardening strategies certainly lend themselves to commercial exploitation. New, allegedly security-enhancing goods and services are constantly being developed for a growing market of people who don't want to become victims, or if victimized once already, don't want to be harmed again.

Ambivalence about Risk Taking

Contradictory messages permeate American culture on the subject of risk taking. On the one hand, the entrepreneurial ideology extols risk taking and generously rewards those business ventures that defy conventional wisdom, survive financial hardships, and thrive in a highly competitive, adverse economic environment. Similarly, cultural heroes are invariably risk takers who overcome overwhelming odds: pioneers, explorers, inventors, private detectives, secret agents, soldiers of fortune, high-stakes gamblers, and other adventurers. On the other hand, middle-class values emphasize control over one's destiny and counsel prudence in the face of grave dangers. Conscientious, responsible, "mature adults" plan, build, invest, and save in order to be prepared for adversity, illness, old age, accidents, or devastating victimizations. They seek out safety, peace of mind, insurance, and protection to guard against unforeseen disasters and avoidable tragedies. The hallmarks of scientific achievement include mastery of events and domination over nature. Technological progress is recognized as the reduction of uncertainty and the attainment of reliable, predictable performance. Autonomy (personal independence) and security are highly desired goals. Underlying all these human aspirations and accomplishments are the notions of reducing or practically eliminating risks.

The ambivalent attitudes toward risks in American culture are mirrored by contradictory responses to victimizations. Some readily rush to the defense of victims while others impulsively criticize them, characterizing victims as risk takers who have lost or failed in their gambits. Their suffering evokes sympathy, but it also invites second-guessing about what, if anything, concerning their attitudes and lifestyles might be altered to avoid future troubles. This line of inquiry leads to a close inspection of the specific acts that immediately preceded the crime, as well as the general routines that define lifestyles. As the victim–offender interaction is reconstructed and scrutinized, exactly how the victim behaved—what he or she said or did—becomes the focus of attention. The keen interest many victimologists have shown in attitudes and actions that increase rather than reduce risks is the subject of the next chapter.

3

The Victim's Role in Crime

THE CONTINUING CONTROVERSY
OVER SHARED RESPONSIBILITY

A man pulls into his driveway, turns off his car's engine, and enters his home. A teenager walks by and spots the car's keys dangling in the ignition switch. He hops behind the wheel and drives off. Was the motorist partly responsible for the crime because he made the thief's task easier? Is victim facilitation a major factor in the high rate of auto theft?

A young woman tries to thumb a ride home from a local beach on a hot summer's day. A young man in a sports car picks up the hitchhiker and interprets her appreciation as a sign of sexual interest. He drives to a deserted parking lot and makes sexual advances. She resists, but he assumes her protests are feigned. When he tries to pin her down, she bolts from the car and runs screaming along the road. Did she contribute to the attempted rape by recklessly placing herself in a dangerous, sexually charged situation? Is victim precipitation a major reason for sexual assaults?

A husband periodically beats his wife over the course of more than twenty years. After each episode, he is contrite and vows to change his "evil ways." But one day he threatens to kill their daughter. When he falls asleep that night, she shoots him and then sets their house on fire. She is arrested and tried for first-degree murder. The jury rejects her contention that she was temporarily insane from terror and that she acted in self-defense to save herself and her daughter. The judge sentences her to life in prison even though she is permanently disabled from his beatings (Browne, 1987). Did the husband instigate his own murder? Is victim provocation a major factor in the slayings of abusive spouses?

Mainstream criminology has consistently ignored the role that victims might play in the consummation of crimes. Victimologists have pledged to correct this imbalance by examining all situations to see whether the people who were harmed might have played some part in their own downfall. Victimologists have thus departed from the classical offender-oriented explanations of crime (in which the act is attributed solely to the free will of the lawbreaker) and have raised the possibility of shared responsibility. That is, victimologists have suggested that, to explain why one person harmed another at a particular time and place, criminal incidents be viewed as the results of a process of interaction between two parties. What has emerged is a dynamic model that takes into account initiatives and responses, actions and reactions, motives and intentions. Several expressions coined by the pioneers in victimology capture their enthusiasm for examining interactions: the "duet frame of reference" (Von Hentig, 1941), the "penal couple" (Mendelsohn, 1956), and the "doer–sufferer relationship" (Ellenberger, 1955). These situational explanations can provide a more complete picture of what happened and thereby represent an improvement over earlier, static, one-sided, perpetrator-centered accounts (Fattah, 1979).

A well-known line of inquiry (albeit a controversial one) within criminology centers upon the differences, if any, between offenders and law-abiding people. Criminologists ask, "What distinguishes the offender from the nonoffender?" In a similar vein, victimologists ask, "What distinguishes the victim from the non-victim? Do victims think or act differently than nonvictims?"

Just posing the question raises the possibility of shared responsibility. Victimologists have borrowed the terminology of the legal system, traditionally used to describe criminals' behaviors, to describe the motives and actions of victims as well. The words *responsibility, culpability, guilt,* and *blame* crop up routinely in studies based on the dynamic, situational, interaction model. In the broadest sense, the concept of shared responsibility implies that victims—as well as offenders—did something "wrong." The victims acted carelessly, foolishly, or even provocatively. Instead of minimizing the risks they faced, these victims maximized them. The circumstances under which they were harmed were partly of their own making. The unfortunate events were preventable. To some degree, such victims can be faulted.

The process of fixing responsibility for crime unavoidably rests on judgments that are subject to question and attack. These judgments are based on values, ethics, prejudices, and allegiances. Much of the crime that plagues everyday life arises out of conflicts between people and groups that have allies and enemies. Long-standing disputes and smoldering struggles that erupt into acts of violence and destruction have caused people to become polarized. Lines have been drawn and sides chosen. When crimes are committed as part of the conflict between family members, neighbors, schoolmates, or coworkers, determinations of responsibility can be made with a considerable degree of objectivity by outsiders and other disinterested parties. But when the criminality arises from conflicts between members of different races, sexes, or social classes, employers and their employees, merchants and their customers, landlords and their tenants, officers and soldiers (superiors and subordinates in general), or "haves and have-nots," assigning responsibility in a scientific, neutral manner is much more difficult. In such cases, people tend to approach the question of responsibility ideologically. Such prejudgment before hearing all the facts—showing a reflexlike empathy toward one side and hostility toward the other—undermines objectivity.

The first few criminologists who were drawn to the study of victims were enthused about the concept of shared responsibility as an overlooked contributory "cause" of crime. By introducing concepts like *victim facilitation, precipitation, provocation, proneness, vulnerability,* and *accountability,* they brought about a more complete—but also a more controversial—picture of crime-producing situations. While victimology has thus enriched criminology, it has also contributed to further schisms. Starting in the 1970s, some criminologists and victimologists began to express concern over the implications of studies into mutual interactions and reciprocal influences of victims and offenders. Those who raised doubts and voiced dissent might be seen to loosely constitute a different school of thought. Just as criminology, with a much longer, richer, and stormier history, has recognizable orientations and camps (for example, in regard to labeling theory and conflict models), so too does victimology have its rifts and factions. To put it bluntly, the victim-blaming tendency within victimology clashes repeatedly with the victim-defending tendency over a great many issues.

In this chapter, the arguments of both sides in the debate over shared responsibility will be presented in a balanced manner. First, to determine what is at stake, the importance of fixing responsibility will be examined. Then the concepts and research findings of those victimologists who have investigated the possibility of shared responsibility, and who believe they have found evidence of it, will be examined. After a general discussion of victim blaming and its opposite, victim defending, the debate between these two schools of thought will be traced in three specific areas: whether some victims of car theft facilitated the crime, whether some rape victims precipitated the attacks upon them, and whether some abusive husbands provoked their wives to slay them. The chapter will conclude with a discussion of the strengths, weaknesses, and limitations of the victim-blaming and victim-defending perspectives.

THE IMPORTANCE OF FIXING RESPONSIBILITY

The question of whether or not and, if yes, to what degree, the victim shares responsibility with the offender for a violation of the law is a crucial one. A number of important decisions that affect the fate of the criminal, the plight of the victim, and the public's perception of the crime problem hinge on determinations of victim responsibility. Whether or not the victim facilitated, precipitated, or provoked the offender is taken into account by policemen, prosecutors, juries, judges, compensation boards, insurance examiners, politicians, and crime control strategists. Victim responsibility arises as an issue at many stages in the criminal justice process: in applications for compensation; in demands for restitution and compensatory damages; in complaints about how crime victims are treated by family, friends, and strangers at home, in hospital emergency rooms, in court, and in the newspapers; and in the development of crime prevention programs and criminological theories.

At every juncture in the operation of the criminal justice system, judgments must be made about the degree of responsibility, if any, the victim bears for what happened. The police confront this issue first. For example, when called to the scene of a barroom brawl, officers must decide whether to arrest one or both or none of the participants and what charges to lodge if they do make arrests. Often the loser is declared the victim, and the combatant still on his feet is taken into custody for assault.

When district attorneys review the charges brought by the police against defendants, they must decide if the complainants were indeed totally innocent victims. If some degree of blame can be placed upon them, their credibility as witnesses for the prosecution becomes impaired. A district attorney may decide that the accused person would probably be viewed (by a jury or a judge) as less culpable and less deserving of punishment and, therefore, has less of a chance of being convicted. Since relatively few cases are ever brought to trial, district attorneys will engage in plea bargaining (accepting a guilty plea to a lesser charge) in cases with a blameworthy victim who would be an unconvincing witness. Such cases might even be screened out, and charges dropped. For instance, a study of files in the District of Columbia during the early 1970s revealed that evidence of victim blameworthiness halved the chances that a case would be prosecuted (Williams, 1976).

Killings that result from the extreme provocations by the deceased persons are likely to be considered justifiable homicides and won't be prosecuted. Different jurisdictions use different standards to determine what constitutes provocation and justification. For example, a study of Houston's murders turned up a figure of 12 percent deemed justifiable, whereas in Chicago only 3 percent of all killings were considered justifiable by the local authorities. It appears that the legal definition of justification was broader in Texas than in Illinois (Block, 1981).

If the provocation by the dead victim is not considered sufficient to make a homicide justifiable, it might be treated as an extenuating circumstance. Evidence of victim provocation can persuade the district attorney to charge the defendant with manslaughter instead of murder. In a homicide or assault case, in order for the charges to be reduced or for the defendant to be acquitted on the grounds of justifiable self-defense, the victim's provocation must have been "adequate." In most states, that means that the defendant's violent responses to the victim's provocations must have occurred during the heat of passion, before there had been a reasonable opportunity for intense emotions to cool (Williams, 1978; Wolfgang, 1958).

If the defendant is convicted, the judge may view the victim's provocation as a mitigating factor that makes a lesser sentence appropriate. In those jurisdictions where restitution by offenders to victims is permitted or even mandated, the culpability of victims can be a cause for reducing the amount of repayment that criminals must undertake. Similarly, the judge or the jury in civil court is likely to consider a victim's blameworthy actions as a reason for reducing the monetary damages a defendant must pay for causing loss, pain, and suffering. Parallel considerations arise when victims of violent crimes apply to a criminal injury compensation board for reimbursement. If the board members determine in a hearing that the victim bears some of the responsibility for the incident, they will reduce the amount of the award or may, in extreme cases of shared guilt and provocation, reject the victim's claims entirely (see Chapter 6).

In some conflicts that erupt after extensive interaction between two mutually hostile parties, the designations "offender" and "victim" simply do not apply. When both people behaved illegally, adjudication under the adversary system may not be appropriate. Neighborhood justice centers have been set up to settle these disputes through mediation and arbitration. Compromise solutions are appropriate when both disputants are to some degree "right" as well as "wrong" (see Chapter 7).

In sum, widely held beliefs and stereotypes about the question of shared responsibility can profoundly shape the way a case is handled within the criminal justice process.

The Possibility of Shared Responsibility

The concept of shared responsibility inspired considerable theorizing and research during victimology's first few decades. Leading figures in the field encouraged researchers to seek out evidence of shared responsibility. Some of their statements appear in Box 3.1.

Victim Facilitation, Precipitation, and Provocation

The notions of victim facilitation, precipitation, and provocation have been derived from the broader theme of shared responsibility to describe the specific, identifiable, blameworthy actions taken by certain individuals immediately before they were harmed. Unfortunately, these three terms have been used somewhat loosely and inconsistently by criminologists and victimologists, to the point that important distinctions have been blurred or buried.

Victim Facilitation   *Facilitation* is a term that ought to be reserved for those situations in which victims unknowingly, carelessly, negligently, and inadvertently make it easier for the criminal to commit a theft. Facilitating victims unwillingly assist the offender and therefore share a minor amount of blame. They increase the risks of losing their property by their own thoughtless actions. If it is assumed that the criminal who steals a careless person's possessions was already on the prowl, looking for opportunities to grab and run, then victim facilitation is not in any sense a root cause of crime. Facilitation is more like a catalyst in a chemical reaction, which, given the right ingredients and conditions, speeds up the interaction. Facilitating victims attract criminally inclined people to their poorly guarded possessions and thereby influence the spatial distribution of crime but not the number of incidents.

BOX 3.1   Expressions of Support for Inquiries into the Victim's Role

---

- A real mutuality frequently can be observed in the connection between the perpetrator and the victim, the killer and the killed, the duper and the duped. The victim in many instances leads the evildoer into temptation. The predator is, by varying means, prevailed upon to advance against the prey. (Von Hentig, 1941:303)

- In a sense, the victim shapes and molds the criminal. Although the final outcome may appear to be one-sided, the victim and criminal profoundly work upon each other, right up until the last moment in the drama. Ultimately, the victim can assume the role of determinant in the event. (Von Hentig, 1948:384)

- Criminologists should give as much attention to "victimogenesis" as to "criminogenesis." Every person should know exactly to what dangers he is exposed because of his occupation, social class, and psychological constitution. (Ellenberger, 1955:258)

- The distinction between criminal and victim, which used to be considered as clear-cut as black and white, can become vague and blurred in individual cases. The longer and the more deeply the actions of the persons involved are scrutinized, the more difficult it occasionally will be to decide who is to blame for the tragic outcome. (Mannheim, 1965:672)

- In some cases, the victim initiates the interaction, and sends out signals that the receiver (doer) decodes, triggering or generating criminal behavior in the doer. (Reckless, 1967:142)

- Probation and parole officers must understand victim-offender relationships. The personality of the victim, as a cause of the offense, is oftentimes more pertinent than that of the offender. (Schultz, 1968:135)

- Responsibility for one's conduct is a changing concept, and its interpretation is a true mirror of the social, cultural, and political conditions of a given era. . . . Notions of criminal responsibility most often indicate the nature of societal inter-relationships and the ideology of the ruling group in the power structure. Many crimes don't just happen to be committed—the victim's negligence, precipitative actions, or provocations can contribute to the genesis of crime. . . . The victim's functional responsibility is to do nothing that will provoke others to injure him [or her], and to actively seek to prevent criminals from harming him. (Schafer, 1968:4, 144, 152)

- Scholars have begun to see the victim not just as a passive object, as the innocent point of impact of crime on society, but as sometimes playing an active role and possibly contributing to some degree to his [or her] own victimization. During the last 30 years, there has been considerable debate, speculation, and research into the victim's role, the criminal-victim relationship, the concept of responsibility, and behaviors that could be considered provocative. Thus, the study of crime has taken on a more realistic and more complete outlook. (Viano, 1976:1)

- There is much to be learned about victimization patterns and the factors that influence them. Associated with the question of relative risk is the more specific question (of considerable importance) of victim participation, since crime is an interactional process. (Parsonage, 1979:10)

- Victimology also postulates that the roles of "victim" and "victimizer" are neither fixed nor

(continued on next page)

BOX 3.1	*continued*

assigned, but are mutable and interchangeable, with continuous movement between the two roles. . . . This position, understandably, will not be welcomed by those who, for a variety of practical or utilitarian reasons, continue to promote the popular stereotypes of victims and victimizers, according to which the two populations are as different as black and white, night and day, wolves and lambs. (Fattah, 1991:xiv)

Calls for Inquiries into the Victim's Role in Specific Crimes

- *Murder:* In many crimes, especially criminal homicide which usually involves intense personal interaction, the victim is often a major contributor to the lawless act. . . . Except in cases in which the victim is an innocent bystander and is killed in lieu of an intended victim, or in cases in which a pure accident is involved, the victim may be one of the major precipitating causes of his own demise. (Wolfgang, 1958:245, 264)

- *Rape:* The offender should not be viewed as the sole "cause" and reason for the offense, and the "virtuous" rape victim is not always the innocent and passive party. The role played by the victim and its contribution to the perpetration of the offense becomes one of the main interests of the emerging discipline of victimology. Furthermore, if penal justice is to be fair it must be attentive to these problems of degrees of victim responsibility for her own victimization. (Amir, 1971:275–276)

- *Theft:* Careless people set up temptation-opportunity situations when they carry their money or leave their valuables in a manner which virtually invites theft by pocket picking, burglary, or robbery. Carelessness in handling cash is so persistently a part of everyday living that it must be deemed almost a national habit. . . . Because victim behavior today is conducive to criminality, it will be necessary to develop mass educational programs aimed at changing that behavior. (Fooner, 1971:313, 315)

Victims cause crime in the sense that they set up the opportunity for the crime to be committed. By changing the behavior of the victim and potential victim, the crime rate can be reduced. Holders of fire insurance policies must meet fire safety standards, so why not require holders of theft insurance to meet security standards? (Jeffrey, 1971:208–209)

- *Burglary:* In the same way that criminologists compare offenders with nonoffenders to understand why a person commits a crime, we examined how the burglary victim and non-victim differ in an attempt to understand the extent to which a victim vicariously contributes to or precipitates a break-in. (Waller and Okihiro, 1978:5)

- *Auto theft:* Unlike most personal property, which is preserved behind fences and walls, cars are constantly moved from one exposed location to another; and since autos contain their own means of locomotion, potential victims are particularly responsible for varying the degree of theft risk by where they park and by the occasions they provide for starting the engine. The role of the victim is especially consequential for this crime; many cases of auto theft appear to be essentially a matter of opportunity. They are victim facilitated. (McCaghy, Giordano, and Henson, 1977:369)

Auto theft and burglary are the property crimes most often cited by victimologists who study the problem of facilitation. A motorist who carelessly leaves the keys dangling in the car's ignition is considered blameworthy of facilitation if a juvenile joyrider impulsively hops behind the wheel and drives off. Similarly, a ransacked home is the price a person might pay for negligence. A residential burglary can be considered victim facilitated if an intruder does not need to break into the premises because a homeowner or apartment dweller left the door unlocked (or, worse yet, ajar) or a window wide open.

By definition, victim-facilitated burglaries are not break-ins but rather acts of trespass that don't require busting down doors or smashing windows. Details about victim-facilitated burglaries appear in the published findings of the yearly *National Crime Victimization Survey*. The survey keeps track of three categories of household (not commercial) burglaries: forcible entries, attempted forcible entries, and unlawful entries without force (which are always counted as completed—not attempted—acts of theft).

In 1992, the *NCVS* estimated that over 4,750,000 household burglaries were carried out (both attempted and completed). Of these, nearly 2,200,000, or almost half (46 percent), were unlawful entries without force. The immediate impulse is to speculate that the total number of burglaries could be cut practically in half if people would take greater care to lock up their homes (at least burglars would have to work harder and, in some cases, would be deterred, thwarted, scared off, or caught red-handed).

According to the breakdowns presented in the 1992 *NCVS*, some kinds of people were more likely to be "guilty" of victim facilitation than others. The overall rate for unlawful entries without force was around 22 for every 1,000 households that year. But the age of the head of the household turned out to be the most important determinant of whether or not someone would be so careless as to facilitate a burglary. The rate for households headed by a teenager was an outrageous 62 per 1,000; by people twenty to thirty-four years old, 30 per 1,000; and senior citizens, a miniscule 11 per 1,000. Another key factor was the number of people in the household: The more people living under the same roof, the more likely carelessness would take its toll. In large families (of six or more) evidently someone was more likely to be lax about security because 41 out of every 1,000 large families suffered an unlawful entry without force that year. People living alone experienced only 15 facilitated burglaries per 1,000 single-person households per year. Rates for families of between two and five members fell in between these two extremes. Region of the country also turned out to be important. Unlawful entries without force were much more of a problem in the West (35 per 1,000) than in the Northeast (13 per 1,000). There was some evidence that people who lived at their current residence for less than two years were more prone to be careless. City dwellers were a bit less likely to take standard precautions than suburbanites and people living in the countryside. Renters were more likely than owners to leave doors and windows open or unlocked. The race and ethnicity of the head of the household hardly mattered: Facilitated burglaries were slightly more common in Hispanic than in either black or white households and slightly less common in "other" families. Finally, the income of the family did not seem to be correlated with the no-force entry rate; the lowest-income families (making less than $7,500 annually) were the most careless, at 34 per 1,000; but the next-to-lowest category (making between $7,500 and $9,999) were the most careful, experiencing only 17 facilitated burglaries per 1,000 per year. The other income groupings had in-between rates (BJS, 1994b).

Since people often talk about the "good old days" when they left their doors unlocked, trends over time might reveal some interesting insights. The findings from the *NCVS* over the years from 1973 to 1992 (BJS, 1994a) appear in the graph in Figure 3.1.

The graph shows a trend that the sellers of alarm systems probably do not want publicized: that (total) burglary rates have dropped substantially (47 percent) over the years. Completed forcible entries (break-ins) declined from about 30 per 1,000 dwellings in 1973 to about 17 per 1,000 in 1992. Unlawful entries without

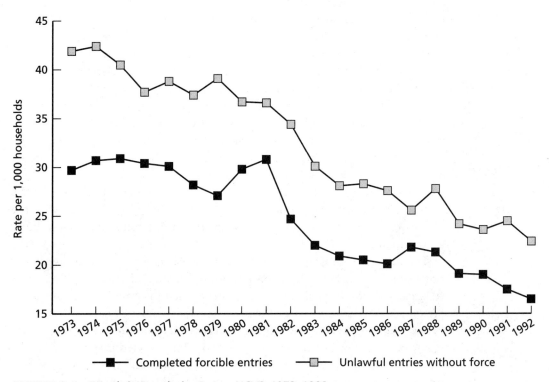

FIGURE 3.1 Trends in Burglaries Rates: *NCVS*, 1973–1992

Note: Only completed burglaries are counted.

Source: BJS, 1994a.

force also dropped sharply, from a little more than 40 to a little more than 20 per 1,000 over the twenty-year time interval. Apparently, security consciousness is more widespread these days: Burglars must work harder because fewer people are making it easy for intruders to come into their homes and steal their possessions.

Victim Precipitation and Provocation   The following case illustrates how easily a perceived affront can escalate into an armed confrontation and end in a fatal showdown:

> **T**wo young men on a popcorn line in a movie theater become embroiled in a dispute over who was there first. One warns the other that he is going out to his car to get his gun. "Go ahead," says his newly made enemy. The man returns to the theater with a revolver and locates his opponent just as the lights go out and the movie begins. The seated man pulls his own gun, fires once, and misses. The man standing over him fires twice, hitting the victim in the head and killing him, and then flees. (James, 1989)

Victimologists have terms to describe such cases: "victim-precipitated," maybe even "victim-provoked" homicides.

Whereas facilitation is a possibility in thefts, charges of precipitation and provocation are directed at victims of violent crimes, such as murder, robbery, assault, and rape. The accusation embedded in the term *precipitation* is that the person who gets hurt significantly contributed to the outbreak of violence. Provocation is even worse than precipitation, because the term implies that the loser is more responsible than the victor for the fight that ensued. The injured party instigated an attack that otherwise would not have taken place. The victim goaded, challenged, or incited a law-abiding person into taking defensive measures in reaction to the victim's aggressive initiatives. When the confrontation is over, the aggressor is the one who is wounded or killed.

Unfortunately, over the years victimologists and criminologists have used the terms *precipitation* and *provocation* loosely, and even interchangeably, obscuring the distinction between less responsibility (precipitation) and more responsibility (provocation).

The first in-depth investigation of what was deemed to be "victim precipitation" centered on homicides committed in Philadelphia from 1948 to 1952 (Wolfgang, 1958). *Precipitation* was the label applied to those cases in which the person who was killed had been the first to use force, either by drawing a weapon, striking the first physical blow during an argument, or in some other way initiating a resort to violence to settle a dispute. Often, the victim and the offender knew each other; some had quarreled previously. Situations that incited the participants to violence included charges of infidelity, arguments over money, drunken brawls, and confrontations over insults and "fighting words." Typical cases drawn from police reports were as follows:

A husband threatened to kill his wife, then attacked her with a knife. In the ensuing struggle, he fell on his own weapon and bled to death.

The person who ended up the victim was the one who had started a barroom shoving match. His friends tried to break up the fight, but he persisted. Finally the tide turned, and the aggressor was knocked down; he hit his head on the floor and died from his injuries.

A man demanded money that he believed was owed to him. The alleged debtor maintained that he had repaid the debt and, incensed over the accusation, drew a knife. The creditor pulled out a gun and shot him as he lunged.

These victim-precipitated cases differ in a number of statistically significant ways from homicides in which the slain people in no way brought about their own demise. Nearly all the precipitative victims were men, whereas a sizable minority of totally innocent victims were women. Conversely, few women committed homicide, but of those that did, a substantial proportion were provoked by the violence of the men they slew. Victim-precipitated killings were carried out by offenders wielding knives or other sharp instruments in more than half the cases, whereas other homicides were due to stabbings in only a third of the cases. Alcohol was used before most killings, but especially before victim-precipitated ones. It turned out that in precipitated homicides, more often than in the killings of totally innocent people, the victim was the one who had been doing the drinking, rather than the offender. Examinations of the victims' past police records revealed that in cases of precipitation, the victim was more likely to have had a prior run-in with the law than in cases of no precipitation. Over a third of the precipitative victims had a history of committing at least one violent offense, as opposed to only a fifth of the blameless victims. Most of the homicides in Philadelphia during that time period were committed by black people against black people; an even higher four out of every five precipitative victims were black.

According to the Philadelphia homicide study, about one murder out of every four in that city during those years could be labeled as victim-precipitated. Hence, the prevailing stereotypes surrounding victims and offenders did not reflect reality in 25 percent of the cases. Widely held images of victims as weak and passive people shrinking from confrontations, and of offenders as strong, brutal, and aggressive people hunting down their prey, didn't fit the facts in one out of every four cases reconstructed in the police department's files. In many of the victim-precipitated homicides, the characteristics of the victims closely resembled those of the offenders. In some cases, two criminally inclined persons clashed, and chance alone determined which one would be designated the victim in their encounter (Wolfgang, 1958).

Some precipitative victims actually may have wanted to die (Wolfgang, 1959). That is, their rash actions and foolhardy initiatives could be interpreted as attempts to commit suicide, as if they had a death wish but could not quite carry it through without help (Reckless, 1967). If the victim's outright dares and subliminal invitations are interpreted within this framework, victim-precipitated homicide is tantamount to suicide (Mueller, in Edelhertz and Geis, 1974). The term *subintentional death* can be applied to all situations in which victims play a contributory role in their own demise, either by exercising poor judgment, by taking excessive risks, or by pursuing a self-destructive lifestyle (Allen, 1980).

This type of speculation, based on unverifiable interpretations of possible motives, is clearly unsympathetic to the dead victims who allegedly manipulated others to kill them. Coupled with the conclusion that a considerable proportion of slain people were largely responsible for their fate, these outlooks foster a tendency to view some victims in a rather harsh light—as troublemakers whose passing away is not a real tragedy.

But this line of thought does raise intriguing questions about whether or not some people want to suffer and be punished and, therefore, consciously or unconsciously enter into risky situations or engineer tragic events that ultimately harm them. This charge is leveled most commonly at people who are victimized repeatedly. In the case of homicide victims, the argument rests on a record of several "near misses" preceding the final violent outburst that took the victim's life.

An equally plausible explanation, which is not psychologically based, is that these precipitative victims didn't want to die but, instead, thought they would emerge from their battles as winners, not losers. Their petty quarrels escalated into life-and-death struggles through a sequence of stages, in which "saving face" played a large part (Luckenbill, 1977). Those who lost the showdowns didn't welcome their fate. What might be misinterpreted as their death wish was really their adherence to the norms of a "subculture of violence" (Curtis, 1974; Wolfgang and Ferracuti, 1967). This willingness to resort to physical combat and to escalate arguments into life-threatening showdowns is not psychopathological but rather learned behavior. Confrontational lifestyles that require a propensity for violence are reported to be most prevalent among young men in poor urban neighborhoods who conform to "the code of the streets" in their quest to prove their manhood and gain their peers' respect (Anderson, 1994). But the reliance on force as a method of solving problems characterizes international politics as much as street-corner life.

Provocation is much worse than precipitation. In extreme cases, the crime would not have occurred if a victim had not instigated or incited an otherwise law-abiding person into committing an illegal act, as the following example illustrates.

A twenty-three-year-old teacher befriends a seventeen-year-old high school student. She implores him to kill her because she is dying from a painful illness and is distraught over divorcing her husband. Reluctantly he agrees to shoot her, but she survives the botched job with a bullet to the shoulder. From her hospital bed, she tries to turn the incident into an example of the need for greater school security, but detectives figure out what really happened, and he is arrested for weapons possession and attempted murder. (Mitchell, 1992)

(Note that according to the law, not all persons wounded or killed by shootings are victims. For example, an armed robber slain in a gun battle with the police would be classified as a dead offender, not a provocative victim. His demise would not be a murder but an act of justifiable homicide, provided that the officer used deadly force appropriately, according to state law and departmental regulations.)

The Frequency of Shared Responsibility in Violent Crimes

The question of the victim's role in cases of street crime was systematically investigated for the first time in the late 1960s by the National Commission on the Causes and Prevention of Violence (NCCPV). As its name suggests, the blue-ribbon commission was searching for the roots of the crime problem and for practical remedies. If large numbers of victims were found to be partly at fault for what happened to them, then changing the behavior of potential victims (that is, the general public) might be a promising crime prevention strategy.

Social scientists working for the commission analyzed a 10-percent sample of all reports contained in police files in seventeen cities. For each type of crime, a definition of "victim precipitation" was derived from previous studies by criminologists and victimologists. Every case in the sample was reviewed, and if there was enough detailed information, a judgment was made about whether or not the victim had shared responsibility with the offender for the crime. Five crimes of violence were examined: criminal homicide (first- and second-degree murder and voluntary or nonnegligent manslaughter), aggravated assault (with the intent to kill or at least inflict severe bodily injury by shooting, stabbing, poisoning, and so on), forcible rape (including attempted rape), and both unarmed and armed robbery (taking anything of value from a person, either through intimidation or by force).

Victim-precipitated homicides (defined as situations in which the person who died was the first to resort to force) accounted for 22 percent of all murder cases in the seventeen cities—but 26 percent in Philadelphia (Wolfgang, 1958) and 38 percent in Chicago (Voss and Hepburn, 1968). About 14 percent of all aggravated assaults (in which the seriously injured victim was the first to use physical force, or offensive language and gestures) were deemed to be victim precipitated. Armed robberies were committed against precipitative victims ("who clearly had not acted with reasonable self-protective behavior in handling money, jewelry, or other valuables") in 11 percent of all the holdups in the seventeen cities—and 11 percent in Philadelphia (Normandeau, 1968). Only 4 percent of the forcible rapes that led to arrests in the seventeen cities were designated as victim precipitated (in which the woman "at first agreed to sexual relations, or clearly invited them verbally and through gestures, but then retracted before the act")—although as many as 19 percent of all sexual assaults were deemed to be precipitated in Philadelphia (Amir, 1967). The commission concluded that instances of victim complicity were not uncommon in cases of homicide and aggravated assault; victim precipitation was less frequent but still empirically noteworthy in robbery; and the issue of shared responsibility was least relevant as a contributing factor in rapes (National Commission on the Causes and Prevention of Violence, 1969b; Curtis, 1974).

Recognizing Complete Innocence and Full Responsibility

Up to this point, the degree of responsibility a victim might share with an offender has ranged from facilitation through precipitation to provocation. But the spectrum of possibilities extends further in each direction, from complete innocence to full responsibility.

Complete Innocence Completely innocent individuals cannot be blamed for what happened to them. As crime-conscious persons, they tried to avoid trouble. They did what they could, within reason, to reduce the risks they faced. (After the fact, it can always be argued that they did not do enough.) In cases of property crimes, these victims took proactive steps to safeguard their possessions in anticipation of the possibility of burglary, larceny, or some other form of theft. They cannot be faulted for negligence, or even passive indifference. In order to deter attack, they sought ways to make the criminals' tasks more difficult (just the opposite of facilitation). They "hardened their targets" by purchasing security devices like special locks and alarm systems. In cases of crimes of violence, they did nothing to instigate otherwise law-abiding people to attack them (no provocation) or to attract assailants to themselves; in fact, they were mindful of threatening situations and took precautions to limit their exposure to dangerous persons (no precipitation).

Full Responsibility If taking precautions and adopting risk-reduction strategies qualifies as the basis for blamelessness and complete innocence, then total complicity becomes the defining characteristic for full responsibility. Logically, a victim can be solely responsible only when there is no offender at all. Victims who bear total responsibility for what happened are by definition really not victims at all. They are offenders posing as victims for some ulterior motive. In cases of property crimes, phony victims are usually seeking either reimbursement from private insurance policies or government aid for imaginary losses. They file false claims and thereby commit fraud. Fake victims may have motives other than financial gain. Some people may claim to be victims to cover up what really oc-curred. For example, a husband who gambled away his paycheck may tell his wife and the police that he was robbed.

Typologies of Shared Responsibility

Previous Efforts A *typology* is a classification scheme that aids in the understand-ing of what a group of people has in common and how it differs from other groups. Researchers have discussed and dismissed the possibility of "born victims" who are doomed from birth to become targets. They have also observed that the social reaction to victimization is not always outrage, empathy, and support but can range from indifference to tacit approval. Some of the types of persons identi-fied in typologies include victims who are "ideal" (above criticism); "culturally le-gitimate and appropriate" (fair game, outcasts); "deserving" (arouse no sympathy); "consenting" (willing); and "recidivist" (chronic) (see Fattah, 1991; also Mendelsohn, 1956; Fattah, 1967; Lamborn, 1968; Schafer, 1977; Sheley, 1979).

Several typologies over the years have been devised to try to illustrate the de-gree of shared responsibility, if any, that victims bear in particular crimes.

A Typology of Auto Theft Victims A typology of different kinds of victims of a single crime, such as burglary or auto theft, makes it possible to derive estimates about the relative proportions of various "types" or groupings of people, what they did "wrong," if anything, and how crime might be prevented.

In the typology of auto theft victims to follow, six types are defined, ranging from those who are totally or largely blameless, through various degrees of shared responsibility—facilitation, precipitation, and provocation—to individuals who are completely responsible (for faking a theft). (See Table 3.1.)

Conscientiously resisting victims are totally blameless and bear no responsibil-ity for the theft of their cars. These unwilling victims tried to protect their autos by scrupulously following the crime-prevention tips suggested by security special-ists. They did all they could to minimize their risks and reduce their vehicle's vul-nerability to attack by purchasing antitheft devices. Yet the defensive measures they adopted proved futile, and they were preyed on by professional thieves who knew how to disarm or circumvent the most sophisticated alarm systems and re-sistant locks.

Conventionally cautious victims relied upon the antitheft features provided by automobile manufacturers as standard equipment. They took the precautions of removing all valuables from sight, rolling up their cars' windows, locking all its doors, and pocketing the keys. Even though they did all they were supposed to do, experienced thieves with the proper tools had no trouble stealing their cars. These victims did nothing "wrong," but since they did not attempt to make their

TABLE 3.1 Types of Victims of Auto Theft

TYPE OF VICTIM	CONSCIENTIOUSLY RESISTING	CONVENTIONALLY CAUTIOUS	CARELESSLY FACILITATING	PRECIPITATIVE INITIATORS	PROVOCATIVE CONSPIRATORS	FABRICATING SIMULATORS
Degree of responsibility	*Totally blameless*	*Largely blameless*	*Partly responsible*	*Substantially responsible*	*Largely responsible*	*Fully responsible*
Actions of victim	Takes special precautions	Takes conventional measures	Facilitates theft through negligence	Precipitates theft by leaving car exposed and vulnerable	Provokes theft by arrangements with criminals	Fabricates theft of nonexistent car
Motivations of victim	Determined to minimize risks	Concerned about risks	Indifferent to risks	Wants car to be stolen	Determined to have car stolen	Seeks to make it look as if car were stolen
Financial outcome after theft	Loses money	Loses money	Loses money	Gains money from insurance coverage	Gains money from insurance coverage	Makes large profit from false claim
Approximate proportion of all victims, currently	55%		20%	25%		
Legal status	Actual victims			Criminals posing as victims to commit insurance fraud		
Extent of attention	Overlooked	Objects of public education campaigns, sometimes scapegoated		Objects of investigations and new legislation		

Source: Adapted from Karmen, 1980.

cars more theft resistant, they can be faulted for not taking the threat of car stealing seriously enough. Thus, they can be considered largely blameless, although
they are not above criticism.

Carelessly facilitating victims set the stage for crimes of opportunity. In many
cases they were victimized by inexperienced thieves and teenage joyriders. They
made the criminals' tasks easier by failing to use the standard anticrime measures
available to them. They left their car doors unlocked or the windows rolled down,
and worst of all, they left their keys inside. They can be considered partly responsible precisely because they did not take precautions. Their thoughtless, negligent
acts and indifferent attitudes were significant contributing factors to their own
losses. However, they were unintentional, unwilling, inadvertent victims who
bear no guilt, legally. (However, rental car companies might hold such customers
financially liable for the cost of the lost vehicles because they left their keys in the
cars [Marriott, 1991].)

Precipitative initiators were knowing and willing victims who intentionally
singled out their vehicles for trouble. They wanted their cars to be stolen because
they were "gas guzzlers" or "lemons." They coldly calculated that they would be
better off financially if they received the "blue book" value as reimbursement from
the insurance company than if they kept their cars or tried to repair them or sell
them. So they took steps that went beyond carelessness. They deliberately left their
car unlocked, with the keys dangling inside it, parked invitingly in a high-crime
area. By maximizing the vulnerability of their auto, they incited would-be thieves
to steal it. But the relationships between the precipitating victims and the criminals
were impersonal; they never met each other despite the symbiosis between them.
These substantially responsible victims, if challenged or investigated, could conceal
their dishonest motives and contend that they were merely negligent motorists
with innocent intentions who had accidentally left their keys in the cars.

Provocative conspirators are largely responsible victims. They contributed so
much to the genesis of the crime that without their instigation the act would not
have taken place. These victims are not really injured parties but accomplices of
thieves. These victims are actually criminals, part of a conspiracy to commit insurance fraud. If the deal was arranged at their initiative (for example, if they offered
money to amateurs or professionals to dispose of their unwanted vehicles), then
they are more guilty than the individuals who drove their cars away. These criminals posing as victims arranged to have their cars "splashed" (driven off a bridge
into deep water), "squished" (compacted, crushed, and then shredded beyond
recognition), or "torched" (set on fire) to collect insurance reimbursement.
Largely responsible victims have the same motives as substantially responsible victims. But the provocative conspirators leave nothing to chance; they know and
pay the criminals who work with them (see Behar, 1993).

Fully responsible victims are not victims at all because they never even
owned cars. They made false claims to defraud insurance companies. They

insured a nonexistent vehicle (a "paper car," or "phantom car") and later reported it stolen to the authorities so that they could collect money. They simulated being a victim and fabricated the entire episode for their own dishonest purposes.

Rough estimates can be derived of the relative proportions of these six types of auto theft victims. Carelessly facilitating victims who leave their keys in their cars make up at most 20 percent of all victims these days (but constituted a higher proportion decades ago; see the discussion later in this chapter). Another 10 percent nationwide, maybe as many as 25 percent in some areas, are suspected of engaging in insurance fraud (Baldwin, 1988; Sloane, 1991; Kerr, 1992). The percentage of conscientiously resisting motorists who did all that could reasonably be expected is more difficult to operationalize and measure. About 6 percent of all cars on the road are protected by alarms, but the percentage of stolen cars with alarms is not known. In addition, owners install a wide variety of other antitheft devices, including steering-wheel locks, tamper-resistant door and ignition locks, ignition kill switches, and fuel cut-off mechanisms (Incantalupo, 1988). If as many as 25 percent of all victims wanted their cars to be stolen (precipitative initiators, provocative conspirators, and fabricating simulators), and another 20 percent are careless facilitators, then conventionally cautious and conscientiously resisting motorists together add up to the remaining 55 percent.

Therefore, the majority of auto theft victims, at least 55 percent and perhaps as many as 70 percent (assuming the lower national estimate for insurance fraud cases), are totally or basically innocent and should not be blamed in any way for their losses.

VICTIM BLAMING VERSUS VICTIM DEFENDING

Arguments that the victims of crime might share responsibility with the offenders for what happened have been characterized as examples of *victim blaming,* which draws upon the concepts of facilitation, precipitation, and provocation as valid descriptions of what some people do "wrong" that gets them into trouble. *Victim defending* questions the logic and usefulness of victim blaming and its preoccupation with shared responsibility, challenging whether certain victims are partly at fault for the crimes committed against them.

When discussing victim blaming and victim defending, it is more useful to discuss the two opposing ideologies, or outlooks, than it is to presume that there are two distinct types of people—victim blamers and victim defenders. Most people are not consistent when they discuss crime: They blame specific individuals but defend others, or they blame certain groups of victims (for example, abusive husbands who get killed by their wives) but not other groups (such as women who have been raped by strangers).

Victim Blaming

Victim blaming casts doubt on the legal categories of "completely guilty" and "totally innocent," alleging that they are potentially misleading descriptions of who did what to whom. Applying such dichotomous labels to real people in actual situations often results in gross simplifications and even distortions of the truth of what happened, according to this view.

Victim blaming proceeds from the assumption that the offender and the victim are sometimes "partners in crime," that a degree of mutuality, symbiosis, or reciprocity may exist between them (Von Hentig, 1948). In such cases, investigating the past police record, possible motives, reputation, and actions of the victim as well as the offender can be justified (Schultz, 1968).

Victimology, despite its aspirations toward objectivity, may harbor an unavoidable tendency toward victim blaming. It is inevitable that an in-depth investigation of the behavior of a victim before, during, and after a crime will turn up rash decisions, foolish mistakes, errors in judgment, and inexcusable carelessness that, with hindsight, can be clearly seen to have shaped the unfortunate outcome. More sophisticated inquiries into the patterns that run through hundreds, perhaps thousands, of confrontations are sure to reveal evidence of what the victims did (or failed to do) that contributed to their own losses and suffering.

Victim blaming follows a step-by-step thought process (see Ryan, 1971). First, the assumption is made that there is something "wrong" with victims. They are thought to differ significantly from people who have never been singled out: Either their attitudes or their behaviors, or both, distinguish them from the unafflicted majority. Second, these presumed differences are said to be the source of the victims' plight. If they were like everyone else, the reasoning goes, they would never be targeted for attack. Third and finally, victims are warned that if they want to avoid trouble in the future, they must change how they think and act. They must abandon the careless, rash, or inciteful behaviors that brought about their downfall.

Victim blaming is widely practiced. It is a popular point of view for several reasons. It provides specific and straightforward answers to troubling questions like "Why did it happen?" and "Why him and not me?" since the focus is on reconstructing the particular sequence of events leading up to the crime. Victim-blaming also has great psychological appeal because it draws on deep philosophical and even theological beliefs concerning why "bad" things happen to seemingly "good" people. In addition, victim blaming readily comes to mind because it is a familiar theme, often voiced spontaneously by wrongdoers and presented even more convincingly by defense attorneys.

An Individualistic Explanation for Social Problems Victim blaming arises from a microscopic, interpersonal, and interactionistic analysis of social problems.

A doctrine of personal accountability underlies victim-blaming explanations. Just as criminals are condemned and punished for their lawbreaking, so too must victims answer for their behavior before and during an incident. In the aftermath of the event, victims may be credited for minimizing the harm they experienced or faulted for errors in judgment that (in retrospect) only made things worse. Such assessments of praise or blame are grounded in the belief that people exercise some substantial degree of control over the course of events in their lives. They may not be totally in command, but they are not powerless or helpless either. If getting into trouble is partly the victim's fault, then escaping harm is also the victim's responsibility. Just as cautious motorists should study the techniques of defensive driving to minimize the risks of getting involved in an accident, crime-conscious people are obliged to review their lifestyles to do what they can, within reason, to increase their personal safety from criminal attack. By following the advice of experts about how to avoid trouble, would-be victims might be able to deter would-be offenders or divert their attention elsewhere. According to this logic, there are many personal solutions to the social problem of crime in the streets. One does not have to go around in resignation, waiting passively to become a statistic.

Victim-blaming arguments can be espoused by people who profess to have the victim's best interests in mind. Social workers, ministers, doctors, teachers, and others in the helping professions are often among the first to blame those who suffer from social problems (like poverty, bad housing, ill health, unemployment, and inadequate education) for bringing about their own downfall. By finding fault with victims' attitudes and actions, sympathetic observers are able to reconcile their own self-interest with their humanitarian impulses. They do not want to criticize a social system that they believe is sound. And they do not want to abandon their commitment to alleviating suffering. Without realizing why, victim blamers feel comfortable with an ideology that stresses that the individual, not society's institutions (organized ways of accomplishing tasks), must change if trouble is to be avoided in the future (Ryan, 1971).

A Comforting Outlook   Victim blaming may result from a fervent belief that justice ultimately prevails in this world. According to the "just-world" outlook, people get what they deserve and deserve what they get. Bad things happen only to evil characters; good people are rewarded for following the rules. Hence, if someone is harmed by a criminal, that person must have done something wrong to deserve such a fate. People who believe that the real world is a just world don't want to find fault with victims if they can help it. They would prefer to blame other people or conditions. But, when put on the spot with other explanations foreclosed, they will blame victims, if only for the sake of their own peace of mind. Imagining a world governed by random events is too disconcerting and threatening for them. The realization that senseless, brutal acts might be inflicted

on anyone at any time is unnerving. The belief that victims did something neglectful, mistaken, or provocative that brought about their misfortune is comforting. It dispels feelings of helplessness and extreme vulnerability and allows the
blamer to be reassured that criminals don't strike out at good people who act
properly (Lerner, 1965; Symonds, 1975).

The Offender's View The offender's view of victims plays a key role in the selection of targets and in the infliction of pain.

> **A** suspect arrested for a series of rapes in a housing development tells detectives
> that "Women get raped because of the way they dress. It does something to a
> man." But his victim-blaming rationale is quickly refuted by a prosecutor, who
> points out that the women who were assaulted were wearing winter coats over
> their business outfits. (Siemaszko, 1994)

Observers often wonder how offenders can be so devoid of feelings of empathy
and pity. Evidently, they have undergone a process of desensitization that reduces
or even eliminates the guilt, shame, remorse, pangs of conscience, and moral inhibitions that would otherwise constrain and beset them. Victim blaming appears
to be a central mechanism of the desensitizing process. By derogating and deni-
grating the victim, juvenile delinquents or adult criminals can picture their harmful acts as justifiable and their choice of an object for injury as legitimate. Acts of
stark cruelty and savagery become possible when the victim is viewed as worth-
less, as less than human, as an appropriate target for venting hostility and aggression, or as an outcast deserving mistreatment (Fattah, 1976, 1979).

To neutralize any sense of guilt, delinquents frequently stereotype their intended victims as having negative traits. They try to dismiss their targets as mere
abstractions (like "the general public" or "the school system"), or they maintain
that the victims were consenting and willing, or they argue that they were justified ("He was asking for it and got what he deserved"). Delinquents disparage the
personal worth of the people they harm ("They are thieves themselves"), or deny
that their actions caused any injuries or losses ("We were just borrowing it, not
stealing it"). In extreme cases, youthful offenders picture the suffering they inflict
as an act of retaliatory justice that ought to be applauded ("We deserve a medal for
doing that") (Sykes and Matza, 1957; Schwendinger and Schwendinger, 1967).

Sometimes defense attorneys persuasively articulate the victim-blaming views
of their clients, especially in high-profile murder cases. A "trash-the-reputation"
(of the dead person) approach coupled with a "sympathy" (for the accused) defense might succeed in swaying a jury and securing an acquittal. This demonize/
humanize strategy relies on the value of pretrial publicity as a way of biasing potential jurors. Despite their claims of wanting a fair trial, both the prosecution and
the defense prefer to seat jurors who, from the outset, are leaning in their direction. In an attempt to win in the court of public opinion, and ultimately in the

courtroom, prosecutors try to plant proconviction biases in people who may be called to jury duty by promoting the government's version of events at press conferences and during interviews right after an arrest and again at indictment, portraying the accused as surely guilty of the crimes of which he or she is charged. Defense attorneys also seek out reporters, to put forward the interpretation that the dead victim was asking for trouble and got what he or she deserved. For example, in cases where children slay their fathers, the dead men may be pictured as brutal abusers and perverse molesters, while their offspring are portrayed as helpless and innocent targets of adult cruelty (Estrich, 1993b; Hoffman, 1994).

Victim Defending

Victim defending rejects the premises of victim blaming and challenges victim blaming over a number of issues.

First of all, victim defending contends that victim blaming overstates the extent to which facilitation, precipitation, or provocation contributes to or explains the genesis of an illegal act. Motivated offenders would have struck their chosen targets even if the victims had not made their tasks easier, or called attention to themselves, or incited their anger. Second, victim defending charges that victim blaming confuses the exception with the rule and overestimates the actual proportion of cases in which facilitation, precipitation, or provocation occurs. Most victims are completely innocent; shared responsibility is unusual, not common. Victim blaming seizes upon the blameworthiness of a relatively small percentage of persons to question the attitudes and behaviors of most victims. For example, a cloud of suspicion hangs over the heads of all motorists whose cars are stolen, even those who took precautions and did not facilitate the criminals' tasks in any way. Third, victim defending opposes the victim-blaming recommendation that victims must change their ways, charging that this advice is unrealistic because it overlooks the cultural imperatives and environmental conditions that largely shape lifestyles. Most people lack the opportunities and resources to alter their means of travel, their hours of work, the company they keep, the schools their children attend, or the neighborhoods in which they live. Recommendations that people give up cherished personal freedoms and sacrifice pleasures for vague promises of enhanced security are likely to be disregarded. Some sharp attacks, from a victim-defending perspective, on victim-blaming notions of shared responsibility, are presented in Box 3.2.

As an outlook, victim defending is clear about what it opposes—victim-blaming; but it is not clear about what it supports, in terms of who or what is to blame. Two tendencies within victim defending can be distinguished. The first can be characterized as *offender blaming*. Offender blaming resists any attempt to shift the burden of full responsibility off of lawbreakers' backs and onto the victims'

BOX 3.2	Criticisms of the Notion of Shared Responsibility

- The concept of victim precipitation has become confused because it has been operationalized in too many different, often incompatible ways. As a result, it has lost much of its usefulness as an empirical and explanatory tool (Silverman, 1974:99).

- The study of victim precipitation is the least exact of the sociological approaches; it is part a priori guesswork and part "armchair detective fun and games" because the interpretation rests in the final analysis on a set of arbitrary standards (Brownmiller, 1975:353).

- A tendency of investigators to assign responsibility for criminal acts to the victims' behavior reinforces similar beliefs and rationalizations held by most criminals themselves.... Scientific skepticism should be maintained regarding the concept of victim participation, especially for crimes of sudden, unexpected violence where the offender is a stranger to the victim (Symonds, 1975:22).

- Victims of crime, long ignored but now the object of special scholarly attention, had better temper their enthusiasm because they may be more maligned than lauded, and their plight may not receive sympathetic understanding. Some victimologists have departed from the humanitarian, helping orientation of the founders of the field and have turned victimology into the art of blaming the victim. If the impression of a "legitimate victim" is created, then part of the burden of guilt is relieved from the perpetrator, and some crimes, like rape for example, can emerge as without either victims or offenders (Weis and Borges, 1973:85).

- Victim precipitation explanations are plagued by the fallacy of circular reasoning about the cause of the crime, suffer from over-simplified stimulus-response models of human interaction, ignore incongruent facts that don't fit the theory, and inadequately explore the victim's intentions (Franklin and Franklin, 1976: 134).

- An analytical framework must be found that salvages the positive contributions of the concept of victim precipitation, while avoiding its flaws—its tendency to consider a victim's provocations as both a necessary and sufficient condition for an offense to occur; its portrayal of some offenders as unrealistically passive; and its questionable moral and legal implications about who is the guilty party (Sheley, 1979:126–127).

- Crime victimization is a neglected social problem in part because victim precipitation studies typically fail to articulate the distress of the victims and instead suggest that some may be to blame for their own plight. The inferences often drawn from these studies—that some individuals can steer clear of trouble by avoiding certain situations—suffer from the "post hoc ergo propter hoc" fallacy of treating the victims' behavior as both necessary and sufficient to cause the crime (Teevan, 1979:7).

- To accept precipitation and provocation as legitimate excuses for attenuating responsibility for violent crime is false, illogical, psychologically harmful to victims, and socially irresponsible. . . . Victim-blaming has been injected into the literature on crime by well-meaning but offender-oriented professionals. It becomes the basis and excuse for the indifference shown to supposedly "undeserving" victims (Reiff, 1979:12,14).

- The eager acceptance of arguments about victim responsibility by scholars and the public alike is undeserved; these accounts of why the crime occurred often lack empirical verification, can lead to cruel insensitivity to the suffering of the victim, and tend to exonerate or even justify the acts of the offenders, especially rapists (Anderson and Renzetti, 1980: 325).

shoulders. Victim defending coupled with offender blaming arises from an application of the doctrine of personal accountability for misbehavior but holds only the aggressors or predators accountable for their behavior.

The second tendency is to link victim defending with *system blaming*. According to the tenets of system blaming, neither the offender nor the victim is the real culprit; both, to varying degrees, are largely products of their culture and social environment. The attitudes and behaviors of both parties have been influenced by parental training (socialization), peer group pressures, media images, criminal justice practices, economic imperatives, and other considerations. Victim defending/system blaming is a more complex and sophisticated outlook than victim defending/offender blaming. According to this more sociological type of analysis, the roots of the crime problem are to be found in the basic institutions upon which the social system is built (among many others, see Franklin, 1978; and Balkan, Berger, and Schmidt, 1980).

So that we can better understand the clash in perspectives between victim blaming and victim defending/offender blaming and victim defending/system blaming, the three fundamental concepts—facilitation, precipitation, and provocation—will be applied to three different types of crime. The question of victim facilitation in automobile theft will be examined first, then the controversy over whether or not some rapes are victim precipitated, and, finally, the possibility that some murdered husbands provoked their wives to slay them.

VICTIM FACILITATION AND AUTO THEFT: IS IT THE CARELESS WHO WIND UP CARLESS?

Some people mistakenly consider auto theft to be the "happy crime" in which no one loses and everyone gains (see Plate, 1975). The thief makes money; the owner gets reimbursed by the insurance company and then enjoys the pleasure of shopping for a new car; the manufacturer gains a customer, who wasn't due back in the showroom for another couple of years; and the insurance company gets a chance to raise the premiums and invest that money in profitable ventures. But in actuality, most victims of auto theft are not pleased, for a number of reasons. First of all, many owners invest a great deal of time, effort, and loving care customizing their vehicles and keeping them in good shape. Second, the shock of not finding the vehicle where it was parked touches off a sense of violation and insecurity that lingers for a long time. Third, not all motorists purchase the optional comprehensive fire and theft coverage, either because they choose not to or cannot afford it. Those that are covered almost always must pay a deductible out of their own pocket, which usually amounts to several hundred dollars, maybe more. Any personal items left in the trunk are lost, as are any expensive add-ons, like tape decks and radar detectors. The loss is always unanticipated, necessitating emergency measures like taking cabs, renting cars, and canceling important appointments. Finally, motorists who collect insurance reimbursement may find that either their premiums are raised or their policies are not renewed.

Car stealing is an old problem. As long ago as 1919, Congress passed the Dyer Act in response to professional thieves who were driving across state borders to evade local police forces. Today, five different motives for car theft can be distinguished. Juvenile joyriding (which the law calls "unauthorized use of a motor vehicle" and treats as a misdemeanor) has been a craze among teenage boys ever since cars were marketed with the message that owning one is a sign of manhood. These amateurs, who seek the status, thrills, and challenge of "borrowing" cars to take their friends for rides, often prey upon careless motorists. But professional thieves don't need to rely on the negligence of drivers. It takes them just a few minutes with the right tools to disarm alarm systems and to defeat standard security hardware like door and ignition locks. These pros, working in league with commercial theft rings, steal cars either to sell or to strip. Steal-to-sell operations ("retagging") alter the car's identity (registration and title documents and vehicle identification number) and then pass it off as a used car. Steal-to-strip operations ("chop shops") dismantle vehicles and infiltrate the crash-replacement parts (sheet metal components like the hood, trunk lid, fenders, and doors) into the salvage and recycling pipelines supplying auto body repair shops. A fourth motive for stealing a vehicle is to use it for temporary or short-term travel, often as a getaway car after committing some other crime, such as robbing a bank. The fifth variety of auto theft is provided as a "service" to the victim. Some owners pay to have their cars disposed of without a trace so that they can collect insurance reimbursement for vehicles they no longer want or can afford to keep (thus they become part of a conspiracy to commit insurance fraud).

Several overall trends are worth noting. Stolen car recovery rates have dropped from over 90 percent in the 1940s and 1950s to about 73 percent in 1992 (according to *NCVS* nationwide figures) and are lower in some cities plagued by commercial rings. Even though a car is the kind of stolen property that is most likely to be returned to its rightful owner, about 30 percent of these "fortunate" motorists who get their vehicles back might be dismayed. What the police retrieve might be unusable—just a stripped hulk of what was formerly a source of pride and joy. The median loss per motor vehicle theft in 1992 was $3,600. The total value of all the unrecovered vehicles that vanished because of the activities of professional rings exceeded $7.8 billion that year (Klaus, 1994). That explains why car owners must pay such high insurance premiums for theft coverage.

Statistics derived from the *NCVS* (BJS, 1994a) indicate that rates of auto theft reached an all-time high in 1991 (22 completed or attempted thefts per 1,000 households). In 1993, nearly 2 million attempted or completed vehicle thefts were reported to interviewers (20 out of every 1,000 households). As for completed thefts, nearly 1,300,000 vehicles were driven away in 1993 (BJS, 1994e). During that year, there were roughly 180 million cars and trucks in operation across the country (about 1 for every American over the age of fifteen) (Hass and Washington, 1994). Mathematically speaking, approximately 1 out of every 150 registered vehicles, or close to 7 out of every 1,000 on the road were stolen that year. (Trends in motor vehicle theft rates over the past few decades appear in Figure 3.2. The top line indicates the yearly rates of all thefts disclosed to survey interviewers, whether successful completions or failed attempts; the bottom line indicates the yearly rates per 1,000 households only for thefts that were successful, from the offender's standpoint.)

As noted in Chapter 2, all people do not face the same chances of being harmed by criminals. In the case of auto theft, differential risks are determined by a number of factors. According to an analysis of over 12 million attempted and completed vehicle thefts disclosed to *NCVS* interviewers between 1973 and 1985, the categories of people who faced the greatest dangers of losing their cars were African Americans and Hispanic Americans, households headed by persons under age twenty-five, apartment dwellers, residents of central-city neighbor-

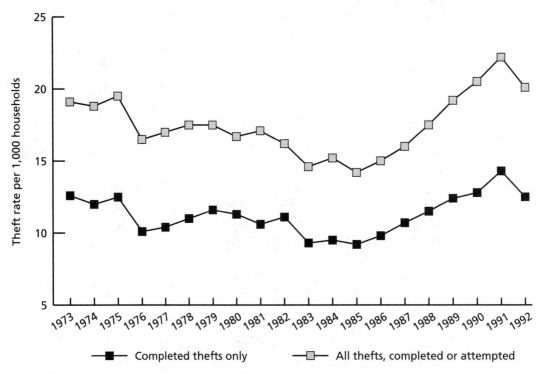

FIGURE 3.2 Trends in Motor Vehicle Theft Rates, *NCVS* Data, 1973–1992

Source: BJS, 1994a.

hoods, and low-income families. The kinds of people whose cars were least likely to be stolen were residents of rural areas, those over fifty-five, and homeowners (Harlow, 1988). Another risk factor was the make, model, and year of the car, since some types are more prized by thieves, are in greater demand in the market for stolen crash parts, or are easier to steal than others (see Clark and Harris, 1992; "NICB Study," 1993; Krauss, 1994). An analysis of insurance records revealed that as cars age, they become more of a target for thieves, especially during their fourth, fifth, and sixth years on the road, for several reasons. If the model lines were not substantially redesigned, then the older cars can be stolen for their parts to repair newer ones. Also middle-aged cars are less likely to be equipped with the latest state-of-the-art antitheft devices. Another reason is that, as cars wear out, their owners have less incentive to maintain security devices in good working order and to vigilantly observe precautions about where they park their less-valuable vehicles. Finally, thieves may also have a learning curve, perfecting their techniques as they become more familiar with a car line's particular antitheft features. Since most cars have a life expectancy of only seven to ten years, owners should never let their guard down ("NICB Study," 1993).

Blaming the Victim for Facilitating the Crime

The question remains, who or what is to blame for the theft of over a million vehicles a year?

Auto theft seems to be the only crime for which there is an organized victim-blaming lobby, a peculiar situation that developed long ago. Composed of representatives of the automakers, insurance companies, and law enforcement agencies, this victim-blaming lobby has castigated motorist carelessness ever since the dawn of the automobile age. As their public pronouncements show, they are quick to fault negligent drivers for facilitating thefts by leaving their vehicles unlocked, or, worse yet, for leaving their keys dangling in their cars' ignition locks. Examples of these public scoldings appear in Box 3.3.

The contribution of victim facilitation to the auto theft rate has usually been measured as the percentage of recovered stolen cars in which there was evidence that the thief had used the owner's keys. Although this methodology has its problems, surveys based on it show a trend that casts doubt on the continued importance of negligence as a factor. Data derived from insurance company records from the 1940s through the 1960s indicate that at least 40 percent and as many as about 90 percent of all thefts were facilitated by victims through carelessness about locks and keys. Since the 1970s, police, FBI, and insurance industry records estimate facilitation to be factor in from 13 percent to 20 percent of all thefts (Karmen, 1979; NIJ, 1984). By the early 1990s, an insurance industry publication reported that only 13 percent of all vehicle thefts were still victim facilitated (National Insurance Crime Bureau, 1993).

BOX 3.3   Examples of "Motorist Blaming"

Source *Affiliation* *Date*	*Statement*
George Henderson Criminologist 1924	Careless owners of automobiles have their cars standing on the street with their engines running, with the magneto key in the locks or entirely unlocked on avenues of the city or in unprotected garages. And in so doing they make life a picnic for the car thief. . . . Nine-tenths of the loss by theft of automobiles is due to the carelessness of the owner (pp. 36, 38).
James Bulger Publicity director Chicago Motor Club 1933	Motorists must be made to realize that they have a responsibility. . . . [They] should make it difficult for a thief to steal a car (p. 810).
Jerome Hall Law professor 1935	Accommodating owners leave doors unlocked, windows open, keys in the switch, and sometimes leave the motor running, all conveniently arranged for automobile thieves who specialize in these easy pickings (p. 269).
August Vollmer Police chief Berkeley, California 1936	No intelligent person would put from $1,000 to $5,000 in good money in the street and expect to find it there an hour later, yet that is exactly what a large number of people do when they leave an automobile in the street without locking it. Even more, not only are they leaving money at the curb but they are also putting four wheels under it to make it easier for the thief to take it (p. 65).
Henry Clement Judge 1946	There must surely be some way to educate Mr. Average careless driver—you and me—to prevent us from stealing our own car (p. 24).
William Davis National Automobile Theft Bureau 1954	What is it about the American public that makes them so disrespectful of their own property as it applies to automobiles? . . . To us the greatest single cause of the theft of these cars is public indifference and irresponsibility (in U.S. Congress, 1954, pp. 383, 385).

(continued on next page)

These estimates support the following analysis: At one time, when the public was less concerned about crime, facilitation may have contributed substantially to the joyriding problem. But teenage amateurs no longer account for most of the car stealing that goes on in cities and suburbs. Professionals, often working for commercial rings that may be affiliated with organized crime syndicates, now represent the greater threat to car owners. As the years roll by, facilitation is declining in significance.

BOX 3.3   *continued*

Source *Affiliation* *Date*	*Statement*
J. Edgar Hoover FBI director 1966	Yet through all this practical, emotional and monetary attachment to the automobile, there emerges convincing evidence that it is one of the motorist's most carelessly neglected possessions (p. 23621).
John Roche President General Motors Corporation 1967	Carelessness by car owners is a major factor in car theft, and a strong educational effort will be required to alert the public to the dangers of theft (p. 7594).
John Damian Vehicle regulations manager Ford Motor Company 1968	Until we can get drivers to stop handing over their cars to thieves, all anti-theft activities are practically useless (in Raskin, 1968:435).
Donald Wolfslayer Assistant chief engineer for security Chrysler Corporation 1975	All the security you put in a car is not going to do a darned bit of good if people are careless. People have to learn to take better care of their autos (in "Offenders Get Wrists Slapped," 1975:2).
Travelers Insurance Company 1977	Will your car be next? It needn't be. Not if you follow these simple precautions. . . . If you're careless about these tips you may wind up carless (pp. 1–2).
Ira Lipman Security industry executive 1982	If people would simply quit leaving their keys in their cars, they would eliminate half of all auto thefts (p. 78).
U.S. News & World Report Magazine column 1992	Take the keys. Obvious? Sure. But 20% of stolen cars are all but given to thieves by owners who leave keys in the ignition ("Where's the Car?" March 30, p. 72).

The Continuing Clash over Carelessness

Even though the proportions of car thefts that are facilitated by motorists have been dropping over the decade, the absolute number remains high. (For example, if 13 percent of nearly 1.3 million completed thefts in 1993 were made easier by the thoughtless behavior of drivers, that means about 170,000 of these acts of car stealing were preventable.)

According to a poll commissioned by insurance companies of 1,000 owners in 1994, evidence persists that motorists are still not doing all they can to safeguard their prized possessions. Nearly 39 percent were "not at all concerned" about having their cars stolen. As for taking precautions, about 76 percent of all owners had not installed an alarm or any other antitheft device in their vehicles. As many as 31 percent conceded that they did not always lock their car doors, and, worse yet, 11 percent confessed that there were occasions when they left their keys in their parked cars (National Insurance Crime Bureau, 1995).

In the case of auto theft, the difference in point of view between victim blaming and victim defending is another example of the half-empty/half-full debate. Victim blaming focuses on the proportion of motorists who still have bad habits; victim defending emphasizes that the overwhelming majority of people whose cars were stolen did nothing wrong. The theft of their cars was not facilitated in any way. These drivers don't have self-defeating attitudes and don't act carelessly. The image of the absentminded owner that is frequently conjured up in victim-blaming arguments is an outmoded stereotype that no longer fits most motorists, according to victim defenders.

VICTIM PRECIPITATION AND RAPE:
WAS IT SOMEHOW HER FAULT?

A man is on trial for rape. His lawyer points out that the alleged victim was wearing a tank top, a lacy miniskirt, and no underpants. The defendant is found not guilty, because, as one juror explains, "We felt she asked for it." The failed prosecution inspires the state legislature to amend the laws governing rape trials to bar defense attorneys from asking complainants about the clothes they were wearing at the time of the incidents. (Merrill, 1994)

Late one night a twenty-two-year-old mother of two enters a bar filled with men. She has a few drinks and flirts with some of the patrons. Suddenly she finds herself held down on a pool table. Six young men force themselves upon her as onlookers cheer them on and she screams and curses. The six men are arrested and put on trial for aggravated rape. Their defense is that she acted seductively and "led them on." The prosecution argues that a sexual assault begins when a man continues after a woman has said "No!" The jury concludes that she did not consent to what they did to her and convicts four of the six. The judge sentences them to terms of from six to twelve years in prison. At a rally held in behalf of the victim, speakers hail the outcome as a symbol that gang rape will not be tolerated as a spectator sport. But at a demonstration protesting the verdicts and sentences, speakers sympathetic to the young men contend, "She got herself raped," "She should have known what she was getting herself into." They hold her largely responsible for enabling the men "to take advantage of her." (Schanberg, 1984; 1989)

A young man convinces a young woman to go back to his apartment after a date. They begin to kiss, but when he makes further sexual overtures she politely whispers "no." He persists, believing that the dating ritual requires the male to be the aggressor and the female to resist, at least at first. He assumes from past experience that "no" means "maybe" and "maybe" means "yes," and that to show she means it when she says "no" a woman must jump up and slap him in the face. When she says she's not ready for "that" yet, he misinterprets her protestation as an invitation to be more assertive. As he climbs on top of her, she becomes petrified that further resistance will be met with violence. The evening ends with the young man perceiving that he ultimately "seduced" her and the young woman feeling that she was violated against her will. She has him arrested. (Dershowitz, 1988)

A paradox surrounds the crime of rape. On the one hand, some women's allegations are sneered at and become the subject of crude jokes. On the other hand, some men are punished so severely that sexual assaults can be considered one of the most terrible and strictly forbidden of all interpersonal crimes. (Between 1930 and 1968, 455 rapists were executed in the United States; when the Supreme Court ruled in 1976 that capital punishment was an excessive penalty for rape, life imprisonment became the maximum sentence.) The paradox arises in part because accusations are subject to interpretations shaped by social attitudes as much as by legal codes, and both attitudes and laws have been changing. What "really happened" is interpreted first by the two people, and then by the police, the prosecutor, the judge, and the jury (as well as the media and the public). Much of the difference of opinion and confusion surrounding controversial cases stem from judgments about whether or not the victim bears any responsibility for the offender's sexual aggression. Charges about shared responsibility can arise in both kinds of forcible rapes: in "classic" (Williams, 1984) or "real rapes" (Estrich, 1986), epitomized by the knife-wielding stranger who leaps out of the darkness in a "blitz attack" to "ambush" and subdue his prey; and in "acquaintance rapes," which arise out of interactions between people who know each other (as friends, relatives, neighbors, classmates, coworkers, or dates). (*Statutory rapes* are distinct from *forcible rapes;* they do not involve violence or threats but are seductions of minors below the age of consent.)

It is not clear from official statistics whether a sexual assault by a male known to the victim is more or less likely than an attack by a complete stranger. According to an analysis of over 500,000 attempted and completed rapes disclosed to *NCVS* interviewers from 1982 to 1984, the attacker was a stranger in 55 percent of the cases (Timrots and Rand, 1987). However, a comparable analysis of *NCVS* data from 1987 to 1991 yielded a somewhat lower figure of 44 percent assaults by strangers (Bachman, 1994a). According to 3,800 police reports from three states in

1991, the girl or woman did not know the assailant in only 28 percent of the cases (Reaves, 1993).

A number of differences stand out when acquaintance rapes are compared to sexual assaults by strangers. Acquaintance rapes are more likely to take place in the victim's home, or nearby, while ambushes by strangers are more likely to occur outdoors or in public places like parks. Strangers are more likely to brandish weapons, and to injure their victims; nonstrangers are more likely to be drunk or high on drugs (Bachman, 1994a). Victims assaulted by someone they know may be more reluctant to report the crime to the police or even to disclose the incident to survey interviewers, for a number of reasons. They may experience a greater sense of shame, guilt, and embarrassment and may feel that they should have been able to prevent the attack. They may wish to protect the identity of the assailant if he is a relative, former friend, boss, or other powerful figure. They may fear reprisals for going to the authorities and may dread that if they do, their account will not be believed (Klaus, DeBerry, and Timrots, 1985). Another important difference is that girls and women raped by acquaintances are much more likely to be blamed than those sexually assaulted by strangers.

The clash between victim blaming and victim defending is particularly sharp in the case of rape. If auto theft provided a clear example of a crime for which there is a well-organized and well-financed group with a vested interest in promoting victim blaming, then rape is the best example of a crime for which there is a vocal and deeply committed victim-defending movement. The controversy erupts over whether certain rapes should be viewed as acts of uncontainable sexual passion that might be victim precipitated or as acts of brutal domination imposed upon unwilling, objectified targets.

A great deal is at stake in the battle for public support between victim blaming and victim defending viewpoints. The problem of rape forces people to choose between two very different courses of action. Who or what has to change—how women behave in the company of men, as victim blaming contends, or how boys are raised to become men and how they are taught to treat girls and women, as victim defending emphasizes? Accepting victim-blaming arguments might lead to the acquittal of certain defendants, but the more socially significant consequence is that this line of thought "excuses" sexist institutions and traditions that are now under attack. Accepting victim-defending arguments leads to the conclusion that sweeping changes in gender relations are needed. To reduce the threat of rape, it is necessary to root out the antifemale biases found within rigid sex roles, prevailing definitions of masculinity and femininity, existing criminal laws and criminal justice practices, and popular culture (Hills, 1981).

Victim-Blaming Viewpoints

Victim-blaming contends that a considerable proportion of rapes are precipitated by what the women wore, said, or did. That means that some females share responsibility with the male offenders for the crimes. They were not singled out for attack by accident or fate. They did something "wrong" and "got themselves raped." Those who share this viewpoint maintain that these girls and women who are partly at fault differ in their attitudes and actions from other females who have not been victimized. Girls and women who have endured precipitated rapes are blamed for singling themselves out for trouble through their own reckless deeds. They are condemned for showing poor judgment and for failing to heed warnings (MacDonald, 1971:79). Their rash actions are said to have attracted violence-prone men and aroused irrepressible passions in them.

The most widely cited (and most heavily criticized) study of victim precipitation in rape was based on data drawn from the files of the Philadelphia police concerning cases reported in 1958 and 1960 (Amir, 1971). The researcher considered precipitation to have occurred whenever a girl's or woman's behavior was interpreted by a teenage boy or man either as a direct invitation to engage in sexual relations that was later retracted (she agreed and then changed her mind, according to him) or as a sign that she would be available if he persisted in his demands (she was saying "no" but meant "yes," in his opinion). Included in this researcher's working definition were acts of commission—like drinking alcohol, or hitchhiking a ride, or using what could be taken as indecent language or gestures—as well as acts of omission—like failing to object strongly enough to his sexually charged overtures. The offender's interpretation was considered to be the crucial element in recognizing a case of victim precipitation. Even if the offender was mistaken in his beliefs about the victim, his perceptions led to actions, and that is what mattered. In the police files, the specific indicators of precipitation were statements by the offender, witnesses, or detectives claiming that "she behaved provocatively," "she acted seductively," "she was irresponsible and endangered herself," or "she had a bad reputation in the neighborhood." Using these criteria, the researcher deemed 19 percent of Philadelphia's forcible rapes to be precipitated. The typical victim, statistically speaking, was a black woman raped by a black man who was known to her as a friend, neighbor, relative, or acquaintance. Comparing victim-precipitated rapes with nonprecipitated rapes, it was found that consuming alcohol was more likely to be a factor, that the victim was more likely to have had a "bad reputation," and that the offender was more inclined to sexually humiliate his victim. A higher percentage of precipitating victims than blameless victims were white females; a higher percentage were teenage girls; and a higher percentage first encountered their assailants at bars or parties (Amir, 1971).

The victim-blaming perspective contends that some young women precipitate rapes because they do not understand—or choose to ignore—the risks involved in certain situations, such as going to bars unescorted or accepting rides home with men they hardly know. They are unaware, naive, or gullible in their dealings with males. They wear clothing or use language that men stereotype as signaling sexual availability. They ignore the dangers that might arise if they are suddenly confronted with a weapon or are overpowered while under the influence of alcohol or some other drug. The reckless behavior of teenage girls is explained as a form of "acting out." These adolescents, especially if they come from poverty-stricken homes and rejecting parents, are said to be seeking protection, attention, love, intimacy, and status through precocious sexuality. As a result, they get involved with older male casual acquaintances and find themselves in situations in which they are forcibly exploited (Amir, 1971; also see Dean and de Bruyn-Kops, 1982).

Two sets of consequences follow if victim-blaming arguments are accepted: If the female can be said to share responsibility for the "tragic misunderstanding," then the male can be considered less guilty and less deserving of severe punishment; and if precipitation is accepted as a common occurrence, then girls and women must be "educated" to prevent "miscommunication," to behave more cautiously, and to avoid the company of potential rapists.

If the victim can be partly blamed, then the crime is not entirely the offender's fault. The legal principle involved is that the female "assumed the risk" of attack when she voluntarily participated in the events leading up to the rape, like hitching a ride or agreeing to drink liquor. Even though the male remains legally responsible, her contributory behavior can provide grounds for granting the benefit of the doubt to the offender. This line of reasoning can influence every stage of the criminal justice system's handling of a case considered to be victim-precipitated (see Schur, 1984). If, after an interrogation of the complainant to determine her background, reputation, actions, and possible motives, the police believe that she contributed to her own victimization, charges may not be pressed. If the police do make an arrest, the prosecutor may decide that the case is "unwinnable," and may therefore drop the charges. If the case is brought to trial, jurors may exercise their discretion in interpreting the facts and may find the assailant guilty of a lesser charge than forcible rape (assault, for example). If the defendant is convicted, the judge may hand down a lenient sentence in view of the mitigating circumstances—her alleged precipitation, provocation, instigation, or misleading seductiveness ("implied consent").

The other major consequence of accepting the victim-blaming point of view is that the burden of preventing rape is shifted from males, the police, or any other responsible parties to the potential targets themselves. Girls and women are told that they may be courting disaster and that it is their obligation to constantly review their lifestyles and to do what they can to minimize their risks and maximize their safety. They are held personally accountable for their own security and are pressured to follow crime prevention tips derived from observations of other females' mistakes. Those who fail to heed the advice, who neglect to take precautions, and who don't draw lessons from the past misfortunes of others are told that they have themselves to blame if they precipitate a rape. Just as the threat of punishment is intended to make would-be rapists think twice before breaking the law, the public humiliation of victim blaming is meant to pressure females to think twice before stepping out of traditional, "sheltered" family roles and activities.

Since controlling the actions of offenders is so difficult, victim blaming seeks to reduce the incidence of rape by influencing the behavior of the potential targets. Girls and women are warned about whom they associate with, what they say in conversations, where they go, and how they dress. Females are urged to communicate clearly, to signal their true intentions, and to avoid teasing or taunting males.

Victim-Defending Perspectives

The traditional victim-blaming views presented above have become highly controversial. Victim defending, which originated from activists in the women's movement, challenges this "conventional wisdom" handed down from generation to generation and provides alternative explanations for why men sexually assault women.

Victim defending rejects as a myth the notion that rapes are acts of lust or outpourings of uncontrollable passion. Rapes are seen as sexual assaults: physical attacks culminating in sexual acts that symbolize domination, conquest, subjugation, and humiliation. The assaults are not triggered by desire and arousal but are motivated by anger, hatred, and contempt for females as depersonalized objects. Using force to control an unwilling partner must not be confused with "making love."

Victim defending questions the applicability of the concept of precipitation, which was originally developed to describe the blameworthy, aggressive initiatives taken by people who start and then lose fights. Although some homicides might be deemed justifiable (cases of self-defense), there is no such thing as justifiable rape (Amir, 1971:266). In victim-precipitated homicides, the person who died was the first to escalate the level of conflict by using physical strength or a weapon; then the survivor resorted to deadly force. Violence incited retaliatory violence. Since the woman does not physically assault the man before he attacks her, the only way to apply the concept of precipitation to rape is to consider the crime as primarily a sexually charged encounter rather than a brutal act of subjugation. Only then can real or presumed sexual advances by the female be considered triggering mechanisms. But there is no justification for the resort to force, no matter what she said, did, or promised. And there is great confusion over what constitutes a sexual overture. Since the female's behavior can be subjected to a wide range of interpretations, whose perceptions should be accepted when deciding if there was precipitation on her part—his? hers? the police's? the jury's? or the researcher's? (see Silverman, 1974; Chappell, Geis, and Geis, 1977; and McCaghy, 1980). The belief that certain rapes are victim precipitated has been dismissed as an ex post facto conclusion that fails to take into account the female's version of the incident (LeGrande, 1973:925), a personification and embodiment of rape mythology, cleverly stated in academic-scientific terms (Weis and Borges, 1973:112); and an academic endorsement of the rapist's point of view that provides an excuse for blaming the victim (Clark and Lewis, 1978).

Victim defending rejects the crime-prevention tips endorsed by victim blaming as ideologically tainted. A woman who abides by the long (and growing) list of recommended self-protection measures ends up resembling the "hysterical old maid armed with a hatpin and an umbrella who looks under the bed each night before retiring." Long a laughable stereotype of prudery, she is now a model of prudence (Brownmiller, 1975:398). Following crime prevention tips means forgoing many of the small pleasures and privileges in life to which men are accustomed (like taking a walk alone at night). Warding off would-be rapists requires women to engage in an extraordinary amount of pretense and deception (like claiming that a boyfriend, husband, or father is nearby). Furthermore, seeking the protection of "trustworthy" men to fend off the unwanted advances of other men undermines the efforts of women to develop their own strengths, self-confidence, self-reliance, and independent networks of mutual support.

Antirape activists have sought not only to defend victims but also to place the burden of blame for recurring outbreaks of male sexual "terrorism" on key social institutions, especially the family, the economy, the military, religion, and the media. Asserting that "the personal is political," they have stressed that apparently private troubles need to be seen as aspects of larger social problems besetting millions of other people. Collective solutions that get at the social roots of male-against-female violence hold out greater promise in the long run than any reliance on individual strategies of risk reduction and self-defense. The cultural practices and traditions that encourage men to be sexually aggressive must be rejected. Attitudes that tacitly excuse acquaintance rape must be changed. The association of domination with eroticism must be discouraged. And men must realize that rape is their problem too.

VICTIM PROVOCATION AND MURDER: IS THE SLAYING OF A WIFE-BEATER EVER JUSTIFIED?

A woman employed by the Navy is married to a military recruiter. Demeaning her as "old, fat, crazy" and friendless, he often slams her up against doors, punches her in the face and kicks her in the stomach. Doctors treat her black eyes, bruises to the neck, and hemorrhages. After each beating, he apologizes, gives her gifts, and takes her on vacations. Envied by other wives, she feels ashamed for not appreciating him. As a career woman in an important position, she feels humiliated and tells no one, not her friends in a church choir, or even her son, why she often wears long sleeves and dark glasses. Eventually she files for a divorce, presses assault-and-battery charges, gets a restraining order, and evicts him from their retirement home. But night after night, he comes back, banging on the windows and doors, trying to force his way in. Sympathizing with her plight, the police officers who repeatedly respond to her calls for help advise her to get a gun. One evening, he barges in brandishing a knife, and she shoots him. Put on trial for first-degree murder, she is painted by the prosecutor as emotionally unstable and twisted by bitterness over the divorce. He asserts that she lured her ex-husband to the house with a phone call as the culmination of a plot to kill him. A hung jury cannot decide her fate, but after another trial she is convicted of second-degree murder. Appeals of the conviction fail, and parole is denied; clemency remains her only hope. (Gibbs, 1993b)

At first it sounds hard to believe: Significant numbers within the victims' rights movement are deeply concerned about the plight of "criminals." They have helped to raise money to pay attorneys' fees and have packed courtrooms to demonstrate their solidarity with the accused. Volunteers have assisted defense lawyers in finding witnesses and in locating psychologists and social workers who can give expert testimony about the desperation that drove them to take another's life. A network of victims' advocates seeks to build public support for freeing certain convicts serving time for murder and manslaughter by repeatedly demonstrating at the gates of prisons. In about twenty states, petition drives are underway, demanding new trials, parole, or pardons. To date, several governors have reviewed scores of cases and granted clemency to at least thirty-five inmates (Schechter, 1982; Johann and Osanka, 1989; Gross, 1992).

This apparently strange twist of events can be easily explained: The cases involve battered women who killed their violent mates. From the standpoint of the law, the dead man is the victim, and the woman who took his life is the offender. But from the perspective of these activists within the battered women's movement, the designations "offender" and "victim" must be rejected as misleading. The persons behind bars are not really criminals and don't belong in confinement. The assaultive husbands, now deceased, are not bona fide victims but simply dead assailants; the battered women are not the aggressors but the genuine victims.

Victim-blaming and victim-defending viewpoints lead to opposite conclusions regarding the tragic endings of these tortured love affairs. Victim defending means siding with the dead man and arguing that his provocations, outrageous as they might have been, were not sufficient to justify her overreactions and that what she did cannot be condoned. Victim defending leads to offender blaming: She must be punished for the terrible crime she committed. On the other hand, victim blaming leads to offender defending, excusing and justifying the actions of the woman.

If the battered woman is believed by the authorities to have acted decisively in a kill-or-be-killed showdown, then no charges will be pressed against her. If, however, she appears to have shot or stabbed him after deliberation or premeditation, she can be indicted for first-degree murder. If there was no evidence of advanced planning, but she did act with malicious intent at the crucial moment, then she may face the lesser charge of second-degree murder. If the prosecutor believes that she killed him in a spontaneous response to intense provocations that incited in her a fit of rage or sheer terror, then she will be indicted for the less serious crime of voluntary manslaughter. If the death of the man is deemed unintentional (because she acted recklessly), then the charge will probably be involuntary manslaughter, which carries the lowest penalties of all, perhaps just probation (Austern, 1987; Bannister, 1992).

The possible outcomes in these cases range from no arrest, to acquittal by a jury of all charges, to conviction for murder or manslaughter and a lengthy term of imprisonment. The usual outcome is for the woman's lawyer to strike a deal with the prosecutor to allow her to plead guilty to a lesser charge with the understanding that the judge will hand down a reduced sentence, usually a prison term followed by parole. In a small proportion of cases, the women elect to stand trial; of those, most argue that they suffered from diminished capacity or temporary insanity at the time of the confrontation. But a growing number raise an affirmative defense against the murder or manslaughter charges and assert that they were compelled to lash out in self-preservation and should not be punished (Browne, 1987).

Wives might kill their husbands for many reasons; to put an end to physical abuse is just one possible motive. Similarly, husbands might murder their wives for a number of reasons. Beating them to death as the culmination of chronic episodes of abuse that intensify over time represents one tragically common outcome. It is not known exactly how many murders fall into the pattern of battered women slaying their violent mates, but the phenomena must be put into perspective. There are clear indications from police records that when it comes to lethal marital disputes, male-on-female violence is the more serious problem: More husbands kill their wives each year than wives kill their husbands (regardless of the motives). During the early 1990s, the ratio was roughly two to one; males killed their female lovers at twice the rate that females killed their male lovers. In 1993, nearly 600 men were slain by their wives or girlfriends. (More than two and one-half times that number, over 1,500 women, were murdered that year by their husbands or boyfriends.) Or, to put it another way, very few battered women (far less than 1 percent annually) kill their abusive mates. Fewer than 600 women (since some murderous wives or girlfriends kill for other motives)—out of several million who are battered each year—respond with deadly force. If there is a trend, it appears that the number of cases of lethal violence by men against the women they once loved is increasing, while killings by women against the men they were romantically involved with may be stabilizing, with male violence as least twice as serious a problem as female violence. (See the data on murders between "lovers" for all kinds of motives, presented in Table 3.2.)

Since husbands (and boyfriends) kill their wives (and girlfriends) much more often than wives (and girlfriends) kill their husbands (and boyfriends), male violence against intimates should be a subject of greater concern than female violence against intimates, but somehow it is the less controversial issue in criminal justice. Put still another way, violence unleashed by intimates poses a clear and

TABLE 3.2 Murders by Intimates

YEAR	WIVES KILLED BY HUSBANDS AND GIRLFRIENDS KILLED BY BOYFRIENDS	HUSBANDS KILLED BY WIVES AND BOYFRIENDS KILLED BY GIRLFRIENDS
1977	1396	1185
1978	1428	1095
1979	1438	1137
1980	1498	1129
1981	1486	1149
1982	1408	1008
1983	1487	1043
1984	1420	897
1985	1480	835
1986	1525	866
1987	1508	824
1988	1592	765
1989	1441	817
1990	1524	797
1991	1528	714
1992	1510	657
1993	1531	591

Source: Zawitz, 1994.

present danger to females but not to males. To illustrate, in 1993, among all female murder victims, a considerable proportion, nearly 30 percent, were slain by husbands or boyfriends. Yet only 3 percent, a small proportion of all male homicide victims, were killed by the females they once were romantically involved with; most men were murdered by other men for some other reason.

As for the way the system handles cases in which one spouse kills the other, there may be evidence of a double standard reflecting gender bias. Just as men who beat the women they live with tend to receive lenient treatment by the legal system, brutal husbands who eventually murder their wives are believed to get less severe sentences than their histories of assaultive conduct merit. But wives who kill their abusive husbands often get lengthy prison terms, even though they have no prior record of violence (Gibbs, 1993b). Perhaps the leniency shown toward the murderous men is due to the widely held assumption that the dead women must have goaded them into fits of rage. Perhaps the harshness meted out to the women who fought back in desperation reflects the belief that females should accept second-class citizenship in a male-dominated world and is meant to serve as a warning to other wives in similar predicaments not to do what these women did (Bannister, 1992).

Victim-Defending Arguments Stressing That the Brutal Man Did Not Deserve to Die

Victim-defending arguments are advanced most clearly by the police who arrest the battered women and by the prosecutors who press charges against them for killing their abusive mates without sufficient legal justification. The reasoning goes as follows: His fits of temper and violent outbursts were wrong, even criminal in nature, but so was her escalation of the level of violence to lethal proportions. She went too far, using criminal violence to halt criminal violence. She did not explore and exhaust all other options open to her before she chose to resort to deadly force. In particular, she should have fled their home, escaped his clutches, and dissolved their relationship. Shooting a man while he is asleep or unconscious is clearly an act of vengeance, motivated more by fury than fear. The battered woman did not fulfill her duty to retreat (and flee) but instead took it upon herself to be the judge, jury, and executioner. Such retaliatory actions cannot be stretched to fit an expanded definition of self-defense predicated upon standards of a reasonable response to an imminent threat.

Furthermore, certain battered women who have killed their mates are not innocent, law-abiding partners who were goaded into defensive action by their brutally aggressive and domineering husbands. When these women killed their husbands, they were not trying to protect their own lives but were engaged in mutual combat. In the final confrontations that ended their stormy relationships, these battered women retaliated in kind, getting even with their husbands for past abuses. They struck back to settle an old score and to punish their husbands for tormenting them. Such attempts by women to "take the law into their own hands" and deliver a dose of "vigilante justice" cannot be permitted. His death must not go unpunished. She must not get away with murder (see Rittenmeyer, 1981; and Dershowitz, 1988). The truth about their relationship up until its final moments will never be known. The dead man's side of the story cannot be told, and the woman's version of the events stands largely unchallenged. Her account of what happened between them over the years is self-serving: He is depicted as uncontrollably, irrationally, chronically, and savagely violent; in her view, the couple's problems were all his fault. This impression is reinforced by her use of the terms *batterer, initiator,* and *aggressor* to describe him, and *target, object,* and *victim* to refer to herself. The explanations of the survivor are partial, biased, imbalanced, and incomplete if the entire burden of responsibility is placed on the deceased party (see Neidig, 1984).

Victim defending concludes with several observations. First of all, courtroom testimony should focus on the woman who did the killing; the dead husband whose reputation is being vilified is not on trial and cannot help counter the negative portrait of him that she is painting. Second, there must be better ways for a decent society to express its outrage at the brutality some women are forced to endure than to symbolically condone homicide and excuse lethal preemptive strikes. Not prosecuting wrongdoers, acquitting defendants who clearly broke laws, or granting clemency to convicts only encourages others to try these drastic solutions (see Caplan, 1991; Frum, 1993; and Gibbs, 1993b).

Victim-Blaming Arguments Emphasizing That the Brutal Man Provoked the Lethal Response

A woman is raped on her way home from work. Twenty years later, she marries a wealthy widower but soon discovers he served two years in prison for murdering his first wife. For ten years, this jealous, possessive man controls her every movement, beats her, makes unreasonable sexual demands, and mocks her lingering rape trauma by repeatedly sneaking up from behind and grabbing her. One day he threatens to do to her what he did to his first wife. When he falls asleep, she shoots him in the head. She is convicted of second-degree murder and sentenced to five years in prison. But with a new lawyer, she appeals, is granted a second trial, and presents a defense of extreme psychological impairment. After the jury becomes deadlocked, she pleads guilty to manslaughter and the judge sentences her to probation. (Abramson, 1994)

Victim-blaming arguments in such cases proceed from the assertion that the dead husband provoked his own demise. In cases of provocation, the person who emerges as the victor was reluctant to fight at the beginning of the abusive relationship. Eventually, however, the individual who winds up as the victim incites this peaceful, law-abiding person into action through inflammatory insults, challenges, threats, gestures, and then physical assaults that cannot be ignored or evaded. Under attack, and facing serious bodily harm, the woman repels the aggressor with self-protective measures. The man dies as a result of an act of self-defense. In these kinds of incidents, the party who should be held responsible is the injured or dead victim who was the loser in the battle he started. He compelled her to kill him to save her own life at a point in their relationship when he was on the verge of murdering her. In a sense, by setting up a life-and-death struggle from which she could extract herself only by resorting to force, he got what he deserved.

Victim blaming asserts that these slain husbands are different from other married men and that their different attitudes and behaviors are the causes of their demise. If they had changed their ways when they had a chance, they would never have met such a fate. Specifically, the men who provoke their spouses to slay them are more abusive than the typical batterer (Browne, 1987). They attack their partners more often and more viciously and are more likely to threaten, and sometimes carry out, sexual assaults (that today are recognized as marital rapes). They tend to drink more heavily and to use illicit drugs more frequently than other batterers. Also, they are more inclined to threaten to kill their wives and to drive them to harbor suicidal fantasies and self-destructive impulses, according to an analysis of forty-one cases (Browne, 1987). In a study of 100 battered women who killed their violent mates compared to 100 who didn't, those who struck back were more socially and economically isolated. They had suffered more severe beatings, their children were more likely to have been physically abused, and their partners were heavier drinkers and drug takers (Ewing, 1987).

In court, in the press, and among observers, the question often arises, "Why didn't she leave him before the fatal showdown unfolded?" Victim-blaming arguments point out that for many of these battered wives, escape was not a realistic option, or that they tried to leave and failed. The question presupposes that fleeing their home would put an end to the dangers she faced. But in many cases, the husband would not let her escape his clutches. Often, a violence-prone husband has a "you belong to me" mentality. Although she feels she can't live with him, he feels he can't live without her. He becomes infuriated by what he perceives to be rejection, abandonment, or desertion. Such a person is likely to stalk his wife, track her down if she is hiding, and use force to bring her back. As a result, the battered woman feels like a captive, trapped in a no-win situation she can't end. Practical considerations might also deter her from trying to escape. Shelters for battered women are few and far between, overcrowded, filled to capacity with waiting lists and time limitations, and just temporary havens at best. Severing an intimate relationship abruptly is difficult when a couple has children, property in common, and intertwined families, friends, daily routines, and jobs. The woman may feel terrified at the thought of having to live on the run like a fugitive and of uprooting her children, and outraged at the "solution" of abandoning her home to the guilty party. And she may know of women who are separated or even divorced but still get beaten by their former husbands (Browne, 1987).

An understanding of "the battered woman syndrome" helps to explain why some women seem stuck in destructive relationships. The syndrome describes the predictable long-term consequences of repeated beatings. The assaults inflict a type of posttraumatic stress disorder of "learned helplessness" that undermines the self-esteem and sense of control of the demoralized and terrorized woman. Gripped by fear, with beatings following a predictable cyclical pattern (the syndrome of tension building/explosion/reconciliation), the woman can believe she is in constant danger, even when he is not on the offensive (Walker, 1984). As a result, she might choose to fight back at a moment when he is not acting in a threatening manner. This can explain why she may seize the element of surprise and strike with whatever weapon is at her disposal when he is distracted, or asleep, or has passed out from too much drinking or drug-taking. Now that the battered woman's syndrome is becoming recognized as a legitimate defense, expert testimony about the cumulative psychological consequences of periodic beatings (explicitly permitted by laws passed in nine states and by Congress; admissible subject to the judge's discretion elsewhere) can help women on trial to explain why they killed a violent mate who was not advancing menacingly at the moment of his death (Kristal, 1991; Sargeant, 1991; and Gibbs, 1993b).

In court, some defendants claim they are "not guilty by reason of diminished capacity or temporary insanity." Pleading insanity means offering an excuse for the act. In using such a defense, the woman concedes that taking the man's life was wrong but argues that she should not be punished for the killing because her mental state was so impaired at the time that she was unable to form criminal intent. Temporary insanity pleas seem most appropriate in cases involving defendants who cannot recall their actions and who are found to be dazed and confused in the aftermath of the confrontation. If acquitted, she need not be confined in a mental institution, since she poses no danger to the community or to herself; the irritant that provoked her out-of-control response has been eliminated (see Bernat, 1992). But legal strategies that rely on convincing a jury of the woman's irrational and pathological behavior shift attention away from the man's provocations and her right to defend herself (Schneider, 1980).

Victim blaming interprets her resort to deadly force as defensive, even if it does not appear so by traditional standards. The legal doctrine of self-defense was developed by men to apply to fights between men and is usually debated and interpreted by men. The classical model posits a clash between two men of roughly equal strength who do not know each other. Self-defense is accordingly defined as the justifiable use of an appropriate amount of force against an adversary by an individual who reasonably believes that he is in imminent danger of unlawful bodily harm, and that the use of such force is necessary to prevent such harm from being inflicted. But this highly subjective male-oriented model with its assumptions and prescriptions needs to be modified when applied to clashes between males and females. For example, a woman can be considered to be acting in self-defense if she uses a weapon like a knife or gun against a man who is unarmed. The rationale is that his hands and feet can be viewed as deadly weapons, since women, and especially battered wives, have been beaten to death by unarmed men. Since women are generally less skilled in combat and tend to be smaller in stature, the use of a deadly weapon is a way of matching but not exceeding his level of violence. A battered woman who resorts to deadly force during the phase of the cycle or syndrome when the husband is just threatening harm but not yet physically attacking also can be considered to be acting in self-defense. Unlike a person confronted by a stranger, she is in a position to know—from many bitter past experiences—that his threats are real and will be carried out. The battered woman learns to recognize the small cues that signal that a beating is imminent, such as subtle changes in the tone of the man's voice or in his facial expressions. Similarly, the woman who strikes out against her assailant during a lull in the ordeal or after an outbreak has peaked can also be considered to be acting in self-defense, because she knows, and is acting on, the patterns in his attacks (Fiora-Gormally, 1978; Jones, 1980; Schneider, 1980; Bochnak, 1981; Thyfault, 1984; Kuhl, 1986; Saunders, 1986; Browne, 1987; Ewing, 1987; Gillespie, 1989; and Bannister, 1992).

Victim-blaming arguments are most convincing to the police, prosecutors, and juries in cases where many of the following elements are present: The battered woman had been threatened many times; beaten repeatedly; rescued by the police from his wrath on several occasions; granted an order of protection; testified in court after pressing charges; sought marital counseling; attempted to escape his clutches; separated from him and filed for divorce; had visible, severe injuries at the time of her arrest; and suffered permanent damage from her wounds after that final deadly confrontation. If a "psychological autopsy" or courtroom reconstruction of the tormentor who provoked his own lover to kill him is presented effectively by a defense attorney with the help of an expert witness testifying about the battered woman's syndrome, the jurors could become so inflamed that they will want to dig up the bully's corpse and kill him all over again (see Sargeant, 1991).

The clash between victim-blaming and victim-defending perspectives illustrates, among other things, that all crimes are socially defined. No act is inherently illegal, even the taking of a life. For example, not every homicide is a murder; each killing of one person by another must be examined and interpreted within its context. Some slayings end up designated as noncrimes: enemy soldiers killed in battle during war, death penalties imposed on convicts lawfully carried out by executioners, justifiable homicides of criminals engaged in shoot-outs with police officers, and, indeed, some deaths of wife-beaters by the targets of their wrath.

BEYOND VICTIM BLAMING AND VICTIM DEFENDING

A review of the three examples presented above uncovers some misleading impressions and some strengths and weaknesses of victim blaming and victim defending.

Contrary to the characterizations of some victimologists, victim blaming is not inherently an exercise in scapegoating or an example of twisted logic and callousness. It all depends on which crime is the focus of attention, who the "real" victims are, and why some people are blaming them. Similarly, victim defending is not invariably a "noble" enterprise engaged in solely by those who champion the cause of the downtrodden.

Hence, victim blamers, as individuals, are not necessarily liberal or conservative, rich or poor, young or old, male or female, or black or white. Sometimes victim blamers "switch sides" and become victim defenders; it depends on the facts of the case and the nature of the crime. Individuals do not line up consistently on one side or the other. Indeed, when the full scope of criminals and victims is taken into account, nearly everyone blames certain victims and defends others.

The strengths of victim blaming and victim defending lie in their advocates' willingness to address actual events, specific criminal acts, and real-life cases. In the course of their debates, victim blamers and victim defenders examine in detail who said and did what to whom, under what circumstances. Victim-blaming and victim-defending arguments bridge the gap between theoretical propositions and abstractions, on the one hand, and how people genuinely think and act, on the other. In dissecting how particular crimes unfolded, victim blamers and victim defenders pay attention to details that otherwise are overlooked.

The most serious drawback of both victim blaming and victim defending is that they tend to be "microscopic" rather than "macroscopic." Victim blamers and victim defenders get so caught up (or bogged down) in the particularities of each case that they tend to ignore the larger social forces and conditions that shape the ideas and behaviors of both criminals and victims. Thus, whenever partisans of the two perspectives clash, they inadvertently let the "system," with its fundamental institutions (established ways of organizing people to accomplish tasks) and culture (way of life) off the hook.

This tendency to parcel out blame between only two parties, the perpetrator and the victim, is reinforced by the way the criminal justice system operates. It isolates conflicts between individuals from the surrounding social context. Rarely are more abstract social forces and conditions considered to be "parties to the crime" and at fault to some degree for what happened. Accordingly, both approaches tend to overlook the many ways in which the economic, political, and legal system, with its underlying institutions (like schools, the military, and the family) and its culture (religious traditions, cherished values) might influence the actors in the drama to play the well-rehearsed roles of offender and victim and to follow a well-known script in an all-too-familiar tragedy.

In the case of auto theft, victim-blaming and victim-defending arguments revolve entirely around the actions of motorists and thieves. What is excluded from the analysis is as important as what is included. A comprehensive analysis of the roots of the problem would include a recognition of how sophisticated and organized commercial thievery has become; how profitable the market for "hot" cars and stolen parts is; how the practices of insurance companies provide incentives for thieves to steal cars and parts; how the operations of salvage yards make it possible for thieves to easily infiltrate black-market parts into the flow of used parts to auto body repair shops; and how inadequacies in record keeping makes it difficult for law enforcement officials to detect and prove thievery (see Karmen, 1980; and NIJ, 1984). It is necessary to go beyond victim blaming and victim defending to realize that the manufacturers bear responsibility for the ease with which their products are taken away from their customers. Year after year, pros continue to brag that they need just a minute or two and an ordinary screwdriver to defeat the standard antitheft locks on the doors and the ignitions of most makes and models (see Kesler, 1992; Behar, 1993; "Auto Theft Alert," 1994; and S. Smith, 1994).

Perhaps victim blaming for auto theft has always been a diversionary tactic, even a form of scapegoating. The most virulent victim-blaming emanated from automobile industry spokespersons, insurance company representatives, and top law enforcement officials. Who or what are they protecting? Certainly, they are not apologists for the lawbreakers—the joyriding juveniles and the professional criminals. Apparently, the attacks on motorists who made their cars easier to steal are intended to draw attention away from the automobile manufacturers who design and sell cars that are so easily stolen! Considerable evidence exists to substantiate the charge that vehicle security (like passenger safety, until recently), has always been assigned a low priority by the Detroit automakers and their foreign counterparts, probably because vehicle thefts stimulate new car sales (see Karmen, 1981a). Vehicle security is likely to remain a problem until manufacturers are compelled by law to install locks that meet minimal standards (in terms of the time and effort required to defeat them) and to post "theft resistance" ratings on new car stickers.

As for the serious problem of forcible rape, victim blamers and victim defenders focus too narrowly on the attitudes and actions of the female targets of male aggression. In the process, they tend to ignore crucial insights into the prevailing cultural prescriptions concerning sex roles, romance, eroticism, and seduction. The possibility that the roots of forced sex lie in the economic, political, and social inequalities between males and females gets lost when the analysis is limited to a reconstruction of the he said/she said interaction.

Similarly, when battered wives become widows by their own deeds, the parceling out of blame should not be limited to just one spouse or the other. If domestic disturbances are to be prevented from escalating to such explosive levels, then effective outside intervention will be necessary. Murders within marriages reflect the failure of criminal justice and social service agencies to provide adequate protection for the victim who ultimately becomes the perpetrator and to provide timely treatment for the abuser who eventually loses his life. Some responsibility for these tragedies also falls on those officials whose traditional notions of sex roles lead them to assign a low priority to cases of family violence, who cling to a "hands off," "settle it yourselves" doctrine, and who discourage the development of adequate refuges to shelter battered women and therapy programs to rehabilitate abusive men.

Victimology complements criminology by drawing attention to "that other party" and thereby corrects the tendency within criminology to fix all attention on the offender. But if victimologists are to contribute significantly to the understanding of the crime problem, they must transcend any inclination to confine their analyses to the interaction between the victim and the offender. An approach that is preoccupied with doling out the proper mix of exoneration and blame to just two people is shortsighted because the influences of social forces and conditions are eliminated from consideration. Given the limited choices of either victim blaming or victim defending, policymakers concerned about crime prevention can attempt to control either would-be offenders or potential victims. But adopting a system-blaming perspective opens up many more promising strategies to reform the social institutions that generate both offenders and victims.

Having to choose between victim blaming and victim defending can be intellectually stifling. In the following satire, a fictional professor of victimology puts forward preposterous victim-blaming proposals in a laughable plan to solve the street crime problem (see the spoof in Box 3.4).

BOX 3.4   Prof Calls for Crackdown on Crime Victims

There is so much talk about crime in the streets and the rights of the criminal that little attention is being paid to the victims of crime. But there is a current of opinion that our courts are being too soft on the victims, and many of them are going unpunished for allowing a crime to be committed against them.

One man who feels strongly about this is Prof. Heinrich Applebaum, a criminologist who feels that unless the police start cracking down on the victims of criminal acts, the crime rate in this country will continue to rise.

"The people who are responsible for crime in this country are the victims. If they didn't allow themselves to be robbed, the problem of crime in this country would be solved," Applebaum said.

"That makes sense, Professor. Why do you think the courts are soft on victims of crimes?"

"We're living in a permissive society and anything goes," Applebaum replied. "Victims of crimes don't seem to be concerned about the consequences of their acts. They walk down a street after dark, or they display jewelry in their store window, or they have their cash registers right out where everyone can see them. They seem to think that they can do this in the United States and get away with it."

"You speak as if all the legal machinery in this country was weighted in favor of the victim, instead of the person who committed the crime."

"It is," Applebaum said. "While everyone is worried about the victim, the poor criminal is dragged down to the police station, booked and arraigned, and if he's lucky he'll be let out on bail. He may lose his job if his boss hears about it and there is even a chance that if he has a police record, it may prejudice the judge when he's sentenced."

"I guess in this country people always feel sorrier for the victim than they do for the person who committed the crime."

"You can say that again. Do you know that in some states they are even compensating victims of crimes?"

"It's hard to believe," I said.

"Well, it's true. The do-gooders and the bleeding hearts all feel that victims of crimes are misunderstood, and if they were treated better, they would stop being victims. But the statistics don't bear this out. The easier you are on the victim, the higher the crime rate becomes."

"What is the solution, Professor?"

"I say throw the book at anybody who's been robbed. They knew what they were getting into when they decided to be robbed, and they should pay the penalty for it. Once a person has been a victim of crime and realizes he can't get away with it, the chances of his becoming a victim again will be slim."

"Why do people want to become victims of crime, Professor?"

"Who knows? They're probably looking for thrills. Boredom plays a part, but I would think the biggest factor is that victims think they can still walk around the streets of their cities and get away with it. Once they learn they can't, you'll see a big drop in crime statistics."

"You make a lot of sense, Professor. Do you believe the American people are ready to listen to you?"

"They'd better be, because the criminal element is getting pretty fed up with all the permissive coddling of victims that is going on in this country."

Source: From "Victim Precipitation," by Art Buchwald. Copyright © *The Washington Post*, February 4, 1969. Reprinted by permission.

4

Victims and the Criminal Justice System: Cooperation and Conflict

Criminologists study the operations of the criminal justice system (law enforcement agencies, prosecutors' offices, courts, corrections departments, and parole authorities). They investigate how the system handles offenders, or more precisely, suspects, defendants, and convicts. Victimologists explore how the system handles victims. Specifically, they examine how the police respond to complainants; how prosecutors, defense attorneys, and judges treat these witnesses for the state; and how corrections officials react to requests by victims. At the conclusion of this step-by-step walk through the system, a fundamental question is addressed: Are all victims handled the same, or are some treated better than others?

This chapter does not discuss the juvenile justice system, which operates according to other principles and treats victims differently, generally worse, because they are not permitted to play much of a role and can exercise fewer options and rights. About one-third of all arrests for street crimes (*UCR* index crimes), particularly offenses against property, involve juveniles younger than eighteen. The victims of these juvenile delinquents face a separate set of problems that are beyond the scope of this chapter.

VICTIMS VERSUS THE CRIMINAL JUSTICE SYSTEM

The criminal justice system is one branch of government that comes under scathing attack from all quarters. Conservatives, liberals, and radicals; feminists; law-and-order advocates; civil rights activists; and civil libertarians all find fault with its rules and procedures. Even officials who run its agencies and shape its daily operations have joined the chorus of critics calling for change:

> If there is one word that describes how the criminal justice system treats victims of crimes and witnesses to crimes, it is "badly." (James Reilly, director of the Victim/Witness Assistance Project of the National District Attorney's Association, 1981:8)

> Crimes that terrorize take many forms, from aggravated assault to petty thievery. But one crime goes largely unnoticed. It is a crime against which there is no protection. It is committed daily across our nation. It is the painful, wrongful insensitivity of the criminal justice system toward those who are the victims of crime. . . . The callousness with which the system again victimizes those who have already suffered at the hands of an assailant is tragic. (Senator John Heinz, sponsor of the Omnibus Victims Protection Act passed by Congress, 1982:A19)

> Without the cooperation of victims and witnesses in reporting and testifying about crime, it is impossible in a free society to hold criminals accountable.

When victims come forward to provide this vital service, however, they find little protection. They discover instead that they will be treated as appendages of a system appallingly out of balance. They learn that somewhere along the way the system has lost track of the simple truth that it is supposed to be fair and to protect those who obey the law while punishing those who break it. Somewhere along the way, the system began to serve lawyers and judges and defendants, treating the victim with institutionalized disinterest. . . . The neglect of crime victims is a national disgrace. (Lois Herrington, chairperson of the President's Task Force on Victims of Crime, President's Task Force, 1982:vi–vii)

The consensus among experts is that the criminal justice system does not measure up to expectations. It fails to deliver what it promises. It does not meet the needs and wants of victims as its "clients" or as "consumers" of its services.

Suppose a person is robbed and injured. What could and should the system do? The police could rush to help the victim and provide whatever physical and psychological first aid might be needed. They could catch the culprit and speedily return stolen goods to the rightful owner. The prosecutor could indict the defendant and press for a swift trial. After securing a conviction, the prosecutor could see to it that the victim's views were fully aired. The judge could hand down a sentence that would satisfy the victim that justice had indeed been done. Correctional authorities could make sure that the probationer, prisoner, or parolee makes court-ordered restitution payments on time, and doesn't harass or harm the person whose complaint set the machinery of criminal justice into motion.

But this scenario frequently does not materialize. Instead of cooperation, conflict pervades relationships between victims and the police, prosecutors, judges, and parole boards who handle their cases.

The account presented in Box 4.1 illustrates how the system routinely mistreated victims in the "bad old days" before the victims' rights movement raised objections and brought about some meaningful reforms. This fictional composite sketch illustrates everything that could possibly go wrong. It was constructed from testimony about real-life ordeals brought to the attention of a presidential task force. Since this account provides a "checklist" of nearly all possible abuses, it can serve as a standard for comparison with current cases to identify just how much progress has been made and exactly what remains to be accomplished. The story follows one woman's plight as her rape is processed as just another case winding its way through the system. The task force pinpointed the various reasons that victims find themselves pitted against the police, the prosecuting attorney working for the government, the defense lawyer acting in behalf of the accused, the judge presiding over the case, the jury sitting in judgment, and the parole board determining the convict's future. This excerpt accentuates the negative by focusing on rape victims because they were and still are the most mistreated of all.

BOX 4.1   The System's Shortcomings, from a Victim's Point of View

The Crime

You are a fifty-year-old woman living alone. You are asleep one night when suddenly you awaken to find a man standing over you with a knife at your throat. As you start to scream, he beats and cuts you. He then rapes you. While you watch helplessly, he searches the house, taking your jewelry, other valuables, and money. He smashes furniture and windows in a display of senseless violence. His rampage ended, he rips out the telephone line, threatens you again, and disappears in the night.

At least you have survived. Terrified, you rush to the first lighted house on the block. While you wait for the police, you pray that your attacker was bluffing when he said he'd return if you called them. Finally, what you expect to be help arrives.

The police ask questions, take notes, dust for fingerprints, make photographs. When you tell them you were raped, they take you to the hospital. Bleeding from cuts, your front teeth knocked out, bruised and in pain, you are told that your wounds are superficial, that rape itself is not considered an injury. Awaiting treatment, you sit alone for hours, suffering the stares of curious passersby. You feel dirty, bruised, disheveled, and abandoned. When your turn comes for examination, the intern seems irritated because he has been called out to treat you. While he treats you, he says that he hates to get involved in rape cases because he doesn't like going to court. He asks if you "knew the man you had sex with."

The nurse says she wouldn't be out alone at this time of night. It seems pointless to explain

that the attacker broke into your house and had a knife. An officer says you must go through this process, then the hospital sends you a bill for the examination that the investigators insisted upon. They give you a box filled with test tubes and swabs and envelopes and tell you to hold onto it. They'll run some tests if they ever catch your rapist.

Finally, you get home somehow, in a cab you paid for and wearing a hospital gown because they took your clothes as evidence. Everything that the attacker touched seems soiled. You're afraid to be in your house alone. The one place where you were always safe, at home, is a sanctuary no longer. You are afraid to remain, yet terrified to leave your home unprotected.

You didn't realize when you gave the police your name and address that it would be given to the press and to the defendant through the police reports. Your friends call to say they saw this information in the paper, your picture on television. You haven't yet absorbed what's happened to you when you get calls from insurance companies and firms that sell security devices. But these calls pale in comparison to the threats that come from the defendant and his friends.

You're astonished to discover that your attacker has been arrested, yet while in custody he has free and unmonitored access to a phone. He can threaten you from jail. The judge orders him not to annoy you, but when the phone calls are brought to his attention, the judge does nothing.

At least you can be assured that the man who attacked you is in custody, or so you think. No one tells you when he is released on his promise to

(continued on next page)

BOX 4.1 *continued*

come to court. No one ever asks you if you've been threatened. The judge is never told that the defendant said he'd kill you if you told or that he'd get even if he went to jail. Horrified, you ask how he got out after what he did. You're told the judge can't consider whether he'll be dangerous, only whether he'll come back to court. He's been accused and convicted before, but he always came to court; so he must be released.

You learn only by accident that he's at large; this discovery comes when you turn a corner and confront him. He knows where you live. He's been there. Besides, your name and address were in the paper and in the reports he's seen. Now nowhere is safe. He watches you from across the street; he follows you on the bus. Will he come back in the night? What do you do? Give up your home? Lose your job? Assume a different name? Get your mail at the post office? Carry a weapon? Even it you wanted to, could you afford to do these things?

You try to return to normal, You don't want to talk about what happened, so you decide not to tell your co-workers about the attack. A few days go by and the police unexpectedly come to your place of work. They show their badges to the receptionist and ask to see you. They want you to look at some photographs, but they don't explain that to your co-workers. You try to explain later that you're the victim, not the accused.

The phone rings and the police want you to come to a line-up. It may be 1:00 A.M. or in the middle of your work day, but you have to go; the suspect and his lawyer are waiting. It will not be the last time you are forced to conform your life to their convenience. You appear at the police station and the line-up begins. The suspect's lawyer sits next to you, but he does not watch the stage; he stares at you. It will not be the last time you must endure his scrutiny.

Charges Are Pressed against a Defendant

You have lived through the crime and made it through the initial investigation. They've caught the man who harmed you, and he's been charged with armed burglary, robbery, and rape. Now he'll be tried. Now you expect justice.

You receive a subpoena for a preliminary hearing. No one tells you what it will involve, how long it will take, or how you should prepare. You assume that this is the only time you will have to appear. But you are only beginning your initiation in a system that will grind away at you for months, disrupt your life, affect your emotional stability, and certainly cost you money; it may cost you your job, and, for the duration, will prevent you from putting the crime behind you and reconstructing your life.

Before the hearing, a defense investigator comes to talk to you. When he contacts you, he says he's "investigating your case," and that he "works for the county." You assume, as he intends you to, that he's from the police or the prosecutor's office. Only after you give him a statement do you discover that he works for the man who attacked you.

This same investigator may visit your neighbors and co-workers, asking questions about you. He discusses the case with them, always giving the defendant's side. Suddenly, some of the people who know you seem to be taking a different view of what happened to you and why.

It's the day of the hearing. You've never been to court before, never spoken in public. You're very nervous. You rush to arrive at 8 A.M. to talk to a prosecutor you've never met. You wait in a hallway with a number of other witnesses. It's now 8:45. Court starts at 9:00. No one has spoken to you. Finally, a man sticks his head out a door, calls out your name, and asks, "Are you the one who was raped?" You're aware of the stares as you stand and suddenly realize that this is the prosecutor, the person you expect will represent your interests.

You only speak to the prosecutor for a few minutes. You ask to read the statement you gave to the police but he says there isn't time. He asks

(continued on next page)

BOX 4.1   *continued*

you some questions that make you wonder if he's read it himself. He asks you other questions that make you wonder if he believes it.

The prosecutor tells you to sit on the bench outside the courtroom. Suddenly you see the man who raped you coming down the hall. No one has told you he would be here. He's with three friends. He points you out. They all laugh and jostle you a little as they pass. The defendant and two friends enter the courtroom; one friend sits on the bench across from you and stares. Suddenly, you feel abandoned, alone, afraid. Is this what it's like to come to court and seek justice?

You sit on that bench for an hour, then two. You don't see the prosecutor; he has disappeared into the courtroom. Finally, at noon he comes out and says. "Oh, you're still here? We continued that case to next month."

You repeat this process many times before you actually testify at the preliminary hearing. Each time you go to court, you hire a babysitter or take leave from work, pay for parking, wait for hours, and finally are told to go home. No one ever asks if the new dates are convenient to you. You miss vacations and medical appointments. You use up sick leave and vacation days to make your court appearances. Your employer is losing his patience. Every time you are gone his business is disrupted. But you are fortunate. If you were new at your job, or worked part-time, or didn't have an understanding boss, you could lose your job. Many victims do.

The preliminary hearing was an event for which you were completely unprepared. You learn later that the defense is often harder on a victim at the preliminary hearing than during the trial. In a trial, the defense attorney cannot risk alienating the jury. At this hearing, there is only the judge—and he certainly doesn't seem concerned about you. One of the first questions you are asked is where you live. You finally moved after your attack; you've seen the defendant and his friends, and you're terrified of having them know

where you now live. When you explain that you'd be happy to give your old address the judge says he'll dismiss the case or hold you in contempt of court if you don't answer the question. The prosecutor says nothing. During your testimony, you are also compelled to say where you work, how you get there, and what your schedule is.

Hours later you are released from the stand after reliving your attack in public, in intimate detail. You have been made to feel completely powerless. As you sat facing a smirking defendant and as you described his threats, you were accused of lying and inviting the "encounter." You have cried in front of these uncaring strangers. As you leave no one thanks you. When you get back to work they ask what took you so long.

You are stunned when you later learn that the defendant also raped five others; one victim was an eight-year-old girl. During her testimony she was asked to describe her attacker's anatomy. Spectators laughed when she said she did not understand the words being used. When she was asked to draw a picture of her attacker's genitalia the girl fled from the courtroom and ran sobbing to her mother, who had been subpoenaed by the defense and had to wait outside. The youngster was forced to sit alone and recount, as you did, each minute of the attack. You know how difficult it was for you to speak of these things; you cannot imagine how it was for a child.

Now the case is scheduled for trial. Again there are delays. When you call and ask to speak with the prosecutor, you are told the case has been reassigned. You tell your story in detail to five different prosecutors before the case is tried. Months go by and no one tells you what's happening. Periodically you are subpoenaed to appear. You leave your work, wait, and are finally told to go home.

Continuances are granted because the courts are filled, one of the lawyers is on another case, the judge has a meeting to attend or an early tennis match. You can't understand why they

(continued on next page)

BOX 4.1 *continued*

couldn't have discovered these problems before you came to court. When you ask if the next date could be set a week later so you can attend a family gathering out of state, you are told that the defendant has the right to a speedy trial. You stay home from the reunion and the case is continued.

The defense attorney continues to call. Will you change your story? Don't you want to drop the charges?

Time passes and you hear nothing. Your property is not returned. You learn that there are dozens of defense motions that can be filed before the trial. If denied, many of them can be appealed. Each motion, each court date means a new possibility for delay. If the defendant is out of custody and fails to come to court, nothing can happen until he is reapprehended. If he is successful in avoiding recapture, the case may be so compromised by months or years of delay that a successful prosecution is impossible. For as long as the case drags on, your life is on hold. You don't want to start a new assignment at work or move to a new city because you know that at any time the round of court appearances may begin again. The wounds of your attack will never heal as long as you know that you will be asked to relive those horrible moments.

No one tells you anything about the progress of the case. You want to be involved, consulted, and informed, but prosecutors often plea bargain without consulting victims. You're afraid someone will let the defendant plead guilty to a lesser charge and be sentenced to probation. You meet another victim at court who tells you that she and her family were kidnapped and her children molested. Even though the prosecutor assured her that he would not accept a plea bargain, after talking with the attorneys in his chambers, the judge allowed the defendant to plead as charged with the promise of a much-reduced sentence. You hope that this won't happen in your case.

The Trial

Finally the day of trial arrives. It is eighteen months since you were attacked. You've been trying for a week to prepare yourself. It is painful to dredge up the terror again, but you know that the outcome depends on you; the prosecutor has told you that the way you behave will make or break the case. You can't get too angry on the stand because then the jury might not like you. You can't break down and sob because then you will appear too emotional, possibly unstable. In addition to the tremendous pressure of having to relive the horrible details of the crime, you're expected to be an actress as well.

You go to court. The continuances are over; the jury has been selected. You sit in a waiting room with the defendant's family and friends. Again you feel threatened, vulnerable, and alone.

You expect the trial to be a search for the truth; you find that it is a performance orchestrated by lawyers and the judge, with the jury hearing only half the facts. The defendant was found with your watch in his pocket. The judge has suppressed this evidence because the officer who arrested him didn't have a warrant.

Your character is an open subject of discussion and innuendo. The defense is allowed to question you on incidents going back to your childhood. The jury is never told that the defendant has two prior convictions for the same offense and has been to prison three times for other crimes. You sought help from a counselor to deal with the shattering effect of this crime on your life. You told him about your intimate fears and feelings. Now he has been called by the defense and his notes and records have been subpoenaed.

You are on the stand for hours. The defense does its best to make you appear a liar, a seductress, or both. You know you cannot relax for a moment. Don't answer unless you understand the question. Don't be embarrassed when everyone

(continued on next page)

BOX 4.1	*continued*

seems angry because you do not understand. Think ahead. Be responsive. Don't volunteer. Don't get tired.

Finally you are finished with this part of the nightmare. You would like to sit and listen to the rest of the trial but you cannot. You're a witness and must wait outside. The jury will decide the outcome of one of the major events of your life. You cannot hear the testimony that will guide their judgment.

The verdict is guilty. You now look to the judge to impose a just sentence.

The Sentence

You expect the sentence to reflect how terrible the crime was. You ask the prosecutor how this decision is reached, and are told that once a defendant is convicted he is interviewed at length by a probation officer. He gives his side of the story, which may be blatantly false in light of the proven facts. A report that delves into his upbringing, family relationships, education, physical and mental health, and employment and conviction history is prepared. The officer will often speak to the defendant's relatives and friends. Some judges will send the defendant to a facility where a complete psychiatric and sociological work-up is prepared. You're amazed that no one will ever ask

you about the crime, or the effect it has had on you and your family. You took the defendant's blows, heard his threats, listened to him brag that he'd "beat the rap" or "con the judge." No one ever hears of these things. They never give you a chance to tell them.

At sentencing, the judge hears from the defendant, his lawyer, his mother, his minister, his friends. You learn by chance what day the hearing is. When you do attend, the defense attorney says you're vengeful and it's apparent that you overreacted to being raped and robbed because you chose to come and see the sentencing. You ask permission to address the judge and are told that you are not allowed to do so.

The judge sentences your attacker to three years in prison, less than one year for every hour he kept you in pain and terror. That seems very lenient to you. Only later do you discover that he'll probably serve less than half of his actual sentence in prison because of good-time and work-time credits that are given to him immediately. The man who broke into your home, threatened to slit your throat with a knife, and raped, beat, and robbed you will be out of custody in less than eighteen months. You are not told when he will actually be released, and you are not allowed to attend the parole release hearing anyway.

Source: Excerpted from the report of the President's Task Force on Victims of Crime, 1982:3–11.

WHAT DO VICTIMS WANT: PUNISHMENT? TREATMENT? OR RESTITUTION?

Why should victims ask that the machinery of criminal justice be set into motion on their behalf? What do they want? What would they like to see done?

The victims' rights movement has sought empowerment. That means the ability to have some input into important decisions at every step along the way. But why demand inclusion? Why insist on having chances to participate at key junctures in the criminal justice process?

Victims can pursue one, or even some combination of three distinct goals. The first is to see to it that the criminal is punished. The second possible objective is to use the justice process as leverage to compel the offender to undergo treatment. The third possible aim is to try to get the court to order the wrongdoer to make restitution.

> **A** small group of women, some of whom had been raped, or whose children had been murdered, demonstrates in favor of a bill before a state legislature that would set up a special prison for serious offenders in which convicts would be forced to perform hard labor for ten hours a day. The proposed prison would stress punishment over rehabilitation by eliminating all educational and vocational training. It would have no gymnasium, no recreational areas, no televisions, and no telephones for inmates. (Hanley, 1994a)

It is punishment that comes to most people's minds first. Most of the deliberations of criminal justice officials concern questions of punishment: who, why, when, where, how much? People have always punished one another, although they have never agreed on their reasons for subjecting deviants to pain and suffering.

Punishment is usually justified on utilitarian grounds as a necessary evil. It is argued that punishing wrongdoers curbs future criminality in a number of ways. The offender who experiences unpleasant consequences learns a lesson and is discouraged from breaking the law again (specific deterrence). Making an example of a convicted criminal also serves as a warning to would-be offenders contemplating the same act (general deterrence). Punishment in the form of imprisonment has been defended as a method of incapacitating dangerous predators so that they can no longer prey upon innocents. Another rationale for punishment by the government is that it heads off vigilantism by angry victims and their supporters.

Punishment has also been justified on nonutilitarian grounds, as a morally sound practice regardless of any value it has in deterring or incapacitating criminals. According to the theory of punishment as retribution, it is fair and just to make offenders suffer in proportion to the suffering they inflicted on others. From biblical times onward, many people have believed in *lex talonis*—retaliation in kind, symbolized by the phrase "an eye for an eye . . ." From this perspective, individuals who harm others must get their "just deserts." Retribution evens the score, rights a wrong, and restores balance to the moral order, as long as the severity of the punitive sanction is in proportion to the gravity of the offense.

The quest for retribution has shaped history. Incorporated into the customs and consciousness of entire groups, classes, and nations, it is expressed in simmering hatreds, longstanding feuds, vendettas, and wars. Revenge fantasies can sustain people and even give purpose and direction to their lives. However, the thirst for vengeance can destroy victims as well, by becoming an obsession. Even when fulfilled, revenge fantasies are rarely as satisfying as had been imagined. Yet for victims to feel a sense of fury and rage toward those who have abused them is entirely human. In the hours and days following a crime, it is psychologically useful and even cathartic for victims to dream of inflicting pain on their offenders. But a chronic preoccupation with striking back and getting even endlessly and needlessly prolongs memories of the victimization. Vengeful victims never break free of the pernicious influence of their victimizers. Survivors learn that the best revenge is to transcend their offender's grip, put the experience behind them, and lead a fulfilling life (Halleck, 1980).

Despite the current popularity of punishment as the antidote to victimization and the cure for crime, the punitive approach has always been controversial and continues to be severely criticized (see Menninger, 1968; Wright, 1973; Prison Research, 1976; Pepinsky, 1991; and Elias, 1993). Utilitarian opponents have documented how ineffective and even counterproductive punishment can be. Civil libertarians have condemned punishment as a tool of domination and oppression, used by tyrants and totalitarian regimes to terrorize their subjects into submission.

Some victims do not look to the criminal justice system to exact revenge in their name. Instead, they want professionals and experts to help offenders become decent, law-abiding citizens. Victims are most likely to press for rehabilitation if their offenders are not complete strangers but lovers, family members, other relatives, neighbors, classmates, or colleagues. Rehabilitation might take the form of counseling, behavior modification, intense psychotherapy, additional schooling, job training and placement, detoxification from addictive drugs, and medical care. Despite the temporary ascendancy of a pessimistic, "nothing works" disenchantment with the ideal of rehabilitation (see Martinson, 1974), "helping" offenders remains as much a part of the system's mission as making them sorry for what they did. Rehabilitation is a long-term strategy that is in the enlightened self-interest of both victims and society. Incapacitation is a short-term strategy that merely buys time and promotes a false sense of security. Victims who overcome their initial emotional outrage over what offenders did to them might become equally infuriated over imprisonment whenever it backfires and drives offenders to new heights of antisocial conduct. Victims could also become dismayed by inept efforts to rehabilitate offenders while they are inmates in jails or prisons, or when they are on probation or parole.

Finally, some victims seek restitution rather than retribution or rehabilitation. They want the system's help to recover their losses and pay their bills. A necessary prerequisite for full recovery, restitution collected from offenders can help to restore victims to the financial condition they were in before the crimes occurred. Once offenders make amends monetarily, reconciliation becomes a possibility.

Whether they desire that something be done to the offender (punishment), for the offender (treatment), or for themselves (restitution), victims want the criminal justice system to react effectively to violations of law. What they don't want is inaction, lack of interest, neglect, abuse, or manipulation.

VICTIMS AND THE POLICE

Police officers are the first representatives of the criminal justice system that victims encounter in the immediate aftermath of crimes.

The police can serve victims in a number of ways. They can respond quickly to calls for help and provide on-the-spot first aid. Detectives can launch thorough investigations and solve crimes by taking suspects into custody, recovering stolen property, and gathering evidence that will lead to convictions in court.

Victims can become bitterly disappointed with the police if officers are slow to arrive, disbelieve their accusations, conduct superficial investigations, don't make arrests, and fail to recover stolen property.

Reporting Incidents

Criminal justice authorities want people to "report, identify, and testify" and have launched nationwide publicity campaigns to promote this theme ("Crime Control Needs," 1985). The fear is that if would-be offenders believe that the people they harm won't complain about their depredations, then the deterrent effect of the risk of getting caught and punished will be undermined. Furthermore, if the police could obtain from the public more complete and accurate information about crime patterns, then they could more effectively anticipate where offenders will strike next. Victims who fail to report incidents forfeit important rights and opportunities, such as eligibility for services and reimbursement of losses through compensation plans, tax deductions, and insurance policies.

Despite these appeals to self-interest and civic responsibility, most individuals do not report incidents in which they were harmed to the police. Only 50 percent of all victims of violent crimes (rape, robbery, assault), and just 30 percent of all victims of thefts of personal property (with or without contact), and 41 percent of thefts of household property (burglaries, larcenies, and thefts of motor vehicles) informed the police about the incidents that they discussed with *NCVS* interviewers in 1992. The combined reporting rate for all the different types of crimes asked about on the survey was 39 percent (Bastian, 1993).

The reporting rates over the years that the *NCVS* surveys have been carried out for each specific type of offense appear in Table 4.1.

Table 4.1 shows that the reporting rates vary substantially by category of crime. Several overall patterns are worth noting. Violent crimes are reported to the police at much higher rates than either personal thefts or household crimes. Victims are more likely to report incidents in which they sustain physical injuries or suffer considerable financial losses. Also (according to figures not appearing in the table), individuals are more inclined to report completed acts than mere attempts. Of all the crimes asked about on the *NCVS*, completed auto theft comes in each year as

TABLE 4.1 Trends in Reporting Crimes to the Police

PERCENTAGE OF VICTIMIZATIONS DISCLOSED TO *NCVS* **INTERVIEWERS THAT WERE ALSO REPORTED TO THE POLICE**

	1973	1974	1975	1976	1977	1978	1979	1980	1981	1982
All crimes	32	33	35	35	34	33	33	36	35	36
Rapes	49	52	56	53	58	49	51	41	56	53
Robberies	52	54	53	53	56	51	55	57	56	56
Aggravated assaults	52	53	55	58	51	53	51	54	52	58
Simple assaults	38	39	39	41	39	37	37	40	39	40
Personal larcenies with contact	33	34	35	36	37	34	36	36	40	33
Personal larcenies without contact	22	24	26	26	24	24	24	27	26	27
Burglaries	47	48	49	48	49	47	48	51	51	49
Household larcenies	25	25	27	27	25	24	25	28	26	27
Motor vehicle thefts	68	67	71	69	68	66	68	69	67	72

	1983	1984	1985	1986	1987	1988	1989	1990	1991	1992
All crimes	35	35	36	37	37	36	37	38	38	39
Rapes	47	56	61	48	52	45	51	54	59	53
Robberies	53	54	54	58	55	57	51	50	55	51
Aggravated assaults	56	55	58	59	60	54	52	59	58	62
Simple assaults	41	40	40	41	38	41	38	42	42	43
Personal larcenies with contact	36	31	33	38	36	35	30	37	38	31
Personal larcenies without contact	26	26	27	28	27	27	29	28	28	30
Burglaries	49	49	50	52	52	51	50	51	50	54
Household larcenies	25	27	27	28	27	26	28	27	28	26
Motor vehicle thefts	69	69	71	73	75	73	76	75	74	75

Note: Figures include reports of both attempts and completed acts.
Source: Bastian, 1993.

the category with the highest reporting rate (about 90 percent). Most car-theft victims inform the police because there is a good chance their stolen vehicles will be recovered, filing a formal complaint is required for insurance reimbursement, and they do not want to be held responsible for any accidents or crimes involving their cars. (It could be assumed that they were behind the wheel.) The lowest reporting rates (about 12 percent of all incidents disclosed to *NCVS* interviewers) are for attempted thefts of personal and household property. Overall, the police tend to find out about half of the more serious violent crimes in a community but do not learn about most of its minor property crimes. As for changes over time, glancing across the rows, it is obvious that no category shows steady or uninterrupted improvement over time. Slight gains are often followed by slight losses. Some reporting rates show considerable variations from year to year. The reporting rate for rapes, for instance, has risen as high as 61 percent and dropped as low as 41 percent. The row labeled "all crimes" shows a trend toward modest increases in overall reporting rates since the surveys were initiated in 1973. Motor vehicle thefts (both attempted plus completed) are reported more often these days than in past decades (Harlow, 1985; Bastian, 1993).

NCVS interviewers ask victims to explain why they did or did not report the incidents to the authorities. When victims do report crimes to the police, their leading reasons are to recover their stolen property and to prevent the offender from harming them again. Victims who do not report crimes to the police tell *NCVS* interviewers that their main reasons are that the offender was unsuccessful and the property was recovered; that it was a private or personal matter (especially for simple assaults); or that they lacked proof. Only a small percentage of all nonreporting victims volunteered that they felt the police would probably be inefficient, ineffective, or insensitively biased (BJS, 1982–1994).

Reporting rates reflect rational decision-making processes and therefore vary by victim characteristics (see Biblarz, Barnowe, and Biblarz, 1984; Greenberg and Ruback, 1984; and Gottfredson and Gottfredson, 1988). In 1992, *NCVS* findings revealed that reporting rates increased with age; teenagers were much less inclined to bring their misfortunes to the attention of the authorities than were older persons. As for income, poor persons were a little more reluctant to call for help than middle-income people. As for race and ethnicity, African Americans were more likely, and Hispanic Americans less likely than other victims to call the police (BJS, 1982–1994).

Accentuating the positive, the data in Table 4.1 show that victims are now reporting a slightly greater proportion of crimes to the police than they did in the not-too-distant past. Stressing the negative, the data also indicate that the police have had only limited success over the last two decades in getting the public to cooperate more closely with law enforcement. This underreporting can be interpreted as a sign that many people remain alienated from a criminal justice system ostensibly set up to help them.

In most jurisdictions, victims are not legally obliged to inform the authorities about crimes committed against them or their property. But if they go beyond silence and inaction and conspire or collaborate in a cover-up to conceal the fact that a law was broken, they can be arrested themselves and charged with "misprison of a felony." The failure of witnesses to report certain kinds of offenses, especially the abuse of a child or an elderly person, is a misdemeanor in many jurisdictions (Stark and Goldstein, 1985).

Responding Quickly

When victims call the police to report a crime, they want officers to spring into action immediately. To meet this challenge, most departments have set up 911 emergency hot lines. The 911 operators function as "gatekeepers," prioritizing requests for help in terms of their degree of urgency (Gilsinan, 1989).

There is reason to believe that a substantial proportion of the public might be dissatisfied with police response times. Starting in the late 1980s, the redesigned *National Crime Victimization Survey* began to ask respondents how long it took the police to arrive after being summoned for help (Whitaker, 1989). The findings from 1990 through 1992 are compiled in Table 4.2. In roughly 90 percent of all calls for help, police departments across the country were able to dispatch an officer to the scene within sixty minutes or less, but in some emergencies, that track record was probably not good enough.

It is possible that cutting police response time might not matter very much, in terms of apprehending more suspects. For fifty years, police departments have been experimenting with ways to arrive at crime scenes faster, but travel time is only one reason for delays. Time is lost most often and more importantly when victims and witnesses hesitate before reporting a crime in progress. There are several reasons for such citizen delay: Onlookers and even participants might be unsure whether or not a crime really occurred; victims and witnesses might want to cope first with emotional conflicts, personal trauma, and physical injuries, and

TABLE 4.2 Police Response Times Reported by Victims of Violent Crimes (Robbery and Assault)

YEAR	POLICE RESPONSE TIMES			
	WITHIN 1 HOUR	WITHIN 10 MINUTES	WITHIN 5 MINUTES	TOTAL
1990	32%	31%	28%	91%
1991	37%	23%	28%	88%
1992	32%	28%	29%	89%

Note: Police response times to calls by rape victims are not available.
Source: BJS, *Criminal Victimization in the United States,* 1990–1992.

thereby regain their composure, before informing the authorities of what happened; or (less frequently) individuals can't find a telephone, or the phone is out of order, or they have no change or don't know the emergency number, or have trouble communicating with the police dispatcher (Spelman and Brown, 1984).

Investigating Complaints

Police officials want the cooperation of persons who report crimes, for without their help the cases are probably not going to be solved. But two areas of conflict between victims and the police can arise at the investigation-of-complaints stage. First, the officers or detectives who respond to the call for assistance might seem remote, uninterested, even unconcerned about the victim's plight. Second, the police may conclude that the complainant's charges lack credibility and may discontinue the investigation.

Some victims might be deterred from seeking assistance by their fear of a type of "police brutality." After the first injury (the suffering inflicted by the criminal), victims are particularly susceptible to a "second wound." Expecting the police to comfort them and help solve their problems, they sometimes find that officers unwittingly make them feel worse. (These slights can also be delivered by care providers, like emergency room personnel, or by friends and relatives.)

In the aftermath of a street crime, victims are likely to feel powerless, disoriented, and infuriated. Fear, guilt, depression, and fantasies of revenge engulf them. Authority figures such as police officers are expected to calm and console the injured parties to help restore their sense of equilibrium and dispel any lingering feelings of helplessness they may have. But if officers act callously and prolong suffering needlessly, victims feel let down, rejected, and betrayed by those they counted on for support (Symonds, 1980b).

Studies of police work suggest that what victims are reacting to is the protective coating of emotional detachment that officers develop to shield themselves from the pain of the human misery they routinely encounter. To avoid "burnout," police officers (like others in "helping" professions) inhibit their impulses to get deeply involved in the cases they investigate. The paramilitary nature of police organizations and the bureaucratic imperatives of specialization and standardization reinforce the inclinations of officers to approach personal tragedies in an impersonal manner. In addition, the "macho" norms of police subculture—with its emphasis on toughness, camaraderie, suspicion of outsiders, inside jokes, graveyard humor, and profound cynicism—put pressure on police officers to act businesslike when dealing with profoundly upsetting situations (Ahrens, Stein, and Young, 1980).

If individual officers appear surprisingly unmoved by the suffering that surrounds them, it might be that they fear "contamination" (Symonds, 1975). People who regularly come into close contact with the casualties of natural and social disasters tend to isolate and ostracize these victims as if they had a contagious disease. Such distancing is a defense mechanism to preserve the helper's faith that ultimately justice prevails: Misfortunes happen only to those who somehow deserve them.

Whether victims expect too much or receive too little, their grievances against the police lead to a "community relations" problem. Administrators of the system have proposed police professionalism as the solution. This involves upgrading the caliber of academy recruits, using psychological tests to weed out potentially brutal or corrupt members of the force, devising regulations and procedures to cover every kind of anticipated emergency, monitoring on-the-job performance, and adding in-service training and specialized squads to handle problems addressed unsatisfactorily in the past.

Some departments have initiated training programs to prepare at least a portion of their force to act differently when they deal with victims with acute needs. Officers and detectives are taught how to administer "psychological first aid" (Symonds, 1980b) to people in distress. They are instructed to respond swiftly, listen attentively, show concern, and refrain from challenging the victims' version of events or judging the wisdom of their reactions while the crime was in progress. Officers are told not to show skepticism because a rape victim is not badly bruised or bleeding, a child did not report a molestation immediately, an elderly person has trouble communicating, or a blind person offers to assist with the identification of a suspect. At the conclusion of the training sessions, the officers are informed that responsiveness to victims carries a high priority within the department and has become a criterion for evaluating performance and a consideration in granting promotions (President's Task Force, 1982).

Notifying the next of kin of murder victims is one of the most emotionally draining tasks in police work. Anecdotal evidence indicates that many officers are inept in delivering bad news in plain language and with compassion. To rectify this problem, some departments have developed guidelines and manuals so that survivors are not further traumatized by memories of clumsy and uncaring acts by officers carrying out their death-notification obligations (Associated Press, 1994e).

According to a survey of over 400 victims in a midwestern city, satisfaction with police services is greater if officers act in a professional manner, if they arrive faster than expected, and if they make a serious effort to investigate property crimes (Brandl and Horvath, 1991). The findings from a survey of over 1,700 victims in two cities suggested that, as time passed from their initial contact with the police, their impressions about the politeness, helpfulness, fairness, and effectiveness of officers improved slightly (Skogan, 1987).

Judging Complaints to Be Unfounded As for the credibility question, when people swear out a complaint, they want officers to accept without question their versions of what transpired. From the police point of view, however, individuals reporting crimes are only complainants, or "presumptive" victims until it is conclusively established that laws were broken and innocent parties were harmed. It is always possible that the person alleging to be a bona fide victim is making a fraudulent claim for some ulterior purpose. People might falsely swear they were harmed by criminals for a number of reasons. They may want to take revenge by getting an innocent person in trouble, or cover up the true circumstances surrounding an event (as, for example, when a husband claims he was robbed to account for the loss of his pay, but he actually spent the money on a prostitute or gambled it away). Some criminals pose as victims in order to commit insurance fraud (and in a scam to get reimbursement for a nonexistent loss, report that a car they never really owned was stolen). From the police point of view, it is essential to screen people who say they have been victimized in order to weed out those cases in which the charges are unfounded. As the following examples demonstrate, on occasion, individuals who tell the police a tale are up to something. They may be seeking attention and sympathy, generating publicity, setting up a scam, manipulating the authorities, or misleading investigators to hide a real crime:

A prominent city official is found bleeding and dazed in his own car. He tells police that he was abducted, assaulted, and driven around by two unknown men. An investigation is launched, but no witnesses come forward. Then the official admits that his wounds were self-inflicted in a failed suicide attempt. When his role in a kickback scandal is revealed, he kills himself by plunging a knife into his chest. (Purnick, 1986)

A distraught young mother tells the authorities that a man with a gun barged into her car at a red light and forced her to drive ten miles before ordering her out and speeding off with her two toddlers still strapped in the back seat. As the mother makes televised tearful appeals, in which she prays along with her family for the safe return of her children, thousands of volunteers from her small hometown join state troopers and FBI agents in combing the countryside in search of the toddlers, her abandoned car, the offender, or any clues. But after she fails several lie detector tests, she breaks down and admits that she is not a victim of a carjacking but the murderer of her own two children, whom she drowned by rolling her car into a lake. (Gibbs, 1994)

Bleeding profusely from a serious bullet wound, a man calls 911 on his car telephone and tells the police that a robber just shot him and his pregnant wife. She dies, as does her unborn baby, but he survives. Under great pressure to solve the case, the police round up scores of suspects (young black men) fitting his sketchy description; eventually detectives make an arrest and announce that the case has been solved. But then the wounded man's brother comes forward and confesses that the shooting was staged: The man murdered his pregnant wife and stole her jewelry in order to collect insurance and then shot himself in the abdomen to make his story about an armed robbery more credible. As the police piece together what really happened, the man posing as a grieving widower commits suicide by jumping off a bridge. (Martz, Starr, and Barrett, 1990)

A ten-year-old who disobeyed his foster parents and went off to play touch football is discovered shoeless, with his pants pulled down, tied to a fence post in an alley. As police officers free him, he tells them that a stranger lured him into a car and then raped him and gives a description of the suspect. Soon, detectives announce that a man has been arrested and is being charged with kidnapping, criminal restraint, and sexual assault. But then the boy recants his allegations and admits he was tied up by three older playmates who were angry at him. He explains that he made up a story because he thought the police and his foster parents wouldn't be sympathetic unless he claimed he was harmed by an adult. The charges against the innocent man are dropped. (Associated Press, 1993a)

The founder and leader of a civilian anticrime subway patrol tells reporters that he was injured when he tried to capture three rapists at a train station. Years later, after a near-death experience (an unsolved shooting), he admits that he conspired with other members of the patrol to stage a series of publicity stunts in order to further the new organization's reputation. (Gonzalez, 1992)

An armored car guard is found tied up. He claims that several robbers took the $8 million he was guarding and bound his wrists and ankles with wire. The police suspect it was an inside job and maintain around-the-clock surveillance on him, his relatives, and his close friends. Cracking under this pressure, one of the robbers confesses and implicates the security guard as a coconspirator. (McFadden, 1993a)

A doctor's wife tells police that a man put a gun to her toddler's head and demanded money after she used an automated teller machine at a suburban bank. Her shocking account touches off a manhunt for the cold-blooded robber. But when the police check with customers who used the ATM immediately before and right after her, they discover that, according to these eyewitnesses, no incident took place. Confronted with these discrepancies, she confesses that she made up a story in order to get her busy husband to pay more attention to her. She is charged with the misdemeanor of filing a false instrument, which carries a penalty of up to one year in jail and a $1,000 fine. (McQuiston, 1994)

Complainants who are not genuine victims are breaking the law. In most states, it is illegal to make false statements to the police "gratuitously" by volunteering unsolicited information. The laws are intended to deter perjury and thereby protect innocent persons from the embarrassment and hardships caused by false accusations. However, to encourage citizen cooperation with law enforcement, most places have adopted a doctrine of witness immunity that shields complainants who furnish information to the police "in good faith" from any subsequent civil lawsuits by innocent persons they mistakenly identified as suspects. But a person who intentionally lodges a false complaint and instigates a wrongful arrest for some improper motive (such as revenge) can be sued for malicious prosecution (Stark and Goldstein, 1985).

Unfounding is a process in which the police completely reject a person's claim about being the victim of a crime. *Defounding* means that detectives believe an offense really did occur but was not as serious as the victim described it (Lundman, 1980). For example, what was reported as a burglary might upon further investigation be classified as an instance of criminal trespass, if nothing of value was stolen, which is a misdemeanor rather than a felony. Just as individuals might have a motive to lodge a false charge, police investigators might have an incentive to declare a report of a crime completely unfounded or to defound it down to a lesser offense. By defounding and unfounding complaints, detectives can improve their personal and their departmental "clearance rates" (percentage of cases solved by arrests) and reduce the number of serious crimes reported within their precinct.

Under pressure to perform, some detectives might disregard legitimate pleas for help by mistakenly unfounding and defounding cases. In Chicago, for example, for more than twenty years, detectives were inclined to dismiss victims' accounts as unfounded because they would receive higher ratings and more promotions if they closed more cases. During this time, the Chicago Police Department dismissed about 21 percent of their major cases as unfounded; according to the FBI, the average rate for other big-city departments was between 1 percent and 2 percent. Auditors reviewing police files came to the conclusion that as many as 40 percent of the rape, robbery, burglary, and theft reports disregarded as unfounded probably did occur, just as the victims claimed. The kinds of cases that were prime candidates for official disbelief involved victims who knew their assailants, were difficult to contact, or did not lose much money ("Chicago Police," 1983; "Burying Crime in Chicago," 1983). In Oakland, California, overworked and understaffed detectives dismissed 24 percent of the rape complaints they received as "unfounded" in the late 1980s. At that time the FBI reported that other departments across the country disbelieved about 9 percent of all rape charges. After a newspaper article questioned why there was such a disparity in the unfounding rate, the police chief conceded that perhaps 200 cases were written-off too quickly and merited reexamination. But detectives advanced several arguments in their own defense. First, they asserted, the nationwide figure of 9 percent was a misleading standard for comparison, since many departments manipulate the unfounding rate to keep it artificially low by classifying cases as "filed pending further investigation" (not officially closed) rather than as "closed due to baseless or false charges." Second, they pointed out that because of budget limitations, the sexual assault unit's six investigators were so swamped with cases that they had to prioritize their workload. They felt pressured to disregard complaints from women who would appear uncooperative, untruthful, or unsympathetic in court, such as prostitutes and drug abusers who would be inclined to lie about the circumstances surrounding the assaults for fear of getting in trouble for solicitation or possession of controlled substances. Finally, the detectives insisted that many of the complainants refused to agree to medical examinations and failed to appear for follow-up interviews, making the investigation of their charges difficult, time-consuming, and unlikely to ultimately lead to convictions (Gross, 1990).

Arresting Suspects

Victims expect thorough investigations, so dissatisfaction can arise whenever detectives deem a complainant's misfortunes to be too minor or too hard to solve to justify the expenditure of the department's limited human resources, time, and money. Some departments even issue directives that specify cut-off points, below which no action will be taken beyond simply making a formal note of the complaint. For example, in Dade County, surrounding Miami, reports about stolen cars were taken only over the telephone and only during certain hours (Combined News Services, 1993). In New York City, a detective from the burglary squad was assigned to a case only if the reported loss exceeded a figure of several thousand dollars (Gutis, 1988). Sometimes, the police might be reluctant to invest much effort if victims are likely to receive insurance reimbursement:

> **A** woman's car is stolen. Several weeks later she receives a bill for her car phone and notices that some calls were placed after the theft. The detective at her local precinct explains that the department doesn't have the time to check out every lead, and since she is entitled to insurance reimbursement, she should forget about recovering her car. But she investigates on her own by calling the number listed on the bill and discovers it is a garage on the other side of town. Returning to the precinct, she asks that a squad car be sent to that address, but the detective insists that following up the lead is the responsibility of the auto squad. The auto squad detective asks why she is so determined to pursue matters if she is insured and refers her back to the precinct. She insists on seeing a lieutenant; he takes down the address and phone number of the garage but advises her that her case was closed and can't be reopened. In a letter to the editor of a newspaper, she writes about how the department gave her the runaround because her loss was covered. (Danziger, 1993)

Many victims discover that with the passage of time their cases are closed even though they remain unsolved. How long a case remains open depends on the workload in the jurisdiction and the seriousness of the offense. If the police are unable to establish the identity of a suspect or cannot obtain sufficient evidence to justify an arrest, then they can exercise their discretion to discontinue any active effort to solve the crime. Victims have no formal means of compelling them to continue to work on it. Dissatisfied complainants have been unable to convince judges to intervene in matters of police discretion unless a pattern of noninvestigation reflects racial or religious discrimination (Austern, 1987). For example, in Milwaukee, a serial killer was captured after he had murdered a victim whose life could have been saved. The scandal led to the appointment of a mayoral commission, which discovered that the police routinely dismissed as unimportant the complaints brought to their attention by members of minority groups (Associated Press, 1991).

On rare occasions, victims who are frustrated by the unwillingness of the police to thoroughly investigate a crime can make a positive contribution by getting involved themselves:

> For four years, people in a small city are terrorized by a rapist who handcuffs women before sexually assaulting them. The parents of one of his victims decide to try to catch him. Imitating the tactics of police decoy squads, the mother makes herself look particularly vulnerable, and frequents the area where her daughter was attacked. Sure enough, one day the rapist returns to this scene of his previous crime and attempts to overpower her. But he is chased off by the father, who, armed with a gun, is watching from a nearby car. The father notes the assailant's license plate number as he drives away, and the police arrest him a few days later. An enraged public hails the parents and condemns the inept sex crimes squad. ("Wholesale Changes," 1988)

Even when the trail of evidence leads to a suspect, an arrest is never automatic. Police officers exercise a great deal of personal and departmental discretion in deciding whom to take into custody and book and whom to let go. The factors that influence these decisions include pressures from colleagues and superiors, the individual predilections of officers, the nature of the offense and the offenders, and the relationship of the victim to the suspect. Victims can become angry when police officers don't arrest the persons they have accused of committing crimes.

One solution for victims is to convince judges to issue arrest warrants (which officers must then carry out) based on their sworn complaints. A second solution is to exercise the do-it-yourself option known as a "citizen's arrest." Private citizens are empowered to use whatever force is necessary to prevent a suspect from escaping until the police arrive to take charge of the situation. Civilians must apprehend their suspects immediately after a crime is committed and must turn their captives over to the authorities without delay. Police officers are generally obligated to accept custody of suspects taken prisoner by victims or bystanders. But citizen arrests are risky ventures. Suspects are likely to resist being captured, endangering victims or bystanders who intervene in their behalf. In cases of mistaken identity, even victims who acted with probable cause and in good faith can be sued in civil court for false arrest and false imprisonment. Police officials generally discourage civilians from thinking of themselves as deputized to make arrests. They point out that citizens who attempt to make arrests lack the lengthy training sworn officers receive in self-defense and the use of firearms and in the application of laws governing arrests and suspects' rights. Since acts of vigilantism can easily evolve out of attempts to make citizen's arrests, law enforcement officials encourage activist-oriented civilians to become involved in police auxiliary units or neighborhood anticrime patrols instead (Hall, 1975; Stark and Goldstein, 1985).

From the victim's point of view, the police have successfully completed their mission when, acting on solid evidence, they take a suspect into custody and charge him or her with a crime. Similarly, from the police department's standpoint, a case is closed when an arrest is made. The police consider the crime solved at that point even if the suspect is not ultimately convicted of the charge originally lodged against him or her. Police departments routinely compile and make public the percentages of crimes reported to them that are solved by arrests. These clearance rates are used to evaluate the performance of individual officers, specialized squads (such as those concentrating on homicide, burglary, and sex crimes), and the department as a whole.

But these same statistics can be interpreted from a different angle and for a different purpose. The proportion of cases that are solved can serve as a rough indicator of the percentage of complainants who have a good reason to be satisfied with the outcome of their cases, at least as far as police performance is concerned.

Each year, in its *Uniform Crime Report,* the FBI calculates the average clearance rates for police departments across the country. Statistics for the past five decades appear in Table 4.3. A glance at the figures for 1993 reveals that the police nationwide are more successful at solving violent crimes than property crimes. Looking at these numbers from the victims' point of view, it is clear that most people who report thefts to the police will not be satisfied with the outcome of their cases; the investigations will be closed before any arrest is made. Put another way, in from 80 percent to 87 percent of the reported cases of larceny, burglary, and motor vehicle theft, the offenders will get away with their

TABLE 4.3   Trends in Clearance Rates: Percentage of Cases Solved

TYPE OF CRIME	1953	1963	1973	1983	1993
Murder	93	91	79	76	66
Rape	78	69	51	52	53
Aggravated assault	75	76	63	61	56
Robbery	36	39	27	26	24
Burglary	27	27	18	15	13
Larceny	20	20	19	20	20
Vehicle theft*	26	26	16	15	14

*Since the 1970s, this category of the *Uniform Crime Report* has included the theft of all motorized vehicles, including trucks, vans, motorcycles, and buses.
Source: FBI, *UCR,* 1954–1994.

crimes and their victims will be frustrated. Most individuals who report robberies will also suffer the aggravation of learning that no one was apprehended for accosting them. Somewhat more than half of all individuals who complain to the authorities that they were raped and/or seriously assaulted can take comfort in knowing that their attackers have been arrested. The highest clearance rates of all are achieved by homicide squads, but even the best detectives who devote considerable time and effort to selected cases manage to figure out who did it in just two thirds of all slayings. Accentuating the negative, that means that just about one in three killers "gets way with murder"! Actually the situation is even worse. Just because someone is arrested and charged by the police with being the perpetrator of a crime doesn't mean that this individual is guilty, or will be prosecuted or convicted. Table 4.3 lists the percentages of cases solved, by type of crime, for ten-year intervals from 1953 to 1993.

The single most important factor in solving crimes, with the obvious exception of murder, is the ability of victims to furnish detectives with clues, leads, and descriptions, or even the names, of suspects. This is why crimes of interpersonal violence are more likely to be solved than offenses against property, which usually take place in the victims' absence (Lundman, 1980).

The statistics summarizing the performance of police departments throughout the country, presented in Table 4.3, point to a disturbing trend. In every one of the seven index crimes (the eighth, arson, is excluded from this compilation) there is a slow but steady drift downward. During the 1950s, practically all murders and most rapes and aggravated assaults were solved. Clearance rates for these three violent crimes and for robberies dropped sharply during the crime wave of the 1960s. During the 1970s and 1980s, the solution rates for rapes and serious assaults remained stable, while the ability of the police to solve murders continued to decline. Burglaries and auto thefts were solved roughly twice as often in the 1950s as in the 1990s; larcenies have always been difficult to solve. Overall, as the years pass, the police are becoming less and less able to clear cases by making arrests. During the early 1990s, clearance rates hit new lows across the board and then stabilized at disappointingly low levels.

Translating these statistical trends into human terms, more and more criminals are getting away with their crimes, and more and more victims have good reason to be dissatisfied with the performance of the police. Decades ago, long before the victims' rights movement began to demand improved services from law enforcement agencies, the police were much more effective at accomplishing their basic task of catching culprits.

When suspects are taken into custody, police officers have a legal obligation to inform them of their Miranda rights. When victims want to be informed of their obligations and opportunities in regard to their cases, they often discover that the police are under no comparable constitutional pressure to read them their "rights." To start with, victims need to know the names and badge numbers of the officer and the detective handling their case, where and when they can be reached, the case identification number, whether or not a suspect has been apprehended, and, if so, whether he or she is being detained in jail or is out on bail. To guarantee these elemental rights, endorsed by the President's Task Force (1982), a number of states have passed statutes that specify that the police must keep victims posted on the status of their cases. In the other states, victims must depend on departmental policies and the good will of individual officers.

Findings from the redesigned *National Crime Victimization Survey* indicate that a large percentage of victims never find out that their cases were solved and arrests were made. In 1986, according to the *NCVS* report, only 15 percent of all robbery victims who reported their incidents to the police eventually learned that a suspect was arrested for robbing them. Yet police departments averaged a clearance rate of 25 percent for robberies that year. Similarly, only 34 percent of aggravated assault victims who reported the crimes to the police were informed about resulting arrests, although police departments solved about 59 percent of all aggravated assault cases brought to their attention that year. The neglect on the part of the police to tell burglary victims that someone was arrested for breaking into and stealing from their homes was even more dramatic: Only 7 percent of all victims were notified, although about 14 percent of all reported burglaries were solved. Motor vehicle theft victims were better informed; of the 15 percent whose cases were solved, 11 percent learned of an arrest (FBI, *UCR,* 1987; Whitaker, 1989).

Recovering Stolen Property

Besides catching the culprits, the police can serve victims by getting back any possessions stolen from them. Just as clearance rates indicate the approximate percentage of victims who receive optimum service in terms of arrests, recovery rates show how often the police succeed in retrieving stolen goods. Unfortunately, unlike clearance rates, recovery rates are not routinely tabulated and published by police departments or the FBI. (In the *UCR,* the FBI does note the overall dollar value of recovered stolen goods for all reported incidents of a particular index crime.) However, interviewers for the *National Crime Victimization Survey* ask respondents whether all or part of the money and property taken from them was recovered (not counting insurance reimbursement). The police recovery rates can then be estimated. But the figures will be biased upward because some victims are able to get back their stolen property through their own efforts (somehow, they knew where to look). Unfortunately, this statistic cannot be refined further to determine what percentage of victims recovered items by themselves and what percentage were given back their stolen goods by the police. Therefore, these rough approximations overestimate the ability of the police to retrieve goods taken from their rightful owners. Furthermore, these estimated rates combine partial and full recoveries, again biasing the statistics upward and presenting the ability of the police to accomplish recoveries as more efficient than it really is. Partial recoveries might not bring much satisfaction to victims. The discovery of a discarded purse emptied of any valuables, for example, or the return of automobile parts with traceable vehicle identification serial numbers on them to a car owner would count as partial recoveries. With these reservations in mind, see Table 4.4 for a compilation of estimated police recovery rates during the 1980s and early 1990s.

The data reveal that this aspect of police work will leave most people who suffered robberies, burglaries, and personal and household larcenies dissatisfied with the outcomes of their cases. The estimated recovery rates are very low, despite the fact that these percentages are overestimates. Only owners of stolen cars are likely to get back some or all of what was taken from them. As for changes over time, the data show mostly downward trends: Fewer and fewer victims are getting their stolen property back as the years go by. Only motor vehicle recovery rates improved, but some unknown proportion of the stolen cars that the police relocated (or that owners found on their own) were surely not in driveable condition.

Even if the police recover stolen property, some victims might not get it back, at least not for a while. Law enforcement agencies have the authority to hold seized items if they are of value in continuing investigations. Prosecutors are allowed to maintain custody of pieces of evidence until after the trial, or even until

TABLE 4.4   Estimated Stolen-Property Recovery Rates

TYPE OF VICTIMIZATION	1980	1981	1982	1983	1984	1985	1986
Robberies	24%	24%	21%	24%	27%	26%	20%
Personal larcenies with and without contact	12	12	12	11	10	11	10
Burglaries	12	12	13	10	10	11	11
Household larcenies	12	13	12	8	9	9	9
Motor vehicle thefts	65	65	63	69	70	70	71

TYPE OF VICTIMIZATION	1987	1988	1989	1990	1991	1992
Robberies	20%	21%	24%	20%	19%	18
Personal larcenies	9	8	8	9	10	9
Burglaries	10	9	10	10	9	10
Household larcenies	8	8	8	8	7	8
Motor vehicle thefts	72	73	66	74	71	72

Notes: Percentages represent the proportions of all cases in which victims get back some stolen items.
Recovery may be total or partial.
An unknown proportion of the recoveries were accomplished by the victims themselves, without the assistance of the police.
Figures were calculated from *NCVS* data on theft losses.
Only incidents that resulted in theft losses were considered.
Source: BJS, *Criminal Victimization in the United States,* 1982–1994.

those convicted have exhausted all appeals. Frustrated victims are now assisted in some states by statutes that compel the police to return stolen property to its rightful owner "expeditiously," as soon as it is no longer needed for law enforcement purposes. In a growing number of jurisdictions, laws direct the police and prosecutors, whenever it is feasible, to promptly photograph the evidence and then return the actual item. But in states without these kinds of procedural directives, the release of property seized as evidence requires the explicit approval of the police department property clerk or the prosecutor's office or even the judge hearing the case. Victims who are denied prompt repossession might have to appeal the decision of the official maintaining custody of the property to some higher criminal justice authority. If the items are damaged, destroyed, or lost by the police property clerk's office or the prosecutor's office, victims can go to civil court to file claims for monetary compensation (Stark and Goldstein, 1985).

Many victims encountered this problem before new procedures were mandated. Thirty-one percent of complainants who had been seriously harmed reported difficulties in getting back stolen property that was being held as evidence in a Wisconsin jurisdiction (Knudten, Knudten, and Meade, 1978). According to a survey conducted in California, in 30 percent of the cases in which stolen property was recovered by the police and used in court as evidence, the items were never returned to their rightful owners (Lynch, 1976).

VICTIMS AND PROSECUTORS

Prosecutors are the chief law enforcement officers within their jurisdictions. They represent and defend the interests of the county, state, or federal government. They also supply the lawyers that represent victims. Therefore, prosecutors' offices can be viewed as public law firms offering free legal services to complainants who are willing to cooperate and testify as witnesses. (County prosecutors are often referred to as "district attorneys" and are elected officials. The lawyers who actually handle criminal cases are called deputy or assistant district attorneys—ADAs.)

Prosecutors can and should serve victims in a number of ways (President's Task Force, 1982): First, these lawyers can keep their clients informed of the status of their cases, from the initial charges lodged against defendants to the parole of convicts. Second, they can help victims to achieve justice by conveying to the attention of the judges their clients' views on questions of bail, continuances, negotiated pleas, dismissed cases and dropped charges, sentences, and restitution arrangements. Third, they can take steps to protect their clients from harassment, threats, injuries, and other forms of intimidation and reprisals. Fourth, they can try to resolve cases as quickly as possible without unnecessary delays and help their clients to minimize losses of time and money by notifying them of required court appearances and scheduling changes. Fifth, they can assist victims in getting back stolen property recovered by the police.

Sometimes prosecutors are able to serve the interests of the government, their own agency, and their victimized client without any conflict. But frequently they cannot do what is best for all of their constituencies. The interests of the government in general, the bureaucracy that employs them, the "consumers" of their services, and their own individual career aspirations may come into conflict. If they must sacrifice the interests of some party, it is likely to be the victim. Victims can feel betrayed if "their" lawyers do not look after their needs and wants. Or, to put it another way, the lawyer assigned by the government—automatically (without choice) and at no cost—might not do a satisfactory job.

Assisting Victims and Other Witnesses for the State

The difficulties, inconveniences, and frustrations faced by victims serving as witnesses for the prosecution have been known for decades (McDonald, 1976). In 1931, the National Commission on Law Observance and Enforcement commented that the administration of justice was suffering because of the economic burdens imposed on citizens who participated in trials. In 1938, the American Bar Association noted that witness fees were deplorably low, courthouse accommodations were inadequate, intimidation went unchecked, and witness time was often wasted. Its report argued that the state had an obligation to ease the sacrifices of witnesses as much as possible. The President's Commission on Law Enforcement and the Administration of Justice reached similar conclusions in 1967. In 1973, the Courts Task Force of the National Advisory Commission on Criminal Justice Standards and Goals noted that the failure of victims and witnesses to appear at judicial proceedings when needed was a major reason for cases being dismissed. Noncooperation was attributed to the high personal costs of involvement incurred by citizens trying to meet their civic obligations.

Victims serving as prosecution witnesses typically were mistreated in these ways: They would be ordered by subpoena to appear at some courtroom, grand jury room, or prosecutor's office. They would wait for hours in dingy corridors or in other grim surroundings. Busy officials would ignore them as they stood around bewildered and anxious. Often, they would never be called to testify or to make statements because of last-minute adjournments. Accomplishing nothing, they would miss work and lose wages, or miss classes at school, or fail to meet their responsibilities at home. In most jurisdictions, they would receive insultingly low witness fees for their time and trouble. In certain metropolitan areas, they would receive no compensation at all because no official informed them of their eligibility and of the proper application procedures. Their experiences could thus be characterized as dreary, time-consuming, depressing, exhausting, confusing, frustrating, and frightening (Ash, 1972).

In 1974, the National District Attorney's Association commissioned a survey to determine the extent to which victims and other witnesses for the prosecution encountered these kinds of problems. Conducted in Alameda County, California, the survey documented that about 12 percent were never notified that an arrest had been made in their case. Nearly 30 percent of all victims never got their property back, even though it had been recovered and used as evidence. About 60 percent of injured victims who were eligible for compensation for unreimbursed losses under a state program were never informed of their right to file a claim. Roughly 45 percent reported that no one had explained to them what their court appearance would entail. Almost 27 percent of all witnesses (including victims) called to court were not subsequently asked to testify. Even though 78 percent lost pay to come to court, about 95 percent received no witness fees. As a final insult, 42 percent were never notified of the outcome of the case (Lynch, 1976).

To address these problems, the Law Enforcement Assistance Administration funded the first Victim-Witness Assistance Projects (VWAPs) through the National District Attorneys Association. Pilot programs were set up in prosecutors' offices in California, Illinois, Utah, Colorado, Kentucky, Louisiana, Pennsylvania, and New York during the mid-1970s (Schneider and Schneider, 1981; Geis, 1983).

Since then, most prosecutors' offices have followed suit. Several assumptions underlie the growth and development of these programs. One is that providing services will elicit greater cooperation from victims and other witnesses: Well-briefed, self-confident witnesses who have been in contact with and benefited from such programs will be more willing to put up with the hardships of testifying in court, leading to lower dismissal rates and higher conviction rates, the standards by which prosecutors' offices are judged. A further assumption is that offering services to a group perceived to be highly deserving of governmental aid will be good for community relations. Public confidence and faith in the criminal justice system will thus be restored, resulting in higher reporting rates within jurisdictions that have assistance programs (Rootsaert, 1987).

Most VWAPs are charged with the laudable but loosely defined mission of helping victims, aiding witnesses, and furthering the goals of law enforcement. Agency personnel intervene as soon as possible after an offense is committed, providing immediate relief to the injured parties through services that include hot lines; crisis counseling; emergency shelter, food, transportation; and immediate lock repairs. Some projects even provide translators, forms for replacing lost documents, and assistance in returning stolen property recovered by the police. Most make referrals to social service and mental health agencies for those needing long-term care and counseling. All programs furnish information about opportunities for reimbursement of losses and eligibility for compensation benefits. A few offer mediation services for victims who seek to reconcile their differences with their offenders. To encourage witness cooperation, pamphlets about the adjudication process (on topics like "What happens in court?" and "Victims' rights") are prepared and distributed. Through a case-monitoring or notification system (involving a series of form letters), the staff keeps victims and other witnesses advised of important developments, such as indictments, postponements and continuances, negotiated pleas, convictions, and acquittals. Linked to the notification system is a telephone alert or "on-call" system, intended to prevent unnecessary trips to court when dates are changed on short notice. (This is also used to save police officers who are needed as witnesses from wasting their time.) Some programs have also set up reception centers (waiting rooms exclusively for prosecution witnesses) in courthouses to provide a secure environment free from any last-minute opportunities for intimidation by offenders and their families and friends. Transportation to and from court, escorts, and child care are frequently available. Help in obtaining witness fees is provided. In some programs, the staff may go so far as to intercede on behalf of victims with employers and landlords and other creditors who might not appreciate the stresses and difficulties faced by witnesses (Schneider and Schneider, 1981; Geis, 1983; Weigend, 1983; and Rootsaert, 1987).

Some signs that VWAPs are reducing the mistreatment of victims are evident. Whereas only 35 percent of the offices of district attorneys routinely notified victims of felonies of the outcomes in their cases in 1974, by 1992 97 percent of these offices did, according to the National Prosecutor Survey Program (Dawson, Smith, and DeFrances, 1993).

The establishment of victim-witness assistance programs has raised some constitutional and ethical questions. To deny services to a victim whose cooperation is not needed (or who wants to pursue a case that the prosecutor's office wants to drop) would be unfair but not illegal, since the aid is granted as a privilege rather than as a right. To deny similar services (free parking, child care, last-minute phone calls canceling a scheduled appearance) to witnesses for the defense would violate notions of fairness within the adversary system. As long as the defendant is presumed innocent unless proven guilty, evenhanded treatment of all witnesses should prevail. Rapport between victims and VWAP personnel that becomes too close can cause another problem: The testimony given in court can be considered "coached" or "rehearsed" to the extent that it departs from the original statements and covers up contradictions in order to make the most convincing case against the defendants.

Protecting Victims Serving as Witnesses for the Prosecution

A man is robbed by three gunmen of $550. He reports the crime to the police and they round up three suspects. After he identifies them as the men who stole his money, he begins to receive death threats. The prosecutor's office suggests various measures to protect him, but he declines the offer. One night, his doorbell rings, and when he answers it, a stranger pulls out a gun and shoots him in the head. ("Warned Not to Testify . . . ," 1991)

Chilling tales like this could dissuade people who are unsure whether to report crimes, press charges, and testify in court.

Offenders may try to intimidate complainants (and other witnesses) from seeking help from the authorities, by issuing threats like, "If you tell, I'll . . ." Since the complainants' perceptions of the risk of cooperation determine whether they will testify in court, the primary responsibility for safeguarding their well-being falls to the prosecutor handling the case (Docksai, 1979). When prosecutors don't react to acts of intimidation, one of the victim's worst fears is confirmed—namely, that the criminal justice system can't provide protection from further harm and that the only way to avoid reprisals is to stop cooperating with it. Anonymous calls in the middle of the night or acts of vandalism are difficult to trace. But, if left unaddressed, these incidents convey the message that complainants are on their own, and they signify to offenders that intimidation is worth a try: It may have the desired effect, and it carries little risk of additional penalties (President's Task Force, 1982).

The actual extent of the intimidation problem is not known. Measuring intimidation is a difficult task, in part because successfully intimidated victims (and witnesses) are afraid to disclose their plight to researchers. Each year, only a small percentage of respondents admit to *NCVS* interviewers that "fear of reprisal" stopped them from informing the police about crimes committed against them. As might be expected, the intimidation rate is higher for crimes of violence than for property crimes; it is a more persistent problem in cases of rape than in robbery and assault. The rates of nonreporting due to fear of reprisal are presented in Table 4.5.

TABLE 4.5   Fear of Reprisal as a Cause of Nonreporting

PERCENTAGE OF NONREPORTING VICTIMS WHO FEARED REPRISALS

TYPE OF CRIME	1980	1981	1982	1983	1984	1985	1986
Rape	12	13	8	8	11	17	12
Robbery	6	6	4	5	3	9	6
Aggravated assault	6	5	5	4	7	6	5
Simple assault	3	3	5	4	4	4	5

TYPE OF CRIME	1987	1988	1989	1990	1991	1992
Rape	21	10	12	8	11	7
Robbery	6	7	4	7	5	6
Aggravated assault	7	5	5	5	7	6
Simple assault	4	4	4	3	3	3

Note: Percentages represent the proportions of respondents citing "fear of reprisal" as their primary reason for not reporting to the police a crime that they were willing to disclose to *NCVS* interviewers.
Source: BJS, *Criminal Victimization in the United States,* 1982–1994.

Other studies have yielded contradictory findings about how often complainants are successfully intimidated by the people they accuse of harming them. In one survey of New Yorkers, about 13 percent of a sample of approximately 1,000 victims confided that their offenders, or their offenders' friends or relatives had attempted to intimidate them, most commonly by verbally threatening them during face-to-face confrontations. Some victims had their property vandalized, but fewer than 1 percent were actually assaulted. The incidents occurred in police stations and courthouses, as well as in the neighborhoods and homes of the victims. The willingness of complainants to cooperate with prosecutors was not seriously undermined by attempts at intimidation, and these attempts did not influence conviction rates to any statistically significant extent (Fried, 1982). But when the same agency conducted another study about ten years later, the researchers came to a different conclusion: attempts to intimidate often succeeded. New Yorkers who were threatened were more than twice as likely to ask that charges be dropped than those who were not contacted by defendants. Individuals who had close prior relations (romantic involvements or family ties) with the people they filed claims against were more likely to be warned about bodily harm or damage to property, to receive menacing looks, or to be assaulted than victims who accused complete strangers ("Study Shows Intimidation," 1990).

(The intimidation problem goes beyond direct threats. Would-be complainants may experience strong pressures from their own families and friends not to come forward and tell the police what happened. Subjected to this kind of "cultural intimidation" by their community, they are forced to either settle the score privately or let the matter rest. Another type of intimidation arises from perceptions rather than overt acts. Victims may be haunted by visions of what offenders might do, even though no specific threats have been made. The thought of exploitative media exposure can also be chilling. Finally, intimidation can be directed against defense lawyers, defendants, and reluctant witnesses in the form of harassment by the authorities, especially in well-publicized and controversial cases. One-sided formulations of the intimidation problem imply that it is improper for anyone other than law enforcement agents to contact witnesses and victims. But defense attorneys must be allowed to, since a person accused of a crime has a constitutional right to confront his or her accusers and put on a vigorous defense against the charges lodged by any witnesses for the prosecution [ABA Committee on Victims, 1979].)

Much of the intimidation problem can be traced to officials who have shirked their responsibilities to victims. Police officers might con victims into cooperating by making empty promises of added protection, knowing full well that their precincts don't have the resources to provide special attention. Prosecutors allow cases to collapse when key witnesses and complainants fail to appear after being subpoenaed (perhaps due to intimidation), because attrition lightens their workload. Judges fail to act for the same reason: Intimidation leads to nonappearance and ultimately dismissals, which reduce caseloads. To reduce fears of reprisal and the effectiveness of acts of intimidation, the American Bar Association Committee on Victims (1979) made the following recommendations: Legislatures should make attempts at intimidation a misdemeanor; police forces ought to setup victim-witness protection squads; judges should issue orders of protection and consider violations of their terms as grounds for contempt of court citations and revocations of bail; if complaining witnesses mysteriously fail to appear when subpoenaed, judges should grant continuances rather than drop all charges against defendants; and prosecutors must avoid carelessly revealing information concerning the whereabouts of victims, even after cases are resolved.

The most extensive governmental response to the threat of reprisals has been the establishment of witness-protection programs on the state and county level. They offer short-term protection until a prosecution and trial is concluded by providing lodging (in hotels or shelters), meals, and security to victims, other witnesses, and their immediate families. These services are intended primarily to safeguard those who are willing to testify against criminal organizations like street gangs and drug trafficking networks. Severely battered women also depend on these temporary services, since they are in the uniquely vulnerable situation of living under the same roof as their assailants. However, inadequate funding limits the ability of prosecutors' offices to offer these protective measures to all who need them (New York State Law Enforcement Council, 1994). The federal Witness Security Program helps individuals who face reprisals for testifying in behalf of the government. The program promises relocation, new identities, new jobs, and moving expenses (Associated Press, 1994i).

Dismissing Charges and Rejecting Cases

Crime victims, police officers, and prosecutors are all supposed to be on the same side within the adversary system. Yet their alliance, based in theory on a common commitment to convict people guilty of crimes, often unravels. Victims may feel rebuffed and abandoned when district attorneys dismiss or reduce charges and counts against suspects. A decision not to go forward means no further official action will be taken, and victims will not achieve the goals they sought when they reported the crime, whether they were looking for maximum punishment as revenge, compulsory treatment of the offenders, or court-ordered restitution. To prosecutors, these decisions that can infuriate victims are unavoidable. It's impossible for prosecutors to fulfill their legal mandate to enforce all laws and seek the conviction of all lawbreakers.

When evaluating the cases brought before them by the police and deciding whether or not to go forward, prosecutors must take into account other considerations besides the victims' wishes. In addition to whether or not the victims want the charges to be pressed or dropped, prosecutors must weigh many factors. What are the chances of conviction rather than acquittal? (Will the case be won or lost?) Are there serious doubts about the guilt of the accused? How credible and how cooperative are the victim and other witnesses? Does the complainant have any improper motives for pressing charges? Is the effort worth the state's limited resources? (How much will it cost, in time and money, to resolve the matter?) Would indictment, prosecution, and conviction of the defendant serve as a general deterrent to others contemplating committing the same type of offense? Would punishment of the offender serve as a specific deterrent to discourage him or her from repeating this illegal act? Would pressing charges and seeking conviction enhance the community's sense of security and confidence in the criminal justice system? Could the accused serve as an informant for the police or as a key witness for the prosecution in other cases if his or her cooperation were secured by lenient treatment in this case? Would pressing or dropping charges set off protests from powerful interest groups in the community? Would a victory in this case substantially advance the careers of the assistant district attorney handling the case and of the prosecutor heading the office? If this office declines to prosecute, would the case be pursued by another branch of government or a different jurisdiction? What diversion programs exist in this jurisdiction to provide alternatives to prosecution and punishment? How are cases of this kind routinely handled in this jurisdiction? (National Advisory Commission, 1973; Sheley, 1979).

When all these factors are taken into account, it is clear that the victim is only one of several key players who influence the decisions of prosecutors. Police officials, other persons in the prosecutor's office, defense attorneys, judges, community leaders, and vocal interest groups all affect prosecutorial decision making.

Cases that have been cleared by arrest might not be pursued for a number of reasons. Prosecutors might screen out cases because of perceived weaknesses that could undercut the chances of conviction. Judges might agree with motions by defense lawyers that the government failed to establish that the defendant committed the crime in question. Judges might throw out cases on their own initiative if they feel that the charges are unprovable. In general, jurisdictions in which prosecutors screen out many cases before going to court have low case-dismissal rates at later stages of judicial proceedings. In jurisdictions in which prosecutors weed out few cases, the rates of dismissal by judges are high. A periodic nationwide survey of case processing revealed that, overall, 49 percent of all cases "solved" by arrest were carried forward (and 6 percent were diverted, 23 percent rejected at screening by prosecutors, and 22 percent dismissed in court by judges, for a total of 51 percent not pursued) during 1981 (Boland and Sones, 1986). By 1988, the percent of all felony arrests carried forward had increased to 55 percent because slightly smaller proportions of "solved" cases were rejected by prosecutors or dismissed by judges (Boland, Mahanna, and Sones, 1992). Still, the outcomes of these cases give a great many victims reasons to be dissatisfied with the adjudication process. (See Box 4.2 for an overview of what happens to felony cases when they reach prosecutors' offices and courthouses across the nation.)

BOX 4.2   What Happens to Cases "Solved" by Arrests?

This diagram or flow chart depicts the typical outcomes of every 100 felony arrests brought forward by the police for prosecution in jurisdictions across the country.

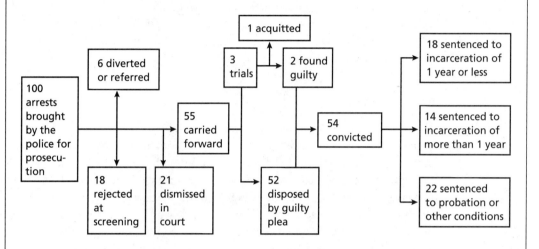

Notes: Some of these cases do not have individual victims, such as arrests for drug selling. Data are drawn from thirty different jurisdictions tracking the outcomes of cases during 1988.
Source: Boland, Mahanna, and Sones, 1992.

A number of factors explain why such a high percentage of cases are dropped at the prosecutorial stage. Limited resources dictate priorities; some types of cases and crimes are deemed trivial and not worth the state's time and money. Also, arrests are based on a much lower standard of proof (probable cause) than that required to secure a conviction (guilt beyond a reasonable doubt). In some jurisdictions, the police devote much more effort to case preparation than in others. Just because a case is cleared (by the arrest of a suspect) doesn't mean that it is ready for presentation to a grand jury for indictment or to a jury for a trial. Prosecutors reject cases at the screening stage (18 percent) or judges dismiss charges at hearings (21 percent) for a number of reasons:

- There might not be sufficient physical evidence to link the defendant to the crime.
- Constitutional guidelines concerning searches and seizures and the questioning of suspects might have been violated by police officers gathering evidence.
- Defendants could be referred to pretrial diversion programs that offer treatment in lieu of punishment.

- Defendants might have pled guilty to other crimes in other cases in return for the dropping of charges and counts.
- Defendants could have been transferred to other jurisdictions to face other charges, usually of a more serious nature.
- Complainants (and other prosecution witnesses) might have failed to appear in court or to have identified the accused in a lineup.
- Complainants could have given inconsistent statements or have had prior relationships with the defendant that undermine the credibility of their testimony for the state (Boland and Sones, 1986).

Negotiating Pleas

The vast majority of cases that are carried forward (not diverted, screened out, or dismissed in court) are resolved through plea negotiations. As the data in Box 4.2 indicates, 52 percent of all felony arrests end up with the accused admitting guilt (possibly just to a misdemeanor, rather than the original felony charge). The term *plea negotiation* refers to the process in which the assistant district attorney and the defense counsel meet to settle a case without having to hold a trial. The typical outcome (of the "bargaining," as most observers and participants derisively refer to the process) is that the defendant agrees to make a public confession of guilt in return for some consideration or concession from the government. The consideration on the part of the state could be the dropping of certain charges (often but not always, the most serious charges carrying the most severe penalties) or the dismissal of particular counts (accusations of harm against specific victims) or a promise or recommendation about a lesser punishment, such as a suspended sentence, probation, a fine, or incarceration for an agreed-upon period of time below the maximum permitted by the law.

The impression implied by the expression *plea bargain*—that defendants who "cop a plea" invariably get a break or good deal that permits them to escape the punishment they deserve—can be erroneous. Police officials and prosecutors routinely engage in "bedsheeting" and "overcharging" in anticipation of the negotiations that will follow. Bedsheeting refers to the prosecutorial practice of charging a defendant with every applicable crime committed during a single incident. For example, an armed intruder captured while burglarizing an occupied home can be held accountable for criminal trespass, breaking and entering, burglary, grand larceny, and carrying a concealed weapon, in addition to the most serious charge of robbery. Overcharging means filing a criminal indictment for an offense that is more serious than the available evidence might support—for example, charging someone with attempted murder after a fistfight. The point is that many of these charges could not be proven in court, but defendants and their lawyers might be too cautious to gamble and call the prosecutor's bluff. For these reasons and others, most accused persons who plead guilty in return for "concessions" receive substantially the same penalties that they probably would have received if convicted after a trial (Rhodes, 1978; Beall, 1980; Katz, 1980). Nevertheless, most victims are convinced that criminals are getting away with something when they accept plea bargains. On the other hand, if all defendants demanded their constitutional right to a trial by jury, the courts would be overwhelmed and paralyzed.

Actually, resolving cases by negotiated pleas rather than by full-scale trials may be in the best interests of certain victims. Besides a sure conviction, plea bargaining spares victims the ordeal of testifying in court and undergoing hostile questioning (cross-examination) by defense attorneys. This is particularly important if the facts of the case portray the complainants in a negative light or reveal aspects of their lives that they do not want to make public and expose to the world through media coverage (especially now that trials can be televised in most states). Concern about the victim having to take the stand is voiced most often in cases of child abuse and rape.

Since doing away with deals and inducements is unrealistic, some victims want to play an active role in the negotiations that resolve their cases. Although victims justify their quest for empowerment by emphasizing that they were the ones directly involved and personally harmed, this demand has evoked considerable resistance.

It is often presumed that the adversarial model characterizes the actual workings of the adjudication process; that in the hard bargaining between prosecution and defense, the assistant district attorney must be able to produce a cooperative witness eager to testify in order to convince the defendant to negotiate a plea and confess guilt to some of the charges. The reality might be that the *courtroom work group* (made up of the judge, assistant district attorney, and defense counsel) has a mutual interest in processing large numbers of cases expeditiously. Victims serving as witnesses for the prosecution are outsiders whose presence and involvement is often unwanted because it might slow down assembly-line practices that resolve cases quickly. Victims see their situations as unique events that deserve careful consideration, not as routine occurrences to be disposed of according to some formula based on the "going rate" (typical penalty or sentence) for the type of crime in question. Victim-witness programs have had little success in improving appearance rates and conviction rates because they have perpetuated the handling of victims as mere witnesses for the prosecution and not as the active participants some would like to be (Davis, 1983; Walker, 1994).

Predictably defense attorneys, prosecutors, and judges make dire predictions about what would happen if victims (and police officers and defendants as well) joined them at pretrial conferences. These insiders contend that the candid discussions necessary to foster settlements would be inhibited by the presence of outsiders; that volatile confrontations between victims and defendants would break out; that both victims and defendants would misconstrue the role of judges and accuse them of improper conduct; and that the dignity of judges would be diminished by their open involvement in negotiations in front of outsiders (Heinz and Kerstetter, 1979). Prosecutors, in particular, feel threatened by the inclusion of victims (whom they supposedly represent, in addition to the state) at such meetings. They object because victims might try to use the administrative machinery as an instrument of personal revenge and might put forward unreasonable demands for the imposition of maximum penalties. Deals would fall through, and risky and costly trials would be necessitated (McDonald, 1976). In general, victims do not have a right to participate in or even be consulted during the process of plea negotiation. Only a few jurisdictions have granted victims a clearly defined role, and most state laws still do not provide them with any formal mechanisms to challenge the decisions of the prosecuting attorneys who act in their name as well as on behalf of "the people." The Supreme Court has issued several rulings that specifically deny complainants any right to challenge the decisions prosecutors make in their cases.

VICTIMS AND DEFENSE ATTORNEYS

Victims and defense lawyers are natural enemies within the adversary system of criminal justice. Lawyers for the accused act as counselors, advising clients about their best interests, the risks they face, and the options they can exercise. Whether hired privately for a fee or provided free to indigents, defense attorneys have a duty to advocate in behalf of their clients. They may deny that their clients are guilty, or they may seek the best deal prosecutors will agree to in plea negotiations. During trials, they pit themselves against the assistant district attorneys and try to cast doubt on the government's version of events. In so doing, they draw on all their skills and training to undermine the impact of the testimony of victims.

Conflicts often break out between victims and defense lawyers over two matters: how long the process takes (and how many court appearances are needed to resolve cases); and the line of questioning directed at victims who testify in court. From the victims' point of view, defense attorneys might engage in two kinds of abusive practices: asking judges for postponements of their clients' cases in order to wear victims down, and using unfair tactics to undermine their credibility when they appear as witnesses for the prosecution.

Postponing Hearings

The problems of court congestion and needless delays have usually been approached from the defendants' standpoint. The Sixth Amendment to the Constitution guarantees accused persons the right to a speedy trial. Many states and the federal government have set limits on the amount of time that can elapse from arrest to trial (not counting continuances requested by defense attorneys). But victims, too, suffer from the uncertainty accompanying unresolved cases and share a common interest with defendants in having legal matters settled in as short a time as possible.

But if their clients are free on bail, defense lawyers may have an incentive to stall proceedings as much as possible to "buy time on the streets." As the delays mount and unnecessary court appearances accumulate, victims (and crucial witnesses) may lose patience with the slow deliberations of the legal system, and their commitment to see the case through to its conclusion may erode. The strategy succeeds if the victims (or other key witnesses) give up in disgust and fail to appear in court as required. For example, a victim who lost her handbag to an unarmed bandit may miss so many days from work that the lost wages far exceed what the robber took, and she will eventually drop out. Stalling for time may also pay off if victims (or other witnesses for the prosecution) forget crucial details, move away, get seriously ill, or die in the interim. At that point, defense attorneys can move for a dismissal of all charges (Reiff, 1979). (Prosecutors can also manipulate continuance provisions for their own ends. If defendants are in jail rather than out on bail, government attorneys may stretch out proceedings to keep them behind bars longer and to pressure them to accept unfavorable plea offers. In the process, the defendants' right to a speedy trial could be violated.)

Postponements can prolong and intensify the suffering of victims. In order to be available if called to testify, they might have to repeatedly arrange for child care, miss school or work, cancel vacations, and break appointments, only to discover (often at the last minute) that the hearings have been rescheduled. To defeat this wear-the-victim-down strategy, some of the motions for postponements by defense attorneys could be opposed more vigorously by prosecutors sensitive to the needs and wants of their clients and rejected by judges if they suspect the requests for continuances are stalling tactics (President's Task Force, 1982). Victim-witness assistance programs operate notification systems to prevent victims from showing up in court on days when hearings have been postponed.

In general, the more serious the charges against the defendant, the longer it takes to resolve the case. Some cases are disposed of quickly in lower courts when, as a result of plea negotiations, felony charges are reduced to misdemeanors. But other cases are handled more judiciously and require preliminary hearings about evidence, grand jury presentations, and bench or jury trials in higher courts. The Offender-Based Transaction Statistics program of the BJS, based on over 500,000 felony cases in eleven states during 1990 yielded these estimates of median case-processing time, by type of crime: homicides took 207 days to be adjudicated; rape charges, 134 days; robberies and kidnappings, about 110 days; and various offenses against property averaged almost 90 days to resolve (Perez, 1994). Cases resolved by negotiated pleas don't take as long as cases resolved by trials, of course. The average time it took to resolve a case from arrest to sentencing when defendants pled guilty was 114 days, and from arrest to sentencing after trials was 241 days, according to data gathered from a national study of thirty jurisdictions in

1988 (Boland, Mahanna, and Sones, 1992). In another study, using 1992 data from the National Judicial Reporting Program's sample of 100 counties, researchers determined that murder cases in state courts took 405 days to be resolved, if a jury trial was held; rape cases brought before juries took 357 days; and robbery cases lasted 280 days from arrest to sentencing after a jury trial. Cases resolved by bench trials took less time, and cases resolved by guilty pleas were wrapped up even more rapidly (Langan and Graziadei, 1995). However, in some high-crime areas, huge backlogs cause even greater delays, prolonging the anxiety of both complainants and defendants waiting to discover the final outcome of their cases.

Cross-Examining Witnesses during Trials

If they can't wear victims down through stalling tactics, defense attorneys will try to discredit them (and other prosecution witnesses) on the stand during the trial so that the jury won't give much weight to their testimony.

Under the adversary system, each side puts forward its own best case and assails the version of events presented by the opposition. Cross-examination is the art of exposing the weaknesses of witnesses. The intent is to impeach their credibility by trapping them into revealing any hidden motives, lapses of memory, unsavory character traits, embarrassing indiscretions, prejudices, incompetencies, or dishonest inclinations. Under the Sixth Amendment to the U.S. Constitution, defendants have the right to confront their accusers. Since the burden of proof falls on the prosecution, and the accused is innocent unless proven guilty, the accuser must be presumed mistaken until his or her credibility is established beyond a reasonable doubt. The defense attorney goes up against a formidable professional foe when the witness for the government is a police officer (although the credibility of police testimony is the subject of much debate). But when the full brunt of the defense's counterattack is directed at discrediting the complainant, the potential for adding insult to injury reaches disturbing proportions. At its best, the confrontation in the courtroom puts the victim-as-eyewitness to the test. At its worst, the victim is set up as a target, to be injured again by being made to look like a liar, a fool, or an instigator who got what he or she deserved.

Trials are relatively rare events, so most victims will never be called upon to testify and undergo cross-examination. As noted in Box 4.2, most cases are resolved through plea negotiation. (Trials involve risks: their outcomes are uncertain. However, statistically, most trials are successful from the point of view of victims and prosecutors: Defendants are found guilty.) The percentage of all criminal indictments that result in trials (either before juries or in bench trials before judges) varies according to two factors: the jurisdiction and the nature of the charges. Some prosecutors are more willing to put defendants on trial than others. Serious felonies are more likely than lesser charges to be resolved through trials. Cases of murder, rape, aggravated assault, and robbery go to trial more often than cases involving lesser crimes. Rape complainants are the most likely to be cross-examined by defense attorneys. In 1992, about 18 percent of all rape convictions were achieved through trials with the help of the complainants' testimony (14 percent before juries, 4 percent in bench trials before judges alone); the remaining 82 percent of all convictions were secured through plea negotiations. As for other violent crimes, 13 percent of all aggravated assault convictions, and 12 percent of all robbery convictions were won through trials rather than by negotiations (Langan and Graziadei, 1995).

Cross-examinations can be ordeals for witnesses. But if defense attorneys were not allowed to sharply question prosecution witnesses, then the right of defendants to try (through their lawyers) to refute the charges against them would be undermined. The concerns of complainants and other witnesses (including witnesses for the defense, who are cross-examined by prosecutors) about being embarrassed under oath on the stand must be balanced against the public humiliation suffered by defendants who are arrested and put on trial. Since defense attorneys have a duty to vigorously represent the best interests of their clients, their courtroom tactics might seem harsh from the victim's point of view. To rattle a witness, discredit damning testimony, and sow seeds of doubt and confusion among jurors, they may have to resort to theatrics and hyperbole. The Code of Professional Responsibility guiding legal strategies permits a zealous defense to gain an acquittal or a lenient sentence but prohibits any line of questioning whose sole aim is to harass or maliciously harm a witness. The experts—and the public—often disagree in specific trials over whether or not a defense attorney (or a prosecutor) crossed the line and acted unethically by badgering and abusing a witness during a cross-examination. The kinds of cases that provoke the greatest controversy are those in which defense attorneys cast aspersions on the character of victims or blame them for their own misfortunes (Shipp, 1987). In murder trials, the families of the deceased find it particularly upsetting if defense attorneys attack the attitudes and actions of the dead persons to try to justify or exonerate the behavior of their clients. Unlike cross-examinations, these attempts to sully the reputation (or "trash the memory") of the dead are peculiarly one-sided affairs, since the subjects of the insinuations cannot rebut the accusations.

A young woman is strangled late at night in a public park by a young man she was dating. He tells police that she died accidently as he protected himself during "rough sex play." His lawyer subpoenas her diary, which he alleges contains graphic descriptions of her aggressive sexual exploits with other men (later it turns out that it doesn't). But some members of the jury are swayed by the defense's arguments. The jury becomes deadlocked for days; before it can render its verdict, a last-minute plea bargain is negotiated that permits the defendant to admit guilt to the lesser charge of manslaughter instead of murder. At a press conference, the father denounces the defense's portrayal of his dead daughter as a bizarre pack of lies. (Hackett and Cerio, 1988; Lander, 1988)

VICTIMS AND JUDGES

Judges are supposed to act as referees within the adversary system. Defendants often consider them to be partisans representing the state and favoring the prosecution. Angry victims, however, frequently see judges as guardians of the rights of the accused rather than protectors of the innocent. Victims who have been mistreated by the offender, the police, the prosecutor, and the defense attorney expect that the judge will finally accord them the justice they seek. But conflicts between victims and judges can erupt over bail decisions and sentencing.

Granting Bail

Police officers often resent bail as a repudiation of the hard work they have put in to apprehend the offenders. To them, releasing defendants on bail is tantamount to turning dangerous criminals loose. Victims can also be outraged by the decisions of judges to grant bail, if they are convinced that the defendants are indeed the culprits.

The Eighth Amendment of the Bill of Rights prohibits the setting of excessive bail. Whether or not it establishes being bailed out as an affirmative right, however, is a subject of scholarly debate and considerable public concern. State and federal courts routinely deny bail to defendants accused of crimes that could carry the death penalty, particularly first degree murder. In noncapital cases, bail can be denied to jailed suspects who have a history of flight to avoid prosecution or who have tried to interfere with the administration of justice (by intimidating a witness or a juror, for example). Otherwise, defendants generally are given a chance to raise money or post bond to guarantee that they will show up for their trial. The amount of bail is usually determined by the judge and is set according to the nature of the offense and the record of the defendant. The prosecutor can recommend a figure. Making bail is a major problem for defendants who are poor and have no prosperous friends or relatives. Across the nation, houses of detention are crammed full with people unable to raise a few hundred dollars to purchase their freedom until their cases are resolved.

The question of bail versus jail raises a number of troubling issues. When accused people are denied bail (preventive detention) or are unable to raise the necessary amount, they are sent to jail and thereby immediately undergo punishment. The living conditions in jails and houses of detention, where persons who have not yet been convicted of any crime are held, are usually far worse than those in prisons, which house convicted felons. Yet the release of a suspected criminal poses a direct threat to the victim who will serve as a witness for the state and a general danger to the community at large (if the accused is genuinely guilty and prone to strike again). One partial resolution of this dilemma is for the judge to state that a condition of bail will be that the defendant must avoid all contacts with the complainant or else forfeit the privilege of pretrial release.

Sentencing Offenders

After a defendant has been convicted, whether by an admission of guilt as part of a negotiated plea or by a jury verdict after a trial, the judge has the responsibility of imposing an appropriate sentence. Judges can exercise a considerable amount of discretion when pronouncing sentences, unless there are mandatory minimums or explicit guidelines.

The substantial variation between judges in the severity of the punishments meted out in comparable cases is termed *sentence disparity.* These differences trouble civil libertarians because the disparities might reflect judges' prejudices, to the extent that they deal more harshly with certain kinds of offenders than with others. Sentence disparity undermines whatever respect convicts might still have for the law and the judiciary since they complain about unjustifiable arbitrariness. Wide ranges are taken by law-and-order advocates as evidence that judges on the low end are too "soft" or "permissive" toward offenders. The wide spectrum of possible punishments that might be handed down inspires the victims' rights movement to press for greater input. Sentences can involve incarceration, fines, enrollment in treatment programs, community service, and obligations to repay victims. The main objectives that guide sentencing are specific deterrence, general deterrence, incapacitation, retribution, rehabilitation, and restitution.

Historically, the exclusion of victims from the sentencing process has been justified on several grounds. If the purpose of punishing offenders is to deter others from committing the same acts, then sanctions must be swift, sure, and predictable, and not subject to uncertainty and modification by the injured parties. If the objective is retribution, then lawbreakers must receive the punishments they deserve, not the penalties their victims request. If the goal of sentencing is to rehabilitate offenders, then the punitive urges of the people they harmed cannot be allowed to interfere with the length and type of treatment prescribed by experts (McDonald, 1979).

The potential impact of victims' desires on sentencing outcomes is limited because many different parties have input. Victims who want to try to determine their offenders' sentences have to compete for influence with other individuals and groups who routinely affect the exercise of judicial discretion. State legislatures pass laws that set maximum and minimum limits for periods of confinement and for fines. Prosecutors make recommendations based on deals arrived at during plea negotiations and draw upon mutual understandings of the appropriate penalty for specific crimes in that jurisdiction at that time (the "going rate"). Defense attorneys use whatever leverage they have on behalf of their clients. Defendants determine their own sentences to some degree by their demeanor, degree of remorse, prior record of convictions, and other mitigating or aggravating personal characteristics. Probation officers conduct presentence investigations and make recommendations to guide judges. Parole boards determine the actual time served when they decide to let convicted felons out of prison ahead of schedule or keep them confined until their maximum sentences expire. Corrections officers influence whether or not convicts earn "good-time" reductions and parole. The news media can shape outcomes by their coverage or lack of it. The public's reactions can affect the handling of cases, prompting either harshness or leniency. And ultimately, state governors can shorten terms of imprisonment (or even stop executions) by issuing pardons or commuting sentences.

Victims can attempt to influence sentences in two ways: either by conveying their requests to judges through written impact statements (or through a variation used in some jurisdictions, statements of opinion), or by expressing their views orally at personal appearances at sentencing hearings ("allocution"). Victim impact statements enable judges to learn about the actual physical, emotional, and financial effects of crimes on the injured parties and their families. Written questionnaires ask (with the threat of penalties for perjury) about any wounds, medical bills, counseling costs, other expenses, insurance reimbursements, and lifestyle changes. Statements of opinion ask victims what they would consider to be appropriate sentences. In most jurisdictions, these statements are incorporated into the presentence investigation reports (PSIRs) prepared by probation officers.

The invention and adoption of impact statements and the granting of the allocution privilege represented important gains for the victims' rights movement. Prior to their acceptance and implementation, victims had to rely on prosecutors to present their views and to fully describe their plight. Direct appeals to judges were thought to undermine the judiciary's professional objectivity by injecting inflammatory emotional considerations into the proceedings. But advocates of victims' rights argued that the situation was unbalanced. Convicted persons did not have to depend solely on their lawyers to speak for them. They were permitted to directly address the court before their sentences were handed down. Yet two lives, the offender's and the victim's, were profoundly shaped by the sentence, which represented an official evaluation of the seriousness of the harm inflicted. Judges couldn't make informed decisions if they heard from only one side—the defendants themselves and their lawyers, families, friends, and other character witnesses. Notions of fairness dictated that suffering individuals also be allowed to write or tell about their experiences before sentences were determined (President's Task Force, 1982).

A nationwide study of how criminal justice officials find out about the harm offenders inflicted on their victims concluded that for judges, the most important source of information was the presentence investigation report, not the prosecutor or the trial testimony. However, the probation officers who prepared the PSIRs obtained much of their information about how seriously victims were harmed from secondhand sources, like police reports and medical records, and not directly from victims through impact statements (Forst and Hernon, 1984).

Just because activists in the victims' rights movement succeeded in securing the right to submit an impact statement or to speak in person at sentencing hearings does not mean that this practice has become widespread and effective. On the contrary, a study carried out in California in 1982 concluded that very few victims took advantage of these opportunities, and when they did, their participation seemed to have very little impact (Villmoare and Neto, 1987).

When a sentence is handed down, it is possible that the victim is misled into thinking that it is more severe than it really is. Therefore, the victims' rights movement has urged states to impose a "truth-in-sentencing" rule which would require judges to calculate and announce the earliest possible date (actual time served) that a convict could be released from confinement, taking into account time off for good behavior behind bars and parole immediately upon eligibility (Associated Press, 1994c). For examples, during the 1980s, felons sent to prison by state court judges across the country served an estimated 38 percent of their maximum sentences. A 1987 federal "truth-in-sentencing" law requires felons to serve at least 85 percent of their court-imposed sentences (parole has been abolished, and the maximum allowable good-time credit is 15 percent) (Langan, Perkins, and Chaiken, 1994).

A study of more than 300 victims of felonies in eight jurisdictions across the country established that most victims were dissatisfied with the sentences judges handed down in their cases. Eighty-six percent agreed with the statement that "guilty offenders are not punished enough" (Forst and Hernon, 1984). This perception that many judges are too lenient is shared by the public at large. Annual nationwide polls ask, "In general, do you think the courts in this area deal too harshly or not harshly enough with criminals?" In 1972, 66 percent of those polled answered "not harshly enough"; by 1976, the number had risen to 81 percent; in 1986, the figure peaked at 85 percent; by 1993, it had declined to 81 percent (Maguire and Pastore, 1994: 194–195).

This widespread impression raises a crucial question: "Just how much punishment is enough?" Victims might feel that the offenders convicted of harming them don't stay in prison long enough, but no formula or equation exists to calculate the gravity of an offense and to translate this rating into the "proper" amount of time the perpetrator should be incarcerated. State legislators, who have the authority to set the upper limits for penalties, can't agree on the maximum length of prison time one person who harms another really deserves. The profound disagreements that divide people over the issue of whether murder should carry the death penalty are well known. Usually overlooked, however, are the dramatic differences in maximum penalties from state to state for lesser crimes like rape, robbery, or burglary. It is impossible to conclude with any degree of objectivity that a particular offender "got off too lightly" when the maximum sentences differ so sharply from one jurisdiction to another (see Katz, 1980).

A bitter controversy erupted over whether victim impact statements should be allowed and whether allocution by members of the immediate family should be permitted during the penalty phase of murder trials (after the defendants have been convicted and face the possibility of execution, in most states).

> **C**aught up in a drug-induced frenzy, a man stabs to death the mother of two toddlers, as well as her two-year-old daughter. During the penalty phase of the trial, the grandmother describes to the jury how the three-year-old boy who survived the attack still cries mournfully for his mother and little sister. The jury sentences the convict to die in the electric chair. (Clark and Block, 1992)

The debate over the admissibility of victim impact information was brought before the Supreme Court. Victims' rights groups and prosecutors' organizations argued that it was illogical to demand that a jury focus all of its attention on the defendant's difficult circumstances and other mitigating factors and ignore the suffering of the deceased's survivors. But civil rights and civil liberties groups argued that the introduction of impact statements could be highly inflammatory and prejudicial in capital cases, diverting the jury's attention toward the victim's character (how much or how little the dead person will be missed and mourned) and away from its duty of evaluating the defendant's blameworthiness and the circumstances surrounding the crime. The first time the high court considered a case that raised the issue, it voted to exclude impact statements; but when the issue came up again, the justices voted that survivors could testify during the penalty phase of a capital case (Clark and Block, 1992).

Victims and the Supreme Court

The U.S. Supreme Court is the highest appellate body in the U.S. judicial system. It is composed of nine judges who are appointed for life by the president with the approval of the Senate. It hears only those cases on appeal from federal and state courts that appear to raise important principles of constitutional law. When a majority of Supreme Court justices (five or more) agree on a decision in a case chosen for review, their ruling sets a precedent that must be followed in all lower courts. These landmark decisions also guide the procedures followed by the police, prosecutors, trial judges, corrections officials, and other agencies within the criminal justice system. Over the past several decades, a number of decisions handed down by the Supreme Court have affected the rights and interests of crime victims (see O'Neill, 1984). Some far-reaching rulings are briefly summarized in Box 4.3.

VICTIMS AND CORRECTIONS OFFICIALS

Corrections officials include jail and prison staffs and probation and parole officers.

As the diagram in Box 4.2 indicated, being placed on probation is the final disposition for 22 percent of all individuals arrested for felonies (and 22 out of every

---

BOX 4.3   Supreme Court Decisions Directly Affecting Victims

**Victims Cannot Compel Prosecutors
to Take Action against Suspects**

A number of decisions handed down in 1967, 1973, 1977, 1981, and 1983 have established that attorneys general and district attorneys have absolute discretion over whether or not to charge defendants with crimes and what charges to press or drop. Victims cannot compel prosecutors to take particular actions, and courts cannot intervene in this decision-making process (see Stark and Goldstein, 1985).

**Victim Impact Statements Can
Be Used in Capital Cases**

In 1987 (*Booth* v. *Maryland*), the Supreme Court overturned a death sentence because the jury, during the penalty phase of the trial, heard a particularly heart-rending impact statement about how the murder of an elderly couple shattered the lives of three generations of their family. The majority ruled that the use of such "inflammatory" impact statements created a constitutionally unacceptable risk that juries might impose the death penalty in an arbitrary and capricious manner, swayed by the standing and reputation of the murdered victims in their communities. The majority believed that the victim's "worth" was not an appropriate factor for a jury to consider when weighing the killer's fate—imprisonment or execution—because it would undermine the guarantee of equal protection (Triebwasser, 1987b).

But in 1991 (*Payne* v. *Tennessee*), the Court reversed itself and ruled that prosecutors could introduce victim impact statements and that the survivors of murder victims could testify. The majority held that courts have always taken into account the harm done by defendants when determining appropriate sentences (Clark and Block, 1992).

**Insufficient Proof That the Lives of Murdered
Black Victims Count for Less**

In 1987 (*McCleskey* v. *Kemp*), in upholding a death penalty conviction, the Supreme Court rejected a statistical analysis that seemed to show that the deaths of black victims were not taken as seriously as the deaths of white victims by criminal justice decision makers—prosecutors, juries, and judges. The court ruled that a pattern in which persons convicted of killing white victims were eleven times more likely to be sentenced to die than those convicted of murdering black victims was not compelling evidence of intentional discrimination in violation of the Eighth and Fourteenth Amendments (Triebwasser, 1987a).

**Offenders Can Escape Paying
Restitution to Victims**

In 1989 (*Pennsylvania Dept. of Public Welfare* v. *Davenport*), the Court ruled 7–2 that if convicts declare bankruptcy, they can avoid paying court-ordered restitution, since restitution obligations are dischargeable debts.

In another case, in 1990 (*Hughey* v. *United States*), the Court ruled that a federal judge cannot order a defendant to pay restitution to a victim if the charge involving that victim was dropped as part of a negotiated plea. The Court based its ruling on a provision of the federal Victim and Witness Protection Act of 1982 (Eddy, 1990).

**Government Has No Constitutional
Duty to Protect Individuals**

In 1989 (*De Shaney* v. *Winnebago County Dept. of Social Services*), six of the nine justices decided that a government agency could not be sued for failing to intervene (in behalf of a child repeatedly beaten and permanently injured by his father) because the state does not have a special obligation to protect individuals from harm by other private persons ("U.S. Supreme Court," 1989).

**Newspapers Can Publish the Lawfully
Obtained Names of Rape Victims**

In 1989, a majority of six justices argued that the First Amendment's guarantee of freedom of the press protected a newspaper from liability for

(continued on next page)

BOX 4.3   *continued*

---

printing the name of a woman who already was identified as a rape victim in publicly available police reports. However, the decision did not declare unconstitutional state laws in Florida, Georgia, and South Carolina that prohibit the publishing of a rape victim's name as an invasion of privacy (Greenhouse, 1989).

Victimized Children Can Testify Via Closed-Circuit Television

In 1990 (*Maryland* v. *Craig*), in a 5–4 decision, the Court held that it was constitutional for a state to pass a law that shields a child who accuses an adult of sexual abuse from a face-to-face confrontation during a trial. The child's testimony and the defense attorney's cross-examination can take place in another room and can be shown to the jury over closed-circuit television if the prosecutor can convince the judge that the young witness would be traumatized by having to testify in the defendant's presence. The majority felt that the state's interest in the physical and psychological well-being of the abused child may outweigh the defendant's Sixth Amendment right to face his or her accuser in person (Greenhouse, 1990).

Rape Victims' Past Can Be Kept Out of Court

In 1991, the Supreme Court ruled by a 7–2 vote that the rape shield laws passed in all fifty states were constitutional. The laws allow judges to suppress as irrelevant attempts by the defense to in-troduce allegations about the past sexual experiences of rape victims (Rauber, 1991).

Victims Can't Easily Claim Income Gained by Notorious Offenders

In 1991 (*Simon & Schuster* v. *New York Crime Victims Board*), the Supreme Court struck down New York's 1977 "Son-of-Sam" statute, which served as a model for forty-one other state laws. The law confiscated fees and royalties offenders gained from selling their inside stories to book publishers or moviemakers and permitted victims to claim that money. The unanimous opinion held that the state's worthwhile goals of ensuring that criminals do not profit from their crimes, and of transferring the proceeds to victims, did not justify infringements on the First Amendment right of free speech (Greenhouse, 1991).

Crimes Motivated by Hatred for the Victim's "Kind" Merit Extra Punishment

In 1993 (*Wisconsin* v. *Mitchell*), the Supreme Court unanimously upheld a state law that imposed harsher penalties on offenders who chose their victims on the basis of race, religion, color, disability, sexual orientation, national origin, or ancestry. The chief justice affirmed that an illegal act motivated by the criminal's hatred for people like the victim was more harmful to the individual, and to society at large, and deserved an enhanced sentence (Greenhouse, 1993).

---

54 who are convicted) or 41 percent of the people found guilty (whether through negotiated pleas or after trials). Eighteen percent are jailed for up to a year (18 out of 54, or 33 percent of all who get convicted) and 14 percent are imprisoned for more than a year (14 out of 54, or 26 percent of all convicts). Therefore, victims whose cases led to "successful prosecutions" are more likely to have contacts with county probation departments than with county jail, state prison, or state parole authorities.

Victims want two things from probation and parole officers. When offenders are placed on probation, or when they are released on parole after serving time in prison, victims want to be protected from any harassment or further harm. They can feel especially endangered by a vengeful violent ex-offender if their cooperation and testimony was a crucial factor leading to conviction. And if making restitution is a condition of probation or parole, victims want to receive the payments they are entitled to on schedule. Probation and parole officers share these goals but often find their caseloads so overwhelming that they cannot effectively keep offenders away from their former victims or see to it that restitution payments arrive on time.

Corrections officials are supposed to safeguard the well-being of victims by keeping them notified of the inmates' whereabouts, according to legislation enacted in more than half the states. Correctional agencies can go further and make sure that prisoners on temporary leave from confinement (on furlough, work release, or educational release) or who escape from an institution do not threaten, track down, stalk, and injure their former victims (National Victim Center, 1990). Conflicts with corrections officials can arise if these responsibilities are not carried out, and victims are shocked to discover that their offenders, especially those guilty of aggravated assault, armed robbery, rape, or sexual molestation, are back on the streets.

Victims and Parole Boards

Statistically speaking, relatively few victims ever deal with members of parole boards because small percentages of offenders are caught, convicted, and sent to prison for years. However, this group of corrections professionals has received a great deal of attention from the victims' rights movement because they determine the fates of inmates who have committed serious felonies.

Parole by definition means early release, before the maximum, full, or upper limit of the judge's sentence has been served. Parole is the earned privilege of conditional liberty, with restrictions on conduct. Prisoners become eligible for parole after serving specific proportions of their sentences, either the minimum or some fraction, often one-third, of the maximum. Of course, parole is not automatic, and many convicts are turned down by parole boards and kept incarcerated after hearings. (However, even without parole, early release is still possible, since most correctional institutions subtract time off for good behavior.) Rule violators (and, of course, parolees who commit new crimes—recidivists) can be arrested and reimprisoned for the remainder of their unexpired full sentences, at the discretion of administrative judges after revocation hearings.

Parole has become an extremely controversial practice, even though its origins date back to the mid-1800s. The rationales for setting up boards to grant the privilege of early release to selected prisoners are that ex-convicts can make a smoother transition from prison life to civilian life with the guidance of parole officers, and that corrections authorities can better manage prisoners as long as the possibility of parole looms as a reward for good behavior. In addition, parole enables authorities to control the flow of prisoners from institutions to ensure that cell space is available for the steady waves of new arrivals sent by the courts.

Prisoners' rights groups have rejected the image of parole as a form of benevolence and as an incentive for rehabilitation. They have criticized the practice as a way of extending the length of time ex-convicts are under governmental control, as a device to prolong punishment, and as a source of anxiety and uncertainty for prisoners. These groups have called for the abolition of the practice of parole and have suggested determinate or fixed sentences of shorter duration as a replacement for indefinite sentences with widely varying minimums and maximums (Shelden, 1982). Law-and-order groups have also demanded an end to the parole system, perceiving it, however, as a source of unwarranted leniency, because it allows dangerous criminals to be let out prematurely. They want parole ended and replaced with definite sentences of longer duration (President's Task Force, 1982). Victims, too, may bitterly resent the practice of parole, since it further reduces sentences of incarceration that they may originally have considered too short.

As a result of the widespread dissatisfaction with parole, the federal prison system and a number of state systems have phased it out. In other jurisdictions, parole is being granted less often. The reliance on parole reached its peak in 1977, when as many as 72 percent of all prisoners returning to society were granted conditional liberty with community supervision. By 1986, the proportion of released prisoners who were let out on parole had dropped to 43 percent (Hester, 1987), and by 1990 the figure stood at 40.5 percent (Jankowski, 1991).

Since 4 out of every 10 prisoners do not serve out their maximum terms, victims retain an interest in exercising their rights before parole boards. Parole boards can serve victims by inviting them to participate in the decision-making process, by warning them in advance that the persons they helped send to prison are being let go, and by ordering the convicts to pay restitution as a condition of release.

As of the start of the 1990s, legislation in thirty-seven states expressly granted victims the right to submit written impact statements, and laws in thirty-four states allowed them to attend the parole hearings and voice their views (National Victim Center, 1990). Through these channels, they might oppose early release on the grounds that, in their opinions, the offender has not been punished sufficiently. Information about the physical, emotional, and financial harm inflicted by the offender could convince members of the board about the severity of the crime. Alternatively, victims might support early release but demand that restitution be one of the conditions, in addition to the usual terms, such as refraining from further illegal activity, avoiding the company of known criminals, abstaining from drinking, and reporting to officers regularly. In some states, restitution is a mandatory requirement for parolees, unless the board excuses them from this obligation.

The potential impact of victim input into parole board decision making is limited, as it was with sentencing. The boards review statements from victims, prosecutors, judges, and other concerned parties. They interview the inmates themselves and review their criminal records and files describing their behavior while in prison. Boards are often subject to intense pressures either to keep convicts confined longer or to let some out ahead of schedule to make room for new arrivals.

AND JUSTICE FOR ALL?

The Fourteenth Amendment to the Constitution promises "equal protection of the law" for all citizens. The standard interpretation of this pledge is that federal and state criminal justice systems ought to regard factors like social class, race, nationality, religion, and sex as irrelevant to the administration of the law. Traditionally, criminologists and political activists have applied this important principle of equal protection to the way suspects, defendants, and convicts are handled by officials and agencies. The main focus of concern has been whether offenders who are poor or members of a minority group are subjected to discriminatory treatment. Until recently, the equally significant question of whether certain kinds of victims are handled in a discriminatory manner has escaped notice.

It is often said that the United States is a country "ruled by laws, not men." This maxim implies that the principles of due process and equal protection limit the considerable discretionary powers of criminal justice officials. Due process means procedural regularity, and equal protection requires that different categories of people be treated similarly. Yet enough discretion remains at each step in the criminal justice process to generate unequal outcomes. Of course, those who exercise discretion can and do defend and justify their actions. Their explanations range from pragmatic considerations about time and money to philosophical rationales about the true meaning of justice. Nevertheless, their actions generate, maintain, and reveal double standards, or, more accurately (since sometimes more than just two distinct groups are involved), "differential handling," or "differential justice."

Recognizing "Second-Class" Treatment

Many social institutions have two or more tracks and deliver unequal services to their clients or consumers. For instance, the health care system does not treat all patients the same: Some get much higher quality medical attention than others. The school system does not provide all students with equal educational opportunities: Some are challenged and nurtured, and they excel, while others are discouraged and neglected, and they fail. A review of how cases are processed by the criminal justice system leads to an inevitable question: Now that victims have rights and are no longer routinely overlooked, are they all treated the same, or do some get much better service than others?

Criminologists have documented the discrepancy between official dogma and actual practices. For example, race and class are supposed to be extraneous factors in a system of "blind justice," but in reality they turn out to be predictors of how officials respond to offenders. When victimologists piece together scattered research findings about how different categories of victims are treated, a comparable picture emerges. Certain victims are more likely to be given what might be termed "VIP" or "red carpet" or "first-class" treatment, while others tend to be neglected or abused and dealt with as second-class complainants by these same agencies and officials. In other words, how a case is handled is determined by who the victim is as well as who the offender is (in addition to the particular circumstances of the crime).

According to a number of independent studies, victims who are totally innocent, from "respectable" backgrounds and privileged groups, are more likely to receive better service from police officers, prosecutors, juries, and judges. Individuals whose backgrounds are "tarnished," or who come from disadvantaged groups, are less likely to get favorable responses from the constituent agencies and officials of the justice system. (See Box 4.4 for a profile of the people who tend to be treated better than others.)

It should come as no surprise that many of the social handicaps that hold people back in other aspects of everyday life also impede their ability to receive fair treatment as crime victims. The same discretionary powers that result in "overzealous" law enforcement in some neighborhoods contribute to "underzealous" enforcement in other neighborhoods. A seemingly pragmatic prosecutorial screening criterion can subvert the intent of justice for all. For instance, the policy in many jurisdictions of not investigating and not pressing charges in minor burglaries (ones that result in losses of less than a certain amount, say $4,000) in effect means that criminals have a license to ransack the homes of the poor without penalty.

Apparently, the claims of victims from discriminated-against groups are not perceived as being entirely legitimate or compelling by those at the helm of the criminal justice system. The credibility of the calls for help from disadvantaged victims is eroded by a belief that these same people are offenders in other incidents. Such stereotypical responses by the authorities poison relations between the two camps. From bitter experience, victims from outgroups, the lower strata, and marginal lifestyles anticipate that their requests for intervention will be greeted with suspicion or even hostility. They expect perfunctory treatment at best. As a consequence, they turn to the criminal justice system only under the most desperate circumstances (Ziegenhagen, 1977).

BOX 4.4   Which Victims Get Better Treatment?

Arrests

Suspects are more likely to be taken into custody if the victims:

- request that the police make an arrest in a deferential, nonantagonistic manner (Black, 1968).
- convince the police officer that they were not involved in any illegal activity themselves before the incident (La Fave, 1965).
- prove to the officer that they are not a friend, relative, or neighbor of the suspect (Black, 1968; Giacinti, 1973; Goldstein, 1960; La Fave, 1965; Reiss, 1971).

Prosecutions

Charges are more likely to be lodged against defendants if the victims:

- are middle-aged or elderly, white, and employed (Myers and Hagan, 1979).
- have high status in the community ("Prosecutorial discretion," 1969).
- are women, and the offender is a male stranger (Myers, 1977).
- are women without a reputation for promiscuity (Newman, 1966).
- are not known to be homosexual (Newman, 1966).
- are not alcoholics or drug addicts (Williams, 1976).
- have no prior arrest record (Williams, 1976).
- can establish that they weren't engaged in misconduct themselves at the time of the crime (Miller, 1970; Neubauer, 1974; Williams, 1976).
- can prove that they didn't provoke the offender (Neubauer, 1974; Newman, 1966; Williams, 1976).
- can show that it wasn't a "private matter" between themselves and a relative, lover, friend, or acquaintance (McIntyre, 1968; Williams, 1976).

- and the offenders are not both black, and the incident is not viewed as "conforming to neighborhood subcultural norms" (McIntyre, 1968; Miller, 1970; Myers and Hagan, 1979; Newman, 1966).

Convictions

Judges or juries are more likely to find defendants guilty if the victims:

- are employed in a high-status job (Myers, 1977).
- are perceived as being young and helpless (Myers, 1977).
- appear "reputable," with no prior arrest record (Kalven and Zeisel, 1966; Newman, 1966).
- had no prior illegal relationship with the defendant (Newman, 1966).
- in no way are thought to have provoked the offender (Kalven and Zeisel, 1966; Newman, 1966; Wolfgang, 1958).
- are white, and the defendants are black (Allredge, 1942; Bensing and Schroeder, 1960; Garfinkle, 1949; Johnson, 1941).
- and the offenders are not both black and are not viewed as acting "in conformity to subcultural norms" (McIntyre, 1968; Miller, 1970; Myers and Hagan, 1979; Newman, 1966).

Punishments

Judges will hand down stiffer sentences to defendants if the victims:

- are employed in a high-status occupation (Myers, 1977; Farrell and Swigert, 1986).
- did not know the offender (Myers, 1977).
- were injured and didn't provoke the attack (Dawson, 1969; Neubauer, 1974).
- are white and the offenders are black (Green, 1964; Southern Regional Council, 1969; Wolfgang and Riedel, 1973; Paternoster, 1984).
- are females killed by either males or females (Farrell and Swigert, 1986).

The way that police and prosecutors respond to murders provides some of the clearest examples of differential handling. When an "important" victim is murdered, the police department comes under tremendous pressure from the media, elected officials, and constituencies within the general public to solve the crime. To give an illustration, a highly publicized robbery and murder of a foreign visitor is so threatening to the multibillion-dollar tourist trade that local business interests and the chamber of commerce will generate tremendous pressure to apprehend whoever is preying upon tourists (see Rohter, 1993b; Boyle, 1994). But when an "ordinary" or even "expendable" person is slain, the overworked and understaffed homicide squad detectives carry out a perfunctory, routine investigation. For example, the fatal shooting of a street-level drug dealer will attract little public notice or official concern (see Simon, 1991). But when a police officer is slain in the line of duty, homicide detectives work day and night, following up every possible lead, in order to catch the killer and send out the message that the death of an officer will not go unpunished. To illustrate how seriously the police take the killing of "one of their own," consider this comparison: In 1992, police forces across the country were able to solve 65 percent of all murders; that same year, they managed to solve 57 out of 62, or 91 percent, of the killings of fellow officers in the line of duty (*Uniform Crime Reports* Section, 1993).

5   Special Kinds of Victims: Problems and Solutions

- **Missing Children**
  The Controversy over Estimates of the Incidence and Seriousness of the Problem ▪ Hunting for Children Who Have Vanished ▪ Victimization Prevention Measures

- **Physically and Sexually Abused Children**
  The Rediscovery of the Problem of Child Abuse ▪ Controversies about Child Abuse ▪ The Controversy over Estimates of the Incidence, Prevalence, and Seriousness of Child Abuse ▪ The Controversy Surrounding Parent-Child Incest ▪ The Furor over Recalling Repressed Memories of Childhood Sexual Abuse ▪ Strange Allegations of Ritualistic Abuse by Satanic Cults ▪ Abused Children and Legal Proceedings ▪ Proactive vs. Reactive Strategies

- **More Casualties of Domestic Violence**
  The Rediscovery of the Problem of Wife Beating ▪ From a Personal Tragedy to a Social Problem ▪ Estimating the Incidence, Prevalence, and Seriousness of Spouse Abuse ▪ Providing Tangible Aid to Victims Who Feel Trapped ▪ Battered Women and the Criminal Justice System: Violence Is Violence—or Is It? ▪ Preventing Battering ▪ The Rediscovery of Other Victims of Batterings ▪ Other Casualties of Intrafamily Violence

- **Victims of Sexual Assault**
  The Rediscovery of the Plight of Rape Victims ▪ "Real Rapes" and "Date Rapes" ▪ The Consequences of Being Sexually Assaulted ▪ Estimating the Incidence, Prevalence, and Seriousness of Rape ▪ How the Criminal Justice System Handles Rape Victims ▪ Crisis Centers: Providing Emergency Assistance ▪ The Problem of Unwanted Publicity and Negative Media Portrayal ▪ Reducing the Threat of Rape ▪ The Rediscovery of More Rape Victims

This chapter examines the plight of missing children, youngsters who are physically and sexually abused, elderly people who are victimized in various ways, battered women, other victims of family violence, and sexual assault victims. The previous chapter looked at the way the criminal justice system handled "ordinary" victims (those harmed by street crimes like robberies, assaults, burglaries, and car thefts). This chapter analyzes the special vulnerabilities and needs of particular groups of victims and explores how the criminal justice system accords them (or is supposed to grant them) special considerations and extrasensitive treatment in some jurisdictions.

In order to overcome their special difficulties, members of these groups have established self-help organizations to fight for policies they perceive to be in their own best interests. Some highly visible movements include the child search movement (to locate missing children); the children's rights movement; the senior citizen's movement to protect the victims of elder abuse; the antirape movement; the battered women's movement; the movement to curb drunk driving; and the civil rights movement against hate groups who commit bias crimes.

One theme that arises over and over again in the examination of the special problems of these particular groups is the ongoing conflict between maximalist alarmists and minimalist skeptics. Maximalists argue that a huge problem has been festering and is now reaching epidemic proportions. They predict dire consequences unless drastic steps are taken. Their outlook can be characterized as "maximalist" because they assume the worst and try to mobilize people and resources to combat this coming crisis. Alarming claims about a dangerous situation that is spiraling out of hand predictably provoke an opposing point of view, which can be termed the "minimalist" outlook. Skeptics who take this stance consider the maximalists' estimates to be unfounded, inflated, and self-serving. (Usually, these skeptics are academic researchers or reporters.) The assessment by minimalists that massive expenditures and emergency measures are not warranted sparks a bitter controversy with maximalists, reflected in their acrimonious debates at conferences and hearings, strident attacks in interviews and articles, and angry exchanges in letters to the editors of newspapers and magazines. The statistics that have generated the most controversy concern the fate of missing children, the real extent of child abuse, the actual prevalence of incest and child molestation, and the frequency of date rape on college campuses.

MISSING CHILDREN

A six-year-old boy wanders over to the toy counter in a department store. A few minutes later his mother realizes he has disappeared. The police launch an intensive search. Two weeks later and one hundred miles away, a fisherman discovers the boy's severed head. The boy's father sets up a group to help locate missing children and becomes a leading figure in the child-find movement. But his son's murder is never solved. (Spitzer, 1986)

A child molester lures a seven-year-old boy into a car by offering him a lift home. He pretends to call the boy's family to secure permission from the parents for the boy to stay with him overnight. Then he convinces the child that his parents don't want him back. For the next seven years the boy lives with this man, who exploits him sexually. He goes to school under a false name but is too scared of a beating to tell his teachers about his plight. But when the kidnapper brings home another young captive, he summons up the courage to go to the police. (Andrews, 1986)

A woman answers an ad in a newspaper for a baby-sitting job. On her first day at work, she runs off with the two-month-old baby girl she is supposed to be tending. The infant's mother calls the police, and with the help of an organization that searches for missing children, she gets the baby's picture aired on a television network news show. An acquaintance of the baby-sitter recognizes the kidnapped victim from the photo shown on TV and calls a hot line. The FBI is notified, follows leads to Florida, recovers the infant unharmed, and reunites her with her mother in Texas. (NCMEC, 1985)

A twelve-year-old girl and her two friends are enjoying a slumber party when they hear a knock on the bedroom door. The girl opens her door and a tall, bearded man wielding a large knife barges in. As her two friends giggle, thinking it is a practical joke, the intruder ties them all up and then carries the twelve-year-old off into the night. The kidnapping galvanizes a sleepy community into action. Waves of volunteers flock to a storefront command center. Thousands of people beg to be assigned some task, like answering telephones or circulating some of the 3 million posters with the victim's picture and a police artist's sketch of the suspect. Shopkeepers close down their stores, and workers give up their vacations to assist the search. A well-known actress donates a huge reward for information leading to an arrest or the safe return of the abducted child ("Kidnapping Summons City to Action," 1993). Two months later, the police arrest a suspect. A crowd gathers for a vigil outside the jail, chanting "Tell the truth and set your conscience free." Shortly afterward, the suspect—who was out on parole after spending fifteen of his last twenty years behind bars for kidnappings, assaults, and burglaries—confesses that he strangled the girl and leads police to her body. (Gross, 1993)

What has happened to children who have mysteriously disappeared? They have vanished, and all that remains are their smiling faces, cropped from snapshots taken in happier times, which now appear on posters, milk cartons, and envelopes containing utility bills. Their frantic, searching parents fear the worst—that they met with foul play and will never be seen or heard from again. Kidnapping embodies a parent's worst nightmare because a routine event in everyday life (like waiting on a corner for the school bus, or taking a ride on a bicycle) can become the starting point for an ordeal that ends in tragedy, when an innocent, helpless child is seized and carried off, never to be heard from again, or turns up dead.

Taking and holding a person against his or her will for some nefarious purpose was recognized hundreds of years ago as a serious crime under English common law. In state and federal statutes today, force is not a necessary element of the crime. The victim can be detained through trickery or manipulation (what is called "inveiglement"). Besides extorting a ransom from some third party, the kidnapper may intend to rob the prisoner (for example, force an adult to withdraw money from an automated teller machine), sexually assault the captive, keep and raise a very young child, or physically injure or even kill the hostage. If the captor makes a ransom demand or transports a captive across state lines, federal statutes are violated and the FBI can enter the manhunt.

At the start of the 1980s, amidst deep-seated concerns about the disintegration of family life, children who disappeared under mysterious circumstances were rediscovered by reporters, politicians, and crusading members of the victims movement. "Missing child" became a household term and a subject of intense concern, if not widespread panic. Sensationalized media coverage, dramatic portrayals in books and films, legislative action, and serious research soon followed. The highlights of this rediscovery process appear in Box 5.1.

The Controversy over Estimates of the Incidence and Seriousness of the Problem

Statistics about missing children measure some of the most heinous crimes imaginable. Yet the true dimensions of this threat were unknown during the 1980s, when the problem was rediscovered. No agency was authorized to keep records of missing child cases, in part because the grouping was not a legal category but rather a media invention that lumped together all situations in which parents did not know where their children were.

The standard source of data about crimes known to the police, the FBI's *Uniform Crime Report,* is of no use because kidnappings are mixed in with other crimes in Part II, under the headings "offenses against family and children" and "all other offenses." The respondents in the *National Crime Victimization Survey* are not asked about kidnappings of members of their households; in fact, the interviewers do not count any crimes committed against persons under twelve. So the only sources of estimates about the number of missing children presumed to be victims of foul play were derived from very limited studies of police files or from projections from surveys of relatively small samples. As a result, throughout the 1980s, a heated debate erupted between maximalist alarmists and minimalist skeptics over what had happened to all those youngsters whose whereabouts were not known to their parents.

BOX 5.1	Highlights of the Rediscovery of the Missing Children Problem

1932 The child of a famous aviator is kidnapped and killed. A man caught with some of the ransom money is executed. State and federal laws are strengthened.

1955 The National Child Safety Council is established as the first private and voluntary organization in the field.

1974 Congress passes the Juvenile Justice and Delinquency Prevention Act, which mandates that runaways be sheltered but not arrested and confined.

1977 California becomes the first of forty-two states to make violating a child custody agreement a felony.

1980 Congress amends the Juvenile Justice and Delinquency Prevention Act to permit the police to detain chronic runaways under court order to return home. Congress passes the Federal Parental Kidnapping Prevention Act, which prohibits state courts from modifying original custody decrees issued after divorces and establishes a locator service that tracks down "fugitive parents" by tracing social security numbers.

1981 A Senate subcommittee holds the first hearings on the problem of missing children.

Child safety groups form a Child Tragedies Coalition.

The mysterious disappearances of twenty-eight youngsters in Atlanta over a two-year period are solved when a young man is convicted of murder.

1982 Congress declares May 25 National Missing Children's Day and passes the Missing Children's Act, which grants searching parents new rights in their dealings with law enforcement agencies.

1983 A TV docudrama about the abduction and murder of a boy named Adam is

viewed by an estimated 55 million people (approximately one out of every four Americans).

1984 Congress passes the Missing Children's Assistance Act, which sets up a National Center for Missing and Exploited Children as a resource base and establishes an advisory board to guide, plan, and coordinate federal efforts.

1985 After a televised documentary, the president appeals to viewers to help find missing children; sixty photos are shown and three children are quickly recovered.

1986 The first annual National Conference on Missing and Exploited Children is held.

1987 A National Association of Missing Child Organizations is formed to share information and maintain professional standards.

A National Resource Facility is opened for public use.

A National Endowment for the Protection of Children is created to raise money for public education, professional training, and services.

1988 Congress amends the Missing Children's Assistance Act to allocate money for establishing and operating clearinghouses on the state level to coordinate local law enforcement, social services, and educational activities.

1990 Congress passes the National Child Search Assistance Act, which requires the police to immediately enter information about a disappearance into their computer networks.

1993 In response to the kidnap-murder of a twelve-year-old girl by a parolee, federal and state lawmakers pass "Three Strikes and You're Out" provisions to incarcerate repeat offenders for life.

Sources: Davidson, 1986; NCMEC, 1987; Howell, 1989; Aunapu et al., 1993.

Maximalists believed that kidnappings had mushroomed to epidemic proportions and that a complacent public needed to become aroused and mobilized. Assuming the worst about these disappearances, maximalist alarmists called for emergency measures to halt the surge in abductions by strangers. Child snatchers, they warned, were everywhere, no youngster was ever completely safe, and parents could never be too careful about taking precautions and restricting their children's activities. This outlook was best illustrated by the remark of a father of a murdered child who told a congressional hearing, "This country is littered with mutilated, decapitated, raped, and strangled children" (see Spitzer, 1986); and a Congressman who in 1981 offered "the most conservative estimate you will get anywhere"—50,000 children abducted by strangers a year (Best, 1989a).

Minimalist skeptics suspected the problem was blown all out of proportion by frantic parents who meant well but were unduly alarmed; by businesses that sought to profit from selling products and services to panicky parents; by journalists willing to sensationalize stories to attract larger audiences; by politicians looking for a surefire cause that would gain them publicity and votes; and by child search organizations seeking recognition, contributions, and funding. Minimalists charged that maximalists were using the broadest possible definitions to generate the largest possible numbers, such as counting suspected runaways and parental abductions (see Schneider, 1987). The minimizing tendency was best summarized by a child welfare advocate who claimed that inflated statistics were being circulated by "merchants of fear" and "proponents of hype and hysteria" who "have foisted on a concerned but gullible American public" what he termed "one of the most outrageous scare campaigns in modern American history" (Treanor, 1986).

By the middle of the 1980s, a striking disparity was evident between the numbers disseminated by maximalist and minimalist sources (see Best, 1989a; Forst and Blomquist, 1991; and Kappeler, Blumberg, and Potter, 1993). Several factors, having to do with police department policies, unclear definitions, and opposite assumptions in the absence of any clues, account for the sharply divergent estimates. For example, one disparity arises from police department practices in turning cases over to the FBI. Some departments are less inclined than others to call for outside assistance and federal intervention; consequently, the FBI does not investigate all the cases in which a stranger might have been involved. The definitions a police department uses in recording crimes can also affect the number of stranger-abduction cases made known to the public. For example, if a child is lured into a car, sexually molested, and then abandoned hours later, how should the incident be classified? Most law enforcement agencies would categorize the incident as a sexual assault for record-keeping purposes, thus inadvertently obscuring the fact that the child was abducted and held against his or her will, albeit for a relatively short period of time. But other agencies, keeping statistics for different purposes, might choose to count the incident as both an abduction and a molestation, since the perpetrator, if caught, could be prosecuted for both crimes.

Assumptions about unsolved cases colored the estimates as well. A missing child might represent a tragic case of stranger-abduction. But he or she is much more likely to be a runaway who will eventually return home voluntarily. (Such children may be victims in a different sense—not of abduction but of sexual or physical abuse. Further, while they are on the run, they are vulnerable to exploitation and criminal victimization.) Some missing children are not runaways, but "throwaways," expelled from their homes by angry or neglectful parents. Most of the children grabbed by adults were not snatched by strangers but taken by a parent disregarding court orders after a bitter custody battle following a divorce or separation. (Parental abductions, of course, can easily be ruled out in many disappearances.) As for all the remaining cases, especially those involving children younger than twelve, assumptions must be made. Maximalists assume that these children were victims of foul play.

Adherents of the maximalist position must be overestimating the real scope of the "stranger-danger" threat to young people, while those of the minimalist position are underestimating it. Their debate demonstrates how important statistics are in bringing social problems to the attention of the media, the public, and policymakers. Many worthy causes compete for media coverage, public concern, and governmental action. The first few crusaders to alert people to the danger of kidnappings by strangers issued press releases with shockingly huge estimates that generated widespread fears. They were the only experts on the subject, since no officials or agencies were charged with keeping track of mysterious disappearances of children across the country. But some journalists and social scientists became skeptical of these statistical projections. Soon, members of the media adopted these misleadingly low official estimates with the same uncritical enthusiasm with which they had earlier accepted the activists' overestimates. Under a cloud of suspicion, representatives of the emerging child-find movement responded in two ways. First, some spokespersons argued that accurate tallies were not needed—one missing child was one too many. Second, they began to redefine the kidnapping problem in broader terms, including parental abductions stemming from custody disputes, attempted abductions that failed, and short-term abductions for the purpose of sexual molestation. Governmental researchers and policymaking task forces have adopted this expanded definition. This capsule history of the controversy confirms these suspicions: Large numbers call attention to neglected social problems more readily than small numbers; figures from official sources carry greater weight than unofficial estimates; and large official estimates are the best of all to galvanize public support and governmental action (Best, 1988; 1989a).

In an effort to try to resolve the maximalist-minimalist debate, the Department of Justice, as mandated by the 1984 Missing Children Act, funded a five-year National Incidence Study of Missing, Abducted, Runaway, and Throwaway Children (NISMART). The data was collected by conducting a telephone survey of nearly 35,000 randomly selected households, by analyzing FBI homicide records and the case files of nonfamily abductions in eighty-three law enforcement agencies in twenty-one randomly selected counties across the nation, and by interviewing runaways and professionals who dealt with them in social service agencies and juvenile facilities. The researchers clarified definitions, consulted with experts, and generated numbers that led them to the conclusion that the term "missing children" caused endless confusion by mixing together five distinct problems that had very different victims, causes, dynamics, and remedies. The worst case scenarios that fit the stereotype of a kidnapping thankfully turned out to be rare occurrences. Family abduction was found to be a much bigger problem than policymakers realized. The number of missing children who turned out to be runaways was about the same in 1988 as it had been in 1975, but up to 20 percent of these homeless youngsters had actually been "thrown out." Finally, the researchers discovered a formerly ill-defined category of apparently missing children who got lost, or were injured and couldn't reach their parents, or failed to clearly tell their caretakers where they were going and when they would return home (Finkelhor, Hotaling, and Sedlak, 1990). The estimated numbers of missing children who turned out to be crime victims appear in Box 5.2.

BOX 5.2   How Often Are Children Kidnapped, and What Happens to Them?

The NISMART study of patterns observed across the nation in 1988 yielded the following estimates of the number of different kinds of victim–offender relationships and the characteristics of abducted children:

200–300 Kidnappings of Children by Adults per Year
(These cases fit the stereotype of a kidnapping: The youngster is detained overnight or longer and/or is transported fifty miles or more. The abductor intends to permanently keep the child, extort a ransom, or commit some other crime, including murder. In most of these extremely serious offenses, the kidnapper is not a complete stranger, but is, instead, a disgruntled former boyfriend of the child's mother, a friend of the family, a neighbor, a baby-sitter, or someone else known by the victim.)

Between 1976 and 1987, as few as about 50 children and as many as around 150 were murdered by kidnappers each year. There was no discernible trend over the twelve-year period. The victims of these kidnappings that ended in homicides tended to be older (ages fourteen to seventeen, female, and from racial minority groups. Overall, teenagers' chances of being kidnapped and murdered during this period were calculated to be seven out of every million; the chances for younger children were one out of a million, per year.

3,200–4,600 Short-Term Abductions by a Nonfamily Member per Year
(These cases meet all the legal elements of kidnapping: a crime by an acquaintance or by a complete stranger who takes the child by force or by deceit into a building, vehicle, or some other

(continued on next page)

BOX 5.2   *continued*

place, and/or detains the child for more than an hour perhaps to commit a sexual assault or molestation.)

About half the victims were twelve years old, or older, and three-quarters were girls. In more than two-thirds of the cases, the youngsters were abducted for sexual purposes. The majority of incidents began in a street setting, involved the use of force, often the brandishing of a weapon, and the ordeal lasted less than a whole day. Black and Hispanic children were disproportionately victimized in these ways.

About 11,500 attempted abductions by strangers per year were reported by caretakers to survey interviewers. In most of these attempts, a passing motorist tried to lure a child into a car, without the use of coercion and without inflicting physical injuries. Most attempts, and probably a substantial number of completed abductions for the purpose of sexual assault, were not reported to the police, generally because the children were ashamed or intimidated.

163,000 Long-Term Abductions by a Family Member per Year

(In these cases a family member, usually a parent, takes the child in violation of a family court decree and tries to conceal the taking and/or the whereabouts of the child and/or moves the child to another state and/or intends to keep the child permanently or alter the custodial arrangements.)

These abductions were most likely to occur during January and August, when school vacations and parental visits end. Most incidents lasted a few days, up to a week. In about 60 percent of these unlawful detentions, the parent with custody rights did not inform the police; lawyers were contacted in 50 percent of the cases. In about 50 percent of these power struggles, the caretaking parent knew where the child was being held but was unable to recover the child from the lawbreaking ex-partner (Finkelhor, Hotaling, and Sedlak, 1990; Forst and Blomquist, 1991).

Patterns from Police Files

An intensive study of police department records for 1984 in Houston, Texas, and Jacksonville, Florida, provided tentative answers to several key questions: What kinds of children are typically the targets of nonfamily abductions? Are they lured or captured by force? When and where are they approached, and where are they taken? How long are they held? What additional crimes are committed against them?

According to the researchers who analyzed more than 200 cases reported to the police in those two cities that year, girls are targeted much more often (in 88 percent of the cases) than boys, although many young males may not tell their parents about the abduction and subsequent molestation, and their parents may not report the incidents to the police. The typical captive was between eleven and fourteen years old. A little more than half (57 percent) of the youngsters were forced to go with their captors (they were intimidated by the sight of a weapon or were physically overpowered), while the remainder were lured or tricked into accompanying their abductors. Most of the victims were taken to secluded spots, either indoors (empty apartments, garages) or outdoors (woods, fields), but a sizable number were kept in a vehicle. Nearly all (98 percent) were released within twenty-four hours. In the majority of the cases (72 percent), the abductor molested the child; in most of the remaining cases (22 percent), the child escaped unharmed from an attempted kidnapping; 4 percent were simply held and then let go; and, tragically, 2 percent were murdered after being sexually assaulted.

The researchers discovered that only 15 percent of the cases involving an abduction were classified by the police as primarily a kidnapping. Most of the cases were filed under the heading of sexual assault and were so categorized on the FBI's *Uniform Crime Report* form (NCMEC, 1986).

Hunting for Children Who Have Vanished

Kidnapping symbolizes the ultimate clash between good and evil: innocent and defenseless little victims in the clutches of ruthless adults. No other group of crime victims has so captured the attention and hearts of the public. Never before has the citizenry's involvement been solicited on such a grand scale as in the campaign to prevent abductions and recover stolen children. Rarely have victims' rights organizations (the child-find groups in the child-search movement) been so instrumental in the drafting of new laws and the reforming of criminal justice procedures. Even though the platitude "children are our most precious resource" was frequently voiced, at the start of the 1980s, there were only a few organizations geared to help locate missing children, staffed by a handful of people with an annual budget of less than $30,000. By the early 1990s, a federally sponsored national center operated a network linking thirty federal agencies, forty-three state clearinghouses, and more than sixty private and nonprofit organizations (Gill, 1989; Aunapu et al., 1993).

Before the advent of child-search organizations, parents were totally dependent on the police to locate and recover their missing children. But the working relationships between parents frantically searching for their missing children and the law enforcement agencies that were supposed to be their allies were frequently strained. The issues that divided them were delays in police response, restricted access to law enforcement computer files, and a reluctance by local authorities to call for nationwide assistance.

When distraught parents turned to missing persons bureaus for help, they expected the police to spring into action by issuing an all-points bulletin describing the child who had disappeared and by launching an intensive search. But many departments followed procedures that dictated that a youngster must have been missing for twenty-four, forty-eight, or even seventy-two hours before an official investigation could be initiated. These waiting periods were based on experiences that indicated the overwhelming majority of cases were not life threatening and would "solve themselves"—the missing youths would turn out to be runaways who would soon return home on their own. But frantic parents condemned such arbitrary delays as endangering the lives of their children and enabling abductors to escape from the local area to other jurisdictions where any call for a manhunt would receive an even lower priority, and interest in the case would be difficult to sustain. The crux of the problem for parents was that the burden of proof fell on them to somehow demonstrate that their children were victims of foul play. In 1990, in response to parental appeals for reform, Congress passed the National Child Search Assistance Act, which prohibited law enforcement agencies from imposing waiting periods before entering the child's description into computer networks linking the FBI's National Crime Information Center, police departments, and the clearinghouses in forty-three states that help to locate and recover missing children (Girdner and Hoff, 1994).

In many states, police officers are now required to take in-service training courses on how to investigate missing children cases and how to interact with their families.

Victimization Prevention Measures

As parents and their children have become more conscious of "stranger-danger," they have incorporated preventive steps into their daily routines in a myriad of ways. In many families and schools, child safety training receives as high a priority as fire safety and traffic safety. Youngsters are instructed by police officers, teachers, and parents, as well as through comic book characters, board games, records, and books, "what to do if. . . ." The training that the children receive in recognizing and rejecting "child lures"—the deceitful tricks abductors use to entice them into their clutches—far exceeds the old warning of "Don't accept candy from strangers." They are taught to distinguish between "good touches" and "bad touches," when to question what adult authority figures tell them to do, and to beware of certain situations and behaviors, as well as specific kinds of persons. The shadow cast by the ominous stranger has eclipsed that cast by the "bomb"— nuclear annihilation—that haunted the imaginations of previous generations (Wooden, 1984).

Victimization prevention strategies take many other forms. Security is incorporated into architectural planning: Playgrounds, schoolyards, and large stores are designed to limit access and escape routes. At the height of the near panic that gripped many families during the mid-1980s, so many new products flooded the market that department stores set up child safety displays. Today, high-tech outlets sell homing devices that trigger alarms when children stray—or are taken—beyond a certain range. Dentists offer to bond microchips containing identifying information to children's teeth. Computer firms can be hired to generate "video portraits" that project how a missing child might look after several years. Shopping centers attract crowds by offering fingerprinting for infants and toddlers.

Understandably, child safety campaigns have provoked a backlash. Some skeptics are concerned about the costs and questionable value of products and services. They take a dim view of commercial outfits that charge for information, devices, and forms of assistance that can be obtained for free from nonprofit child-find organizations or the police. They are suspicious of the motives of the many corporations that have made tax-deductible contributions to child-search projects; amidst the hoopla over short-lived, staged events they get free publicity and cultivate good public relations. Civil libertarians fear that the intense concern about stranger-danger will undermine citizens' reluctance to allow government bureaucracies to maintain fingerprints and photographs on file, which could be another step toward a "Big Brother" police state. Other critics worry about the potential social and psychological costs of certain victimization prevention measures. They wonder whether an anxious, suspicious, and dependent generation will be cheated out of a carefree childhood and will grow up obsessed by security considerations and burdened by adult responsibilities prematurely. And, of course, social scientists properly question whether the child safety measures really work as intended, or fail to be effective, or, worse yet, have unanticipated negative side effects (see Karlen et al., 1985; Andrews, 1986; Gill, 1987, 1989; and Adler, 1994).

PHYSICALLY AND SEXUALLY ABUSED CHILDREN

The Rediscovery of the Problem of Child Abuse

For centuries, parents were permitted to beat their children in the name of imposing discipline. Religious and legal traditions legitimized parental violence toward youngsters as a necessary, even essential technique of child rearing (unless permanent injury or death resulted; then the problem was labeled "cruelty to children").

The "House of Refuge" movement of the early 1800s was the first to intervene in behalf of beaten and neglected children; its priority was to prevent such children from growing up to be delinquents. Young victims were removed from their homes and hangouts and placed in controlled environments with youthful vagrants and lawbreakers. In the late 1800s, the Society for the Prevention of Cruelty to Animals undertook responsibility for rescuing children from heartless employers and uncaring foster parents. Its offshoot, the Society for the Prevention of Cruelty to Children, used the police powers it was granted to place victimized poor children from big-city slums in institutions. During the early 1900s, the "child savers" movement, organized to set up separate courts and reform schools for juveniles, was motivated by the same fear: that neglect and abuse caused delinquency and criminality later in life (Pfohl, 1984). (This concern about abused children growing up to become abusers and victimizers themselves continues to inspire a great deal of theorizing and research; see, for example, Gray, 1986; Wyatt and Powell, 1988; Barringer, 1989; and Widom, 1989.)

It was not until the early 1960s that pediatric radiologists (doctors who study X rays of childhood injuries) sparked the rediscovery of physical abuse. Apparently, other physicians were inhibited from exposing the consequences of severe beatings by their face-to-face dealings with brutal parents, by the norm of confidentiality between doctors and patients, and by their reluctance to get embroiled in the criminal justice process. Pediatric radiologists, on the other hand, had few direct contacts with parents and desired greater recognition within the medical profession. Therefore, they were willing to set into motion the process of labeling abuse as a deviant behavior, and encouraging legislation against it, by alerting colleagues and the public to the "battered child syndrome" (Pfohl, 1984). The syndrome was identified as a cyclical pattern, in which abuse was perpetrated by parents who had been beaten themselves as children. In the typical case, the victim was younger than three years old and suffered traumatic injuries to the head and to long bones; and the parents claimed that the wounds were caused by an accident and not a beating. News media coverage of "horror stories" (describing unusual injuries or dramatic circumstances that evoke strong condemnations) helped to galvanize a social movement. Initially, journalists focused on battering, but they soon broadened their inquiries to include cases of gross neglect, emotional cruelty, and eventually sexual exploitation and incest. Coverage of these human interest stories fit the organizational needs not only of the news media to attract readers and viewers but also of professional and occupational groups and private and nonprofit agencies seeking more recognition for their missions and secure funding (Johnson, 1989).

Social workers, women's organizations, public health associations, and law enforcement groups joined doctors to help raise public consciousness about the suspected dimensions of the problem. Between 1962 and 1966, laws forbidding parents from abusing their children were passed in all fifty states (Pfohl, 1984). As requirements for reporting cases of apparent abuse to child welfare and protection agencies were imposed on doctors, teachers, and others throughout the country, a debate broke out—and still rages today—over whether such parents are "sick" and need "treatment" (the medical model) or are "criminals" who deserve punishment (the law enforcement model).

In 1974, Congress passed the Child Abuse Prevention and Treatment Act, amending it in 1978. In the act, *neglect* was defined as abandonment, refusal to provide needed personal or medical care, inadequate supervision, tolerance of chronic truancy, and denial of nurturing and affection. *Abuse* was defined as physical assault (punching, scalding, suffocating), extended confinement, and sexual exploitation (use for pornographic purposes, impairment of morals, prostitution, incest, fondling, sodomy, intercourse, and statutory rape) (Irwin, 1980). During the 1980s, the focus of attention of an indignant public, researchers, and practitioners shifted from physical maltreatment to sexual abuse (Milner, 1991). In 1989, the United Nations amended earlier international declarations dating back to 1924 and 1959 and adopted "The Convention on the Rights of the Child." The member states that ratified the convention pledged to take all appropriate legislative, administrative, social, and educational measures to protect youngsters less than eighteen from all forms of physical and mental violence, injury, or abuse. The convention promised that governments would promote the physical and psychological recovery and social reintegration of victimized children, and would enable them to be heard at any judicial and administrative proceedings affecting their welfare (NOVA, 1991).

The problem of child abuse always has been of great concern to victimologists. Victimologists want to know what percentages of cases go unreported and unattended, how the abused youngsters are handled by the authorities, and whether treatments are effective. To anticipate and thereby prevent future cases of abuse, victimologists want to discover the risk factors that indicate which children face the gravest dangers. For example, an inquiry carried out by the National Center on Child Abuse and Neglect verified the suspicion that children with physical, emotional, and mental disabilities are maltreated by their primary caretakers, generally their mothers, at an unusually high rate. Disabled children are physically abused at twice the rate of other youngsters, sexually abused nearly twice as often, and emotionally neglected almost three times as frequently (Associated Press, 1993b). Research into the backgrounds of physically abused children indicates that beatings are more likely to occur in dysfunctional families racked by a combination of symptoms of marital discord: where the two parents fight viciously (partner abuse); one or both of the parents are currently substance abusers (drug takers and/or alcoholics); the mother was raised by a substance-abusing parent; and the mother was often beaten while she was growing up (Salzinger, Feldman, and Hammer, 1991).

It is generally believed that children from poverty-stricken families face the greatest risk of being neglected and/or physically and/or sexually abused (DeConcini, 1989). It is possible, however, that because the problems of poor families are more likely to come to the attention of social welfare agencies and the police, the concentration of abuse cases in lower socioeconomic neighborhoods indicated by official statistics and agency files might be misleading. Yet, in a study of how police officers exercised their discretion about whether to report suspected cases of child abuse, researchers discovered that officers were more likely to overlook signs of possible abuse in low-income minority families because of prejudicial beliefs that violence and promiscuity are "normal" among the poor and that minority youths need sterner discipline (Willis and Wells, 1988).

The consequences of being abused also concern victimologists. Studies of sexually abused youngsters indicate that they may suffer complicated, far-reaching, and long-lasting problems. A review of the literature written by therapists turned up seven groupings of adverse effects. Affective problems were evidenced by guilt, shame, anxiety, fear, depression, anger, low self-esteem, concerns about secrecy, feelings of helplessness, and an inordinate need to please others. Physical repercussions included genital injuries, unwanted pregnancies, venereal diseases, loss of appetite, sleep disruptions, and bed-wetting. Cognitive effects took the form of shortened attention spans and troubles concentrating. Behavioral symptoms materialized as hostile-aggressive acting out, tantrums, drug taking, delinquency, withdrawal, and repetitions of the abusive relationship. Self-destructive impulses were manifested as suicidal thoughts and attempts and self-mutilations. Psychopathological repercussions took the form of neuroses, character disorders, psychotic thought patterns, and multiple personalities. Finally, sexual abuse created sexual disorders in the form of age-inappropriate sexual knowledge, talk, and activities. Since sexual abuse can range from a single molestation to an ongoing incestuous relationship, each youngster will exhibit a different set of symptoms, and no specific problem or repertoire of behaviors definitively and conclusively indicates that a child has been abused (Yapko and Powell, 1988; Whitcomb, 1992).

Controversies about Child Abuse

Most people harshly condemn the mistreatment of children and feel that the perpetrators of serious abuse or neglect should be severely punished. Yet, despite this overarching consensus, public opinion is sharply divided over a number of issues relating to physical and sexual abuse (see Gardner, 1994; de Koster and Swisher, 1994).

The first surrounds victimization statistics. Some people believe that the tremendous increase in the number of reported cases of child maltreatment indicate that the authorities are finally beginning to confront an epidemic of hidden criminality directed against helpless children that adults were always afraid to acknowledge. But others believe that an avalanche of false accusations is vastly inflating the official figures kept by agencies, yielding a mistaken impression that children are being abused like never before.

A second set of controversies revolves around the question of credibility. Some argue that children don't lie about such serious matters as sexual molestation, and the presumption should be that a child's testimony is as credible as an adult's. Others contend that many allegations by young people are outright fabrications, complete delusions, or serious distortions and exaggerations of the truth, often the result of adult influence, suggestions, and coaching. This controversy over credibility takes on particular bitterness in three contexts: when allegations of sexual abuse arise in the midst of custody battles between parents; when adults claim they can now recall long-suppressed memories of childhood molestations; and when charges are made about cults abusing youngsters during religious rituals.

A third set of disputes arises over the way the fact-finding and truth-seeking process is carried out. Some argue that brutal abusers and cunning pedophiles are getting away with their crimes to such a degree that the criminal justice process must adopt dramatically different procedures to handle child witnesses. Others charge that these reforms are going too far and are trampling the constitutional rights of the adults to effectively defend themselves in court. Although most allegations might be true, all charges are surely not true, so an unacceptably large number of innocent people are being falsely accused and, worse yet, mistakenly convicted, which is a terrible miscarriage of justice (Gardner, 1990; Feher, 1992).

The Controversy over Estimates of the Incidence, Prevalence, and Seriousness of Child Abuse

Data about the yearly incidence and lifetime prevalence of child maltreatment cannot be found in the usual statistical sources, the FBI's *UCR* and the BJS's *NCVS*. Murder is the only crime category in the *UCR* for which the age of the victim is reported, but not all homicides against youngsters are carried out by abusive parents or other caretakers. The *NCVS* keeps track of the age of victims, but it does not ask respondents about any illegal acts committed against persons younger than twelve. Therefore, two other sources must be tapped: the National Incidence Study (NIS) sponsored by the National Center on Child Abuse and Neglect, a division of the U.S. Department of Health and Human Services; and the annual reports of the American Humane Association (AHA)(NCCAN, 1978).

The NIS survey has been carried out twice, in 1980 and again in 1986. Researchers contacted child protective service agencies, schools, hospitals, police departments, and courts in a randomly selected number of counties in various states. The working definition of "child maltreatment" on the questionnaire was: A situation where, through purposive acts or marked inattention to the child's basic needs, behavior of a parent (or substitute caretaker) caused foreseeable and avoidable injury or impairment to a child, or materially contributed to an unreasonable prolongation or worsening of an existing injury or impairment. Knowledgeable respondents were asked to provide data about all the standard categories of child maltreatment: child abuse (defined as physical assaults, sexual exploitation, and emotional abuse) and child neglect (defined as physical neglect, emotional neglect, and educational neglect [failure to send to school]). The 1980 survey projected an incidence rate of 10.5 cases of maltreatment (of all types) for every 1,000 children under eighteen in the country (which equals a little more than 1 percent of all youngsters per year). Of all the categories of abuse, physical assault was the most common, and sexual abuse was the least common, with emotional abuse somewhere in between. The rates of abuse varied dramatically by income: In desperately poor families, the rate of maltreatment (of all kinds) was 27 of every 1,000 children under eighteen each year; in middle-class homes, the rate was only 3 children out of every 1,000 per year. (It is likely that much more maltreatment by middle-class parents is covered up or not reported than among the poor. But abuse and neglect does appear to be more of a problem in low-income households.) During the six years between surveys, the substantiation rate rose from 43 percent to 53 percent; in other words, a higher proportion of cases were deemed to be "validated" or worthy of official action in 1986 than in 1980 (Garbarino, 1989; Finkelhor, 1990).

The AHA comes out each year with a report called the National Study of Child Abuse and Neglect. It counts all cases reported to and accepted by official protective services agencies in about 80 percent of the states. The reports to agencies came from law enforcement (the police, probation departments), medical personnel (hospitals, doctors), and private citizens (friends, neighbors, relatives, even parents). The AHA data show an upward trend in the total number of cases of maltreatment known to the authorities (some of which eventually will be labeled as "unsubstantiated"). (See the graph in Figure 5.1, which shows the increased number of reported cases over the years since the data-gathering process began in 1976.) The AHA data also provide the basis for some profiles: The typical victim who sustained major physical injuries was a five-year-old white boy beaten by his own father; the typical victim of sexual maltreatment was a nine-year-old white girl molested by her own father (Garbarino, 1989).

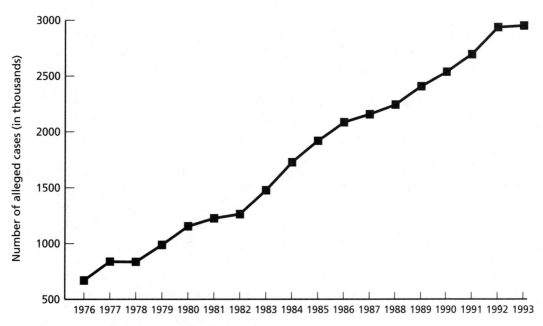

FIGURE 5.1   Trends in Reports of Child Abuse

Notes: Numbers are in thousands. Includes cases of physical and sexual abuse, or neglect, later deemed to be "unfounded."

Source: Information supplied by states to the American Humane Association and compiled by the National Committee for the Prevention of Child Abuse (NCPCA, 1993).

An Epidemic of Abuse or Just a Deluge of Reports? Experts disagree over the answers to two questions: How common is child abuse? and Is it rapidly increasing or remaining fairly constant? (Few observers would argue that rates actually are decreasing.)

As for how common child abuse might be, widely varying estimates appear in the literature. Two opposite points of view can be discerned; as before, they will be labeled the maximalist alarmist and minimalist skeptical perspectives. The maximalist point of view contends that the time has come to reject the reluctance of earlier generations to face the facts and to recognize the enormity of the developing crisis. Parents are abusing and neglecting their children in record numbers, and exploitive adolescents, pedophiles (child molesters), and other abusers are preying upon youngsters with impunity. From the minimalist standpoint, huge numbers of honestly mistaken and maliciously false allegations are mixed in with true disclosures, making the problem seem worse than it really is and fueling the impression that it is spiraling out of control.

Maximalist alarmists put forward strong arguments and marshall appalling statistics to support their case that child abuse is becoming all too common (see Finkelhor, 1990; Ceci and Bruck, 1993):

- Incidence rates based on statistics from official sources are really gross underestimates. A presumably huge but unknown number of episodes are never reported to the authorities—not by the victimized child, the other parent, another relative, or a neighbor. Cherished beliefs about family privacy and parental rights still overshadow concerns about the welfare and protection of little children.
- Many professionals fail to file the mandatory official reports when they suspect child abuse, preferring instead to pressure adults in troubled families to enter counseling, drug treatment, or other programs (Whitcomb, 1992).
- Many cases of reported abuse are mistakenly screened out and dismissed as "unproven" by child welfare agencies that do not have sufficient time, money, and staff to do the thorough investigations necessary to verify the charges. Just because a report is deemed to be "unsubstantiated" due to a lack of sufficient evidence to meet stringent legal standards of proof does not mean it is untrue; classifying a report as "unfounded" certainly does not mean it is completely baseless or intentionally, maliciously false.
- Violence against children (ranging from minor acts like throwing an object to severe extremes like using a knife or gun) seems to be the norm, occurring in more than 60 percent of all intact (two-parent) American families each year, according to the findings of a telephone survey of over 1,400 parents (Straus and Gelles, 1986).

- As for forcible rapes of little girls younger than twelve, the BJS estimated that about 17,000 sexual assaults took place during 1992, accounting for 16 percent of all reported rapes. Most of the assailants were nonstrangers, and 20 percent were the girls' fathers (Langan and Harlow, 1994).
- Of the approximately one million confirmed maltreatment cases in 1993, 47 percent of the children experienced physical neglect, 25 percent suffered physical abuse, and 15 percent endured sexual abuse. The remaining 13 percent were harmed by parental abandonment, emotional neglect, and other forms of maltreatment, according to reports compiled by the National Committee for the Prevention of Child Abuse (NCPCA) (Edmonds, 1994).
- About 1,300 children died from physical abuse or neglect during 1993. About 90 percent were age five or younger (Edmonds, 1994).
- As for physical abuse prevalence rates, as many as 30 percent of very poor children are beaten or neglected at least once, but often chronically, while they are growing up (Garbarino, 1989).
- As for sexual abuse prevalence rates, the percentage of girls who are molested during their childhood might be as high as 38 percent (if peer exploitation is included) (Russell, 1984), even 62 percent (counting male exhibitionism) (Wyatt, 1985); and of boys, 31 percent (see Peters, Wyatt, and Finkelhor, 1986). Between 4 percent and 16 percent of women in various surveys reported a childhood sexual experience with a relative, and about one girl in every 100 endured sexual contacts with her father or stepfather (Herman, 1981; Russell, 1986).
- As for trends, abuse rates increased 50 percent between 1985 (30 reports for every 1,000 children, nationally) and 1993 (45 reports per 1,000), according to NCPCA figures (Edmonds, 1994).

Minimalist skeptics make the following arguments to back up their contention that child abuse is much less widespread than the maximalist alarmists believe (see Besharov, 1990; Wexler, 1990; and Ceci and Bruck, 1993):

- The definition of child maltreatment has been expanding and diluting. Minor instances of bad parenting (like excessive spankings), which were justifiably overlooked in the past, are now being routinely reported. All physical discipline does not automatically qualify as child abuse. For example, in a 1977 ruling, the Supreme Court held that corporal punishment in school (within reasonable limits, by designated personnel, with parental approval) is not unconstitutional. Some researchers apply the term *abuse* to what the majority considers "normal discipline" involving corporal punishment, instead of reserving it for clearly inappropriate violence.

No state prohibits, and five states expressly permit, parents to use "reasonable corporal punishment" when disciplining their children (see Pagelow, 1989).

- Incidence rates based on official statistics are grossly inflated overestimates, since many reports are never finally "validated" conclusively. "Unfounded" reports (also called "unsubstantiated" or "not indicated" cases) are dismissed or closed when, after an investigation, there is insufficient legally admissible evidence on which to proceed. The glut of unfounded allegations is caused by the public's emotionally driven desire to "do something" about child abuse, coupled with the media's sensationalistic coverage of a formerly taboo topic, plus the "take no chances" overzealousness of professionals facing mandatory reporting requirements. The high unfounding rate in many child protection agencies is due in part to a lack of screening of calls to hotlines; a willingness to follow up anonymous tips, some of which may be deliberately and maliciously false; a proclivity to investigate and act when a child seems to be in imminent danger even if no actual harm has been inflicted; an acceptance of complaints from estranged spouses locked in custody battles; and a reliance on "behavioral indicators" as possible symptoms of abuse (in the absence of corroboration in the form of statements by the victim or eyewitnesses, or physical evidence) when actually these same behaviors (such as extreme shyness or unusual friendliness) can result from other situations (Besharov, 1987).
- As for incidence rates, fewer than 1 percent of all children in the United States were sexually abused in 1991 (Robin, 1991).
- As for prevalence rates, the percentage of females who suffer childhood sexual abuse could be as low as 7 percent (Siegel, Sorenson, Golding, Burnham, and Stein, 1987); for males, as low as 3 percent (see Peters, Wyatt, and Finkelhor, 1986).
- As for trends, researchers carrying out a National Family Violence Re-Survey noted a substantial decline in disclosures of "very severe violence" (biting, kicking, punching, beating up, using weapons like a knife or gun) by parents against their children in 1985 compared to 1975. The incidence rate dropped from 36 cases of "very severe violence" to 19 cases for every 1,000 families in the ten-year period, a nearly 50 percent drop (Straus and Gelles, 1986).

Some of the contradictory findings that fuel the debate between maximalist alarmists and minimalist skeptics are probably the result of methodological inconsistencies. For example, consider the confusion over whether the incidence of physical abuse is rising or falling. The impression that the frequency of physical abuse is going up is derived from the National Incidence Survey, which is based on reports by child protection professionals who used a broader definition of physical abuse and a narrower age range (infants and toddlers under the age of three were not counted). The impression that the rate of physical abuse is going down comes from the National Family Violence Re-Survey, which was directed only at parents and was conducted over the telephone, using a narrower definition of physical abuse, but applied to children of all ages, even infants. Therefore, it is likely that this set of contradictory findings is attributable to differences in methodology in how cases of abuse were discovered, how abuse was defined, and what age group was included and excluded from the sample. Similar measurement problems plague the other studies that yield opposing impressions (Mash and Wolfe, 1991).

When children are victimized, they are often too young and too intimidated to report their problems to the authorities. Therefore, in every state, a wide array of professionals (especially doctors, nurses, dentists, social workers, teachers, child-care workers, and law enforcement officers) now have the duty to report suspected cases of neglect and abuse to the proper authorities (and they face civil and criminal penalties if they are grossly negligent). In about twenty states, these mandatory reporting requirements are imposed on all adults, not just those who routinely come into contact with children as part of their occupation. And in all jurisdictions, any person can file a report, often anonymously, to a "tip" hotline. As a result of these mandatory reporting laws, as well as public awareness campaigns, the number of suspected cases of maltreatment—physical abuse, sexual abuse and exploitation, physical neglect, and emotional abuse—has soared. Of course, wrong decisions and mistakes happen; professionals and members of the public fail to report about children who need protection, or they file reports about children who are really not in danger. When failure to report occurs, children face grave dangers. When unwarranted reports are filed, agencies waste their limited resources, and the reputations of innocent parents are called into question.

The factors that contribute to child abuse are intensifying alcohol and drug problems among adults, a rising rate of teenage motherhood, and a growth in the number of poverty-stricken families ("Child Abuse Reports," 1988). The factors that decrease child maltreatment are upturns in the nation's economy, a trend toward marrying later in life and having fewer children, greater public awareness and condemnation of abuse, improved treatment and prevention programs, and more shelters for battered women and their offspring (Jennings, 1986; Straus and Gelles, 1986).

The Controversy Surrounding Parent-Child Incest

The incest taboo, which prevails in nearly all societies, forbids reproductive sexual relations between members of the same family (other than husband and wife). Incest was traditionally viewed as an activity that was so repulsive and heinous that it must be extremely rare, occurring perhaps in one family out of a million (Weinberg, 1955). But a careful review of the records maintained by child protection agencies in Boston from 1880 to 1930 revealed that even back then, in 10 percent of the violence-scarred troubled families, incest was occurring. Almost all the perpetrators were older male relatives, usually fathers, but also stepfathers, uncles, and older brothers; nearly all the victims were young girls (Gordon, 1988). Today, adult-child incest and, in particular, man-girl sexual contact has been rediscovered as a problem and is acknowledged to be more widespread than was ever thought or feared.

Now, two intense controversies have broken out over the real extent of parent-child incest, especially father-daughter sexual contacts. One controversy surrounds charges of child molestation that arise during divorce proceedings, or shortly afterward; and the other surrounds charges leveled by children—many years later—against their parents.

Accusations Made during Divorce Proceedings and Custody Battles

When allegations surface during the height of a divorce and tug-of-war over a child, two camps quickly emerge. People on one side argue that since there are no outsiders who witness violations of the incest taboo within the home, these "family secrets" usually are not exposed unless the parents break up. People on the other side contend that baseless allegations are being taken too seriously, and the resulting investigations ruin the lives of innocent parents, usually fathers.

In the mid-1980s, an organization was formed to provide support to adults who insisted they were falsely accused. They nicknamed their predicament as the "SAID syndrome": sexual allegations in divorce ("False Accusations," 1989). Their contention is that in most of these cases, a spiteful mother has pressured her daughter to echo a totally fictitious story about molestation that never occurred. Spreading this vicious lie is a vindictive ploy to discredit her former husband so that the court will issue an order to prevent the little girl's father from having further contact with her as she grows up (Fahn, 1991; Sheridan, 1994).

Charges are deemed to be "unsubstantiated" in these civil proceedings if the preponderance of the evidence is insufficient to affirmatively conclude that the girl was sexually molested by the defendant. The investigators for the child protective services agency who interview the girl and her parents to evaluate the family dynamics and home environment often feel a need to quickly resolve the matter to minimize the strain on all three parties. In many jurisdictions, they are too overburdened by huge caseloads to carry out a thorough investigation. The caseworkers may lack the assessment skills and interviewing techniques necessary to elicit crucial testimony. Faced with a father who vehemently denies everything, an intimidated and confused child torn by divided loyalties, and a lack of corroboration by witnesses, the investigators may have little choice but to write that it was unlikely that abuse occurred. However, their conclusion might be attributed more to the constraints of time, money, and training than to the merits of the case. An "unproved" charge is not necessarily "untrue" (Fahn, 1991).

Although feelings run high on both sides of this controversy, it is usually not an issue in divorce proceedings. In one study of over 6,000 cases in seven family court jurisdictions, allegations of sexual abuse by a parent were raised in from 2 percent to 10 percent of all disputes over custody and visitation rights (Nicholson, 1988).

The Furor over Recalling Repressed Memories of Childhood Sexual Abuse

A prosecutor cross-examining a man accused of molesting his three-year-old daughter suddenly becomes nauseous and dizzy. Fragmented memories flash before her. She begins to pound on the witness stand and screams, "These men just get away with it! The law never does anything!" After the judge jails her for two days for contempt, she enters therapy. She begins to remember being repeatedly molested by both her older brother and her father, although they deny it. To break the conspiracy of silence around childhood incest, she teams up with several other lawyers to draft new legislation to enable grown children to sue their molesters many years after the alleged incident occurred. (Mithers, 1990)

A thirty-four-year-old man accuses a highly respected Catholic cardinal of seducing him seventeen years earlier when he was a junior in high school and considering entering the priesthood. After launching a $10 million civil suit and publicly humiliating the clergyman (who denied everything), the man confesses that he cannot remember the specific details of the incident, loses faith in the reliability of his vague memories unearthed during hypnosis, and drops the charges. (Woodward, Annin, and Cohen, 1994)

Sigmund Freud, the founder of modern psychology, originally believed that many of his adult patients diagnosed as suffering from "hysteria" were desperately trying to repress memories of childhood sexual abuse. But after several years of psychoanalyzing his clients, he arrived at the conclusion that his patients' suspicions about being molested when they were very young were actually fantasies of incestuous desires, which were strictly taboo. Ever since then, the question of memory loss and recovery (amnesia and delayed recall) has been controversial, and grownups who claim they were molested as infants, toddlers, or very young children generally have not been believed. But starting in the 1980s, a memory-recovery movement emerged to help adult "survivors" (as they prefer to be called) of childhood incest and molestations. The movement is a coalition of victims, support groups, authors of self-help handbooks, and therapists who practice what might be called memory-retrieval techniques. How many thousands of clients have become convinced that they were previously sexually abused is difficult to estimate, since most do not make their suspicions public. With the encouragement of a national center for civilly prosecuting cases of child sexual abuse, about 7,000 lawsuits have been filed for monetary damages for pain and suffering brought about by incidents allegedly carried out years earlier. Some suits arise from claims that Cub Scouts were molested by their scoutmasters or altar boys fondled by priests, but in the typical case, the plaintiff is a woman who believes she was forced to endure incestuous acts perpetrated by her father. In about a quarter of these suits, both parents stand accused. Meanwhile, the older adults targeted by these suits have organized a foundation to defend themselves against these charges arising from what they brand as a "false memory syndrome." Some defendants are filing countersuits against their accusers for defamation of character. Some former patients who have recanted their exhumed "memories" are bringing malpractice suits against the therapists who persuaded them to view themselves as incest victims (Horn, 1993; Woodward, Annin, and Cohen, 1994).

Incest is always difficult to prosecute because the case usually lacks eyewitnesses or tangible evidence and, therefore, hinges entirely on the child's contentions against the adult's denials. When children grow older, it is usually too late to bring criminal charges. In most states, the statute of limitations for felonies runs out five years after the abuse is committed. Therefore, adults who now think they can recall memories of incest they had been trying to forget throughout their childhood are seeking to punish their tormentors in a different arena, civil court, via lawsuits for monetary damages. In twenty-one states, legislatures have recognized the possibility of "delayed discovery" and the legitimacy of the demands by incest victims for some avenue of redress. In these jurisdictions, the lawmakers lengthened the statute of limitations for filing civil lawsuits (which used to expire a few years after the youth reached the age of majority, generally at eighteen) to several years after the victim recalls the abuse (which could be as long as twenty or thirty years, even more, after the crime). This reform can be considered proplaintiff (provictim, but antidefendant) because the purpose of a statute of limitation is to protect the accused from having to fight allegations that are so old that he can't remember where he was and what he did, and witnesses he could call in his defense have moved away or died (Mithers, 1990).

The aftershocks of childhood incest can be devastating. Youngsters reportedly suffer from clinginess, loss of appetite, nightmares, bed-wetting, inappropriate sexual preoccupations and knowledge, and post-traumatic stress disorder. As they grow older, they are more prone than others to alcohol and drug abuse, reckless promiscuity, sexual dysfunctions, eating disorders, depression, guilt, self-hatred, self-mutilation, and suicidal impulses. However, there is no one symptom that crops up in a majority of sexually abused children. What's more, although these symptoms are consistent with abuse, they don't constitute legal proof that incest definitely occurred; other problems can bring about these same disorders (Kendall-Tackett, Williams, and Finkelhor, 1993). Successful patients progress through several stages, proceeding from initial denial, to suspicions, to realization (after considerable self-examination, probing, dredging up, and digging). Survivors come to recognize that many others have shared their fate. They join support groups and undergo therapy involving hypnosis, psychoactive drugs that serve as truth serums (such as sodium amytal), age regression, guided fantasy, automatic writing, suggestive and leading questions, group support, training tapes, and self-help manuals. When adults suspect unspeakable acts were foisted on them as children, these unsettling hunches are usually well-founded: They have been expending great mental energy to unconsciously block, blot out, or deny any recollection of their "terrible secrets," but a flood of these dammed-up memories eventually is unleashed (Bass and Davis, 1992; Terr, 1994).

A maximalist-minimalist type of controversy has broken out over this issue. The maximalist alarmist perspective held by many members of the recovery movement argues that the thousands of people now recalling childhood sexual abuse (including celebrities and other public figures) and the growing number of plaintiffs currently launching lawsuits represent just the tip of the iceberg. Maximalists believe that there are many more victims who will never become aware of the true source of their misery and anguish and will go through life blaming themselves for their emotional distress. Maximalists believe that false memories and baseless accusations are rare (Maltz and Holman, 1986; Bass and Davis, 1992; and Herman, 1992). Adherents of the minimalist skeptical perspective concede that until the 1980s, the sexual abuse of children, particularly by parents, went largely underreported and unprosecuted. But skeptics question whether a genuine medical breakthrough and a sound psychological diagnosis account for the current flood of accusations from individuals who claim they can now remember what they were trying so hard to forget. Skeptics suspect that certain intervention techniques do not unearth buried memories but actually invent "pseudomemories" that are delusions arising from the therapist's repetition of persuasive suggestions. As a result, certain practitioners who are so intent on unlocking repressed memories are misguiding some of their patients who are burdened by confusing emotions. Furthermore, minimalists charge that the maximalist alarmist definition of what behaviors constitute "violations," which are then characterized as "childhood sexual abuse," is much too inclusive (for example, unwanted kisses and hugs, or lack of respect for personal privacy). Similarly, too many of the vague symptoms on the lengthy checklists in self-help manuals are interpreted as likely signs of childhood sexual abuse—everything from ordinary physical ailments (headaches, stomach pains, dizziness) and common emotional problems (general malaise, alienation, low self-esteem, and phobias) to specific attitudes and behaviors (like feeling powerless or having difficulties in maintaining long-term relationships). As a result of these overly broad definitions and unwarranted assumptions about the origins of these symptoms, many vulnerable patients end up deceiving themselves; they come to believe that they can remember awful events that never really happened (Goldstein, 1993; Ofshe and Watters, 1993; Loftus and Ketcham, 1994; Pendergrast, 1994; and Yapko, 1994).

The debate over claims of therapeutic breakthroughs on the one hand vs. charges of planted suggestions and intense coaxing on the other has become acrimonious in the 1990s. The possibility of repressed memories is increasingly addressed in incest support groups, the recovery movement, confessions and revelations by well-known figures, tabloid exposés and talk-show conversations, made-for-television movies, magazine cover stories, popular psychology best sellers, family therapy journals, computer bulletin boards, and in the testimony of expert witnesses during civil lawsuits. Maximalists denounce skeptics who question the authenticity of some claims about vivid and precise memories as "enemies" of incest survivors. Minimalists dismiss the many testimonials about long-forgotten episodes of childhood sexual abuse as part of a modern-day "witch hunt," reflecting a jump-on-the-bandwagon phenomenon and a passing fad. Some psychologists and psychiatrists voice concerns that the furor surrounding symptom-producing traumatic memories is undermining the reputation of the entire profession of clinical therapy and causing genuine victims to be scoffed at as misguided. Some feminists support the memory-recovery movement as a sociopolitical force that could help put an end to the sexual exploitation of children and the subordination of women. They interpret the resistance as a backlash, just another tactic in the longstanding tradition of silencing and denying in which what women say about their oppression within the family is dismissed, belittled, and derided. But other feminists argue that the tendency of the incest survivor movement to blame so many problems that crop up in women's lives on some clearly identifiable villain who might have committed sexual offenses long ago has the counterproductive political consequence of shifting the focus of activism from seeking sweeping social changes to pursuing individual recovery and private retribution (see Darnton, 1991; Chira, 1993; Horn, 1993; and Tavris, 1993).

Strange Allegations of Ritualistic Abuse by Satanic Cults

A deputy sheriff is arrested and charged with sexually abusing his two daughters, now eighteen and twenty-two. Soon the charges emanating from the devoutly religious twenty-two-year-old (who has a history of making unsubstantiated complaints about sexual abuse) grow to alarming proportions: She claims to have attended 850 satanic rituals and to have watched 25 babies being sacrificed and then cannibalized. Eventually, both daughters, the mother, and then even the father, can visualize being present at these ceremonies where members of a sadistic devil-worshipping cult forced the women to perform sexual acts with goats and dogs. The father is grilled by his police department colleagues and quickly confesses but then hires a new lawyer and tries to withdraw his guilty plea. But it is too late, and he is convicted of six counts of child molestation. His older daughter demands that he receive the stiffest punishment possible, and the judge sentences him to twenty years in prison. (Wright, 1994)

One of the most peculiar debates between maximalists and minimalists has revolved around allegations of predatory acts carried out by members of satanic cults. Maximalist believers circulate frightening accounts about bizarre "wedding" ceremonies in which covens of witches and devil worshippers chant, wear costumes, take drugs, sacrifice animals, and even allegedly mutilate, torture, and murder newborn infants or children. In its most extreme form, the charge is that satanic cults engage in baby breeding and kidnapping for the purposes of human sacrifices and cannibalism. Maximalists promote fantastic claims that thousands disappear and are killed this way each year. People who come forward and say they survived ritual abuse (often young women making retrospective claims after undergoing psychotherapy) tell tales of being fondled, raped, sodomized, and exploited as objects in sexual games and pornographic films. Usually, the scenarios they recall involve groups of adults, sometimes including members of their families, abusing several very young children at the same time. Although the alleged victims complain that they encounter skepticism or even outright disbelief, some law enforcement agencies have taken their charges seriously. Newsletters, conferences, and training sessions have been organized for detectives, social workers, child welfare investigators, and therapists. Responding to a public outcry, several state legislatures have outlawed the "ritual mutilation" of innocents during religious initiation rites (see Bromley, 1991; Richardson, Best, and Bromley, 1991; Lanning, 1992; Shapiro et al., 1993; and Sinason, 1994).

Minimalist skeptics point out that the scare developed after bizarre charges about teachers practicing witchcraft at a California preschool generated one of the longest and costliest trials in American history (but no convictions). To investigate the deluge of claims, researchers sponsored by the National Center on Child Abuse and Neglect surveyed more than 11,000 psychiatrists, psychologists, clinical social workers, district attorneys, police executives, and social service agency administrators during 1993. The respondents told the survey interviewers that over 12,000 accusations of ritual abuse had been brought to their attention, but that not one case had been proven in which a well-organized, intergenerational ring of satan worshippers had sexually molested, tortured, or killed children in their homes or schools. All the study could unearth were some cases in which lone individuals or couples carried out abusive rituals or perpetrated crimes in the name of religion (Goleman, 1994). Minimalists attribute the panic about a secret network that preys upon the young to sensationalism by the tabloid press and irresponsible talk shows that operate in a climate of widespread and deep-seated anxieties concerning brainwashing techniques of mind control, cultlike religious groups, the breakdown of traditionally structured families, the redefinition of

male and female roles, youthful experimentation with sex and drugs, and a growing reliance on abortion and on day-care services for preschoolers. Fears about
well-financed, hidden cells of satanic infiltrators seem to have replaced communist
subversives as the forces of an evil underworld in the latest versions of conspiracy
theories. Although many people now claim to have witnessed, participated in, and
survived these devilish rituals, skeptics argue that their credibility is as questionable as that of the hundreds of people who swear they have been abducted by
aliens from outer space or who say they can remember events from their "past
lives" as different people, now dead (Bromley, 1991; Richardson, Best, and Bromley, 1991; Lanning, 1992).

Abused Children and Legal Proceedings

Intrafamily abuse cases traditionally were handled by child welfare protective services, family courts, and the juvenile justice system. As more and more cases were
brought to criminal court, a long-standing dilemma became acute: In trying to
protect the child from further abuse, the judicial proceedings could inadvertently
compound the youngster's trauma. It became clear that the adult-oriented criminal justice system was not designed to address the emotional, psychological, and
physical needs of victimized youth. As key witnesses for the prosecution, they often found the setting to be hostile and the proceedings to be confusing, meaningless, and frightening (Munson, 1989).

Taking the Best Interests of the Child into Account It is clear that a victimized child needs a "friend" or "advocate" who will provide support and advice
during legal proceedings, especially when the accused offender is a parent. The
law has recognized the inability of the government's prosecutor to play this role
and has created a special position, called the guardian *ad litem* (GAL), to look after
"the best interests of the child." The Child Abuse Prevention and Treatment Act
enacted by Congress in 1974 required that youngsters be provided with a guardian *ad litem* if their cases were heard in family court. The Victims of Child Abuse
Act of 1990 went further and recommended the provision of GALs to young
complainants when their alleged offenders were put on trial for more serious
charges in criminal court. By 1990, fifteen states had passed laws mandating the
appointment of GALs in criminal proceedings. Usually, these court-appointed
advocates are attorneys, but in some states they can be specially trained volunteers.
Their duties include accompanying the child to legal proceedings and helping the
child get needed social, mental health, and medical services. In criminal proceedings against an abuser, the GAL is supposed to serve as counselor, interpreter, de-
fender against system-induced trauma (insensitive handling), monitor, coordinator, advocate (of rights to privacy, protection from harassment), and spokesperson
(about wishes, fears, and needs). In some states, guardians *ad litem* assist the child

in preparing a victim–impact statement and can submit their own recommendations to the court about what would be best for the child's welfare (Whitcomb, 1992).

Handling Charges of Abuse The creation of the role of guardian *ad litem* has dramatized the importance of a much larger question: What are the victim's best interests? When victims are too young to be capable of defining for themselves what they consider to be in their best interests, it is up to guardians *ad litem* to advocate in their behalf. But what are the options, opportunities, perils, and pitfalls of various courses of action?

Two official responses are possible in cases of physical or sexual abuse. One is to handle parental wrongdoers as subjects for treatment and rehabilitation, viewing their acts as possibly caused by psychological disturbances. The other is to react to the incident as a violation of law and turn the case over to the criminal justice system. These two alternatives reflect opposing philosophies. Mental health professionals like psychiatrists, psychologists, counselors, and social workers tend to see criminal proceedings as unproductive, inhumane, damaging to both victims and perpetrators, and inappropriate in all but the most horrendous cases. Police officials and prosecutors tend to resent therapeutic approaches that, in their view, coddle offenders and excuse their antisocial conduct. But in recent years the alternatives have become intertwined, as criminal proceedings have been used to compel abusers to undergo court-mandated and supervised treatment programs as a condition of pretrial diversion or probation (see Berliner, 1987; Harshbarger, 1987; and Newberger, 1987).

Children as Witnesses Historically, when children were drawn into the adult court system as complaining witnesses, the proceedings were inherently biased against their participation. Their testimony was automatically suspect, and their legitimate unique needs were routinely overlooked. Only recently has the view been widely accepted that victimized children have special problems requiring special handling.

A girl is accidentally switched at birth in a hospital and years later becomes caught up in a bitter and highly publicized six-year custody battle between her biological parents and the couple who raised her. At one point in the proceedings, she alleges that the father who reared her since birth sexually abused her for years. Later, she admits to investigators that she is lying. (Associated Press, 1994h)

Nineteen children between the ages of three and five testify at the trial of their nursery school teacher that she abused them sexually. They tell the jury that over a period of seven months, during nap time, this twenty-two-year-old woman (who received an excellent evaluation and a promotion) inserted knives, forks, spoons, and Lego blocks into them. Some testify that they all played games naked and she made them drink urine, eat feces, and defecate on her. Although no staff members saw, heard, smelled, or suspected anything suspicious, and no parent ever detected any evidence of strange behavior, the jury believes the children. Three years after the alleged incidents, the ten-month trial ends, and the teacher is convicted on 115 counts of sexual abuse and sentenced to forty-seven years in prison. But five years later, the conviction is overturned on appeal when a three-judge panel rules that prosecution interviewers pressured the little complainants to confirm the charges with bribes and threats and that the judge shed his mantle of impartiality when he coaxed the young witnesses to testify against her (over closed-circuit TV) in his chambers while they were sitting on his lap and whispering into each other's ears. The prosecution decides not to retry the case, in part because some parents conclude that putting their now-teenage children back on the witness stand will be too stressful. (Manshel, 1990; Nieves, 1994)

An estimated 20,000 children are called upon each year to testify in legal proceedings stemming from allegations of sexual abuse, and as many as 80,000 more are questioned by investigators annually about possible molestations (Goleman, 1993). As a result, whether or not children tend to tell the truth or are prone to concoct stories has become an emotionally charged issue with significant legal repercussions. Would youngsters lie about such important matters? Is there a kernel of truth to most revelations, whether spontaneously volunteered or coaxed out of children, or do hysterical parents and overzealous investigators set off witch hunts and fall for hoaxes?

Ever since the Salem witch trials of 1692 (in which a number of girls made fantastic claims, which they publicly recanted several years later, after the "witches" were executed), the testimony of children has been viewed with skepticism. Now, social scientists are conducting experiments to determine just how accurate and complete the memories children acquire, retain, and retrieve can be. Because of their immaturity, very young children suffer from cognitive limitations that can undermine their credibility: They think in very concrete terms and have trouble understanding generalizations; they do not organize their thoughts logically and recount stories sequentially; their inability to properly locate events in space, distance, and time makes it difficult for them to be sure about "where" and "when" something happened; they tend to assume that adults know the whole story, so their partial answers are satisfactory; they have short attention spans; and they may be uncomfortable confiding in strangers who intimidate them (Whitcomb, 1992).

Two distinct points of view characterize the debate over the issue of credibility (see Ceci and Bruck, 1993). At one extreme is the proprosecution/provictim "believe the children" position that youngsters are generally competent witnesses about events that happened to them weeks or months earlier, are resistant to suggestions, and do not conjure up claims about abuse, especially sexual molestations and assaults, that didn't happen. Furthermore, some investigators are not surprised if a child retracts an accusation that rings true. They point out that the social reaction to a disclosure often creates chaos. For example, a girl who reveals an incestuous relationship will be rejected and branded a liar by her father who faces disgrace and imprisonment; her mother might become hysterical and enraged; her siblings might be furious about the disruption of their family life; caseworkers and detectives will become intrusive. The girl will feel she is being blamed for provoking the crisis and could recant her original charges in a vain attempt to restore some semblance of normality (Whitcomb, 1992).

At the other extreme is the prodefendant position that reserves judgment about the credibility of children who testify as witnesses for the prosecution and views their versions of events with initial skepticism. This point of view assumes that children are extremely vulnerable to coaching and manipulation by adults, easily confusing fantasy with reality, and that their testimony is usually no longer trustworthy once they have been subjected to intensive questioning by caseworkers, detectives, prosecutors, and parents who strongly believe that abuse has occurred. If the authority figures, who are attempting to "validate" their preconceived notion of what may have happened, keep repeating the "right answers," which are embedded in the slanted questions, and even go so far as to pressure the youngster to confirm what other children have already disclosed, then the youngster may eventually be swayed and regurgitate the adults' suspicions back to them, as if these events actually took place. The contention is that when a high-pressure interviewing technique is imposed upon a hypersuggestible youngster, the result can be the creation of a "false memory" that could fuel a baseless charge against an innocent adult and, ultimately, lead to a wrongful conviction. According to skeptics critical of certain child abuse convictions (such as the one involving the nursery school teacher, cited above), the scenario proceeds as follows: The initial charge is usually lodged by an unstable or vengeful adult. It is believed by detectives and social workers. These authority figures make the alleged victim undergo intrusive medical examinations. Then the child is asked to act out what "really" happened using "anatomically correct" dolls with enlarged genitals. The investigators keep asking leading questions until the child follows the cues and confirms the accusations.

Contradictory findings about the reliability of children's claims have filled the forensic literature since the mid-1970s. Some studies conclude that youngsters can be swayed only about minor details, but others indicate that repeated interrogations during legal proceedings can coerce children to make up tales that they believe are memories. Professionals who look into and report about instances of suspected maltreatment must be scrupulous about carrying out two legal obligations simultaneously: promoting the best interests of their young clients while safeguarding the legal rights of the grown-ups they investigate (Ceci and Bruck, 1993).

Ever since the landmark decision of the Supreme Court in 1895 (*Wheeler* v. *United States*), whenever children appeared in court as complaining witnesses (or eyewitnesses), they had to pass pretrial competency tests unless they were over the age of fourteen. They had to show that they understood the difference between truth and falsehood, appreciated the seriousness of the oath to swear to tell the truth, and could remember details of past events. Nearly one hundred years later, Congress passed a federal statute (The Victims of Child Abuse Act of 1990) that reversed the presumption; now children are presumed to be competent witnesses, unless there is evidence to the contrary. Following the federal government's lead, in forty-four of the fifty states special requirements for children who testify have been removed. In the remaining six, children must demonstrate their competency before they are allowed to testify. However, in most courtrooms across the country, the judge evaluates the competency of young children before a trial. Child welfare advocates welcome these reforms because they believe most children in abuse cases don't lie (Whitcomb, 1992). But civil libertarians are concerned that the presumption of competency might undermine a defendant's right to a fair trial (Austern, 1987; Dershowitz, 1988).

When children testify in court, another question that always arises is whether the proceedings will add to their suffering. To avoid further traumatizing victimized youngsters, the idea of developing a special courtroom setting and protocol was raised (Libai, 1969). The idea quickly caught on.

The right to a public trial has always been viewed as a safeguard for defendants against judicial misconduct and governmental persecution. However, the prospect of testifying in front of a crowded courtroom can be a great deterrent to a youthful complainant. In particular, the spectacle of describing in intimate detail what happened during an episode of sexual abuse is so potentially disturbing to a sensitive youngster that exceptions to the public nature of a trial have been legislated. In fourteen states, judges have the authority to bar spectators from the courtroom during the testimony of a child who claims to have been sexually abused. In twenty-six states, the release of identifying information by the news media about a complainant in a sexual abuse case is severely limited (Whitcomb, 1992).

The Sixth Amendment guarantees all defendants in criminal trials the right to confront their accusers. In theory, looking the defendant in the eye as an accusation is repeated in court has traditionally been considered a test of a complaining witness's truthfulness. But when little children are the complainants, they often dread seeing the accused in person. For many years, what prosecutors did to avoid last-minute intimidation when the youngster took the stand was to position themselves in such a way as to block the child's view of the defendant. Other prosecutors simply instructed their witness to look at someone in the spectator section during the testimony, preferably toward a supportive person like a family member or victim advocate. More overt physical methods to protect sensitive complainants from the direct gaze of defendants, such as using a screen or one-way glass, or having the children turn their backs, were considered to violate the face-to-face requirement of the confrontation clause's concerns for truthfulness. With the advent of modern video technology, particularly closed-circuit television (one-way and two-way) and videotaping, more options developed. To avoid intimidation and the heightened anxiety caused by the presence of jurors and other courtroom personnel, forty-six states now allow the young complainant to be questioned in another room using two-way, live closed-circuit television. To spare the child the ordeal of reliving unpleasant experiences in front of strangers, most of these states permit testimony and cross-examination videotaped at depositions, grand jury proceedings, or preliminary hearings to be used in trials. In 1990, the Supreme Court ruled (in *Maryland* v. *Craig*) that these alternatives to direct confrontation were constitutionally permissible under certain circumstances (Whitcomb, 1992).

Hearsay is usually not admissible during trials because statements made out of court are not made under oath or subject to cross-examination. Yet in child abuse cases, what the youngster says before legal proceedings are initiated may be very compelling evidence. For example, the casual, innocent remark of a very young and immature little girl might be a surprisingly graphic description of a sexual act that should be unknown or unfamiliar to her. Therefore, in the "interest of justice" in twenty-eight states, special exceptions to the hearsay rule enable witnesses to tell the court what apparently sexually abused children have told them. In 1980, the Supreme Court ruled (in *Ohio* v. *Roberts*) that a statement made by a complainant who does not testify at the trial can be used as evidence if it falls under one of the rules for hearsay exceptions or meets a reliability test (Whitcomb, 1992).

In the late 1970s, investigators began to use anatomically detailed dolls (with genitalia) to facilitate and enhance interviews with children who were suspected to have been sexually abused. The rationale was that the presence of a doll would make the interview seem less formal and stressful; enable children with limited vocabularies or suffering great embarrassment to demonstrate what happened to them; and permit the information to be disclosed without any reliance on leading questions. Congress endorsed the use of dolls as demonstrative aids during interviews and court proceedings in the Victims of Child Abuse Act of 1990, and eight states have followed suit. But some critics point out that experiments have shown that even children with no suspected history of abuse play with the anatomically intriguing dolls in a sexually suggestive way that could falsely imply inordinate interest in sexuality (see Whitcomb, 1992).

Other reforms that are less controversial and more often implemented include allowing children to use drawings to describe what happened to them, interviewing victims in decorated playrooms at police stations rather than in dingy, bare-walled interrogation rooms ("Child Abuse Victims," 1989), modifying the courtroom's protocol and seating arrangements to make the setting less imposing, giving child witnesses a tour of the courthouse to orient them to the setting, enrolling them in brief "court schools," which explain the role of key figures and the procedures that will be followed, permitting them to have a supportive person at their side, and using a single, trained interviewer to elicit all their testimony. To limit the length of the ordeal of going to trial, some jurisdictions give child abuse cases a high priority in scheduling and try to avoid continuances that cause stressful delays (Whitcomb, 1986).

A number of recent innovations are intended to alleviate the suffering of abused children. In many jurisdictions, the medical, mental health, treatment, and legal aspects of abuse cases are now coordinated by child protection teams composed of professionals from different disciplines. Information-sharing procedures eliminate unnecessary interviews. Public funds cover the costs of physical and mental health examinations. Caseworkers from protective services agencies and law enforcement officers are empowered to take children endangered by their environment into emergency custody. Because confused and intimidated youngsters often do not inform anyone of their plight for years, many states have extended their statutes of limitations so they do not begin until the victim reaches a more mature age (Howell, 1989).

The Victims of Child Abuse Act of 1990 granted youngsters the right to submit victim impact statements to judges in a manner appropriate for their age and stage of personal development. States that are following the federal government's example are permitting children to send handwritten letters, or even drawings, to the sentencing judge.

The "funnel" model of the criminal justice system best describes how child abuse cases are handled. Although the system potentially has a huge caseload to tackle, cases are "lost" or "weeded out" at each stage, until there are very few left at the end of the process. Conviction and punishment of the abuser turns out to be a rare event. (See the statistics in Box 5.3.)

Proactive vs. Reactive Strategies

Strategies to prevent children from being abused take many forms. They range from screening potential child-care workers for known molesters, to setting up "help lines" and crisis nurseries where parents can drop off their children if they feel they are about to lose control, to organizing self-help Parents Anonymous support groups for abusers and offering child-rearing courses for new parents (Irwin, 1980).

The problem of child maltreatment raises many profound issues. Although all would agree that proactive, preventive strategies are as important as reactive, criminal justice responses, people are sharply divided over the proper role of government in the balance between social nurturance and social control. In reply to

---

BOX 5.3   The Criminal Justice System's Handling of Child Abuse Cases

---

Very few agencies keep records to track the progress of cases of child physical and sexual abuse in their local jurisdictions. Various studies based on limited samples have yielded statistics that give some impression of what happens at each stage, but huge variations by jurisdiction are evident.

Roughly 39 percent of child abuse cases reported to law enforcement agencies result in arrests.

About 63 percent of all cases referred by law enforcement for prosecution are filed (accepted, taken forward, charges pressed). Between 7 percent and 33 percent are then dismissed by a judge. The major reasons for prosecutors to decline to file charges and for judges to dismiss cases are the same: noncooperation by the complainant or the child's family. Less frequently, cases do not get

filed or later get dismissed because the child protection agency worked out a solution, the suspect cannot be located, corroborating evidence is lacking, the child is considered to be too young or too incompetent to testify, or the child has recanted the earlier accusations or has given inconsistent accounts.

About 75 percent of cases that are filed and not dismissed lead to convictions (but as few as 50 percent and as many as 93 percent). These convictions are usually obtained through plea negotiations (from as few as 33 percent of such cases to as many as 87 percent).

About 64 percent of convicted offenders are sentenced to a period of incarceration (but as few as 38 percent of such cases and as many as 78 percent).

Sources: Chapman and Smith, 1987; Whitcomb, 1988, 1992.

---

the question "Whose children are they?" one long-standing answer is that children belong to, or are the property of, their parents. But another way of looking at youngsters is to see them as "junior" citizens: Parents have custody of them, but the larger community has "visiting rights." In extreme cases, the community might even assert "joint custody" and violate the privacy of the family and the rights of parents. Government agencies step in as parents-of-last-resort when a clear and present danger to the child is evident. Yet, in an age when the social conditions experienced by children are generally deteriorating (in terms of reduced parental involvement and support and increased exposure to deprivation and violence), stepped-up efforts to criminalize the maltreatment of children may not do much to stem the growth of the problem (Garbarino, 1989). On the other hand, the price for inaction or minimal reaction on the part of the authorities—child protection agencies and family courts—in the name of family preservation, can be death. For example, during 1993, a check of the case files showed that 42 percent of the nearly 1,300 children who died from physical abuse or neglect were living in families that had been investigated for maltreating them (Edmonds, 1994).

MORE CASUALTIES OF DOMESTIC VIOLENCE

When child abuse is committed by a parent (as opposed to some other caretaker, such as a preschool teacher in a day-care center), it can be considered a type of "domestic" or within-the-family victimization. Besides child abuse, other forms of violence that break out between members of the same household include parent-adolescent strife, partner abuse (by a spouse or lover), elder abuse, and sibling abuse.

The Rediscovery of the Problem of Wife Beating

In her autobiography, the daughter of a prominent political figure reveals that she endured many vicious beatings by her first husband, a police officer, shortly after they got married. During fits of jealous rage, he would punch and kick her in the head so brutally that she fantasized about killing him. But when she picked up his service revolver, she found she was incapable of pulling the trigger. She told her coworkers, friends, and parents that her cuts and swellings were due to accidents. Her father, a former president of the United States, finally discovers the truth about her "bruises from accidents" when he reads her book. (Bruni, 1989)

The rediscovery of the plight of battered wives during the 1970s shattered the illusion of "domestic tranquillity"—that women were safe from harm as long as they remained at home, protected by their husbands from the vicious dog-eat-dog world raging outside their doors. Once it was realized that a "silent crisis" marred the lives of many women and that the perpetrators were the men they married, not menacing strangers, the "look-the-other-way," "mind-your-own-business," "hands-off" policy toward "lovers' spats" that took place "behind closed doors" could no longer be justified (see Straus, 1978; Pagelow, 1984a, 1984b; Gelles and Cornell, 1990; Straus and Gelles, 1990; Dobash and Dobash, 1992).

Early on in the rediscovery process, news media coverage generated stereotypes of the typical victim–offender relationship. According to a content analysis of stories and reports in widely read magazines during the rediscovery phase of the 1970s and 1980s (Loseke, 1989), journalists depicted wife beating in ways favorable to a provictim, prowoman analysis. Abusers were typically described as "supermacho types" who followed conventional sex-based role prescriptions. They were said to believe that they had a right to discipline and control their wives and to beat back any challenges to their manly privileges. Just as these wife beaters were portrayed as stereotypically "masculine," the targets of their wrath were pictured as stereotypically "feminine." Battered wives were reported to believe that a woman's place was in the home—selflessly devoted to their husbands, dependent on them as breadwinners, and deferential to their rightful authority. Several themes ran through most of the articles: that wife abuse is everyone's concern because it occurs at all levels of society, although it is harder to detect in affluent, high-status families; that it is a social problem, afflicting millions, and is not just a personal or individual source of trouble burdening only a few unfortunate women; that the victims did not deserve or provoke the abuse heaped upon them; that the consequences were serious, even life threatening; and that this crisis in a fundamental social institution, the family, demanded public attention and governmental action, from social programs to criminal justice solutions. Most articles identified the cause of the problem as an outgrowth of unjust gender relations, buttressed by an ideology that proclaimed that men are superior to women and perpetuated by socialization practices that exhorted boys to be aggressive, tough, and powerful and girls to be passive, submissive, and supportive.

From a Personal Tragedy to a Social Problem

For centuries, legal traditions granted the man, as "head of the household," whose "home was his castle," the "right" to "discipline" his wife and children "as he saw fit," since they were regarded as his "property" or "chattel." This prescription became the basis in English common law (which was accepted into American jurisprudence) for a nonintervention stance that denied women equal protection under law. Such institutionalized indifference was legally permissible since it was a wife's duty to "love, honor, and obey" her husband. Indeed many "victims" did not even define their beatings as crimes and did not consider themselves victims, if they accepted the prevailing ideology (echoed by authority figures, friends, and parents) that they had "stepped out of line" and "had it coming," and "got what they deserved." Such traditional thinking made the marriage license a husband's "hitting license."

A mistaken impression prevails that the issue of spouse abuse was first raised in the 1970s, primarily by feminists intent on exposing the weaknesses and cruelties of the system of male dominance known as patriarchy. Actually, there were two previous periods of concern about family violence in American history.

As early as the mid-1600s, the Pilgrims who settled in New England officially recognized the possibility that wives could be victims of assault by their husbands, that husbands could be brutalized by their wives, that children could be harshly mistreated by their parents, and that incestuous sexual relations could be imposed upon youngsters. Guided by religious teachings about the virtues of harmonious family life and the sins of disobeying authority, the Puritans in Plymouth Colony and Massachusetts Bay Colony passed the first laws anywhere in the world forbidding verbal or physical abuse between family members. Wife beating was punishable by a fine or a whipping; the sentence for husband abuse was up to the judge; child abuse (called "unnatural severity") carried a fine, but incest, when discovered, could result in execution by hanging, as the Bible recommended. Even though conformity to all laws was insisted upon and intervening into a neighboring family's affairs was expected, none of these laws were vigorously enforced. Only on very rare occasions were wives brought to court for verbally abusing ("nagging") their husbands. Husbands rarely were fined and almost never whipped for beating their wives (some charges were dropped when judges decided wives had provoked their husbands' wrath). Wives who complained that their husbands beat them often recanted their accusations when they got to court; no case of child abuse was ever prosecuted, and no one was ever put to death for incest, according to court records from these New England colonies. Apparently, these laws strictly served a symbolic function, outlining rights and responsibilities and setting limits. Puritan teachings held that God ruled the state, the state supervised the family, and the husband headed the household. The occasional use of force to discipline a wife (what they called "moderate correction" within "domestic chastisement") was permissible within reasonable limits (as long as the beating caused no permanent damage). The expression "rule of thumb" in those days was a guideline that prohibited men from using sticks thicker than their thumbs to beat their wives whose "provocations" included "passionate language" (scolding) or refusing to engage in sexual relations. The desire to reinforce patriarchal control, uphold parental rights, and shore up the nuclear family necessitated that laws criminalizing abuse within families would be rarely enforced and that "sinners" would receive lenient sentences. The most effective restraints on male violence were informal means of social control—community disapproval plus pressures from the wife's parents, and in extreme cases, divorce (Rhode, 1989; Pleck, 1989).

The second wave of concern about family violence developed in the late 1800s. Reformers argued in favor of the principle that the government had a responsibility to enforce morality as codified in law. Fears of immigrants, drifters, and the growing "dangerous classes" of criminals and delinquents in the urban industrial centers fueled this movement for change. Societies for the Prevention of Cruelty to Children (SPCC) were set up across the country. Temperance advocates hammered away at the evils of drinking by emphasizing how wives and children were abused by drunkards who wasted their time and money in saloons. Some women's rights activists contended that fining and jailing were insufficient to deter wife beating and called for the restoration of the whipping post. (Public flogging had been abandoned in most states about 100 years earlier, after the American Revolution, as an uncivilized and barbaric form of corporal punishment.) Other feminists sought ways to help battered wives get orders of protection and divorces (Pleck, 1989).

The third wave of reform and victim-support activities was spearheaded by feminists in the women's liberation movement in the early 1970s. Wife beating symbolized women's oppression within the family, and the lack of responsiveness on the part of the men who ran the criminal justice system demonstrated the institutionalized discrimination women faced in everyday life. Projects like setting up shelters for battered women typified the tangible aid, victim empowerment, and independent self-help that women could achieve if they acted collectively. A battered women's movement developed out of this third wave of concern about family violence.

The battered women's movement encountered resistance and opposition at first because of the widespread acceptance of victim-blaming arguments that portrayed beaten wives in an unsympathetic light. Many people, including some counselors and family therapists, believed that a high proportion of beatings were unconsciously precipitated or even intentionally provoked. Those wives who were said to be responsible for stirring up their husbands' wrath were negatively stereotyped as "aggressive," "masculine," and "sexually frigid." Their husbands were categorized as "shy," "sexually ineffectual," "dependent and passive," and even as "mothers' boys." The dynamics of their conflict was thought to start when a badgered husband tried to please and pacify his querulous and demanding wife. But eventually her taunts and challenges provoked an explosion, and he lost his self-control (for example, see Snell, Rosenwald, and Roby, 1964; and Faulk, 1977). Activists in the battered women's movement pointed out that this victim-blaming outlook failed to condemn the violence and implied that it was not a matter for the police and courts; it pictured the husband's main problem as his weakness rather than his assaultiveness; it identified the wife's main problems as her domineering nature, her coldness, and her secret masochistic cravings for suffering; and it placed the burden of change on the woman, and not the man, the community, and the social structures that maintain male dominance (see Schechter, 1982; and Beirne and Messerschmidt, 1991).

The battered women's movement succeeded in replacing this victim-blaming outlook with a victim-defending one. Therapists working with victims and couples now recognize a cycle of violence accompanied by "learned helplessness," which has been termed "the battered woman's syndrome." Battering often follows a pattern. After the initial "honeymoon" part of their courtship, the cycle is marked by three phases: tension building; the battering; and the tranquil, loving aftermath. During the first phase, the aggressor hurls insults and threats while his docile target tries to appease him in a vain attempt to stave off violence and preserve their relationship. She tries to rationalize her mate's behavior and conceal it from others, inadvertently isolating herself from potential rescuers. As her sacrifices to make peace fail, the second, acute stage unfolds: He goes on a rampage and savagely assaults her, inflicting injuries that shock and confuse her. Feeling trapped, she acts submissively as part of a defense mechanism to prevent an escalation of his attacks. The third phase is marked by an illusion of resolution and tranquillity. He expresses shame and remorse, apologizes, pledges it won't happen again, and acts tenderly. Unwilling to confront the seriousness of her plight, blaming herself for his loss of control, and believing she can head off his assaults in the future, she decides not to seek outside help or to leave him, and she acts in a forgiving manner. But over time, his attacks increase in frequency and ferocity. He expresses less contrition and she feels less confident about being able to defuse his anger. He rachets up his efforts to dominate her life, and she feels more isolated, helpless, and trapped (Walker, 1984).

Estimating the Incidence, Prevalence, and Seriousness of Spouse Abuse

"I never reported it . . . I was intimidated, ashamed. I had nowhere to go. I had five children to raise. I was told that if I ever left, he would find me and kill me," said the police chief of a small rural department, who suffered broken bones, burns, and stab wounds in a series of beatings that began two weeks after she got married. ("Police Chief," 1993)

As the terms *partner abuse, spouse abuse, wife beating,* and *woman battering* became part of everyday vocabulary, a number of questions arose, such as "What kinds of families were wracked by these problems?" At first, there were only media images and personal revelations (true confessions), but this kind of anecdotal evidence might be very unrepresentative and misleading. Atypical cases, like the one cited above involving a high-ranking law enforcement official, make the news, but what kinds of women are usually the objects of their lovers' wrath?

The myth that very few husbands beat their wives was hard to dispel as long as official statistics revealed only the tip of the iceberg. Once the battered women's movement organized "speakouts," where victims revealed their plight to audiences of sympathetic strangers, it became evident that partner abuse can arise in all kinds of families, regardless of class, race, and religion. However, the statistical profile of a couple in which the woman is at risk for a severe beating is as follows (the more factors that fit, the higher the risk): The family income is less than $15,000 a year. She is young, unemployed, poorly educated, and lives with but is not married to a man of a different religious or ethnic background. He is between the ages of eighteen and thirty, is unemployed or working in a blue-collar job, did not graduate from high school, beats his children, and abuses alcohol and illicit drugs. His parents were violent toward each other, and he grew up in a rough neighborhood. She suffers from isolation, low self-esteem, passivity, dependence, and an inordinate need for attention, affection, and approval. He is impulsive, jealous, and possessive and also suffers from a low sense of self-worth. His violent outbursts are often triggered by feelings of rejection and abandonment. The threat of a separation or her moving out are interpreted as "provocations" because he feels he is losing control of her. If he owns a gun, goes on drinking binges, disregards restraining orders, and stalks her, she may be in grave danger (Ingrassia and Beck, 1994; Goleman, 1995a).

To measure the incidence, prevalence, and seriousness of the problem, a basic methodological issue must be resolved: Exactly what behaviors and which victim–offender relationships are included and excluded? Social workers, family therapists, feminists, psychologists, criminologists, victimologists, police officers, and prosecutors have tried to define a set of actions that are described by several terms with similar and overlapping but not identical meanings: *partner abuse* (which refers to all male and female violence arising from intimate romantic relationships); *spouse abuse* (which includes only male and female victims who are legally married); *domestic disturbances* (a police expression) involving members of the same household; *domestic violence* (which might be interpreted more broadly, to involve children, siblings, elders, and other relatives living under the same roof); *wife abuse* (which embraces only married female victims); and *woman battering* (which includes all female victims). The most inclusive definitions would count all assaults committed by persons who are currently romantically involved (whether legally married or not) plus attacks by ex-spouses and former lovers.

As for the actions that should be labeled as abusive, violent, or assaultive, considerable disagreement arises over where to draw the line between inclusion and exclusion. Many people approve of, tolerate, or are resigned to some "normal" level of quarreling and fighting among partners in romantic relationships. Although there is no standard definition, a good working definition would take into account the seriousness of the assault, the assailant's intentions, the actual physical injury inflicted, the depth of psychological trauma, and the specific acts. These acts can cover the entire gamut of behaviors comprising simple and aggravated physical assaults, ranging from pushing and shoving, pulling and dragging, shaking, ripping clothing, hitting with an open hand, punching with a closed fist, choking, kicking and stomping, throwing an object, threatening with a weapon to wounding the opponent with a weapon like a knife or gun. The full continuum of physical injuries sustained by victims includes bruises and swellings, cuts and scratches, dizziness, sprains, burns, loss of vision or hearing, fractures, concussions, and more serious wounds. Emotional harm, on the other hand, is not so easily characterized (see Loseke, 1989; Rhodes, 1992).

Obviously, it is difficult to accurately measure how often and how seriously couples who are married or living together (cohabiting) hurt each other. With the passage of time since the rediscovery of the problem, the definitions of what constitutes abuse, battering, beating, and violence have changed. There are differences among these terms, shades of meaning, connotations, and ambiguities that lead to almost endless confusion and permit observers to draw very different conclusions. For example, if abuse is recognized only when a victim is physically injured and not just "attacked," then very different estimates of the incidence rate can result. Since most physical assaults do not bring about visible injuries, the estimate of how frequently partners attack each other can be twenty times higher than how often partners injure each other. If "physical injury" is taken to be the defining criterion, then domestic violence is overwhelmingly a male-on-female crime; but if "attacks" are counted, then females attack their male partners almost as often as males attack their female lovers (Straus, 1991). (Put succinctly, many men who are attacked are not wounded; assaults by males tend to result in injuries more often than assaults by females.) Clearly, which definition is used by the researcher dramatically shapes the numbers and the interpretation of the statistics.

Another issue concerns where to draw the line between "minor violence" and "criminal violence." Beating one's partner with a weapon (club, bottle) surely is criminal violence; using a lesser object (stick, belt) is also, by most people's definitions; but what about punching with a closed fist or just slapping with an open hand? The lack of public consensus can be called "normative ambiguity" (Straus, 1991), and it reflects the distinction some would make between conflicts that occur within the family and fights between strangers. The cultural support that still exists for using force to settle family quarrels has important policy implications. If all physical attacks between spouses were criminalized— judged by the same standards (rules, expectations) as those used to identify assaults between nonfamily members—and were potentially subject to the same penalties, then currently the majority of outbursts of spouse abuse go unreported, unprosecuted, and unpunished.

Abuse, assault, battering, and domestic violence are all evaluative concepts because each contains a definition of behavior that is morally wrong (Straus, 1991). But ideas about what actions are improper and unacceptable vary from time to time and place to place and group to group. Some researchers are now counting not only physical assaults (or violent acts), and/or injuries (wounds), but also verbal assaults (threats, maybe even vicious name-calling). If the definition of abuse is expanding over time to embrace all expressions of oppressive, domineering behavior that harm the target physically, mentally, or financially, then it is mushrooming well beyond its original meaning, becoming highly subjective, and losing precision and comparability.

Reliable sources of data about spouse abuse are difficult to find. For cases of child abuse, compulsory reporting laws have been passed in every state, and datagathering clearinghouses have been established. But for spouse abuse, no comparable reporting and compiling systems yet exist. The FBI's Uniform Crime Reporting System is of little use, because assaults between intimates are not recorded in a separate category from other assaults. The BJS's *National Crime Victimization Survey* attempts to measure the disclosure by household members of assaults committed against them by partners. But it produces a serious undercount because most "victims" don't consider themselves to have been "criminally" harmed by an "offender" in the legal sense, unless they were seriously injured or the perpetrator was a former partner (after separation, divorce). Of course, many incidents are not disclosed if the assailant is present when the victim is being interviewed. Researchers studying *NCVS* findings from 1978 to 1982 determined that only about half of all batterings were reported to the police. The main reasons cited for informing the authorities were to end the attack, to keep it from happening again, and to get the offender in trouble so that he would be punished. The leading reasons for not calling for help were the women's beliefs that these incidents were private and personal matters, that the crime wasn't important enough, that the police wouldn't or couldn't assist them, and that they would be subject to reprisals if they dared to seek outside protection. *NCVS* data indicate that women who report being assaulted by a mate one year are likely to report being physically abused again in later years. Police files reveal that the cycle of violence tends to escalate in frequency and severity over time (Langan and Innes, 1986).

Given the limitations of these two official sources of crime statistics, researchers have had to devise their own measurement scales and carry out their own surveys or turn to fragmentary sources (like records kept by hospital emergency rooms and police departments). But using a possibly biased source can strongly skew the results of a study. For example, research based on files about women seeking assistance or treatment often is not generalizable ("the clinical fallacy") because the sample is not representative of the entire population saddled with the problem (Straus, 1991).

Despite all these methodological problems, a number of statistical findings indicate that domestic violence is a serious problem:

- At least 6 million women are physically abused one or more times each year (using the criterion of even just one incident of minor violence, such as being slapped). Using a more restrictive definition of serious assaults (being kicked, punched, choked, or attacked with a weapon), at least 1.8 million women are severely victimized yearly. The average victim was assaulted six times during the year, according to projections from a 1985 national family violence survey (described above), which used the "Conflict Tactics Scale." (Straus, 1991)
- Although simple assaults are most common, about a third of the violent outbursts described to *NCVS* interviewers would be classified by the police as more serious felonies—aggravated assaults, rapes, even robberies. (Langan and Innes, 1986)
- About one million women each year seek medical attention for wounds inflicted by a male partner: husband, ex-husband, boyfriend, former lover. Somewhere between 22 percent and 35 percent of all visits by women to hospital emergency rooms are to treat injuries resulting from a partner's assault. The beatings pregnant women receive cause more birth defects than all the diseases combined for which children are immunized. Domestic violence poses the single greatest threat of injury to women between the ages of fifteen and forty-four, taking a greater toll than automobile accidents, robberies, and cancer combined. About a third of all female

murder victims are killed by "intimates" (their spouses, former husbands, or lovers), over 1,400 a year. The social costs of domestic violence, in terms of health care, social services, and criminal justice outlays, add up to between $5 and $10 billion dollars a year. (Senate Committee on the Judiciary, 1993; Gibbs, 1993b)

- About 6 percent of 13,000 new mothers in four states conceded to interviewers that they were physically injured by their husbands or partners during their pregnancy. The greatest risks are faced by younger women who are not formally married, poorly educated, living in crowded households, and unable to get prenatal care. (Hilts, 1994)
- The rate of domestic violence in military families (about 18 confirmed cases of spouse abuse per 1,000 couples per year) is about double that of civilians, according to a survey of 55,000 soldiers at forty-seven bases. (Schmitt, 1994)

As for trends, domestic violence may be declining in frequency. Researchers found in a 1975 survey of 2,000 married couples that over one-fourth (28 percent) admitted that one partner (usually the husband) had physically assaulted the other at least once since their wedding. A decade later, however, researchers using the same definitions in interviews (but this time with a larger representative sample of over 6,000 married and cohabiting couples) uncovered evidence that serious incidents of spouse abuse may be subsiding rather than intensifying. In the 1975 survey, roughly 4 couples out of every 100 admitted having at least one serious outbreak of violence within the year; by 1985, the rate had declined to about 3 couples per 100. Serious incidents were defined as those involving kicking, hitting with a fist, biting, beating up, or using or threatening to use a gun or knife during a dispute. The overall incidence rate, which included less serious instances of slapping, shoving, pushing, and throwing things was estimated to be about 16 percent of all married and cohabiting couples. The prevalence rate was 33 percent for one or more incidents involving violence during the lifetime of the marriage or cohabiting relationship. These surveys also indicated that women tended to be as willing as men to use force. But much of the women's "violence" could be interpreted as acts of self-defense or retaliation against male initiatives rather than as acts of aggression, and many of their "attacks" did not physically injure their male partners (Straus and Gelles, 1986).

Providing Tangible Aid to Victims Who Feel Trapped

The question "Why does she stay if he is so brutal?" has been traditionally dismissed with the victim-blaming rejoinder that being regularly beaten must somehow fulfill a pathological need of hers. For example, battered women have been accused of being masochistic and enjoying feeling miserable, or of looking forward to the passionate sex that supposedly follows a violent outburst when a "repentant" husband asks her for forgiveness (see Paglia, 1994). Today, researchers and advocates have discovered a number of plausible reasons why women stay with their violent mates, repeatedly enduring the cycle of battering/reconciliation/battering. Some feel dependent, dread being alone, and despair that they have nowhere to go and no one to turn to for aid and comfort. They are intimidated, even terrorized, and fear reprisals if they dare to try to escape their possessive and controlling husbands obsessed with a "You belong to me!" and "If I can't have you, no one can!" mentality (many of the worst attacks, even slayings, erupt after separation). They worry about their children's welfare (psychological damage, loss of financial support, custody and visitation issues). Some still love their tormentors and invoke higher loyalties (a commitment to the institution of marriage, and to the vows they took—"for better or worse, in good times and in bad") and, because of cultural and religious traditions, are ashamed of the stigma (of "abandoning or deserting a husband" and of a "failed marriage"), or believe they should stand by their men and try to help to cure them (attributing their whole "mess" to external causes, like alcoholism or unemployment or job-related stress). Finally, trying to escape from a batterer's clutches is a risky course of action. Many women are beaten when they try to break up or after they separate from their abusive partners (Frieze and Browne, 1991; Steinman, 1991; Barnett and LaViolette, 1993; and Kirkwood, 1993).

From its inception, the battered women's movement's first priority was to provide tangible aid at a time of great need. Just as the antirape movement set up crisis centers to offer immediate support to victims of sexual assaults, the anti-battering movement established shelters for women to seek refuge. In 1974, following the lead of feminists in England a few years earlier, women in St. Paul, Minnesota, transformed an old house used for meetings into the first shelter in the United States (Martin, 1976).

These "safe houses" offer a number of services to their residents. First and foremost, they provide short-term room and board in a secure setting for victims who are in continuing physical danger. Most also furnish emergency clothing and transportation. Through self-help groups, the women can give one another emotional support when grappling with transitional issues, particularly about whether to try to sever or salvage their relationships with abusers. Counselors discuss legal issues (such as pressing charges; obtaining court orders of protection; and the complexities of separation, divorce, child custody, and alimony), educational matters (such as returning to school and retraining for displaced homemakers), and vocational opportunities (including job hunting) with those seeking temporary shelter. Hotline staffers instruct victims where to go, since the locations of shelters are kept secret to protect the residents from vengeful mates. Through outreach activities, staff members raise public awareness about the needs for empowering these otherwise dependent women and for reforming the criminal justice and social service systems (Warrior, 1977; Neidig, 1984; Dutton-Douglas and Dionne, 1991).

Although the first safe houses were initially set up as independent self-help projects and were staffed by volunteers, many people quickly agreed that local governments had a responsibility to establish permanent shelters run by social service agencies. By 1987, approximately 1,200 battered women's shelters were operating across the country. Most were overcrowded, underfunded, and understaffed, according to the National Coalition Against Domestic Violence (Abrams, 1987). Those who were turned away or whose time ran out faced the same limited choices that battered women confronted before there was a movement to shelter them: to return home and face renewed attacks or seek temporary respite with friends, relatives, or parents. As government-sponsored shelters spread during the 1980s, a backlash against them emerged. "Profamily" organizations sought to limit local, state, and federal funding for shelters, and police referrals of victims to them. These critics contended that shelter workers tended to be "homewreckers" who contributed to the breakup of marriages by encouraging victims to divorce their abusive husbands (Stone, 1984; Pleck, 1989). Actually, most women who took refuge in a shelter eventually returned to live with their abusive mates again, and many of them suffered additional beatings, according to limited follow-up studies by researchers attempting to assess the effectiveness of this method of intervention with women facing grave risks (see Dutton-Douglas and Dionne, 1991).

The battered women who flee their violent mates and seek refuge in government-sponsored shelters tend to be the poorest and most desperate of all, as might be anticipated. Two surveys of women seeking shelter yielded estimates that they were suffering between sixty and seventy beatings per year, whereas the average victim endured six per year. They also differed from the "norm" in another way: These routinely beaten women rarely dared to fight back (see Straus, 1991).

Battered Women and the Criminal Justice System: Violence Is Violence—or Is It?

A woman is beaten by her husband hundreds of times. She divorces him and then testifies against him in court. He is sent to prison and vows to get even with her some day. A note is placed in his file that she must be warned before he is released from custody. One day he is let out for a brief furlough but she is not contacted. He catches her by surprise at home and murders her. (Pollitt, 1989)

A major objective of the battered women's movement has been to convince the public and criminal justice officials that wife beating should be regarded as a crime and not as a private lover's quarrel. Until activists launched consciousness-raising efforts, wife beating was viewed as special in the negative sense—different than other assaults, not a "real crime" and not a problem that could be resolved effectively through the criminal justice process. The long arm of the law shouldn't reach into the home and intrude into family quarrels between adults, many people argued, unless the situation was life threatening. Movement activists who spurred on the rediscovery of the plight of battered women insisted that batterings were serious and widespread enough to be considered a "silent crisis" or "epidemic." They pointed out that fights between partners could have grave consequences when left to fester and smoulder. Assaults could escalate in intensity and lead to severe injuries, even to death, usually of the victim, less often of the tormentor. Furthermore, they pointed out that children, viewing their parents acting brutally toward each other, could mistakenly come to believe that the use of physical force to settle disputes is appropriate and acceptable and would perpetuate a cycle of violence when they grew up and got married (see Schechter, 1982).

Historically, women seeking relief from the criminal justice system were routinely maltreated, discouraged, and disappointed. Wife beating cases were heard in lower courts, police courts (proceedings held in police stations), alderman's courts (at the neighborhood level), and family courts (civil proceedings dedicated to preserving the marriage). A double standard prevailed, in which an assault by an intimate was not considered a real crime, and, therefore, did not merit the same attention as an attack of equal ferocity launched by a complete stranger. Arresting the aggressor was taken as a risky strategy that could cause him to escalate his level of violence against the woman who turned him in and got him in trouble. Prosecution was written off as a waste of precious resources, time, and effort, since the victim often changed her mind about pressing charges, forgave her assailant, and bailed him out of jail. Incarceration was dismissed as counterproductive since locking up the breadwinner meant he could not provide for his wife and children (Pleck, 1989).

People concerned about the problem of spouse abuse are still divided over how best to respond to the plight of battered women: whether to pursue a legalistic course of action that depends on a quick resort to criminal justice solutions; or to follow a "preserve the family" approach that primarily relies on social agencies to provide effective services and turns to the police and courts only in extreme cases, as a last, desperate measure after all else has failed (see Saunders, 1986; Fagan, 1988; Gondolf, 1988; Ohlin and Tonry, 1989; Pleck, 1989; Buzawa and Buzawa, 1990; and Hilton, 1993).

The "preserve the family" (family systems model or the social service strategy) way of handling domestic violence was favored in the 1950s and 1960s, and was funded by the U.S. Department of Justice. It proposes that the primary objective of any outside intervention should be to restore harmony to the marriage. That means salvage the relationship, keep the family intact, heal its wounds, and foster its nurturing potentials. Social programs and agencies are counted upon as the appropriate providers of these services. Couples locked into ongoing violent conflicts need to see marriage counselors who can mediate their disputes and build on the underlying strengths of their relationship. Really dangerous and brutal men are referred to behavioral therapy programs to learn to control their anger. Advocates of this therapeutic, nonadversarial, pro-reconciliation approach contend that many battered women are not totally innocent victims; some are partly to blame for being the first to resort to force or for provoking their husband's wrath; and some battered wives want to try to save their marriages. Such cases of shared responsibility are not well handled by the courts, within the straightjacket of a victory/defeat contest that emphasizes total guilt or complete innocence, conviction or acquittal. Bringing the police, prosecutors, and judges in to help "settle" bitter fights between husbands and wives rarely works satisfactorily and should be considered only as a last resort, when all other options and programs have been tried and have failed. Turning to the courts to solve family problems can waste the government's scarce resources, undermine family cohesion (trigger a separation and ultimately a divorce), escalate conflict levels (provoke retaliatory violence), and end up as self-defeating (punishing the women and her children as well as the aggressor).

The ideological underpinnings justifying this "preserve-the-family" approach include a concern for domestic privacy and for the sanctity of the family, and a disdain for government "interference" in personal matters between intimates. But this reliance on social service agencies and mediation has been criticized for trivializing or condoning what might be serious violence, for assuming shared responsibility, and for disregarding glaring inequalities in power relations between the spouses. The notion of "privacy" has been selectively applied and interpreted to mean that criminally assaulted victims do not merit protection by the state because their problem is deemed to be "individual," "personal," and "peculiar"; this stance denies the reality that wife beating is clearly a pervasive and serious public issue, a social problem inextricably connected to family life and gender relations (Schneider, 1991).

The legalistic approach, currently in favor, argues that violence is violence, regardless of who the offender is and what his relationship to the victim might be. Criminalizing spouse abuse entails arresting the aggressor, prosecuting the case as an assault, and convicting and punishing the wrongdoer with a fine and/or a jail term coupled with compulsory treatment. The approach rests on these tenets: Separate the parties, rescue and protect the victim, punish and then rehabilitate the aggressor. The philosophical underpinnings of the legalistic approach are that the state has a responsibility to enforce public morality as codified in law, and that the government has a duty to intervene when innocent, vulnerable victims are in danger and reach out to the authorities for help. Adherents of this approach fault the criminal justice system for not taking violence between intimates as seriously as violence between strangers. Too often, assailants are not arrested; or, if the police take them into custody, charges are not filed or are later dropped; or, if prosecutors achieve convictions, judges impose very lenient sentences. Proponents of the legalistic approach advocate reliance on the civil remedy of an order of protection (also called a restraining order), which is backed up by criminal penalties to discourage a batterer from harassing and striking the victim again. If a judge's order of protection is violated and a beating occurs, the police should follow a policy of mandatory arrest. A specially trained prosecutor should vigorously press charges against the assailant and seek court-ordered treatment as a condition of probation or in addition to jail time, depending on the severity of the incident and the frequency of recidivism (Fagan, 1988; Gondolf, 1988).

Although the letter of the law has been changed in every state over the last century, making wife beating a crime, the spirit of the law remains ambivalent. In the past, the intent behind the law permitting husbands to beat their wives was to compel women to endure their lot and preserve their marriages by forgiving and forgetting. Today, such tolerance of abuse and resignation by women in the face of alternatives is viewed as pathological (Browne, 1987).

The Police Response The first dilemma facing a battered woman is whether or not to call the police. If she opts for bringing in outside assistance to force her attacker to cease, he might get arrested. Being taken into custody might "teach him a lesson," but it also could further provoke his anger and result in reprisals later.

Most of the episodes in which the police are called to break up a fight involve lower-income people, which might indicate that spouse abuse is associated with poverty and joblessness. Researchers conducting a study in Minneapolis when the unemployment rate was 5 percent found that 60 percent of the violent men that the police had to restrain were unemployed. On the other hand, higher-income persons may be reluctant to call the police to quell family fights (Sherman and Berk, 1984).

Intervening between husbands and wives has always been an unpleasant, thankless, and dangerous assignment for police. In the past, departmental policies stressed preserving the peace. The preferred course of action for officers who responded to calls about domestic disturbances was to pressure the participants to call a halt, and then "kiss and make up." If that failed, the police might insist that the enraged man exit the premises until he regains his composure ("take a walk and don't come back until you have cooled off"). Officers routinely failed to advise victims of their rights to file complaints because they identified with their male counterparts and assumed that the females either provoked the fights or subconsciously enjoyed the beatings. Only as a last resort, if the women's injuries were so severe as to require surgical sutures (the "stitch rule"), would officers make an arrest (Rhode, 1989).

An experiment conducted in Minneapolis during the early 1980s indicated that arrested offenders were about half as likely to assault their partners again as those men who only were forced to leave their homes to cool off or who had their disputes mediated by officers (Sherman and Berk, 1984). But complicated and apparently contradictory findings derived from five replication studies carried out during the late 1980s and early 1990s have cast doubt on the effectiveness of the Minneapolis study's implication that a mandatory arrest policy is the best way to handle disturbance calls. Getting arrested may serve as a deterrent to married men with jobs (who have a high stake in conformity), but it seems to be counter-productive and increase the likelihood of recidivism among unemployed men who are not married to the women they beat (Sherman, Berk, and Smith, 1992; Berk, Campbell, Klap, and Western, 1992).

Supporters of proarrest policies believe that punishing these aggressors is morally and legally appropriate, that arresting them will teach them a lesson and deter them from assaulting their wives again, deter other men from behaving similarly, and provide a legal basis for compelling them to undergo treatment for their violent tempers. Critics of this change in policy argue that police officers should exercise their discretion on a case-by-case basis. They point out that the arrested men may unleash greater violence against their wives or lovers after they are released; that the victims are likely to change their minds and refuse to sign complaints or follow through and press charges, perhaps out of fear of reprisals; that some battered women are not innocent victims but share responsibility for provoking their mates and for escalating the violence; and that compelling officers to make arrests in such volatile situations endangers their safety (Sherman, 1986; and Bouza, 1991).

Before the late 1970s, police officers were not allowed to make an arrest for a misdemeanor without a warrant issued ahead of time by a judge unless the simple assault was committed in their presence. But now, they can protect a victim by making an arrest if there are visible signs of injury, if a dangerous weapon was involved, if they believe the violence will continue after they depart, if they have prior knowledge of the offender's predilection for violence, or if an order of protection was violated (Bouza, 1991). By 1988, many states had passed provictim legislation improving police practices. In thirty-nine states, police are empowered to make a probable cause warrantless arrest for a domestic violence misdemeanor; in thirty-eight states, the victim does not have to be married to the offender to receive this protection; in twenty states, officers must write up a complete report; in fifteen states, departments must develop and implement training courses about how to handle domestic disturbances; in sixteen states, officers must transport injured victims to a nearby hospital; in eleven states, the police are authorized to supervise the eviction of abusers from their strife-torn homes; and in twenty-seven states, officers are required to inform victims of their legal rights by reading or presenting a written list (Hendricks, 1992).

Although the law is now supposed to be on the side of battered women, in some jurisdictions glaring problems remain. According to a study in 1989 of police files in Washington, D.C., in over 85 percent of the calls in which the woman was found bleeding from her wounds, the police did not arrest the man (Senate Committee on the Judiciary, 1993). In another evaluation of the implementation of a presumptive arrest policy, the abuser was taken into custody in only 18 percent of the cases (Bouza, 1991; Steinman, 1991; Ferraro, 1992; Miller, 1992).

A comprehensive provictim policy goes beyond the single issue of "to arrest or not to arrest" and requires more extensive community services, in the form of prosecutorial follow-through, emergency shelters, support groups for the women and therapeutic programs for the men (Bowman, 1992).

The Prosecutorial Response The next set of dilemmas a battered woman faces concerns prosecution: Should she keep up the pressure and get him into further trouble, thereby jeopardizing the continuation of the relationship? Or should she withdraw her complaint and permit her violent mate to come home? Historically, many prosecutors have discouraged women from pressing charges because they are concerned about their office's conviction rates and don't want to be committed to pursuing cases that are difficult to prove. They also have viewed domestic violence cases as minor disputes that are private matters that don't merit expenditures from their tight budgets and should be diverted into mediation (since many spouses presumably share responsibility for the bitter quarrels with their assailants, or they want to try to salvage the relationship). A woman might anticipate that punishing her mate will be counterproductive, hurting her and their children as well, or she may fear his fury when he is released, or she may prefer that he receive treatment rather than punishment. In some jurisdictions where spouse abuse is handled punitively, prosecutors have simplified procedures for filing complaints, set up special units staffed with specially trained assistant district attorneys, provided supportive victim/witness assistance programs and advocates, and devised more sentencing options. In other jurisdictions, most domestic violence cases are dismissed; of the remainder, most are bargained down to lesser offenses, and most of these convictions result in a sentence of probation, perhaps coupled with mandatory participation in some aggression-control program. Because many women change their minds about pressing charges, or are manipulated or intimidated by their violent mates to drop the charges, some jurisdictions have established procedures to go forward without the victim's testimony by relying solely on the evidence (911 tapes of calls for help; eyewitness accounts; hospital reports; incriminating statements by the defendants). Other jurisdictions have gone as far as mandating victim cooperation and threaten women with contempt-of-court proceedings if they set the legal machinery into motion and then decide they don't want to follow through and testify. However, the absence of the accuser usually results in dropped charges, dismissed cases, or the acquittal of the accused (Bouza, 1991; Cahn and Lerman, 1991; and Ferraro, 1992).

The Judicial Response The final set of obstacles facing victims arises from their attempts to get the courts to act in their best interests. Judges seeking to dispose of cases and clear their calendars are reluctant to clog up the system with long and drawn-out spouse abuse cases. But there are a number of steps dedicated judges can take to assist victims: accede to their wishes that bail be made low—or kept high—or revoked if reprisals occur; speed up case processing by avoiding continuances; and exercise their authority to issue "orders of protection" or "restraining orders," which are intended to shield victims from further attacks. These court orders, available in forty-nine states, are supposed to grant victims immediate relief by enjoining abusers from entering the battered woman's sphere of activity. A judge's order can evict and bar an assailant from their shared residence; prohibit any contacts, threats, harassment, or stalking; limit his supervised child visitation rights; require him to pay child support; and compel him to enter treatment. In the interest of the victim's immediate safety, a temporary order of protection can be handed down in the defendant's absence, if there is insufficient time to grant notice and hold a hearing. (After a proceeding where both parties have an opportunity to present their cases, the temporary order may become permanent for up to a year.) Since the orders are issued in civil court, the aim is separation of the disputants and not punishment, and the standard of proof is a preponderance of the evidence, and not guilt beyond a reasonable doubt. Violating a court order of protection can be a civil or a criminal offense that subjects the trespasser to immediate arrest. However, criminal justice officials and advocates for battered women have serious doubts about whether orders of protection are now, or can ever be, truly effective. In theory, stay-away orders straddle the middle ground between inaction (no arrest, dropped charges, probation) and overreaction (incarceration that results in escalating tensions, a criminal record and diminished job opportunities, and reduced financial support for the family). In practice, the greatest problem is that civil orders are not vigorously enforced by many police departments, especially in high-crime urban areas (Finn, 1991; Ferraro, 1992).

Preventing Battering

As always, reliance on criminal justice solutions may bring about temporary relief in specific cases and may even resolve particular conflicts among certain couples, but working with abusers and their victims does not address the root causes of the problem in the first place.

According to activists in the battered women's movement, it is a mistake to attempt to "pathologize" spouse abuse as a problem that burdens just a limited number of mentally disturbed couples. But it is also incorrect to try to normalize family violence as an inevitable by-product of unavoidable conflicts that occasionally arise in every intimate relationship.

Social scientists have developed a number of competing explanations to account for the widespread problem of partner abuse (see Gelles, 1987; Hotaling et al., 1988).

Those who apply *exchange theory* start out with the explanation that in couples, each partner supplies the other with valued services and benefits. The problem arises when a domineering person employs force to obtain his goals and discovers that the gains outweigh the losses (getting rough pays off). In nuclear families, where couples live in isolation from the scrutiny and support of others, the benefits of violence can exceed the costs because the authorities are reluctant to violate the privacy of intimates. Similarly, a *resource theory* analysis proposes that decision-making power within a family flows from the income, property, contacts, and prestige that each partner contributes to the relationship. Because men have advantages in the outside economy, they command much more power in most families, leaving the women in a subordinate and therefore vulnerable position. According to the *subculture-of-violence theory,* battering occurs more often in the homes of poorer people because the ready resort to physical force to settle disputes is more acceptable to them than among the middle classes, who purportedly believe in negotiation and compromise. The problem of male violence, according to *social learning theory,* arises because acting aggressively is generally taught and encouraged, along with female passivity and resignation, as part of sex role socialization. Intergenerational transmission of wife beating occurs when boys grow up watching their fathers beat their mothers during times of stress or bouts of heavy drinking (see Viano, 1992).

But the real underlying problem might go much deeper than just the way boys and girls are raised and could be rooted in the traditions of patriarchy (a system of male dominance), according to *feminist theory.* The division of domestic labor in families places the husband in the dominant role, assigning him male prerogatives, and the wife in a subordinate position, burdening her with female duties. These distinctions are legitimized by religion and the state, as symbolized by the wife's marriage vows to "love, honor, and obey" her husband. Some couples are on a collision course whenever the "head of the household" feels that his wife's assertions of independence are threatening his privileges and social status as protector and provider, and he may interpret the marriage license as his license to hit her, in order to regain control. In other couples, overly dependent, passive, and submissive wives serve as inviting targets for displaced aggression and misplaced blame. They seem resigned, crushed, and defeated and have learned to feel helpless and trapped because escape seems impossible: emotionally destructive to the children; economically disastrous; and likely to trigger more violence. In a society controlled by giant corporations and huge government bureaucracies, some men seize upon domination over their wives and children as a substitute for real autonomy. As long as women with children are financially dependent upon men, and both sexes are raised to expect male aggression and female passivity, woman battering will persist as a serious social problem (see Dobash and Dobash, 1979; Schechter, 1982; Walker, 1984; Yllo and Bograd, 1988; and Rhode, 1989).

The Rediscovery of Other Victims of Batterings

Once violence within intimate relationships was recognized as a widespread problem, two other rediscoveries became predictable. First, in some relationships, the predominant problem is female violence more than male aggression. Second, partner abuse is not limited to heterosexual couples; it can also occur in intimate relations between members of the same sex.

The Controversy Surrounding Battered Husbands Starting in the late 1970s, several social scientists began to challenge the dogma that all initiators are male and all victims female. They reported that their data on family violence had uncovered an overlooked but serious aspect of spouse abuse: husband beating. Survey findings revealed that there was some truth to the old images of wives slapping their husbands' faces, or chasing them with a frying pan, or throwing dishes at them: Women attacked the men in their lives (by slapping, kicking, biting, punching, throwing something, or threatening with a weapon) about as often as the men assaulted the women they professed to love (see Steinmetz, 1978a; Straus and Gelles, 1986). But skeptics argued that the sequence of events was not recorded in the surveys cited above and that much of the self-reported "violence" by women was probably unleashed in response to male provocations, or was carried out in self-defense, and did not qualify as aggressive initiatives. Because men tend to be bigger and stronger than their mates, their use of physical force is far more likely to bring about serious injuries. Perhaps for every battered woman there exists a beaten man, when it comes to "moderate aggression" (pushing and shoving). But the overwhelming majority of instances of "severe aggression," in which someone winds up in a hospital emergency room, are male-on-female offenses. Therefore, husband abuse should not be mistakenly "equated" with wife abuse, and a recognition that men can be battered too should not be used to undercut the urgency of stopping the battering of women (see Pleck et al., 1978; Lewin, 1992; Cose, 1994). Furthermore, most of the small number of women who are convicted in court of domestic violence offenses against their mates and are sent to batterer treatment programs were probably falsely accused. Their male partners lied, denied, and minimized their own use of force in the relationship and pretended to be victims when they were actually perpetrators (Zorza, 1994).

Genuinely battered men face several unique problems. First of all, if they reveal their plight, they face either disbelief or mockery (unless they are elderly or physically infirm). Since men traditionally are supposed to be physically adept and to "take charge of situations," for battered husbands to publicly admit that their wives get the best of them in family fights is to confess that they are not living up to these "manly" standards. Their failure to measure up to the "head of the household" stereotype might add to their confusion and distress from their special stigma, as well as inhibit them from reporting the abuse and seeking help. Their understandable reluctance to call the police after a beating (in anticipation of an insensitive response, if not outright contempt or even getting arrested based on stereotypical assumptions) as well as their fear of ridicule if they confide in their family or friends can only contribute to their sense of isolation. Second, if they overcome their feelings of inadequacy, self-loathing, and shame and dare to reveal their plight, they do not have access to the same resources now available to battered women, especially support groups, professional counseling, and temporary shelters. The only sanctuary for battered men in the country, established in St. Paul, Minnesota, in 1993, housed over fifty men in its first six months. However, these battered husbands have one crucial advantage compared to battered wives: Their ability to support themselves financially probably encourages many of them to leave the troubled relationship. And when they separate, they are rarely stalked, brought back, and beaten again (Chavez, 1992; Lewin, 1992; and Cose, 1994).

Battering within Same-Sex Relationships The second inevitable rediscovery was the recognition that physical fighting can mar the intimate relationships between gay men and between lesbians as well. Understandably, there was reluctance and resistance to any public disclosure about partner abuse in same-sex love affairs, for two reasons: Some feared that it would fuel homophobia; others were concerned that domestic violence would be reconceptualized as an outgrowth of the way power and privilege are exercised in the roles partners play in intimate relationships rather than a result of the oppression that arises strictly from gender differences. Partner abuse in gay and lesbian relationships is estimated to occur at least as frequently as violence within heterosexual relationships. For example, physical violence in relationships between gay males may injure as many as 500,000 persons annually. However, gay and lesbian victims have discovered they have fewer options and legal rights, in terms of pressing charges, seeking shelter, or obtaining restraining orders, than do their heterosexual counterparts. As a result, they often turn to programs intended to assist victims of hate crimes such as gay bashings committed by strangers (Island and Letellier, 1991; King, 1993; and Renzetti, 1992).

Other Casualties of Intrafamily Violence

Several other victim–offender relationships within the realm of intrafamily violence are being rediscovered and explored. Besides child abuse and spouse abuse, victimologists are carrying out research into elder abuse, sibling abuse, adolescent abuse by parents, and parent abuse by adolescents.

Elder Abuse *NCVS* data (BJS, 1994c) confirm the suspicion that elderly people are the least likely of all age groups to become victims of violence, personal theft, and household crimes, largely because of the precautions they take. But starting in the 1970s, victimologists and senior citizen advocates began to delve into other ways that older people are made to suffer by younger people (see Goldsmith and Goldsmith, 1976; Boston, 1977; Center, 1980; and Hochstedler, 1981). Elder abuse was rediscovered after child abuse and spouse abuse. Once the term was coined, the problem began to receive the attention it merited from geriatric social workers and law enforcement professionals, as well as researchers (see Quinn and Tomita, 1986; Breckman and Adelman, 1988; and Steinmetz, 1988b).

Elder abuse is defined as patterns of neglect, as well as acts of intentional harm. Neglect is recognized as failure to provide medical care, food (leading to malnutrition), clothing, and shelter; failure to protect from health and safety hazards; and failure to assist with personal hygiene. Acts of intentional harm take the form of either physical, psychological, or financial abuse. Physical abuse includes inflicting beatings; using unreasonable restraints; perpetrating sexual assaults; or withholding food, water, or medication. Psychological abuse refers to threatening, harassing, frightening, or otherwise verbally assaulting an elder or withholding emotional support. Financial abuse takes the form of outright theft, extortion, fraud, embezzlement, or misuse of the elder's funds (House Subcommittee, 1992). Domestic elder abuse is perpetrated by persons who provide care to elderly people who live at home. Institutional elder abuse is committed by individuals, such as employees of nursing homes, who have a contractual obligation to tend to the needs of older persons (McGrath and Osborne, 1989).

In 1992, a congressional committee reported an estimate that as many as 1.5 million older Americans (about 5 percent of all senior citizens) were subjected to physical, psychological, or financial abuse or suffered serious, even life-threatening neglect (House Subcommittee, 1992). The offender is most commonly a close relative, especially a grown child, spouse, or sibling. Less often, the abuser is a son- or daughter-in-law, grandchild, niece, nephew, or friend and neighbor. The typical victim is a frail, ailing woman more than seventy years old. In most cases, the victim and the abuser live in the same household in social isolation from friends, neighbors, and kin who might otherwise informally deter the abuse. The abusers tend to be overburdened care givers who become depressed and hostile at the long-term prospects of tending a mentally and physically impaired, isolated, and dependent individual. When homebound parents are physically beaten or financially exploited, sons are the most likely culprits; when daughters and daughters-in-law are abusive, their maltreatment usually takes the form of emotional and physical neglect. Mistreatment by home health aides and nursing home staff members is also suspected to be commonplace (Pagelow, 1989).

The underreporting of incidents of elder abuse remains a serious problem and accounts for the current lack of reliable data. Congressional investigators estimated that only about 16 percent of abused elderly persons dared to bring their plight to the attention of the proper authorities. Mandatory reporting laws, similar to those that require disclosure of suspected cases of child abuse, are being imposed on health care professionals, especially doctors, generating upwardly spiraling statistics, and overwhelming caseloads for geriatric social workers (Editors, *New York Times,* 1991).

Abuse of Adolescents by Parents Two problems held back the rediscovery that adolescents can be abused by their parents. First of all, the abuse of youngsters between twelve and eighteen was often overlooked entirely or else was subsumed under the heading "child abuse" and then neglected in favor of a focus on the very young and totally defenseless. Second, some attempts to define and measure abuse became confusing because of the cultural ambivalence about the extent of children's rights as opposed to parents' rights, and the thin line between physical abuse and physical discipline. Adolescents are not viewed as helpless or particularly vulnerable the way infants, toddlers, and youngsters under twelve are. The same force that, if used against a little child might produce an injury, might not seriously wound a teenager. The overt consequences of psychological abuse and emotional neglect become less detectable as adolescents mature into independent young adults. Many adults consider parental wrath to be justifiable if there is "sufficient provocation"—that is, if a beaten teenager is argumentative, defiant, "incorrigible," or "out of control" (see Lourie, 1977; Libbey and Bybee, 1979; and Pagelow, 1989).

Attempts to measure the frequency of adolescent abuse have yielded estimates that from one-fifth to almost one-half of all cases of child maltreatment known to social service agencies at various times during the 1970s and 1980s involved youths between twelve and seventeen. Parents use more severe forms of violence against their older children. As a result, teenagers tend to suffer more serious injuries than younger children. Their suffering usually comes to light when they are reported by their parents or their teachers to the authorities for disobedience or "acting out" behavior, or are referred to counselors for "emotional problems." Girls are more likely than boys to be physically, sexually, and emotionally abused, while boys are more often emotionally and educationally neglected. As boys grow older, the power differential between parents and sons decreases, and abuse declines. As girls become sexually mature and seek greater independence, the power differential between parents and daughters remains, leading to conflicts as parents impose restraints backed up by force. Sons who strike back get into legal trouble for assault, while girls seek to escape a repressive household by running away, acting promiscuously, or taking drugs. The majority of abused teenagers are white, from lower-income families where they are either the only child or one of four or more children. Their abusive parents tend to be middle-aged, are often stepparents, and are going through their own midlife crises. Their excessive violence ranged from hair pulling, slapping, and choking to beating and threatening with a knife or gun, to using a weapon (see Pagelow, 1989).

Abuse of Parents by Adolescents When teenagers batter their parents, the adults tend to feel ashamed and wish to keep the matters private, so there is a high rate of underreporting. In many cases, the violence directed at caretakers can be seen as an outgrowth of the violence parents previously visited upon their children. In that sense, an intergenerational cycle of violence has been set into motion. Mothers and stepmothers are more likely to be the injured parties than fathers or stepfathers. But male parents are more likely to be the targets of extreme violence, perhaps in retaliation for abuse or in self-defense against an attack. Physically aggressive fathers with drinking problems are the most common victims of severe injuries or even lethal force by sons who view themselves as protectors of their mothers and siblings. In the rare cases in which a daughter is involved in the murder of a parent, the actual killer is usually a male she recruited for the deed. Although increased attention is now paid to cases in which children kill their abusive parents, the number of parricides remained fairly constant during the 1980s (see Steinmetz, 1978b; Straus, Gelles, and Steinmetz, 1980; Lubenow, 1983; Pagelow, 1989; and Mones, 1991).

Sibling Abuse When brothers and sisters fight each other, their rough mistreatment is often disregarded as a "normal" expression of sibling rivalry. Sons are more violent than daughters, and all-boy families are the most violent of all. The use of force to resolve quarrels breaks out more often between siblings than between parents, or between parents and children. Older youths may not only physically assault but also sexually abuse younger siblings. The younger child generally does not tell anyone about the incidents for fear of being blamed, or not being believed, or of suffering reprisals (see Straus, Gelles, and Steinmetz, 1980; Pagelow, 1989; and Wiehe, 1990).

Sibling-on-sibling violence stands out because it is the most frequent type of assault and yet the least studied, which evidently reflects the difference between the priorities of researchers and the concerns of youngsters. In terms of a typology of victimization during childhood, violence between siblings can be classified as "pandemic" (occurs in the lives of a majority of children as they grow up), along with the incidence of a robbery, theft, vandalism of a possession, assault by a peer, and physical punishment by a parent. Less frequent in the lives of most children, but of greater severity, are victimizations that can be classified as "acute," including serious physical abuse and neglect, sexual abuse and molestation, and abduction by a family member. "Extraordinary" victimizations are the third category, which afflict a small number of children but with disastrous consequences: kidnapping by a stranger, forcible rape, death from child abuse, and murder. Much more professional and public attention has been paid to the extraordinary and acute types of victimizations than to the pandemic ones, to date. A more developmental approach is needed, one that explores the changing vulnerability of children to abuse by family and nonfamily members as they pass through different stages of immaturity and dependency (Finkelhor and Leatherman, 1994).

VICTIMS OF SEXUAL ASSAULT

The Rediscovery of the Plight of Rape Victims

Forcible rape is surely one of the most heinous violent crimes imaginable, and yet for centuries people reacted to this crime in inconsistent ways. In the past, rape was frequently handled as an offense that harmed the interests of a father or husband rather than the emotional and physical health of the girl or woman herself. Sometimes the unproven charge of rape provoked public outrage and demands for severe punishment, even execution—if the victim was a "chaste" woman from a higher social status and the offender was a complete stranger to her, and from a lower social status. In still other cases, if the victim was a "loose" woman, her claims that she was coerced into engaging in sex were usually discounted or even mocked. It was not until the start of the 1970s that rape victims were rediscovered by feminists fighting for the rights of women to control their own bodies (reproductive rights via contraception and abortion) and to resist sexual exploitation and domination. The provictim antirape movement exposed a legacy of injustice, routine abuse, and systematic neglect: Because of class, race, and gender discrimination, most offenses went unreported and unpunished. These feminists argued that rape was more than a personal tragedy—it was a social problem and a political issue. They interpreted sexual assaults as skirmishes in what had been traditionally referred to as the "unending battle of the sexes": as persistent acts of terrorism that intimidate all women and serve to keep them in their "proper place"—outside of male territory but subordinate to males (dependent upon "good" men for protection against "bad" men). As a crime, rape symbolized how a man could abuse his power differential—his superior physical force, often backed up with a weapon, to have his way sexually. As a legal matter, the handling of rapes dramatized how the men who ran the criminal justice system could not be trusted to act in behalf of the interests of victimized women. The relationship between the two parties (especially their social class, race/ethnicity, and prior contacts) often diverted attention away from the coerciveness of the sexual assault (see Russell, 1975; Griffin, 1979; Rhode, 1989; and Muehlenhard et al., 1992).

Through consciousness-raising groups and public speakouts, the antirape movement redefined the prevailing image of the crime and of its victims. Over the ages, rape had been pictured as an act of lust and an outpouring of uncontrollable sexual urges. Such a view seems plausible only if the physical injuries sustained by these "objects of desire" are totally ignored. The violence surrounding the sexual act—before, during, and after—betrays its true nature: an assault upon the victim's dignity and personhood for the purpose of domination and subjugation. The attacker reveals his hatred and contempt for all females, and certainly not his "passion" or "love" for a particular girl or woman.

"Real Rapes" and "Date Rapes"

Rape is generally defined as unlawful sexual intercourse ("carnal knowledge") by a male without the female's consent. Taking sexual advantage by penetrating a female who is unable to give meaningful consent because she is drugged, drunk, or unconscious (whether or not this altered state was induced by the offender) is classified as "simple rape." In contrast, "forcible" rape takes place if the target reasonably fears bodily harm if she refuses to acquiesce. "Aggravated" rape involves more than one assailant, and/or the use of a weapon, and/or the infliction of additional wounds besides the unwanted penetration. Other, less severe acts (for example, unwelcomed sexual contacts like fondling) are considered sexual assaults of a lesser degree. (Statutory rape is an illegal act in which a minor below the legal age of consent voluntarily engages in sexual intercourse.)

Although all sexual acts involving coercion of an unwilling person can be classified as sexual assaults in terms of the law, not all of these acts qualify as "real rapes" in terms of public opinion. Surely, widespread confusion over what constitutes "real rape" accounts for some of the controversy that today surrounds the handling of certain rape cases. Many people have trouble distinguishing sexual violence from "engaging in sex." As a result, when a woman summons up the courage to go public and claims to have been sexually assaulted (and, in "completed" rapes, penetrated against her will), some people might conjure up images of "lovemaking" rather than "forcible bodily invasion."

"Real rapes" (in the language of sociology, "ideal types"—in the sense that they are the clearest examples) are readily identifiable without question or doubt. Real rapes, in which an unsuspecting female is ambushed by a blitz attack, have several features: The offender is a complete stranger to the victim. He is heavily armed and leaps out of the darkness to surprise his prey. The victim is completely virtuous and above suspicion—perhaps too young, too old, or too inexperienced to be faulted in any way for attracting his attention. At the time, she is engaged in some "wholesome" activity that can't be criticized. Even though she faces grave dangers, she dares to fight back, resists to her utmost, and suffers severe physical injuries in a futile attempt to fend him off. Eyewitnesses glimpse parts of the struggle and hear her cries for help. As soon as she escapes from his clutches, she reports the crime to the police. Detectives find forensic evidence that backs up all her charges—that she was caught off guard, confronted with a weapon, brutally assaulted, overpowered, and forced to yield. Finally, when captured, the assailant, obviously a deeply disturbed predator, quickly confesses (see Estrich, 1986). Few people would have any difficulty conceding that a "real rape," one that mirrors many of these characteristics, is one of the worst experiences a woman can suffer. Detectives, prosecutors, juries, and judges agree that victims of such heinous crimes deserve to be treated with dignity and sensitivity within the criminal justice process and that such dangerous offenders must be removed from society and severely punished.

The problem for most rape victims is that the facts in their cases usually fall short, in one way or another, of the unambiguous standards that characterize a "real rape." As a result, the accusers' versions of events are likely to be questioned when essential elements are missing (for example, no brandishing of a weapon, no infliction of physical injuries, no ferocious struggle or desperate screams, and/or no corroboration by eyewitnesses or forensic tests). Doubts quickly surface if some crucial defining features of "real rapes" are missing (perhaps the victim knows the offender, or she fails to meet the old-fashioned criteria of "virtuous," or she does not report the attack for days or weeks). As a result, the man she accuses is less likely to be arrested, prosecuted, and convicted.

Consider a case like the following real-life, headline-generating story involving a young man from a prominent family who was eventually acquitted of all charges:

> **A** man meets a woman late at night at a fashionable cocktail lounge. They share some drinks, dance, and flirt. She returns to the oceanfront home where he is vacationing and they take a walk on the deserted moonlit beach at three in the morning. They embrace, he sheds his clothes, takes a brief swim, and then . . . throws her down on the sand, overpowers her, and violates her. (Gibbs, 1991)

Some would argue that if forced intercourse is preceded by a series of consensual acts with sexual overtones, her "contributory behavior" makes the nature of the crime less serious and it should be penalized less severely than an ambush attack. Others insist that it makes no difference if the victim and the offender knew each other and interacted warmly, even passionately, prior to the incident. The encounter cannot be written off as a case of miscommunication, or a terrible misunderstanding, or an instance of a woman having regrets for the way she behaved the night before. What counts is that she was stripped of control, denied the right to make a crucial decision, and compelled to submit to someone else's sexual demands (Gibbs, 1991). Until the late 1980s, most prosecutors would be very reluctant to move forward, press charges, and go to trial on a case like this—with no eyewitnesses, no bruises from a beating, no signs of a fierce struggle. Yet forced sex arising out of a date or from a nonsexual interaction with an acquaintance meets the legal definition of rape, which hinges on the use of physical coercion against a nonconsenting person, and not on the previous relationship between the accuser and the accused (Estrich, 1993a).

The Consequences of Being Sexually Assaulted

Rape victims have been studied more intensively than any other kind of crime victims. The aims of these studies have been to assess the nature of the suffering inflicted on them (see Girelli et al., 1986) and to discover ways of helping them to recover from the aftershock (see McCahill, Williams, and Fischman, 1979; APA Task Force, 1984; Burt and Katz, 1987; and Allison and Wrightsman, 1993). Being raped is almost always shattering to the victim, at least for a time. The ordeal challenges and may even transform her identity and the assumptions she makes about the world. The emotional impact is manifested largely as fear, anxiety, depression, sexual dysfunction, and feelings of isolation. The social impact shows up as the loss of any sense of invulnerability and immortality: the destruction of any sense of predictability within her environment and of the meaningfulness of events in her life; and a decline in her own sense of self-worth. The tribulation of being treated as an object instead of a person may plunge her into a "rape crisis syndrome." The acute initial phase of this syndrome lasts for about two or three weeks immediately following the sexual attack. The typical short-term reactions to being violated and humiliated are revulsion, shock, anger, fury, self-recrimination, fear, sorrow, and total disorientation. Victims often suffer from an inability to sleep, nausea, and tension headaches. The second phase, in which the victim's personality reintegrates, can last much longer and is characterized by recurring nightmares, defensive reactions, and strains in relationships with men. Many victims try to reorganize their daily lives by changing jobs, moving to a new location, dropping out of college, and limiting personal contacts. Lingering effects often include loss of sexual desire and the development of phobias—fear of being indoors as well as going outdoors, of being alone as well as being in crowds, and of persons approaching from behind (Burgess and Holmstrom, 1974).

Such reactions are now recognized as manifestations of a larger phenomenon besetting all kinds of victims who endure events that go beyond the range of usual tragic experiences: post-traumatic stress disorder (PTSD). People who reexperience their crises over and over again in daydreams, flashbacks, or nightmares are suffering from PTSD. Other symptoms include a desire to avoid things that remind one of the trauma, feeling different, a general lack of interest or enthusiasm, an inability to concentrate, and increased irritability (Williams, 1987). Focusing on the consequences of the crime for the person turned into a sex object dispels any notions that rape is an act of passion rather than of control and that the unwilling targets somehow invite, secretly desire, and deserve such treatment.

Even though most rapes are not completed (according to the *NCVS*, about two-thirds are not), females who thwart their assailants' intentions still suffer serious psychological scars. In fact, according to the results of a telephone survey carried out in South Carolina, women who endured attempted rapes were more likely to contemplate suicide and to try to kill themselves than women who suffered completed rapes (perhaps because of a fear of the unknown) (Kilpatrick, 1985).

Estimating the Incidence, Prevalence, and Seriousness of Rape

Victimologists and criminologists routinely point out that official statistics usually do not accurately indicate how many crimes of a specific kind are committed each year; but when it comes to rape, it is particularly likely that even the most carefully derived estimates could be way off.

The crucial question is, even if the yearly statistics are flawed, what is the trend? Is the rate of rape increasing, decreasing, or remaining about the same (albeit intolerably high)?

The official figures from the two government sources, the FBI's *UCR* and the BJS's *NCVS*, are both indisputably incomplete. The *UCR* statistics are gross underestimates, as always, because only rapes reported to the police are counted; surely some large percentage of victims do not tell the authorities. (According to the findings of the *NCVS* over the years, around half of all victims who were willing to discuss incidents with survey interviewers did not report the crimes to the police.) The statistics compiled by the *NCVS* are supposed to circumvent this problem of nonreporting to the police, since all incidents are counted, whether or not an official complaint was filed. But a new methodological question arises: "What percent of people who are raped are willing to disclose this information to government interviewers?" It's likely that the manner in which the data is gathered for the *NCVS* discourages some individuals from revealing what happened to them. Even though confidentiality is pledged, anonymity is compromised by face-to-face questioning; surely some girls and women are very reluctant to speak openly about such incidents, especially in the presence of other family members. Some respondents might feel uncomfortable discussing such a sensitive subject with any stranger, especially a male interviewer, particularly if his age, class, or ethnicity differ from that of the respondent. Some incidents that could legally be classified as rapes may not be defined as crimes by the females who experienced them, especially if the aggressor was an acquaintance and/or he used force or made threats but was not brutally violent. Screening questions are worded in roundabout ways; the term "sexual attack" is used but not spelled out graphically with examples. The survey's working definition excludes disclosures about marital rapes; acts of forcible sodomy to other parts of the body; and incidents in which the perpetrator took advantage of a person's intoxicated state, mental illness, or mental retardation. Finally, "series victimizations"—repeated rapes (generally by an intimate or acquaintance) are not counted as separate incidents (Koss, 1992).

The overall impact of all these methodological shortcomings of the BJS's victimization surveys is an underdetection of rapes in general, and acquaintance rapes in particular. Estimates derived from studies carried out by independent researchers suggest that the actual incidence of rape might be many times higher than the *NCVS* estimate of about 1 female per 1,000 per year. One telephone survey discovered that about 7 women per 1,000 suffer a completed rape each year (attacks on children and adolescents were not estimated; however, 61 percent of the respondents disclosed that they had been sexually assaulted before they were eighteen years old, so the overall incidence rate would be even higher for females of all ages, not just adult women). As for the victim–offender relationship, again official figures may be misleading if survey respondents are more inclined to reveal attacks by strangers. Females are much less likely to be attacked by a complete stranger than to be overpowered by someone they know and trust—an acquaintance, male relative, father or stepfather, boyfriend or former boyfriend, or husband or ex-spouse (Kilpatrick, 1992; Koss, 1992).

To sum up, these methodological issues account for the substantial disagreements in the estimated number of rapes from different sources. For example, during 1990, about 103,000 attempted and completed rapes were committed, according to police files compiled by the FBI's *UCR*. A larger number, about 130,000 girls over eleven and women, suffered attempted and completed rapes that year, according to the BJS's *NCVS*. But perhaps as many as 683,000 women were forcibly raped during that same year, according to projections from an unusually focused and frank telephone survey of a representative national sample of 4,000 adult females (Kilpatrick, 1992).

To address some of the methodological criticisms leveled by researchers against the way the FBI's *UCR* and the BJS's *NCVS* attempt to measure the incidence of rape, both data-collecting systems were changed. As of 1991, a new *National Incident Based Reporting System (NIBRS)* definition replaced the old, narrow *UCR* guideline of "carnal knowledge of a female forcibly and against her will." The FBI's *NIBRS* now counts sexual assaults directed against males and broadens the definition to keep track of incidents in which the person was not violated by force but was unable to give consent because of either a temporary or permanent mental or physical incapacity (due, for example, to unconsciousness). In addition, acts of forcible sodomy that don't involve intercourse, sexual assaults carried out with an object, and forcible fondling are noted and tabulated. In 1992, the *NCVS* expanded its data-gathering approach by adding screening questions inquiring about any unwanted or coerced sexual contacts (short of rape) that involved threats or attempts to cause harm. Also, interviewers were instructed to present "cues" that might jog the respondents' memories so they could recall and disclose more of these sex offenses.

Trends in Rape Rates, According to the Two Official Sources of Data
Further discrepancies and confusion arise when the estimated number of rapes each year is plotted on graphs to reveal changes over time.

According to the FBI's *UCR,* the trend since the 1960s is alarmingly upward. The number of rapes reported to the police has increased nearly every year, with few exceptions, and is reaching new highs in the 1990s. There is no sign that the crime is being brought under control. (See the graphs in Figures 5.2 and 5.3.)

But according to the *NCVS*, the number of rapes disclosed to survey interviewers goes down and up from year to year in a rather unpredictable way. In gen-

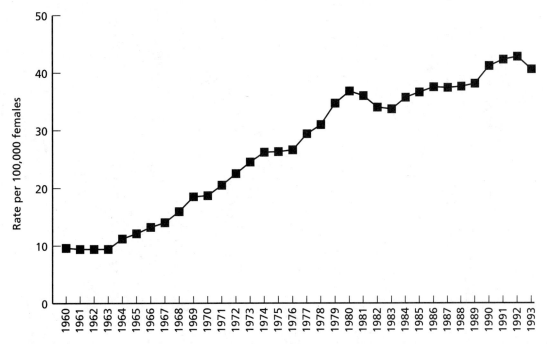

FIGURE 5.2 Trends in Rape Rates, *UCR,* 1960–1993

Note: Only incidents reported to the police are counted. Includes attempts as well as completed acts.

Source: FBI, *UCR,* 1960–1993.

eral, there appears to be a downward trend. After reaching a low in 1990, the number of disclosed rapes shot up in 1991, but then dropped to an all-time low (since the survey was initiated in 1973) in 1992. Therefore, the impressions from the two sources are exactly opposite. Rapes are becoming more frequent according to police reports and becoming less frequent according to survey disclosures. It is difficult to determine which trend best reflects reality. The *NCVS* statistics indicating a downward trend could be misleading if the underlying method of eliciting information from the people in the sample is seriously flawed. Survey interviewers do not directly and bluntly ask the respondents if they were "raped" during the past year. The BJS's discreet approach to such a sensitive topic might lead to underreporting if actual victims do not want to reveal their problems, or to overreporting if misguided nonvictims describe incidents that fall short of meeting the legal criteria defining the crime of rape (Eigenberg, 1990). The *UCR* statistics showing an upward trend could be inaccurate if more and more women are coming forward over the years to report rapes that in the past were not brought to the attention of the police. In particular, it is possible that public attitudes toward women raped by nonstrangers are improving, so victims of sexual assaults by dates and acquaintances are becoming less reluctant to report these kinds of offenses to the authorities (Orcutt and Faison, 1988). (However, there is no steady increase in

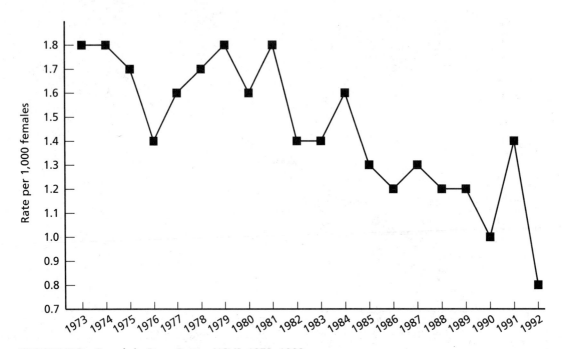

FIGURE 5.3 Trends in Rape Rates, *NCVS*, 1973–1992

Note: Only incidents disclosed to survey interviewers are counted. Includes attempts as well as completed acts.

Source: BJS's *NCVS*, 1973–1992.

rape reporting rates, according to *NCVS* figures; refer back to Table 4.1, which presents the percentages of rapes revealed to interviewers that were also reported to the police since the early 1970s.) It is also possible that police departments are taking the allegations of rape complainants more seriously and are investigating, documenting, and recording these kinds of incidents more carefully than in the past (Jensen and Karpos, 1993).

Although the *NCVS* figures are surely underestimates, the differential risks of being raped derived from the yearly survey are worth analyzing. The figures that appear in Table 5.1 reveal that different categories of females face different levels of risk. The statistical portrait indicates that unmarried, unemployed, black, teenage girls and young women who live in large cities and have low incomes are most at risk (Harlow, 1991).

An analysis of rapes reported to *NCVS* interviewers from 1987 to 1991 (Bachman, 1994a) revealed that the attacks were more likely to take place after dark but before midnight. Assaults were more likely to be committed by someone known to the victim (55 percent) than by a complete stranger (44 percent). Rapes committed by strangers were more likely to occur in some open area or public place than at or near the victim's home.

TABLE 5.1 Differential Risks of Being Raped

	ANNUAL RAPE RATE PER 1,000 FEMALES
All females	1.6 for every 1,000
By age:	
12–15	2.3
16–19	4.8
20–24	4.1
25–34	2.3
35–49	0.6
50–64	0.2
65 and over	0.1
By race and ethnicity:	
White	1.5
Black	2.7
Other	1.8
Hispanic	1.5
By marital status:	
Married	0.5
Widowed	0.4
Divorced or separated	4.3
Never married	3.5
By employment status:	
Employed	1.7
Unemployed	6.2
Keeping house	0.8
Going to school	3.8
By income:	
Low	2.7
Middle	1.2
High	0.8
By area of residence:	
Central cities	2.5
Suburbs	1.4
Nonmetropolitan areas	1.1

Notes: Estimated rates were derived from an analysis of 2,515,200 rapes (832,200 completed and 1,683,000 attempted) reported by respondents to *NCVS* interviewers from 1973 until 1987.
Source: Harlow, 1991.

The Controversy over Date Rape on College Campuses In the early 1990s, a controversy broke out over the actual incidence of date rape, especially on college campuses (see Warshaw, 1988; Schreiber, 1990; Bohmer and Parrot, 1993; Faludi, 1993; and Leone and de Koster, 1995). Antirape activists took a maximalist stance and launched educational campaigns alerting students, parents, and college administrators to what they perceived to be an epidemic of sexual assaults in dorms, fraternity houses, and off-campus apartments. Their minimalist critics charged they were disseminating inflated risk estimates by loosely applying the serious term *rape* to much less serious, regrettable, or equivocal sexual encounters. "Real" forcible rapes after dates appeared to be rare and isolated events. Minimalists pointed out that despite widespread rape awareness programs, government surveys monitoring crime on campus revealed that very few students ever filed complaints about being raped after a date.

Advocates of the maximalist position put forward the following arguments: The pervasiveness of the date rape crisis was not being recognized because these offenses are reported even less often than sexual assaults by strangers, since the young women fear they will be harshly judged, condemned, and slandered. The only way to accurately estimate the true dimensions of the problem is through anonymous questionnaires in which respondents who disclose intimate details about their upsetting sexual confrontations are assured of confidentiality. In the 1980s, carefully constructed and administered surveys documented how common coerced sex really was. For example, in one widely cited survey, over 3,000 women students at 32 colleges were presented with scenarios that described sexual assaults as defined by recently reformed state statutes. Respondents could identify elements of the crime that resembled their own experiences, such as being plied with liquor until judgment was so impaired that "consent" was meaningless, being physically held down, or being forced to surrender from arm twisting. From the survey's findings, the researcher estimated that about 166 out of every 1,000 female students (a shocking 17 percent) suffered one or more attempted or completed rapes per year. Fewer than 5 percent reported the assault to the police, about 5 percent sought solace at a rape crisis center, and almost half told no one at all about what happened. In 84 percent of the cases, the victim knew the offender; in 57 percent, he was a date. Projecting a yearly incidence estimate into a lifetime prevalence estimate indicates that as many as 1 in 4 college-aged young women might have experienced an attempted rape or a completed rape since she was fourteen years old (Koss et al., 1987; Koss and Harvey, 1991).

Followers of the minimalist position make the following countercharges: Many of the "date rapes" included in the count by maximalists actually fall into a gray area between sexual assault and consensual sex and should be excluded. Cases in which a young woman felt pressured into agreeing to engage in sex, or had lost good judgment because of drinking or drug taking, or wanted to say "No!" but was not assertive enough to stop the young man's advances were classified as rapes by maximalists adopting a definition that was too broad and vague. If the woman was "given" alcohol or drugs by the man prior to intercourse, that does not mean she was "intentionally incapacitated" as the law requires for prosecution and conviction. Verbal coercion, manipulation, deception, false promises, and betrayal—all of which are nonviolent tactics in the male arsenal of "seduction"—are errone-ously equated with "being forced to give in" but are not the same as physical as-sault, the use of a weapon, or a credible threat. Most of the women deemed vic-tims by the maximalist researchers did not consider themselves to have been raped, and over 40 percent of them dated their supposed assailants again and engaged in intercourse again with them. The *NCVS* survey figure that one female in a thou-sand is raped or fends off a would-be rapist each year is much closer to the truth and puts the problem in its proper perspective. By overestimating the date rape problem, maximalists were manufacturing a crisis in order to further certain social policies such as increased funding and training programs. Their political agenda was unnecessarily alarming women, trivializing those "real" rapes that are genu-inely brutal, undermining the credibility of real complainants, and unfairly por-traying all male–female relationships as inherently antagonistic and fraught with danger. Promoting such a negative image of sexuality stigmatizes normal hetero-sexual intercourse as criminal conduct unless explicit, unambiguous consent is se-cured from the female partner before each escalation in intimacy. The presumed adversarial model of bold male initiatives and timid female resistance denies the re-ality of female desires and portrays women as naive, helpless, vulnerable, and in need of strictly enforced protective codes of appropriate sexual behavior, more than equal rights. The underlying politics of the antidate rape movement actually sets back the cause of women's equality, minimalists contended (see Gilbert, 1991; Podhoretz, 1991; Crichton, 1993; Hellman, 1993; and Roiphe, 1993).

Regardless of the actual dimensions of the threat, the tactics to discourage date rapes must be different from those employed to prevent stranger rapes (for ex-ample, securing campus buildings against intruders). Efforts by college administra-tions include holding dating workshops during freshman orientation week, com-plete with reenactments of dangerous situations and role-playing exercises led by seniors; setting up rape crisis centers and fostering a climate of openness on cam-pus that encourages students to report offenses and seek help; and issuing student-government approved guidelines and handbooks for completely consensual sexual conduct, with violations punishable by expulsion by a campus judicial committee (Crichton, 1993; and Bohmer and Parrot, 1993).

How the Criminal Justice System Handles Rape Victims

Before public consciousness was raised by the antirape movement, complainants who courageously reported sex crimes were socially stigmatized. The old-fashioned notion was that "good girls don't get raped, so those who do must have somehow done something to deserve their fate." Even if an unquestionably in-nocent victim was taken against her will, she was callously looked down upon as being "defiled" and "devalued" by the experience. Those who dared to press charges were often told that their cases were unprosecutable—"unwinnable," given the unreasonably stringent legal standards required for conviction. However, as the public grew alarmed about an apparent upsurge in sexual violence, legislators became more willing to change sexist laws that reflected the moral strictures of the past. State by state, beginning with Minnesota in 1974, statutes were rewritten as the analysis put forward by feminists gained acceptance and as more women became lawyers and legislators, reforming the legal system from within, as well as pressuring it from without (Largen, 1987).

The laws passed over the centuries and amended by judges' case-by-case decisions (common law), were not intended, and never functioned, to guarantee the safety, freedom of movement, and peace of mind of women. The choice of terms like *fallen, ravaged,* and *despoiled* to describe rape victims betrayed the attitudes of men toward girls and women: that they were the "property" of their fathers or husbands who lost "market value" if they were "violated." Rape laws reflected and reinforced the prevailing double standards regarding appropriate forms of sexual conduct and sex-based roles for females and males (Le Grande, 1973). Built-in antivictim biases that shaped the way cases were investigated and prosecuted were most evident in the corroboration rule, the resistance requirement, and the practice of inquiring into the victim's sexual history.

Over the decades, the provictim antirape movement has tried to eliminate these unfair roadblocks on the path to justice. Today, cautious optimists emphasize how much progress has been made in dismantling the institutionalized discrimination that put victims at such an unusual disadvantage in the not-too-distant past (see Fairstein, 1993). Skeptics point out how many traditional antivictim practices still need to be reformed within the justice system. The degree of success of efforts by the antirape movement can be evaluated with reference to the following criteria: improvements in public attitudes regarding a woman's right to sexual autonomy, free from coercion; gains in the willingness of victims to report the crimes and press charges; declines in the perceptions of complainants that the entire fact-finding and decision-making process is painful and degrading; and increases in the rates of arrest, prosecution, conviction, and incarceration of rapists (see Goldberg-Ambrose, 1992; Spohn and Horney, 1992).

The Controversy over Unfounded Accusations   Rape has always been in a class by itself, unlike any other crime, in one peculiar way: There always has been great concern about false accusations. Even though knowingly and maliciously filing a false complaint with the police and having someone falsely imprisoned are punishable acts no matter what the crime, fears about baseless charges in rape cases have been so great that special safeguards were built into the laws in the past.

Two types of errors are always possible, honest mistakes and deliberate acts of perjury intended to hide the truth. A complainant in any kind of criminal case, acting in good faith, can make a terrible mistake and identify the wrong person—

some innocent stranger—as the perpetrator. In the case of rape, confusion and distress can lead to an honest error that is especially damaging, as the following two cases illustrate:

A college student tells the police that she was raped outside her dormitory late one night. She identifies a graduating senior in engineering who is a basketball star as her attacker by selecting his picture from the school yearbook and then pointing him out in a police lineup. The rape charge polarizes the campus, in part because he is black and she is white. His supporters view him as a victim of an injustice; at rallies, they argue that the woman and the police, in their rush to find the culprit, are having trouble distinguishing one black man from another. Her supporters march in solidarity with all women who have been assaulted and then disbelieved when they come forward and ask for help. He is arrested, then released on bail, but is barred from the campus except to attend classes and use the library. She returns to her home to study for her final exams. When a number of credible alibi witnesses testify that the accused was far away from the campus that night, the prosecutor drops the charges against him and closes the case for lack of additional evidence or investigatory leads. (Lyall, 1989)

A hitchhiker is picked up by a man with a beard wearing a three-piece suit. He drives the young woman down a dirt road, pulls over, overpowers and rapes her, and then kicks her out. She goes to the police and identifies her attacker from a "photo lineup"—a collection of mug shots that the detectives show her. The young man insists he is innocent but is convicted largely on the basis of her testimony. But several months after the trial, the police uncover evidence that links someone else to a series of rapes, including this one. When detectives show the complainant the new suspect's picture, she immediately recognizes him and then breaks into tears, crying "Oh my God, what have I done?" The mistakenly accused and convicted man is soon released from prison but his life is in shambles: He has no money left because of legal fees; he has lost his job and good reputation; and his fiancée has broken off their engagement. He sues the authorities but dies from a heart attack shortly before being awarded a settlement of $2.8 million. (Goleman, 1995b)

Fraudulent accusations are even more of a concern than mistaken identifications. The fear is that a dishonest girl or woman could attempt to deceive the authorities and knowingly lodge a fake charge against an innocent man for some ulterior purpose—perhaps to punish her former lover, to provide a "don't-blame-me" explanation for an embarrassing pregnancy or venereal disease, or to hide the truth for some other reason. Widely held negative stereotypes and suspicions about manipulative or vengeful women obviously fuel these fears. To justify the routine skepticism that many rape complainants receive in press accounts, police stations, prosecutors' offices, and courtrooms, cases like the following are often cited:

A secretary working for a prominent law firm goes to the sex crimes squad and tells detectives in a calm and forthright manner that a senior partner raped her when they were working alone in the office late one night. When questioned, the attorney denies he raped her but admits to carrying on a discreet affair with her, telling his wife he was working late or traveling overnight on business trips. He claims that when she demanded that he leave his family and move in with her, his refusal provoked her to threaten to kill herself, kill his wife, or kill him. Confronted by detectives with his version of events—that a "scorned woman" was making up terrible charges to get even with him for dashing her dreams of upward mobility—she initially denies the charges. But when the police dig up hotel bills and airline ticket receipts documenting their secret trysts together, she confesses that her vengeful claim was intended to cost him his prestigious job and his marriage. (Fairstein, 1993)

A fifteen-year-old black girl is discovered in an apparent state of shock curled up in a plastic garbage bag. She does not say much to police officers or doctors, but according to her relatives and her lawyers she had been kidnapped and repeatedly raped for several days by four white men who appeared to have police affiliations. Her explosive charges divide the public along racial lines. A special grand jury is impaneled by the state's attorney general to look into the accusations and to explore the possibility of an official cover-up; it concludes that there is insufficient evidence to charge anyone with a crime. Months later, the girl's boyfriend claims that she told him that she and her mother made up the whole story so that her stepfather would not beat her for staying out late. Unfortunately, an aunt who believed the story contacted the news media, which sensationalized the incident into headlines for months. (Payne, 1989; Taibbi and Sims-Phillips, 1989)

The "Scottsboro Boys" case stands out in history as the most notorious example of what appears to be a false accusation of rape for some malicious purpose. The trumped-up charges were made for political reasons. In the Old South, white women were often pressured by white men to falsely accuse black men of rape so that the alleged suffering of the victims could be seized upon to justify the execution or lynching of the accused individuals and, by extension, to rationalize the segregation and repression of all black men (Sagarin, 1975). The controversy surrounding the way the defendants in this case of "Southern racial justice" were "railroaded in a kangaroo court" without lawyers and sentenced to die led to a Supreme Court decision *(Powell v. Alabama,* 1932) that established the right of persons accused of capital crimes to be represented by competent counsel.

The task confronting detectives and prosecutors is to weed out the very few false claims (about a consensual act that is later characterized as forced; or about a totally fabricated incident that never took place) from the overwhelming majority of genuine charges. The dishonesty of a few does not justify systematically mistreating all complainants as liars (Fairstein, 1993). The task for criminologists and victimologists is to determine how often baseless charges are lodged and whether false accusations are really more common in rape cases than in other crimes.

Credible statistics about the percentage of complaints that turn out to be "definitely" baseless are hard to find. The FBI's *UCR* reported that, in 1966, local police forces across the country, after a preliminary investigation, had declared 20 percent of all rape complaints unfounded and, in 1976, 19 percent. During 1991, 1992, and 1993, the FBI estimated that only about 8 percent of all rape complaints were classified as unfounded (compared to about 2 percent of all complaints about other index crimes). However, the designation "unfounded" is not synonymous with "false accusation." Some of the cases in this category were deemed by the police to be unprovable in court, but that doesn't mean that the complainants were deliberately committing perjury or imagining things. Social workers at a hospital and a police sex crime unit have estimated the false complaint rate to be only 1 or 2 percent (Bode, 1978).

In sum, fake reports about sexual assaults that never happened lodged by dishonest complainants posing as victims are very rare, but the havoc they wreak is very real and pervasive: Highly publicized instances fan smoldering traditional doubts that cast a cloud of suspicion over all legitimate victims who demand to be taken seriously.

Detectives often operated on the presumption that false cries of forcible rape were the rule and not the exception. For example, many police departments routinely administered lie detector tests to check a complainant's credibility. Since the prospect of submitting to a polygraph test of questionable reliability loomed as an added indignity and served as a further deterrent to reporting crimes and pressing charges, groups in the antirape movement (who are convinced the problem of false allegations is greatly exaggerated) went to court to get injunctions against the practice. The President's Task Force on Victims of Crime (1982) recommended that procedures that reflected routine distrust of complainants be abandoned, and a number of states have specifically outlawed polygraph testing of complainants.

Unusually stringent standards of proof were intentionally crafted into rape laws in order to make it particularly difficult to secure convictions. The men who wrote the laws and administered the legal system considered these difficult-to-surmount hurdles to be safeguards against miscarriages of justice. But from the genuine innocent victim's standpoint, these "safeguards" loomed as major obstacles that discouraged and thwarted her pursuit of justice. From a feminist perspective, these obstacles represented a clear case of institutionalized sexism.

The exceptionally high standards of proof required in rape cases took several forms: demands for evidence that the female did not willingly consent to engage in sex; a requirement that her testimony be corroborated (backed up in some independent way); and a tradition that she undergo particularly vigorous cross-examination by a defense attorney at the trial. At the end of a trial, a judge often delivered a "cautionary instruction" to the jury before they began their deliberations, reminding them of the traditional assumption that the woman's charges might be completely false. Often quoted is an English judge who, in 1671, cautioned that although it is easy to accuse a man of rape but hard to prove the charge, it is even harder for an innocent man to defend himself and clear his name.

The Accuser vs. the Accused In the prosecution of rape cases, the rights of the accused man are directly pitted against the rights of the accusing woman. According to the Sixth Amendment, he has a right to wage (through his attorney) a vigorous defense. According to recent victims' rights legislation and rewritten rape laws, she has a right to be taken seriously and treated with respect on and off the witness stand. Observing the rights of both parties requires a delicate balancing act that has not been resolved yet.

Males accused of committing a forcible rape can pursue one of several possible defense strategies. The first is to argue that the complaining witness has made a terrible error, accusing an innocent man of committing a crime carried out by someone else—the "mistaken identity" defense. The second is to deny that the accused engaged in sexual acts with the complainant—the "it-never-happened defense." This stand requires a direct attack on the alleged victim's credibility and motivation, charging that she made up a completely false story for some deceptive reason. The third defense is to concede that the accused engaged in sexual intercourse with the complainant but to argue that she agreed at the time; afterward, she changed her mind, considered it a rape, and had him arrested—the "consent" defense.

The issue of consent is central to any rape complaint, since "willingness" or at least "voluntary compliance" is what distinguishes making love from being sexually assaulted. The victim must convince the police, the prosecution, and ultimately a jury that she did not freely agree to engage in sex but was forced to submit by her attacker. The burden of proof shifts onto the woman, who must present a compelling account that she in no way encouraged, enticed, or misled the man she is accusing of violating her against her will. The prosecutor must establish beyond a reasonable doubt that she was forced—hit, knocked down, pinned down, overpowered, or threatened with serious bodily harm. The prosecutor must also show that she is a person to be believed, a woman of integrity and impeccable character, who has no motive to distort the truth. To stir up reasonable doubts, the defense will pursue a strategy of impeaching her credibility by attacking her virtue. The goal is to sow the seeds of reasonable doubt among jurors by asserting that she consented at the time but later regretted her decision and lodged false charges. To undermine her credibility as the star witness for the prosecution, the defense attorney often pursues a "nuts and sluts" strategy, portraying her as a mentally unstable liar and/or as a sexually promiscuous willing partner. To counter such personal attacks, the prosecutor must argue that the defense attorney is turning the tables and is putting the victim on trial, humiliating her again, this time in court, in front of the jury. From the complainant's point of view, some reasonable limits should be placed on the defense's cross-examination so it doesn't become a degrading spectacle. But from the defendant's point of view, it is only fair that she answer probing questions about her sexual involvements in the past and her mental health, if he is to have a fighting chance in this credibility contest to clear his name and expose the falseness of her charges against him (Estrich, 1993b; Vachss, 1993).

Rape Shield Laws To screen out improper lines of questioning regarding the issue of consent, from the mid-1970s to the mid-1980s legislatures in almost every state passed rape shield laws. Generally, shield laws say that the defense cannot introduce evidence about an accuser's past sexual conduct unless the woman has previously been convicted of prostitution, or has had consensual sex before with the defendant, or has an obvious motive to lie. Procedural guidelines provide for a hearing in the absence of the jury, spectators, and the press to permit the judge to determine whether or not the defense counsel's allegations about the woman's past should be aired in open court. Staunch supporters of shield laws want more restrictions on the ability of defense attorneys to raise credibility issues and cite several justifications: to encourage victims to go to the authorities for help by assuring them that their privacy will be respected; to spare complainants the embarrassment of having the most intimate details of their sex lives made public and used against them in court; to dispel the fallacy that "if she consented in the past she probably consented this time too"; and to prevent juries and judges from being distracted by allegations about the complainant's past affairs when they should be focusing on the allegations about the defendant's use of force. Critics of shield laws want fewer restrictions and argue that the laws deny the accused the right to effectively confront his accuser and therefore to have a fair trial on a "level playing field." Higher-court decisions have held that most inquiries into the woman's reputation for "chastity" have little relevance for determining consent (Stark and Goldstein, 1985; Austern, 1987; Lewin, 1993b).

Force and Resistance In the not-so-distant past, to convict a rapist, a woman had to convince a jury that she forcefully resisted to her utmost and ceased struggling only because she feared she would be killed or seriously injured. The justification cited for requiring such proof of resistance was that it indicated the victim's state of mind (unwillingness) and refuted the defendant's claims that he reasonably believed his partner was just feigning reluctance and was actually willing to engage in sex. Legal reforms enacted in most states no longer require the woman who wants to press charges to risk her life fending off her attacker. A reasonableness standard stipulates that the degree of resistance considered to reflect nonconsent can depend on the circumstances. A strong statement or an unambiguous act is sufficient to show lack of consent in the face of overwhelming force or an intimidating weapon. The woman does not even have to fight back, or scream, or try to flee. Evidence that the accused possessed a weapon or that the victim was physically injured is also sufficient to establish nonconsent (Robin, 1977; Stark and Goldstein, 1985; Austern, 1987).

A survey of 4,000 women interviewed over the telephone about completed rapes discovered that about 70 percent reported no additional physical injuries, 24 percent said they suffered additional minor injuries, and 4 percent sustained serious wounds in addition to being penetrated against their will (Kilpatrick, 1992).

Although the proportion of women who are killed after being raped is extremely small (far less than 1 percent), the proportion of murdered women who were raped before they were killed is not so small. An analysis of female homicide victims in California during 1988 revealed that 6.5 percent had been sexually assaulted before they were murdered (Sorenson and White, 1992).

How the victim reacts can profoundly influence the outcome of a sexual assault. Her behavior—either submission or resistance—affects the attacker's decisions about whether to try to complete the act and about how much force to use to subdue her. Some victims are still blamed for not resisting fiercely enough.

Between 1987 and 1992, most assailants were unarmed (about 21 percent had guns, knives, or other sharp instruments). Most of the victims who took some type of self-protective action, such as yelling for help or fighting back, reported to NCVS interviewers that it helped the situation (61 percent) rather than made it worse (17 percent) (Bachman, 1994a).

The victims who resisted improved their chances of thwarting the rapists' aims of completing the act, but they also increased their risks of suffering additional injuries. One-third of the nonresisting victims were wounded in addition to being sexually assaulted, whereas two-thirds of the victims who used self-defense measures were physically hurt—bruised, cut, scratched, even stabbed or shot, according to a study of NCVS data from the late 1970s (McDermott, 1979). In a study of about 125 women who were assaulted by rapists, the best strategy turned out to be a "dual verbal defense" of calling out for help while simultaneously attempting to reason with, plead with, or threaten the attacker. Nearly all the women who physically resisted their assailants reported that their actions only made the men angrier, more vicious, and more violent (Cohen, 1984).

Studies assessing the relative effectiveness of various responses have generated mixed, confusing, and perhaps impractical recommendations. It is impossible to predict the outcome of a particular assault, given the complex web of factors involving the offender, his intended victim, and their situation at that moment. Girls and women under attack—and those who would advise them how to behave during the confrontation—face an unavoidable dilemma: Resistance may foil a rape but may further endanger their physical well-being. But at least one factor in the equation has changed to the advantage of victims. Whether or not fierce resistance "within reason" is the best strategy under all circumstances, it is no longer required to justify an arrest and prosecution.

The apparent acquiescence of some victims can be readily explained. The primary reaction of nearly all rape victims is to fear for their lives, according to interviews conducted at a hospital emergency room (Burgess and Holmstrom, 1974). Therefore, some victims are simply immobilized by terror, shock, and disbelief. Faced with the prospect of death or severe physical injury, many conclude that their only way out is to "strike a bargain" or a tacit "understanding" with the attacker, and trade submission for survival (to exchange sexual violation for some sort of pledge that they won't be killed, savagely beaten, or cruelly disfigured). There is, of course, no guarantee that compliance will minimize physical injury. The rapists do not have to keep their promises (Brownmiller, 1975).

Corroboration An aspect of the law in most states that made rape charges very difficult to prove beyond a reasonable doubt was the corroboration requirement, which demanded that the prosecution discover independent evidence to back up the key elements of the victim's account. Derived hundreds of years ago from the evolution of British common law, the corroboration requirement assumed that the complainant's accusations alone were not credible without some other form of substantiation. Corroboration can take the form of medical and forensic evidence gathered by a doctor; torn clothing; other signs of a struggle; the testimony of an eyewitness or a third party like a police officer, a family member, or a friend who had been promptly told about the assault; and the physical condition of the victim. The belief that the woman's word alone should not be enough to secure a conviction in court was based on several concerns: that some females might accuse males falsely; that males charged with rape were socially stigmatized immediately; and that conviction carried serious penalties, including, until recently, execution. But the corroboration requirement was criticized as being patently unfair for putting rape victims in the unique position, compared to complainants of other kinds of assaults, of being automatically distrusted without additional "real proof." Now, to strike a balance, most state laws no longer require corroboration, unless the victim is a minor, was previously intimate with the accused, did not promptly report the crime to the authorities, or provides a version of events that is inherently improbable and self-contradictory (Robin, 1977; Stark and Goldstein, 1985; and Austern, 1987).

Arrest, Prosecution, and Adjudication In order for a crime to be solved, it must first be reported. But most rapes are not reported to the police, according to findings from the *National Crime Victimization Survey*. Some victims tell *NCVS* interviewers about sexual assaults committed against them about which they never told the police. The reasons females cited most often for not informing the authorities were that they feared reprisals, considered the incident to be a private or personal matter, or felt that they lacked proof. Women who reported the offenses to the police most often said they did so to be rescued, to prevent the rapist from harming them again or attacking someone else, and to get him in trouble so that he would be punished. Women are more likely to go to the authorities if the assailant used a weapon or if they were physically wounded and require medical care for their injuries. About half the perpetrators were known to their targets. Whether or not the offender was a complete stranger, an acquaintance, or an intimate did not seem to affect the decision to report or not report the crime to the police, according to *NCVS* findings (BJS, 1994b). Of course, some victims do not want to discuss sexual assaults committed against them with *NCVS* interviewers either. The question arises, How many rapes are not reported to the police and not disclosed to the *NCVS*? Researchers attempting to find out about unreported rapes conducted a telephone survey of over 4,000 women (which asked unusually explicit questions about forced penetrations and other sexual assaults) concluded that the reporting rate to the police may actually be as low as 16 percent. After the attack, the victims' greatest concerns, which influenced reporting decisions, were that her family would find out; other people would find out; she would be blamed for what happened; and that she would contract AIDS, another venereal disease, or become pregnant (Kilpatrick, 1992).

Over the years since the *NCVS* started in 1973, the rate at which women report rapes to the police has hovered around 50 percent, ranging from a low of 41 percent in 1980 to a high of 61 percent in 1985 (see Table 4.1 in Chapter 4). There does not appear to be a pronounced upward trend toward higher rates of reporting, despite many public relations efforts to encourage more victims to come forward (such as poster campaigns and special hotline numbers), and several reforms (like safeguarding a woman's privacy by not publicly identifying her; and establishing rape crisis centers at hospitals and on campuses).

In order to improve the solution rate and to prevent victims from being treated insensitively, some police departments have set up sex crimes squads with specially trained detectives. Despite these measures, aggregate clearance rates for police departments across the nation show no improvement in recent years (see Table 4.3 in Chapter 4). In fact, the percentages of cases that were solved each year were much higher in the past, even though most of the reported rapes in those days involved attacks by strangers (such cases are more difficult to solve than sexual assaults by persons known to the victim).

Victims of acquaintance rapes face more obstacles within the criminal justice system than victims of stranger rapes. Although acquaintance rapes are still grossly underreported (see Kanin, 1984; Estrich, 1986), they comprise a rapidly growing proportion of all cases brought to the attention of staffers at rape crisis centers and prosecutors within specialized sex-crimes units. However, attrition rates for acquaintance rape cases are substantially higher than for stranger rape cases. Victims are more inclined to ask that charges be dropped, and prosecutors are less willing to press charges because they fear juries will find "reasonable doubts" and not convict defendants (Mansnerus, 1989; LaFree, 1989).

In an effort to increase the conviction rate, some district attorneys have established sex-crimes prosecution units with specially trained lawyers. Traditionally, prosecutors whose performance was judged on the basis of their won/lost records preferred offering lenient pleas rather than going to trial, unless the complainant fit the narrow stereotype of a "good woman." The kinds of victims who are believed by jurors and arouse their sympathy are wives and mothers who are attractive but not too "sexy," well educated, articulate, and visibly upset but not hysterical while testifying (Vachss, 1993).

Most rape cases, like other felonies, are resolved through plea negotiations. The percentage of rape cases that go to trial varies greatly by jurisdiction (in 1981: San Diego, 2 percent; Manhattan, 12 percent; Los Angeles, 20 percent; St. Louis, 23 percent; Washington, D.C., 32 percent). In general, however, defendants in rape cases are more willing to have their charges resolved by jury trials than defendants in other crimes except homicide (Boland and Sones, 1986).

Besides the creation of special investigation and prosecution squads, a number of other reforms have been enacted to try to increase the arrest, prosecution, conviction, and incarceration rates. In most jurisdictions, the chances of conviction in sexual assault cases have been enhanced by new legal codes and sentencing structures which specify gradational levels of seriousness (from improper sexual contact to forcible rape), each carrying a corresponding penalty (Bienen, 1983; Largen, 1987). In many courtrooms, evidence of rape trauma syndrome can be introduced during trials to account for behavior on the victim's part (concerning reporting delays or failure to actively resist), which in the past would have undermined her credibility.

And yet, despite these many reforms and attempts at improving the criminal justice system's handling of rape cases, most attackers are never arrested, prosecuted, convicted, and certainly not incarcerated. According to one study, for every 100 rape arrests, 76 defendants are prosecuted (and 24 find the charges against them dropped); of these 76 charged, 50 are convicted; of these 50 convicted, 42 are sentenced to jail or prison, but only 29 face a sentence of more than one year behind bars (Lisefski and Manson, 1988). This funneling or shrinkage (many cases enter the system at the outset; few offenders wind up in prison at the end of the case processing) has shown up to even greater degrees in other studies. According to a survey of criminal justice agencies in states that together contain more than half of the nation's population, more than half (54 percent) of all rape prosecutions result in either a dismissal before trial or an acquittal after a trial. As for sentencing outcomes, about 21 percent of convicted rapists are granted probation, and another 24 percent are sent to county jails for up to eleven months, so nearly half (45 percent) of all offenders found guilty of rape are not sent to prison. Factoring in unsolved crimes and unsuccessful prosecutions, the accused assailant serves some time in state prison in only about 1 out of every 10 rapes that were reported to the police. When the rapes that go unreported are factored in, along with the cases handled by the system, then only about 2 out of every 100 rapists goes to prison for more than one year (Senate Judiciary Committee, 1993).

Crisis Centers: Providing Emergency Assistance

No matter how poorly (or how well) the criminal justice system handles rape cases in the long run, victims of sexual assault need immediate aid in the short run. Starting in 1972, feminist activists began to provide concrete emergency assistance to women who had just been raped. The first crisis centers (also known as distress or relief centers) were set up in Berkeley, California, and Washington, D.C. These independent self-help projects were intended to provide an alternative to the very limited services available through the police, at hospital emergency rooms, and through mental health centers. They also became organizing bases for the nationwide antirape movement.

Rape crisis centers provide a variety of services. Usually, a twenty-four-hour telephone hotline puts victims in contact with advocates who are standing by to help. The center's staff members are available to accompany women to hospital emergency rooms to collect forensic evidence and to receive first aid, and to police stations or prosecutor's offices to file complaints and make statements. Individuals may receive peer counseling, as well as participate in a support group. Referrals are made to other community agencies that provide social services. Some centers conduct in-service training to sensitize doctors, nurses, police officers, and assistant district attorneys about the needs and problems of the rape victims they encounter. Most undertake educational campaigns to raise public consciousness about the realities of sex crimes and the plight of sexually assaulted women. Frequently, centers offer self-defense courses for women and children.

Many staff members at the original crisis centers were former victims who shared a commitment to many of the themes embodied in the protest movements of the 1960s and early 1970s. From the feminist movement came the conviction that rape was primarily a women's issue, best understood and more effectively dealt with by women than by male authorities. A distrust of remote bureaucracies and of control by professionals who claim to know what is best for their clients was derived from the youthful counterculture of the 1960s, which spawned "crash pads" (emergency shelters), drop-in centers (for counseling and advocacy), and free clinics (for drug-related health crises) in "hippie" neighborhoods. The New Left's emphasis on egalitarianism, volunteerism, and collective action led to grass-roots, community-based projects stressing self-help and peer support, and to symbolic confrontations with the power structure (demonstrations at police stations and trials).

With the passage of time, however, rifts developed within many rape crisis centers. More pragmatic and less ideological staffers challenged the fundamental principles of these nonprofit, nonbureaucratic, nonhierarchical, nonprofessional, nongovernmental organizations. They pressed for a more service-oriented approach that would avoid militancy and radical critiques, improve chances for funding, increase referrals from hospitals and police departments, and permit closer cooperation with prosecutors. To the founders of the centers, such changes represented a co-optation by the establishment and a retreat from the original mission (see Amir and Amir, 1979; and Largen, 1981).

The Problem of Unwanted Publicity and Negative Media Protrayal

Fears of public exposure and of being blamed discourage some women from turning to the criminal justice system for help. From the victims' point of view, reporters and editors have trouble covering rape cases without inflicting further harm.

Since the middle of the 1800s, newspapers have regularly featured stories about violent crimes but they rarely covered rapes until the 1930s "Scottsboro Boys" case. For a number of years, the only cases that aroused media interest were those that resulted in lynchings, in which a black man accused of raping a white woman was murdered by a white mob. Even today, according to a content analysis of the news media coverage of several highly publicized cases, the mainstream media are still preoccupied with the rape of white women, continue to sensationalize interracial cases involving a black defendant and a white victim, and rarely devote attention to sexual assaults upon black women. Journalists tend to stereotype victims as either "virgins" (pure and innocent, who are ravaged by beastial males) or "vamps" (wanton and sexually provocative, who arouse male lust). By assigning blame to one party or the other, crime reporters assume the responsibilities of judges and juries. The victim is likely to be portrayed as a vamp if the defendant is an acquaintance; no weapon is brandished; they are both from the same ethnic group and social class; and she is young, considered attractive, and doesn't live with her family (Benedict, 1992).

When a girl or woman lodges charges of sexual assault against a man, like any other complainant of any other crime, her name appears in police and court documents. The question then arises of whether her identity should be revealed in press accounts of the case.

In four states, laws prohibit the press from publishing the name of the victim in a sex crime; elsewhere, most newspapers, magazines, and radio and television stations have adopted a policy of self-restraint that shields the injured person from unwanted public exposure.

The arguments in favor of keeping the victim's name out of the media's coverage center on the potential for additional harm to the victim and the chilling effect on other women who are considering going to the authorities for help. The long-standing ethical norm of concealing the name of a complainant who wishes to remain anonymous developed out of a realization that rapes are not like other crimes. Victims are more likely to be in an emotionally fragile state, afflicted by post-traumatic stress, nervous breakdowns, and suicidal impulses. Publicly identified rape victims have always been discredited, stigmatized, scandalized, mocked, scorned, and even harassed. Harsh victim-blaming accusations are particularly likely and especially painful psychologically. Therefore, revealing her name against her will is a humiliating second violation that is likely to prolong her suffering. Furthermore, other rape victims who see how powerless she was to prevent her name and intimate details from being publicized might be discouraged from reporting similar incidents to the police. Therefore, media self-censorship is the way to respect a victim's privacy rights, unless she chooses to go public and speak out about the attack (Pollitt, 1991; Young, 1991).

The arguments in favor of disclosing victims' names appeal to the principles of the public's right to know, the defendant's right to a fair trial, and the news media's right to be free from censorship. Media outlets have an obligation to disseminate all relevant and newsworthy facts. Accusations from anonymous sources are contrary to American jurisprudence. The accused—who is presumed to be innocent unless proven guilty—endures humiliation from the publicity surrounding the case; to deter untrue allegations, the accuser's name should be revealed as well. People with knowledge about her credibility might come forward with information about her background and character that could aid the defense of a falsely accused man. Finally, shielding victims from exposure implies that being forced to submit to a sexual act is something to be ashamed of, like a "dirty" secret; in the long run, routinely giving faceless victims a human identity might diminish the persisting stigma (see Dershowitz, 1988; Cohen, 1991; Kantrowitz et al., 1991).

In a public opinion poll conducted right after a controversial 1991 "outing" of the complainant in a high-profile case involving the relative of a politically powerful family, 77 percent of those surveyed said that the media should not reveal the names of rape victims; 86 percent felt that being publicly identified imposes special hardships; and 86 percent predicted that other women would be less likely to report being raped if they knew their names would be released by the press (Kantrowitz et al., 1991).

Reducing the Threat of Rape

Over the years, three approaches have been developed to cut down the prevalence of sexual assaults. The oldest (and now subject to vehement denunciation) is the "blame the victim, she's responsible for what happened" approach that unjustly faults the attitudes, words, and actions of the girl or woman attacked by the violent boy or man. Following the logic of this approach, women must stop precipitating rape through careless, reckless, or even provocative behavior. Instead, these would-be targets must learn to take precautions to reduce the risks they face in a dangerous world. One alternative perspective is the "blame the offender, it's all his fault" approach that views sexual assaults as pathological acts by mentally disturbed individuals. If deranged sexual predators are the source of the problem, then criminal justice strategies that remove these dangerous deviants from circulation (incapacitation via incarceration, followed by rehabilitation) are the solution. But a third approach, more sociologically based because it emphasizes the wide variety of offenders, motives, targets, and victim–offender relationships, considers rape to be the outgrowth of social conditions, especially patriarchy (rule by men), male chauvinist (superiority) ideology, traditional gender-based roles, and prevailing patterns of socialization (how children are raised). If this analysis is correct, then criminal justice "solutions" can only keep a lid on a potentially explosive situation. Deterrence through punishment attempts to teach the men who are not mentally disturbed a lesson they won't forget and to make negative role models out of them to serve as a warning to other men contemplating sexual assaults (so they will "think twice," consider the likelihood of imprisonment, and decide not to act out their oppressive fantasies). But many rapists escape the punishment they deserve; at best, an efficient criminal justice system weeds out assailants and brings them under control one at a time, after they have struck and harmed the targets of their wrath. If social conditions breed generation after generation of sexually aggressive and exploitive men, then the only viable strategy is to eradicate these root causes of the problem. That means doing something about the encouragements to commit rape that pervade contemporary culture: the glorification of the coupling of sex and violence in popular music lyrics, movies, pornography, and other forms of entertainment, as well as advertising (promoting violence as "sexy" and sexual desire as something to be expressed forcefully rather than tenderly); and the general indoctrination of boys and men to look disdainfully at girls and women as little more than objects for gratifying sexual urges (see Buchwald, Fletcher, and Roth, 1993).

The Rediscovery of More Rape Victims

Sexually Assaulted Males   The rape of a male by a female is presumed to be extremely rare. The molestation of boys by men has been of great concern for a long time (see Maghan and Sagarin, 1983; and Porter, 1986). But the rape of an adult man by another male (or by a gang of boys or men), although rarely discussed, can and does happen. This was such a taboo subject that many state laws ignored the possibility and defined rape strictly as a crime perpetrated against females. In 1986, however, Congress passed a bill revising federal rape statutes (which govern the handling of sexual assaults committed on federal property, such as in federal prisons). Among other changes, the law redefined rape as a gender-neutral offense; in other words, victims and perpetrators both could be of either sex ("Federal Rape Laws," 1986). This official recognition that males could be rape victims paved the way for their rediscovery, including efforts to estimate the scope of the problem and to devise effective ways of easing their suffering.

The first rough estimates for all kinds of sexual assaults attempted or completed against males appeared in a study of the findings of annual *National Crime Victimization Surveys* conducted between 1973 and 1982. During those ten years, about 1.5 million females were estimated to be victims of attempted and completed rapes. Almost 125,000 male rape victims were projected for that same time period. Hence, the problem females faced was about twelve times greater, numerically speaking (Klaus, DeBerry, and Timrots, 1985). In 1992, the proportion of all rapes reported to *NCVS* interviewers that were perpetrated against males over age eleven remained at about this same level, 8 percent (BJS, 1993). Similarly, 9 percent of all reported rapes during 1991 in three states were male-on-male (0.8 percent were female-on-female, and 0.2 percent were female-on-male), according to the first analysis of more detailed data gathered by the FBI's new *UCR* National Incident Based Reporting System method (Reaves, 1993). Records kept by rape crisis centers indicated that about one caller out of every ten was a victimized male. But these measures of the incidence of male-on-male rapes are probably gross underestimates because they exclude the thousands of sexual assaults committed in institutional settings like jails, prisons, and reform schools. Sexual violence among inmates is now a well-known problem (see Lockwood, 1980) that is routinely dramatized in movies about life behind bars.

Seven recent immigrants who drive unlicensed passenger vans come forward and file formal complaints alleging that they were sodomized at gunpoint by a police officer in uniform. After an exhaustive investigation that lasts almost two years and involves hundreds of interviews and conflicting expert testimony about lie detector tests and rape trauma syndrome, the district attorney concludes that the incidents never took place. The police department claims that the drivers concocted the bizarre charges to get rid of a zealous officer who issued thousands of tickets to illegal van operators. The complainants charge that by dropping the criminal investigation, the authorities are covering up the truth in order to preserve the image of the police department and undermine their pending $120 million civil lawsuit against the city. (Firestone, 1994)

Male rape victims have discovered that they are subjected to the same kind of disbelief, scorn, and insensitive treatment today that female victims endured routinely in the not-so-distant past. They are often blamed for their own misfortunes, stereotyped as homosexual (the majority are exclusively heterosexual), disparaged as not being "real men" for not resisting to the utmost and for not thwarting their attackers, and accused of secretly enjoying the experience. Although males and females suffer in similar ways, experiencing bouts of depression, flashbacks, recriminations, nightmares, and an overwhelming sense of vulnerability, males are more visibly angry and more preoccupied with fantasies of revenge. In a few large cities, they have set up self-help support groups. Impressionistic evidence indicates that male rape victims experience more force and brutality, are held captive for a longer period, and are subjected to more acts of sexual humiliation. Evidently, sexual assaults against both males and females are expressions of culturally induced drives toward domination and subjugation within a society that prizes exercising power over other people (Krueger, 1985; White and Wesley, 1987).

Wives Raped by Their Husbands The antirape movement argued that all kinds of forced sex should be outlawed, regardless of who the aggressor is and what his relationship to the victim might be. This view led to the rediscovery that rape can occur even between husbands and wives; despite the religious blessings, government license, and marriage vows, a wife retains the right to say "No!" to her husband. The forcible rape of a spouse first became explicitly recognized as a crime in 1975, when South Dakota legislators rewrote the state's statutes and rejected the common-law "exception" (or exemption from arrest) that granted husbands the right to virtually unlimited sexual access (Russell, 1982). By 1990, in every state, the immunity extended to a husband no longer applied if his wife had separated from him and filed for divorce; in many states, the husband could be arrested and prosecuted even if the couple was living together, if he used a weapon, or took advantage of his mentally or physically incapacitated wife who was unable to give meaningful consent (Russell, 1990). According to projections from a telephone survey, more than 1,100,000 women who are currently married have been forcibly raped one or more times by their husbands (Crime Victims Research and Treatment Center, 1992). Various surveys have found that between 10 percent and 15 percent of all wives concede that they have been physically forced to submit to the sexual demands of their husbands. An even higher proportion of women, 15 percent to 25 percent, report that they were raped by an ex-husband (Finkelhor and Yllo, 1985). If researchers could develop methods to achieve full disclosure, marital rape might turn out to be more common than all other kinds of rapes combined (ambush attacks by strangers, acquaintance rapes, date rapes). Raped wives are also battered wives in most cases. They are beaten periodically and raped repeatedly over the years; and many beatings include acts of sexual abuse as well. Raped wives endure many of the same problems that burden women who were sexually assaulted by nonintimates. They are physically injured, psychologically scarred, and personally humiliated (Bowker, 1983). Wives whose husbands force them to submit to sexual acts are the least likely of all sexual assault victims to report the incidents, to be believed by the authorities, to have their cases adjudicated, and to secure convictions. Between 1978 and 1985, only 118 husbands were prosecuted across the country, although 104 of them (90 percent) were convicted, according to a report by a national clearinghouse on marital rape (Barden, 1987).

6

Repaying Victims

The human costs of crime cannot be measured in dollars and cents. Receiving reimbursement can't erase victims' mental anguish and physical damage. Nevertheless, restoration of financial health is an achievable goal and a necessary first step on their road to recovery. For offenders, repaying those they harmed is one of the few tangible ways in which they can try to make amends for the havoc they have caused. Seeing to it that reimbursement takes place is one concrete way that members of a society can collectively demonstrate their care and concern about other people's economic well-being. And, by helping individuals get back on their feet financially, government officials can "do something" about a seemingly insoluble crime problem.

Victims suffer monetarily when offenders vandalize or steal property, take cash, inflict wounds that require medical attention and interfere with work, and cause trauma that necessitates psychological care. Survivors suffer financially when lawbreakers kill persons others depended on for economic support. Victims and survivors can seek to recover their financial losses in a number of ways. Making the offender pay is everyone's first choice, embodying as it does the most elemental notion of justice. Judges in criminal court can order convicts to make restitution; judges and juries in civil court can compel defendants to pay damages. Another possible source of reparations might be a grossly negligent third party, such as an enterprise or a governmental agency that bears some responsibility for the criminal incident. Insurance coverage can also be a source of repayment, as can state and federal compensation programs that may cover certain expenses and losses. Finally, in rare instances, victims might be able to deprive offenders of any money the latter make from telling a sensationalized "inside story" of their exploits.

This chapter explores all these means of monetary recovery: court-ordered restitution; lawsuits for damages; third-party civil suits; private insurance policies; government compensation plans; and acts prohibiting criminals from profiting from their notoriety.

GAINING RESTITUTION FROM OFFENDERS

Back to Basics?

A patient's bankbook is stolen by her home health aide, who withdraws $400 from the account. When the aide returns the money to the patient, the judge dismisses the charges. (Editors, *New York Times,* 1987)

An ice-skating rink is broken into and vandalized by three teenagers. They steal money from a concession cash register and start a fire that results in damages exceeding $20,000. Charged with larceny, wanton destruction of property, and arson, they are given two-year suspended sentences and ordered to work full-time for up to four months repairing and repainting the property they destroyed. (Klein, 1988)

A gas station attendant is robbed by a young man wielding a knife. The robber is sentenced to serve thirty days in jail, repay $95 to the attendant, perform eighty hours of unpaid community service work for a local church, and remain under house arrest in the evening. (Taylor, 1983)

An elderly lady is run over by a drunken driver with a previous DWI conviction. Found guilty of criminally negligent homicide, he is not given the usual sentence of one year in jail. Instead, he is ordered to spend sixteen weekends behind bars; to pay $4,000 to the woman's family; and to perform 1,250 hours of community service by visiting nursing homes, giving lectures to youth on the perils of mixing drinking with driving, and accompanying the local volunteer fire department to the scene of every serious auto accident. (Wexler, 1984)

These examples of "alternative," "creative," or "constructive" sentences herald a renewed interest in restitution.

As they finish serving their time behind bars, convicts are told that they have paid their debt to society. But their victims often wonder, "How about the debt owed me?"

Advocates of restitution argue that it's time to get back to basics. The financial health of victims shouldn't be neglected or sacrificed by a system ostensibly set up to deliver justice for all. Criminal acts are more than symbolic assaults against abstractions like the social order or public safety; real flesh-and-blood people suffer losses. Offenders shouldn't be prosecuted solely on behalf of the state or "the people." Fairness demands that victims be "made whole again"— restored to the financial condition they were in before the crime occurred (see Abel and Marsh, 1984).

Restitution and compensation are alternative methods of repaying losses. *Restitution* is the responsibility of offenders; *compensation* is the financial obligation of government-run funds or private insurance companies. Restitution takes place whenever offenders return stolen goods to their rightful owners, hand over equivalent amounts of money to cover out-of-pocket expenses, or perform direct personal services to those they have harmed. Community service is designed to make amends to society as a whole by benefiting some worthy cause or group. "Symbolic restitution" (Harris, 1979) to substitute victims seems appropriate when society as a whole has been menaced, when the immediate casualties can't be found, or when the victims don't want to accept the offenders' aid. "Creative restitution" (Eglash, 1977), an ideal solution, comes about when offenders, on their own initiative, go beyond what the law or their sentence requires, exceed other people's expectations, and leave the victims better off than they were before the crimes took place.

Usually, wrongs are righted in a straightforward manner. Litterbugs clean up the mess they have made. Adolescent graffiti artists scrub off their spray-painted signatures. Burglars repay cash for the loot they have carted away. Embezzlers return stolen funds to the company. Occasionally, "client-specific" punishments are imposed, tailored to fit the crime, the criminal, and unmet community needs. For example, a drunken driver does several months of voluntary labor in a hospital emergency room to see, firsthand, the consequences of his kind of recklessness. A lawyer caught defrauding his clients avoids disbarment by spending time giving legal advice to needy individuals too poor to pay for it. A young purse snatcher who preys on the elderly is ordered to work weekends at a nursing home. Such sentences anger those who are convinced that imprisonment is the answer and fervently believe "If you do the crime, you must do the time." But imaginative dispositions that substitute restitution for locking up criminals are favored by reformers who want to reduce jail and prison overcrowding, cut the tax burden of incarceration, and shield first-time and minor offenders from the corrupting influences of the prison subculture ("Fitting Justice?" 1978; "When Judges Make the Punishment Fit the Crime," 1978; and Seligmann and Maor, 1980).

The Rise, Fall, and Revival of Restitution

The idea of making criminals repay their victims is an ancient one. But spontaneous acts of revenge predated the invention of restitution. During the millennia before governments, laws, and criminal justice systems, the gut reaction to attack was to seek to "get even" with aggressors by injuring them physically in ferocious counterattacks and by taking back things of value. But as groups accumulated riches and primitive societies established rules of conduct, the tradition of retaliatory violence gave way to negotiation and reparation. For the sake of community harmony and stability, compulsory restitution was institutionalized in ancient societies. The law of Moses of the Hebrews instructed that an assailant repay an injured person for any losses due to recuperation from a serious wound. Mosaic law also required that a thief hand over to a victim five oxen for every one stolen. The Code of Hammurabi granted a victim as much as thirty times the value of any goods stolen or damaged. Under Roman law, a thief had to pay the victim double the value of what he stole if he was caught in the act; if he escaped and was captured later, he owed the victim three times the value of what he took; and if he used force to commit the theft, the robber had to repay the injured party four times as much as he stole. Under the "Dooms" of King Alfred in England during the ninth century, each tooth knocked out of a person's mouth by an aggressor required a payment of a different amount, depending upon its location (Peak, 1986).

These reimbursement practices went beyond the simplistic formula of "an eye for an eye and a tooth for a tooth." Restitution was intended to satisfy any thirst for vengeance, as well as to repay losses. These transactions involving goods and money were designed to encourage lasting settlements ("composition") between the parties that would head off any further strife (Schafer, 1970).

By the ninth century in Britain, an offender was supposed to restore peace and harmony by offering two separate payments—a "bot" (or "bote") to the victim and a "wer" (or "wergild") to the victim's kin. An official list spelled out exact penalties for specified acts. Private retaliation was permissible only if the offender refused the victim's demands for repayment. Anyone in the community could kill such an outlaw who rejected the chance to make amends.

But fragmentary historical records confirm the suspicion that in a society with sharply defined classes, restitution worked to the advantage of the upper classes. If they were powerful enough, guilty parties could scoff at the claims of their social "inferiors." If compelled to settle accounts, the affluent could easily make fiscal atonement for even the most outrageous breaches of law through relatively inconsequential composition payments of gold, cattle, land, or other valuables. On the other hand, offenses by the marginal against the mighty were not so readily resolved. The amounts specified were often beyond the resources of the common folk. Those who could not meet their obligations were branded as outlaws or were forced to sell themselves into virtual slavery. Restitution functioned as one of many mechanisms that made the rich richer and the poor poorer (Geis, 1977).

Restitution practices changed as the power of the feudal aristocracy and of nation-states consolidated. Royal officials drew up regulations to formalize the process of redressing grievances between subjects. Public involvement in what were formerly considered private matters was justified on several grounds: to more effectively preserve peace; to curb brutality, extortion, and exploitation of the weak by the strong; and to raise revenue for the Crown. Offenders found themselves obligated to repay the state for its services, as well as to reimburse their victims for their losses. The nobility extracted a "wite" as a fee for supervising reconciliation between the two parties and for guaranteeing protection to the offenders from any retaliation by the victims or their kin. By the twelfth century, the victim's bot and the kin's wer were shrinking, while the wite paid to the treasury was growing.

The expansion of the state's interest in resolving criminal matters was solidified with the emergence of a category of "bootless" crimes considered so heinous that no transfer of money could restore social equilibrium; the offender had to pay in blood. As the concept evolved, representatives of the government, as protectors of the "king's peace" and "public order," began to define the state as the injured party in most crimes. Governmental demands to punish and collect fines from transgressors soon crowded out the victim's right to recover damages. Under a law of forfeiture, the Crown could seize whatever property a felon owned (Mueller and Cooper, 1973; Younger, 1977).

In America before the Revolution, criminal acts were viewed primarily as conflicts between individuals. Police departments and public prosecutors did not exist yet. A victim in a city could call night watchmen for help, but they might not be on duty, or the offender might flee beyond their jurisdiction. If a victim sought the aid of a sheriff, he had to pay a fee. If the sheriff located the alleged perpetrator, he would charge extra to serve a warrant against the defendant. With the suspect in custody, the victim had to hire a lawyer to draw up an indictment. Then the victim either prosecuted the case personally or hired an attorney for an additional fee to handle the prosecution. If the accused was found guilty, the victim could gain substantial benefits. Persons convicted of theft were required to pay their victims three times as much as they had stolen. If the thieves could not hand over such amounts, they were assigned to their victims as servants until their debts were paid off. If the victims wished, they could sell these indentured servants for a hefty price and had one month in which to find a buyer. After that, they were responsible for the costs of maintaining the offenders in jail; if they didn't pay, the convicts were released.

In the years following the American Revolution, the procedures governing criminal charges set up by the British in the thirteen colonies were substantially reorganized. Reformers were concerned about the built-in injustices in a system in which only wealthy victims could afford to purchase law enforcement by hiring sheriffs, private detectives, bounty hunters, and attorneys, and by posting rewards. To promote equality, state and local governments hired public prosecutors. Prison systems were constructed to house offenders. Crimes were redefined as acts against the state. The redress of individual grievances was no longer regarded as the primary function of court proceedings (McDonald, 1977). A distinction developed between *crimes* and *torts*. Crimes were offenses against the state, and torts were the corresponding wrongful acts against specific persons. Criminals were forced to "pay their debt to society" through fines and periods of confinement. Victims who wanted to compel offenders to repay their personal debts were shunted away from criminal court to a separate arenas, civil courts, where lawsuits were resolved.

As restitution faded, leading figures in legal philosophy and criminology called for its revival. In 1516, in his book *Utopia,* Sir Thomas More proposed that offenders labor on public works projects. The English utilitarian philosopher Jeremy Bentham advocated mandatory restitution for property offenses. A French jurist developed a plan in 1847 that combined restitution with compensation from state funds. A number of criminologists introduced restitution resolutions at international prison congresses around the turn of the century. Enrico Ferri raised the issue in Italy in the 1920s, and the penal reformer Margery Fry rekindled support for restitution in England during the 1950s (Jacob, 1977; Schafer, 1970).

In the United States, restitution has been ordered more often and for a longer period of time in the juvenile justice system. The oldest existing repayment program for victims harmed by delinquents was initiated in Florida in 1945. The earliest community service program was set up in South Dakota in 1965. A Minnesota program established in 1972 was the first to allow youthful offenders to perform direct services for victims instead of paying them cash; it also pioneered mediation sessions as a way of reconciling the two parties. Hundreds of juvenile restitution projects were started during the 1970s and 1980s (Warner and Burke, 1987).

In 1967, the President's Commission on Law Enforcement and the Administration of Justice recommended more frequent restitution by convicts and suggested the repeal of laws passed during the Great Depression that crippled prison industries by restricting the sale of products made by inmates. During the 1970s, the American Law Institute, the American Bar Association, and the National Advisory Commission on Criminal Justice Standards and Goals approved of a greater reliance on restitution, as did the U.S. Supreme Court. Reform groups, like the American Correctional Association and the National Moratorium on Prison Construction, also favored restitution, along with governmental organizations such as the National Association of Attorneys General and the Office for Victims of Crime of the U.S. Justice Department. In 1982, the President's Task Force on Victims of Crime recommended that judges routinely impose restitution, or else state for the record why they didn't. The Federal Victim/Witness Protection Act of 1982 removed restrictions that had limited restitution to a condition of probation within the federal judicial system. In forty-six states, common-law traditions permitting restitution have been formally codified to facilitate the imposition of repayment schedules as a condition of probation or parole. In twenty-three states, restitution is mandatory, unless a judge excuses an offender from this obligation and states the reasons why in writing. The National Institute of Justice projected that many more restitution programs could be established or expanded at little additional cost to local communities. Yet the implementation of restitution remains the exception rather than the rule in most jurisdictions (McDonald, 1988; Leepson, 1982; Harland, 1983; Herrington, 1986; National Victim Center, 1992b).

Since the late 1970s, a number of surveys have confirmed that the general public, and victims in particular, support the imposition of restitution as a fair and fitting sanction, usually as a condition of probation or parole and as a substitute for incarceration, especially for nonviolent offenders guilty of committing crimes against property (Galaway, 1992).

The ground swell of support for its revival is due to a recognition of the glaring inadequacies of private insurance coverage, governmental compensation plans, and civil lawsuits as means of recovering losses. Yet the principles underlying restitution are deceptively simple. For when theory is translated into practice, thorny problems arise at every turn. Enthusiasm over restitution today is reminiscent of the unfounded optimism that greeted earlier "sweeping reforms" that ostensibly would restore equity and bring about justice—reforms like the substitution of imprisonment for corporal and capital punishment, the establishment of a treatment-oriented juvenile justice system to supplant a punitive one, and the replacement of fixed-term sentences with indeterminate ones based on individual progress toward rehabilitative goals.

Divergent Goals, Clashing Philosophies

Restitution is often overlooked as an option because other considerations come first: punishing offenders to teach them a lesson and to deter potential criminals from following their example; treating offenders so that they can be released back into the community as rehabilitated; or incapacitating offenders believed to be dangerous by confining them.

Some advocates of restitution have been advancing this ancient practice as a new form of punishment, while others tout it as a new method of rehabilitation. Still other champions of restitution emphasize its potential for resolving tensions and its beneficial impact on the financial well-being of victims. As a result, groups with divergent aims and philosophies, while pushing restitution, are pulling at newly established programs from different directions (Galaway, 1977).

Restitution as a Means of Repaying Victims Those who advance restitution primarily as a way of helping victims (see Barnett, 1977; and McDonald, 1978) argue that the present punitively oriented criminal justice system offers victims few incentives to get involved. Those who cooperate with the police and prosecutors incur additional losses of time and money for their trouble (for example, while attending lineups and appearing in court). They also run the risk of suffering reprisals from offenders. In return, they get nothing tangible—only the sense that they have discharged their civic duty by assisting in the apprehension, prosecution, and conviction of a dangerous person, a social obligation that goes largely unappreciated. The only satisfaction the system provides is revenge. But when restitution is incorporated into the criminal justice process, cooperation really pays off.

If the primary goal of restitution is to see to it that victims get repaid, then they should be able to negotiate the arrangement, in terms of the total amount of money and the schedule of payments. Reimbursement should be as comprehensive as possible. The criminal ought to pay back all stolen cash plus the current replacement value of any lost or damaged property, any outstanding medical bills stemming from crime-related injuries (including psychological wounds attended to by therapists), any wages lost because of absence from work (including sick days or vacation time used up during recuperation or while cooperating with the police and prosecutors), plus any crime-related miscellaneous expenses (such as the cost of renting a car to replace one that was stolen or the expense of hiring a baby-sitter when testifying in court). Repayment should be as prompt as possible, since victims foot the bill in the interim.

Restitution as a Means of Rehabilitating Offenders Advocates of restitution as a means of rehabilitation (see Prison Research, 1976; and Keve, 1978) argue that instead of being punished, wrongdoers must be humanized and sensitized to the disruption and distress that their illegal actions have caused. By learning about their victims' plight, they come to realize the injurious consequences of their deeds. By expending effort, sacrificing time and convenience, and performing meaningful tasks, they begin to understand their personal responsibilities and social obligations. By making fiscal atonement or contributing services, they can feel cleared of guilt, morally redeemed, and reaccepted into the fold. Through their hard work to defray their victims' losses, they can gain a sense of accomplishment and self-respect from their legitimate achievements. They may also develop work skills, self-discipline, and valuable on-the-job experience as they earn their way back into the community.

If restitution is to be therapeutic, offenders must perceive their obligations as logical, relevant, just, and fair. They must be convinced to voluntarily shoulder the burden of reimbursement because it is in their own best interest as well as being "the right thing to do." However, offenders probably will define their best interest as minimizing any penalty for their lawbreaking. This includes minimizing restitution, even if it is offered as a substitute for serving time behind bars. Offenders will underestimate the suffering they have caused, while victims may tend to overestimate their losses and want to extract as much as they can from offenders (see McKnight, 1981). The sensibilities of offenders must be taken into account, since their willingness to make amends is the key to the success of this "treatment."

Restitution as a Means of Reconciling Offenders and Their Victims

Some advocates of restitution view the process primarily as a vehicle for reconciliation. Reconciliation is achieved when two parties who have been locked in an escalating conflict settle their differences through negotiation. In situations of shared responsibility, restitution might be mutual, with each of the disputants reimbursing the other for damages inflicted during the period of destructive quarreling. Admittedly guilty perpetrators and the innocent persons they harmed are brought together for face-to-face meetings in the presence of trained mediators at victim–offender reconciliation programs. Both parties have to consider the restitution agreement they decide upon to be fair and constructive if a lasting peaceful settlement is to emerge. (The philosophy and operating principles of "restorative justice," which relies heavily on restitution, are discussed in Chapter 7.)

Restitution as a Means of Punishing Offenders

Those who view restitution primarily as an additional penalty (see Schafer, 1977; and Tittle, 1978) argue that for too long offenders have been able to shirk this responsibility to victims. First, convicts should suffer incarceration to pay their debt to society for violating norms that embody cherished values and maintain social stability. Next, they should undertake strenuous efforts to repay the specific individuals they harmed. Only then can their entanglement with the criminal justice system come to an end.

Those who promote restitution as a means of repaying victims, or as a way of rehabilitating offenders, or as the basis for bringing about mutual reconciliation can come into conflict with people who advocate restitution as a means of punishment and deterrence. The problem with using restitution as an additional penalty is that it delays repayment for many years. Since few convicts can earn decent wages behind prison walls, the slow process of reimbursement cannot begin until the period of incarceration is over, either when the sentence expires or upon the granting of parole. When punishment takes priority over reimbursement, the victims' financial needs, the offenders' therapeutic needs, and the community's need for harmony are subordinated to the punitive interests of the state. As long as prison labor is unchallenging and poorly paid, restitution and incarceration will be incompatible.

Objections to Emphasizing Restitution   The major argument against making victim reimbursement the primary consideration in criminal justice proceedings was articulated in a 1986 Supreme Court decision: The operations of the system are intended to benefit society as a whole, not just the injured party. Reimbursing victims cannot interfere with other, more important societal goals, like deterring would-be offenders, incapacitating dangerous persons, or rehabilitating lawbreakers in treatment programs. Subordinating these other sentencing objectives to restitution would reduce the criminal justice system to a mere debt-collection agency catering to victims, according to this traditional point of view (Triebwasser, 1986).

The imposing of community service obligations, as a form of restitution benefiting agencies, organizations, institutions, and whole neighborhoods, has also drawn criticism as an abuse of judicial activism. Guidelines in most jurisdictions specify that offenders cannot be put to work on behalf of profit-making enterprises or tax-paying organizations. But beyond that, judges can force people on probation or parole to labor on behalf of what they consider to be noble causes, worthy charities, or deserving individuals. In the process of defining and assigning "good works," judges go beyond the legitimate mission of a criminal justice system within a pluralistic society and jeopardize their neutrality within the political patronage process (Czajkoski and Wollan, 1986). Through their ingenuity in devising individualized "creative sentences," some judges thwart guidelines intended to make sentences more consistent, predictable, and proportionate (Von Hirsch, 1988).

Unresolved Issues

Some key questions about restitution remain unanswered because of the divergent goals of its advocates (see Edelhertz, 1977; Galaway and Hudson, 1975; Hudson and Chesney, 1978; Gottesman and Mountz, 1979; and Harland, 1979, 1981a).

One issue is whether restitution is appropriate in cases of shared responsibility. If the victim is partly to blame for what happened (as in an aggravated assault that was provoked), it would seem fair to require less-than-full restitution by the offender. But if partial restitution is the solution to cases of shared responsibility, then offenders have an incentive during the negotiation of restitution contracts to derogate victims as having asked for trouble and having deserved their fate. This incentive undermines the therapeutic aspect of making amends as a means of reconciliation. On the other hand, if the victim's precipitation or provocation is disregarded as a mitigating factor, the offender will consider the terms of the settlement unjust.

Another question is whether receiving restitution should be considered a privilege enjoyed by some or a right guaranteed to all. If getting reimbursed becomes a right upon conviction, then victims deserve institutionalized input so that they can present their bills and defend their financial interests. Prosecutors, judges, and probation and parole officers would have to cede some of their discretionary authority, which they are reluctant to do.

A final thorny question concerns the appropriateness of financial repayments as a way of making up for the physical, emotional, and economic damage inflicted during acts of violence. Most people think about restitution in relation to thefts. If robbers, assailants, rapists, and murderers are eliminated from consideration, then the numbers of cases suitable for restitution are slashed dramatically. Although crimes against property outnumber crimes against persons by a ratio of about nine to one, most property crimes are never solved, whereas a sizable proportion of violent crimes are cleared by arrest. The history of restitution shows that, at various times and places, payment schedules have been worked out to resolve nearly every kind of offense, including the most vicious killings. In tort law (civil proceedings), monetary values have been calculated for all sorts of injuries, from loss of prestige to loss of life. In some cases, victims (and their kin or survivors) might demand restitution from violent offenders, but in other cases, the injured parties might not want to accept, or permit, restitution as a means of making amends for acts of cruelty and brutality.

Economic Ironies

Since the street crime problem is, in large part, an outgrowth of economic ills, it is no surprise that solutions involving restitution collide with economic realities. Repayment takes time and costs money. Restitution is predicated on work. Offenders must have, must be helped to find, or must be given jobs. These jobs must pay reasonably well, to permit restitution installments to be deducted from total earnings. But the U.S. economy cannot provide decent jobs for all who want to earn a living. Besides chronic unemployment, there is a permanent shortage of positions in government and industry that pay adequate wages.

Many dilemmas arise when restitution programs are considered within this context of intense competition and relative scarcity: If a job is found or created, then the prospects for the successful completion of the restitution obligation are increased. Otherwise, unemployed, down-and-out street criminals are denied a chance to make amends. If the wages are low, then the repayment cannot be completed within a reasonable amount of time. If nearly all of the offender's earnings are confiscated and handed over to the victim, then commitment to the job and to repaying the debt is jeopardized. If the job is demeaning, then its therapeutic value as a first step in a new lifestyle built on productive employment is lost. If the job is temporary, only for the duration of the restitution obligation, then the risk of returning to a career of crime is heightened. But if the job found or created for the offender is permanent and pays well, then observers might justifiably object. To some, it will appear that criminals are being rewarded, not punished, for their misdeeds. Law-abiding people desperately seeking work particularly will resent any policy that seems to put offenders at the head of the line. Trade union members rightfully will fear that convict labor could replace their civilian labor over the long run. But if offenders are put to work in large-scale prison industries, then business interests will complain about unfair competition. If adolescents owing restitution are too young to receive working papers, then a job in private industry would violate child labor laws. Only unpaid community service would be permissible. If large numbers of youngsters are put to work cleaning streets, repairing park facilities, maintaining public beaches, and so on, municipal workers might feel that their jobs are being farmed out to troubled youth. If the community service work is extremely unpleasant, exhausting, or dangerous, then restitution becomes a smoke screen for forced labor, chain-gang style.

When both the offenders and the victims are hard-pressed to make ends meet, restitution seems most appropriate. But if the offenders are penniless while the victims are affluent, then restitution smacks of exploitation—taking from the poor and giving to the rich. If the offenders are well-off and are allowed to make restitution by drawing on their wealth, instead of by working, they will appear to be "buying their way out of trouble." If poor people without marketable job skills are kept in prison and denied the opportunity to make restitution as a condition of probation or parole, such discrimination against an entire class of criminals would be a violation of the equal protection clause of the Fourteenth Amendment. Yet, when the criterion "perceived ability to repay" determines eligibility, the typical participant in a restitution program turns out to be a white, middle-class, first-time property offender, and the most common recipient of reimbursement is a business (Hudson and Chesney, 1978).

Opportunities Versus Obstacles

Opportunities   Advocates of restitution point out that it is an extremely flexible sanction that is not being used to its full potential within the criminal justice system. Restitution is possible at every juncture, from the immediate aftermath of the crime up until the final moments of parole supervision following a period of imprisonment. (See Figure 6.1, which illustrates how restitution can be introduced at each stage in the criminal justice process.)

As soon as an offender is apprehended, an informal restitution arrangement can settle the matter. The victim might negotiate directly with the offender or with a representative. For example, a storekeeper might order a shoplifter to put the stolen item back on the shelf and never return to the premises; parents might offer to pay for their son's act of vandalism in spray-painting on a neighbor's fence. In most states, however, serious offenses cannot be resolved informally. It is a felony for an injured party to demand or accept any payment as "hush money" to cover up a violation of the law, or in return for not pressing charges, or as a motive for discontinuing cooperation with the authorities in an investigation or prosecution. A criminal act is an offense against the state in addition to a particular person and cannot be settled privately (Laster, 1970).

If a suspect is arrested, an agreement can be worked out through a diversion program as an alternative to formal prosecution. If a defendant is indicted, the district attorney's office can make restitution a condition for dismissing formal criminal charges. Once prosecution is initiated, restitution can be part of a plea bargain struck by the defense lawyer and the district attorney, wherein the accused concedes guilt in return for lesser penalties. Restitution is particularly appropriate as a condition of probation or of a suspended sentence. If incarcerated, an inmate can repay the victim from wages earned from labor in prison, from an outside job while on work release, or while residing at a halfway house. After serving time, restitution can be included as a condition of parole.

Restitution contracts can be administered and supervised by parties concerned about the crime problem: community groups, private and nonprofit charitable and religious organizations, juvenile courts, adult criminal courts, probation departments, corrections departments, and parole boards.

Obstacles As promising as restitution is, it is not the answer for most victims. Only a small percentage will ever collect anything. The problem is directly comparable to the quest for satisfaction from retribution. Just as most criminals escape punishment, most also evade restitution obligations. The situation has been labeled "funneling," or "shrinkage," and has been likened to a leaky net. At the outset, many cases are appropriate for restitution. But after these cases have been processed through the criminal justice system, only a relative handful of victims receive full or even partial restitution. All the other cases (offenders) have slipped through the net (see Figure 6.2 for an explanation of how and why so many "escape" their financial obligations).

A large proportion of cases immediately drop out of the picture because victims do not report the incidents to the police. In the remaining cases, the majority of offenders get away with their crimes because clearance rates are so low, especially for burglaries, car thefts, and other forms of stealing (which would be so

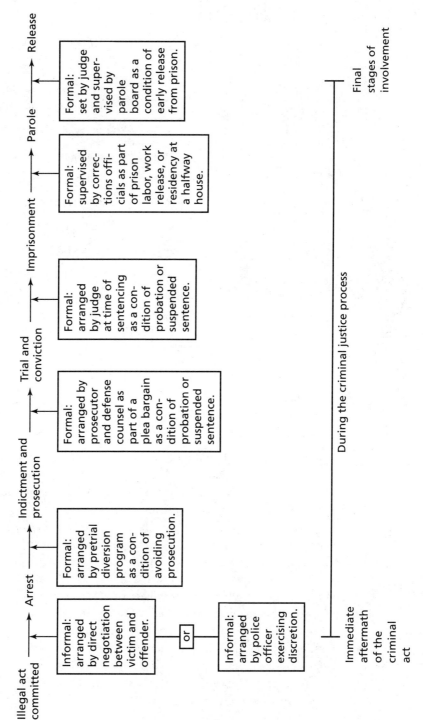

FIGURE 6.1 Opportunities for Restitution

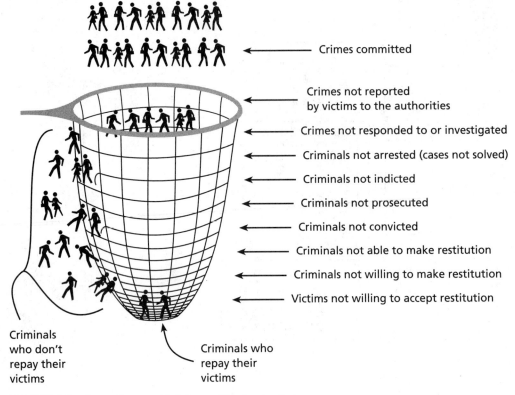

Crimes committed

Crimes not reported by victims to the authorities

Crimes not responded to or investigated

Criminals not arrested (cases not solved)

Criminals not indicted

Criminals not prosecuted

Criminals not convicted

Criminals not able to make restitution

Criminals not willing to make restitution

Victims not willing to accept restitution

Criminals who don't repay their victims

Criminals who repay their victims

FIGURE 6.2   Funneling, or Shrinkage: The Leaky Net

appropriately resolved by restitution). Hence, at the outset of the criminal justice process, most victims have already been eliminated from any chance of receiving reimbursement. Of the relatively small number of crimes that are solved, problems arise during the adjudication process. The overwhelming majority of cases (upwards of 90 percent in many jurisdictions) are resolved through plea bargains, which involve dropping charges or dropping counts. Many victims are eliminated from consideration for these reasons. Some cases that go to trial result in acquittals, and some convictions are reversed on appeal. Of those who are convicted or who plead guilty, many are not willing or able to shoulder financial obligations. Prisoners granted parole have trouble finding any work, let alone a job that pays enough to allow them to make meaningful payments after all their other deductions. Finally, most jurisdictions lack both a tradition of ordering restitution and a mechanism for monitoring and enforcing such arrangements. Even when a restitution program is operating within a jurisdiction, actually collecting the funds awarded to victims remains a major challenge (Harland, 1983; McGillis, 1986).

In sum, given all these difficulties, although restitution is often morally appropriate and theoretically possible, statistically speaking, it is not probable. According to a study of felony sentences handed down in state courts during 1992, restitution was ordered, in addition to a prison sentence, in a small proportion of all convictions for violent crimes (for murder, 8 percent; rape and robbery, 12 percent; aggravated assault, 18 percent); and in a larger proportion of all convictions for property crimes (for burglaries, 24 percent, and for fraud, 35 percent) (Langan and Graziadei, 1995).

Evaluating Restitution Programs

Despite the limitations, conflicting priorities, dilemmas, and ironies discussed above, restitution is under way in many jurisdictions. The programs responsible for facilitating and supervising restitution obligations are being evaluated. The challenge in evaluation is to adequately define the specific goals of the programs and then to devise appropriate criteria to measure degrees of success and failure. Victim-oriented goals involve making the injured parties "whole again" by enabling them to collect full reimbursement and regain peace of mind (restoration of victims' psychological well-being; recovery from emotional stress and trauma). Offender-oriented goals involve identifying signs of rehabilitation and preventing recidivism. System-oriented goals include reducing case-processing costs, relieving taxpayers of the financial burden of compensating victims, alleviating jail and prison overcrowding through alternative sentences, and improving citizen cooperation by providing material incentives for participating in the criminal justice process (McGillis, 1986).

There are so many different aims and touted benefits that no sweeping conclusions about the effectiveness of the programs now in operation can be drawn. An offender-oriented evaluation found lower rates of recidivism among those delinquents who were ordered to pay restitution by juvenile courts in Utah in cases of robbery, assault, burglary, theft, auto theft, and vandalism (Butts and Snyder, 1992). One victim-centered evaluation of four programs with reputations for being successful uncovered considerable dissatisfaction with the amount imposed, the rate of repayment, and the total actually handed over. Most of the recipients believed that officials in the two probation departments, the prosecutor's office, and the victim service agency that administered the programs could have done more to involve them in determining the size of the award, to keep them posted about developments, and to help them collect the full amount due. The average reimbursement owed was about $250; the losses stemmed primarily from larcenies and burglaries, but also from robberies and assaults, along with some traffic-related offenses and acts of fraud like passing bad checks (Davis, Smith, and Hillenbrand, 1992).

The compliance rate with restitution orders is frequently low. Although restitution is imposed most often as a condition of probation, if probationers knowingly and willingly fail to keep up with the agreed-upon payment schedule, their conditional liberty is not likely to be taken away. Judges are not inclined to revoke probation because they are more concerned with jail overcrowding and with being fair toward probationers (Davis, Smith, and Hillenbrand, 1992). If probationers make good-faith efforts to meet their obligation (by seeking employment, borrowing money, or selling off assets) but fail to pay off their debts in full, revocation would violate their Fourteenth Amendment rights, according to a Supreme Court ruling. If convicts can demonstrate an "inability to pay" an "unreasonable" or "unduly burdensome" restitution order, judges can reduce the amount due, stretch out the installments, or suspend the payment schedule entirely. In some jurisdictions courts can authorize an extension of probation or parole supervision, but in most places restitution arrangements cannot be enforced as effectively as judgments handed down in civil courts, through the garnishing of wages and the seizing and selling of assets (National Victim Center, 1992b). Some states place limits on the total amount that can be extracted (for example, $5,000 for felonies, $1,000 for misdemeanors, $2,500 for parental responsibility for damages inflicted by juveniles) (Roy, 1990).

Those victims and their advocates who have become impatient and dissatisfied with the task of improving criminal court-ordered restitution have begun to explore another avenue for reimbursement: lawsuits in civil court.

WINNING JUDGMENTS IN CIVIL COURT

The Revival of Interest in Civil Lawsuits

Looking for a Halloween costume party in a suburban neighborhood, a sixteen-year-old exchange student from Japan dressed up as a disco dancer rings the wrong doorbell. A woman opens the door, becomes frightened by the sight of the stranger, slams it shut, and yells to her husband to get his gun. He grabs his revolver, opens a side door and shouts "freeze!" Apparently not understanding the meaning of the colloquialism, the student moves forward and is shot and killed. A jury acquits the homeowner of manslaughter, deeming the killing a justifiable homicide, understanding how the man might have felt he was under attack and in imminent danger. After the disappointing verdict comes down in criminal court, the boy's parents sue the homeowner in civil court. The civil judge who hears the case (without a jury) rules that there was no justification whatsoever for the shooting and awards more than $650,000 in damages and funeral costs to the student's parents. (Nossiter, 1994b)

A young black man is accosted by members of the Ku Klux Klan, kidnapped at gunpoint, beaten, and then hung from a tree. Two Klansmen are convicted of the racially motivated lynching. The victim's mother hires a lawyer experienced in civil rights cases to sue the Klan, not for money or even for revenge, but to shut it down by taking away its resources. A civil jury awards her $7 million, entitling her to ownership of the Klan chapter's headquarters building. (Kornbluth, 1987)

A growing number of victims are no longer content to simply let prosecutors handle their cases in criminal court. They have discovered that they can go after their alleged wrongdoers and pursue their interests in another, separate arena: civil court. Criminal proceedings are intended to redress "public wrongs" that threaten society as a whole. As a result, the economic interests of victims seeking restitution from convicts are necessarily routinely subordinated to the government's priorities, whether probation, incarceration, or execution. Injured parties seeking financial redress are directed to civil court. There, they can launch lawsuits designed to remedy "private wrongs" arising from violations of law.

Activists in the victims' movement want to call attention to these legal rights and opportunities. Litigation is a largely overlooked battlefield in the legal struggle waged by victims against those who harmed them. Offenders can be held accountable in both criminal and civil courts. Guilty verdicts in criminal courts cost offenders their freedom; successful judgments in civil courts cost offenders their money. Lawsuits can be successful even if charges are never filed, or if the alleged perpetrator is found "not guilty" after a trial in criminal court. To make lawsuits an occupational hazard and a deterrent for habitual criminals, centers for legal advocacy and technical assistance are springing up in a number of cities (Barbash, 1979; Carrington, 1986; Carson, 1986; and National Victim Center, 1993).

The Litigation Process

Civil suits can involve claims for punitive damages as well as compensatory and pecuniary damages. Awards for compensatory damages (repayment of expenses) and pecuniary damages (to cover lost income) are supposed to restore victims to their former financial condition (make them "whole" again). They can receive the monetary equivalent of stolen or vandalized property; wages lost because of missing work; projected future earnings that, because of injuries inflicted by the offender, won't materialize; and outlays for medical and psychiatric care (hospital bills, counseling expenses); plus recompense for physical pain and mental suffering (resulting from loss of enjoyment, fright, nervousness, grief, humiliation, and disfigurement). Punitive damages might be levied by the court to make a negative example out of offenders who deliberately acted maliciously, oppressively, and recklessly (Stark and Goldstein, 1985; Brien, 1992).

In civil courts, victims can sue offenders for a number of torts: wrongful death, which enables survivors to collect compensation for the loss of a loved one without justification or legitimate excuse; assault, which covers intentionally threatening acts sufficient to cause fear of immediate bodily harm; battery, which involves intentional, harmful, physical contact that is painful, injurious, or offensive; trespass, which refers to the intentional invasion of another person's land; conversion of chattel, which is intentionally stealing or destroying someone's possessions or property; false imprisonment, which occurs against the person's will, such as during a hostage taking or rape; and infliction of emotional distress through extreme or outrageous conduct (Stark and Goldstein, 1985; Brien, 1992).

Civil actions commence when the person who was harmed (called the *plaintiff,* or the *second party)* formally files a *complaint,* which includes a brief statement of the legal issues, a description of the injuries and damages sustained, and a summary of the relevant facts of the case. This legal document must be physically handed to the *defendant* (also called the *first party),* along with a *summons* requiring a response to the allegations within a stated period of time. The accused wrongdoer submits an answer admitting to the charges or, more likely, contesting them and issuing a defense, and perhaps even launching a *countersuit.* In preparing for a trial to resolve the claims, both parties engage in a process called *discovery,* in which they exchange written replies to questions (*interrogatories*), documents, and sworn statements of eyewitnesses (including police officers). The typical outcome, just as in criminal proceedings, is a negotiated compromise agreement. But if an *out-of-court settlement* cannot be reached, the accused exercises his or her right to a trial under the Seventh Amendment, and the victim has his or her day in court. After considerable delays because of congested court calendars, the trial is held before twelve or, in some states, six jurors, or perhaps only in front of a judge. After opening statements by both attorneys, witnesses testify and are cross-examined, and physical evidence is introduced. Then the attorneys sum up their arguments, and the jury retires, deliberates, and renders its verdict after a simple majority vote over the two versions of events. The jury awards *damages* if it finds for the plaintiff. The losing party is likely to appeal the decision, and a higher court can overturn the trial court's verdict if errors in procedural law are discovered, or if the jury acted contrary to the evidence (Stark and Goldstein, 1985).

Litigation in civil court usually follows rather than precedes adjudication in criminal court. Victims usually wait, since the evidence that is introduced during the criminal proceedings can be used again in the lawsuit and generally is sufficient to establish that a tort occurred. Furthermore, if the civil action is filed too early, the defense attorney will use this fact to try to undermine the victim's credibility as a witness for the prosecution, claiming that the testimony is motivated by potential financial gain. But if the civil action is not filed for years, the *statute of limitations* might run out, and it will be too late to sue the defendant. For example, lawsuits alleging assault in most states must be filed within two years, before vivid memories fade and material evidence is lost or destroyed (Brien, 1992).

Possibilities and Pitfalls from the Victim's Point of View

Victims considering civil litigation must weigh the advantages and disadvantages of this course of action. One reason civil lawsuits are relatively uncommon is that most victims conclude that the benefits are not worth the costs. In addition, many injured parties are unfamiliar with this option.

Civil lawsuits have several attractions (see Stark and Goldstein, 1985; and Brien, 1992). First and foremost, victims can seize the initiative, haul their assailants into court, bring them to the bar of justice, and sue them for all they can get. In criminal cases, prosecutors exercise considerable discretion and make all the important decisions, even in jurisdictions where victims have the right to be informed and consulted. In civil cases, victims can regain a sense of control and feel empowered. It is up to them whether to sue and whether to accept an out-of-court settlement. Plaintiffs can present their own cases in small-claims courts, which have simplified procedures designed to expedite trials. Plaintiffs seeking larger amounts of money can hire attorneys of their own choosing and can participate in preparing the case and developing the strategy in anticipation of the trial.

Second, victims can achieve full reimbursement through lawsuits. Plaintiffs can collect punitive damages far in excess of their actual out-of-pocket expenses. Defendants' assets, including homes, cars, savings accounts, investments, and inheritances, can be attached (confiscated), and their wages can be garnished (seized). Most attorneys accept cases on a contingency basis and don't charge victims unless they win.

Third, winning a judgment in civil court is easier than securing a conviction in criminal court because the standard of proof is lower or less demanding. In civil court, conflicting claims are decided by a preponderance of the evidence (the winning side is the one that presents the more convincing arguments), not by guilt beyond a reasonable doubt (proving the charges to a moral certainty). Therefore, a civil suit following a conviction in criminal court is likely to succeed because the same evidence and testimony can be used again. An acquittal in criminal court does not rule out civil action, because a jury still might decide in favor of a plaintiff who presents a more persuasive case than the defendant. Even if the prosecutor drops the criminal charges that were initially lodged by the police, a plaintiff might win if the evidence that turned up during the criminal investigation is presented in civil court. Since defendants in civil court do not face imprisonment or execution, constitutional protections are less stringent than in criminal court. Defendants cannot "plead the Fifth Amendment" and refuse to testify on the grounds of self-incrimination. Rules of evidence are more flexible and, for example, allow the plaintiff to reveal the defendant's prior convictions for similar acts, a disclosure that wouldn't be permissible in criminal court. If plaintiffs win awards but defendants are unwilling to pay up voluntarily, sheriffs and marshals can be enlisted to enforce the courts' judgments by seizing contested assets or property (which can be sold at public auctions to raise cash).

Finally, successful suits can make victims feel vindicated: The judges and jurors sided with them, accepted their version of events, and rejected the defendants' denials, excuses, or rationalizations. Reimbursement is soothing and revenge is sweet. Victims teach perpetrators the lesson that crime does not pay and that wrongdoers ultimately will be held liable for their misdeeds.

> **A** fourteen-year-old boy tells his father that he was sexually molested on a number of occasions by a rock music superstar. The family sues the performer in civil court for sexual battery, seduction, willful misconduct, intentional infliction of emotional distress, fraud, and negligence. At first the superstar's lawyers contend that the father is trying to extort money, but then they work out an out-of-court settlement involving millions of dollars. In return, the family of the unidentified boy drops the lawsuit. Although the district attorney vows that the criminal investigation will go on, and the family says the teenager is cooperating with the authorities, without his testimony there is no prosecution. (Weinraub, 1994)

Despite these promising possibilities, however, a number of drawbacks deter most victims from pursuing civil actions, for several reasons (see Stark and Goldstein, 1985; and Brien, 1992). Civil proceedings are independent of criminal proceedings. The entire case must be fought all over again in the courtroom, this time at the victim's expense, without the backing of the government and its enormous resources. Victims have to put their lives "on hold" for years while the litigation process slowly drags on. Cases involve motions, hearings, conferences, depositions, interrogatories, negotiations, trials, and appeals. In the meantime, plaintiffs (and defendants as well) undergo an ordeal punctuated by moments of suspense, anxiety, frustration, despair, and humiliation. Despite their opposing interests and simmering mutual hostility, the warring parties must keep in contact with each other, at least through their respective lawyers, for months or even years after criminal proceedings end. If negotiations fail, and last-minute out-of-court settlements are beyond reach, victims must relive the crime once again on the stand. After testifying, they must submit to a withering cross-examination by the defense attorney that could raise questions of shared responsibility, damage the victims' reputation, and expose the most intimate details of their backgrounds, lifestyles, injuries, losses, and suffering. Win or lose, civil suits may take years to be resolved. The backlogs and delays in civil court are worse than those in criminal court, because litigation has become such a popular way to settle disputes.

Victims run the risk of being sued themselves. Countersuits by defendants against plaintiffs fit into a strategy of harassment and intimidation intended to force victims to drop charges or accept unfavorable out-of-court settlements. The defendants are likely to allege contributory negligence (the injured party was partly responsible for what happened), or victim provocation, or consent by the plaintiff to the action causing harm (that is, the plaintiff assumed the risk; for example, a woman alleging rape was drinking heavily and agreed to go to the man's apartment).

Top-notch lawyers, who in the adversary system of civil proceedings are said to be as important a factor as the facts of the case, probably won't be interested unless huge sums of money are at stake. If they are victorious, their contingency fees may range as high as one-third to one-half of the money awarded to the plaintiff. Win or lose, victims may have to pay for litigation costs other than their attorney's services, such as filing fees, deposition costs, and the expenses incurred in obtaining expert testimony.

Most discouraging of all is the collection problem. Even in victory there can be defeat. Most street criminals don't have what lawyers call "deep pockets" (substantial assets, like homes, cars, jewelry, bank accounts, stocks, bonds, or business interests). On the contrary, many are virtually "judgment-proof"—broke and with no prospects of coming into money from careers or inheritances. It will be hard for the victims' attorneys to recover any money without incurring great expenses if the offenders have spent or hidden the spoils of their crimes.

Records on the successes and failures of victims who have sued offenders in civil courts have not been systematically compiled. The actual dollar amounts of some out-of-court settlements are kept confidential. However, advocacy groups are urging victims to consider exercising this option if the identity and whereabouts of the offender are known, if restitution is not forthcoming from criminal court proceedings, and if compensation is not available from insurance companies or government-administered funds. Civil suits are the only means of redress when the entire injury and loss is intangible and subsumed under the heading of "pain and suffering." Lawsuits are still possible in cases in which victims failed to take reasonable precautions for their own protection, since the victims' contributory negligence is not a legal defense for those who intentionally inflicted harm. Of course, the prospects for a meaningful judgment are promising only when offenders have substantial assets or incomes. Since few street criminals who commit acts of violence or theft meet these criteria, attorneys within the victims' rights movement have developed a strategic alternative: lawsuits against financially sound third parties.

Collecting Damages from Third Parties

Even when the perpetrators of a crime are known to be judgment-proof, victims still have a chance to recover their losses. Instead of suing those who directly inflicted the injuries, they can go after third parties, either individuals or entities such as businesses, institutions, or government agencies. The twist in these civil suits is to allege that a third party is partly to blame for the victim's misfortunes. The legal theory behind the current wave of third-party suits parallels traditional notions of "negligence." The plaintiff argues that the defendant (the third party) had a duty or obligation, that there was a breach of this duty, and that this breach proximately caused injury to the plaintiff. The plaintiff tries to prove that the third party's negligence put the criminal in a position to single out the plaintiff and harm him or her (Carrington, 1977).

Third-party suits can be of two types. The first type is directed against enterprises like private businesses—for example, landlords, innkeepers, and department stores. The second type is aimed at custodial agencies and officials of the criminal justice system, such as parole boards, prison wardens, probation officers, and directors of mental institutions.

Whereas suing offenders is reactive (benefiting victims after they have been harmed), third-party civil suits can be both reactive and proactive. If for no other motive than their own enlightened self-interest, the private enterprises and governmental bodies that are the targets of these kinds of suits are compelled to take reasonable and necessary precautions to prevent further crimes for which they can be sued again. By discouraging the indifference and negligence that facilitate predatory acts, third-party civil suits contribute to security consciousness and crime prevention (Carrington, 1986).

Suing Private Enterprises The following landmark cases of successful suits in the 1970s have served as models for many subsequent claims.

A well-known singer is raped in a motel by an unknown assailant who has entered her room by jiggling the lock on sliding glass terrace doors. Badly shaken by the experience and unable to appear on stage, the singer sues the motel chain for lost earnings. Her attorney argues that the motel has shown gross negligence in maintaining security for its guests by failing to provide adequate door locks. A jury renders a verdict in her favor of $2.5 million. The motel chain agrees to a settlement by not appealing the verdict and pays her $1.5 million. (Barbash, 1979; Rottenberg, 1980)

A security guard at a drive-in hamburger stand is shot in the head during a robbery. He doesn't sue the offender or his employer (the restaurant). Instead, his attorney argues successfully that the store that sold the robber the bullet, a branch of a major department store chain, is guilty of gross negligence. The guns and ammunition department routinely ignored an obscure state law that requires two citizens to vouch for the identity of the purchaser of bullets. (Barbash, 1979; Rottenberg, 1980)

Third-party suits against private enterprises can take several forms (Austern, 1987). Lawsuits can allege that landlords are liable for crimes committed against their tenants, because of inadequate lighting or locks; that hotels and motels are liable for assaults and thefts committed against guests, because of lax security measures (such as failure to install closed-circuit television monitors, to store room keys safely, or to hire guards); that college administrations are responsible for failing to correct security lapses that reasonable and prudent persons would realize endanger students in campus buildings and dormitories; that banks, stores, shopping malls, and theaters are liable for failure to provide ordinary care to protect customers from robbers and thieves; that common carriers (bus, train, or airplane companies) are liable for failure to furnish customary forms of protection for passengers on vehicles or at stations and platforms; and that employers who negligently hire known felons and put them in positions of trust and responsibility are liable if they commit crimes during the course of their work.

Third-party lawsuits against businesses have established new definitions of corporate responsibility and financial liability. The suits never accuse the defendant (business) of intentionally harming the plaintiff, because the executives in charge probably never met the victim and were two or three steps removed from the criminal action. What is alleged is that the defendant's gross negligence and breach of responsibility created a climate that made the criminal's task easier and the incident predictable (Carrington, 1977, 1978).

Victims can win if they can prove in civil court that the third party did not act to prevent a reasonably foreseeable crime. To prevail, the attorney must convincingly demonstrate that the defendant chronically disregarded complaints, did not post warnings, chose not to rectify conditions and improve security, and did not offer the degree of protection expected by community standards. Most claims fail to meet this test, but the few that successfully do can contribute to the improvement of public safety in places like shopping centers, bus terminals, parking lots, hotels, and apartment complexes (Brien, 1992).

A young woman moves into a townhouse and asks the superintendent to install a "night latch," a lock that can be opened only from the inside. But the management refuses her request, declaring that it needs to have access to all units. Six months later, she is awakened when an intruder puts his hand over her mouth. He sexually assaults her, burglarizes her home, and takes her to an automatic teller machine to withdraw cash. As a reward for her cooperation, he explains how he broke into the management's office, rifled through an unlocked file cabinet, discovered where single women lived, and took her key from a board where all the tenant's keys were hanging with identifying tags. She sues the management for negligence and the jury awards her a judgment of $17 million. (Balleza, 1991)

As attorneys are honing their skills at "security litigation" seminars, landlords and businesses are scrambling to make their premises "suit-proof" even if they cannot be crime-proof (Purdy, 1994). Since many lawsuits against property owners are settled out of court, reliable figures about their rate of occurrence and success are hard to find. One estimate from a sample of court records turned up 186 suits against property owners from 1958 to 1982. A later study established that the rate has increased, locating 267 third-party suits from 1983 to 1992. Almost half of all the suits were launched by rape victims (Deutsch, 1994).

Suing Governmental Bodies Successful third-party lawsuits against criminal justice agencies and custodial officials, like the two 1970s landmark cases described below, are less common than suits against private enterprises.

> **A** fourteen-year-old girl is abducted from a private school, tied to a tree, molested, and then left to freeze to death. The man who kills her had previously attacked another girl from the same school in that way. He had been committed for treatment while under confinement at a nearby psychiatric institute. The victim's parents sue the mental hospital, a psychiatrist, and a probation officer for arranging the release of the offender into an outpatient program without first receiving court approval. They win a judgment of $25,000. (Carrington, 1977, 1978)

> **A** convict with a record of forty felony convictions and seventeen escape attempts is permitted to participate in a "take-a-lifer to dinner" program at a prison in Washington. After eating at the home of a prison baker, he escapes, commits an armed robbery, and kills a man. The victim's widow sues the warden both personally and in his official capacity, in addition to the state of Washington, for gross negligence. Her attorney argues that the warden didn't have legislative authority or administrative permission from his superiors to let the inmate out that night. She wins a judgment of $186,000, which the state does not appeal. (Barbash, 1979; Rottenberg, 1980)

In a few states, governmental bodies cannot be sued even when the negligence of officials clearly contributed to the commission of crimes; the agents and agencies are protected by the English common-law doctrine of "sovereign immunity." Most states and the federal government permit citizens to sue, but impose limitations (like financial caps and exemption from punitive damages) and invoke special procedures.

The basic charge in civil actions against the government is gross negligence. The plaintiffs allege that officials severely abused their discretionary authority. The crimes are said to have happened because official inaction or incompetence facilitated the offenders' inclinations to harm innocent parties (Austern, 1987; Carrington, 1978).

The specific charges in third-party liability lawsuits against governmental agencies and officials fit under a number of headings (Austern, 1987). Claims against the police can allege "nonfeasance": that officers failed to act to protect individuals to whom they owed a special duty, such as witnesses for the prosecution. Claims can also allege police "malfeasance": that officers acted carelessly or inattentively as victims got hurt.

A husband stabs his wife thirteen times. Nearly a half-hour later, when the police arrive in response to her earlier call for help, he kicks her in the head, then drops their son on her unconscious body, and kicks her again. As he wanders around screaming, he is finally restrained and taken into custody. After eight days in a coma and several months in a hospital, she sues the city, three police chiefs, and twenty-nine officers. Her lawsuit alleges that, because her assailant was her husband, the police failed to provide her with equal protection under the law, as guaranteed by the Fourteenth Amendment, by handling her numerous calls for help over the years differently. A jury finds the police negligent for failing to protect her and awards her $2.3 million. The city appeals, and she settles for $1.9 million out of court. (Gelles and Straus, 1988)

When dangerous prisoners are not adequately supervised or are let go as the result of an administrative error, and then they inflict harm, suits can allege "wrongful escape." When dangerous convicted criminals are released and then injure persons whom they had previously publicly threatened, suits can be filed for "failure to warn." Claims can also allege "wrongful release" when, through gross negligence on the part of officials, a convicted criminal is granted conditional release (like probation, parole, or furlough) from a jail, prison, or mental institution and then commits a foreseeable crime.

A mental patient walks out of a minimum-security state psychiatric hospital and wanders into a small town. He buys a hunting knife and then, for no apparent reason seizes a passerby on a crowded street—a nine-year-old-girl—and stabs her more than thirty times. He is found not guilty of murder by reason of insanity. The girl's parents sue the state for failing to protect their daughter from this man. Originally the lawyer for the state argues that the suit should be dismissed because the government is not responsible for the child's death since the mental patient chose her at random, so there was no way to know in advance that he posed a threat to her safety. But then the state agrees to a $1.5 million out-of-court settlement, compensating the mother for the emotional harm of witnessing her daughter's murder, and pledging to improve security at state mental hospitals. (Hays, 1992)

Suits against custodial officials and agencies raise important issues. The U.S. Supreme Court ruled in 1980 that neither the Constitution nor the Civil Rights Act of 1964 give the survivors of a murder victim the right to sue a state parole board (Carrington, 1980). In upholding the doctrine of sovereign immunity from liability, the justices of the Court argued that government has a legitimate interest in seeking to rehabilitate criminals. All the treatment alternatives to totally incapacitating convicts through maximum-security confinement involve a gamble with the public's safety. Halfway houses, therapeutic communities, work release, educational release, furloughs, probation, and parole—all grant conditional liberty to known offenders.

Underlying a charge of "abuse of discretionary authority" and "gross negligence" is the assumption that dangerousness can be predicted. It usually can't be, with any statistical certainty. Some patients and inmates thought to be dangerous turn out to be well-behaved, and some individuals on conditional liberty who were rated as posing a low risk act viciously. What is predictable is that successful third-party lawsuits by victims against custodial officials and agencies will have a chilling effect on wardens, psychiatrists, parole boards, and others who make decisions regarding confinement versus release. What might develop in these therapeutic relationships is a type of defensiveness comparable to the defensive medicine practiced by doctors afraid of malpractice suits. Fear of legal and financial repercussions could dominate professional judgments and record keeping. Rehabilitation programs could be severely constrained. Eligible convicts could be barred from such programs because administrators wouldn't want to jeopardize their own careers by releasing them from total confinement. Qualified professionals could be deterred from taking such jobs because of exposure to personal liability lawsuits, unless states protect such custodial employees under a doctrine of sovereign immunity.

On the other hand, vulnerable members of the general public need lawsuits as a vehicle to exert some leverage over justice officials and unresponsive bureaucracies. And aggrieved parties need a way to hold grossly negligent agency officials accountable, as well as a mechanism to recover losses inflicted by dangerous criminals who should not have been left unsupervised. Third-party lawsuits seem to be the appropriate remedy. These civil suits are helping to establish a proper balance between two conflicting policy objectives: enhancing public safety in the long run by rehabilitating offenders through the judicious granting of conditional liberty, and maintaining public safety in the short run by incapacitating and incarcerating individuals believed to be dangerous to the community.

COLLECTING INSURANCE REIMBURSEMENTS

Private Crime Insurance

Private insurance companies are innocent third parties that can quickly and routinely reimburse victims for their losses. The positive aspect is that a prudent policyholder can be protected against the threat of financial loss. The drawbacks are that a company must be found that is willing to issue a policy (some people in high-crime areas have trouble finding an insurer), and that a potential target must be willing and able to pay for the coverage (many people are aware of life's dangers but do not have the disposable income to afford the "luxury" of purchasing insurance).

Cautious individuals can take out coverage to protect themselves against a wide variety of hazards. For example, life insurance policies can pay sizable sums to survivors of murder victims. Some policies (which cost more) contain a "double indemnity" clause, which pays survivors twice as much if the policyholder dies from an accident, including a criminally inflicted injury. Coverage can also be purchased to offset lost earnings (income maintenance) and expenses due to medical bills (health insurance). Property can be insured against loss or damage. Car and boat insurance covers losses due to theft, vandalism, and arson. Home insurance covers losses due to burglary, some larcenies (of items on porches or in yards, for example), vandalism, arson, and robbery (if the confrontation occurs within the home). Some companies sell robbery insurance that covers losses of valuables like jewelry no matter where the crime occurs. A few companies offer protection to businesses whose executives might be kidnapped and held for ransom.

Patterns of Loss, Recovery, and Reimbursement Data from victimization surveys confirm some commonsense predictions about insurance coverage and recovery. First, some types of coverage are more common than others. More people are insured against medical expenses than against property losses. Medical costs are potentially more devastating, and health coverage is often a fringe benefit of full-time jobs. Second, higher-income people are more likely to buy crime insurance than lower-income people (even though poorer people are exposed to more risks and may suffer higher victimization rates). Third, large losses are more likely than small ones to be reimbursed through insurance claims. Many policies have "deductible" clauses, which stipulate that the victim must bear the first $100 or $250 (or some other sum) of the losses and cannot file a claim unless the out-of-pocket expenses exceed this figure (Harland, 1981a).

Statistics derived from the *National Crime Victimization Surveys* indicate that most losses from property crimes do not result in insurance reimbursement. Those whose cars are stolen are the most likely to receive cash settlements. A small proportion of families who suffer household burglaries and larcenies are covered. An even smaller fraction of persons who are robbed or pickpocketed are insured against such losses.

Studies concerning patterns of burglary loss, coverage, and recovery show that both the average amount stolen and the percentage of victims insured are positively correlated with family income. That means the average value of stolen cash and valuables lost in a burglary increases as the victim's family income goes up; and that families that earn more are more likely to be insured than lower-income households. In one study during the 1970s, only one family in ten was insured in the lowest income category, whereas about half of all families in the higher-income category were covered. (Presumably, the rich were fully insured, but that data was unavailable.) Stolen goods are rarely recovered, by the police or by victims themselves. People who lose a lot have a slightly better chance of recovering all or part of their property than individuals who lose a little (whose cases are assigned very low priorities by the police and whose lost goods are difficult to positively identify and return). For losses of less than $100, insurance is of no use, probably because of deductible clauses. In sum, although a small number of families recover substantial amounts of what they originally lost, insurance provides relief for relatively few burglary victims (Skogan, 1978; Harland, 1981a).

Federal Crime Insurance

Insurance companies make profits in two ways: They adjust their rates continuously so that they take in more in premiums than they pay out in claims, and they invest the money paid in by policyholders in order to collect interest, dividends, and rents. To contain costs and limit payouts, companies raise their rates, place caps on reimbursements, impose sizable deductibles, and exclude certain kinds of common losses.

One irony of the insurance-for-profit business is that those who face the greatest risks are sometimes denied coverage. The insufficiency and unfairness of private insurance underwriting practices first received public attention during the late 1960s. The National Advisory Panel on Insurance in Riot-Affected Areas, part of the National Advisory Commission on Civil Disorders, was appointed by President Johnson in 1967 to examine the plight of inner-city residents and businesses that had suffered losses during ghetto rebellions. The panel cited a general lack of insurance availability as a contributing factor in urban decay—the closing of businesses, the drying up of jobs, the abandonment of buildings, and the exodus of residents from high-crime areas. In 1968, Congress followed some of the panel's recommendations and granted relief to victims of insurance "red-lining" (an illegal, discriminatory practice that results in denial of coverage). The Department of Housing and Urban Development Act set up Fair Access to Insurance Requirements (FAIR) plans to make sure that property owners were not denied fire damage coverage solely because the neighborhood had a high rate of arson cases. In 1970, Congress amended the 1968 act to permit the federal government to offer "affordable" burglary and robbery insurance directly to urban homeowners, tenants, and businesses in locales where such coverage from private companies was either unavailable or exorbitantly expensive. Federal intervention into the insurance market to assist actual and potential crime victims was viewed as a last resort (Bernstein, 1972).

The Federal Emergency Management Agency (FEMA) currently runs the Federal Insurance Administration. During 1993, over 16,700 policies were in effect in areas where the government concluded that there was a critical problem in crime insurance availability. About 83 percent of the policies were taken out to protect residences, with the remainder covering commercial enterprises against losses arising from robberies and burglaries. The government took in over $4,750,000 in premiums and paid out over $3,100,000 in claims. The roughly 800 claimants collected an average of less than $4,000 each (Maguire and Pastore, 1994).

Once the government began to sell insurance coverage, it became reasonable to ask whether public reimbursement funds could be set up to bail out families that faced economic ruin because they were not willing or able to take out insurance, or were not adequately protected, especially against huge medical bills and lost earnings. Public insurance plans have been devised to aid such persons. They are called victim compensation programs.

RECOVERING LOSSES FROM COMPENSATION PROGRAMS

Reimbursement from Government Funds

Most street crime victims never receive criminal court–ordered restitution for one obvious reason: Their offenders were not caught and convicted. For a parallel reason, most victims never collect civil court–ordered judgments: Their perpetrators cannot be identified or located and successfully sued. Furthermore, rarely can any third party be held partly responsible for the incident and sued for its liability. Given the inadequacy of most people's insurance coverage when major disasters strike, the only remaining hope for monetary recovery lies with a different sort of third party, a state compensation fund. Reimbursement from a government fund appears to be the only realistic method for routinely restoring individuals to the financial condition they were in before the crime occurred.

A middle-aged man is blinded by assailants, who are caught, convicted, and imprisoned. On their release, they are ordered by the court to pay restitution to their victim for the loss of his eyesight. Under the arrangement, it will take 442 years for the victim to collect the full amount due him. (Fry, 1957)

A Good Samaritan comes to the aid of two elderly women who are being harassed by a drunken youth on a subway train. As his wife and child watch in horror, the man is stabbed to death by the drunk. The killer is captured and sentenced to from twenty years to life in prison. The widow is forced to send her child to live with her mother while she goes to work to pay off bills. ("The Good Samaritans," 1965)

A man shot during the course of a robbery is awarded $30,000 for unpaid medical bills and $12,000 for wages lost because of his injuries. He receives $600 a month until he is able to go back to work. (New York State Crime Victims Board, 1988)

The widow of a murder victim is granted $1,500 for funeral expenses and $15,000 for loss of support. She collects $1,000 a month in death-benefits until a maximum of $20,000 in payments is reached. (New York State Crime Victims Board, 1988)

The first two cases, which took place, respectively, in England in 1951 and in New York City in 1965, dramatized the need for special funds to compensate victims for devastating losses. The remaining two cases, from a state-run compensation program, illustrate the kinds of aid that are now available. Money can't erase painful memories or cure lingering emotional and physical wounds. Payments are stopgap measures that counteract the effects of crime without touching its roots. Yet reimbursement can ease the suffering of victims. It is the easiest, simplest, and most direct way of speeding a victim's recovery.

The History of Victim Compensation by Governments

The earliest reference to governmental compensation for crime victims can be found in the ancient Babylonian Code of Hammurabi (about 1775 B.C.), which is considered to be the oldest written body of criminal law. The code instructed territorial governors to replace a robbery victim's lost property if the criminal was not captured; in the case of a murder, the governor was to pay the heirs a specific sum in silver from the treasury. In the centuries that followed, restitution replaced compensation by the state. But during the Middle Ages, routine restitution also faded away, leaving the victim with little redress except to seek to recover losses by suing the offender in civil court.

Interest in compensation revived when the prison reform movement in Europe during the 1800s focused attention on the suffering of convicts and, in so doing, indirectly called attention to the plight of their victims. Jeremy Bentham, a major figure in the classical school of criminology, argued that those who had been victimized, either in their person or their fortune, should not be abandoned to their fate. The society to which they had contributed, and which ought to have protected them, owed them an indemnity. The three leading criminologists of the rival Italian positivist school, Cesare Lombroso, Enrico Ferri, and Raffaele Garofalo, also endorsed compensation (and restitution) at several International Penal Congress meetings held at the turn of the century. But these resolutions did not lead to any concrete actions.

Legal historians have uncovered only a few instances of special funds set aside for crime victims—one in Tuscany after 1786, another in Mexico starting in 1871, and one beginning in France in 1934. Switzerland and Cuba also experimented with victim compensation (MacNamara and Sullivan, 1974; Schafer, 1970; Silving, 1959).

Margery Fry, an English magistrate, is widely acknowledged as the prison reformer who sparked the revival of interest in compensation in Anglo-Saxon legal systems in the late 1950s. Because of her efforts, in 1963 a government commission investigated different schemes for reparations, and in 1964 Britain set up its program. Several Australian states and Canadian provinces followed suit during the next few years. The most complete protection in the Western world is offered in New Zealand, which in 1972 abolished the victim compensation program it had pioneered in 1963 and absorbed it within a universal accident insurance system.

Everyone in New Zealand is covered for losses arising from any kind of misfortune, including crimes. The nature of the event, the reason it occurred, and the responsibility for it do not affect the compensation decisions (European Committee on Crime Problems, 1978; Meiners, 1978).

The Debate over Compensation in the United States

In the late 1950s, the question of compensation that was under consideration in England surfaced in American law journals. Initially, distinguished scholars raised many objections to the idea of government aid to crime victims. But support for the notion of compensation grew when Supreme Court Justice Arthur Goldberg argued that society should assume some responsibility for making whole again those whom the law had failed to protect. Soon, some well-known political figures of the period came to accept the proposition that special funds to repay victims should be set up. Their enthusiasm was in accord with the liberal political philosophy embodied in President John Kennedy's "New Frontier" and President Johnson's "Great Society": that government programs should be designed to try to solve persistent social problems.

The proposals of elected officials, the suggestions of legal scholars and criminologists, and the pressures of coalitions of interest groups were necessary but not sufficient to trigger legislatures into action. Widely publicized incidents of brutality and tragedy supplied the missing ingredient of public support in the first few states to experiment with compensation schemes. In 1965, California initiated a repayment process as part of its public assistance system. In 1966, New York created a special board to allocate reimbursements. In 1967, Massachusetts designated certain courts and the state attorney general's office as grantors of financial aid to victims.

Starting in 1965, Congress began to debate the question of federal encouragement of and assistance to state compensation programs. No lobby emerged to pressure elected officials to vote against compensation plans. Even private insurance companies did not feel threatened by the potential loss of business. At hearings, the idea of compensation was endorsed by spokespersons for the American Bar Association, the International Association of Chiefs of Police, the National District Attorneys' Association, the U.S. Conference of Mayors, the National League of Cities, the National Conference of State Legislatures, existing state compensation boards, judges' organizations, senior citizens' groups, and the National Council on Crime and Delinquency ("Crime Control Amendments," 1973; Edelhertz and Geis, 1974; "Crime Victims' Aid," 1978; Meiners, 1978). The pros and cons of governmental compensation raised many vital political, philosophical, and pragmatic issues (see Childres, 1964; Schultz, 1965; Wolfgang, 1965; Brooks, 1972; Geis, 1976; Meiners, 1978; Carrow, 1980; U.S. House Committee on the Judiciary, 1980; Gaynes, 1981; and Elias, 1983a).

The most compelling rationales advanced by advocates presented compensation as either an additional type of social insurance; as a way of meeting an overlooked governmental obligation to all citizens; or as a means of assisting individuals facing financial ruin.

Proponents of the "shared risk" rationale viewed compensation as part of the safety net of the comprehensive social insurance system that has been developing in the United States since the Great Depression of the 1930s. All public welfare insurance programs are intended to enable people to cope with the hazards that threaten stability and security in everyday life. Health expenses are addressed by Medicaid and Medicare; disability and untimely death by Social Security; on-the-job accidents by workers' compensation; and loss of work and earnings by unemployment compensation. The premiums for these state-run compulsory insurance plans are derived from taxation. Criminal injury insurance, like the other types of coverage, provides "equal protection" against dangers that are reasonably certain to harm some members of society but that are unpredictable for any individual. All taxpayers contribute to the pool to spread the costs, and, therefore, everyone is entitled to reimbursement.

The "government liability" rationale argued that the state is responsible for the safety of its citizens because it monopolizes, or reserves for itself, the right to use force to suppress crime and to punish offenders. Since individuals are not allowed to carry deadly weapons around routinely for their own defense, and settling serious criminal matters privately is forbidden, the government has made it difficult for victims to defend themselves and recover their losses. Therefore, within the social contract, the state becomes liable for damages when its criminal justice system fails to fulfill its obligation to its citizens. By the logic of this argument, all victims, regardless of their economic standing and the type of loss they have suffered, ought to have a right to compensation.

Those taking the "social welfare" approach held that the state has a humanitarian responsibility to assist victims, just as it helps other needy and disadvantaged groups. The aid is given as a symbolic act of mercy, compassion, and charity (and not as universal insurance coverage or because of any legal obligation). According to this theory, receiving compensation is a privilege, not a right, so eligibility and payment amounts can be limited.

Besides these rationales, several additional arguments were advanced to encourage public acceptance of compensation. Some sociologists and criminologists contended that the "system" (the social institutions, economic and political arrangements, prevailing relationships within society) generates crime by perpetuating bitter competition, poverty, discrimination, unemployment, and insecurity, which breed greed, desperation, and violence. Therefore, society, through its governmental bodies, owes crime victims compensation as a matter of social justice. Some advocates contrasted the attention accorded to criminals with the neglect shown toward their innocent victims. They charged that it was blatantly unfair to attend to many of the medical, educational, vocational, legal, and emotional needs of criminals (albeit minimally, and sometimes against their will) at public expense and yet leave injured victims to fend for themselves. Compensation partly corrected this "imbalance." Finally, some pragmatists anticipated that the prospect of compensation would induce more victims to cooperate with the authorities by pressing charges and testifying against their assailants.

Some skeptics and critics rejected the notion of government intervention on both philosophical and practical grounds. The earliest opponents of importing this British Commonwealth practice to America denounced what they considered to be the spread of "governmental paternalism" and "creeping socialism." They contended that taxpayer-funded crime insurance undermined the virtues of rugged individualism, self-reliance, personal responsibility, independence, saving for emergencies, and calculated risk taking. They considered any expansion of the welfare state and the growth of new, expensive, and remote bureaucracies to be greater evils than the neglect of crime victims. They contended that private enterprise could write more effective and efficient policies than governmental bodies for individuals and families who had enough prudence and foresight to purchase protection before tragedy struck. Other opponents worried that criminal injury insurance, like fire, auto, and theft coverage, was vulnerable to fraud. Deserving applicants would be hard to distinguish from manipulators who staged incidents, inflicted their own wounds, and padded their bills. Finally, certain critics did not dispute the merits of compensation programs but objected to their establishment and expansion on financial grounds. They argued that it was unfair to compel taxpayers to repay the losses of victims as well as foot the bill for the costs of the police, courts, and prisons. To accommodate this objection, state programs have come to rely more and more on money raised from "offenders" (including traffic law violators).

A statistical analysis of congressional votes on bills between 1965 and 1980 revealed that Democrats, particularly liberal Democrats, tended to favor allocating federal aid to reimburse crime victims. Republicans, especially conservative Republicans, tended to oppose spending federal tax dollars on state compensation programs. The exceptions to these patterns were usually conservative Democrats, generally from southern states, who sided with conservative Republicans against compensation plans, and some liberal Republicans, often from northern states, who joined with liberal Democrats in support of these provictim legislative initiatives. In other words, ideology proved to be a better predictor of voting behavior than party affiliation (Karmen, 1981b).

In 1984, Congress finally reached a consensus about the appropriate role for the federal government on the question of compensation and passed a Victims of Crime Act (VOCA), ending nearly twenty years of floor debates, lobbying, political posturing, maneuvering, and last-minute compromises. VOCA established a fund within the U.S. Treasury, collected from fines, penalties, and forfeitures.

Administered by the attorney general, the money is earmarked to subsidize state compensation funds and victim assistance services, and to aid victims of federal crimes (Peak, 1986). In 1989, VOCA guidelines were revised to encourage state programs to expand their coverage and to resemble each other more closely. Providing federal matching funds worked out as intended: Every state had set up a compensation program by 1993 (Maine and South Dakota were the last to join in).

How Programs Operate: Similarities and Differences

In all of the fifty states, plus the District of Columbia, the question of whether to compensate victims has been resolved. But the programs vary in a number of ways, reflecting the diversity in the traditions, populations, crime rates, and resources of the states and the differing rationales on which the programs were based.

Certain requirements are the same in each state (see Parent, Auerbach, and Carlson, 1992). All of the programs grant reimbursements only to "innocent" victims. Compensation board investigators always look for evidence of "contributory misconduct." If it is established that the individual was partly to blame for getting hurt, the grant can be reduced in size or disallowed entirely. For example, applicants would not be repaid if they were engaging in an illegal activity when they were injured (such as getting shot while holding up a liquor store, getting robbed while buying drugs, or being beaten after agreeing to perform an act of prostitution). Most boards would rule victims of barroom brawls as ineligible if they had been drinking, uttered "fighting words," and thereby provoked the fracas in which they got seriously injured. Applicants can appeal claims that were denied.

Another common feature is that the programs deal only with the most serious crimes that result in physical injury, psychological trauma, or death: murder, rape, assault, robbery, child sexual abuse, child physical abuse, spouse abuse, other types of domestic violence, and also hit-and-run motor vehicle collisions and crashes caused by drunk drivers. Most do not repay people for property that is damaged or lost in thefts, burglaries, or robberies (unless they are elderly or the possessions are "essential," like hearing aids or wheelchairs). Only "out-of-pocket expenses" (bills not paid by collateral sources, such as Medicaid, or private insurance, like Blue Cross) are reimbursed. The payments can be for medical expenses (to doctors, emergency rooms, clinics, hospitals), for mental health services (to psychiatrists, counselors, therapists), and for earnings lost because of missed work. The families of murder victims are eligible for assistance with reasonable funeral and burial costs and for a death benefit or pension for surviving dependents to compensate for the loss of financial support. Each program requires that all parts of a claim be fully documented with bills and receipts.

All the programs prohibit double recoveries. Any money collected from insurance policies or other government agencies is deducted ("subrogated") from the compensation board's final award. In the statistically unusual cases in which offenders are caught, found guilty, and forced to pay restitution, this money is also subtracted from the award.

In every state, the applicant must report the crime promptly to the police and cooperate fully with any investigation and prosecution, but the assailant does not have to be caught and convicted.

Despite sharing these basic features, the fifty state programs differ in a number of ways: how long victims can wait before telling the police about the crime (from one day, in Iowa, to three months, in New Jersey, with a mode of three days); how long victims can take before applying for reimbursement (from six months, in Iowa, to three years, in Rhode Island, with a mode of one year); how much victims can collect (maximum awards of $1,000, in Georgia, to $50,000, plus limitless medical expenses, in New York, with modes at $10,000 and $25,000); whether the program will grant an emergency loan before fully investigating a case; and whether lawyers can be hired to present cases and collect fees.

Eligibility rules differ slightly from state to state. For example, survivors of murder victims (who can apply for reimbursements of customary funeral costs and perhaps loss of financial support) include parents, siblings, and in-laws in some programs, but most limit coverage to children and spouses. In 1988, amendments to the Victim of Crime Act mandated that eligibility in all states be extended to victims of domestic violence, people hurt by drunk driving crashes, and nonresidents (visitors and commuters). On the other hand, whole groups of people can be automatically ruled ineligible. In each state the list varies. Law enforcement officers and fire fighters are generally excluded because they are covered by workers' compensation. In some jurisdictions, prison inmates, parolees, probationers, ex-convicts, and members of organized crime are eliminated from consideration.

A number of trends in compensation regulations are worth noting. Initially, the money given out by compensation programs came from general revenues, which essentially means from taxpayers. The trend since the 1970s is to rely more heavily on funds derived from "penalty assessments" or "abusers' taxes" (more than half of the programs now get all or part of their money this way). These funds are raised from fines and surcharges levied on persons convicted of traffic violations, misdemeanors, and felonies, plus, in some states, taxes imposed on the earnings of offenders on work release, and from collateral forfeited by defendants who jump bail. In these states, "criminals" as a class are being held responsible for providing reimbursement to victims in general. Offender-funded compensation programs reflect a larger trend, compelling convicts to shoulder all kinds of financial obligations, including restitution, halfway house room and board, fines, court costs, and supervision fees. Before the 1980s, in about one-third of the states, only claimants who faced severe financial hardships could pass a "means test" to become eligible for reimbursement. By the end of the 1980s, only eleven programs still required their investigators to establish a victim's compelling financial need before granting an award. Another change over time has been to extend coverage to include losses resulting from pain and suffering, child care, cleaning up the crime scene, and replacing essential personal property like wheelchairs and hearing aids. Some programs are broadening eligibility to include incest victims, victims of sexual assault who escaped without physical injuries, elderly victims of burglaries, and parents of missing children. Encouraged by VOCA's financial support, eight states have recognized the need to raise the upper limits for awards because of substantial hikes in the cost of living. In the other states with frozen maximum benefits, compensation payments are failing to keep up with the rate of inflation. Minimum loss requirements and deductible provisions (usually of $100), designed to eliminate minor claims, are being scrapped, and persist in only eighteen states (NOVA, 1988; Parent, Auerbach, and Carlson, 1992).

Monitoring and Evaluating Compensation Programs

A man and his girlfriend have an argument at 4 o'clock in the morning. They drive a short distance from her mother's house to sort things out and park in a well-lighted area. A man approaches the car, sprays the couple with Mace, shoots the man in the neck with a pellet gun, and then forces them to get out of the car, strip naked, and run away. The suspect is later apprehended and pleads guilty to committing a series of sexual assaults and robberies in that neighborhood. The male victim misses four months of work because of medical complications and submits a claim for $1,638. Unfortunately, he lives in a state with a backlog of 6,000 cases. Currently it takes the compensation board about a year to decide whether to reimburse a victim and another year until it sends out a check. More than two years pass, and the man still waits to find out whether he will receive any money. Then the board sends him a letter that asks why he was sitting in a parked car so early in the morning. (Sanderson, 1994)

Many of the arguments about the "rightness" of compensation hinge on judgments about what type of financial help crime victims require and on assumptions about the ability of programs to meet these needs. Now that a number of states have operated programs for many years, a substantial body of data has become available for analysis. Program evaluations reveal how well compensation boards are meeting their goals and can provide benchmarks to justify or rule out new procedures and requests for more funds. Assessments of the efficiency of administrative practices contribute to efforts to eliminate delays, minimize overhead, and iron out inequities. Evaluation is especially important as a means of improving service delivery during periods when the public clamors for additional government aid but is not willing to pay the taxes for it.

When it comes to evaluation, the striking differences between state programs can be considered an asset. Each jurisdiction can be regarded as a "social laboratory" within which an experiment is in progress. From this viewpoint, various approaches to achieving the same ends are being tested to determine which works best.

Assessing whether compensation programs are succeeding or failing in their mission requires that their goals be stated clearly and precisely. In the 1960s, the early advocates of reimbursing victims from government-administered funds had ambitious goals and made optimistic (and perhaps unrealistic) pronouncements. Certainly their lofty, noble, charitable, and humanitarian aims of substantially alleviating economic suffering have not been realized. Data that either support or refute this charge can be derived from two kinds of assessments: process evaluations and impact evaluations.

Uncovering How Programs Work *Process evaluations* are focused on the programs' internal operations and monitor variables like productivity, overhead costs, and decision-making patterns. Process evaluators also develop profiles of the typical claimants and recipients of awards. Analyzing data bearing on these questions allows evaluators to provide useful feedback to administrators and board members about the trends and patterns that characterize their efforts.

Two process evaluations of a sample of the fifty state funds in operation at the end of the 1980s (Parent, Auerbach, and Carlson, 1992) and the start of the 1990s (Sarnoff, 1993) shed some light on various aspects of how compensation programs really work.

During fiscal year 1988, the programs in the survey's sample received over 92,000 claims and granted aid to nearly 66,000 people, paying out more than $125 million. They took in more than $165 million. Of that revenue, most (62 percent) was raised from fines and penalty assessments levied on law violators of all kinds (including traffic infractions); 22 percent of the income was derived from general appropriations (taxes) and the remaining 15 percent from the federal government in accord with the Victims of Crime Act. Most (85 percent) of the claims concerned drunk driving collisions, homicides, rapes, robberies, aggravated assaults, and child abuse cases. Very few claims arose from spouse abuse. The volume of cases handled per year varied dramatically by population size and crime rate. Workloads ranged from 62 claims (Wyoming) to over 33,000 (California) during fiscal 1988. Case-processing time, measured as the average amount of time it took to resolve a claim, ranged from one month (Utah, Washington, West Virginia) to two years (Rhode Island), with a mean of eighteen weeks. In the interim, these applicants probably suffered bouts of anxiety from uncertainty and felt strong pressures from creditors. In thirty-three states, small emergency awards between a few hundred and a few thousand dollars were permissible. Some programs seemed to be run a lot more efficiently than others. Administrative costs as a percentage of total expenditures averaged about 16 percent, but ranged from a low of 3 percent (in Missouri) to a high of 31 percent (in Wyoming, with its small caseload; however, New York, with the second-highest workload, had the second-highest overhead, spending 26 cents of every dollar on administration).

As for decision-making patterns, denial rates indicated that some boards are much stricter than others. The proportion of applicants who were turned down ranged from a low of 11 percent (Pennsylvania) to a high of 76 percent (Virginia); overall, about 36 percent get nothing and 64 percent receive some financial assistance. Denials can be for "technical reasons," such as failure to supply sufficient documentation of expenses; and for "fault," such as the stigmatizing moral judgment that the victim was "guilty" of contributory misconduct. Fault denials that rejected victims' assertions of complete innocence ranged from 0 percent (Wyoming) to 48 percent (Virginia). Some boards seem more generous, while others are determined to refute the charges that they "give money away" and are vulnerable to fraud and abuse. The average award ranged from a low of nearly $700 (Arizona) to a high of roughly $9,000 (Rhode Island, where attorney's fees are covered). The rate of compensation, calculated as a proportion (crimes actually compensated compared to all reported crimes committed in that state that year that potentially would have been eligible for compensation) also showed tremendous variation, and ranged from a low of 1 percent (Michigan) to a high of 91 percent (Minnesota), and averaged out at 19 percent.

The total number of unserved victims a year in the late 1980s was estimated to be about 90,000, or about 55 percent of the almost 170,000 potentially eligible persons (innocent, injured, facing expenses, uninsured). In other words, despite outreach efforts (such as public service announcements and posters in police stations and hospital emergency rooms), more than half of all possible beneficiaries do not know their rights and/or do not even file a claim. Some state program administrators estimated that 67 percent, maybe even 95 percent of eligible victims do not apply for financial aid. Of course, if more eligible persons were aware of their rights and did seek reimbursement, the state funds would take even longer to process their claims and either would have to cut back on the average size of awards or turn down a greater proportion of applicants, unless the directors could somehow raise more money (Parent, Auerbach, and Carlson, 1992; Sarnoff, 1993). Setting up storefront offices to accept claims from people living in high-crime areas might help to achieve the objective of reaching the maximum number of deserving individuals in the most effective and efficient manner possible (McCormack, 1991).

The findings from process evaluations about insufficient funding and inadequate outreach confirm that compensation plans are failing to live up to their humanitarian commitments. Because of their limited budgets, many boards have low visibility or even face prohibitions against advertising. Lack of interest on the part of police, prosecutors, and hospital emergency room personnel might also be a continuing problem. Some injured parties might be deterred by complex filing procedures and detailed probes into their personal finances (to prevent fraud). Others are discouraged when they hear about high rejection rates, long waits, and disappointingly small awards. Even with low rates of applications and awards, underfunded programs can run out of money before the year is over (McGillis and Smith, 1983; Sanderson, 1994).

Measuring the Effects of Programs Studies are carried out to compare a program's intentions with its actual accomplishments. These *impact evaluations* reveal the consequences of a program for its clients and the community. To determine whether or not compensation really eases the financial stress experienced by crime victims, the ratio of award payments to submitted losses can be calculated. To assess a program's impact on the participation of compensated victims in the criminal justice system, those who did and did not receive aid can be compared with regard to their attendance rates as witnesses in police lineups and court proceedings.

The diversity of structures and procedures in different state programs provides opportunities to test out which arrangements work best under which conditions. The findings of research and evaluation studies can have important consequences for the future of compensation. Determining successes and failures can help to resolve the ongoing debates over the pros and cons of compensating crime victims with public funds and the merits and demerits of particular rules and practices (Chappell and Sutton, 1974; Carrow, 1980).

The findings of several impact evaluations do not support the hypothesis that the prospect of reimbursement would increase the public's degree of cooperation with law enforcement. When the reporting rates for violent crimes in states with programs were compared with the rates in states without programs (in the 1970s), no appreciable differences were found in the extent to which victims in cities told the police about their misfortunes (Doerner, 1978). A comparison of the attitudes of claimants in Florida who were granted awards versus those whose requests were denied revealed that getting repaid did not significantly improve victims' ratings of the performance of the police, prosecutors, or judges (Doerner and Lab, 1980).

More information is needed about the impact of board decisions on the psychological and economic well-being of victims. Applicants who were rejected because of what they perceived as mere "technicalities" (like waiting too long before filing) might feel cheated. Regulations that imply that whole categories do not deserve assistance can intensify distress levels. Insensitive treatment, background investigations, extensive delays, and partial reimbursements can make even successful claimants feel victimized once again (McGillis and Smith, 1983). One researcher who evaluated the New York and New Jersey programs concluded that claimants ended up more alienated from the criminal justice system than nonclaimants. Instead of reducing public discontent with the police and courts, compensation programs provoked additional frustrations. Applicants' expectations probably rose when they first learned about the chance of reimbursement, but these hopes were consistently dashed when most claimants, for a variety of reasons, were turned down entirely or awarded insufficient funds to cover all documented expenses. Three-quarters indicated that they would not apply for compensation again if they were victimized a second time, largely because of their displeasure over delays, eligibility requirements, their treatment by program administrators, incidental expenses, inconveniences, and, ultimately, the inadequacy of their reimbursements (Elias, 1983a).

The enactment of victim compensation programs might have been merely an exercise in "symbolic politics" (Elias, 1983b, 1986), a cynical view that accuses certain politicians of voting for programs that look impressive on paper because they want to appear to be "doing something" for victims but won't allocate the necessary resources to make the promise a reality. Nevertheless, the public is favorably impressed by the foresight and concern shown by policymakers and legislators toward victims. Unaware that the majority of claimants are turned down and that the remainder are largely dissatisfied with the extent of reimbursement, people are led to believe that an effective safety net has been set up to cushion the blows of violent crime. At their current insufficient levels of funding, compensation programs serve more to pacify public opinion than to genuinely restore victims to their previous financial condition.

CONFISCATING PROFITS FROM NOTORIOUS CRIMINALS

A lone gunman terrorizes New Yorkers, committing a series of ambushes that leaves six people dead and a number of others wounded. Dubbed the "Son of Sam" as well as the "44-Caliber Killer" by the media, he is eventually caught, convicted, and sentenced to a lifetime behind bars. From his cell, he grants interviews to writers and accumulates about $90,000 in royalties from publishers. The victims he shot and the families of the people he killed sue him to prevent him from profiting from his notoriety. Eight years later his attorneys arrive at a settlement: All the money will be divided among those he harmed, and they will share any additional earnings he might receive. (Associated Press, 1984a)

A robber enters a bank but bungles the job and winds up taking four employees hostage when his escape route is blocked by police. After a siege, they are released, and he is captured, convicted, and imprisoned. Hollywood producers pay him $100,000 for the rights to depict his exploits in a movie entitled *Dog Day Afternoon*. The money is seized by the New York State Crime Victims Board and apportioned out to his kidnap victims, his lawyers (to whom he owed fees), and his former wife (for alimony and child support payments). (Roberts, 1987)

For a handful of victims or their survivors, one option for recovering losses remains: going after the profits made by offenders who sell their firsthand accounts of how and why they committed their crimes. In a few cases each year, offenders cash in on the sensationalism surrounding their highly publicized crimes. The question that arises is whether victims can take these "fruits of crime" away from offenders. Uncertainty has reigned since 1991 when the U.S. Supreme Court struck down laws that enabled the authorities to seize these ill-gotten gains and turn them over to the individuals who directly suffered because of the convicts' depredations.

In 1977, the New York State legislature passed a forfeiture of assets bill in anticipation that a vicious serial killer (cited in the first example above) might be showered with lucrative offers for book contracts, movie rights, and paid appearances to tell his inside story once he was captured (ironically, this offender never tried to cash in). After that, forty-two states and the federal government enacted similar "Son of Sam" laws to head off the financial exploitation of crimes by their perpetrators. Public opinion backed this legislative trend; in one poll, 86 percent of the respondents favored laws that took profits from notoriety away from criminals and distributed the money to victims (National Victim Center, 1991a).

These statutes went after financial gains, in the form of fees, advances, and royalties, from any reenactments of the heinous deeds in movies, memoirs, books, magazine articles, tape recordings, phonograph records, radio programs, television shows, or other forms of entertainment. If offenders (accused or convicted) were paid for expressing their thoughts, opinions, or feelings about their depredations, or for giving graphic descriptions, their income could be seized by the government and placed in an escrow account before they could spend it. For five years, individuals who had incurred direct physical, mental injuries, or financial losses could argue in civil court that were entitled to a portion of the money. In some states, any leftover funds not awarded in damage lawsuits could revert back to the offenders. But in other jurisdictions, the remaining money could have been used to cover unpaid attorneys' fees plus the court costs of the prosecution or to replenish the state's victim compensation fund (Stark and Goldstein, 1985; NOVA, 1988). The legal issues became very complicated when the offenders were not guilty of predatory street crimes with specific victims but of political crimes or white-collar crimes or vice crimes like running prostitution rings or trafficking in drugs.

Notoriety-for-profit laws were primarily symbolic gestures to drive home the message that "crime doesn't pay"; secondarily, they were intended to facilitate the handing over of money to innocent victims. Yet, from the outset, these laws were controversial. Critics argued that the confiscation of payments by government had a chilling effect on the First Amendment's guarantee of freedom of expression. In 1991, all the justices of the Supreme Court agreed, and by a vote of 8 to 0, struck down New York's law and all the others like it. In a unanimous opinion (*Simon and Schuster* v. *New York Crime Victims Board*), the Court recognized that states had an undisputed compelling interest in depriving offenders of the fruits of crime and were pursuing a worthwhile goal in trying to transfer the proceeds from criminals to their victims. However, it argued, enacting these state laws unfairly singled out a convict's "speech-derived income" for a special tax burden and thereby established an inhibiting financial disincentive to create or publish works with a particular content. Publishers, moviemakers, and civil libertarians hailed the Court's landmark ruling as a victory for authors and their audiences and noted that a substantial body of worthwhile literature and redeeming commentary by notable prisoners might never had been written if these laws were on the books. Victim advocates denounced the Court's decision as a blow to victims' rights and undertook the task of redrafting provisions about lawsuits, statutes of limitation, fines, forfeitures, and escrow accounts so that they would meet constitutional standards (Fein, 1991).

7

Future Directions

- **Toward Greater Formal Legal Rights within the Criminal Justice System**
Rights Gained at the Expense of Offenders ▪ Rights Gained at the Expense of the System ▪ Rights Gained at the Expense of Either Offenders or the System or Both

- **Toward Informal Justice: The Restorative Approach**
The Search for Peace ▪ The Reliance on Mediation ▪ How Reconciliation Programs Work ▪ Evaluating Efforts at Reconciliation ▪ Pros and Cons from the Victim's Point of View

- **Toward Informal Justice, Vigilante Style**
Vigilantism's Frontier Origins ▪ Confusing Vigilantism with Legitimate Acts of Self-Defense ▪ Would Potential Victims Be Better Off If They Were Armed? ▪ The Drift Back toward Vigilantism

Several contradictory tendencies characterize the current period. On the one hand, a successful campaign is under way to expand the formal legal rights that assure that victims will be treated with fundamental fairness within the criminal justice system. Activists and advocacy groups within this rights movement want to empower victims so they can exercise greater influence over how their cases are resolved.

On the other hand, some individuals and groups are moving away from the arena of formal legal rights. This tendency toward informalism contains within it two opposite currents. One leads participants on a quest for nonlegalistic and nonadversarial ways to settle differences between people embroiled in conflicts. Within this new paradigm of "restorative justice," victim–offender reconciliation is the goal, restitution arranged through mediation is the method, and a neighborhood justice center or community-based program is the setting that substitutes for criminal court. This tendency is spurred on by a belief that it is hopelessly unrealistic to attempt to make an intransigent criminal justice system more responsive and accountable to the ostensible "clients" or "consumers" of its services. But an opposite current within informalism rejects this peacemaking approach and reverts back to earlier, more violent methods of handling criminal matters. It is the revival of the vigilante tradition of the Old West and Deep South, in which victims and their allies use force to retaliate against alleged offenders.

Together, these three tendencies will shape how victims and offenders will interact in the near future.

TOWARD GREATER FORMAL LEGAL RIGHTS WITHIN THE CRIMINAL JUSTICE SYSTEM

The struggle to gain formal legal rights has been a powerful moving force throughout history. The concept of *rights* implies both an escape from oppression and exploitation and greater independence and autonomy. A number of social movements seeking freedom, liberation, empowerment, equality, and justice have sought greater rights for their constituencies. The most well-known include the civil rights, women's rights, workers' rights, students' rights, children's rights, gay rights, patients' rights, and prisoners' rights movements. The victims' rights movement of the 1970s through the 1990s falls within this same reformist tradition. To *reform* simply means to improve by correcting faults and ending abuses. Many people agree that the way victims are handled within the criminal justice system needs to be reformed.

The term *victims' rights* has been applied to a wide variety of pledges, guarantees, remedies, and opportunities.

The legal rights of journalists, political activists, criminal defendants, and prisoners have been derived from the safeguards specified in the first ten amendments to the U.S. Constitution, which taken together are referred to as the Bill of Rights. But the framers of the Constitution did not enumerate any rights for crime victims. The entitlements, privileges, benefits, options, and practices commonly subsumed under the heading of "victims' rights" have been derived from several different sources. A few rights originated as idiosyncratic policies adopted by certain caring and innovative officials, such as police chiefs, district attorneys, and trial judges. Other rights were derived from case law based on court decisions. The remainder were established by laws passed by city and county governments, statutes enacted by state legislatures, acts approved by Congress, and referenda placed on the ballot by advocacy groups and endorsed by voters. As a result, an inconsistent, nonuniform "crazy quilt" of rights has developed that varies markedly from state to state, jurisdiction (county or municipality) to jurisdiction, and even courthouse to courthouse. However, one trend is clear: With the passage of time, victims' rights have been increasing and expanding geographically. A self-reinforcing cycle can be recognized: As more victims become aware of their rights and begin to exercise them, these rights become more accepted and honored within the criminal justice system, encouraging victims and their allies to raise new demands for further rights (Stark and Goldstein, 1985; Viano, 1987).

In the early 1980s, activists and advocacy groups raised the possibility of changing the Sixth Amendment to the Constitution to provide a legal basis for protections and rights, especially after a presidential task force recommended rewording it in 1982. But in 1986, reformers decided that the plan to amend the U.S. Constitution should be put aside in favor of a strategy of securing amendments to state constitutions. An opinion poll carried out at the start of the 1990s turned up overwhelming public support: 90 percent of the respondents said they would probably or definitely support an amendment to their state's constitution (NVC, 1991b). By 1992, this approach had succeeded in thirteen states, although the percentage of the voters that ratified the amendment was usually considerably less than 90 percent (NVC, 1992a). The common threads running through these amendments are that victims should be treated with fairness, compassion, and respect and should have the right to be informed about, to be present at, and to be heard at all critical stages of the criminal justice process. Also, since 1980, in almost every state, legislatures have passed packages of statutes termed a *victim's bill of rights.* Their provisions most often promise these rights: to be notified about and to participate in judicial proceedings, to promptly get back stolen property that was recovered, to be protected from intimidation and harassment, and to receive restitution or compensation.

The rights that crime victims have fought for—and in many places won—are so numerous and varied that they must be categorized or grouped for comparison and analysis. One way to categorize these newly achieved rights is to note which groups of victims directly need, want, and benefit from a specific right. For example, in 1984, Wisconsin was the first state to adopt a Child Victim's Bill of

Rights. Among other provisions, it stipulated that all legal proceedings must be carefully explained to the young complainant in language he or she can understand. Today, in many jurisdictions, abused children are entitled to have their testimony videotaped so they can be spared the ordeal of being examined and then cross-examined in open court in front of the accused and a room full of strangers.

Another way to keep track of rights is to note at which stage of the criminal justice process the rights can be exercised. For example, the right to be protected from reprisals needs to be asserted as soon as a complaint is filed with the police; the right to be present at all court proceedings as long as the presiding judge approves begins at arraignment when bail is considered; the right to make one's views about sentencing known to the judge can be exercised immediately after a conviction via an impact statement; and the right to address the parole board arises years after the convict has been imprisoned.

Still another way to classify victims' rights is to note "at whose expense" they were gained. Conflicts between individuals, groups, and classes permeate society. Rights gained by one group or class enhance its position vis-a-vis its rivals (competitors, opponents, or adversaries). For example, students' rights (to appeal low grades, for instance) might be secured at the expense of the prerogatives of faculty members. Workers' rights to organize a union and strike might be established to the detriment of owners and managers. Women's rights to be seriously considered for jobs from which they were formerly excluded might be expanded at the expense of men. The rights of racial minorities (for example, to sit in any seat on buses or at lunch counters, or to vote in elections) might be gained at the expense of a discriminatory racial majority. (Of course, a persuasive argument can be made that the entire society benefits when students, workers, women, and minorities receive fair treatment.)

If this group conflict model is accepted, then three categories of victims' rights can be discerned: those gained at the direct expense of "criminals" (more accurately: suspects, defendants, and prisoners); those gained at the expense of the criminal justice system (the privileges and convenience of law enforcement, judicial, and corrections officials and agencies); and those gained at the expense of either offenders or officials, depending on how victims exercise their new powers.

Rights Gained at the Expense of Offenders

Some assert that victims' rights ought to be gained at the expense of offenders' rights; too much concern has been shown for the "rights of criminals," they say, and not enough for the plight of the innocent people they harm. In the ongoing battle between lawbreakers and law-abiding citizens, somehow the "bad guys" gained certain advantages within the legal system over the "good guys." To restore some semblance of evenhandedness to the scales of justice, which have been tipped or tilted in favor of criminals, some of the "antivictim" advantages offenders have accumulated must be taken back. According to this analysis, victims need rights to match, counter, or even "trump" the rights of criminals. In this context, reform means reversing previous court decisions and legal trends, shifting the balance of power away from wrongdoers and toward injured parties (see Hook, 1972; Carrington, 1975; and the President's Task Force, 1982).

The head-on collision between victims' rights and offenders' rights can be very sharp. For example, to protect a victim's privacy and head off possible attempts at intimidation and reprisals, the defense attorney (and simultaneously, the accused) could be prevented from learning the phone number and address of the complainant, except under extraordinary circumstances. Similarly, to make lawsuits more attractive and effective, plaintiffs can be allowed to go after any and all assets owned by defendants and not just the proceeds from the specific crime (for instance, some offenders may suddenly inherit money, which could then be taken away). Also, to make it easier for victims to sue offenders, the time limit for launching a civil lawsuit for damages can be extended from one year to seven years (see Shelton, 1992). To alleviate some of the fears burdening sexual assault victims, convicted sex offenders can be compelled to undergo AIDS tests, even if that undermines their privacy rights. (However, the screening for HIV positive antibodies cannot indicate if a molester or rapist contracted the disease afterward, and whether the infection was transmitted during the assault. To be sure, the victim must undergo periodic tests ["AIDS Tests," 1993].)

Those who emphasize punishing the offender as a way of vindicating the victim assume that the interests of victims and government officials largely coincide: apprehension, prosecution, conviction, and imprisonment. Victims' rights gained at the expense of their offenders would include provisions that would raise the conviction rate of the suspects complainants accuse, close any legal "loopholes" that enable these defendants to escape their "just deserts," increase the likelihood of incarceration of convicts victims want to see locked up, and eliminate any "unwarranted" acts of leniency toward these prisoners whom victims want to suffer. In 1982 the President's Task Force on Victims of Crime proposed a number of recommendations along these lines, and some were enacted that same year in California when voters passed Proposition 8, which its sponsors called a Victim's Bill of Rights. (Some of the provisions that fit within this punitive/retributory framework and have been characterized as "provictim" reforms are listed in Table 7.1.)

Critics of this approach to enhancing victims' rights at the expense of the rights of suspects, defendants, and convicts raise a number of objections. First, they argue that making inmates suffer more does not make victims suffer any less (Fatah, 1986). Second, they charge that many of these measures do not really empower victims but actually strengthen the government's ability to control its citizens. Antidefendant, propolice and proprosecutor measures undermine the principles cherished by civil libertarians who fear a development of an out-of-control

TABLE 7.1 Victims' Rights Gained at the Expense of Suspects, Defendants, and Prisoners

SUBJECT	RIGHT OF VICTIMS
Denial of bail	To be protected from suspects whose pretrial release on bail might endanger them
Protection from further harm	To be reasonably protected during the pretrial release period from the accused through orders of protection and by increased penalties for acts of harassment and intimidation
Defenses	To be assured that defendants cannot avoid imprisonment by pleading "not guilty by reason of insanity," through the substitution of "guilty and mentally ill," which requires treatment in a mental institution followed by incarceration in prison
Counseling	To be assured that statements divulged to counselors remain confidential if requested by the defense during the discovery phase of court proceedings
Evidence	To be assured that defendants cannot benefit from the exclusion of illegally gathered evidence, by having all evidence obtained by the police in good faith declared admissible in trials
Offender's age	To be assured that juvenile offenders do not escape full responsibility for serious crimes, by having such cases transferred from juvenile court to adult criminal court
Restitution	To receive mandatory repayments from convicts who are put on probation or parole unless a judge explains in writing the reasons for not imposing this obligation
Appeals	To appeal sentences that seem too lenient
Notoriety for profit	To have any royalties and fees paid to notorious criminals confiscated and used to repay victims or to fund victim services
Abuser's tax	To have penalty assessments collected from felons, misdemeanants, and traffic law violators to pay for victim services, compensation, and assistance programs

Sources: BJS, 1988; MADD, 1988; NOVA, 1988.

police state: that an accused person is to be considered innocent unless proven guilty, and that the burden of proof falls on the state. These due-process safeguards are subverted when defendants are denied pretrial release, when illegally obtained evidence is used against them, and when the victims' thirst for revenge (for example, as expressed in impact statements) is manipulated by the government to enhance its punitive powers (see Henderson, 1985; Hellerstein, 1989; Hall, 1991; and Abramovsky, 1992). Finally, critics point out that these opportunities to press for institutionalized revenge benefit only a small proportion of all victims—only those fortunate ones whose reported cases are solved and then prosecuted vigorously and successfully. For the overwhelming majority of property crime victims and for many victims of violence, rights gained at the expense of "criminals" are empty rights, since in their cases no one will even be arrested.

Rights Gained at the Expense of the System

Some rights that victims gain will come at the expense of justice system officials and agencies. People advancing these rights argue that for far too long those in positions of authority and public trust have neglected the needs and wants of their ostensible clients. Agencies and officials have obligations to complainants even if they cannot catch or convict their offenders. Society, or, more precisely, the social system, is partly at fault for the crime problem that plagues individuals. The state, therefore, is obligated to minimize suffering and to help innocent injured parties get back on their feet and become whole again through government intervention. A preoccupation with punishing lawbreakers must not overshadow the need for assisting and supporting the individuals they harm. New laws must guarantee that the criminal justice officials and agencies will meet standards of fair treatment that respect the dignity and privacy of victims. Since extra effort, time, and money must be expended to provide services that were not formerly available on a routine basis, these rights can be considered to have been gained by victims at the expense of the prerogatives, convenience, and budgets of criminal justice officials and agencies.

For example, in some states, prosecutors are required to provide victims with written materials about all their rights. Also, in most states, sexual assault victims are no longer charged for the costs of medical examinations to collect evidence of rape; the police department or the district attorney's office now pays that bill.

Rights gained by victims at the expense of officials and agencies first were enacted in 1980, when Wisconsin's legislature passed the nation's first bill of rights for victims and witnesses. In 1982, the President's Task Force on Victims of Crime endorsed similar proposals, which were incorporated into federal statutes when Congress approved of the Victim and Witness Protection Act. Many states have granted similar rights, either through specific laws or more comprehensive victims' bill of rights packages. (See the provisions listed in Table 7.2.)

Some critics of these rights gained at the expense of officials and agencies contend that notification, protection, and intercession requirements increase the justice system's fiscal burdens and workloads and thus interfere with its priorities of concentrating on the handling of offenders. But other critics believe that the pledges of fair treatment do not go far enough, pointing out that notification is no substitute for actual participation. For example, being informed of the results of a bail hearing, plea negotiation session, or parole board meeting falls far short

TABLE 7.2 Victims' Rights Gained at the Expense of Criminal Justice Agencies and Officials

SUBJECT	RIGHT OF VICTIMS
General rights	To be "read their rights" as soon as a crime is reported, or to be provided with written information about all obligations, services, and opportunities for protection and reimbursement
Case status	To be kept posted about any progress in their cases; to be advised when arrest warrants are issued or suspects are taken into custody
Court appearances	To be notified in advance of all court proceedings and of changes in required court appearances
Secure waiting areas	To be provided with courthouse waiting rooms separate from those used by defendants, defense witnesses, and spectators
Employer intercession	To have the prosecutor explain to the complaining witness's employer that the victim should not be penalized for missing work because of court appearances
Creditor intercession	To have the prosecutor explain to creditors like banks and landlords that crime-inflicted financial losses necessitate delays in paying bills
Suspect out on bail	To be notified that a suspect arrested for the crime has been released on bail
Negotiated plea	To be notified that both sides have agreed to a plea of guilty in return for some consideration
Sentence and final disposition	To be notified of the verdict and sentence after a trial, and the final disposition after appeals
Work release	To be notified if the convict will be permitted to leave the prison to perform a job during specified hours
Parole hearings	To be notified when a prisoner will be appearing before a parole board to seek early release
Pardon	To be notified if the governor is considering pardoning the convict
Release of a felon	To be notified when a prisoner is to be released on parole or because the sentence has expired
Prison escape	To be notified if the convict has escaped from confinement
Return of stolen property	To have recovered stolen property that has been held as evidence returned expeditiously by the police or prosecution
Compensation	To be reimbursed for out-of-pocket expenses for medical bills and lost wages arising from injuries inflicted during a violent crime

Sources: BJS, 1988; MADD, 1988; NOVA, 1988.

of actually being there to advocate in behalf of one's perceived best interests; and being there and speaking out is no guarantee of being taken seriously and having an impact.

Rights Gained at the Expense of Either Offenders or the System or Both

The boldest demands raised by advocacy groups within the victims' rights movement concern the question of power. Some victims want to influence the outcome of the criminal justice process at various important stages. Instead of being relegated to the role of passive observers, they want to be active participants in the events that shape their lives. People with this point of view believe that victims should be present and heard whenever offenders are present and heard.

Any participatory rights victims gain may come at the expense of either offenders or agency officials, or both, depending on how the victims use their newly authorized levers for influence.

Resistance to the implementation and expansion of these rights can come from different quarters, depending upon how victims are viewed. They can be seen as allies of the government and as junior partners "on the same side" as the police and the prosecution in the adversarial system. Therefore, empowering them means strengthening the ability of the government to arrest, detain, convict, and punish persons accused of wrongdoing. Enhancing the powers of a potentially repressive state apparatus will provoke opposition from civil libertarians concerned about safeguarding constitutional rights and maintaining checks and balances. But if victims are visualized as independent actors, or as clients or consumers of criminal justice services, then they may not agree with the course of action taken by their ostensible allies—government officials and agencies. Empowering them might provoke resistance from professionals who fear that their personal privileges will be jeopardized, or their agency's mission will be compromised, or the public interest will be undermined (see Karmen, 1992).

It is often asserted or assumed that victims primarily want retribution. If retribution is their highest priority, then they are likely to seize every opportunity to press for harsher handling of offenders. For example, fearing reprisals, complainants might urge that suspects not be granted pretrial release. Bitter victims might insist that defendants not be offered concessions or considerations in return for guilty pleas, that sentences imposed on convicts be as severe as the law allows, and that parole boards reject prisoners' petitions for early release.

On the other hand, at least in certain cases, victims may have a different priority. For example, their greatest concern may be securing treatment for a violence-prone lover or therapy for a drug abuser who is a relative, neighbor, or a former friend. If so, then they might favor diversion of the case from the criminal justice system to allow the offender to enter a rehabilitation program. Then again, victims preoccupied with receiving full and prompt reimbursement of their financial losses might favor an alternative to incarceration, such as restitution as a condition of probation.

Victims and criminal justice officials might find themselves at odds over how to handle particular cases. For example, a victim might press for diversion while the assistant district attorney seeks a conviction through plea negotiation. Or a victim might argue for probation with restitution while the prosecutor demands time behind bars, but the judge leans toward a stiff fine. When such conflicts arise, it becomes evident that the participatory rights of victims are gained at the expense of criminal justice officials as well as offenders; that the preferences of the officials and the priorities of their agencies might occasionally have to be compromised or sacrificed to appease persistent victims. Thus, the involvement of victims as an additional party in the decision-making process constrains the free exercise of discretion formerly enjoyed by prosecutors, judges, and parole boards.

The three critical junctures for victim input are during plea negotiations, at sentencing hearings after conviction (whether arrived at through trials or negotiated pleas), and at parole board hearings.

As for plea negotiations, victims have never been granted veto power over the deals worked out by assistant district attorneys and defense lawyers. But in many states, they have been given a voice, or consultive role, as the out-of-court settlements are hammered out.

Opportunities for victims to influence the outcome of sentencing decisions take two forms. In the less active (and probably less effective) approach, victims are allowed to submit a written statement. Victim-impact statements are objective assessments of the crime's economic, medical, and emotional consequences. They are prepared by probation officers and presented to judges as part of the pre-sentencing investigation report in nearly all states. Victim statements of opinion, written recommendations regarding appropriate sentences, can be submitted to judges in most states. The more active alternative is to allow the victim to appear in person in court. This opportunity to speak out before the judge sentences the offender, called allocution, is also permitted in most states. Similarly, victims can make their views known to parole boards in two ways, by submitting an impact statement or through allocution during the hearing (NOVA, 1988).

Guarantees about participatory rights raise several questions. Should such formal guarantees also be extended to individuals who do not fit the profile of the innocent, law-abiding adult victim of a serious crime? For example, should assault victims from "unsavory backgrounds" (such as street gang members, drug dealers, mobsters, and prostitutes) be permitted a say in plea negotiations and sentencing? If so, should their requests carry less weight? Should people who represent the victim, in their capacity as the legal guardian of a minor or as survivors, lawyers, or volunteer advocates be granted consultive rights during plea negotiations and allocution rights before sentencing and parole decisions? Should participatory rights be restricted to victims of serious crimes like felonies, or even more narrowly, only to persons injured by serious violence? And what happens when these participatory rights are violated? What remedies do victims have when criminal justice agencies fail to involve them in the decision making (or don't live up to the standards for fair treatment)? Anticipating this issue, legislators include in most of these amendments a provision stating that "nothing in this statute shall be construed as creating a cause of action against the state, a county or municipality, or any of its agents." Such clauses bar lawsuits to secure money damages or to overturn unfavorable decisions by victims whose rights were not respected. Under the separation-of-powers doctrine, however, judges could order executive agencies to comply with policies created by legislative bodies, directing criminal justice officials to honor the rights of victims who bring suits (Stark and Goldstein, 1985; NOVA, 1988).

The lack of enforcement mechanisms highlights another related problem: the absence of clear lines of responsibility for implementation. Which officials or agencies can be held accountable for keeping victims informed of their rights? For example, does the duty of notifying the victim about the right to allocution before sentencing fall to the police officer who files the initial complaint, to the assistant district attorney who prosecutes the case, to the probation officer who prepares the presentence report, or to the clerk in the office of court administration who schedules the postconviction hearing? And how many times must the responsible official attempt to contact a victim before giving up and declaring that a good-faith effort was made to involve him or her in the sentencing process?

One way to make sure that victims find out about all their rights and exercise them as best they can is to provide them with the services of knowledgeable consultants who understand how the criminal justice process really works and how to make the system responsive to their clients' needs. Although advocates are available at rape crisis centers, shelters for battered women, prosecutors' offices, and family courts (guardians *ad litem* for abused children), no jurisdiction has yet institutionalized advocacy by assigning a knowledgeable consultant to each complainant who wants one, in the same way that lawyers are routinely provided to all suspects, defendants, and convicts (see Karmen, 1995).

One measure that would substantially empower complainants would be to permit them to hire their own private prosecutors to handle plea negotiations and trials (as is the practice in other countries, and used to be allowed in colonial America). However, if this reform were implemented, some would be able to afford this "personalized justice" while others couldn't, so the gap in the way cases are resolved and the way both indigent victims and offenders are treated could grow wider, intensifying the double standard.

Social scientists have yet to evaluate the effectiveness of most of the informational and participatory rights that have been granted in recent years. Criminologists and victimologists are sure to discover evidence of "differential handling" or "differential access to justice": that certain groups of people are more likely than others to be informed of their rights, to exercise them, and to use them effectively to influence the decision-making process (see Karmen, 1990).

Does institutionalized indifference toward the victims' plight still pervade the justice system? The answer seems to be a qualified "yes," according to some preliminary findings culled from evaluation studies. Only 3 percent of victims who reported offenses to the police told *NCVS* interviewers in 1991 that they had contact with or received advice or help from any office, agency, or program set up to serve them (Dawson, Smith, and DeFrances, 1993). Reportedly, many victims are never informed of their rights to be kept posted about progress in their cases and about court dates (Webster, 1988); about filing impact statements that might influence sentences (Wells, 1990) and parole board decisions (NVC, 1991b); and about the release of the felons they helped to send to prison (Cuomo, 1992; Dawson, Smith, and DeFrances, 1993). Left to fend for themselves, most fail to appear and speak out at sentencing hearings (Forer, 1980). Those that did exercise their allocution rights to voice their opinions in person exerted very little influence, especially when convicts faced determinate (fixed) sentences. The discretionary authority of judges was limited, and they had many additional factors besides victims' recommendations to take into account (Villmoare and Neto, 1987; Walsh, 1992).

The courtroom work group of "insiders"—prosecutors, defense attorneys, and judges—tends to frustrate attempts by "outsiders"—victims, their advocates, and lawmakers—to influence their rapid, assembly-line processing of cases. These key courtroom figures usually have developed a consensus about the appropriate "going rate" (sentence) for various crimes at particular times and places (Walker, 1994). To the extent that the courtroom insiders are able to resist the "interference" by outsiders to alter the going rate, victims will find the use of their participatory rights an exercise in futility (see Ranish and Shichor, 1985).

In fact, some activists within the victims' rights movement are pessimistic and cynical about the much-heralded "reforms" that supposedly have empowered victims. Victims still have no constitutional standing, which means that they cannot go to civil court and sue for monetary damages if their rights are ignored or violated, and they cannot veto decisions about bail, sentences, and parole that are made in their absence, without their knowledge and consent (Gewurz and Mercurio, 1992). Pledges that the rights of victims to fair treatment will be carefully carried out by officials might prove to be mere "lip service," "paper promises," and "cosmetic changes" without much substance (Gegan and Rodriguez, 1992; Elias, 1993).

TOWARD INFORMAL JUSTICE:
THE RESTORATIVE APPROACH

The Search for Peace

A teenager shoots a police officer, paralyzing him for life. Seven years later, the youth is released from prison but is quickly arrested and reincarcerated when the authorities realize they have made a miscalculation and he has another 600 days to serve. From his wheelchair, the officer tells a reporter, "If this is the first time he sampled freedom in years, he must be beside himself." The officer reveals that over the years he has been in touch with his attacker through letters and phone calls and now forgives him and wishes to meet with him when he is released. He notes, "How many people who have done worse things have spent that long, seven years, in jail?" (Duggan, 1994; Faison, 1994)

A front-desk clerk in a hotel is shot in the back by an armed robber. The assailant is caught, convicted, and sentenced to prison for a term of twelve to twenty-five years. With the bullet still lodged in his body, the clerk is unable to go through the day without anxiety attacks, get through the night without bad dreams, keep his hotel job, or continue his other career as a runner. But he is willing to meet with the robber and talk about the shooting at a face-to-face meeting arranged by the prison staff. The event is cathartic for the clerk, who is then able to go on with the rest of his life. He testifies in favor of releasing the robber on parole and helps the robber's family to line up a room in a halfway house and a job for his former nemesis. (Associated Press, 1994g)

Even in these cynical times, when calls for rehabilitating criminals are greeted with skepticism while demands for punishing them receive such enthusiastic support, a significant proportion of victims don't want to manipulate the system to make their offenders suffer. Given the chance, they may opt to take part in a process whose goal is a cessation of hostilities and a sense of closure, in which both parties put the incident behind them and go on with their lives. These are the aims of restorative justice, an alternative paradigm that is gaining many new adherents. It draws upon the nonpunitive approaches of peacemaking, mediation, negotiation, dispute resolution, conflict management, and restitution. Its goal is to use informal methods to bring about lasting settlements that reconcile offenders with their victims and communities.

To a large extent, advocates of restorative justice are trying to salvage and revitalize some of the best traditions that were used centuries ago to repair the social damage caused by criminal acts, before the state asserted its authority to dominate the justice process. Long ago and far away, legal systems such as that in England before the Middle Ages were victim-focused and restitution-oriented. Detailed "price lists" had been worked out specifying how much the wrongdoer had to pay the injured party for each kind of loss imaginable. But priorities shifted dramatically when the aristocracy discovered that the legal process could be used to control the populace. Laws were passed that proclaimed that any disturbance of the peace (such as murder, robbery, insurrection, or counterfeiting) threatened the king and was a matter for the Crown to resolve. The king and his government symbolically displaced the victimized individual as the injured party, and the courts were transformed from a forum to settle disputes between specific persons into an arena for ritualized combat between representatives of the state and of the accused. If the prosecution succeeded, the state inflicted pain upon its vanquished opponents in order to teach them not to break the law again (specific deterrence) and to make examples of them to serve as a warning to others (general deterrence). Later, prisons were invented to serve these purposes, as well as to take troublemakers out of circulation to protect the public (incapacitation) and to force maladjusted persons to undergo compulsory treatment (rehabilitation). The government often extracted a fine or seized property from offenders, but it never shared the spoils with victims. The overriding concern of the authorities was to impose the appropriate punishment, not to restore the victims' well-being. In effect, this paradigm shift resulted in a justice process that was state-centered, offender-focused, and punishment-oriented, rather than injury-centered, victim-focused, and restitution-oriented.

Centuries later, some reformers are trying to reinvigorate some earlier insights about the real meaning of justice. They argue that achieving "genuine justice" requires that something be done for the victim and not just to the offender. They point out that reparations not only help victims to recover from the aftershocks of predatory incidents but also enable harmony to be restored to the entire afflicted community. The government, through its criminal justice agencies, can strive to maintain order and protect lives and property; but only the community, through its local institutions and traditions, can further the healing process (Van Ness, 1990; Wright, 1991).

Pilot programs to test whether mediated restitution arrangements could lay the groundwork for reconciliation were pioneered in Canada in the mid-1970s and Indiana in 1978. Members of the Mennonite religious sect were among the first enthusiastic supporters of this healing process. Their experimental project served as a model for others to replicate and modify, just as the penitentiary, invented by the Quakers as a nonviolent alternative to corporal and capital punishment in the early 1800s, was copied by governments worldwide. By 1994, over 125 Victim–Offender Reconciliation Programs (VORPs) were operating in twenty states, handling about 16,000 cases a year. In most jurisdictions, the programs were administered by private nonprofit agencies and focused on resolving cases of property crime referred by the courts (Coates, 1990; Umbreit, 1994).

Several assumptions guided these early efforts: First of all, street crimes are best viewed as conflicts between individuals rather than as affronts to an abstraction such as society or the state. The most appropriate way to respond to such violations of an innocent person's well-being is to be restorative rather than punitive. Whenever possible, victims and offenders should be empowered to resolve their own differences. To heal their emotional wounds, both the victim and the offender need to directly participate in negotiated settlements. Restitution (whether in monetary payments or direct personal services) is a symbolic gesture toward reconciliation and a prerequisite for reacceptance of the offender by the entire community. And finally, advocates believe that a neutral third party from a private nonprofit agency can facilitate and oversee the process of forgiveness better than an agent of the state (such as a prosecutor, judge, or probation officer) who coerces both parties to agree to certain terms (Umbreit, 1989; 1990). However, programs seeking to achieve reconciliation via restitution are being set up by juvenile corrections agencies and probation departments and are becoming acceptable to a growing number of judges in juvenile and criminal courts (Umbreit and Coates, 1993; Umbreit, 1995).

The Reliance on Mediation

Two college roommates decide that they will no longer share their off-campus apartment. They argue bitterly over who owns the television set that they purchased jointly. One night the roommate who moved out returns to the apartment and takes the set. When the other student discovers that the TV was removed, he calls the police.

Two suburban homeowners continually quarrel over a parking spot on the street between their houses. One slashes the tires of the other's car. In retaliation, his neighbor sets a fire in his garage.

Two boys are in love with the same girl. After a high school prom they fight, and one boy's tooth is broken.

Two friends spend an evening drinking and playing poker. One accuses the other of cheating, throws the deck of cards in his face, grabs all the money, and storms out.

The development of methods of "alternative dispute resolution" (ADR) has furthered interest in reconciliation programs relying upon mediated restitution agreements. Originally, mediation was embraced as a way of resolving interpersonal conflicts reflecting shared responsibility, as illustrated by the hypothetical cases above. Calling the police/ pressing charges/ and prosecuting in court was considered to be an inappropriate procedure for handling minor violations of the law stemming from ongoing relationships in which each person did something "wrong" to antagonize, provoke, and harm the other. Mediation was viewed as preferable to adjudication, since it could lead to a compromise settlement that might satisfy both parties and resolve their dispute once and for all.

Mediation, one of several techniques for resolving conflicts, lies in the middle of a continuum bounded by conciliation and arbitration. Conciliation simply requires a go-between to facilitate the flow of information from one disputant to another. Arbitration is a process in which a neutral individual is called in to break a deadlock. The arbitrator plays an active role as fact finder and then, after hearing presentations from both sides, imposes a fair, final, legally binding decision. Mediation requires direct negotiations between disputants. The mediator, a neutral person, helps the feuding parties arrive at a mutually acceptable compromise by promoting discussion, soliciting viewpoints, and helping uncover areas of common interest.

A "multidoor courthouse" is a place where these alternative ways of settling conflicts are made available. Disputants take their cases to an intake/diagnosis/referral unit, where a screening specialist decides upon the most appropriate method of resolving the conflict: conciliation, mediation, arbitration, or adjudication within the criminal justice system (Roehl and Ray, 1986).

To secure a niche within the criminal justice process, advocates of dispute resolution through mediation argued that the process of adjudication under the adversarial system had been tried and tested for centuries and was unsatisfactory for many types of cases. They likened the adversary system that underlies criminal and civil proceedings to a "zero-sum game." At each stage, points are won by one party at the expense of the other. The rules of evidence may prevent the disputants and witnesses from telling the whole story. Both sides are preoccupied with determining guilt and influencing the degree of severity or leniency of the sentence. At the end of the contest, there must always be a winner and a loser. The victorious side is pleased with the outcome, while the defeated side is embittered. The two parties may leave court just as they arrived, locked in conflict, hostile toward each other, sometimes even more alienated and polarized than at the outset (Wright, 1989).

At neighborhood justice centers practicing alternative dispute resolution techniques, hearings are scheduled at the convenience of the participants, not the staff. The use of private attorneys is discouraged. The rules of evidence are minimized. Witnesses are not sworn in. Mediators do not wear robes or sit above others. Nontechnical language is used, and only limited records of the proceedings are kept. The "moot model" of informal justice rejects the constraints of a guilty-innocent, wrong-right, pin-the-blame/deny-responsibility framework. With the mediator as a referee, the disputants educate each other by presenting their own versions of their conflict. The intent is to look to the future rather than to dwell on the past. The ultimate goals are to reconcile the estranged parties and repair rifts within their community (Prison Research, 1976; Wright, 1985).

Neighborhood justice centers were not demanded by activists in the victims' rights movement. In fact, the use of informal negotiations to settle the conflicts underlying criminal acts initially conjured up the unfavorable image of an unwilling, trembling victim being forced to shake hands with a smirking, unrepentant offender. The impetus for developing this additional forum came from other constituencies (Umbreit, 1987). Attempting to streamline the judicial process, court administrators sought ways of weeding out the minor criminal cases that clogged their calendars. Judges, including the justices of the Supreme Court, encouraged experiments in conflict resolution, hoping to find a way to make fighting it out in public, in court, at hearings and trials, at great expense, a last resort. Police and prosecutors endorsed the removal of what they considered "junk" cases from their workloads. From their point of view, too many people wasted their time trying to resolve personal matters. They argued that the machinery of criminal justice should not be used to settle petty squabbles between people with prior relationships but should be reserved to deal with real crimes, those involving serious injuries inflicted by strangers and those involving large financial losses. Prosecutors complained that a great many victims decided to drop charges, or failed to appear in court to testify, when their offenders were family members, loved ones, former friends, classmates, colleagues, or neighbors. Anticipating that these complainants would change their minds shortly after having their offenders arrested, prosecutors disposed of their "garbage" cases quickly, either by dropping the charges completely or by plea bargaining them down (Silberman, 1978; Ray, 1984).

The first experiments with alternative techniques for resolving conflicts of both a civil and a criminal nature were launched at the start of the 1970s in Philadelphia and Columbus, Ohio. The Law Enforcement Assistance Administration (LEAA) provided seed money to cover the start-up costs of other programs. The majority were sponsored by and attached to a criminal justice agency (such as a court or prosecutor's office); the others were run by private nonprofit organizations like the American Arbitration Association or the Institute for Mediation and Conflict Resolution (IMCR), by a community group like the local bar association, or by some county or municipal governmental body. The kind of sponsorship that a center was under profoundly shaped the way it conducted its business and the types of cases it accepted. (See Alper and Nichols, 1981; Freedman and Ray, 1982; McGillis, 1982; Goldberg, Green, and Sander, 1985; and Harrington, 1985.)

In 1980, Congress passed the Dispute Resolution Act authorizing the creation of a national clearinghouse to conduct research and disseminate information about "storefront" justice. In 1981, New York became the first state to fund new and existing programs. In 1984, the entire branch of social science known as conflict resolution received much-needed recognition, legitimation, and support when Congress earmarked money within the huge military budget for establishing a United States Institute of Peace. Courses on the techniques, strategies, and philosophies of conflict resolution and peacemaking are now offered in schools

and colleges and in training programs for lawyers, police officers, and other criminal justice personnel (Volpe, 1989).

The kinds of cases considered appropriate for conflict resolution have grown
steadily since the first projects were initiated. Originally, guidelines restricted the
types of cases referred to neighborhood justice centers to noncriminal quarrels
between people with ongoing relationships. Then the scope of eligible cases was
broadened to include such misdemeanors as harassment, simple assault, petty larceny, and vandalism, in which the disputants had committed retaliatory acts
against each other as part of a simmering feud. Such cases of shared responsibility
were not suitable for criminal justice processing because the adversary framework
imposed a "winner take all" format that resulted in an undeserved victory for one
party and an unjust defeat for the other. Over the years, the nature of the relationship between the victim and the offender, rather than the nature of the offense,
became the single most important criterion for diverting cases out of the criminal
justice system and into ADR. Hence, violence unleashed by offenders who knew
their victims were addressed at neighborhood justice centers. Eventually, even acts
of violence perpetrated by complete strangers (such as unprovoked assaults) were
considered appropriate cases for face-to-face meetings. Currently, some programs
even bring together for group sessions victims whose cases were never solved and
offenders convicted of harming people who don't wish to participate (Wright,
1985, 1989; Umbreit, 1989).

How Reconciliation Programs Work

Most programs treat reconciliation as a process with four distinct phases: case selection; preparation for mediation; mediation and negotiation; and the follow-up
period. The healing process begins when a case manager screens cases and finds
ones that seem suitable. Next, a trained mediator (either a staff member or a volunteer) contacts the complainant and then the accused in order to explain the
mechanics of the program, discuss the nature of the charges, and test their willingness to participate in a face-to-face encounter. If they both agree, the mediator
meets with each side separately, and then brings the two disputants together (perhaps at the victim's home, or at the jail where the defendant is being detained, or
at the program's office). During their meeting, both parties vent their emotions
and share their reactions to the crime and the way it was handled by the criminal
justice system. After that, they focus on the damage that was done and hammer
out a mutually acceptable arrangement in which the offender pledges to make
amends. After the meeting, the mediator remains in contact, monitoring and supervising the acts of restitution, verifying that the written contract is completely
fulfilled. The agreement usually requires that the wrongdoer make payments from
earnings, perform useful and needed personal services, or undertake community
service work to benefit some charity. In some jurisdictions the negotiations are

held prior to adjudication, as part of a strategy of pretrial diversion, while in other places the programs handle cases only after convictions are attained. The wrongdoers are both delinquents sent from juvenile court and adult criminals. The offenses are usually burglaries and other thefts, acts of vandalism, instances of shoplifting, and minor assaults (Galaway, 1987; Coates, 1990; Umbreit, 1990, 1994).

Evaluating Efforts at Reconciliation

In theory, at least, victim–offender reconciliation offers advantages to victims, offenders, and crime-plagued communities. For victims, these programs provide a safe, secure setting for confrontations with those who harmed them. In the presence of trained and skilled intermediaries, victims get an opportunity to release pent-up feelings and ask troubling questions. Besides having the opportunity for emotional catharsis, victims ought to be able to leave the negotiations with a satisfactory restitution agreement in hand. For offenders, the encounter offers an occasion to accept responsibility, express remorse, and ask for forgiveness. Probably more important to most perpetrators is the chance to substitute restitution obligations for prison time. For the community, the pragmatic benefit is that negotiated settlements relieve court backlogs and jail and prison overcrowding and eliminate the need to build more cells to confine greater numbers of convicts at the taxpayers' expense. A less tangible but significant spiritual dividend is the fostering of an atmosphere of tolerance, understanding, and redemption within the community (Coates, 1990; Umbreit, 1990; Viano, 1990).

Several evaluations of different restitution/reconciliation programs across the country shed some light on a number of interesting questions. As for the willingness of victims to meet with their perpetrators (juveniles placed on probation for property crimes), the percentages ranged from 54 percent to 90 percent. Reportedly, nearly 95 percent of the meetings led to a mutually acceptable agreement. The average amount of money the offenders pledged to pay to victims ranged from about $175 to $250. The proportion of the contracts that were carried out to the victims' satisfaction ranged from a low of 52 percent in one program to a high of 91 percent in another. In general, the research findings showed that many victims volunteer to participate in face-to-face confrontations, very few mediation sessions become emotionally explosive, and most victims are not vindictive and do not make unreasonable demands (Galaway, 1987). Another evaluation of four mediation projects attached to juvenile courts uncovered high levels of client satisfaction, approaching 80 percent of the victims and nearly 90 percent of the offenders. Roughly 85 percent of the participants felt that the process of mediation was fair to both parties. Before meeting their offenders in person, nearly 25 percent of the victims confided that they were afraid of being preyed upon again by the same individual; after the mediation session ended, only 10 percent still harbored that fear. Over 80 percent of the delinquents successfully completed their negotiated restitution arrangements, compared to 58 percent for similar offenders who were ordered to make restitution by juvenile court judges who didn't directly involve victims or use mediation. As for recidivism, the juvenile offenders who passed through mediation committed fewer and less-serious offenses than a control group of their peers during the one-year follow-up period (Umbreit, 1994). Victim dissatisfaction surfaces in those programs that fail to follow up to see to it that restitution pledges are fulfilled (Coates and Gehm, 1989).

According to several evaluations that compared cases handled at selected ADR programs to similar cases adjudicated in court, mediators received higher ratings for "fairness" than judges. Most disputants reported that they left the neighborhood justice centers believing that their differences had been settled. The compromise solutions worked out at centers were adhered to more faithfully than dispositions imposed by criminal or civil court judges (Cook, Roehl, and Sheppard, 1980; Davis, Tichane, and Grayson, 1980; Garofalo and Connelly, 1980).

Proponents of mediation in pursuit of reconciliation interpret these findings as evidence of a solid, positive track record. They conclude that the experimental stage can be judged a success and that the time has come for a substantial reallocation of resources that would enable these programs to handle many more cases. They point to polls which demonstrate that considerable public support favors restitution as an alternative to imprisonment, at least for cases involving property crimes (Galaway, 1987, 1989).

Pros and Cons from the Victim's Point of View

For victims of minor offenses who are embroiled in ongoing conflicts for which they admittedly bear some responsibility, alternative dispute resolution offers several advantages over adjudication in criminal or civil court. If they don't want an arrest to be made or charges to be pressed, they now have the additional option of bringing their problems to a neighborhood justice center. Incidents that otherwise would be too trivial to interest the police or prosecutors can be addressed. Smoldering tensions that might flare up again and result in a spiral of violence and retaliation can be smothered. Individuals who dread the public spectacle of testifying and of being cross-examined in open court can choose to hold hearings behind closed doors. They can represent themselves rather than accept the services of a prosecutor who looks after the state's interests or, in civil court, a private attorney who is only after a share of the money. Informal justice has proven to be speedier, cheaper, and more accessible than formal proceedings. Cases are handled sooner, cost less in terms of time and money, and are heard at times and places convenient to the participants. The settlement can be seen as a vindication if the other party apologizes in writing and undertakes restitution as an admission of responsibility. Such settlements can provide a sound basis for reconciliation for people who want to—or have to learn to—get along with each other in the future within their community.

Because the moot model consciously abandons the presumptions of guilt and innocence that underlie the labels "offender" and "victim" and terms both parties "disputants," a completely innocent victim might find informal justice unsatisfactory. The complainant's conduct is more open to scrutiny, especially in the absence of rules governing evidence and cross-examination. The notion of shared responsibility is frequently invoked by mediators, who view disputes as outgrowths of misunderstandings and the pursuit of self-interest by both parties. To reach a compromise, complainants might be pressured to concede more responsibility, fault, or involvement than they feel they should. The entire notion of compromise solutions as a means of achieving reconciliation rests on the practice of both parties giving in, to varying degrees, from their original demands. Complainants who insist that they are absolutely blameless can feel cheated that their cases have been diverted from the criminal justice system, because this symbolizes a withdrawal of governmental support (prosecutorial power) from their side.

For those victims who are intent on revenge, the greatest drawbacks of alternative dispute resolution, mediation, and restitution are that these processes are not punishment oriented. Neighborhood justice centers and victim–offender reconciliation programs are not authorized to convict offenders, publicly humiliate them with the stigma of the label of "criminal," fine them, or confine them in a penal institution (Garofalo and Connelly, 1980).

Several potential problems could plague ADR and VORP programs in the near future. Overly enthusiastic staff members and mediators might pressure victims to participate and make them feel that they "must" end up forgiving and reconciling with their offenders. If caseloads grow too large, mediators might be inclined to adopt an assembly-line approach to speed up the process and avoid backlogs. Worse yet, overworked staff members might be tempted to eliminate the face-to-face mediation session entirely, in order to more quickly "dispose" of a large case load. Originally, the cases considered suitable for mediation/restitution/reconciliation involved petty nonviolent offenses against property. Program staff members acceded to this limitation in order to perfect their techniques, avoid controversy, and maintain funding and referral sources. But now legislators and judges seem increasingly willing to send conflicts marred by violence to mediation. Some of these more serious cases don't fit the mediation format; the harm cannot be repaired through restitution; and any thought of reconciliation is out of the question. But other tough cases will require more time to resolve, more professionally trained mediators, a greater commitment of resources, and more support from social service and criminal justice agencies (Coates, 1990; Umbreit, 1990).

The number of cases directed to neighborhood justice centers and victim–offender reconciliation programs will grow because there is a movement toward informality throughout the criminal justice system. In practice, informality is marked by a preference for unwritten, flexible, commonsense, discretionary procedures tailored to fit particular cases. As an ideology, informality is characterized by an antipathy toward rigid hierarchy, bureaucratic impersonality, and professional domination. The growing interest in informal justice is fostered by several beliefs: that centralized governmental coercion has failed as an instrument of social change; that people must solve their own problems in decentralized, community-controlled settings; that nonstranger conflicts ought to be diverted from the formal adjudication process whenever possible; that both punishment and rehabilitation have failed to "cure" offenders; and that criminal justice officials and agencies primarily serve the state's interests, or their own, to the detriment of both offenders and victims. Enthusiasm for informal alternatives is fed by perceptions that the crime rate is rising while criminal courts are paralyzed, civil courts are swamped with frivolous lawsuits, and prisons and jails are dangerously overcrowded. As a pragmatic response to such economic and political realities, informality beckons as a solution to the government's fiscal crisis. Neighborhood justice centers and victim–offender reconciliation programs can relieve the overburdened criminal justice system at a time when calls for more services are clashing with demands for less taxation. However, the critics of informality warn that under the guise of cutting back on formal governmental intervention into everyday life, the coercive apparatus of the state can be extended in new ways over more people by handling cases that otherwise would be dropped or dismissed for being too trivial, too tangled (in terms of who was right and who was wrong), or too weak to adjudicate in court (Abel, 1982).

TOWARD INFORMAL JUSTICE, VIGILANTE STYLE

The owner of a grocery parks his car outside his store. Later, he spies a man breaking into it, so he grabs a pistol and, joined by an employee with a bat, runs outside. They beat the unarmed car thief and then shoot him. The grocer and his assistant are arrested for murder. ("Car Thief Slain," 1988)

A teenager waiting for a train is robbed of his gold jewelry by six young men. The next night, the teenager spots the gang of robbers at the same station. He comes up to them and says cryptically, "Remember me?" They don't recognize him and look puzzled, until he pulls out a revolver and starts shooting. He wounds three and then flees. When the injured youths tell the police the full story about why they were shot, they are arrested for confessing to the robbery that apparently provoked the victim's wrath. He is never found. (Marriott, 1989)

A young man accused of killing a teenage boy at a party is in court for his eleventh pretrial hearing. Infuriated by what he considers to be the slow pace of justice, the father of the slain adolescent enters the courthouse and shoots the defendant in the back, in plain view of a crowd of lawyers and off-duty detectives. Put on trial for attempted murder, the father is acquitted because the jurors agree with him that the defendant posed a threat to him and his remaining children. But the jury convicts the father of the misdemeanor of illegally possessing a pistol. (Tomasson, 1991)

A drug addict snatches a $20 bill from a woman in a bakery. She screams as he flees, but a crowd forms and takes after him. More than a dozen people kick the thief and beat him with sticks and their fists. He is rescued by two detectives but later dies. Two men and five teenagers are arrested for manslaughter. Despite substantial evidence, the district attorney drops most of the charges. A prominent lawyer representing one of the defendants argues that the prosecutor's actions vindicate the crowd's belief that they did what was appropriate under the circumstances. (Hays, 1988)

There is a kind of "informal justice" that is entirely different from the peacemaking through mediation that is offered at neighborhood centers. It is a type of "conflict resolution" that relies on the use of force, not negotiation. It has a long and bloody history, and its goal is not reconciliation but retaliation. This outlawed alternative to formal case processing within the criminal justice system embodies a "do-it-yourself" approach. In common parlance, it is dubbed "back-alley justice," "curbstone justice," "street justice," or "frontier justice." To government officials, criminologists, and victimologists, it is the modern-day expression of that old-fashioned impulse called *vigilantism*.

Although statistics are not available (no government agency or private research group keeps track of such outbreaks), cases of vigilante violence seem to be infrequent these days. Nevertheless, clear-cut examples usually attract extensive media coverage and become well known. Most of the reported incidents fit into one of three categories (see Shotland, 1976): victims unleashing more force than the law permits under the doctrine of self-defense (first example above) or avenging an earlier incident (second example); retaliatory actions carried out in behalf of victims by family members or close friends (third example); or spontaneous mob actions in which a crowd responds to a victim's plea for help and gets carried away (fourth example).

But if vigilantism is defined broadly as "taking the law into one's own hands" by physically punishing suspected transgressors, then it may be more common than initially realized. Many, if not most, instances of vigilantism are never detected, recorded, investigated, or prosecuted, since victims and their allies (relatives, or members of a crowd) don't want the authorities to find out their real intentions. Bystanders who spontaneously intervene to break up a crime in progress, to rescue a person in trouble and catch an assailant, might get swept away by a mob mentality or crowd psychology and feel compelled to "get in a few good licks" to punish the offender right then and there. Similarly, some incidents in which officers use excessive force to take resisting or unruly suspects into custody are commonly called cases of "police brutality" but might really be outbreaks of police vigilantism (Kotecha and Walker, 1976). When innocent victims gain the upper hand during confrontations, they too may overreact and use more force than the law allows, not only to subdue their attackers but also to make them pay, on the spot, for their attempted crimes. Additionally, many schoolyard fights and barroom brawls probably are motivated by a victim's desire to settle a score with some bully or aggressor. Surely some family fights are fueled by a yearning for personal vengeance. An unknown proportion of the battered wives who fight back or even kill their tormentors go beyond the legal limits of self-defense and launch preemptive strikes to forestall another beating or unleash retaliatory violence to get back for a previous one. A few cases even have come to light in which physically and sexually abused children grow up and slay their cruel parents. Criminals can be vigilantes too: They routinely resort to violence to settle their disputes precisely because they cannot bring their private problems and business quarrels to the police, prosecutors, and courts without incriminating themselves. Vigilantism breaks out whenever street gangs engage in drive-by shootings to retaliate for an ambushing of one of their members, or when mobsters hire hit men to "whack" some enemy in a rival crime family during a mob war over turf, or when drug dealers eliminate someone who cheated or stole from them. Vigilantism is also part of the ideology of right-wing extremist groups, such as the Ku Klux Klan, neo-Nazis, racist skinheads, and citizens' militia (see Madison, 1973; Burrows, 1976; Lasch, 1982; and King, 1989), since they openly proclaim their intention to revive the "night rider" tradition to "rid society of undesirable elements," "troublemakers," "corrupt officials," and "traitors."

Vigilantism's Frontier Origins

Vigilantism is a worldwide phenomenon. (In some countries, it takes the form of "death squad" disappearances—killings by out-of-uniform soldiers and police officers; in other societies, the impulse is expressed through mob attacks culminating in "necklacings" with burning tires.) In the United States, vigilantism has a long and bloody history, especially in the Old West and the Deep South. It started out in colonial times as a frontier reaction to marauding bands of desperadoes in South Carolina. In Virginia in the late 1700s, a "vigilance committee" led by a Colonel Lynch developed a reputation for the public whippings it staged. Its escalating violence against lawbreakers gave rise to the terms *lynch law* and *lynchings*.

From 1767 to 1909, 326 short-lived vigilante movements peppered American history, mostly as Western frontier phenomena, claiming 729 lives (Brown, 1975). From 1882 until as recently as 1951, spontaneous lynch mobs killed 4,730 people, mostly black men, particularly in rural areas of the Deep South (Hofstadter and Wallace, 1970).

Over the course of American history, the vigilantes' call to action was issued whenever "honest, upright citizens" became enraged and terrified about what they considered to be an upsurge of criminality and a breakdown of law and order. Closely identifying with victims, vigilantes feared that they were next if they didn't take drastic measures. Hence, "red-blooded, able-bodied, law-abiding" men banded together and pursued outlaws who were threatening their families, property, and way of life. Vigilance committees, led by individuals from the local power elite, with a solid middle-class membership, tended to go after people at the bottom of the social hierarchy. They lashed out at alleged cutthroats, bushwhackers, road agents (robbers), cattle rustlers, horse thieves, and desperadoes of all kinds. They also crusaded against people they maintained were troublemakers, parasites, drifters, idlers, sinners, "loose" women, "uppity" members of subjugated groups, "outside agitators," and "subversives" with anarchist and communist leanings. The targets of their wrath were blacklisted, banished (run out of town), flogged (whipped), tarred and feathered, mutilated, and sometimes brutally murdered (Burrows, 1976).

Very few of these self-appointed executioners ever got into legal trouble for their lawless deeds. Vigilantes portrayed themselves as true patriots and dedicated upholders of moral codes and sacred traditions. The manifestos of vigilance committees were crowned with references to "the right to 'revolution,'" "popular sovereignty," and personal survival as "the first law of nature." Just as they held criminals fully accountable for their transgressions, these rugged individualists held themselves personally responsible for their own security. If duly constituted authority could not be relied on for protection, they would shoulder the burden of law enforcement and the obligation to punish offenders. The vigilante credo boils down to a variation on "the end justifies the means"—breaking the law is necessary in order to preserve the rule of law. Most vigilante actions were defended as avenging victims and punishing common criminals. But in retrospect, other reasons may have been paramount. Teaching lawbreakers a lesson and making an example out of them to deter other would-be offenders was the goal the men in the mob attacks cited to rationalize their own criminality. Vigilantes probably had ulterior motives as well: to quash rebellions; to reassert control over rival racial, ethnic, religious, or political groups; to intimidate subordinates back into submission; and to impose the dominant group's moral standards on outsiders, newcomers, and marginal members of the community (Brown, 1975).

Today, vigilantism is argued about much more than it is carried out. The label "vigilante" (a term formerly accepted with pride, but now hurled as an epithet) crops up occasionally in accounts about citizen anticrime activities; usually, the word is used for shock value by journalists and public officials. When civilians fortify their homes and stockpile weapons, that is not vigilantism (although some groups warn that they will resort to vigilantism if a crisis develops and the government becomes paralyzed or collapses). When neighbors organize citizen patrols and ride around in cars equipped with two-way radios, that's not vigilantism either. (The first such crime-watch patrol in 1964 in a Brooklyn community was quickly dubbed a "vigilante group" by politicians and police officials, but the concerns of the authorities have subsided. Federal money has sponsored such local efforts to supplement law enforcement, and police departments have provided training and equipment to civilian patrols.) Tenant and subway patrols (like the "Guardian Angels") also have been mischaracterized as vigilante groups. They are not, so long as they confine their activities to reporting incidents, helping victims, and making citizen's arrests of suspects. If they do not cross the line and dish out "back-alley justice," then they are not vigilantes (Marx and Archer, 1976).

Confusing Vigilantism with Legitimate Acts of Self-Defense

A sixth-grader is going door to door, selling chocolates for a school fund-raiser. A man sitting on his porch agrees to buy some candy and invites the girl inside while he gets some money. But then he whips out a knife and threatens to kill the eleven-year-old if she doesn't undress. As he throws her on a couch, she snatches the knife away from him, slashes him on the hand, kicks him in the stomach, and bolts out the front door. Within minutes, the man (who previously served time for raping a ten-year-old relative) is placed under arrest for attempted aggravated sexual assault, assault with a deadly weapon, and kidnapping. (Smith, 1994)

A man is walking to a store late on a Saturday night to buy a pack of cigarettes. He is accosted by two teenagers, nineteen and fifteen, who put a handgun to his head and demand his wallet. Instead, he pulls out his own pistol and shoots them both. Even though they die, and their weapon turns out to be a pellet gun, he is charged only with possession of an unlicensed revolver, a misdemeanor for which he is later put on probation. (Jones, 1993)

A businessman shoots a reputed member of organized crime who is trying to extort protection money from him. Placed on trial for murder, the businessman is condemned by the prosecutor for firing an "outrageously excessive" number of shots, eighteen in all, leaving the alleged gangster "perforated like a piece of Swiss cheese." But a jury acquits him of all charges, accepting his lawyer's contention that he acted in self-defense and was "on automatic pilot." (Fraser, 1991)

The ultimate right of an individual is to not be victimized at all. Victims under attack are entitled by law to defend themselves. Self-defense should not be confused with vigilantism.

According to responses provided to *NCVS* interviewers in 1992, most victims of violent attacks (in 60 percent of all robberies, 74 percent of all assaults, and 80 percent of all rapes) took measures to protect themselves. Their reactions included screaming for help, running away, reasoning with or threatening the offender, resisting and trying to capture the assailant, and counterattacking with or without a weapon. Willingness to take self-protective measures did not seem to vary by race, sex, or prior relationship (stranger or nonstranger) but was dependent upon age (older victims were less likely to put up a struggle). Males were more likely to try to fight back to resist and capture an assailant, while females were more inclined to call for help or threaten the attacker. More victims reported that their self-protective measures helped the situation (by enabling them to avoid injury altogether, or at least to prevent further injury) rather than hurt it (by making the attacker angrier and more aggressive). Only about 1 percent of all victims reported that they counterattacked by drawing their own weapon (BJS, 1994b).

The statutes governing fighting back in self-defense are not worded the same in each state because they have been shaped by four different rationales. According to a punitive rationale, using force against an attacker is permissible because any harm the aggressor suffers is deserved. Under the rationale of necessity, the use of violence is excused when a victim fearing great harm has no choice but to resort to force as a means of self-protection. According to the individualist rationale, a citizen does not have to yield or concede any territory to those who would encroach on his or her autonomy. Under the social rationale for self-defense, resistance to attack is justified as a way of preserving order (Fletcher, 1988a).

In general, the right to self-defense is formulated as the permissible use of reasonable force to protect one's life (or that of an innocent third party) from an adversary whom one reasonably believes is threatening harm. Several qualifications within the law are intended to restrain victims in order to discourage needless escalations of violence that can place them in greater danger or imperil bystanders, or to prevent terrible misunderstandings that can cause innocent people to be mistaken for dangerous offenders. If a person who meant no harm is hurt or killed, the individual who made the mistake can be held responsible for assault or murder.

The first restriction is that the threat posed by an aggressor must be imminent. The intended victim may not use force if the would-be aggressor issues a conditional threat (if . . . then) or a future threat (the next time . . .). The second qualification is that if the assailant retreats, removing the victim from imminent danger, force may no longer be used. (In some states, the victim must try to evade a confrontation or attempt to escape before resorting to deadly force.) Third, the victim's belief that harm is imminent must be reasonable. A "reasonable person" takes into account the size of the adversary, the time of day, the location, the presence or absence of a weapon, and similar factors. Fourth, the degree of force the victim uses to repel the attack must be in proportion to the threat of injury or death posed by the aggressor. Finally, the timing of the victim's action must be appropriate. A preemptive strike, initiated (too soon) before the presumed attacker makes his or her intentions known, is illegal. A retaliatory strike, made (too late) after the incident is over, also exceeds the limits of self-defense (see Austern, 1987; and Fletcher, 1988a).

In every state, the law permits innocent victims to use deadly force to defend themselves. Statutes passed by state legislatures usually spell out the circumstances under which victims of particular crimes can try to wound or kill their adversaries. For example, whether or not citizens are entitled by law to unleash deadly force to protect their homes and property varies dramatically from state to state. In most jurisdictions, intruders guilty of forcible entries into dwellings can be shot; in nine states, however, victims must be threatened or actually attacked before they can use lethal force against criminals who invade their home. Trespassers are generally not considered to pose a grave peril and therefore cannot be shot. Only seven states authorize citizens to use some degree of physical force to protect their property from thieves (BJS, 1988).

Would Potential Victims Be Better Off If They Were Armed?

Offenders armed with handguns committed over 930,000 violent crimes during 1992, including over 13,000 murders, nearly 12,000 rapes, almost 340,000 robberies, and more than 560,000 assaults, according to *NCVS* projections. Overall, between 4 and 5 out of every 1,000 persons age twelve and over were confronted by a gun-wielding offender during that year. Young men confronted armed adversaries more often than any other group. The gravest risks were faced by young black males between sixteen and nineteen (40 per 1,000, compared to 10 per 1,000 for white youth the same age), followed by young black men between twenty and twenty-four (29 per 1,000, compared to 9 per 1,000 for white men in their early twenties) (Rand, 1994b).

In response to the threat posed by gun-toting offenders, many people have armed themselves in self-defense. Surveys going back to 1959 have confirmed that about half of all American households own at least one gun. It is estimated that there are as many as 70 million pistols, 130 million rifles and shotguns, and 1 million assault weapons in circulation. These 200 million firearms in private arsenals add up to more than double the total that were in nonpolice/nonmilitary hands in 1970, when federal gun control laws first became a major political issue. Nearly one-half (45 percent) of all these gun owners cite self-protection as one of the main reasons for acquiring firearms. Almost 75 percent of respondents in a 1994 poll said it was "OK" for people to have a gun in their homes, but only roughly 20 percent approved of carrying a concealed weapon (Morganthau and Shenitz, 1994; Witkin, 1994). Yet, in response to an "arm yourself in self-defense" movement, a growing number of state legislatures are passing "right-to-carry" bills, which enable ordinary citizens to pack concealed handguns as they lead their everyday lives. In these states, pistol permits are easily obtainable, provided that the applicant is "of good character" and doesn't have a record of arrests and convictions or a documented history of mental illness. About 1 percent to 4 percent of the residents have been issued permits in states with lax right-to-carry laws. In the other states, citizens have to prove that they have a compelling need to be armed, and local police chiefs, sheriffs, and judges decide who gets the limited number of permits (Verhovek, 1995).

Obviously, people are sharply divided over the issue of armed self-defense. The debate revolves around the question of whether intended victims would be better off or worse off if they were in a position to draw their own guns when threatened or under attack. One side sees guns as "equalizers" that can save innocent lives and pushes for policies that provide ready access to firearms for law-abiding, responsible adults. The other side seeks to further restrict gun availability because firearms are seen as "facilitators" that cause minor conflicts to escalate into deadly confrontations; these weapons are considered more dangerous to the individuals who wield them than to their opponents at whom they take aim. Both sides in the debate admit there is a trade-off between appropriate self-defense uses and improper uses (accidental shootings, shootings of the wrong person by mistake, using firearms to commit suicide, and using guns for criminal purposes), but differ on whether the costs on balance outweigh the benefits.

The defenders of gun ownership consider keeping a firearm at home and carrying a legally registered handgun to be a rational response or antidote to the threat of violent crimes. They offer several arguments in favor of arming for self-protection. First, the likelihood that intended targets would be armed and prepared for battle might dissuade some potential predators from even trying to break the law. Second, the mere sight of a firearm in the hands of the target may abort the plans of a would-be offender. Third, when a crime is in progress, recourse to a firearm may enable a victim to drive off an attacker and thwart his criminal intentions. Fourth, an armed, law-abiding citizen could capture and hold an assailant at bay until the police arrive. Finally, in a life-or-death struggle, a gun can serve as an equalizer, improving the victim's odds of surviving a confrontation with a dangerous foe.

Although self-defense is a commonly cited reason for purchasing a gun, victims rarely are in a position to draw a gun during a confrontation. According to data from the *NCVS*, people under attack from assailants and robbers pull out a gun to threaten or to shoot in self-defense in just 1 percent of all cases, about 70,000 incidents per year (Roth, 1994). But gun ownership advocates dismiss this official estimate as misleadingly low and suspect that many respondents are reluctant to tell the full story of how they repelled the attacker to interviewers working for the government. Findings extrapolated from other surveys (based on much smaller samples), indicate that it's possible that guns protect their owners between 800,000 and 2,450,000 times a year. The mere presence of the gun deters the assailant from striking in 3 out of every 4 incidents. The gun is fired but no one is shot in most of the remaining (23 percent) confrontations. In only 2 percent of the standoffs does the attacker get shot. About 1 in 6 of the gun owners who brandished or fired their weapons reported that they believed their defensive use of it saved their lives or the lives of people they were trying to protect. Putting these estimates into perspective, its possible that guns are used in self-defense by intended victims more often than they are used to commit crimes by predators. The number of lives saved by guns might exceed the number of lives lost annually. And the crime-inhibiting effect of gun ownership by prospective victims might counterbalance the crime-generating effect of gun ownership by criminally inclined persons (Kleck, 1991; Will, 1993; and Witkin, 1994).

In 1989 the FBI's *UCR* began to keep track of the number of justifiable homicides (killings in self-defense) by police officers and by private citizens. The data show an upward trend and a pattern in which officers slay more criminals than civilians do each year. Currently, people under attack (civilian and police, combined) put an end to the lives of over 800 offenders annually. Considering that over 24,000 people are murdered yearly, justifiable homicides (which are not classified by the FBI as murders) account for about 3 percent of all crime-related violent deaths. Most of these legally excusable deaths are from gunfire (see Table 7.3).

Some advocates of armed self-defense and self-reliance go so far as to argue that intended victims have a "moral responsibility" to fight back in defense of their property, lives, families, and communities. To do this effectively, law-abiding citizens need to be trained and to be equipped with "equalizers" (guns). The existence of the police does not relieve individuals of their obligation to protect themselves, and officers cannot reasonably be depended upon to serve as personal bodyguards. Readiness to resist an assault on one's dignity is a prerequisite for self-respect, as well as a deterrent to crime (Snyder, 1993; Will, 1993).

Advocates of armed self-defense like to cite examples like the following that indicate how guns can be used successfully to protect life and property:

A man breaks into a home and badly beats a teenage girl. Emotionally devastated, she drops out of school. Many years later, another intruder enters her home and

TABLE 7.3 Justifiable Homicides by Police Officers and Private Citizens

	NUMBER OF KILLINGS IN SELF-DEFENSE	
YEAR	BY POLICE OFFICERS	BY PRIVATE CITIZENS
1988	343	238
1989	363	273
1990	385	328
1991	367	331
1992	418	351
1993	455	356

Source: FBI, *UCR*, 1989–1993.

threatens her family. This time, she gets her semiautomatic rifle out of the closet. Hearing the sound of her loading her weapon, the intruder curses and runs away. (Seelye, 1995).

Two customers enter a jewelry store and suddenly pull guns and announce a stickup. As one robber holds a gun to the owner's head, the latter's son emerges from the back room with his licensed pistol. The robbers turn and fire at him, but miss; he shoots back, mortally wounding one and frightening off the other. ("The Armed Citizen," 1991)

On the other side stand critics of the domestic arms race. They believe that although many people conjure up fantasies about how drawing a gun will save them, the reality is that gunfire claims many innocent lives. Gun control advocates bring up horror stories like the following, which illustrate how individuals mistakenly perceiving themselves to be in grave danger fire their guns in error, causing avoidable tragedies and needless deaths:

A truck driver and his wife come home at midnight and hear a noise in their daughter's room. The man grabs a loaded revolver he keeps handy and enters the darkened room. His fourteen-year-old daughter springs out of the closet and yells "Boo!" Even though she has played this practical joke several times before during the day, he reacts instantaneously and shoots in her direction, because she was supposed to be sleeping over at a friend's house. She cries out in pain but tells her father she is only wounded in the arm; when she dies from a bullet through her neck, the devoted and doting father is devastated. The local sheriff deems the incident an accident and does not file charges. (Nossiter, 1994a)

Late one night, a toddler crawls out of his bed and goes into the living room to watch the blinking colored lights on his family's Christmas tree. His actions set off an alarm on a motion detector. His stepmother awakens, grabs a handgun and fires at what she believes is a burglar. The three-year-old boy is shot in the head under the tree and dies. His death is ruled an accident. (Associated Press, 1994f)

A shopkeeper and his two relatives hide in the darkness, with guns drawn, lying in wait, as once again a burglar dares to enter their store after it closes, this time by climbing in through a broken window. Meanwhile, out on the street, plainclothes detectives spot the illegal entry and burst in through the back door. Mistaking the detectives for more criminals, the store owner opens fire. Believing they have stumbled upon a gang of well-armed burglars, the police fire back. When the shooting stops, both the shopkeeper and the burglar are dead. The officers arrest the two surviving relatives for possession of unlicensed firearms. (McKinley, 1991)

Homicide—in most cases from being shot—is now the third leading cause of death for children between the ages of five and fourteen. Over 5,300 youngsters were killed by gunfire in 1991 alone, about one every two hours. As access to guns increased dramatically between 1979 and 1991, nearly 50,000 children and teenagers died from bullet wounds inflicted from homicides, suicides, and accidental shootings ("Report," 1994). Each year, about 1,500 to 2,000 unintentional deaths due to firearms are recorded (approximately 40 percent of these fatal accidents stem from hunting mishaps). These accidental deaths from gunplay comprise about 2 percent of all fatal accidents. About 15,000 suicides are carried out annually with firearms. Adding in the more than 15,000 murders that are committed with revolvers, rifles, and shotguns, the toll of gun-related deaths exceeds 30,000 people a year, which amounts to between 1 percent and 2 percent of all deaths from any cause. In addition, each year about 70,000 people are shot during crimes, constituting roughly 2 percent of all victims who face armed aggressors (Roth, 1994; Wright, 1995). In 1993, 70 percent (the highest percent ever recorded) of all murder victims, more than 17,000 people, were killed by gunfire, amounting to about 6.7 persons per 100,000 per year (FBI, 1994). A disproportionate share of the people who died from bullet wounds were young black males between the ages of fifteen and twenty-four (BJS, 1994d).

Gun control advocates argue that owning a firearm for self-defense actually heightens risks and leads to a false sense of security. They point to studies that seem to show that keeping a gun at home, instead of protecting the members of a household, increases the likelihood that someone will be killed there. According to a study of 420 homicides committed in the homes of victims who had access to guns, the majority (77 percent) were slain by a spouse, other family member, or someone else they knew; only a small proportion (4 percent) were murdered by complete strangers (the remaining cases, 19 percent, were not solved). The highest risks of being shot to death at home are faced by people who keep one or more guns at home; live in a rental unit; and either live alone or with someone who was previously arrested, uses illicit drugs, hits others, or was hurt in a family fight (Kellerman, in Leary, 1993).

Similar studies have concluded that loaded guns are more likely to be used to slay family members than intruders. The availability of handguns causes ordinary fights between family members, former friends, and neighbors to escalate into deadly encounters. More people die in one year from handgun accidents than are killed over several years by home-invading burglars and robbers. In shoot-outs with armed offenders, victims lose more often than they win. In some confrontations, attackers may wrest the gun away and shoot victims with their own weapons. Firearms also facilitate suicides by deeply depressed individuals. Skeptics conclude that the gravest threats to members of a household come from within, not from outsiders; and therefore, on balance, the risks that arise from access to guns substantially outweigh the benefits (see Wright, Rossi, and Daly, 1983; Kates, 1986; Zimring, 1986; Green, 1987; and Witkin, 1994).

The Drift Back toward Vigilantism

As she leaves her apartment building to go to work, a mother of nine children is robbed of her jewelry by two men. Shaken and crying, she runs back upstairs to describe her assailants to her family. Three of her teenage sons rush out and spot a suspect lounging on a park bench. They confront him, and a struggle ensues. As the suspect apparently reaches for a weapon, one of the brothers fatally stabs him. Although the dead man had a reputation as a person who robbed to get money for drugs, the police found no weapon of his at the crime scene. When the eighteen-year-old brother is arrested for first-degree manslaughter, his neighbors sign petitions in his behalf and take up a collection to hire a good defense lawyer. But after a grand jury refuses to indict the brother, the district attorney feels compelled to warn the public not to interpret this decision "as a green light for people to take the law into their own hands." (James, 1990)

A ten-year-old girl is abducted from her bedroom at four in the morning. Twelve hours later, she comes running back to her apartment and tells her father that a notorious neighbor kidnapped and raped her. The father and some friends surround the accused man and begin to pummel and stomp him. In a fit of rage, the father stabs him. When the police arrive, the father is arrested along with the suspect. The district attorney presses charges to demonstrate that vigilantism will not be tolerated. But while the father is held overnight in the police station, officers visit his cell to shake his hand. When he is released on very low bail by a sympathetic judge, his neighbors hail him as a hero and take up a collection to pay for his legal expenses. Complete strangers who saw him on television stop him on the street to express their approval of what he did. ("Street Sentence," 1983; Winerip, 1983)

A man is in court, accused of molesting several young boys. Detecting a smirk on his face as she walks forward to take the witness stand, the mother of one of the boys pulls out a gun and shoots him in the back of the head five times. When she is arrested and put on trial for murder, some people rally to her side. Picturing her as a heroic figure who rose up in righteous indignation in defense of her child, they send telegrams offering their support and raise money for her defense. But others are skeptical of her portrayal as an anguished parent pushed to the breaking point by an arrogant offender who was about to be coddled by an ineffectual judicial system. When they learn that she waited two years for the chance to shoot the alleged pederast, was high on methamphetamine that day, and had a past conviction for auto theft herself, they view her more like a drug-addled ex-con with a score to settle. Convicted of voluntary manslaughter, she is sentenced to ten years in prison by a judge who categorizes her courtroom gunplay as an "execution" that was an intentional and intolerable assault on the justice system. The sentence is hailed by the prosecutor, who interprets it as affirming the message that one must not take the law into one's own hands. But her supporters urge clemency so she can be freed to lead a crusade to change the way child molesters are handled by the legal system. (Kincaid, 1993; Associated Press, 1994d)

A violent man with a record of at least eighteen arrests terrorizes his neighbors in a small farming community. One day, a crowd surrounds the bully's pickup truck as he travels down the main street. Someone shoots him. Even though he is murdered in front of sixty townspeople, no eyewitness cooperates with an FBI investigation, and no one is ever arrested for the crime. Leading citizens, including the mayor, marshal, prosecutor, and minister, publicly affirm that the dead man got what he deserved. (Galliher, Kunkel, and Hobbs, 1986)

Self-defense involves the use of force to prevent a crime from being completed or to rescue an intended victim from harm. Vigilantism involves the use of force to punish an offender after a crime has been completed. The distinction between defensive force and retaliatory violence can be expressed in plain English (rather than in legal jargon) as a deceptively simple formula: Any person who is in immediate danger of death or serious bodily harm may use any means necessary to stave off the attack, but once the threat has passed, the victim may not use force to exact revenge. But such distinctions are more easily drawn in classrooms and textbooks than in real-life confrontations. In actual cases, difficult questions must be resolved: "What was the nature of the threat?" "Did the victim reasonably fear serious bodily harm or even death?" "Was the response proportionate to the perceived threat, or did the victim overreact?" "Had the threat abated by the time the victim resorted to force?"

Police officers grapple with these questions first when they decide whether or not to make an arrest. Prosecutors confront these issues when they determine what charges, if any, to lodge against an intended victim who has emerged victorious from a battle with an offender. If the case goes to trial, jurors, acting as the conscience of the community, must arrive at a verdict by answering such hypothetical questions as "What would I have done under similar circumstances?" "Does the abuse the victim endured excuse his or her violent reaction?" "Did the aggressor get what was coming to him or her?" and "What message should the verdict give to the public?" Juries retain the right to "nullify" legal principles, disregard the limits placed by the law on the use of force in self-defense, and render a verdict based on their own interpretations of what is reasonable and appropriate under particular circumstances (Dershowitz, 1988). The acceptance by juries of "abuse excuse" defenses—that the person on trial is more a victim than a perpetrator and therefore should not be punished—reflects both a growing intolerance toward crime and a yearning to regain control over the immediate environment, by drastic measures if necessary, especially when the criminal justice system seems to be incapable of providing adequate protection (Dershowitz, 1994).

When individuals accused of vigilante actions are not arrested, or are not vigorously prosecuted, or are acquitted by a jury after a trial, commentators try to decipher the meaning or message: Was the person who was accused of dispensing street justice vindicated by public opinion as doing the right thing? Was the prosecution, representing the criminal justice system and the government, repudiated? Were the laws restraining the use of force rejected? Various interpretations are possible when persons charged with vigilante violence are not punished for their questionable deeds (see Bahr, 1985; Zimring, 1987; and Dershowitz, 1988).

Vigilantism seems to appeal to many people on a gut level. A steady stream of extremely popular movies have capitalized on the theme of personal vendettas and "getting even." Even though the plots are transparent and the thirst for revenge is quenched by the end of the story, audiences stand up and cheer as victims strike back and make vicious thugs pay in blood for their cruel misdeeds.

In public opinion polls conducted during the early 1990s, from about one-quarter to about one-third of the people who were questioned expressed support for frontier-style justice. When asked in a survey (NVC, 1991a) whether vigilantism is ever justified, 33 percent answered "Yes!" while 61 percent said "No!" and 6 percent were not sure. In another public opinion poll (Roper, in Maguire, Pastore, and Flanagan, 1993: 194), respondents were asked whether or not the situation (police not being around when innocent victims need them) has reached the point at which it is necessary for citizens to take the law into their own hands to protect themselves from attack in any way they can. Overall, 26 percent replied, "Yes, it is necessary," while 66 percent declared "No, it is wrong," with 8 percent saying they didn't know. Support for taking the law into one's hands (how respondents interpreted that phrase is not clear) was higher among men (30 percent) than women (22 percent); among people from thirty to forty-four years old (30 percent) than among persons over 60 (19 percent), with the level of support for people in other age groups somewhere between 19 percent and 30 percent; and among southerners (31 percent) more than residents of other regions, especially northeasterners (17 percent). Differences in opinion by education, income, occupation, and political party affiliation were not as pronounced.

Genuine vigilantism of the Old West and Deep South varieties may make a comeback if victims and their supporters conclude that only civilian violence can quell criminal violence.

Opportunistic politicians seeking to ride the provictim, and anticrime vote to higher office have rekindled the vigilante impulse with their inflammatory rhetoric. Their use of the metaphor of "waging war on crime" has become a household phrase. In this "war," victims are obviously the casualties, the "criminal element" is cast as the enemy, the streets are the battlefields, and criminal justice personnel serve as the troops. Alarmist pronouncements that the "war" is being "lost" because the criminal justice system has "broken down" spread panic. Charges that the government is "paralyzed" and unwilling to act, that police are "handcuffed" by needless rules, that judges are "too soft," and that prisoners are "coddled" prompt distraught victims and their allies to mobilize their own forces lest they be overrun. As the situation seems to grow more desperate, violent actions loom as reasonable solutions to stave off military defeat and to rout the enemy.

The emotional attraction of the vigilante "solution" to the street crime problem rests on the notion that retaliation-in-kind is what "justice" is all about. Offender rehabilitation, restitution, and reconciliation are out of the question. Because the criminal justice system cannot impose "appropriate" far-ranging punishments that directly match the suffering inflicted by offenders, it consistently fails to deliver payment-in-blood "justice" to victims and their supporters. As the gulf widens between the harsh punishments some people are calling for and the actual penalties that the system metes out, street justice gains appeal as being better than no justice at all in some circles.

At present, the impulse toward vigilantism is held in check by two counter-ideologies. Law enforcement officials and responsible figures in government, embracing the tenets of professionalism, reject vigilantism out of a conviction that experts, not ordinary citizens, ought to control the criminal justice process. They urge citizens to allow the proper authorities and courts to handle cases and to reject any do-it-yourself impulses. Civil libertarians marshal even stronger arguments. They insist that due process safeguards and constitutional guarantees must be adhered to faithfully, to make sure that innocent individuals are not falsely accused and then subjected to the passions of mob rule.

A mother warns a fourteen-year-old boy to leave her thirteen-year-old son alone. He says he does not know what she is talking about. Believing that he is the neighborhood bully who stole her son's watch, she shoots him in the groin. She is arrested and charged with assault and possession of a deadly weapon. (Pierre-Pierre, 1993)

A woman, holding her hand over her bruised eye, is accompanied by a crowd of men who are looking for the person who assaulted her. They come upon a man drinking a bottle of beer, begin to question him, and then rough him up. Although the woman screams to them "That's not the guy!" they continue to pummel him and then break the bottle over his head. As they melt away, realizing they attacked the wrong man, he dies from his wounds. Later, neighbors discover that the original fight stemmed from a drug deal that went sour. (Newman, 1992)

A crowd of fifty teenagers masses in response to a rumor (which later proves false) that a girl from their suburban high school had been raped. Intent on retaliating, they pile into cars and invade an adjoining neighborhood, spoiling for a fight. Several fist fights break out, and some youths are injured by rocks and bottles. Then the suburban teenagers break out baseball bats, corner about fifteen parochial high school boys, and beat one sixteen-year-old to death. Six students from the mob who really don't know each other and have not been in serious trouble before are arrested, charged with murder, tried as adults, and face possible execution. (Janofsky, 1994)

"Do-it-yourself justice" has been criticized as too swift, too sure, and too informal—victims and their accomplices dispense with all the rules of the criminal justice "game" and assume the roles normally played by the police, prosecutor, judge, jury, and ultimately, executioner. The delicate balance between the rights of victims and of accused persons, hammered out through centuries of conflict and compromise, is overturned, and suspects are presumed to be guilty no matter how loudly they assert their innocence. The history of vigilantism is littered with cases of mistaken identity, in which the wrong person was made to pay a high price for someone else's misdeeds.

Street justice has also been denounced as too harsh. Physical punishments, including death, are imposed in the heat of the moment for offenses that merit lesser penalties under the law. Unlike the other kind of informal justice, restorative justice, arrived at through mediation and restitution at reconciliation programs, street justice is not directed toward a peaceful resolution of an antagonistic relationship through negotiation and compromise. On the contrary, the vigilante's intent is to forcefully settle matters in a manner that mirrors the original act in which one person harms another, except that the roles are reversed.

The widely used phrase "taking the law into one's own hands" does not capture the essence of this reaction to crime. Vigilantes don't "take" the law; they break the law. They don't use force in self-defense, which is legal; they unleash retaliatory violence in order to inflict physical punishment, which is illegal. Their disdain for the "technicalities" of due process mocks the entire criminal justice system. Unleashed in the name of restoring law and order, vigilantism undermines the legal system and sends shock waves through the social order by trampling on the Bill of Rights. In trying to vindicate victims, vigilantes create new ones.

From an academic standpoint, the study of vigilantism leads victimology full circle, right back to its ancestral origins in criminology. Through vigilantism's role reversals, victims become lawbreakers, physically harming individuals whom they suspect previously made them suffer. Offenders, formerly enjoying the advantage within the relationship, are compelled to experience firsthand what it is like to be on the receiving end of criminal violence. But trading places—transforming victims into offenders and offenders into victims—is no solution to the crime problem. In an ironic twist, by retaliating against the wrong person or unleashing excessive force, vengeful victims open themselves up to the risk of being sued in civil court and prosecuted in criminal court. There are too many offenders already. Vigilantism just adds to their ranks.

References

Abel, C., and Marsh, F. (1984). *Punishment and restitution: A restitutionary approach to crime and the criminal.* Westport, CT: Greenwood Press.

Able, R. (1982). *The politics of informal justice: Vol. 1. The American experience.* New York: Academic Press.

Abramovsky, A. (1992). "Victim impact statements: Adversely impacting upon judicial fairness." *St. John's Journal of Legal Commentary* 8(1) (Fall): 21–35.

Abrams, A. (1987). "Sharing sorrow: Shelter helps turn victims into survivors." *New York Newsday,* December 21, pp. 2, 40.

Abramson, L. (1994). "Unequal justice." *Newsweek,* July 25, p. 25.

Acker, J. (1992). "Social sciences and the criminal law: Victims of crime—plight vs. rights." *Criminal Law Bulletin* 28: 64–77.

Adler, J. (1994). "Kids growing up scared." *Newsweek,* January 10, pp. 43–50.

Ahrens, J., Stein, J., and Young, M. (1980). *Law enforcement and victim services.* Washington, DC: Aurora Associates.

"AIDS tests for rapists." (1993). *Crime Victims Digest* 4 (April): 9.

Akiyama, Y. (1981). "Murder victimization: A statistical analysis." *FBI Law Enforcement Bulletin,* March, pp. 8–11.

Allbritten, R., and Allbritten, W. (1985). "The hidden victims: Courtship violence among college students." *Journal of College Student Personnel* 26: 201–204.

Allen, H., Friday, P., Roebuck, J., and Sagarin, E. (1981). *Crime and punishment: An introduction to criminology.* New York: Free Press.

Allen, N. (1980). *Homicide: Perspectives on prevention.* New York: Human Sciences Press.

Allison, J., and Wrightsman, L. (1993). *Rape: The misunderstood crime.* Newbury Park, CA: Sage.

Allredge, E. (1942). "Why the South leads the nation in murder and manslaughter." *Quarterly Review* 2: 123–134.

Alper, B., and Nichols, L. (1981). *Beyond the courtroom.* Lexington, MA: Lexington Books.

American Academy of Pediatrics (AAP). (1985). *Child sexual abuse.* Elk Grove Village, IL: Author.

American Bar Association (ABA). (1987). *Dispute resolution program directory.* Washington, DC: Author.

American Bar Association (ABA) Committee on Victims. (1979). *Reducing victim/witness intimidation: A package.* Washington, DC: ABA.

American Psychological Association (APA) Task Force on Victims of Crime and Violence. (1984). *Final report.* Hyattsville, MD: APA.

Amir, D., and Amir, M. (1979). "Rape crisis centers: An arena for ideological conflicts." *Victimology* 4(2): 247–257.

Amir, M. (1967). "Victim precipitated forcible rape." *Journal of Criminal Law, Criminology, and Police Science* 58: 493–502.

———. (1971). *Patterns in forcible rape.* Chicago: University of Chicago Press.

Anderson, E. (1994). "The code of the streets." *Atlantic Monthly,* 273(5) (May): 81–94.

Anderson, M., and Renzetti, C. (1980). "Rape crisis counseling and the culture of individualism." *Contemporary Crises* 4(3) (July): 323–341.

Andrews, L. (1986). "Are we raising a terrified generation?" *Parents Magazine,* December, pp. 139–142, 228–230.

"The armed citizen." (1991). *American Rifleman,* September, p. 6.

Ash, M. (1972). "On witnesses: A radical critique of criminal court procedures." *Notre Dame Lawyer* 48 (December): 386–425.

Associated Press. (1984a). "Victims to get 'Son of Sam' cash." *New York Times,* September 20, p. B3.

————. (1984b). "Wounded ice cream vendor robbed by children." *New York Times,* July 15, p. A21.

————. (1991). "Milwaukee panel finds discrimination by police." *New York Times,* October 16, p. B8.

————. (1993a). "Boy recants rape account, freeing suspect." *New York Times,* May 28, p. B6.

————. (1993b). "A disabled child is seen more likely to be abused." *New York Times,* October 7, p. A21.

————. (1993c). "High murder rate for women on job." *New York Times,* October 3, p. A29.

————. (1993d). "Survey finds school violence hits 1 in 4 students." *New York Times,* December 17, p. A37.

————. (1994a). "As cities reach record numbers of killings, youths play grim role." *New York Times,* January 1, p. A7.

————. (1994b). "Author's mugging one for the book." *Long Island Newsday,* June 12, p. A10.

————. (1994c). "Courts in New Jersey adopt 'truth in sentencing' rule. *New York Times,* April 26, p. B7.

————. (1994d). "Mother gets 10 years for slaying molester suspect." *New York Times,* January 8, p. A7.

————. (1994e). "Notifying the next of kin: The worst job is often poorly done." *New York Times,* June 12, p. A35.

————. (1994f). "A parent kills child mistaken for a burglar." *New York Times,* December 6, p. A18.

————. (1994g). "Shot victim helps robber gain freedom." *New York Times,* May 15, p. A42.

————. (1994h). "Switched-at-birth girl recants accusations." *New York Times,* September 27, p. A20.

————. (1994i). "Witness intimidation is called a growing problem." *New York Times,* August 7, p. A30.

Aunapu, G., Epperson, S., Kramer, S., Lafferty, E., and Martin, K. (1993). "Robbing the innocents." *Time,* December 27, p. 31.

Austern, D. (1987). *The crime victim's handbook.* New York: Penguin.

"Auto theft alert." (1994). *CAR (Citizens for Auto-Theft Responsibility) Newsletter,* Fall, p. 7.

Ayres, B. (1994). "Big gains are seen in battle to stem drunk driving." *New York Times,* May 22, pp. A1, A24.

Bachman, R. (1992). *Crime victimization in city, suburban, and rural areas: A National Crime Victimization Survey report.* Washington, DC: U.S. Department of Justice.

————. (1994a). *Violence against women: A National Crime Victimization Survey Report.* Bureau of Justice Statistics. Washington, DC: U.S. Department of Justice.

————. (1994b). *Violence and theft in the workplace. BJS Crime Data Brief.* Washington, DC: U.S. Department of Justice.

Bahr, R. (1985). "The threat of vigilantism." *Kiwanis,* May, pp. 20–24.

Baldwin, J. (1988). "Car thefts (33 a day) becoming an ugly fact of life." *New York Times,* May 8, sec. 12, p. 2.

Balkan, S., Berger, R., and Schmidt, J. (1980). *Crime and deviance in America: A critical approach.* Belmont, CA: Wadsworth.

Balleza, M. (1991). "Many rape victims finding justice through civil courts." *New York Times,* September 20, pp. A1, B7.

Bannister, S. (1992). "Battered women who kill their abusers: Their courtroom battles." In R. Muraskin and T. Alleman (Eds.), *It's a crime: Women and justice* (pp. 316–333). Englewood Cliffs, NJ: Regents/Prentice Hall.

Barbash, F. (1979). "Victim's rights: New legal weapon." *Washington Post,* December 17, p. 1.

Barden, J. (1987). "Marital rape: Drive for tougher laws is pressed." *New York Times,* May 13, p. A16.

Barnett, O., and LaViolette, A. (1993). *It could happen to anyone: Why battered women stay.* Newbury Park, CA: Sage.

Barnett, R. (1977). "Restitution: A new paradigm of criminal justice." In R. Barnett and J. Hagel (Eds.), *Assessing the criminal: Restitution, retribution, and the criminal process* (pp. 1–35). Cambridge, MA: Ballinger.

Barringer, F. (1989). "Children as sexual prey, and predators." *New York Times,* May 30, pp. 1, A16.

Bass, E., and Davis, L (1992). The courage to heal: A guide for women survivors of child sexual abuse (3rd ed.). New York: Harper Collins.

Bastian, L. (1993). *Criminal victimization 1992. Bureau of Justice Statistics Bulletin.* Washington, DC: U.S. Department of Justice.

Bastian, L., and Taylor, B. (1991). *School crime: A National Crime Victimization Survey Report.* Washington, DC: U.S. Department of Justice.

Beall, G. (1980). "Negotiating the disposition of criminal charges." *Trial,* October, pp. 10–13.

Beck, M., Rosenberg, D., Chideya, F., Miller, S., Foote, D., Manly, H., and Katel, P. (1992). "Murderous obsession." *Newsweek,* July 13, pp. 60–62.

Behar, R. (1993). "Car thief at large." *Time,* August 16, pp. 47–48.

Beirne, P., and Messerschmidt, J. (1991). *Criminology.* San Diego: Harcourt Brace Jovanovich.

Benedict, H. (1992). *Virgin or vamp: How the press covers sex crimes.* New York: Oxford University Press.

Bensing, R., and Schroeder, O. (1960). *Homicide in an urban community.* Springfield, IL: Charles C Thomas.

Berk, R., Campbell, A., Klap, R., and Western, B. (1992). "The deterrent effect of arrest in incidents of domestic violence: A Bayesian analysis of four field experiments." *American Sociological Review* 57 (October): 698–708.

Berke, R. (1989). "Capital offers unlimited turf to drug dealers." *New York Times,* March 28, pp. 1, A16.

Berliner, L. (1987). "Commentary: Editor's introduction." *Journal of Interpersonal Violence* (March): 107–108.

Bernat, F. (1992). "Book review: 'Representing . . . battered women who kill' by Johann and Osanka." *Justice Quarterly* 9(1) (March): 169–172.

Berns, W. (1994). "Getting away with murder." *Commentary* (97)4 (April): 25–29.

Bernstein, G. (1972). "Statement." In U.S. Senate, *Report on the federal crime insurance program.* Committee on the Judiciary, Subcommittee on Criminal Laws and Procedures, 1st sess. (pp. 521–529). Washington, DC: U.S. Government Printing Office.

Berreby, D. (1988). "The ordeal of the credit fraud victim." *New York Times,* September 4, Sec. 3, p. 4.

Berry, J. (1992). *Lead us not into temptation.* New York: Doubleday.

Besharov, D. (1987). "Federal action urged to protect rights of parents accused of child abuse." *Crime Victims Digest,* November, pp. 5–6.

———. (1990). *Recognizing child abuse: A guide for the concerned.* New York: Free Press.

Best, J. (1988). "Missing children, misleading statistics." *Public Interest* (Summer): 84–92.

———. (1989a). "Dark figures and child victims: Statistical claims about missing children." In J. Best (Ed.), *Images of issues: Imagining contemporary social problems* (pp. 21–37). New York: Aldine de Gruyter.

———. (Ed.). (1989b). *Images of issues: Imagining contemporary social problems.* New York: Aldine de Gruyter.

Best, J., and Luckenbill, D. (1982). *Organizing deviance.* Englewood Cliffs, NJ: Prentice-Hall.

Biblarz, A., Barnowe, J., and Biblarz, D. (1984). "To tell or not to tell: Differences between victims who report crimes and victims who do not." *Victimology* 9(1): 153–158.

Bienen, L. (1983). "Rape reform legislation in the United States: A look at some practical effects." *Victimology* 8(1): 139–151.

Birkbeck, C. (1983). " 'Victimology is what victimologists do.' But what should they do?" *Victimology* 8(3–4): 270–275.

Black, D. (1968). *Police encounters and social organization.* Unpublished doctoral dissertation, University of Michigan, Ann Arbor.

Block, R. (1981). "Victim-offender dynamics in violent crime." *Journal of Criminal Law and Criminology* 72: 743–761.

Block, R., Felson, M., and Block, C. (1985). "Crime victimization rates for incumbents of 246 occupations." *Sociology and Social Research* 69(3): 442–449.

Block, R., and Skogan, W. (1986). "Resistance and nonfatal outcomes in stranger-to-stranger predatory crime." *Violence and Victims* 1(4) (Winter): 241–254.

Bochnak, E. (Ed.). (1981). *Women's self-defense cases: Theory and practice.* Charlottesville, VA: Michie Co. Law Publishers.

Bode, J. (1978). *Fighting back.* New York: MacMillan.

Bohmer, C., and Parrot, A. (1993). *Sexual assault on campus: The problem and the solution.* New York: Lexington Books.

Boland, B., Mahanna, P., and Sones, R. (1992). *The prosecution of felony arrests, 1988. Bureau of Justice Statistics Report.* Washington, DC: U.S. Department of Justice.

Boland, B., and Sones, R. (1986). *BJS special report: Prosecution of felony arrests, 1981.* Washington, DC: U.S. Department of Justice.

Boston, G. (1977). *Crimes against the elderly: A selected bibliography.* Washington, DC: National Criminal Justice Reference Service.

Bouza, A. (1991). "Responding to domestic violence." In M. Steinman (Ed.), *Woman battering: Policy responses* (pp. 191–203). Cincinnati: Anderson.

Bowker, L. (1983). "Marital rape: A distinct syndrome?" *Social Casework* (June): 340–350.

Bowman, C. (1992). "The arrest experiments: A feminist critique." *The Journal of Criminal Law and Criminology* 83(1): 201–208.

Boyer, D., and James, J. (1983). "Prostitutes as victims." In D. MacNamara and A. Karmen (Eds.), *Deviants: Victims or victimizers?* (pp. 109–146). Newbury Park, CA: Sage.

Boyle, P. (1994). "Travel industry launches drive to protect tourists." *New York AAA Motorist,* April, pp. 1, 18.

Brandl, S., and Horvath, F. (1991). "Crime victim evaluation of police investigative performance." *Journal of Criminal Justice* 19: 109–121.

Breckman, R., and Adelman, R. (1988). *Strategies for helping victims of elder mistreatment.* Newbury Park, CA: Sage.

Brien, V. (1992). *Civil legal remedies for crime victims.* (Office for Victims of Crime bulletin). Washington, DC: U.S. Department of Justice.

Briere, J. (1992). *Child abuse trauma: Theory and treatment of the lasting effects.* Newbury Park, CA: Sage.

Bromley, D. (1991). "The satanic cult scare." *Society* (May–June): 55–66.

Brooks, J. (1972). *Criminal injury compensation programs: An analysis of their development and administration.* Unpublished doctoral dissertation. Ann Arbor, MI: University Microfilms.

Brown, R. (1975). *Strains of violence: Historical studies of American violence and vigilantism.* New York: Oxford University Press.

Browne, A. (1987). *When battered women kill.* New York: Free Press.

Brownmiller, S. (1975). *Against our will: Men, women, and rape.* New York: Simon & Schuster.

Bruni, F. (1989). "Maureen Reagan reveals husband beat her." *New York Post,* April 3, p. 9.

Buchwald, A. (1969). "Victim precipitation." *Washington Post,* February 4, p. 23.

Buchwald, E., Fletcher, P., and Roth, M. (1993). *Transforming a rape culture.* Minneapolis: Milkwood Editions.

Buckley, W. (1994). "Excelsior the counterculture." *On the Right* (syndicated column). *Islamorada* (Florida) *Free Press,* December 21, p. 30A.

Bulger, J. (1933). "Automobile thefts." *Journal of Criminal Law, Criminology, and Police Science* 23: 806–810.

Bureau of Justice Statistics (BJS). (1974–1994). *Criminal victimization in the United States, 1973–1992.* Washington, DC: U.S. Department of Justice.

———. (1982–1994). *Criminal victimization in the United States, 1980, 1981 . . . 1992.* (Annual reports). Washington, DC: U.S. Department of Justice.

———. (1988). *Report to the nation on crime and justice* (2nd ed.). Washington, DC: U.S. Department of Justice.

———. (1994a). *Criminal victimization in the United States: 1973–1992 trends.* Washington, DC: U.S. Department of Justice.

———. (1994b). *Criminal victimization in the United States, 1992.* Washington, DC: U.S. Department of Justice.

———. (1994c). *Elderly crime victims.* Washington, DC: U.S. Department of Justice.

———. (1994d). *Firearms and crimes of violence: Selected findings from national statistical series.* Washington, DC: U.S. Department of Justice.

———. (1994e). *Crime rate essentially unchanged last year.* (Press release). Washington, DC: U.S. Department of Justice.

Burgess, A., and Holmstrom, L. (1974). "Rape trauma syndrome." *American Journal of Nursing* 131: 981–986.

Burrows, W. (1976). *Vigilante!* New York: Harcourt Brace Jovanovich.

Burt, M. (1983). "A conceptual framework for victimological research." *Victimology* 8(3–4): 261–268.

Burt, M., and Katz, R. (1987). "Dimensions of recovery from rape." *Journal of Interpersonal Violence* 2(1) (March): 57–81.

"Burying crime in Chicago." (1983). *Newsweek,* May 16, p. 63.

Butts, J., and Snyder, H. (1992). *Restitution and juvenile recidivism: OJJDP Update on Research.* Washington, DC: U.S. Department of Justice.

Buzawa, E., and Buzawa, C. (1990). *Domestic violence: The criminal justice response.* Newbury Park, CA: Sage.

Cahn, N., and Lerman, L. (1991). "Prosecuting woman abuse." In M. Steinman (Ed.), *Woman battering: Policy responses* (pp. 95–113). Cincinnati: Anderson.

"California study finds victims' rights bill has not put an end to all plea bargaining." (1985). *Crime Victims Digest,* November, p. 5.

Caplan, G. (1991). "Battered wives, battered justice." *National Review,* February 25, pp. 15–20.

Carrington, F. (1975). *The victims.* New Rochelle, NY: Arlington House.

———. (1977). "Victim's rights litigation: A wave of the future?" *University of Richmond Law Review* 11(3): 447–470.

———. (1978). "Victim's rights: A new tort." *Trial,* June, pp. 39–41.

———. (1980). "Martinez ruling won't bar suits on negligent custodial releases." *National Law Journal* (February 11): 26.

———. (1986). "Preventing victimization through third-party victims' rights litigation." *Networks* (newsletter of the National Victims Center, Fort Worth, Texas) 1(1) (June): 7.

Carrow, D. (1980). *Crime victim compensation: Program model*. Washington, DC: U.S. Department of Justice.

Carson, E. (1986). "Crime victims strike back with civil lawsuits for compensation." *NOVA Newsletter,* September, pp. 1–2, 4.

"Car thief slain—pair charged." (1988). *New York Post,* April 19, p. 10.

Ceci, S., and Bruck, M. (1993). "Suggestibility of the child witness: A historical review and synthesis." *Psychological Bulletin* 113(3): 403–439.

Center, L. (1980). "Victim assistance for the elderly." *Victimology* 5(2): 374–390.

Chapman, J., and Smith, B. (1987). *Child sexual abuse: An analysis of case processing.* Washington, DC: American Bar Association.

Chappell, D., Geis, R., and Geis, G. (1977). *Forcible rape: The crime, the victim, and the offender.* New York: Columbia University Press.

Chappell, D., and Sutton, P. (1974). "Evaluating the effectiveness of programs to compensate victims of crime." In I. Drapkin and E. Viano (Eds.), *Victimology: A new focus* (vol. 2, pp. 207–220). Lexington, MA: D. C. Heath.

Chavez, J. (1992). "Battered men and the California law." *Southwestern University Law Review* 22: 239–256.

"Chicago police found to dismiss cases erroneously." (1983). *New York Times,* May 2, p. A20.

"Child abuse reports rise 2%." (1988). *Law Enforcement News,* May 15, pp. 1, 12.

"Child abuse victims get help through interior decor." (1989). *Law Enforcement News,* May 15, pp. 1, 12.

Childres, R. (1964). "Compensation for criminally inflicted personal injury." *New York University Law Review* 39: 455–471.

Chilton, R. (1987). "Twenty years of homicide and robbery in Chicago: The impact of the city's changing racial and age composition." *Journal of Quantitative Criminology* 3(3): 195–206.

Chira, S. (1993). "Sexual abuse: The coil of truth and memory." *New York Times,* December 5, p. E3.

Clark, C., and Block, T. (1992). "Victim's voices and constitutional quandries: Life after *Payne v. Tennessee.*" *St. John's Journal of Legal Commentary* 8(1) (Fall): 35–64.

Clark, J. (1994). "Crime in the 90's: It's a blast." *Law Enforcement News,* March 15, pp. 1, 7.

Clark, L., and Lewis, D. (1978). *Rape: The price of coercive sexuality.* Toronto: Women's Press.

Clark, R., and Harris, P. (1992). "Auto theft and its prevention." In M. Tonry (Ed.), *Crime and justice: A review of research,* vol. 16 (pp. 1–54). Chicago: University of Chicago Press.

Clement, H. (1946). "Stealing your own car." *FBI Law Enforcement Bulletin,* April, pp. 21–34.

Coates, R. (1990). "Victim-offender reconciliation programs in North American: An assessment." In B. Galaway and J. Hudson, (Eds.), *Criminal justice, restitution and reconciliation* (pp. 125–134). Monsey, NY: Willow Tree Press.

Coates, R., and Gehm, J. (1989). "An empirical assessment." In M. Wright and B. Galaway (Eds.), *Mediation and criminal justice: Victims, offenders, and community* (pp. 251–263). Newbury Park, CA: Sage.

Cohen, L., and Felson, M. (1979). "Social change and crime rate trends: A routine activity approach." *American Sociological Review* 44: 588–607.

Cohen, L., Kluegal, J., and Land, K. (1981). "Social inequality and criminal victimization." *American Sociological Review* 46: 505–524.

Cohen, P. (1984). "Resistance during sexual assaults: Avoiding rape and injury." *Victimology* 9(1): 120–129.

Cohen, R. (1991). "Should the media name the accuser when the crime being charged is rape?" *New York Times,* April 21, p. E4.

Cohn, E., Kidder, L., and Harvey, J. (1978). "Crime prevention vs. victimization prevention: The psychology of two different reactions." *Victimology* 3(3): 285–296.

Collins, J., McCalla, M., Powers, L., and Stutts, E. (1988). *OJJDP update on research: The police and missing children—Findings from a national survey.* Washington, DC: U.S. Department of Justice.

Combined News Services. (1993). "NYC man slain on Florida highway." *New York Newsday,* September 27, p. 17.

Conklin, J. (1975). *The impact of crime.* New York: Macmillan.

Cook, P. (1985). "Is robbery becoming more violent? An analysis of robbery murder trends since 1968." *Journal of Criminal Law and Criminology* 76(2): 480–490.

———. (1987). "Robbery violence." *Journal of Criminal Law and Criminology* 78(2): 357–377.

Cook, R., Roehl, J., and Sheppard, D. (1980). *Neighborhood justice centers field test.* Washington, DC: U.S. Department of Justice.

Cose, E. (1994). "Truths about spouse abuse." *Newsweek,* August 8, p. 49.

Crichton, S. (1993). "Sexual correctness: Has it gone too far?" *Newsweek,* October 25, pp. 52–56.

"Crime control amendments." (1973). *Congressional Quarterly Almanac* 29: 370–372.

"Crime control needs citizens to do their part in helping." (1985). *Crime Victims Digest,* August, pp. 1–2.

"Crime victims' aid." (1978). *Congressional Quarterly Almanac* 34: 196–198.

Crime Victims Research and Treatment Center. (1992). *The national women's study.* Charleston: Medical University of South Carolina.

Cuomo, M. (1992). "The crime victim in a system of criminal justice." *St. John's Journal of Legal Commentary* 8(1) (Fall): 1–20.

Curtis, L. (1974). "Victim precipitation and violent crime." *Social Problems* 21: 594–605.

Czajkoski, E., and Wollan, L. (1986). "Creative sentencing: A critical analysis." *Justice Quarterly* 3(2) (June): 215–229.

Danziger, L. (1993). "New York, car theft capital of the world." *New York Times,* March 2, p. A21.

Darnton, N. (1991). "The pain of the last taboo." *Newsweek,* October 7, pp. 70–72.

Davidson, H. (1986). "Missing children: A close look at the issue." *Children Today,* July-August, pp. 26–30.

Davis, R. (1983). "Victim/witness noncooperation: A second look at a persistent phenomenon." *Journal of Criminal Justice* 11: 287–299.

Davis, R., Kunreuther, F., and Connick, E. (1984). "Expanding the victim's role in the criminal court dispositional process: The results of an experiment." *Journal of Criminal Law and Criminology* 75(2): 491–505.

Davis, R., Smith, B., and Hillenbrand, S. (1992). "Restitution: The victim's viewpoint." *The Justice System Journal* 15(3): 746–758.

Davis, R., Tichane, M., and Grayson, D. (1980). *Mediation and arbitration as alternatives to criminal prosecution in felony arrest cases: An evaluation of the Brooklyn Dispute Resolution Center (first year).* New York: Vera Institute of Justice.

Dawson, J. (1993). *Murder in large urban counties, 1988. Bureau of Justice Statistics Special Report.* Washington, DC: U.S. Department of Justice.

Dawson, J., and Langan, P. (1994). *Murder in families: BJS Special Report.* Washington, DC: U.S. Department of Justice.

Dawson, J., Smith, S., and DeFrances, C. (1993). *Prosecutors in state courts, 1992. Bureau of Justice Statistics Bulletin.* Washington, DC: U.S. Department of Justice.

Dawson, R. (1969). *Sentencing: The decision as to type, length, and conditions of sentence.* Boston: Little, Brown.

Dean, C., and de Bruyn-Kops, M. (1982). *The crime and the consequences of rape.* Springfield, IL: Charles C Thomas.

Deane, G. (1987). "Cross-national comparison of homicide: Age/sex-adjusted rates using the 1980 U.S. homicide experience as a standard." *Journal of Quantitative Criminology* 3(3): 215–227.

DeConcini, D. (1989). "National child abuse prevention month." *Crime Victims Digest* 6(2): 4–5.

De Koster, K., and Swisher, K. (Eds.). (1994). *Child abuse: Opposing viewpoints.* San Diego: Greenhaven Press.

Del Castillo, V., and Lindner, C. (1994). "Staff safety issues in probation." *The Justice Professional* 8(2): 37–54.

Demaris, A. (1992). "Male versus female initiation of aggression: The case of courtship violence." In E. Viano (Ed.), *Intimate violence: Interdisciplinary perspectives* (pp. 111–120). Washington, DC: Hemisphere Publishing.

Dershowitz, A. (1988). *Taking liberties: A decade of hard cases, bad laws, and bum raps.* Chicago: Contemporary Books.

———. (1994). *The abuse excuse and other cop-outs, sob stories and evasions of responsibility.* Boston: Little, Brown.

Deutsch, C. (1994). "Victims of violence increasingly hold landlords liable for crimes." *New York Times,* June 3, p. B8.

Dillon, S. (1994). "Report finds more violence in the schools." *New York Times,* July 7, pp. B1, B7.

Dobash, R. P., and Dobash, R. E. (1979). *Violence against wives: The case against patriarchy.* New York: Free Press.

———. (1992). *Women, violence, and social change.* New York: Routledge.

Docksai, M. (1979). "Victim/witness intimidation: What it means." *Trial,* August, pp. 51–54.

Dodge, R. (1988). *BJS bulletin: The seasonality of crime.* Washington, DC: U.S. Department of Justice.

Doerner, W. (1978). "An examination of the alleged latent effects of victim compensation programs upon crime reporting." *LAE Journal* 41: 71–80.

Doerner, W., and Lab, S. (1980). "Impact of crime

compensation on victim attitudes toward the criminal justice system." *Victimology* 5(2): 61–77.

Duggan, D. (1994). "Not his day: Error in math puts cop's shooter back in prison." *New York Newsday,* March 11, pp. 3, 44.

Dunlap, D. (1994). "Survey details gay slayings around U.S." *New York Times,* December 21, p. D21.

Dutton-Douglas, M., and Dionne, D. (1991). "Counseling and shelter services for battered women." In M. Steinman (Ed.), *Woman battering: Policy responses* (pp. 113–130). Cincinnati: Anderson.

Ebony Magazine. (1979). *Black on black crime* (Special issue, August).

Eddy, D. (1990). "Supreme Court decides cases involving VOCA, restitution, child witnesses, sobriety checkpoints." *NOVA Newsletter* 14(3): 6.

Edelhertz, H. (1977). "Legal and operational issues in the implementation of restitution in the criminal justice system." In J. Hudson and B. Galaway (Eds.), *Restitution in criminal justice* (pp. 63–76). Lexington, MA: Lexington Books.

Edelhertz, H., and Geis, G. (1974). *Public compensation to victims of crime.* New York: Praeger.

Editors, *New York Times.* (1987). "Paying victims, freeing prisoners." *New York Times,* July 7, p. A26.

———. (1991). "Help for the terrified elderly." *New York Times,* April 2, p. A18.

Edmonds, P. (1994). "One million young victims and counting." *USA Today,* April 7, p. 2A.

Edwards, B. (1994). Humorous news item. May 4 broadcast of "Morning edition." National Public Radio.

Eglash, A. (1977). "Beyond restitution: Creative restitution." In J. Hudson and B. Galaway (Eds.), *Restitution in criminal justice* (pp. 91–100). Lexington, MA: Lexington Books.

Eigenberg, H. (1990). "The *National Crime Survey* and rape: The case of the missing question." *Justice Quarterly* 7: 655–671.

Elias, R. (1983a). *Victims of the system: Crime victims and compensation in American politics and criminal justice.* New Brunswick, NJ: Transaction Books.

———. (1983b). "The symbolic politics of victim compensation." *Victimology* 8(1): 210–219.

———. (1986). *The politics of victimization: Victims, victimology and human rights.* New York: Oxford University Press.

———. (1993). *Victims still: The political manipulation of crime victims.* Newbury Park, CA: Sage.

Ellenberger, H. (1955). "Psychological relationships between the criminal and his victim." *Archives of Criminal Psychodynamics* 2: 257–290.

Estrich, S. (1986). *Real rape.* Cambridge, MA: Harvard University Press.

———. (1993a). "Balancing act." *Newsweek,* October 25, p. 64.

———. (1993b). "The sympathy defense." *New York Times,* October 24, p. E15.

European Committee on Crime Problems. (1978). *Compensation of victims of crime.* Strasbourg, Austria: Author.

Ewing, P. (1987). *Battered women who kill: Psychological self-defense as legal justification.* Lexington, MA: D.C. Heath.

Fagan, J. (1988). "Contributions of family violence research to criminal justice policy on wife assault: Paradigms of science and social control." *Violence and Victims* 3(3): 159–186.

Fagan, J., Piper, E., and Cheng, Y. (1987). "Contributions of victimization to delinquency in inner cities." *Journal of Criminal Law and Criminology* 78(3): 586–611.

Fahn, M. (1991). "Allegations of child sexual abuse in custody disputes: Getting to the truth of the matter." *Family Law Quarterly* (Summer): 16–21.

"A fair chance for young black men." (1989). *New York Times,* April 4, p. A26.

Fairstein, L. (1993). *Sexual violence: Our war against rape.* New York: William Morrow.

Faison, S. (1994). "In a mistake, officer's attacker is briefly freed." *New York Times,* March 11, pp. B1, B2.

"False accusations of abuse devastating to families." (1989). *Crime Victims Digest* 6(2): 4–5.

Faludi, S. (1993). "Whose hype?" *Newsweek,* October 25, p. 61.

Farrell, R., and Swigert, V. (1986). "Adjudication in homicide: An interpretive analysis of the effects of defendant and victim social characteristics." *Journal of Research in Crime and Delinquency* 23(4) (November): 349–369.

Fattah, E. (1967). "Towards a criminological classification of victims." *International Criminal Police Review* 209: 162–169.

———. (1976). "The use of the victim as an agent of self-legitimation: Toward a dynamic explanation of criminal behavior." In Emilio Viano (Ed.), *Victims and society* (pp. 105–129). Washington, DC: Visage.

———. (1979). "Some recent theoretical developments in victimology." *Victimology* 4(2): 198–213.

———. (1986). *From crime policy to victim policy.* New York: St. Martin's Press.

———. (1990). "Victims and victimology: The facts and the rhetoric." *International Review of Victimology* 1(1): 43–66.

———. (1991). *Understanding criminal victimization: An introduction to theoretical victimology.* Scarborough, Ontario: Prentice-Hall Canada.

———. (1992a). *Towards a critical victimology.* New York: St. Martin's Press.

———. (1992b). "The need for a critical victimology." In E. Fattah (Ed.), *Towards a critical victimology* (pp. 3–28). New York: St. Martin's Press.

Faulk, M. (1977). "Men who assault their wives." In M. Roy (Ed.), *Battered women: A psycho-sociological study of domestic violence* (pp. 119–126). New York: Van Nostrand.

Federal Bureau of Investigation (FBI). (1954–1994). *Uniform crime report: Crime in the United States* (selected years, 1953–1993). Washington, DC: U.S. Government Printing Office.

Federal File. (1994). "Bureau of Justice Statistics report." *Law Enforcement News,* April 30, p. 7.

"Federal rape laws revised: Now apply to male victims." (1986). *Crime Victims Digest,* November, p. 10.

"The Feds make it official: For many, the workplace is a dangerous place to be." (1993). *Law Enforcement News,* December 15, p. 5.

Feher, T. (1992). "The alleged molestation victim, the rules of evidence and the Constitution: Should children really be seen and not heard?" In E. Fattah (Ed.), *Toward a critical victimology* (pp. 260–282). Englewood Cliffs, NJ: Prentice-Hall.

Fein, E. (1991). "Decision praised as a victory for free speech rights." *New York Times,* December 11, p. B8.

Felson, M. (1994). *Crime and everyday life.* Thousand Oaks, CA: Pine Forge Press.

Ferraro, K. (1992). "Cops, courts, and woman battering." In P. Bart and E. Moran (Eds.), *Violence against women: The bloody footprints* (pp. 165–176). Newbury Park, CA: Sage.

Ferrigno, R. (1987). "How foreign diplomats get away with crime." *New York Newsday,* October 2, p. 81.

Fingerhut, L., Ingram, D., and Feldman, J. (1992a). "Firearm and non-firearm homicide among persons 15 through 19 years of age." *Journal of the American Medical Association* 267(22) (June 10): 3048–3053.

———. (1992b). "Firearm homicide among black teenage males in metropolitan counties: Comparison of death rates in two periods, 1983 through 1985 and 1987 through 1989." *Journal of the American Medical Association* 267: 3054–3058.

Finkelhor, D. (1990). "Is child abuse overreported?" *Public Welfare* 48(1) (Winter): 20–30.

Finkelhor, D., Hotaling, G., and A. Sedlak (1990). *Missing, abducted, runaway, and thrownaway children in America: First report.* Washington, DC: U.S. Department of Justice, Office of Juvenile Justice and Delinquency Prevention.

Finkelhor, D., and Leatherman, J. (1994). "Victimization of children." *American Psychologist* 49(3) (March): 173–183.

Finkelhor, D., and Yllo, K. (1985). *License to rape: Sexual abuse of wives.* New York: Holt, Rinehart & Winston.

Finn, P. (1991). "Civil protection orders: A flawed opportunity for intervention." In M. Steinman (Ed.), *Woman battering: Policy responses* (pp. 155–190). Cincinnati: Anderson.

Fiora-Gormally, N. (1978). "Battered wives who kill: Double standard out of court, single standard in?" *Law and Human Behavior* 2(2): 133–136.

Firestone, D. (1994). "Van drivers' charges of rape against officer called false." *New York Times,* December 16, pp. B1, B4.

Fisher, I. (1992). "Man shoots assailant, then tries to save him." *New York Times,* March 15: A33.

"Fitting justice? Judges try 'creative' sentences." (1978). *Time,* April 24, p. 56.

Fletcher, G. (1988a). *Bernhard Goetz and the law on trial.* New York: Free Press.

———. (1988b). *A crime of self-defense: Bernhard Goetz and the law on trial.* Chicago: University of Chicago Press.

Flynn, E. (1982). "Theory development in victimology: An assessment of recent progress and of continuing challenges." In H. Schneider (Ed.), *The victim in international perspective* (pp. 96–104). Berlin: de Gruyter.

Follingstad, D., Rutledge, L., McNeill-Harkins, K., and Polek, D. (1992). "Factors related to physical violence in dating relationships." In E. Viano (Ed.), *Intimate violence: Interdisciplinary perspectives* (pp. 121–135). Washington, DC: Hemisphere Publishing.

Fooner, M. (1971). "Money and economic factors in crime and delinquency." *Criminology* 8(4) (February): 311–320.

Forer, L. (1980). *Criminals and victims: A trial judge reflects on crime and punishment.* New York: Norton.

Forst, G., and Hernon, J. (1984). *NIJ research in brief— The criminal justice response to victim harm.* Washington, DC: U.S. Department of Justice.

Forst, M., and Blomquist, M. (1991). *Missing children: Rhetoric and reality.* New York: Lexington Books.

Franklin, B. (1978). *The victim as criminal and artist: Literature from the American prison.* New York: Oxford University Press.

Franklin, C., and Franklin, A. (1976). "Victimology revisited." *Criminology* 14(1): 125–136.

Fraser, C. (1991). "18-shot killing is ruled by jury as self-defense." *New York Times,* July 5, p. B3.

Freedman, L., and Ray, L. (1982). *State legislation on dispute resolution.* Washington, DC: American Bar Association.

Fried, J. (1982). "Intimidation of witnesses called widespread." *New York Times,* May 2, p. S1.

Friedman, L. (1985). "The crime victim movement at its first decade." *Public Administration Review* 45 (November): 790–794.

Friedrichs, D. (1983). "Victimology: A consideration of the radical critique." *Crime and Delinquency* 29(2) (April): 280–290.

Frieze, I., and Browne, A. (1991). "Violence in marriage." In L. Ohlin and M. Tonry (Eds.), *Crime and justice: A review of research, Volume 11: Family violence* (pp. 163–218). Chicago: University of Chicago Press.

Frum, D. (1993). "Women who kill." *Forbes Magazine,* January 18, pp. 20–24.

Fry, M. (1957). "Justice for victims." *London Observer,* November 10, p. 8. Reprinted in *Journal of Public Law* 8 (1959): 191–194.

Fuller, R., and Myers, R. (1941). "The natural history of a social problem." *American Sociological Review* 6 (June): 320–328.

Furstenberg, F. (1972). "Fear of crime and its effect on citizen behavior." In A. Biderman (Ed.), *Crime and justice* (pp. 52–65). New York: Justice Institute.

Galaway, B. (1977). "The uses of restitution." *Crime and Delinquency* 23(1): 57–67.

———. (1987). "Victim-offender mediation as the preferred response to property offenses." In E. Viano (Ed.), *Crime and its victims: International research and public policy issues* (pp. 101–111). New York: Hemisphere.

———. (1989). "Prospects." In M. Wright and B. Galaway (Eds.), *Mediation and criminal Justice: Victims,*

offenders and community (pp. 270–275). Newbury Park, CA: Sage.

———. (1992). "Restitution as innovation or unfilled promise?" In E. Fattah (Ed.), *Toward a critical victimology* (pp. 347–371). New York: St. Martin's Press.

Galaway, B., and Hudson, J. (1975). "Issues in the correctional implementation of restitution to victims of crime." In J. Hudson and B. Galaway (Eds.), *Considering the victim: Readings in restitution and victim compensation* (pp. 351–360). Springfield, IL: Charles C Thomas.

———. (Eds.). (1981). *Perspectives on crime victims.* St. Louis, MO: C.V. Mosby.

Galliher, J., Kunkel, K., and Hobbs, D. (1986). "Media explanations of small-town vigilante murder." *Contemporary Crises* 10: 125–136.

Garbarino, J. (1989). "The incidence and prevalence of child maltreatment." In L. Ohlin and M. Tonry (Eds.), *Crime and justice: A review of research, Volume 11: Family violence* (pp. 219–262). Chicago: University of Chicago Press.

Gardner, R. (1990). *Sex abuse hysteria: Salem witch trials revisited.* Cresskill, NJ: Creative Therapeutics.

———. (1994). "Belated realization of child sex abuse by an adult." In K. de Koster and K. Swisher (Eds.), *Child abuse: Opposing viewpoints* (pp. 217–223). San Diego: Greenhaven Press.

Garfinkle, H. (1949). "Research note on inter- and intra-racial homicides." *Social Forces* 27 (May): 370–381.

Garofalo, J. (1981). "Victimization surveys: An overview." In B. Galaway and J. Hudson (Eds.), *Perspectives on crime victims* (pp. 98–103). St. Louis, MO: C. V. Mosby.

———. (1986). "Lifestyles and victimization: An update." In E. Fattah (Ed.), *From crime policy to victim policy* (pp. 135–155). New York: St. Martin's Press.

Garofalo, J., and Connelly, K. (1980). "Dispute resolution centers: Part 1—Major features and processes; Part 2—Outcomes, issues, and future directions." *Criminal Justice Abstracts,* September, pp. 416–610.

Gartner, A., and Riessman, F. (1980). "Lots of helping hands." *New York Times,* February 19, p. A22.

Gartner, R. (1990). "The victims of homicide: A temporal and cross-national comparison." *American Sociological Review* 55(1) (February): 92–106.

Gaynes, M. (1981). "New roads to justice: Compensating the victim." *State Legislatures,* November-December, pp. 11–17.

Gegan, S., and Rodriguez, N. (1992). "Victims' roles in the criminal justice system: A fallacy of empowerment." *St. John's Journal of Legal Commentary* 8(1) (Fall): 225–250.

Geis, G. (1976). "Compensation to victims of violent crime." In R. Gerber (Ed.), *Contemporary issues in criminal justice* (pp. 90–115). Port Washington, NY: Kennikat.

———. (1977). "Restitution by criminal offenders: A summary and overview." In J. Hudson and B. Galaway (Eds.), *Restitution in criminal justice* (pp. 147–164). Lexington, MA: Lexington Books.

———. (1983). "Victim and witness assistance programs." In *Encyclopedia of Crime and Justice* (pp. 1600–1604). New York: Free Press.

Geller, W. (1992). "Put friendly-fire shooting in perspective." *Law Enforcement News,* December 31, p. 9.

Gelles, R. (1987). *The violent home.* Newbury Park, CA: Sage.

Gelles, R., and Cornell, C. (1990). *Intimate violence in families* (2nd ed.). Newbury Park, CA: Sage.

Gelles, R., and Straus, M. (1988). *Intimate violence.* New York: Touchstone Books.

Gewurz, D., and Mercurio, M. (1992). "The victims' bill of rights: Are victims all dressed up with no place to go?" *St. John's Journal of Legal Commentary* 8(1) (Fall): 251–278.

Giacinti, T. (1973). *Forcible rape: The offender and his victim.* Unpublished master's thesis. Ann Arbor, MI: University Microfilms.

Gibbs, N. (1991). "When is it rape?" *Time,* June 3, pp. 38–40.

———. (1993a). "Hell on wheels." *Time,* August 16, pp. 44–46.

———. (1993b). "Til death do us part." *Time,* January 18, pp. 38–45.

———. (1994). "Death and deceit." *Time,* November 14, pp. 43–48.

Gilbert, N. (1991). "The phantom epidemic of sexual assault." *The Public Interest* 103 (Spring): 54–65.

Gill, J. (1987). "Let's stop fingerprinting kids." *New York Newsday,* August 14, p. 94.

———. (1989). "Missing-kids' groups foster fear rather than facts." *New York Newday,* April 11, p. 65.

Gillespie, C. (1989). *Battered women, self-defense, and the law.* Columbus: Ohio State University Press.

Gilsinan, J. (1989). "911 and the social construction of reality." *Criminology* 27(2): 329–344.

Girdner, L., and Hoff, P. (1994). *Obstacles to the recovery and return of parentally abducted children: Research summary.* Washington, DC: U.S. Department of Justice.

Girelli, S., Resick, P., Dvorak, S., and Hutter, C. (1986). "Subjective distress and violence during rape: Their effects on long term fear." *Victims and Violence* 1(1): 35–46.

Goldberg, S., Green, E., and Sander, F. (1985). *Dispute resolution.* Boston: Little, Brown.

Goldberg-Ambrose, C. (1992). "Unfinished business in rape law reform." *Journal of Social Issues* 48(1): 173–185.

Goldsmith, J., and Goldsmith, S. (1976). *Crime and the elderly: Challenge and response.* Lexington, MA: D. C. Heath.

Goldstein, E. (1993). *Confabulations: Creating false memories, destroying families.* Boca Raton, FL: SIRS Books.

Goldstein, J. (1960). "Police discretion not to invoke the criminal process." *Yale Law Journal* 69 (March): 543–594.

Goleman, D. (1993). "Studies reveal suggestibility of very young as witnesses." *New York Times,* June 11, pp. A1, A23.

———. (1994). "Proof lacking for ritual abuse by satanists." *New York Times,* October 31, p. A13.

———. (1995a). "An elusive picture of violent men who kill their mates." *New York Times,* January 15, p. A22.

———. (1995b). "Studies point to flaws in lineups of suspects." *New York Times,* January 17, pp. C1, C7.

Gondolf, E. (1988). "The state of the debate: A review essay on woman battering." *Response* 11(3): 3–8.

Gonzalez, D. (1992). "Sliwa admits faking crimes for publicity." *New York Times,* November 25, pp. B1, B2.

Goodman, R., Mercy, J., Loya, F., Rosenberg, M., Smith, J., Allen, N., Vargas, L., and Kolts, B. (1986). "Alcohol use and interpersonal violence: Alcohol detected in homicide victims." *American Journal of Public Health* 76(2): 144–148.

"The Good Samaritans." (1965). *New York Times,* November 20, p. 34.

Gordon, L. (1988). *Heroes of their own lives: The politics and history of family violence, Boston, 1880–1960.* New York: Viking.

Gottesman, R., and Mountz, L. (1979). *Restitution: Legal analysis.* Reno, NV: National Council of Juvenile and Family Court Judges.

Gottfredson, M., and Gottfredson, D. (1988). *Decision making in criminal justice: Toward the rational exercise of discretion* (2nd ed.). New York: Plenum.

Governor's Task Force on Bias-Related Violence. (1988). *Final Report*. Albany, NY: Author.

Graham, E. (1993). "Education: Fortress academia sells security." *Wall Street Journal,* October 25, p. B1.

Gray, E. (1986). *Child abuse: Prelude to delinquency?* Washington, DC: U.S. Department of Justice.

Gray, J. (1993). "New Jersey court says victims of car chases cannot sue police." *New York Times,* July 29, pp. B1, B6.

Grayson, B., and Stein, M. (1981). "Attracting assault: Victims' nonverbal clues." *Journal of Communications* 31: 65–70.

Green, E. (1964). "Inter- and intra-racial crime relative to sentencing." *Journal of Criminal Law, Criminology, and Police Science* 55 (September): 348–358.

Green, G. (1987). "Citizen gun ownership and crime deterrence: Theory, research, and policy." *Criminology* 25(1) (February): 63–82.

Greenberg, M., and Ruback, R. (1984). "Elements of crime victim decision making." *Victimology* 10(1): pp. 600–616.

Greenhouse, L. (1989). "Supreme court roundup: First Amendment protects paper that named rape victim, justices rule." *New York Times,* June 22, p. B9.

———. (1990). "Child abuse trials can shield witness." *New York Times,* June 28, pp. A1, B8.

———. (1991). "High court upsets seizing of profits of convict's books." *New York Times,* December 11, pp. A1, B8.

———. (1993). "Justices uphold stiffer sentences for hate crimes." *New York Times,* June 12, pp. A1, A8.

Griffin, S. (1979). *Rape: The power of consciousness*. New York: Harper & Row.

Gross, J. (1990). "203 rape cases reopened in Oakland as the police chief admits mistakes." *New York Times,* September 20, p. A13.

———. (1992). "Abused women who kill now seek way out of cells." *New York Times,* September 15, p. A16.

———. (1993). "California town mourns abducted girl." *New York Times,* December 6, p. A12.

Gutis, P. (1988). "New head of police speaks out." *New York Times,* April 10, sec. 12, p. 2.

Hackett, G., and Cerio, G. (1988). "When the victim goes on trial." *Newsweek,* January 18, p. 31.

Hall, D. (1975). "The role of the victim in the prosecution and conviction of a criminal case." *Vanderbilt Law Review* 28(5): 932–985.

———. (1991). "Victims' voices in criminal court: The need for restraint." *American Criminal Law Review* 28: 233–243

Hall, J. (1935). *Theft, law, and society*. Boston: Little, Brown.

Hall, T. (1990). "Fatal accidents are down as U.S. becomes vigilant." *New York Times,* October 7, pp. A1, A32.

Halleck, S. (1980). "Vengeance and victimization." *Victimology* 5(2): 99–109.

Hanley, R. (1994a). "Crime victims call for hard labor." September 28, p. B6.

——— R. (1994b). "Three lives converge in a killing." *New York Times,* January 5, p. B6.

Harland, A. (1979). "Restitution statutes and cases: Some substantive and procedural restraints." In B. Galaway and J. Hudson (Eds.), *Victims, offenders, and restitutive sanctions* (pp. 151–171). Lexington, MA: Lexington Books.

———. (1981a). *Restitution to victims of personal and household crimes*. Washington, DC: U.S. Department of Justice.

———. (1981b). "Victim compensation: Programs and issues." In B. Galaway and J. Hudson (Eds.), *Perspectives on crime victims* (pp. 412–417). St. Louis, MO: C. V. Mosby.

———. (1983). "One hundred years of restitution: An international review and prospectus for research." *Victimology* 8(1): 190–202.

Harlow, C. (1985). *Reporting crimes to the police. BJS special report*. Washington, DC: U.S. Department of Justice.

———. (1987). *Robbery victims. BJS special report*. Washington, DC: U.S. Department of Justice.

———. (1988). *Motor vehicle theft. BJS special report*. Washington, DC: U.S. Department of Justice.

———. (1991). *Female victims of violent crime. BJS special report*. Washington, DC: U.S. Department of Justice.

Harrington, C. (1985). *Shadows justice: The ideology and institutionalization of alternatives to court*. Westport, CT: Greenwood Press.

Harris, M. (1979). *Sentencing to community service*. Washington, DC: American Bar Association.

Harshbarger, S. (1987). "Prosecution is an appropriate response in child sexual abuse cases." *Journal of Interpersonal Violence* (March): 108–112.

Hass, N., and Washington, F. (1994). "A new lease on life." *Newsweek,* April 4, pp. 42–43.

"Hawaii return-witness program turns tide against crime." (1982). *Criminal Justice Newsletter,* June 7, p. 1.

Hays, C. (1988). "Charges dropped against seven in fatal beating." *New York Times,* June 28, p. B1.

———. (1992). "Family to get $1.5 million in slaying by mental patient." *New York Times,* July 29, p. B6.

Heinz, A., and Kerstetter, W. (1979). "Pretrial settlement conference: Evaluation of a reform in plea bargaining." *Law and Society Review* 13(2): 349–366.

Heinz, J. (1982). "On justice to victims." *New York Times,* July 7, p. A19.

Hellerstein, D. (1989). "The victim impact statement: Reform or reprisal?" *American Criminal Law Review* 27: 390–434.

Hellman, P. (1993). "Crying rape: The politics of date rape on campus." *New York Magazine,* March 8, pp. 32–37.

"Help for the terrified elderly." *New York Times,* April 2, p. A18.

Henderson, G. (1924). *Keys to crookdom.* New York: Appleton.

Henderson, L. (1985). "Victim's rights and wrongs." *Stanford Law Review* 37: 937–1021.

Hendricks, J. (1992). "Domestic violence legislation in the United States: A survey of the states." In E. Viano (Ed.), *Intimate violence: Interdisciplinary perspectives* (pp. 213–228). New York: Hemisphere.

Herman, J. (1981). *Father-daughter incest.* Cambridge, MA: Harvard University Press.

———. (1992). *Trauma and recovery.* New York: Basic Books.

Herrington, L. (1982). "Statement of the chairman." In the President's Task Force on Victims of Crime, *Final report* (pp. vi–vii). Washington, DC: U.S. Government Printing Office.

———. (1986). "Dollars and sense: The value of victim restitution." *Corrections Today,* August, pp. 156–160.

Hester, T. (1987). *BJS bulletin: Probation and parole, 1986.* Washington, DC: U.S. Department of Justice.

Hickey, E. (1991). *Serial murderers and their victims.* Pacific Grove, CA: Brooks/Cole.

Hills, S. (1981). *Demystifying deviance.* Englewood Cliffs, NJ: Prentice-Hall.

Hilton, N. (1993). *Legal responses to wife assault: Current trends and evaluation.* Newbury Park, CA: Sage.

Hilts, P. (1994). "6% of women admit beatings while pregnant." *New York Times,* March 3, pp. A1, A23.

Hindelang, M., Gottfredson, M., and Garofalo, J. (1978). *Victims of personal crime: An empirical foundation for a theory of personal victimization.* Cambridge, MA: Ballinger.

Hinds, M. (1988). "The new fashioned way to steal money: Fake credit." *New York Times,* December 31, p. A28.

Hochstedler, E. (1981). *Crime against the elderly in twenty-six cities.* Washington, DC: U.S. Department of Justice.

Hoffman, J. (1994). "May it please the public: Lawyers exploit media attention as a defense tactic." *New York Times,* April 22, pp. B1, B7.

Hofstadter, R., and Wallace, M. (1970). *American violence: A documentary history.* New York: Knopf.

Holloway, L. (1994). "Impersonators bearing badges of dishonor." *New York Times,* November 12, pp. B1, B28.

———. (1995). "Despite the bitter cold, many homeless resist the shelters." *New York Times,* February 8, p. B3.

Holmes, R. (1994). *Murder in America.* Newbury Park, CA: Sage.

Holmes, R., and DeBurger, J. (1988). *Serial murder.* Newbury Park, CA: Sage.

"Homicide also up sharply in NYC and other areas." (1988). *Law Enforcement News,* December 31, p. 1.

Hook, S. (1972). "The rights of the victims: Thoughts on crime and compassion." *Encounter,* April, pp. 29–35.

Hoover, J. (1994). *Technical background on the redesigned National Crime Victimization Survey.* Washington, DC: U.S. Department of Justice, BJS.

Hoover, J. E. (1966). "The car theft problem: How you can help beat it." *Congressional Record: Senate,* September 22, p. 23621.

Horn, M. (1993). "Memories lost and found." *U.S. News & World Report,* November 29, pp. 52–63.

Hotaling, G., Finkelhor, D., Kirkpatrick, J., and Straus M. (1988). *Coping with family violence: Research on policy perspectives.* Newbury Park, CA: Sage.

House Subcommittee on Health and Long-Term Care, Select Committee on Aging. (1992). *Hearings on elder abuse.* Washington, DC: U.S. Department of Justice.

Howell, J. (1989). *Selected state legislation: A guide for effective state laws to protect children* (2nd ed.). Washington, DC: National Center for Missing and Exploited Children.

Hudson, J., and Chesney, S. (1978). "Research on restitution: A review and assessment." In B. Galaway and J. Hudson (Eds.), *Offender restitution in theory and action* (pp. 131–148). Lexington, MA: Lexington Books.

Hudson, J., and Galaway, B. (1975). *Considering the victim: Readings in restitution and victim compensation.* Springfield, IL: Charles C Thomas.

Hughes, R. (1993). *Culture of complaint: The fraying of America.* New York: Oxford University Press.

Hunzeker, D. (1992). "Stalking laws." *National Conference of State Legislatures' State Legislative Report,* 17(19): 1–6.

Incantalupo, T. (1988). "Auto alarms: Keeping the thieves at bay." *New York Newsday,* April 22, p. 49.

Inciardi, J. (1976). "The pickpocket and his victim." *Victimology* 1(3): 446–453.

Ingrassia, M., and Beck, M. (1994). "Patterns of abuse." *Newsweek,* July 4, pp. 26–33.

Irwin, T. (1980). *To comabat and prevent child abuse and neglect.* New York: Public Affairs Committee.

Island, D., and Letellier, P. (1991). *Men who beat the men who love them.* New York: Harrington Park Press.

Jacob, B. (1977). "The concept of restitution: An historical overview." In J. Hudson and B. Galaway (Eds.), *Restitution in criminal justice* (pp. 45–62). Lexington, MA: Lexington Books.

James, G. (1988). " Serious crime up 3.4 % in New York City. " *New York Times,* March 23, pp. Bl, B6.

———. (1989). "Movie fan is killed in theater argument over a popcorn line." *New York Times,* July 4, p. 33.

———. (1990). "Bronx jurors fail to indict in slaying." *New York Times,* November 28, pp. B1, B3.

———. (1993). "Finding help in New York: Step 1, smash a police car." *New York Times,* June 14, p. B4.

Jankowski, L. (1991). *Probation and parole, 1990. Bureau of Justice Statistics Bulletin.* Washington, DC: U.S. Department of Justice.

Janofsky, M. (1994). "The 'why' of youth's fatal beating in Philadelphia is elusive." *New York Times,* December 5, p. A16.

Jeffrey, C. (1971). *Crime prevention through environmental design.* Beverly Hills, CA: Sage.

Jennings, K. (1986). "Dispute on abuse survey." *New York Newsday,* August 12, p. D3.

Jensen, G., and Brownfield, D. (1986). "Gender, lifestyles, and victimization: Beyond routine activity." *Violence and Victims* 1(2): 85–99.

Jensen, G., and Karpos, M. (1993). "Managing rape: Exploratory research on the behavior of rape statistics." *Criminology* 31: 363–385.

Johann, S., and Osanka, F. (1989). *Representing battered women who kill.* Springfield, IL: Charles C Thomas.

Johnson, G. (1941). "The Negro and crime." *Annals of the American Academy of Political and Social Science* 217: 93–104.

Johnson, J. (1989). "Horror stories and the construction of child abuse." In J. Best (Ed.), *Images of issues: Typifying contemporary social problems* (pp. 5–19). New York: Aldine de Gruyter.

Jones, A. (1980). *Women who kill.* New York: Fawcett Columbine Books.

Jones, C. (1993). "Man released in killing of 2 in Brooklyn." *New York Times,* November 16, pp. B1, B3.

"Justice by the numbers." (1993). *Law Enforcement News,* December 31, p. 27.

Kalish, C. (1988). *BJS special report: International crime rates.* Washington, DC: U.S. Department of Justice.

Kalven, H., and Zeisel, H. (1966). *The American Jury.* Boston: Little, Brown.

Kanin, E. (1984). "Date rape: Unofficial criminals and victims." *Victimology* 9(1): 95–108.

Kantrowitz, B., Starr, M., and Friday, C. (1991). "Naming names." *Newsweek,* April 29, pp. 27–32.

Kappeler, V., Blumberg, M., and Potter, G. (1993). *The mythology of crime and criminal justice.* Prospects Heights, IL: Waveland.

Karlen, N., Greenberg, N., Gonzalez, D., and Williams, E. (1985). "How many missing kids?" *Newsweek,* October 7, pp. 32–33.

Karmen, A. (1979). "Victim facilitation: The case of auto theft." *Victimology* 4(4): 361–370.

———. (1980). "Auto theft: Beyond victim blaming." *Victimology* 5(2): 161–174.

———. (1981a). "Auto theft and corporate irresponsibility." *Contemporary Crises* 5: 63–81.

———. (1981b). *Crime victims and Congress.* Paper presented at the meeting of the Academy of Criminal Justice Sciences, Philadelphia, February.

———. (1989). "Crime victims and the news media: Questions of fairness and ethics." In J. Sullivan and J. Victor (Eds.), *Annual editions: Criminal justice 1988–1989* (pp. 51–57). Guilford, CT: Dushkin Publishing Group.

———. (1990). "The implemetation of victims' rights: A challenge for criminal justice professionals." In R. Muraskin (Ed.), *Issues in justice: Exploring policy issues in the criminal justice system* (pp. 46–57). Bristol, IN: Wyndham Hall.

———. (1992). "Who's against victims' rights? The nature of the opposition to pro–victim initiatives in criminal justice." *St. John's Journal of Legal Commentary* 8(1) (fall): 157–176.

———. (1995). "Towards the institutionalization of a new kind of justice professional: The victim advocate." *The Justice Professional* 9(1): 1–16.

Kates, D. (1986). *Firearms and violence: Issues of public policy.* New York: Ballinger.

Katz, L. (1980). *The justice imperative: An introduction to criminal justice.* Cincinnati: Anderson.

Kelly, R. (1983). "Addicts and alcoholics as victims." In D. MacNamara and A. Karmen (Eds.), *Deviants: Victims or victimizers?* (pp. 49–76). Newbury Park, CA: Sage.

Kendall-Tackett, K., Williams, L., and Finkelhor, D. (1993). "Impact of sexual abuse on children: A review and synthesis of recent empirical studies." *Psychological Bulletin* (January).

Kerr, P. (1992). "Blatant fraud pushing up the cost of car insurance." *New York Times,* February 6, pp. A1, D6.

Kesler, J. (1992). *How to keep your car from being stolen.* Houston, Texas: Shell Oil Company.

Keve, P. (1978). "Therapeutic uses of restitution." In B. Galaway and J. Hudson (Eds.), *Offender restitution in theory and action* (pp. 59–64). Lexington, MA: Lexington Books.

"Kidnapping summons city to action." (1993). *New York Times,* October 15, p. A24.

Kilpatrick, D. (1985). "Survey analyzes responses of female sex assault victims." *Crime Victims Digest,* February, p. 9.

———. (1992). *Rape in America.* Fort Worth, TX: National Victim Center.

Kincaid, J. (1993). "Purity, pedastry and a fallen heroine." *New York Times,* June 1, p. A17.

King, P. (1993). "Not so different, after all." *Newsweek,* October 4, p. 75.

King, W. (1989). "Violent racism attracts new breed: Skinheads." *New York Times,* January 1, p. A35.

Kirkwood, C. (1993). *Leaving abusive partners.* Newbury Park, CA: Sage.

Klaus, P. (1994). *Costs of crime to victims. BJS crime data briefs.* Washington, DC: U.S. Department of Justice.

Klaus, P., DeBerry, M., and Timrots, A. (1985). *BJS bulletin: The crime of rape.* Washington, DC: U.S. Department of Justice.

Kleck, G. (1991). *Point blank: Guns and violence in America.* New York: Aldine de Gruyter.

Kleck, G., and DeLone, M. (1993). "Victim resistance

and offender weapon effects in robbery." *Journal of Quantitative Criminology* 9(1): 55–81.

Klein, A. (1988). *Alternative sentencing.* Cincinnati: Anderson.

Knudten, M., Knudten, R., and Meade, A. (1978). "Will anyone be left to testify?" In E. Flynn and J. Conrad (Eds.), *The new and the old criminology* (pp. 207–222). New York: Praeger.

Kolarik, G. (1992). "Stalking laws proliferate." *ABA Journal* (November): 35–36.

Koppel, H. (1987). *Lifetime likelihood of victimization: Bureau of Justice Statistics technical report.* Washington, DC: U.S. Department of Justice.

Kornbluth, J. (1987). "The woman who beat the Klan." *New York Times Magazine,* November 1, pp. 26–39.

Koss, M. (1992). "The underdetection of rape: Methodological choices influence incidence estimates." *Journal of Social Issues* 48(1): 61–75.

Koss, M., Gidyez, C., and Wisniewski, N. (1987). "The scope of rape: Incidence and prevalence of sexual aggression and victimization in a national sample of higher education students." *Journal of Consulting and Clinical Psychology* 55: 162–170.

Koss, M., and Harvey, M. (1991). *The rape victim: Clinical and community interventions.* Newbury Park, CA: Sage.

Kotecha, K., and Walker, J. (1976). "Vigilantism and the American police." In J. Rosenbaum and P. Sederberg (Eds.), *Vigilante politics* (pp. 158–174). Philadelphia: University of Pennsylvania Press.

Krauss, C. (1994). "New York car theft draws police priority." *New York Times,* January 23, pp. 21, 26.

Kristal, A. (1991). "You've come a long way baby: The battered woman's syndrome revisited." *New York Law School Journal of Human Rights* 9: 111–116.

Krueger, F. (1985). "Violated." *Boston,* May, pp. 138–141.

Kuhl, A. (1986). "Implications of justifiable homicide verdicts for battered women." *Response* 9(2): 6–10.

La Fave, W. (1965). *Arrest: The decision to take a suspect into custody.* Boston: Little, Brown.

LaFree, G. (1989). *Rape and criminal justice.* Santa Fe: University of New Mexico Press.

Lamborn, L. (1968). "Toward a victim orientation in criminal theory." *Rutgers Law Review* 22: 733–768.

———. (1985). "The impact of victimology on the criminal law in the United States." *Canadian Community Law Journal* 8: 23–43.

Land, K., McCall, P., and Cohen, L. (1990). "Structural

covariates of homicidal rates: Are there any invariances across time and social space?" *American Journal of Sociology* 95(4) (January): 922–963.

Lander, E. (1988). "Rough sex defense assailed." *New York Newsday,* May 11, p. 26.

Laner, M., and Thompson, J. (1982). "Abuse and aggression in courting couples." *Deviant Behavior* 3: 229–244.

Langan, P. (1985). *BJS special report: The risk of violent crime.* Washington, DC: U.S. Department of Justice.

Langan, P., and Graziadei, H. (1995). *Felony sentences in state coursts, 1992. Bureau of Justice Statistics Bulletin.* Washington, DC: U.S. Department of Justice.

Langan, P., and Harlow, C. (1994). *BJS crime data brief: Child rape victims, 1992.* Washington, DC: U.S. Department of Justice.

Langan, P., and Innes, C. (1986). *BJS special report: Preventing domestic violence against women.* Washington, DC: U.S. Department of Justice.

Langan, P., Perkins, C., and J. Chaiken. (1994). *Felony sentences in the United States, 1990. Bureau of Justice Statistics Bulletin.* Washington, DC: U.S. Department of Justice.

Lanning, K. (1992). *Child sex rings: A behavioral analysis.* Arlington, VA: National Center for Missing and Exploited Children.

Largen, M. (1981). "Grassroots centers and national task forces: A herstory of the anti-rape movement." *Aegis* 32 (Autumn): 46–52.

———. (1987). "A decade of change in the rape reform movement." *Response* 10(2): 4–9.

Lasch, C. (1982). "Why the 'survival mentality' is rife in America." *U.S. News & World Report,* May 17, pp. 59–60.

Laster, R. (1970). "Criminal restitution: A survey of its past history and analysis of its present usefulness." *University of Richmond Law Review* 5: 71–98.

Leary, W. (1993). "Guns in home? Study finds it a deadly mix." *New York Times,* October 7, p. A18.

Lederer, L. (1980). *Take back the night.* New York: Morrow.

Lederman, D. (1994). "Crime on the campuses." *Chronicle of Higher Education,* February 2, A31–A42.

Leepson, M. (1982). "Helping victims of crime." *Editorial Research Reports* 1(17): 331–344.

LeGrande, C. (1973). "Rape and rape laws: Sexism in society and law." *California Law Review* 61: 919–941.

Lehnen, R., and Skogan, W. (1981). *The national crime survey: Working papers: Vol. 1. Current and historical perspectives.* Washington, DC: U.S. Department of Justice.

Leo, J. (1994). "Watching 'As the jury turns.' " *U.S. News & World Report,* February 14, p. 17.

Leone, B., and de Koster, K. (1995). *At issue: Rape on campus.* San Diego: Greenhaven Press.

Lerner, M. (1965). "Evaluation of performance as a function of performer's reward and attractiveness." *Journal of Personality and Social Psychology* 1: 355–360.

Letkemann, P. (1973). *Crime as work.* Englewood Cliffs, NJ: Prentice-Hall.

Levin, J., and McDevitt, J. (1993). *Hate crimes: The rising tide of bigotry and bloodshed.* New York: Plenum.

Levine, J. (1976). "The potential for crime overreporting in criminal victimization surveys." *Criminology* 14(2): 307–331.

Lewin, T. (1992). "Battered men sounding equal-rights battle cry." *New York Times,* April 20, p. A12.

———. (1993a). "New laws address old problem: The terror of a stalker's threats." *New York Times,* February 8, pp. A1, B10.

———. (1993b). "Rape and the accuser: A debate still rages on citing sexual past." *New York Times,* Feb. 12, p. B16.

Libai, D. (1969). "The protection of the child victim of a sexual offense in the criminal justice system." *Wayne Law Review* 15: 977–1032.

Libbey, P., and Bybee, R. (1979). "The physical abuse of adolescents." *Journal of Social Issues* 35(2): 101–126.

Lindner, C., and Koehler, R. (1992). "Probation officer victimization: An emerging concern." *Journal of Criminal Justice* 20(1): 53–62.

"Line-of-duty deaths continue their upward trend in the '90s." (1994). *Law Enforcement News,* January 15, p. 5.

Lipman, I. (1982). "Ways to protect yourself from burglars, muggers." *U.S. News & World Report,* December 13, pp. 77–78.

Lisefski, E., and Manson, D. (1988). *BJS bulletin: Tracking offenders, 1984.* Washington, DC: U.S. Department of Justice.

Lockwood, D. (1980). *Prison sexual violence.* New York: Elsevier.

Loftin, C. (1986). "The validity of robbery-murder classifications in Baltimore." *Violence and Victims* 1(3): 191–202.

Loftus, E., and Ketcham, K. (1994). *The myth of repressed memory: False memories and allegations of sexual abuse.* New York: St. Martin's Press.

Loseke, D. (1989). "Violence is 'violence' . . . or is it? The social construction of 'wife abuse' and public policy." In J. Best (Ed.), *Images of issues: Typifying contemporary social problems* (pp. 191–206). New York: Aldine de Gruyter.

Lourie, I. (1977). "The phenomenon of the abused adolescent: A clinical study." *Victimology* 2(2): 268–276.

Lubenow, G. (1983). "When kids kill their parents." *Newsweek,* June 27, pp. 35–36.

Luckenbill, D. (1977). "Criminal homicide as a situated transaction." *Social Problems* 25: 176–186.

Lundman, R. (1980). *Police and policing: An introduction.* New York: Holt, Rinehart & Winston.

Lundsgaarde, H. (1977). *Murder in space city: A cultural analysis of Houston homicide patterns.* New York: Oxford University Press.

Lurigio, A. (1990). *Victims of crime: Problems, policies and programs.* Newbury Park, CA: Sage.

Lyall, S. (1989). "Rape charge is dropped in case at L. I. School." *New York Times,* May 11, p. B1.

Lynch, R. (1976). "Improving the treatment of victims: Some guides for action." In W. MacDonald (Ed.), *Criminal justice and the victim* (pp. 165–176). Beverly Hills, CA: Sage.

Lynn, W. (1981). "What scientists really mean by 'acceptable risk.' " *U.S. News & World Report,* March 30, p. 60.

MacDonald, J. (1971). *Rape: Offenders and victims.* Springfield, IL: Charles C Thomas.

MacNamara, D., and Sullivan, J. (1974). "Making the victim whole: Composition, restitution, and compensation." In T. Thornberry and E. Sagarin (Eds.), *Images of crime: Offenders and victims* (pp. 79–90). New York: Praeger.

Madison, A. (1973). *Vigilantism in America.* New York: Seabury Press.

Maghan, J., and Sagarin, E. (1983). "Homosexuals as victimizers and victims." In D. MacNamara and A. Karmen (Eds.), *Deviants: Victims or victimizers?* (pp. 147–162). Newbury Park, CA: Sage.

Maguire, K., and Pastore, A. (1994). *BJS sourcebook of criminal justice statistics—1993.* Washington, DC: U.S. Government Printing Office.

Maguire, K., Pastore, A., and Flanagan, T. (1993). *Bureau of Justice Statistics Sourcebook of Criminal Justice Statistics—1992.* Washington, DC: U.S. Department of Justice.

Maier, T. (1984). "Teller hands it over, loses job." *Long Island Newsday,* June 8, p. 4.

Makepeace, J. (1981). "Courtship violence among college students." *Family Relations* 30: 97–102.

Maltz, W., and Holman, B. (1986). *Incest and sexuality: A guide to understanding and healing.* New York: Free Press.

Mannheim, H. (1965). *Comparative criminology.* Boston: Houghton Mifflin.

Manshel, L. (1990). *Nap time.* New York: Kensington.

Mansnerus, L. (1989). "The rape laws change faster than perceptions." *New York Times,* February 19, Sec. 5, p. 20.

Margolick, D. (1994). "Does Mrs. Bobbitt count as another battered wife?" *New York Times,* January 16, p. E5.

Marriott, M. (1989). "With a 'Remember me?' man shoots 3 in subway." *New York Times,* June 12, p. B2.

———. (1991). ". . . And thefts bedevil car renters." *New York Times,* November 16, p. 48.

Martin, D. (1976). *Battered wives.* San Francisco: Glide.

———. (1989). "The line of duty: Special officers help their own." *New York Times,* June 7, p. B1.

Martinson, R. (1974). "What works—questions and answers about prison reform." *Public Interest* 35 (Spring): 22–54.

Martz, L., Miller, M., Hutchinson, S., Emerson, T., and Washington, F. (1989). "A tide of drug killing." *Newsweek,* January 16, pp. 44–45.

Martz, L., Starr, M., and Barrett, T. (1990). "A murderous hoax." *Newsweek,* January 22, pp. 16–21.

Marx, G., and Archer, D. (1976). "Community police patrols and vigilantism." In J. Rosenbaum and P. Sederberg (Eds.), *Vigilante politics* (pp. 129–157). Philadelphia: University of Pennsylvania Press.

Mash, E., and Wolfe, D. (1991). "Methodological issues in research on physical child abuse." *Criminal Justice and Behavior* 18(1) (March): 8–29.

Mathews, A. (1993). "The campus crime wave." *New York Times Magazine,* March 7, pp. 38–47.

Mawby, R., and Walklate, S. (1993). *Critical victimology: International perspectives.* Newbury Park, CA: Sage.

Maxfield, M. (1987). "Household composition, routine activity, and victimization: A comparative analysis." *Journal of Quantitative Criminology* 3: 301–320.

Mayhew, P., and Hough, M. (1988). "The British crime survey: Origins and impact." In M. Maguire and J. Pointing (Eds.), *Victims of crime: A new deal?* (pp. 156–163). Philadelphia: Open University Press.

McCaghy, C. (1980). *Crime in American society.* New York: Macmillan.

McCaghy, C., Giordano, P., and Henson, T. (1977). "Auto theft: Offenders and offense characteristics." *Criminology* 15 (November): 367–385.

McCahill, T., Williams, L., and Fischman, A. (1979). *The aftermath of rape.* Lexington, MA: Lexington Books.

McCormack, R. (1991). "Compensating victims of violent crime." *Justice Quarterly* 8(3): 329–346.

McDermott, J. (1979). *Rape victimization in 26 American cities.* Washington, DC: U.S. Government Printing Office.

McDonald, D. (1988). *NIJ crime file study guide: Restitution and community service.* Washington, DC: U.S. Department of Justice.

McDonald, W. (1976). "Criminal justice and the victim." In W. McDonald (Ed.), *Criminal justice and the victim* (pp. 17–56). Beverly Hills, CA: Sage.

———. (1977). "The role of the victim in America." In R. Barnett and J. Hagel III (Eds.), *Assessing the criminal: Restitution, retribution, and the legal process* (pp. 295–307). Cambridge, MA: Ballinger.

———. (1978). "Expanding the victim's role in the disposition decision: Reform in search of rationale." In B. Galaway and J. Hudson (Eds.), *Offender restitution in theory and action* (pp. 101–110). Lexington, MA: Lexington Books.

———. (1979). "The prosecutor's domain." In W. McDonald (Ed.), *The prosecutor* (pp. 15–52). Beverly Hills, CA: Sage.

McFadden, R. (1993a). "Armored car suspect confirmed inside job." *New York Times,* February 5, pp. B1, B4.

———. (1993b). "A stranger is stabbed saving a life." *New York Times,* May 14, p. B3.

McGillis, D. (1982). "Minor dispute processing: A review of recent developments." In R. Tomasic and M. Feeley (Eds.), *Neighborhood justice: Assessment of an emerging idea* (pp. 60–76). New York: Longman.

———. (1986). *NIJ issues and practices: Crime victim restitution: An analysis of approaches.* Washington, DC: U.S. Department of Justice.

McGillis, D., and Smith, P. (1983). *Compensating victims of crime: An analysis of American programs.* Washington, DC: U.S. Department of Justice.

McGrath, K., and Osborne, M. (1989). "Redressing violence against elders." *NOVA Newsletter* 13(2): 1, 4, 5.

McIntyre, D. (1968). "A study of judicial dominance of the charging decision." *Journal of Criminal Law, Criminology, and Police Science* 59 (December): 463–490.

McKinley, J. (1991). "Merchant and burglar die in police shootout." *New York Times,* May 3, p. B3.

McKnight, D. (1981). "The victim-offender reconciliation project." In B. Galaway and J. Hudson (Eds.), *Perspectives on crime victims* (pp. 292–298). St. Louis, MO: C.V. Mosby.

McLarin, K. (1994). "Fear prompts self-defense as crime comes to college." *New York Times,* September 7, pp. A1, B11.

McQuiston, J. (1994). "Woman says police forced her to deny holdup report." *New York Times,* February 21, p. B4.

Meiners, R. (1978). *Victim compensation: Economic, political and legal aspects.* Lexington, MA: D. C. Heath.

Mendelsohn, B. (1940). "Rape in criminology." Translated and cited in S. Schafer (1968), *The victim and his criminal.* New York: Random House.

———. (1956). "The victimology." *Etudes Internationales de PsychoSociologie Criminelle,* July, pp. 23–26.

Menninger, K. (1968). *The crime of punishment.* New York: Viking Press.

Merrill, L. (1994). "A defense that won't go away." *New York Daily News,* April 7, p. 6.

Messner, S., and Golden, R. (1992). "Racial inequality and racially disaggregated homicide rates: An assessment of alternative theoretical explanations." *Criminology* 30(3) (Aug.): 421–447.

Messner, S., and Tardiff, K. (1985). "The social ecology of urban homicide: An application of the 'routine activities' approach." *Criminology* 23: 241–267.

Miers, D. (1989). "Positivist victimology: A critique." *International Review of Victimology* 1: 3–22.

Miethe, T., Stafford, M., and Sloane, D. (1990). "Lifestyle changes and risks of criminal victimization." *Journal of Quantitative Criminology* 6(4): 357–375.

Miller, F. (1970). *Prosecution: The decision to charge a suspect with a crime.* Boston: Little, Brown.

Miller, S. (1992). "Arrest policies for domestic violence and their implications for battered women." In R. Muraskin and T. Alleman, (Eds.), *It's a crime: Women and justice* (pp. 334–359). Englewood Cliffs, NJ: Regents/Prentice Hall.

Milner, J. (1991). "Introduction: Current perspectives on physical child abuse." *Criminal Justice and Behavior* 18(1) (March): 4–7.

Mitchell, A. (1992). "Strange school ties: A near fatal student-teacher pact." *New York Times,* October 23, p. B3.

Mithers, C. (1990). "Incest and the law." *New York Times Magazine,* October 21, pp. 44–63.

Mones, P. (1991). *When a child kills: Abused children who kill their parents.* New York: Simon & Schuster.

Moore, E., and Mills, M. (1990). "The neglected victims and unexamined costs of white collar crime." *Crime and Delinquency* 36(3): 408–418.

Moore, L. (1985). "Your home: Make it safe." *Security Management,* March, pp. 115–116.

Morganthau, T., and Shenitz, B. (1994). "Too many guns? Or too few?" *Newsweek,* August 15, pp. 44–45.

Mothers Against Drunk Driving (MADD). (1988). "Victim rights: How far have we come?" *Maddvocate,* Spring, p. 13.

Muehlenhard, C., Powch, I., Phelps, J., and Giusti, L. (1992). "Definitions of rape: Scientific and political implications." *Journal of Social Issues* 48(1): 23–44.

Mueller, G., and Cooper, H. (1973). *The criminal, society, and the victim.* Washington, DC: National Criminal justice Reference Service.

Munson, D. (1989). *The child victim as a witness: OJJDP update on research.* Washington, DC: U.S. Department of Justice.

Mydans, S. (1994). "The other Menendez trial, too, ends with the jury deadlocked." *New York Times,* January 29, pp. A1, A8.

Myers, M. (1977). *The effects of victim characteristics on the prosecution, conviction, and sentencing of criminal defendants.* Unpublished doctoral dissertation. Ann Arbor, MI: University Microfilms.

Myers, M., and Hagan, J. (1979). "Private and public trouble: Prosecutors and the allocation of court resources." *Social Problems* 26(4): 439–451.

Myrdal, G. (1944). *An American dilemma: The Negro problem and modern democracy.* New York: Harper & Row.

National Advisory Commission on Criminal Justice Standards and Goals. (1973). *The courts.* Washington, DC: U.S. Government Printing Office.

National Center for Child Abuse and Neglect (NCCAN). (1978). *Child sexual abuse: Incest, assault and sexual exploitation.* Washington, DC: U.S. Department of Health, Education, and Welfare.

National Center for Missing and Exploited Children (NCMEC). (1985). "Safe recovery of baby girl tribute to partnership in missing child search." Press release, December 16.

———. (1986). *State legislation to protect children: An update on the nation's progress to implement effective laws preventing child victimization.* Washington, DC: Author.

———. (1987). *Accomplishing great things.* Washington, DC: Author.

National Commission on the Causes and Prevention of Violence (NCCPV). (1969a). *Crimes of violence.* Washington, DC: U.S. Government Printing Office.

———. (1969b). *The offender and his victim.* (Staff report by D. Mulvihill, L. Curtis, and M. Tumin). Washington, DC: U.S. Government Printing Office.

National Committee for Prevention of Child Abuse (NCPCA). (1993). *Current trends in child abuse reporting and fatalities.* Chicago: National Committee.

National Crime Prevention Institute. (1978). *Understanding crime prevention.* Louisville, KY: Author.

National Institute of Justice (NIJ). (1984). *Vehicle theft prevention strategies.* Washington, DC: U.S. Government Printing Office.

National Insurance Crime Bureau. (1993). "The public speaks out on fraud and theft." *Spotlight on Insurance Crime* 2(3) (Winter): 1–2.

———. (1995). "Eye on insurance crime." *Spotlight on Insurance Crime* 3(3) (Winter): 8–9.

National Organization for Victim Assistance (NOVA). (1988). *Victim rights and services: A legislative directory—1987.* Washington, DC: Author.

———. (1989). "Bipartisan victim rights bill introduced in U.S. Congress." *NOVA Newsletter* 13(3): 1, 5.

———. (1991). "U.N. convention on the rights of the child." *NOVA Newsletter* 15(1): 1–9.

National Victim Center (NVC). (1990). *Crime victims and corrections.* Fort Worth, TX: Author.

———. (1991a). *America speaks out: Citizens' attitudes about victims' rights and violence.* Fort Worth, TX: NVC.

———. (1991b). *National victim services survey of adult and juvenile corrections and parole agencies.* Final report. Fort Worth, TX: NVC.

———. (1992a). *Infoline: Constitutional rights for crime victims.* Fort Worth, TX: NVC.

———. (1992b). "Restitution statutes." *Infoline* 1(58): 1–4.

———. (1993). *Civil justice for crime victims.* Fort Worth, TX: NVC.

Neidig, P. (1984). "Women's shelters, men's collectives and other issues in the field of spouse abuse." *Victimology* 9(3–4): 464–476.

Neubauer, D. (1974). *Criminal justice in middle America.* Morristown, NJ: General Learning Press.

"The new American epidemic." (1994). *Law Enforcement News,* November 30, p. 7.

Newberger, E. (1987). "Prosecution: A problematic approach to child abuse." *Journal of Interpersonal Violence* (March): 112–117.

Newman, D. (1966). *Conviction: The determination of guilt or innocence without trial.* Boston: Little, Brown.

Newman, M. (1992). "Gang fatally beats a mistaken target, Bronx witness says." *New York Times,* August 20, pp. A1, B3.

Newman, O. (1972). *Defensible space: People and design in the violent city.* London: Architectural Press.

"New studies say single crime can inflict $41,000 in injury." (1994). *Crime Victims Digest* 11(1) (January): 9.

New York Police Department (NYPD), (1992). *Auto theft: A growing business.* New York Police Department Auto Crime Division.

New York State Crime Victims Board. (1988). *Annual report, 1987–88.* Albany, NY: Author.

New York State Law Enforcement Council. (1994). *Legislative proposals, 1994.* New York: Author.

"NICB study shows vehicle theft trends." (1993). *Corporate Security Digest* 6(31) (August 3): 1–2.

Nicholson, E. (Ed.). (1988). *Sexual abuse allegations in custody and visitation cases.* Washington, DC: American Bar Association.

Nieves, E. (1994). "Prosecutors drop charges in abuse case from mid-80s." *New York Times,* December 3, pp. A25, A29.

Normandeau, A. (1968). "Patterns in robbery." *Criminologica,* November, pp. 2–15.

Nossiter, A. (1994a). "A daughter's death, a father's guilt." *New York Times,* November 10, p. A24.

———. (1994b). "Judge awards damages in Japanese youth's death." *New York Times,* September 16, p. A12.

O'Brien, R. (1985). *Crime and victimization data.* Beverly Hills, CA: Sage.

Ochberg, F. (1978). "The victim of terrorism: Psychiatric considerations." *Terrorism, An International Journal* 1(2): 147–167.

"Offenders get wrists slapped: Car thefts total a million a year." (1975). *Salem* (Massachusetts) *News,* October 2, p. 2.

Ofshe, R., and Watters, E. (1993). *Making monsters: False memories, psychotherapy, and sexual hysteria.* New York: Scribners.

Ohlin, L., and Tonry, M. (1989). "Family violence in perspective." In L. Ohlin and M. Tonry (Eds.), *Crime and justice: A review of research, Volume 11: Family violence* (pp. 1–18). Chicago: University of Chicago Press.

O'Neill, T. (1984). "The good, the bad, and the Burger court: Victims' rights and a new model of criminal review." *Journal of Criminal Law and Criminology* 75(2): 363–387.

Onishi, N. (1994). "Stray gunfire kills man in Bronx." *New York Times,* May 26, p. B3.

Orcutt, J., and Faison, R. (1988). "Sex-role attitude change and reporting of rape victimization, 1973–1985." *Sociological Quarterly* 29: 589–604.

Pagelow, M. (1984a). *Family violence.* New York: Praeger.

———. (1984b). *Women battering: Victims and their experiences.* Beverly Hills, CA: Sage.

———. (1989). "The incidence and prevalence of criminal abuse of other family members." In L. Ohlin and M. Tonry (Eds.), *Crime and justice: A review of research, Volume 11: Family violence* (pp. 263–313). Chicago: University of Chicago Press.

Paglia, C. (1993). Interview on CBS's *Sixty Minutes.* August 1.

———. (1994). *Vamps and tramps.* New York: Vintage.

Parent, D., Auerbach, B., and Carlson, K. (1992). *Compensating crime victims: A summary of policies and practices.* Washington, DC: U.S. Department of Justice.

Parsonage, W. (Ed.). (1979). *Perspectives on victimology.* Beverly Hills, CA: Sage.

Paternoster, R. (1984). "Prosecutorial discretion in requesting the death penalty: A case of victim based racial discrimination." *Law and Society Review* 18: 437–478.

Payne, L. (1989). "Her boyfriend says: Tawana made it up." *New York Newsday,* April 27, pp. 1, 3.

Peak, K. (1986). "Crime victim reparation: Legislative revival of the offended ones." *Federal Probation,* September, pp. 36–41.

Pendergrast, M. (1994). *Victims of memory: Incest accusations and shattered lives.* San Francisco: Upper Access.

Pepinsky, H. (1991). "Peacemaking in criminology and criminal justice." In H. Pepinsky and R. Quinney (Eds.), *Criminology as peacemaking* (pp. 299–327). Bloomington: Indiana University Press.

Perez, J. (1994). *Tracking offenders, 1990. Bureau of Justice Statistics Bulletin.* Washington, DC: U.S. Department of Justice.

Perez-Pena, R. (1993). "Victim sues to prevent crime from paying $4.8 million." *New York Times,* December 16, p. B3.

Peters, D., Wyatt, G., and Finkelhor, D. (1986). "Prevalence." In D. Finkelhor (Ed.), *A sourcebook on child sexual abuse* (pp. 50–60). Beverly Hills, CA: Sage.

Pfohl, S. (1984). "The discovery of child abuse." In D. Kelly (Ed.), *Deviant behavior* (pp. 45–65). New York: St. Martin's Press.

Pierre-Pierre, G. (1993). "Brooklyn woman arrested in shooting of teenager." *New York Times,* July 31, p. A25.

Plate, T. (1975). *Crime pays.* New York: Simon & Schuster.

Pleck, E. (1989). "Criminal approaches to family violence, 1640–1980." In L. Ohlin and M. Tonry (Eds.), *Crime and justice: An annual review of research, vol. 11: Family violence.* (pp. 19–57). Chicago: University of Chicago Press.

Pleck, E., Pleck, J., Grossman, M., and Bart, P. (1978). "The battered data syndrome: A comment on Steinmetz' article." *Victimology* 2(4): 680–684.

Podhoretz, N. (1991). "Rape in feminist eyes." *Commentary,* October, pp. 30–36.

"Police chief and others do not fit victim stereotypes." (1993). *Crime Victims Digest,* September, pp. 6–7.

Pollitt, K. (1989). "Violence in a man's world." *New York Times Magazine,* June 18, pp. 16, 20.

———. (1991). "Naming and blaming: The media goes wild in Palm Beach." *The Nation,* June 24, pp. 833, 847–852.

Porter, E. (1986). *Treating the young male victim of sexual assault: Issues and intervention strategies.* Syracuse, NY: Safer Society Press.

President's Task Force on Victims of Crime. (1982). *Final report.* Washington, DC: U.S. Government Printing Office.

Press, A., Copeland, J., Contreras, J., Camper, D., Agrest, S., Newhall, E., Monroe, S., Young, J., and Mattland, T. (1981). "The plague of violent crime." *Newsweek,* March 23, pp. 46–54.

Press, A., McCormick, J., and Wingert P. (1994). "Overview: A crime as American as a Colt .45." *Newsweek,* August 15, pp. 22–43.

Prestia, K. (1993). *Chocolates for the pillows—Nightmares for the guests.* Silver Spring, MD: Bartleby Press.

Prison Research and Action Project. (1976). *Instead of prisons.* Genesee, NY: Author.

"Prosecutorial discretion in the initiation of criminal complaints." (1969). *Southern California Law Review* 42 (Spring): 519–545.

Purdum, T. (1986). "Link is sought in 5 City U. robberies." *New York Times,* February 19, p. B3.

———. (1988). "The reality of crime on campus." *New York Times Education Supplement,* Sec. 12, April 10, pp. 47–51.

Purdy, M. (1994). "Workplace murders provoke lawsuits and better security." *New York Times,* February 14, pp. A1, B5.

Purnick, J. (1986). "Manes retracts story and says he cut himself." *New York Times,* January 22, p. 1.

Quinn, M., and Tomita, S. (1986). *Elder abuse and neglect: Causes, diagnosis, and intervention strategies.* New York: Springer.

Rand, M. (1993). *Crime and the nation's households, 1992. Bureau of Justice Statistics Bulletin.* Washington, DC: U.S. Department of Justice.

———. (1994a). *Carjacking: Bureau of Justice Statistics crime data brief.* Washington, DC: U.S. Department of Justice.

———. (1994b). *Guns and crime.* Bureau of Justice Statistics Crime Data Brief. Washington, DC: U.S. Department of Justice.

Ranish, D., and Shichor, D. (1985). "The victim's role in the penal process: Recent developments in California." *Federal Probation,* March, pp. 50–56.

Raskin, L. (1968). "A heist a minute." *Nation,* April 7, pp. 434–436.

Rauber, M. (1991). "Rape victims get a legal break." *New York Post,* May 21, p. 22.

Ray, L. (1984). "Dispute resolution: 'A muffled explosion.' " *NIJ Reports* 185 (May): 9.

Reaves, B. (1993). *National incident-based reporting system: Using NIBRS data to analyze violent crime. Bureau of Justice Statistics Technical Report.* Washington, DC: U.S. Department of Justice.

Reckless, W. (1967). *The crime problem.* New York: Appleton-Century-Crofts.

Reiff, R. (1979). *The invisible victim.* New York: Basic Books.

Reilly, J. (1981). "Victim/witness services in prosecutor's offices." *The Prosecutor,* October, pp. 8–11.

Reiman, J. (1990). *The rich get richer and the poor get prison: Ideology, class, and criminal justice* (3rd ed.). New York: Wiley.

Reiss, A. (1971). *The police and the public.* New Haven, CT: Yale University Press.

———. (1981). "Toward a revitalization of theory and research on victimization by crime." *Journal of Criminal Law and Criminology* 72(2): 704–713.

———. (1986). "Official and survey statistics." In E. Fattah (Ed.), *From crime policy to victim policy* (pp. 53–79). New York: St. Martin's Press.

Renzetti, C. (1992). *Violent betrayal: Partner abuse in lesbian relationships.* Newbury Park, CA: Sage.

"Report finds 'Crisis of children killing children.'" (1994). *Crime Victims Digest,* (January), p. 3.

Rhode, D. (1989). *Justice and gender: Sex discrimination and the law.* Cambridge, MA: Harvard University Press.

Rhodes, N. (1992). "The assessment of spousal abuse: An alternative to the conflict tactics scale." In E. Viano (Ed.), *Intimate violence: Interdisciplinary perspectives* (pp. 27–36). Washington, DC: Hemisphere Publishing.

Rhodes, W. (1978). *Plea bargaining: Who gains? Who loses?* (PROMIS Research Project No. 14). Washington, DC: Institute for Law and Social Research.

Richardson, J., Best, J., and Bromley, D. (Eds.). (1991). *The satanism scare.* New York: Aldine de Gruyter.

Riedel, M. (1987). "Stranger violence: Perspectives, issues, and problems." *Journal of Criminal Law* 78(2): 223–259.

Riedel, M., and Mock, L. (1985). *NIJ report: The nature and patterns of American homicide.* Washington, DC: U.S. Government Printing Office.

Rittenmeyer, S. (1981). "Of battered wives, self-defense and double standards of justice." *Journal of Criminal Justice* 9 (5): 389–396.

Roberts, A. (1990). *Helping crime victims.* Newbury Park, CA: Sage.

Roberts, S. (1987). "Criminals, authors, and criminal authors." *New York Times Book Review,* March 22, pp. 1, 34–35.

———. (1989). "When crimes become symbols." *New York Times,* March 7, Sec. 4, pp. 1, 28.

Robin, G. (1977). "Forcible rape: Institutionalized sexism in the criminal justice system," *Crime and Delinquency,* April, pp. 136–152.

Robin, M. (1991). "The social construction of child abuse and 'false allegations.'" *Child and Youth Services* 15, 1–34.

Roche, J. (1967). "Statement to Senate." *Congressional Record: Senate,* March 22, p. 7594.

Roehl, J., and Ray, L. (1986). "Toward the multi-door courthouse: Dispute resolution intake and referral." *NIJ Reports* 198 (July): 2–7.

Rohter, L. (1993a). "Fearful of tourism decline, Florida offers assurances on safety." *New York Times,* September 16, p. A14.

———. (1993b). "Tourist is killed in Florida despite taking precautions." *New York Times,* September 9, p. A16.

Roiphe, K. (1993). *The morning after: Sex, fear, and feminism on campus.* Boston: Little, Brown.

Rootsaert, D. (1987). *A prosecutor's guide to victim/witness assistance.* Alexandria, VA: National District Attorneys Association.

Rose, V. (1977). "Rape as a social problem: A by-product of the feminist movement." *Social Problems* 25 (October): 75–89.

Rosenthal, E. (1990). "U.S. is by far the homicide capital of the industrialized nations." *New York Times,* June 27, p. A10.

Ross, R., and Staines, G. (1972). "The politics of analyzing social problems." *Social Problems* 20 (Summer): 18–40.

Roth, J. (1994). *Firearms and violence.* National Institute of Justice Research in Brief. Washington, DC: U.S. Department of Justice.

Rottenberg, D. (1980). "Crime victims fight back." *Parade,* March 16, pp. 21–23.

Roy, S. (1990). "Offender-oriented restitution bills: Bringing total justice to victims?" *Federal Probation,* September, pp. 30–35.

Russell, D. (1975). *The politics of rape: The victim's perspective.* New York: Stein & Day.

———. (1982). *Rape in marriage.* New York: Macmillan.

———. (1984). *Sexual exploitation: Rape, child molestation, and workplace harassment.* Newbury Park, CA: Sage.

———. (1986). *The secret trauma: Incest in the lives of girls and women.* New York: Basic Books.

———. (1990). *Rape in marriage.* Bloomington: Indiana University Press.

Ryan, W. (1971). *Blaming the victim.* New York: Vintage.

Sachs, A. (1994). "Now for the movie." *Time,* January 31, p. 99.

Sagarin, E. (1975). "Forcible rape and the problem of the rights of the accused." *Intellect,* May-June, pp. 515–520.

Salzinger, S., Feldman, R., and Hammer, M. (1991). "Risk for physical child abuse and the personal consequences for its victims." *Criminal Justice and Behavior* 18(1) (March): 64–81.

Sanchez, R. (1994). "Fake cops' crime wave." *Long Island Newsday,* January 28, p. 31.

Sanderson, B. (1994). "Crime compensation little and late in N.J." *Bergen County Sunday Record,* November 6, pp. A1, A16.

Sargeant, G. (1991). "Battered woman syndrome gaining legal recognition." *Trial* 27(4) (April): 17–20.

Sarnoff, S. (1993). *A national study of policies and administrative methods of state crime victim compensation programs.* Unpublished doctoral dissertation, Adelphi University School of Social Work.

Saunders, D. (1986). "When battered women use violence: Husband-abuse or self-defense?" *Victims and Violence* 1(1): 47–59.

Savitz, L. (1982). "Official statistics." In L. Savitz and N. Johnston (Eds.), *Contemporary criminology* (pp. 3–15). New York: Wiley.

———. (1986). "Obscene phone calls." In T. Hartnagel and R. Silverman (Eds.), *Critique and explanation: Essays in honor of Gwynne Nettles* (pp. 149–158). New Brunswick, NJ: Transaction Books.

Sawyer, S. (1987). "Law enforcement officers and their families face special difficulties when victimized." *NOVA Newsletter,* 11(11) (November): 1–2.

Schafer, S. (1968). *The victim and his criminal.* New York: Random House.

———. (1970). *Compensation and restitution to victims of crime* (2nd ed.). Montclair, NJ: Patterson Smith.

———. (1977). *Victimology: The victim and his criminal.* Reston, VA: Reston Publishers.

Schanberg, S. (1984). "The rape trial." *New York Times,* March 27, p. A31.

———. (1989) "We should be outraged at all rapes." *New York Newsday,* April 28, pp. 94–95.

Schechter, S. (1982). *Women and male violence.* Boston: South End Press.

Scherer, J. (1982). "An overview of victimology." In J. Scherer and G. Shepherd (Eds.), *Victimization of the weak: Contemporary social reactions* (pp. 8–30). Springfield, IL: Charles C Thomas.

Schmitt, E. (1994). "Military struggling to stem an increase in family violence." *New York Times,* May 23, pp. A1, A12.

Schneider, A. (1981). "Methodological problems in victim surveys and their implications for research in victimology." *Journal of Criminal Law and Criminology* 72(2): 818–830.

Schneider, A., and Schneider, P. (1978). *Private and public-minded citizen responses to a neighborhood crime prevention strategy.* Eugene, OR: Institute of Policy Analysis.

———. (1981). "Victim assistance programs." In B. Galaway and J. Hudson (Eds.), *Perspectives on crime victims* (pp. 364–373). St. Louis, MO: C.V. Mosby.

Schneider, E. (1980). "Equal rights to trial for women: Sex bias in the law on self-defense." *Harvard Civil Rights and Civil Liberties Review* 15: 623–647.

———. (1991). "The violence of privacy." *The Connecticut Law Review* 23: 973–999.

Schneider, H. (Ed.). (1982). *The victim in international perspective.* New York: Walter DeGruyter.

Schneider, P. (1987). "Lost innocents: The myth of missing children." *Harper's Magazine,* February, pp. 47–53.

Schreiber, L, (1990). "Campus rape." *Glamour,* September, pp. 23–26.

Schultz, L. (1965). "The violated: A proposal to compensate victims of violent crime." *St. Louis University Law Journal* 10: 238–250.

———. (1968). "The victim-offender relationship." *Crime and Delinquency* 14: 135–141.

Schur, E. (1984). *Labeling women deviant: Gender, stigma, and social control.* New York: Random House.

Schwendinger, H., and Schwendinger, J. (1967). "Delinquent stereotypes of probable victims." In M. Klein (Ed.), *Juvenile gangs in context* (pp. 92–105). Englewood Cliffs, NJ: Prentice-Hall.

———. (1974). "Rape myths in legal, theoretical, and everyday practice." *Crime and Social Justice* 1: 18–26.

Seelye, K. (1995). "A life saved, a life lost: Gun issue gets personal." *New York Times,* April 1, p. A26.

Seligmann, J. and Maor, Y. (1980). "Punishments that fit the crime." *Newsweek,* August 4, p. 60.

Senate Committee on the Judiciary (1993). *Report: The violence against women act of 1993.* Washington, DC: U.S. Senate.

Senate Judiciary Committee (Majority Staff) (1993). *The response to rape: Detours on the road to equal justice.* Washington, DC: U.S. Senate.

Sexton, J. (1994). "Brooklyn drivers fear reckless young guns." *New York Times,* December 3, pp. A1, A26.

Shapiro, L., Rosenberg, D., Lauerman, J, and Sparkman, R. (1993). "Rush to judgment." *Newsweek,* April 19, 54–60.

Shelden, R. (1982). *Criminal justice in America: A sociological approach.* Boston: Little, Brown.

Sheley, J. (1979). *Understanding crime: Concepts, issues, decisions.* Belmont, CA: Wadsworth.

Shelton, S. (1992). "New law curbs inmates' book, movie profits." *Long Island Newsday,* August 14, p. 22.

Sheridan, R. (1994). "The false child molestation outbreak of the 1980s: An explanation of the cases arising in the divorce context." In K. de Koster and K. Swisher (Eds.), *Child abuse: Opposing viewpoints* (pp. 48–55). San Diego: Greenhaven Press.

Sherman, L. (1986). *NIJ crime file: Domestic violence.* Washington, DC: U.S. Department of Justice.

Sherman, L., and Berk, R. (1984). "The specific deterrent effects of arrest for domestic assault." *American Sociological Review* 49 (April): 261–272.

Sherman, L., Berk, R., and Smith, D. (1992). "Crime, punishment, and stake in conformity: Legal and informal control of domestic violence." *American Sociological Review* 57 (October): 680–690. Washington, DC: Police Foundation.

Sherman, L., Gartin, P., and Buerger, M. (1989). "Hot spots of predatory crime: Routine activities and the criminology of place." *Criminology* 27(1) (February): 27–40.

Sherman, L., Steele, L., Laufersweiler, D., Hoffer, N., and Julian, S. (1989). "Stray bullets and 'mushrooms': Random shootings of bystanders in four cities, 1977–1988." *Journal of Quantitative Criminology* 5: 297–316,

Shipp, E. (1987). "Defense lawyers' tactics: Unfair or just aggressive?" *New York Times,* April 21, pp. BI, B4.

Shotland, L. (1976). "Spontaneous vigilantism: A bystander response to criminal behavior." In J. Rosenbaum and P. Sederberg (Eds.), *Vigilante politics* (pp. 30–44). Philadelphia: University of Pennsylvania Press.

Siegel, J., Sorenson, S., Golding, J., Burnham, M., and Stein, J. (1987). "The prevalence of childhood sexual assault." *American Journal of Epidemiology* 126: 1141–1153.

Siemaszko, C. (1994). "Blaming rape victims: Women's dress invites attack, suspect says." *New York Daily News,* April 7, p. 6.

Silberman, C. (1978). *Criminal violence, criminal justice.* New York: Random House.

Silberman, M. (1995). *A world of violence: Corrections in America.* Belmont, CA: Wadsworth.

Silverman, R. (1974). "Victim precipitation: An examination of the concept." In I. Drapkin and E. Viano (Eds.), *Victimology: A new focus* (pp. 99–110). Lexington, MA: D. C. Heath.

Silving, H. (1959). "Compensation for victims of criminal violence—a roundtable." *Journal of Public Law* 8: 236–253.

Simon, D. (1991). *Homicide: A year on the killing streets.* New York: Fawcett Columbine.

Sinason, V. (1994). *Treating survivors of satanist abuse.* New York: Routledge.

Singer, S. (1981). "Homogeneous victim-offender populations: A review and some research implications. *Journal of Criminal Law and Criminology* 72(2): 779–788.

———. (1986). "Victims of serious violence and their criminal behavior: Subcultural theory and beyond." *Violence and Victims* 1(1): 61–70.

Skogan, W. (1978). *Victimization surveys and criminal justice planning.* Washington, DC: U.S. Government Printing Office.

———. (1981a). "Assessing the behavioral context of victimization." *Journal of Criminal Law and Criminology* 72(2): 727–742.

———. (1981b). *Issues in the measurement of victimization.* Washington, DC: U.S. Department of Justice.

———. (1986). "Methodological issues in the study of victimization." In F. Fattah (Ed.), *From crime policy to victim policy* (pp. 80–116). New York: St. Martin's Press.

———. (1987). "The Impact of police on victims." In E. Viano (Ed.), *Crime and its victims: International research and public policy issues* (pp. 71–77). New York: Hemisphere.

Skogan, W., and Maxfield, M. (1981). *Coping with crime: Individual and neighborhood reactions.* Beverly Hills, CA: Sage.

Sloane, L. (1991). "Rising fraud worrying car insurers . . ." *New York Times,* November 16, p. 48.

Smith, B. (1985). "Trends in the victims' rights movement and implications for future research." *Victimology* 10(1–4): 34–43.

Smith, B., Sloan, J., and Ward, R. (1990). "Public support for the victim's rights movement: Results of a statewide survey." *Crime and Delinquency* 36(4): 488–502.

Smith, K. (1994). "Outrage over new attack by freed N.J. kid molester." *New York Post,* September 19, p. 6.

Smith, M. (1988). *Coping with crime on campus.* New York: American Council on Education (ACE).

Smith, S. (1994). "Have screwdriver, will steal." *Car and Driver,* July, pp. 157–167.

Smith, S., and Freinkel, S. (1988). *Adjusting the balance: Federal policy and victim services.* New York: Greenwood Press.

Snell, J., Rosenwald, R., and Robey, A. (1964). "The wifebeater's wife: A study of family interaction." *Archives of General Psychiatry* 11 (August): 107–112.

Snyder, J. (1993). "A nation of cowards." *The Public Interest,* (Spring).

Sorenson, S., and White, J. (1992). "Adult sexual assault:

Overview of research." *Journal of Social Issues* 48(1): 1–8.

Southern Regional Council. (1969). *Race makes the difference: An analysis of sentence disparity among black and white offenders in southern prisons.* Atlanta: Author.

Sparks, R. (1981). "Multiple victimization: Evidence, theory and future research." *Journal of Criminal Law and Criminology* 72(2): 762–778.

Spector, M., and Kitsuse, J. (1987). *Constructing social problems.* New York: Aldine de Gruyter.

Spelman, W., and Brown, D. (1984). *NIJ report: Calling the police: Citizen reporting of serious crime.* Washington, DC: U.S. Department of Justice.

Spitzer, N. (1986). "The children's crusade." *Atlantic,* June, pp. 18–22.

Spohn, C., and Horney, J. (1992). *Rape law reform: A grassroots revolution and its impact.* New York: Plenum.

Stark, J., and Goldstein, H. (1985). *The rights of crime victims: An American Civil Liberties Union handbook.* New York: Bantam Books.

Steinman, M. (1991). "The public policy process and woman battering: Problems and pitfalls." In M. Steinman (Ed.), *Woman battering: Policy responses* (pp. 1–18). Cincinnati: Anderson.

Steinmetz, S. (1978a). "The battered husband syndrome." *Victimology* 2(4): 499–509.

———. (1978b). "Battered parents." *Society* 15(5): 54–55.

———. (1988). *Duty bound: Elder abuse and family care.* Newbury Park, CA: Sage.

Stephens, M. (1988). *A history of the news.* New York: Penguin.

Stets, J., and Pirog-Good, M. (1987). "Violence in dating relationships." *Social Psychology Quarterly* 50: 237–246.

Stillman, F. (1987). *NIJ Research in brief. Line-of-duty deaths: Survivor and departmental responses.* Washington, DC: U.S. Department of Justice.

Stone, L. (1984). "Shelters for battered women: A temporary escape from danger or the first step toward divorce?" *Victimology* 9(1): 284–289.

Straus, M. (1978). "Wife beating: "How common and why?" *Victimology* 2(4): 443–458.

———. (1991). "Conceptualization and measurement of battering: Implications for public policy." In M. Steinman (Ed.), *Woman battering: Policy responses* (pp. 19–42). Cincinnati: Anderson.

Straus, M., and Gelles, R. (1986). "Societal change and change in family violence from 1975 to 1985." *Journal of Marriage and the Family* 48: 20–30.

———. (1990). *Physical violence in American families.* New Brunswick, NJ: Transaction.

Straus, M., Gelles, R., and Steinmetz, S. (1980). *Behind closed doors: Violence in the American family.* New York: Doubleday.

"Street sentence: Vigilante justice in Buffalo." (1983). *Time,* August 15, p. 15.

"Study shows intimidation of witnesses affects verdicts." (1990). *New York Amsterdam News,* October 3, p. 18.

Sullivan, A. (1993). "Gay values, truly conservative." *New York Times,* February 9, p. A21.

Sykes, C. (1992). *A nation of victims: The decay of the American character.* New York: St. Martin's Press.

Sykes, G., and Matza, D. (1957). "Techniques of neutralization: A theory of delinquency." *American Sociological Review* 22: 664–670.

Symonds, M. (1975). "Victims of violence: Psychological effects and after-effects." *American Journal of Psychoanalysis* 35(1): 19–26.

———. (1980a). "Acute responses of victims to terror." *Evaluation and Change* (special issue): 39–42.

———. (1980b). "The 'second injury' to victims." *Evaluation and Change* 7(1): 36–38.

Taibbi, M., and Sims-Phillips, A. (1989). *Unholy alliances.* San Diego: Harcourt Brace.

Tardiff, K., Gross, E., and Messner, S. (1986). "A study of homicides in Manhattan, 1981." *American Journal of Public Health* 76(2): 139–145.

Task Force on Assessment. (1967). "The victims of crime." In The President's Commission on Law Enforcement and Administration of Justice, *Task force report: Crime and its impact—an assessment* (pp. 80–84). Washington, DC: U.S. Government Printing Office.

Tavris, C. (1993). "Beware the incest survivor machine." *New York Times Book Review,* January 3, pp. 1, 16–17.

Taylor, B. (1989). *Redesign of the national crime survey.* Washington, DC: U.S. Department of Justice.

Taylor, R. (1983). "Beyond bars: Instead of jail, one county in New York imposes sentences of work, reparations, or 'house arrest.'" *Wall Street Journal,* December 23, p. 28.

Teevan, J. (1979). "Crime victimization as a neglected social problem." *Sociological Symposium* 25: 6–22.

Terr, L. (1994). *Unchained memories: True stories of traumatic memories, lost and found.* New York: Basic.

Thomason, T., and Babbili, A. (1987). *Crime victims and the news media.* Fort Worth: Texas Christian University Department of Journalism.

Thompson, M. (1984). "MADD curbs drunk drivers." *Victimology* 9(1): 191–192.

Thyfault, R. (1984). "Self-defense: Battered woman syndrome on trial." *California Western Law Review* 20: 485–510.

Timrots, A., and Rand, M. (1987). *BJS special report: Violent crime by strangers and non-strangers.* Washington, DC: U.S. Department of Justice.

Timrots, A., and Snyder, E. (1994). *Drugs and crime facts, 1993.* Drugs and crime data center and clearinghouse. Washington, DC: U.S. Department of Justice, BJS.

Tittle, C. (1978). "Restitution and deterrence: An evaluation of compatibility." In B. Galaway and J. Hudson (Eds.), *Offender restitution in theory and action* (pp. 33–158). Lexington, MA: Lexington Books.

Toby, J. (1983). "Violence in school." In M. Tonry and N. Morris (Eds.), *Crime and justice: An annual review of research* (Volume 4) (pp. 1–47). Chicago: University of Chicago Press.

Tomasson, R. (1991). "Man acquitted in shooting at courthouse." *New York Times,* July 26, pp. B1, B16.

Travelers Insurance Company. (1977). "Your car's a steal in more ways than one." Hartford, CT: Author.

Treanor, W. (1986). "The missing children's act has been misused, abused." *Juvenile Justice Digest,* August 25, pp. 7–10.

Trescott, P. (1987). *Diplomatic crimes.* Washington, DC: Acropolis Books.

Triebwasser, J. (1986). "Court says you can't run from restitution." *Law Enforcement News,* June 28, pp. 6, 8.

———. (1987a). "Court leaves death penalty alive and well." *Law Enforcement News,* June 9, p. 5.

———. (1987b). "Victims' non-impact on sentence." *Law Enforcement News,* September 29, p. 5.

Turner, J. (1990). "Preparing individuals at risk for victimization as hostages." In E. Viano (Ed.), *The victimology handbook: Research findings, treatment, and public policy* (pp. 217–226). New York: Garland.

Umbreit, M. (1987). "Mediation may not be as bad as you think; some victims do benefit." *NOVA Newsletter,* March, pp. 1–2, 6.

———. (1989). "Violent offenders and their victims." In M. Wright and B. Galaway (Eds.), *Mediation and criminal justice: Victims, offenders and community* (pp. 99–112). Newbury Park, CA: Sage.

———. (1990). "Victim-offender mediation with violent offenders: Implications for modifications of the VORP model." In E. Viano (Ed.), *The victimology*

handbook: Research findings, treatment, and public policy (pp. 337–352). New York: Garland.

———. (1994). "Victim empowerment through mediation: The impact of victim offender mediation in four cities." *Perspectives* (American Probation and Parole Association), Special Issue (Summer), pp. 25–28.

———. (1995). "Restorative justice: Implications for organizational change." *Federal Probation* 59 (1, March): 47–54.

Umbreit, M., and Coates, P. (1993). "Cross-site analysis of victim-offender mediation in four states." *Crime and Delinquency* 39: 565–585.

Uniform Crime Reports Section. FBI. (1993). *Law enforcement officers killed and assaulted, 1992.* Washington, DC: U.S. Department of Justice.

U.S. Attorney General's Advisory Board on Missing Children. (1986). *America's missing and exploited children: Their safety and their future.* Washington, DC: U.S. Department of Justice.

U.S. Congress Senate Committee on the Judiciary. Subcommittee to Investigate Juvenile Delinquency. (1954). *Hearings.* 83rd Cong., 2nd sess., January 15. Washington, DC: U.S. Government Printing Office.

U.S. House Committee on the Judiciary. (1980). *Victims of Crime Act of 1979: Report together with dissenting and separate views.* 96th Cong., 2nd sess., February 13. Washington, DC: U.S. Government Printing Office.

"U.S. Supreme Court holds: No constitutional duty to protect." (1989). *NOVA Newsletter* 13(2): p. 6.

Vachss, A. (1993). *Sex crimes.* New York: Random House.

Van Ness, D. (1990). "Restorative justice." In B. Galaway and J. Hudson, (Eds.), *Criminal justice, restitution and reconciliation* (pp. 7–14). Monsey, NY: Willow Tree Press.

Verhovek, S. (1995). "States seek to let citizens carry concealed weapons." *New York Times,* March 6, pp. A1, B8.

Viano, E. (1976). *Victims and society.* Washington, DC: Visage.

———. (1983). "Victimology: The development of a new perspective." *Victimology* 8 (1–2): 17–30.

———. (1987). "Victim's rights and the constitution: Reflections on a bicentennial." *Crime and Delinquency* 33: 438–451.

———. (1989). "Victimology today: Major issues in research and public policy." In E. Viano (Ed.), *Crime and its victims: International research and public policy issues* (pp. 3–16). New York: Hemisphere Publishing.

———. (1990a). Introduction, "Victimology: A new focus of research and practice." In E. Viano (Ed.), *The victimology handbook: Research findings, treatment, and public policy* (pp. xi–xii). New York: Garland.

———. (1990b). "The recognition and implementation of victim's rights in the United States: Developments and achievements." In E. Viano (Ed.), *The victimology handbook: Research findings, treatment, and public policy* (pp. 319–336). New York: Garland.

———. (1992). "Violence among intimates: Major issues and approaches." In E. Viano (Ed.), *Intimate violence: Interdisciplinary perspectives* (pp. 3–12). New York: Hemisphere.

Villmoare E., and Neto, V. (1987). *NIJ research in brief: Victim appearances at sentencing under California's victims' bill of rights.* Washington, DC: U.S. Department of Justice.

Vollmer, A., and Parker, A. (1936). *The police and modern society.* San Francisco: University of California Press.

Volpe, M. (1989). "The police role." In M. Wright and B. Galaway (Eds.), *Mediation and criminal justice: Victims, offenders and community* (pp. 229–240). Newbury Park, CA: Sage.

Von Hentig, H. (1941). "Remarks on the interaction of perpetrator and victim." *Journal of Criminal Law, Criminology, and Police Science* 31 (March-April): 303–309.

———. (1948). *The criminal and his victim: Studies in the sociobiology of crime.* New Haven, CT: Yale University Press.

Von Hirsch, A. (1988). "Punishment to fit the criminal." *The Nation,* June 25, pp. 901–902.

Voss, H., and Hepburn, J. (1968). "Patterns in criminal homicide in Chicago." *Journal of Criminal Law, Criminology, and Police Science* 59: 499–508.

Walker, L. (1984). *The battered woman syndrome.* New York: Springer.

Walker, S. (1982). "What have civil liberties ever done for crime victims? Plenty!" *ACJS (Academy of Criminal Justice Sciences) Today,* October, pp. 4–5.

———. (1994). *Sense and nonsense about crime and drugs: A policy guide* (3rd ed.). Belmont, CA: Wadsworth.

Walklate, S. (1991). "Researching victims of crime: Critical victimology." *Social Justice* 17(3): 25–42.

Waller, I., and Okihiro, N. (1978). *Burglary: The victim and the public.* Toronto: University of Toronto Press.

Walsh, A. (1992). "Placebo justice: Victim recommenda-tions and offender sentences in sexual assault cases." In E. Fattah (Ed.), *Toward a critical victimology* (pp. 295–311). New York: St. Martin's Press.

Walsh, M., and Schram, D. (1980). "The victim of white collar crime: Accuser or accused." In G. Geis and E. Stotland (Eds.), *White collar crime* (pp. 32–51). Beverly Hills, CA: Sage.

"Warned not to testify, theft victim is shot." (1991). *New York Times,* June 25, p. B5.

Warner, J., and Burke, V. (1987). *National directory of juvenile restitution programs.* Washington, DC: U.S. Department of Justice.

Warrior, B. (1977). "Transition house shelters battered women." *Sister Courage* (Boston), February, p. 12.

Warshaw, R. (1988). *I never called it rape.* New York: Harper & Row.

Webster, B. (1988). *Victim assistance programs report in-creased workloads.* National Institute of Justice, Re-search in Action. Washington, DC: U.S. Department of Justice.

Weigend, T. (1983). "Problems of victim/witness assis-tance programs." *Victimology* 8(3): 91–101.

Weinberg, S. (1955). *Incest behavior.* New York: Citadel Press.

Weinraub, B. (1994). "Michael Jackson settles suit for sum said to be in millions." *New York Times,* January 26, pp. A1, A18.

Weis, K., and Borges, S. (1973). "Victimology and rape: The case of the legitimate victim." *Issues in Criminol-ogy* 8(2): 71–115.

Wells, R. (1990). "Considering victim impact: The role of probation." *Federal Probation,* September. pp. 26–29.

Wertham, F. (1949). *The show of violence.* New York: Doubleday.

Wexler, R. (1984). "Genesee justice." *Empire State Report,* March, pp. 43–46.

———. (1990). *Wounded innocents: The real victims of the war against child abuse.* Buffalo: Prometheus Books.

"When judges make the punishment fit the crime." (1978). *U.S. News & World Report,* December 11, pp. 44–46.

"Where's the car?" (1992). *U.S. News & World Report,* March 30, p. 51.

Whitaker, C. (1989). *BJS special report: The redesigned National Crime Survey: Selected new data.* Washington, DC: U.S. Department of Justice.

———. (1990). *Black victims. Bureau of Justice Statistics*

Special Report. Washington, DC: U.S. Department of Justice.

Whitcomb, D. (1986). *NIJ research in action: Prosecuting child sexual abuse: New approaches.* Washington, DC: U.S. Department of Justice.

———. (1988). *Evaluation of programs for the effective prosecution of child physical and sexual abuse.* Washington, DC: Institute for Social Analysis.

———. (1992). *When the victim is a child* (2nd ed.). Washington, DC: Office of Justice Programs.

White, J., and Wesley, J. (1987). "Male rape survivors: Guidelines for crisis counselors." *Crime Victims Digest,* April, pp. 3–6.

Whitman, H. (1951). *Terror in the streets.* New York: Dial Press.

"Wholesale changes in staffing, training ordered for Columbus PD sex-abuse unit." (1988). *Law Enforcement News,* October 31, p. 3.

Widom, C. (1989). "Child abuse, neglect, and violent criminal behavior." *Criminology* 27(2): 251–270.

———. (1992). "The cycle of violence." *NIJ Research in Brief* (October). Washington, DC: U.S. Department of Justice.

Wiehe, V. (1990). *Sibling abuse: Hidden physical, emotional, and sexual trauma.* Lexington, MA: Lexington Books.

Wilbanks, W. (1987). *The myth of a racist criminal justice system.* Pacific Grove, CA: Brooks/Cole.

Will, G. (1993). "Are we a nation of cowards?" *Newsweek,* November 15, pp. 93–94.

Williams, K. (1976). "The effects of victim characteristics on the disposition of violent crimes." In W. McDonald (Ed.), *Criminal justice and the victim* (pp. 172–214). Beverly Hills, CA: Sage.

———. (1978). *The effects of victim characteristics on judicial decisions: PROMIS research project report.* Washington, DC: Institute for Law and Social Research.

Williams, L. (1984). "The classic rape: When do victims report." *Social Problems,* 31: 459–467.

Williams, T. (1987). "Post traumatic stress disorder: Recognizing it, treating it." *NOVA Newsletter,* February, pp. 1–2, 7.

Willis, C., and Wells, R. (1988). "The police and child abuse: An analysis of police decisions to report illegal behavior." *Criminology* 26(4): 695–714.

Winerip, M. (1983). "Rape case: Vengeance and furor." *New York Times,* August 1, p. B1.

Witkin, G. (1994). "The great debate: Should you own a gun?" *U.S. News & World Report,* August 15, pp. 24–31.

Wolff, C. (1993a). "Former police officer stabbed while intervening in an attack." *New York Times,* May 19, p. B3.

———. (1993b). "Hostages mean hard lessons for police." *New York Times,* February 7, p. A37.

———. (1993c). "Massive cabdriver protest of 35 killings snarls traffic." *New York Times,* October 27, pp. B1, B4.

Wolfgang, M. (1958). *Patterns in criminal homicide.* Philadelphia: University of Pennsylvania Press.

———. (1959). "Suicide by means of victim precipitated homicide." *Journal of Clinical and Experimental Psychopathology and Quarterly Review of Psychiatry and Neurology* 20: 335–349.

———. (1965). "Victim compensation in crimes of personal violence." *Minnesota Law Review* 50: 229–241.

Wolfgang, M., and Ferracuti, F. (1967). *The subculture of violence: Towards an integrated theory in criminology.* London: Tavistock.

Wolfgang, M., and Riedel, M. (1973). "Race, judicial discretion, and the death penalty." *Annals of the Academy of Political and Social Science* 407 (May): 119–133.

Wood, N. (1990). "Black homicide—a public health crisis: Introduction and overview." *Journal of Interpersonal Violence* 5: 147–150.

Wooden, K. (1984). *Child lures: A guide to prevent abduction.* St. Louis: Ralston Purina.

Woodward, K., Annin, P., and Cohen, A. (1994). "Was it real or memories?" *Newsweek,* March 14, pp. 54–55.

Woodward, K., Friday, C., Quade, V., and Sparkman, R. (1993). "The sins of the fathers . . ." *Newsweek,* July 12, p. 57.

Wright, E. (1973). *The politics of punishment.* New York: Harper & Row.

Wright, J. (1995). "Guns, crime, and violence." In J. Sheley (Ed.), *Criminology: A contemporary handbook* (2nd ed.) (pp. 495–514). Belmont, CA: Wadsworth.

Wright, J., Rossi, P., and Daly, K. (1983). *Under the gun: Weapons, crime, and violence in America.* New York: Aldine.

Wright, L. (1994). *Remembering satan.* New York: Knopf.

Wright, M. (1985). "The impact of victim-offender mediation on the victim." *Victimology* 10(1): 630–646.

———. (1989). "Introduction." In M. Wright and B.

Galaway (Eds.), *Mediation and criminal justice: Victims, offenders and community* (pp. 1–13). Newbury Park, CA: Sage.

———. (1991). *Justice for victims and offenders.* Philadelphia: Open University Press.

Wyatt, G. (1985). "The sexual abuse of Afro-American and white American women in childhood." *Child Abuse and Neglect* 9: 507–519.

Wyatt, G., and Powell, G. (1988). *Lasting effects of child sexual abuse.* Newbury Park, CA: Sage.

Yapko, M. (1994). *Suggestions of abuse: True and false memories of childhood sexual trauma.* New York: Simon & Schuster.

Yapko, M., and Powell, G. (1988). *Lasting effects of child sexual abuse.* Newbury Park, CA: Sage.

Yllo, K., and Bograd, M. (1988). *Feminist perspectives on wife abuse.* Newbury Park, CA: Sage.

Young, M. (1991). "NOVA protests NBC's 'Naming Names.'" *NOVA Newsletter,* 15(4): 1.

Younger, E. (1977). Introduction to the American Bar Association, *Victims of crime or victims of justice?* (pp. 1–5). Washington, DC: Author.

Zawitz, M. (1994). *Domestic violence: Violence between intimates. Bureau of Justice Statistics selected findings.* Washington, DC: U.S. Department of Justice.

Ziegenhagen, E. (1977). *Victims, crime, and social control.* New York: Praeger.

Ziegenhagen, E., and Brosnan, D. (1985). "Victim responses to robbery and crime control policy." *Criminology* 23(4): 675–695.

Zimring, F. (1986). *NIJ crime file study guide: Gun control.* Washington, DC: U.S. Department of Justice.

———. (1987). "Why the Goetz verdict was not a landmark precedent." *New York Times,* June 21, p. E20.

Zimring, F., and Zuehl, J. (1986). "Victim injury and death in urban robbery: A Chicago study." *Journal of Legal Studies* 15(1) (January): 1–40.

Zorza, J. (1994). "Women rarely batter men except when abused themselves." *New York Times,* February 17, p. A22.

Name Index

Subject Index